To Speak with Cloth

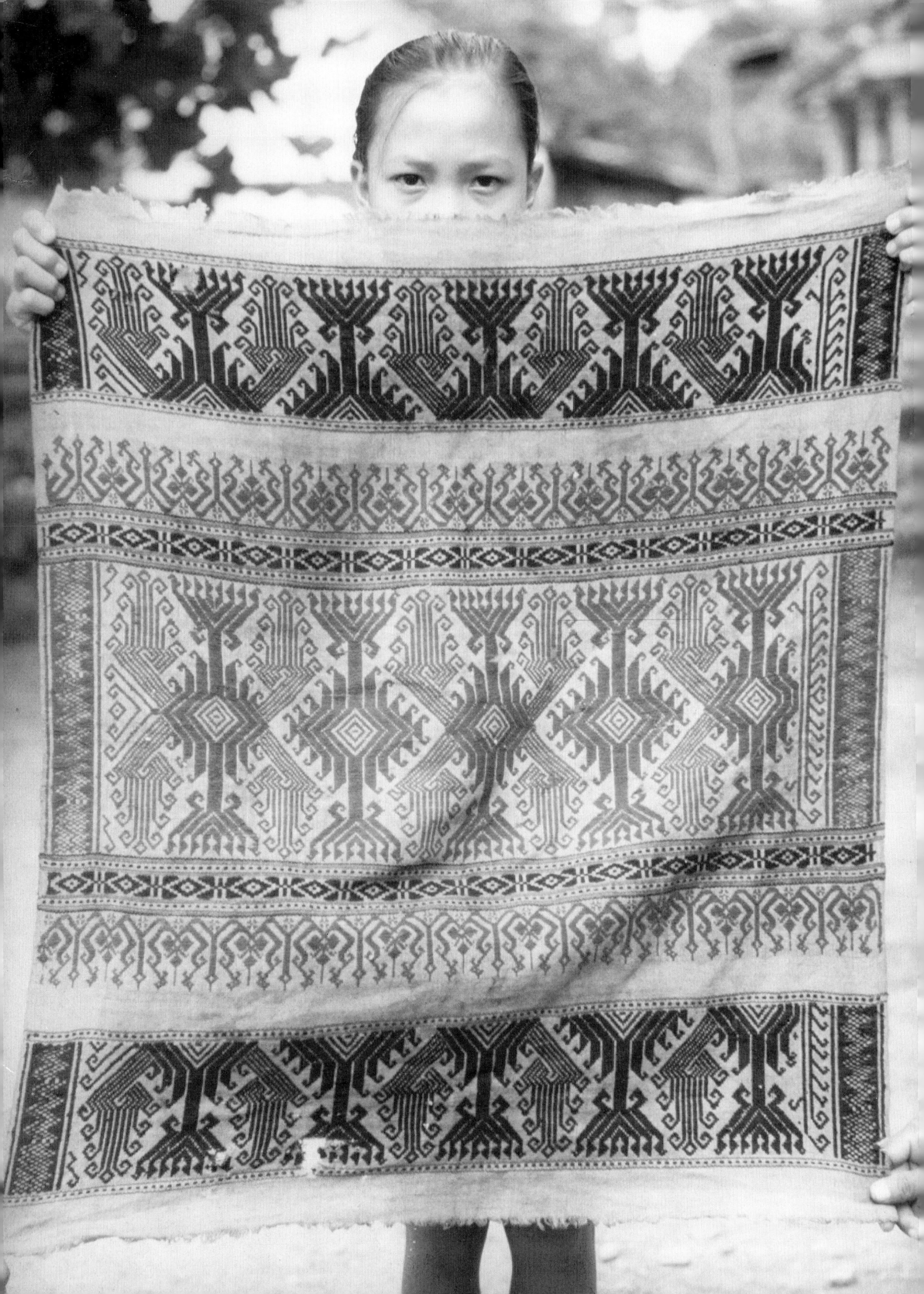

To Speak with Cloth
Studies in Indonesian Textiles

Mattiebelle Gittinger, Editor

MUSEUM OF CULTURAL HISTORY
University of California, Los Angeles

This publication was supported by funding from
The National Endowment for the Humanities,
The Ahmanson Foundation, and Manus, the support
group of the UCLA Museum of Cultural History.

*Cover (softbound version): Three-panel bridewealth cloth
from Atadéi (detail of Plate 5).
UCLA Museum of Cultural History X81.15030.*

Frontispiece: A tampan *photographed in the Talang Padang
region of South Sumatra in 1971.*

ISBN 0-930741-17-X (softbound)
ISBN Standard Book Number 0-930741-18-8 (hardbound)

Library of Congress Card Catalog Number 89-050052

Museum of Cultural History
University of California, Los Angeles
405 Hilgard Avenue
Los Angeles, California 90024

© 1989 Regents of the University of California. All rights reserved.

Printed in Japan.

Contents

Foreword	6
Preface	7
Color Plates	9
Map of Indonesia	24
Flags and Half-Moons Tanimbarese Textiles in an "Engendered" System of Valuables Susan McKinnon	27
The Bridewealth Cloth **of Lamalera, Lembata** Ruth Barnes	43
Textiles of West Sumba Lively Renaissance of an Old Tradition Danielle Geirnaert	57
Foreign Textiles in Sahu Culture Leontine E. Visser	81
Batik Patterns **of the Early Nineteenth Century** Anthony Forge	91
Dye Process and Life Sequence The Coloring of Textiles in an East Javanese Village Rens Heringa	107
Political Motives The Batiks of Mohamad Hadi of Solo Robyn J. and John R. Maxwell	131
Batiks in the Central Javanese **Wedding Ceremony** Judi Achjadi	151
The Sacred Cloths of the Toraja Unanswered Questions Hetty Nooy-Palm	163
A Sacred Cloth of Rangda *Kamben Cepuk* of Bali and Nusa Penida Marie-Louise Nabholz-Kartaschoff	181
Ceremonial Attire in Nias Jerome Feldman	199
Batak Bags in Weft Twining Rita Bolland	213
A Reassessment **of the *Tampan* of South Sumatra** Mattiebelle Gittinger	225
Glossary	240
Bibliography	242
Contributors	253

Foreword

The UCLA Museum of Cultural History was established in 1963 to consolidate the University's various departmentally dispersed collections of non-Western art and archaeology. Among the important materials to enter the new museum was the Katharane E. Mershon collection of Indonesian textiles originally assembled in the 1930s. With that as a foundation, George R. Ellis, Associate Director of the Museum from 1975 to 1981, built the holdings into a significant, broad-based collection from this nation of 6,000 islands. This process was assisted by Elizabeth and Richard Rogers, who generously funded most of the textile acquisitions as part of their ongoing and vital support for the Museum and its programs. In 1985 the Museum mounted the first major exhibition from our Indonesian collections. It was titled *The Eloquent Dead: Ancestral Sculpture of Indonesia and Southeast Asia,* and was accompanied by a publication of the same name, edited by Dr. Jerome Feldman.

With its commitment to Indonesian arts well established, the Museum invited Dr. Mattiebelle Gittinger, Research Associate for Southeast Asian Textiles at The Textile Museum, Washington, D.C., to author a publication on some facet of this area of study. She suggested an anthology of essays addressing current research interests on Indonesian textiles and selected an outstanding group of internationally recognized scholars to contribute to the project. The Museum would like to thank Dr. Gittinger for her considerable efforts in bringing this volume to fruition. Her energetic involvement in Indonesian textile studies has clearly established her as one of the leading scholars in that field. We are also most grateful to the contributors whose careful and detailed research made this publication possible. Their thoughtful work and patience are sincerely appreciated.

Others deserve recognition too. As a research associate here, Roy Hamilton provided critical expertise in the cataloguing of our Indonesian textile holdings. Two other members of the Museum staff should be singled out for their efforts on this volume. Henrietta Cosentino edited the essays with insight and handled the difficult logistics of working with authors literally scattered across the planet. Danny Brauer created the handsome design for the publication and organized the details of its production. Together they accomplished the Museum's transition to computerized "desktop publishing." It is always a pleasure to work with such engaging professionals.

It is anticipated that this will be the first in a series of volumes devoted to various facets of Indonesian textiles. At the same time it will be the last publication to appear under our current name and to be produced out of our Haines Hall quarters. Shortly we will move into the new building specifically designed to house the Museum. At the end of 1990, when we reopen and resume our exhibition and publication programs, we will celebrate our new home as The Fowler Museum of Cultural History.

Christopher B. Donnan, Director
Doran H. Ross, Associate Director

Preface

These thoughtful studies assess textiles and their role in discrete micro-environments of Indonesia. Most are built on the authors' prolonged experience in those environments and each reflects an intense consideration of the problem addressed. Previous publications on Indonesian textiles tended to be broadly based, generalizing about many cloth types from various parts of the archipelago. Often that vagueness was unavoidable because field data either did not exist or failed to address in any detail the questions presented by the textiles. Happily, now that textiles are increasingly recognized as primary source material, researchers are asking the questions and obtaining the answers that reveal, even more convincingly, how remarkable and important they are in the socio-religious scene of Southeast Asia. While this volume is selective in its subject matter, the essays contribute to a deeper understanding of textiles throughout the archipelago.

Many of those dealing with islands other than Java enumerate the textile types and decorative means for the area. These are much more than mere lists. Rather they are logical ways to organize an inventory of form and function with interpretations that address both the past and the present. Such a comprehensive approach within the context of this rapidly changing archipelago will be applauded by scholars and connoisseurs alike. In an era when the textile craft is rapidly disappearing, Danielle Geirnaert's documentation from West Sumba will come as a surprise to most readers who, at best, may be familiar only with fabric from the Kodi region. She portrays an area in which textile manufacture and usage continue to be an evolving and complex phenomenon. Hers is the first work to enumerate the textile forms from this region of Sumba.

The role of gender (and relative gender) as the differentiating factor controlling the creation, use, and exchange of textiles in many Indonesian societies has been recognized for many years. This matrix, in which bride-givers supply female textile gifts in exchange for the male goods of the bride-takers, is elaborated in the essays of Susan McKinnon and Ruth Barnes, who examine it within the particular societal expressions of the peoples of Tanimbar and Lembata. McKinnon, using this balanced exchange as the normal "given," is able to interpret apparently ambiguous social phenomena. Other ethnographers may want to look closely at her approach as a potential model.

Some of these micro-studies provide evidence once again of the importance of symmetries, reversal of symmetries, and odd and even continuities. The textile medium lends itself to this type of manipulation; how deeply these elements can penetrate the structure of a textile is exemplified by Barnes's elaboration of detail integral to the creation of textiles from Lembata. The essays of Geirnaert and of Leontine Visser touch on this subject as well.

Visser addresses the problem of ritually important textiles among a non-textile-producing people, the Sahu of Halmahera. She demonstrates that the society selected them not at random, but rather for their properties, which served symbolic roles. Her conclusions as to their source, together with significant evidence contained in the essays by Geirnaert and Barnes, point toward south Sulawesi as the dispersal point for certain textiles and textile techniques. This possibility, too, will be a subject for future research.

Two of the essays bring order and detail to textiles that were formerly categorized in a very general manner. Hetty Nooy-Palm returns to the topic of the *maa'* and *sarita* from the Toraja of Sulawesi. She further specifies the types of sacred cloths and offers photographic evidence of the manner in which certain of them were imitated in The Netherlands. Marie-Louise Nabholz-Kartaschoff imposes order on the array of cotton weft ikat textiles once solely attributed to Nusa Penida. She shows that some of these textiles were made on Bali and proposes a hierarchy of textile types. She also discusses, and in some instance is able to illustrate, the specific ritual use appropriate to these.

The number of essays addressing issues dealing with batik increased as the book evolved. To a great degree this reflects a growing awareness on the part of textile scholars that batik has more to say than is suggested by initial consideration. The Javanese certainly realized this; it took longer for others. Anthony Forge's detective work on the Sir Thomas Stamford Raffles material in the Museum of Mankind has produced a previously undocumented puppet form and the earliest known visual records of particular batik patterns. This evidence will prompt us to reassess our dating of certain pattern developments; it also provides new source material for additional studies. Rens Heringa's contribution offers fresh understanding of how raw materials enter into the symbolism of batik patterned cloth. While it is coastal custom she records and interprets, her work opens new ways of considering batik elsewhere in Java. Robyn and John Maxwell's essay on one artist's use of batik for recent political expression amply demonstrates how enduring this medium has been even into the contemporary scene.

The essays by both Judi Achjadi and Jerome Feldman consider the cosmological symbolism inherent in the parts and the whole of ritually appropriate costume, although they interpret this symbolism from radically different societies. Achjadi considers the formal Javanese bridal costume and its significance within the marriage ritual. Feldman's material stems from the vigorous societies traditional to the island of Nias. He details costume parts, suggests their symbolic values and articulates interesting contrasts between hard and soft costume. Achjadi's material has been gathered over years of living on Java and innumerable discussions with local "marriage counselors." It makes accessible the fine details of Javanese custom associated with the marriage ritual.

Well known for her meticulous analysis and diagrammatic renderings of textile structures, Rita Bolland turns her analytical focus to a group of rare twined bags once made by the Batak of Sumatra. Her work reveals a painstaking art long vanished from the ethnographic scene, but it also gives us a textile form made, very probably, by men—a rare occurrence in the Indonesian world where, traditionally, textile labor is women's. It seems too late to prove conclusively that these bags were the work of men. However, with previously published work and the information presented here by Geirnaert relating to West Sumba, there seems little doubt that for part of the archipelago, at least, weft twining was originally a male occupation. It should be recognized as one more of the intriguing details of the textile arts in this ethnographic field.

My own essay interprets a Sumatran textile form with the aid of textiles woven on mainland Southeast Asia. Whether the hypothesis is accepted or not, the article expresses my belief that certain customs associated with cloth on the mainland will ultimately lead to an understanding of what are now enigmatic details in the textiles and textile usage in the insular world of that region. In a larger perspective, the conclusion I hope will be drawn from the entire collection of essays is that textiles deserve to be considered as valuable primary source material, subject to as much scrutiny as kinship structures for the anthropologist and ancient chronicles for the historian.

Mattiebelle Gittinger
Washington, D.C.

Color Plates

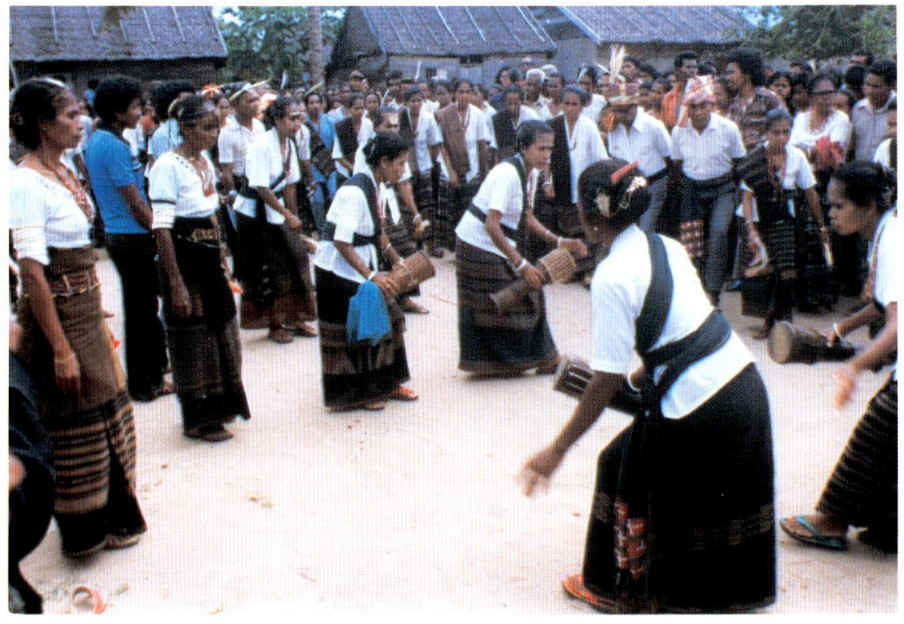

Plate 1 (left). Women dancing in their village of Latdalam, on the southwest coast of Yamdena. The antique sarongs they are wearing are more typical of those to be found in southern Yamdena and Selaru. Some of the women have loincloths tied over their blouses. Tanimbar, 1980.

Plate 2 (below). A striped sarong (bakan maran) with a "full rainbow" pattern, from the village of Olilit on the southeast coast of Yamdena, Tanimbar. Collection of Susan McKinnon.

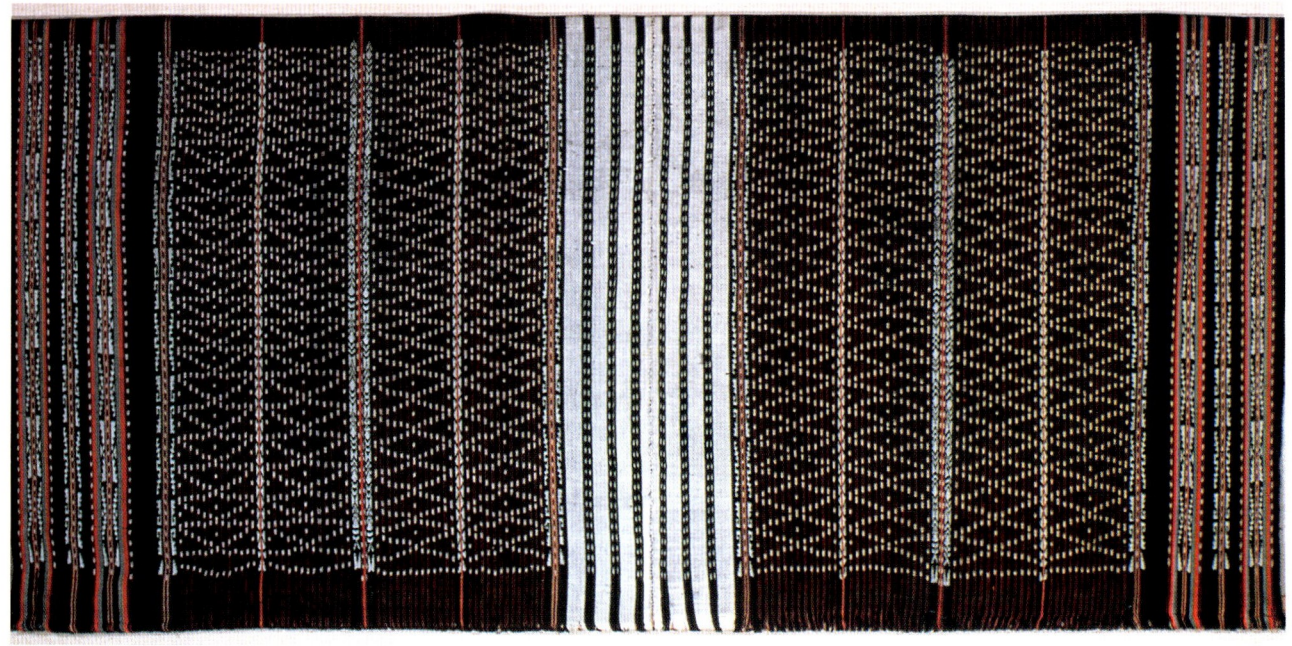

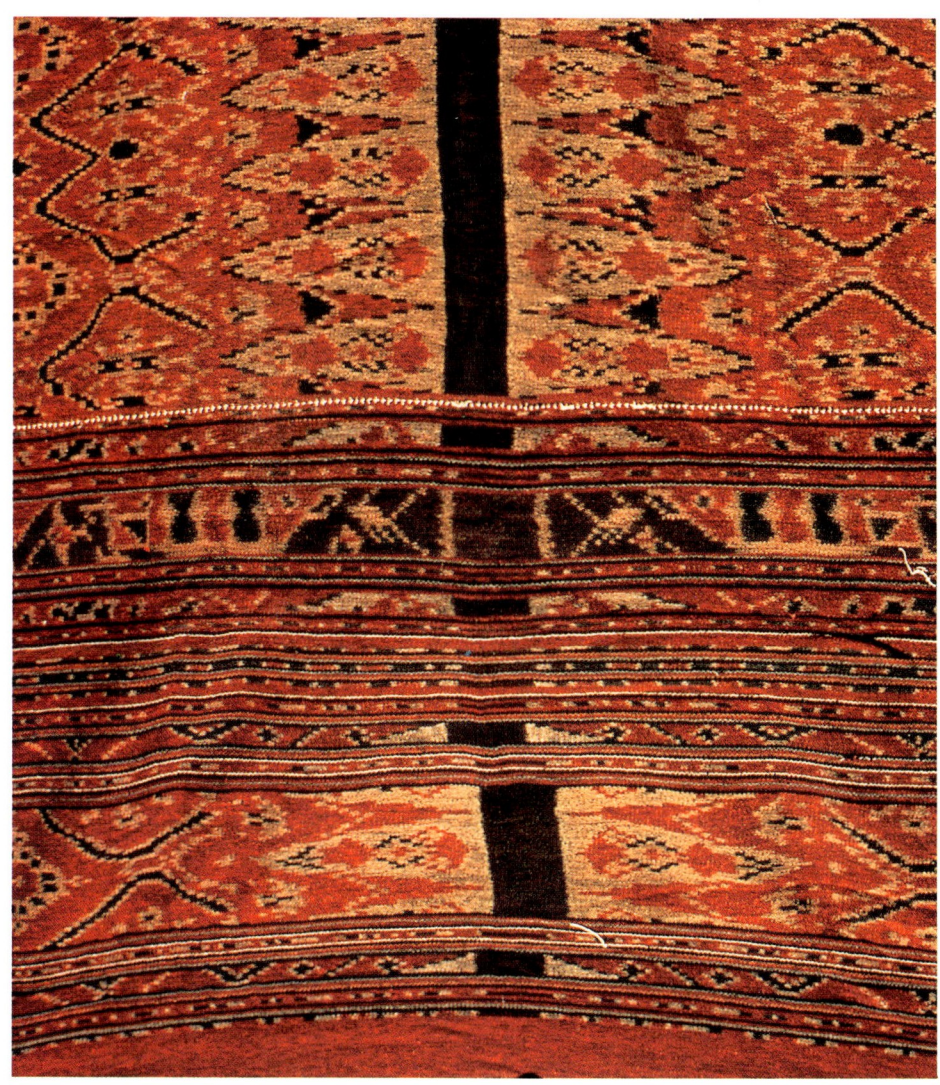

Plate 3. Detail of a three-panel bridewealth cloth from Lamalera, known there as kewatek nai telo. *The patterns of the lower panel* (hebā) *show the boat* (téna), *the manta ray* (moku), *and the shark* (iu), *as well as a single width of the linked pattern* (beléré) *which appears again in the central panel* (tukā), *above. Outer panel weft: approximately 60 cm. Central panel: weft, approximately 40 cm., warp, approximately 125 cm. (circular, only half visible). Lamalera, Lembata, 1979. Also shown in Figure 4, p. 46.*

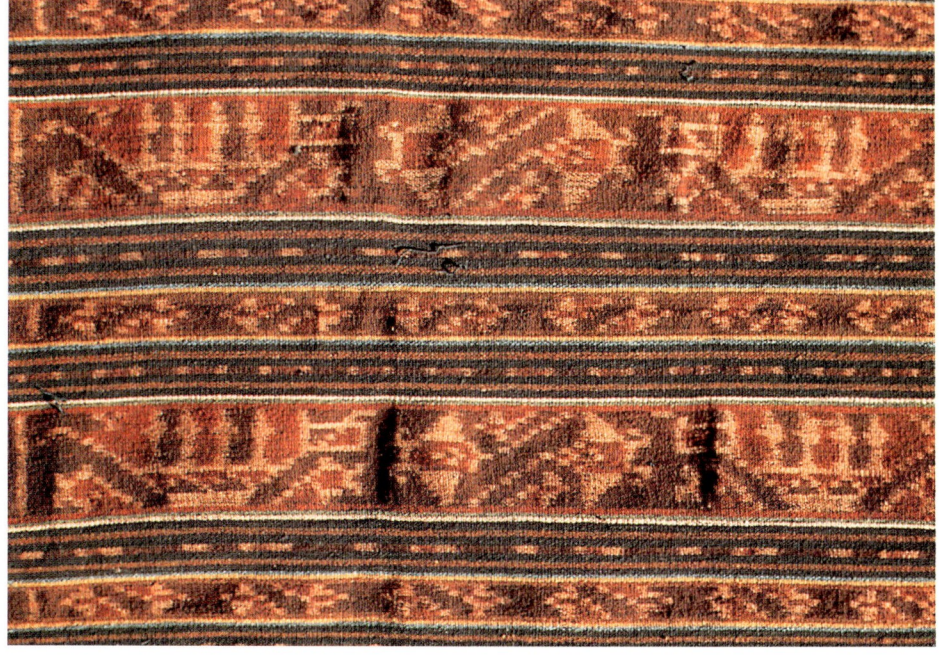

Plate 4 (left). Detail of a shouldercloth (senai) *with boat* (téna) *and manta ray* (moku) *patterns. Lamalera, Lembata, 1982. Also shown in Figure 9, p. 48.*

Plate 5 (opposite). Three-panel bridewealth cloth from Atadéi, Lembata, known there as petak haren nai telo. *The two outer panels show the manta ray* (moku) *and star* (sirété) *patterns; on the central panel is the design called* menué, *named for the swift, a thread-winding device. The open warp area has been cut. UCLA Museum of Cultural History X81.1503.*

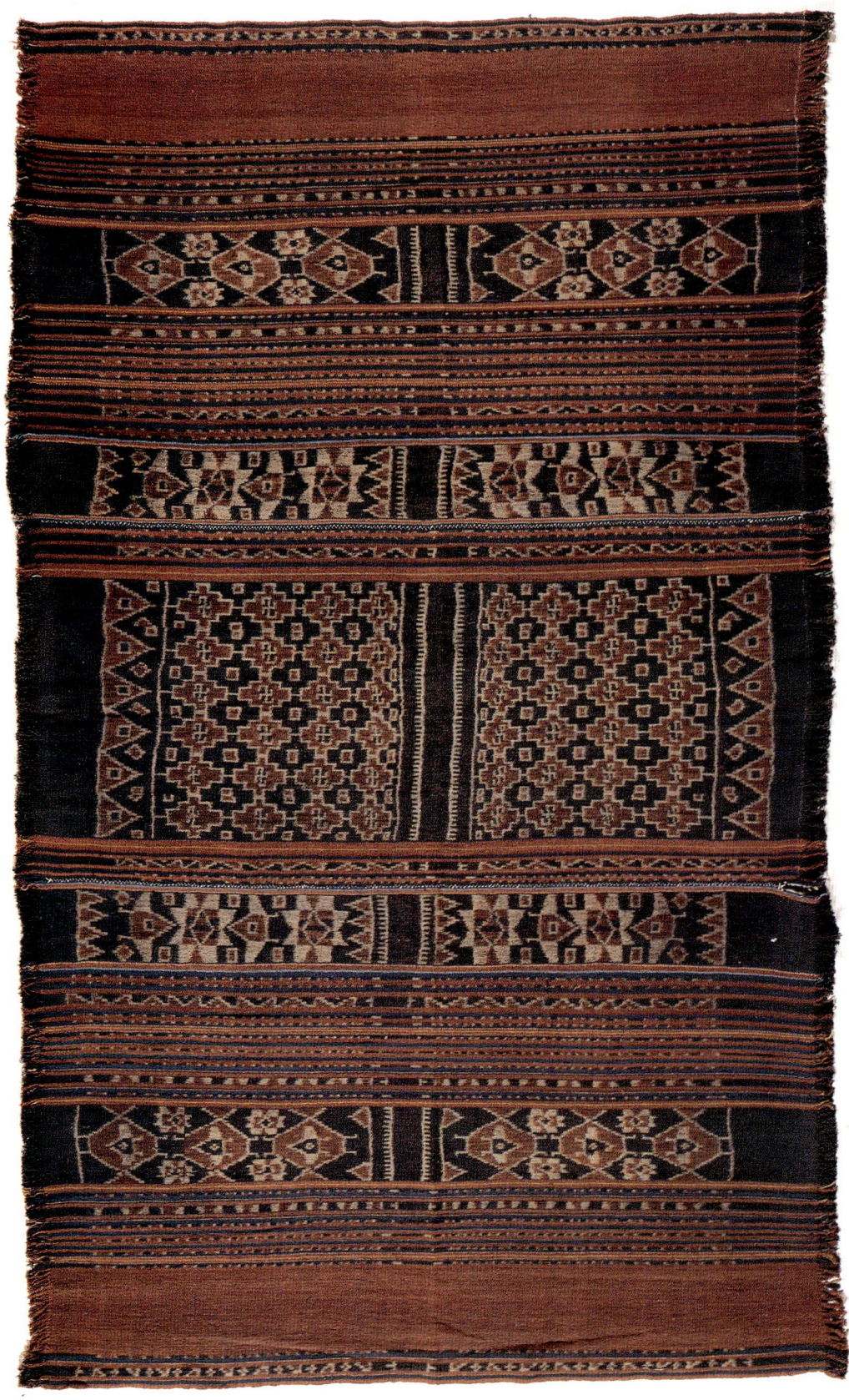

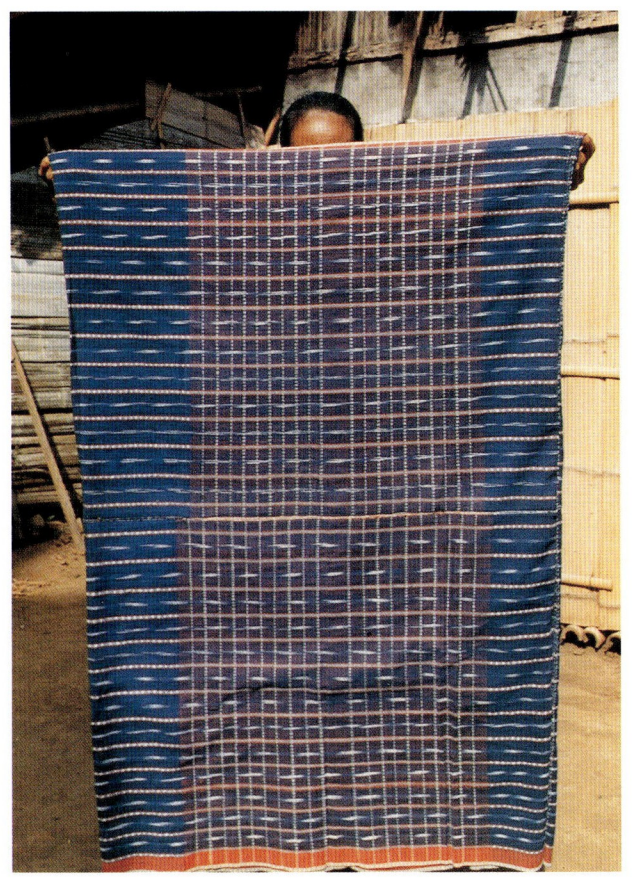
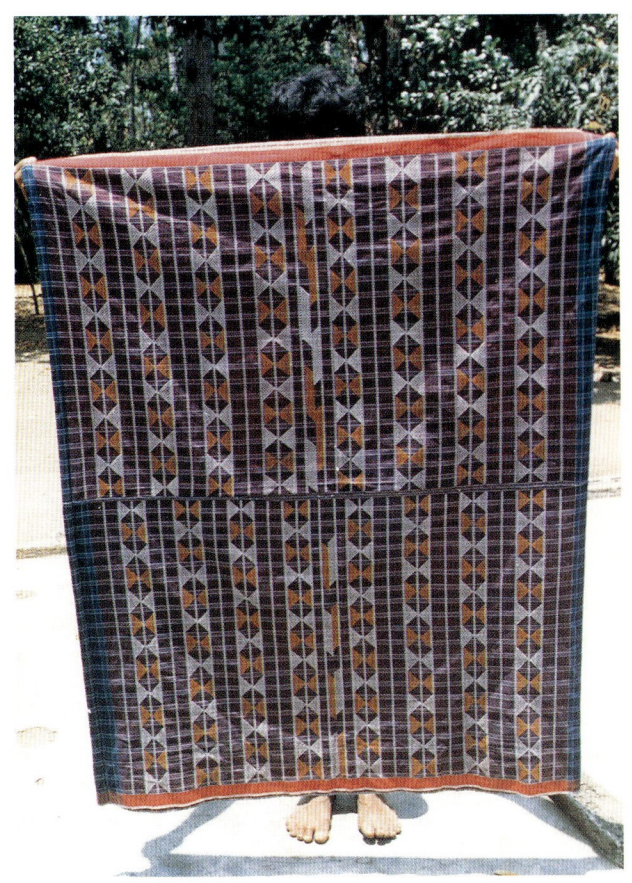
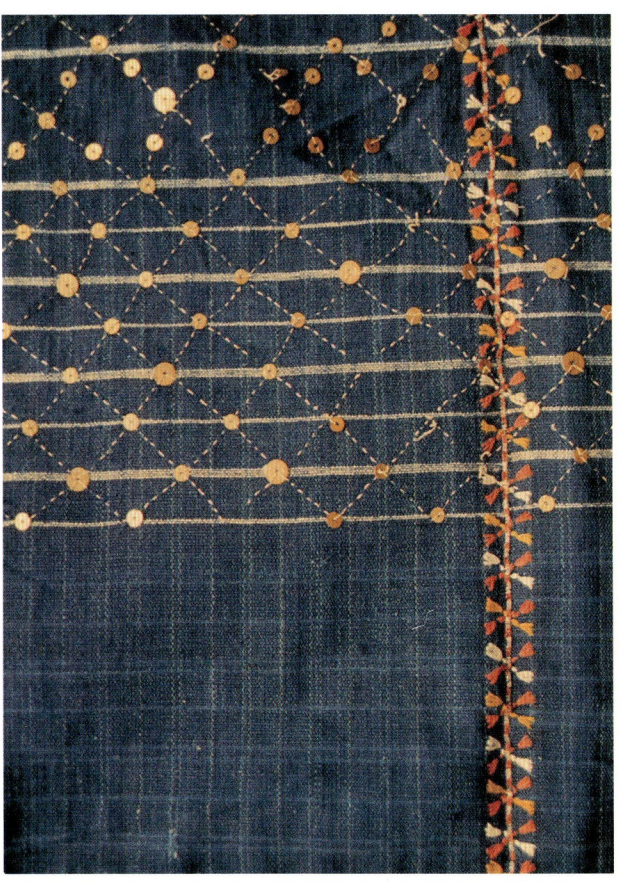
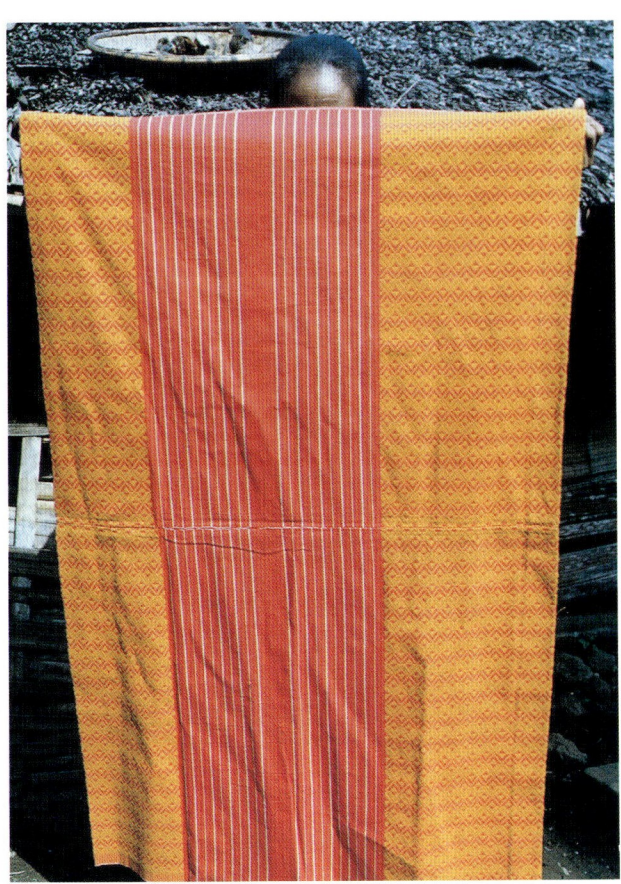

12

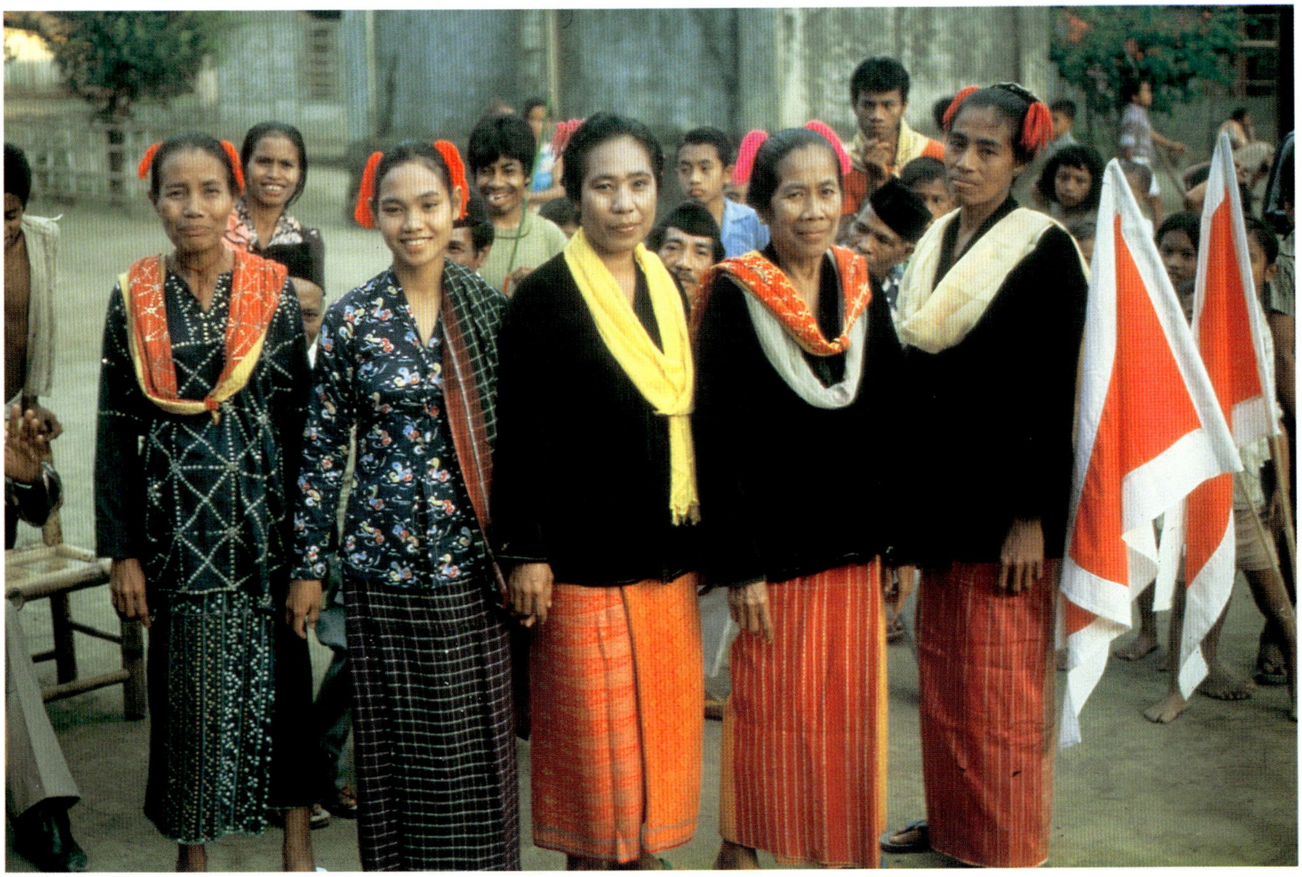

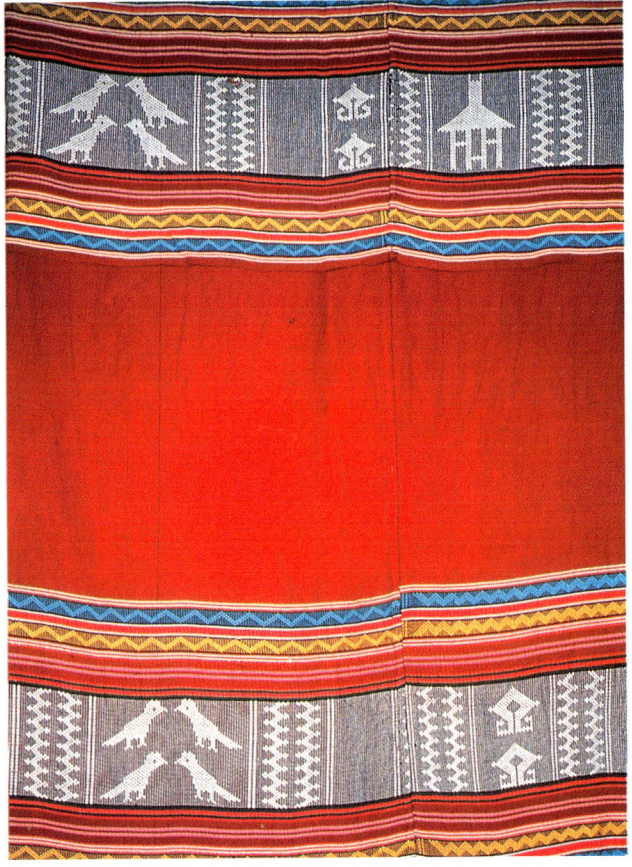

Facing page, clockwise from upper left:

Plate 6. Indigo ikat sarong, ba'a boba, *with supplementary weft lines in the central design area or "head." Awer, Halmahera, 1982.*

Plate 7. Woven sarong, ba'a boba, *in which the heads of the two panels are asymmetric. Awer, Halmahera, 1982.*

Plate 8. Woven sarong, ba'a suje, *with supplementary weft patterns in head and body, and white lines in the head. Awer, Halmahera, 1982.*

Plate 9. Detail of an embroidered cloth with mica spangles. Awer, Halmahera, 1982.

This page:

Plate 10 (above). Sahu women, dressed for the harvest festival, wear a variety of costumes, including indigo sarongs used the first and second nights of the festival, and red-and-yellow sarongs worn the first day, together with black velvet jackets and, at far left, a mica-embroidered one. Their costumes are further embellished with shouldercloths called kalaotala, *consisting of two embroidered kerchiefs* (tuala suje) *knotted together in one corner and worn over the breast. Skirtcloths, from left to right:* ba'a boba, kain mandar, ba'a grem, ba'a suje, ba'a suje. *Tarau'u, Halmahera, 1980.*

Plate 11 (right). Back portion of a Lolinese lambelekko *skirt. Motifs include, left to right: birds, very popular in West Sumba; the golden ear pendant* (mamuli); *and the Sumbanese house with peaked roof (top right). Waikabubak, Loli, West Sumba, 1984.*

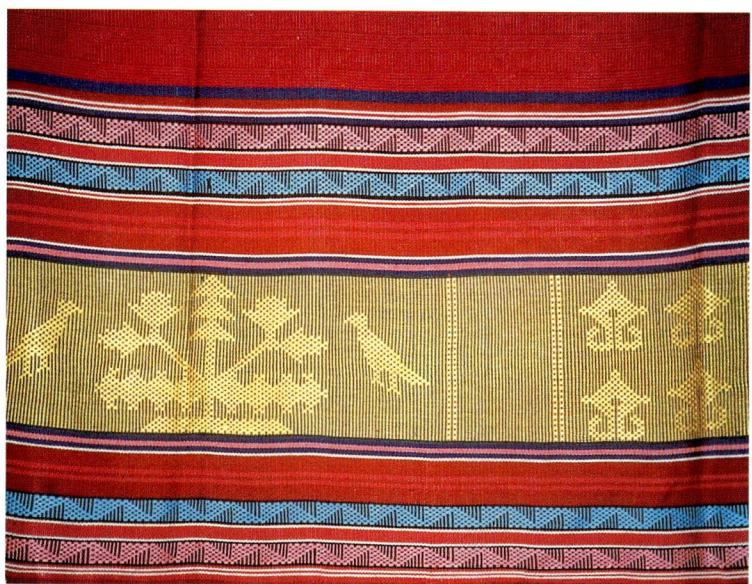

Plate 12. Detail of a Lolinese lambelekko *border. The "flower bowl" has probably been copied originally from a European cross-stitch pattern book. Waikabubak, Loli, West Sumba, 1984.*

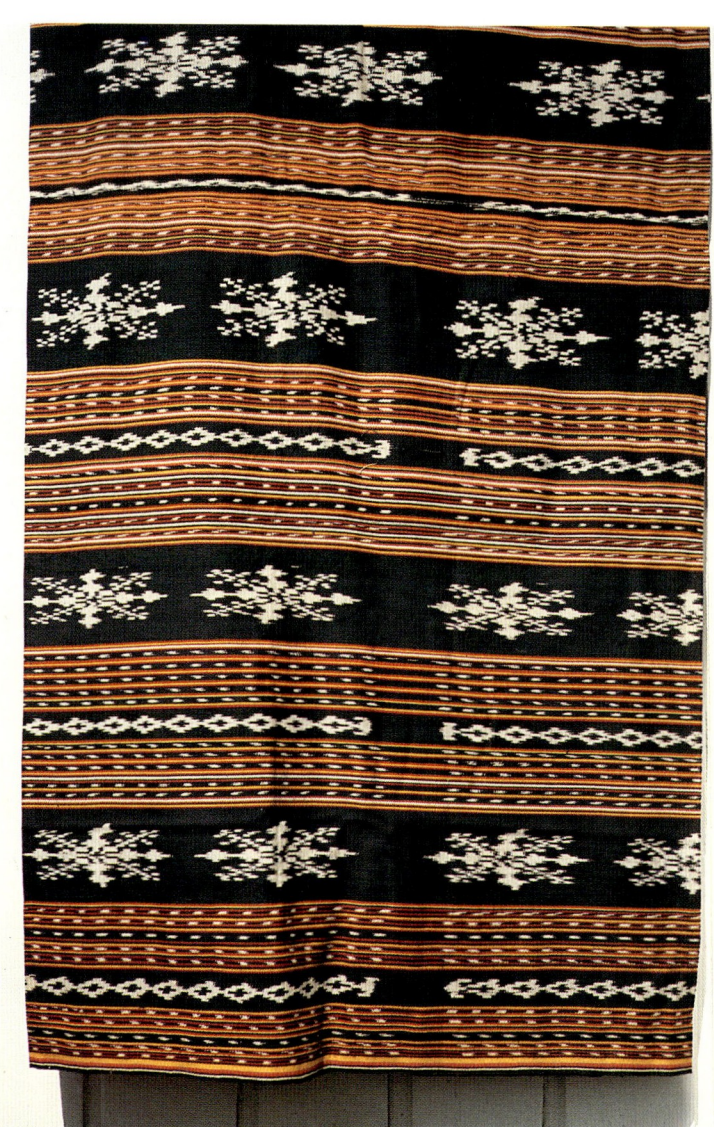

Plate 13. Modern Laboyan ikat skirt, made of machine-spun yarns dyed in natural indigo. White flower patterns and narrow stripes of imported red and yellow thread (benang jawa) *contrast with the background of dark blue. Near Kabukarudi, Laboya, West Sumba, 1983.*

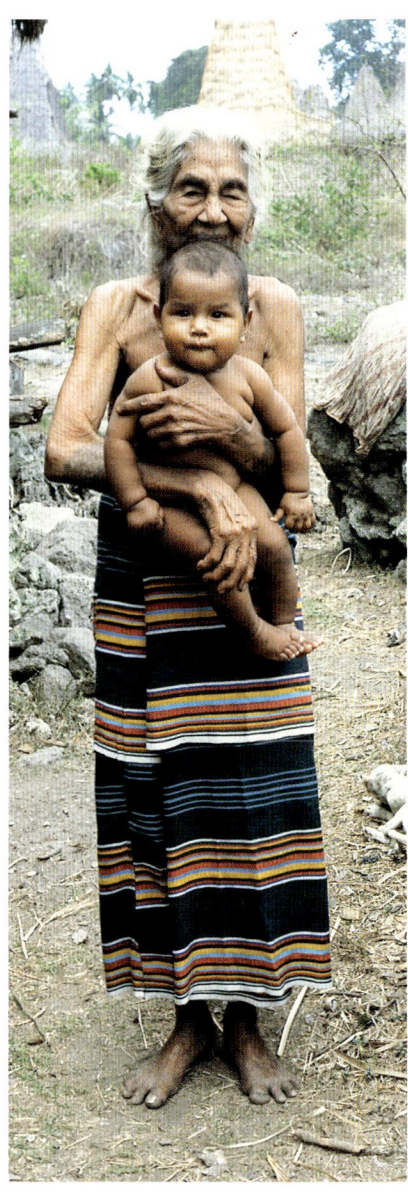

Plate 14. An old Kodinese lady wearing a lau gundu of handspun yarns dyed with natural indigo. Near Tossi, Kodi, West Sumba, 1982.

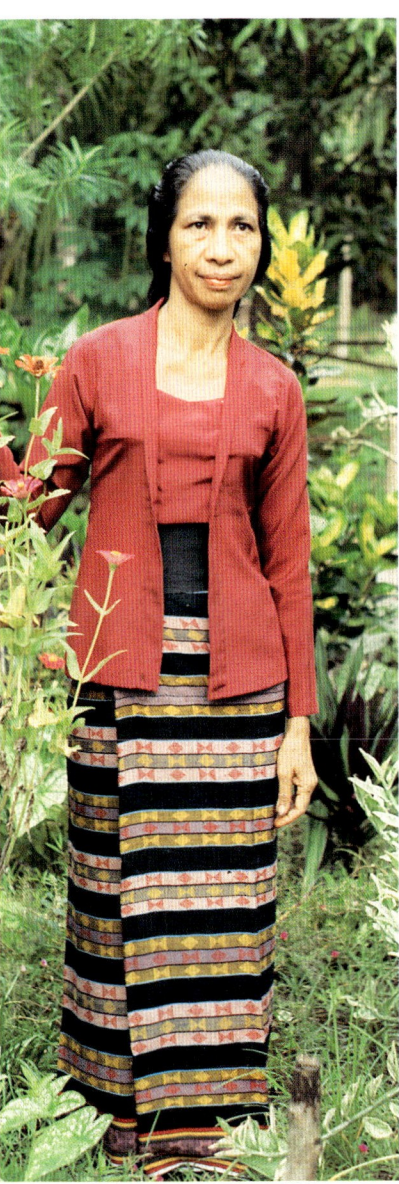

Plate 15. Nyonya Lien, wife of the late Raja of Kodi, wearing a Kodinese lambalekko with butterfly (kabebo) motifs. Note how it differs from Lolinese lambelekko. Bondokodi, Kodi, West Sumba, 1982.

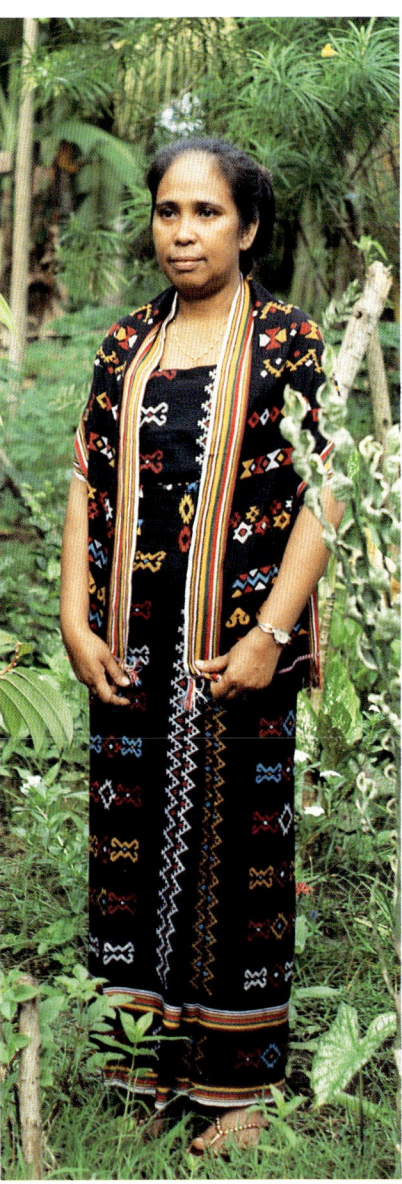

Plate 16. A young Laboyan woman attending a wedding ceremony. Near Padedewatu, Laboya, West Sumba, 1986.

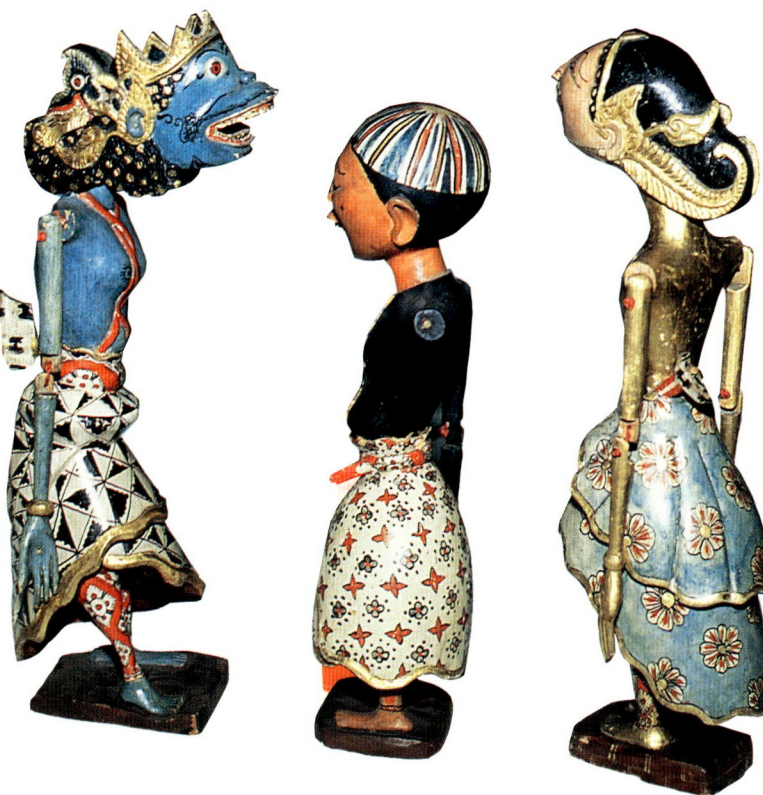

Plate 17. Puppets Nos. 448, 420, and 442 (left to right) from the Raffles collection. Left is the King of Blambangan. Despite his royal regalia—notably a fine crown, with a backward-facing Garuda head and gold-speckled hair—his vile nature is indicated by his hideous head, large mouth with huge teeth (albeit of gold), bug eyes, and skin color. His kain is in the pattern called slobok djamang and he has patola leggings; the remains of a kris scabbard project from the back of his waist. Center is presumably a commoner. He wears a cloth pattern here classified as ceplok, a sleeved jacket, and a skull cap showing polychrome rays. Right, "...ing Setro son to Patih Lungin...," wears a cloth of probable Indian origin with a lavendar field, now faded; his headdress is lower aristocracy, and the remains of a kris scabbard projects from his waist. British Museum 1859.12.28.448, 420, 442.

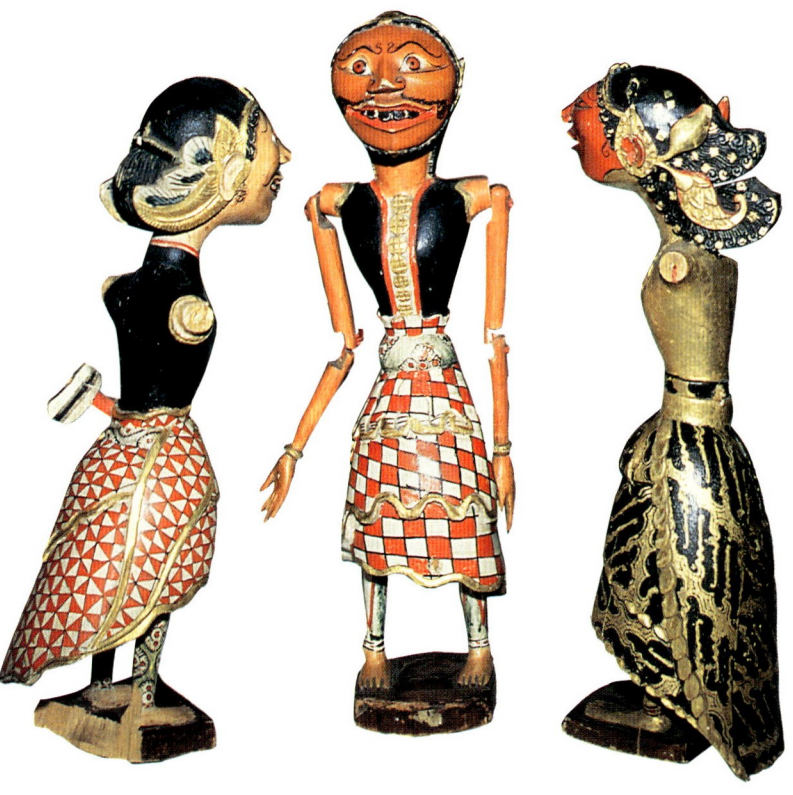

Plate 18. Puppets Nos. 422, 417, and 440 (left to right) from the Raffles collection. A young aristocrat with a retainer and a patih. Left, "Kebo Pengtajur," wears a cloth with poleng triangles in red and white, a sleeveless jacket, and a moderate winged headdress. A kris scabbard projects from his waist band. Center, "Angkat-buto Patih of Blambangan" wears poleng in red and white, a sleeveless jacket with elaborate buttons, and a skullcap. His large round eyes and coarse teeth indicate his vulgar (kasar) nature. Right, "Menak Kindah" in the register, wears an elaborately wrapped cloth with a parang design in prada on indigo. His large winged headdress and gold-speckled luxuriant hair confirm the high status indicated by his bare gold torso and refined eyes. British Museum 1859.12.28.422, 417, 440.

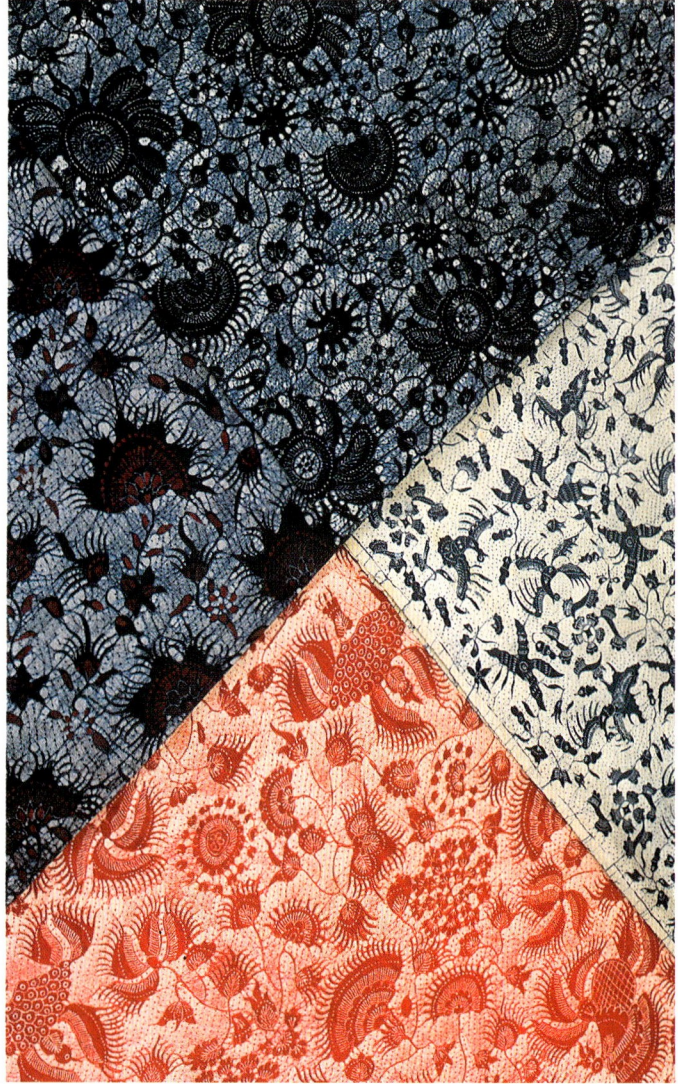

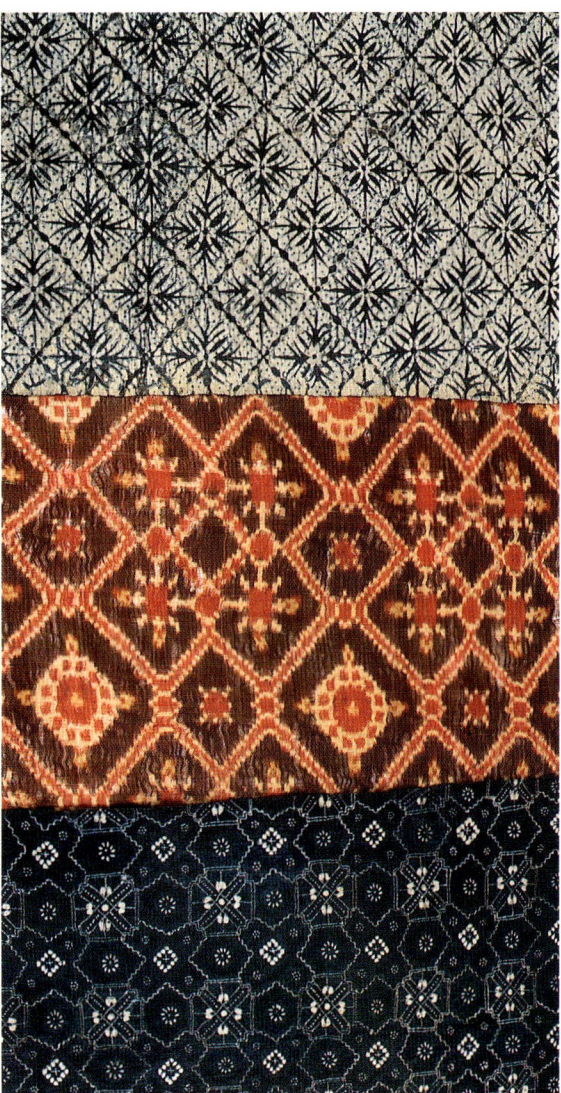

Plate 19. Horizontal series of colored cloths from northeastern Java. Clockwise, starting from the East:

a) Putihan, *the protective cloth. The motif is* laseman *(i.e. in the style of Lasem, a village near Kerek). Collection of R. Heringa.*

b) Bangrod, *the cloth for daughters, brides, and young husbands. The motif is* laseman. *Collection of R. Heringa.*

c) Pipitan, *the wraparound skirt for mothers. The motif is* kembang waluh *(pumpkin flower). This profuse creeper is strongly associated with fertility; its fruit is known as "water container." Collection of R. Heringa.*

d) Irengan, *the shouldercloth for grandmothers. The motif is* kenanga ginubah *(concealed* kenanga*). The* kenanga *flower is often used in grave offerings. But the "flowers" on this cloth are actually birds. Collection of R. Heringa.*

Plate 20. Vertical series of ritual cloths from northeastern Java. From top to bottom:

a) Putihan, *the Upper World cloth. The motif is* panji lori *(banner with small wooden clubs). Others call this motif* panji serong *(diagonal banner). Its meaning is unclear. Collection of R. Heringa.*

b) Cinde, *a patola type for commoner use. From Bühler and Fischer 1979:106-7.*

c) Irengan, *the Lower World cloth. The motif is* kelapa senkantet *(hanging coconuts). The coconut grew out of the head of Dewi Sri and as such has procreative associations. Collection of R. Heringa.*

17

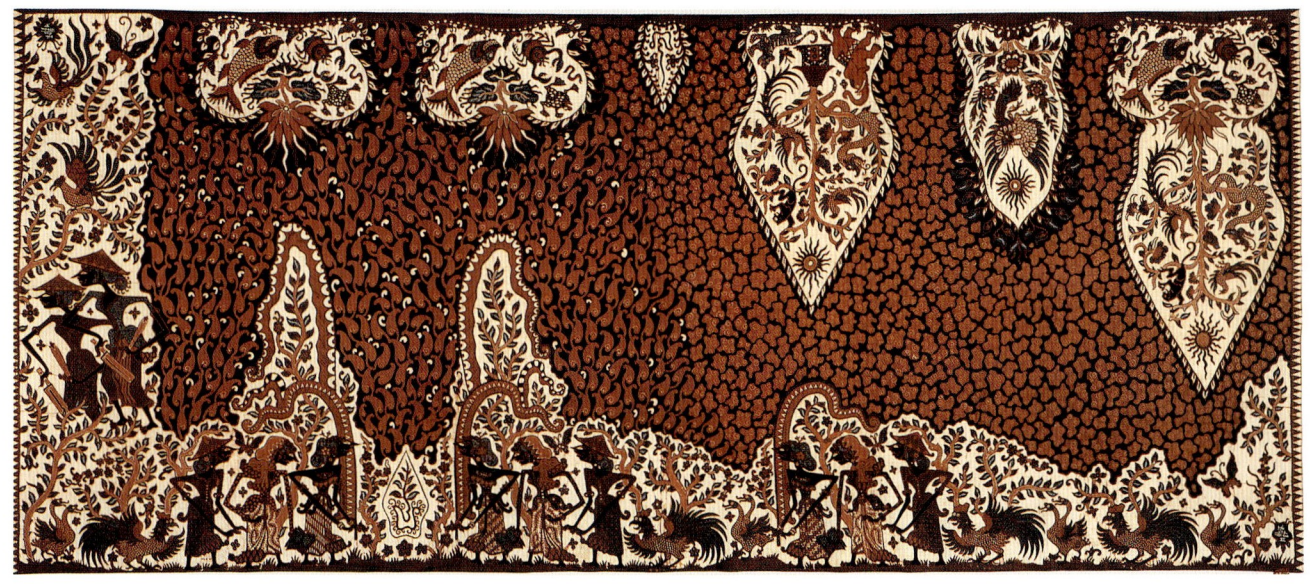

Plate 21. "Srikandi Gerwani" (Srikandi as Goddess of the Indonesian Women's Movement). Batik skirtcloth (kain panjang) designed by Mohamad Hadi. Solo, Java, 1964. Cotton, natural dyes. 251.5 x 106.0 cm. Purchased from Gallery Shop Funds, 1984. Australian National Gallery, Canberra, 1984.3065.

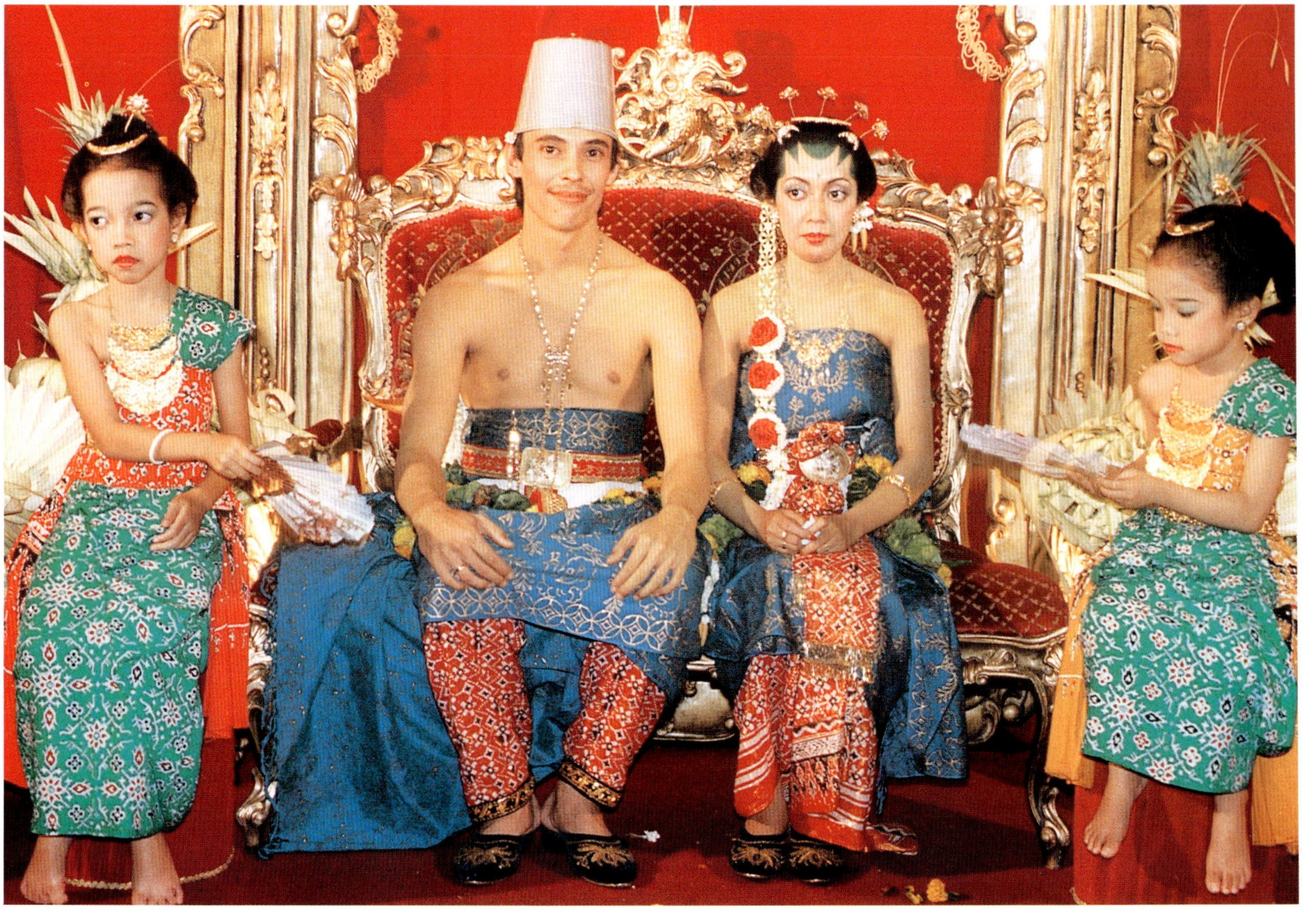

Plate 23. A bridal couple sits on formal settee flanked by little girls in traditional costume. They are clothed in a multitude of fertility and cosmic symbols. The significance of the costume is not diminished by today's cheaper textiles. Jakarta, Java, 1984.

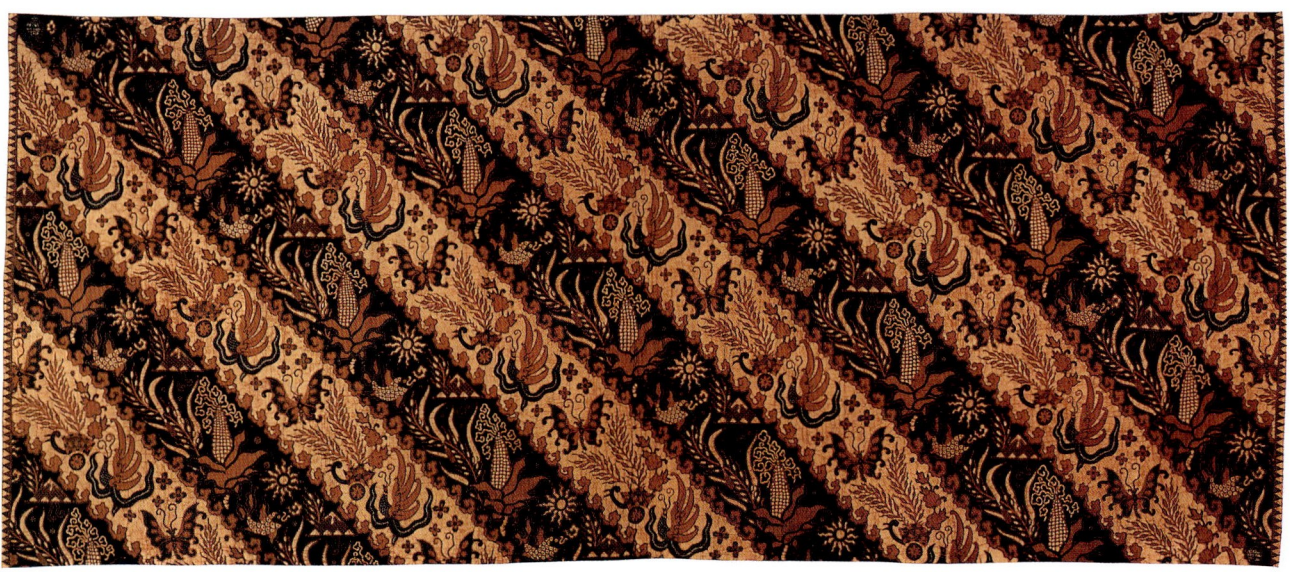

Plate 22. "Jembatan Mas" (The Golden Bridge). Batik skirtcloth (kain panjang), *designed by Mohamad Hadi. Solo, Java, 1965. Cotton, natural dyes. 105.5 x 256.0 cm. Australian National Gallery, Canberra, 1987.1056. See also Figure 10.*

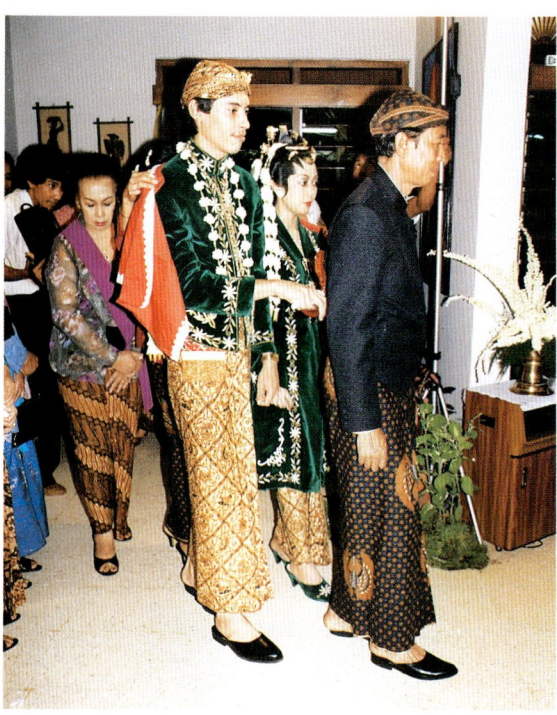

Plate 24. In the course of the panggih *ceremony, the newly "reborn" bridal couple is led by the bride's father and "carried" in a red-and-white* sindur *cloth by her mother. Today the velvet jacket and batik skirt are worn at the religious and traditional rites, while the formal* dodot ageng *is donned for the evening reception (given by the bride's parents) following the* panggih. *This is a reverse of traditional usage. Jakarta, Java, 1984.*

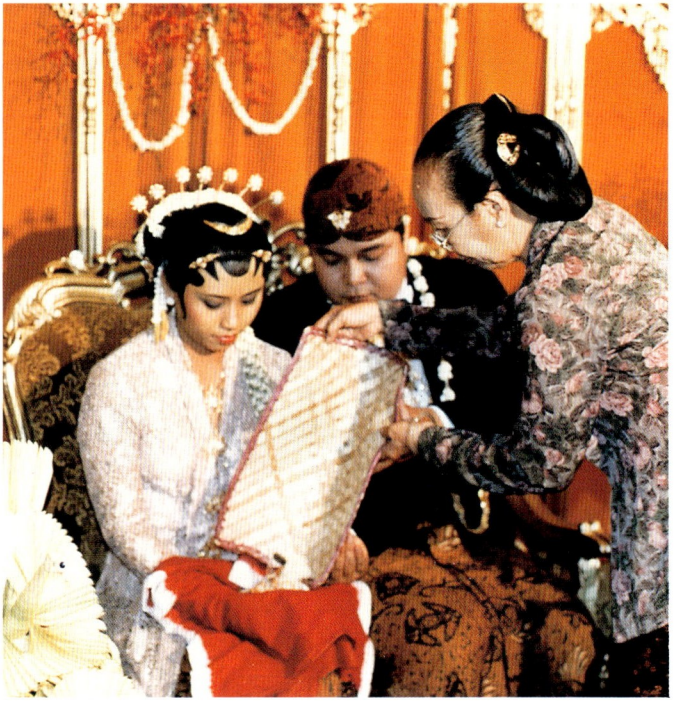

Plate 25. In the ritual pouring of wealth, or kacar-kucur, *the bridegroom endows his bride with "all his wealth." Coins, rice, soya beans and other symbolic items are poured out of a magically empowered pad (*klasa bangka) *into a sacred red-and-white cloth (*sindur) *held in the bride's lap. Jakarta, Java, 1984.*

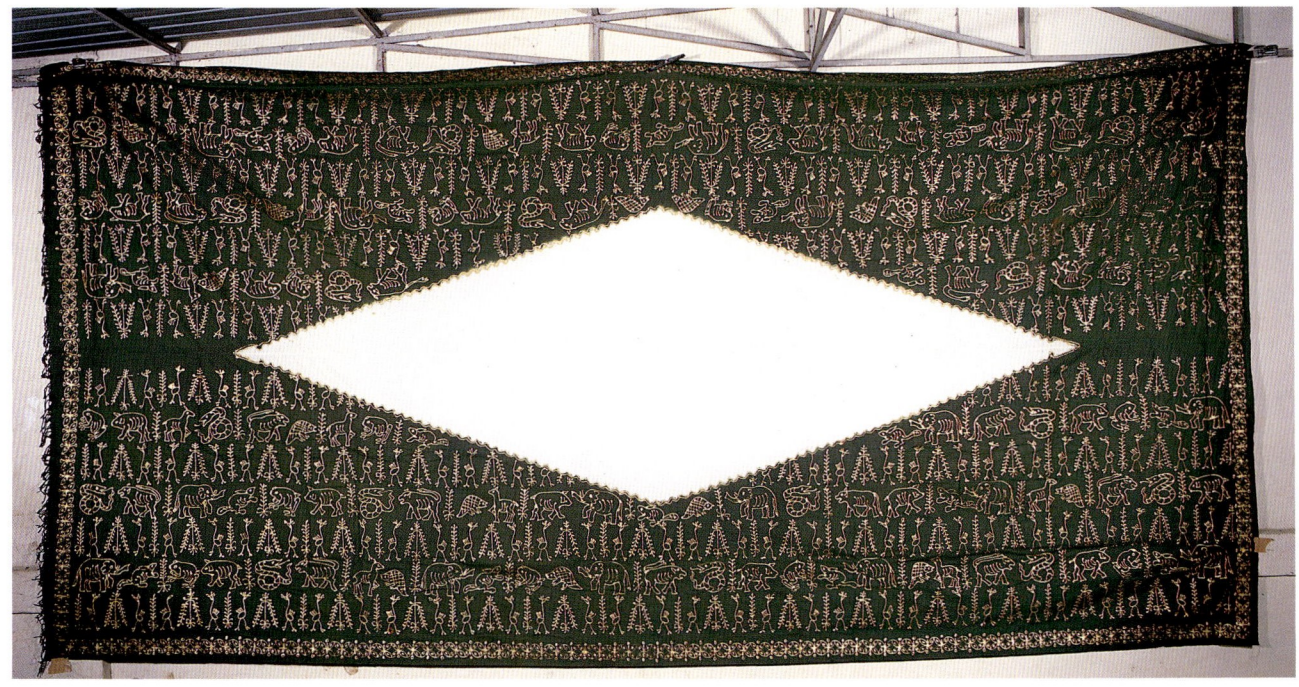

Plate 26a. Wedding cloth in the collection of Princess Kus Supijah, daughter of Paku Buwana XII. The cloth, called dodot bangun tulak alas-alasan, *is decorated with gold-leafed outlines of animals and trees representing forest life, and an uncolored diamond-shaped centerfield. On one end of the cloth the warp threads have been left unwoven to form a fringe. Photographed in Jakarta, Java, 1987.*

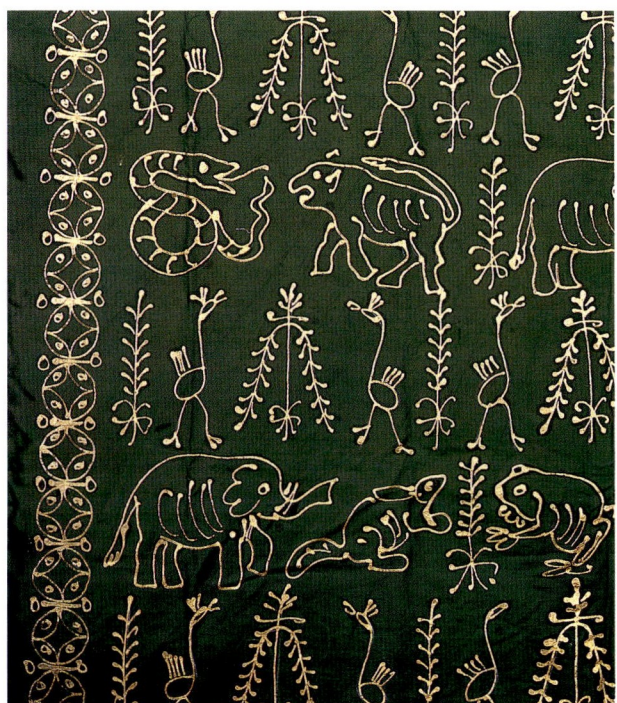

Plate 26b. Detail of the Javanese wedding cloth seen in Plate 26a shows the main motif: a small tree with the two outermost branches bent down to form the slopes of the cosmic mountain.

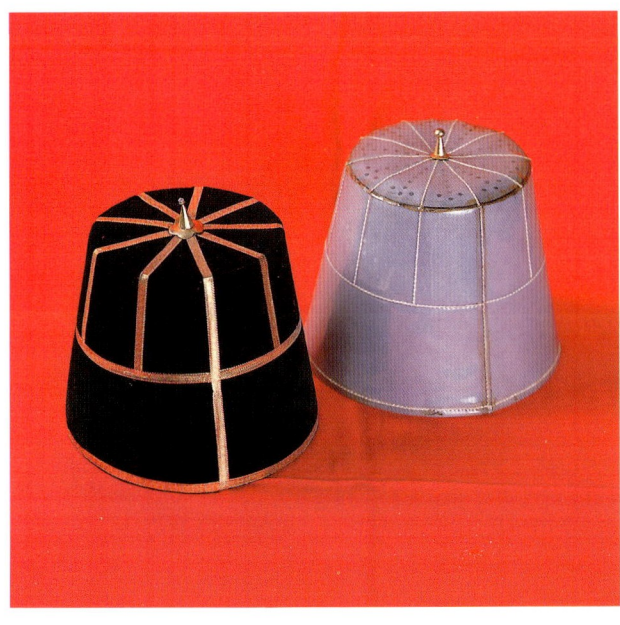

Plate 27. The crown of a bridegroom's kuluk *cap is decorated with lines radiating out from the center like the rays of the sun. These caps were photographed in Jakarta, Java, in 1987.*

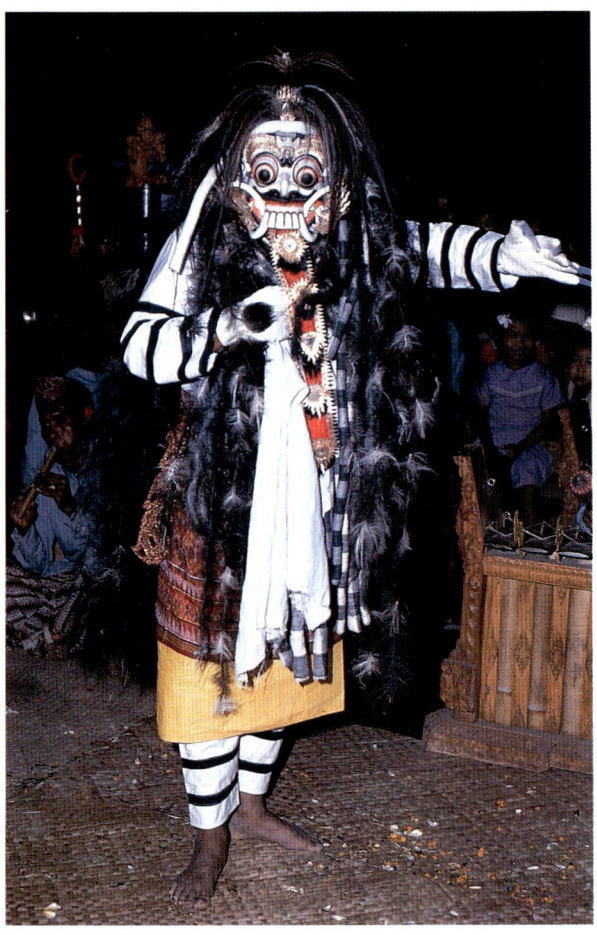
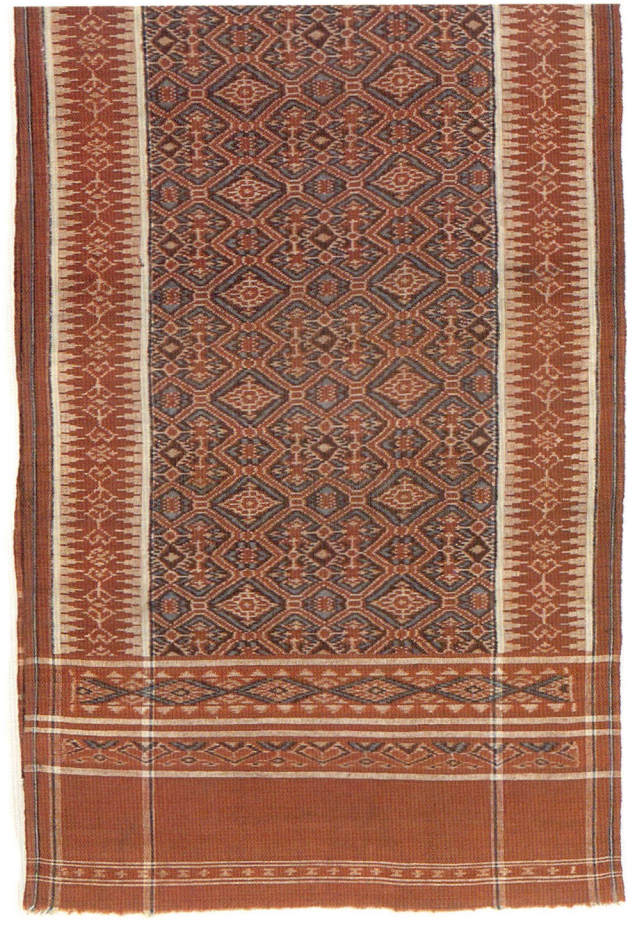
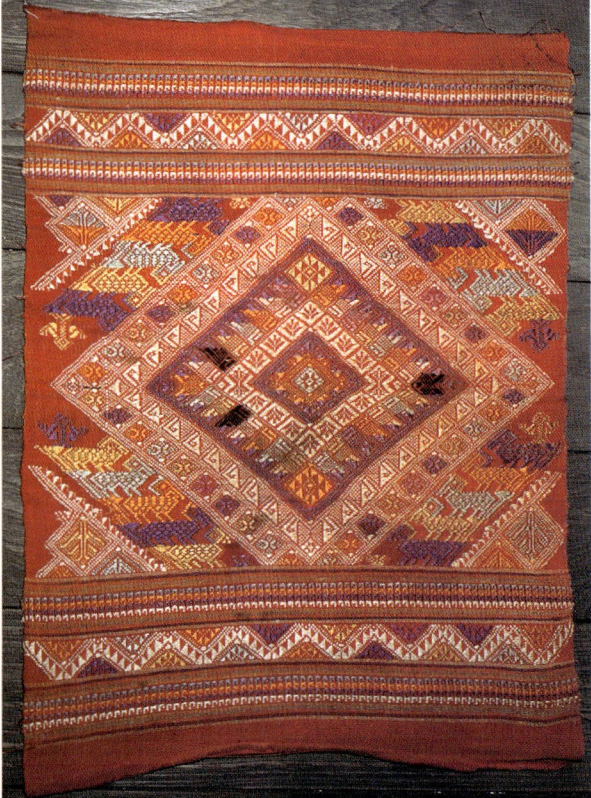

Plate 28 (above left). The witch Rangda wearing a sacred cloth (kamben cepuk) as wraparound skirt. Saba, South Bali, 1970s.

Plate 29 (above right). Sacred cloth with lotus motif (kamben cepuk padma). West Bali, probably Kerambitan. Museum für Völkerkunde, Basel, IIc 14203.

Plate 30 (left). In Thailand gifts to monks are presented on small woven squares known as phaa chiit. This example derives from a Lao source. Collection of Khun Nisa Shaenakul, Bangkok, Thailand.

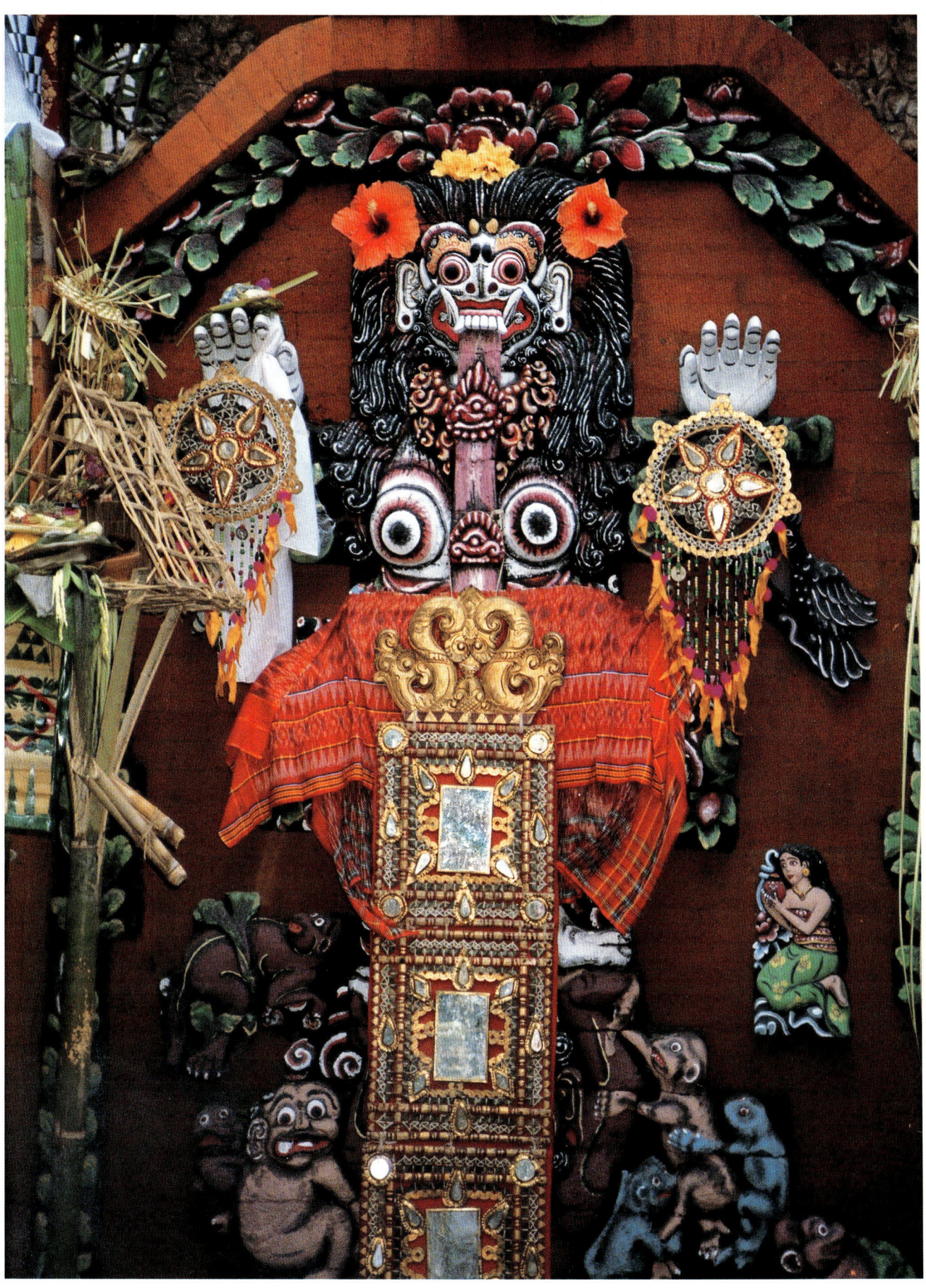

Plate 31 (opposite). The central shrine (gedogan) for the goddess Betari Durga, at the inauguration of the newly renovated temple Pura Kalyangan Setra in the village of Intaran. The relief of Durga (and Rangda) is decorated with two sacred cloths (kamben cepuk), arranged like a wraparound skirt. Near Sanur, South Bali. June 22, 1988.

Plate 32 (right). Purse for betel nut (bola nafo) in South Nias style. Also recorded as bola ni'o tarawa, "purse in a lace pattern" (Fischer 1909: xxxviii, 4). Rijksmuseum voor Volkenkunde, Leiden, No. 115/3. Gift to the museum by C. De Grijs in 1870.

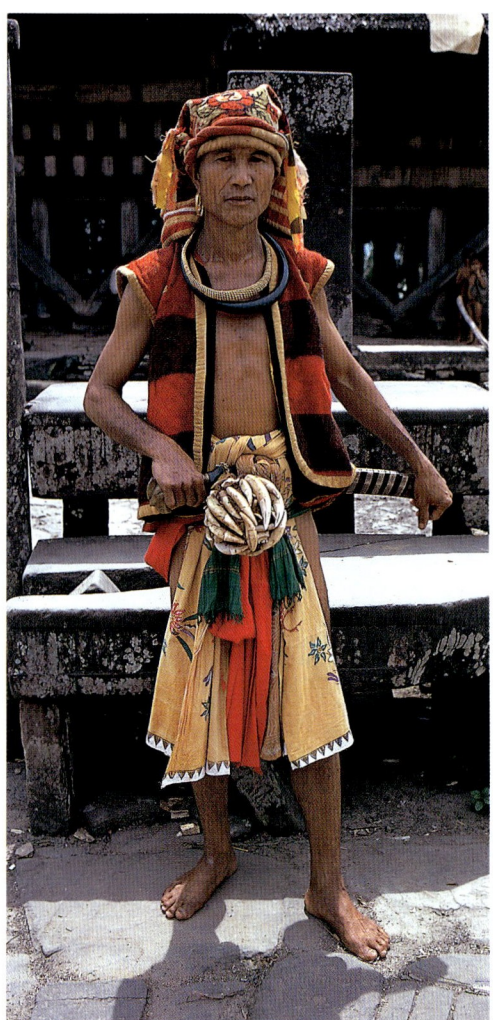

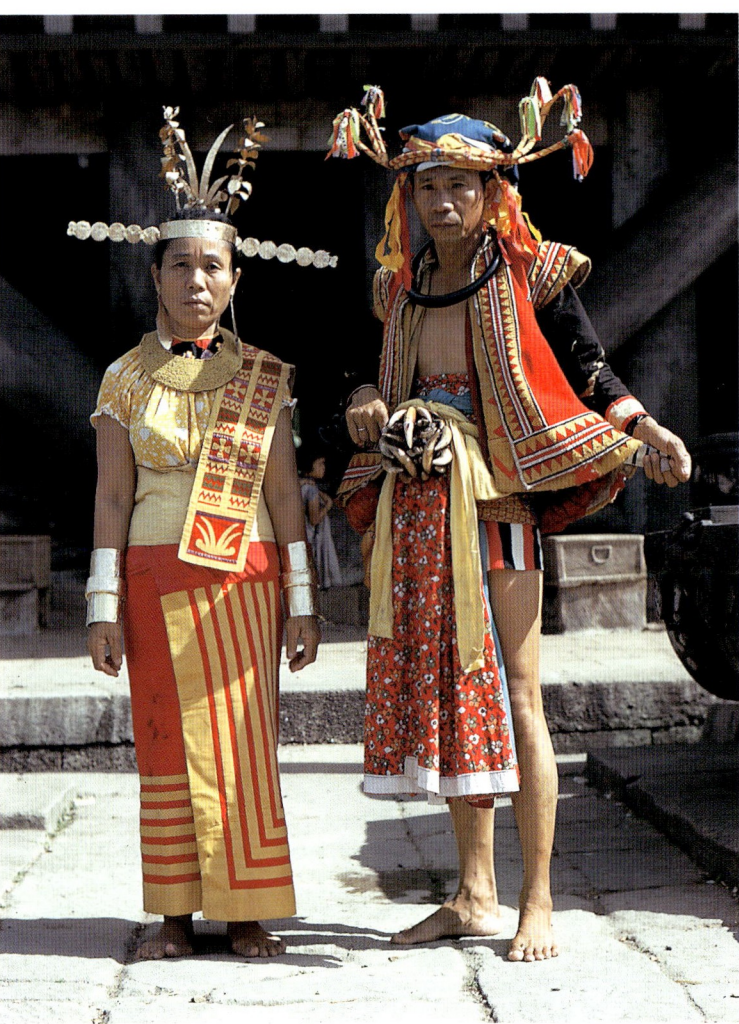

Plate 33. A man in ceremonial attire wearing golden ornaments stands in front of the ruler's clothes rack (naha gamagama nama). Hiliamaetaniha village, South Nias, 1974.

Plate 34. Contemporary attire worn by Ama Bazanalui Fau and his wife, the late Ina Sarifiti Nehe, of Bawömataluo village. She wears a lembe over her shoulder. Her husband, who is a relative of the man seen in Figure 9, wears a modern adaptation of the traditional headdress; but as can be seen, golden ornaments have disappeared from Nias ceremonial dress. South Nias, 1974.

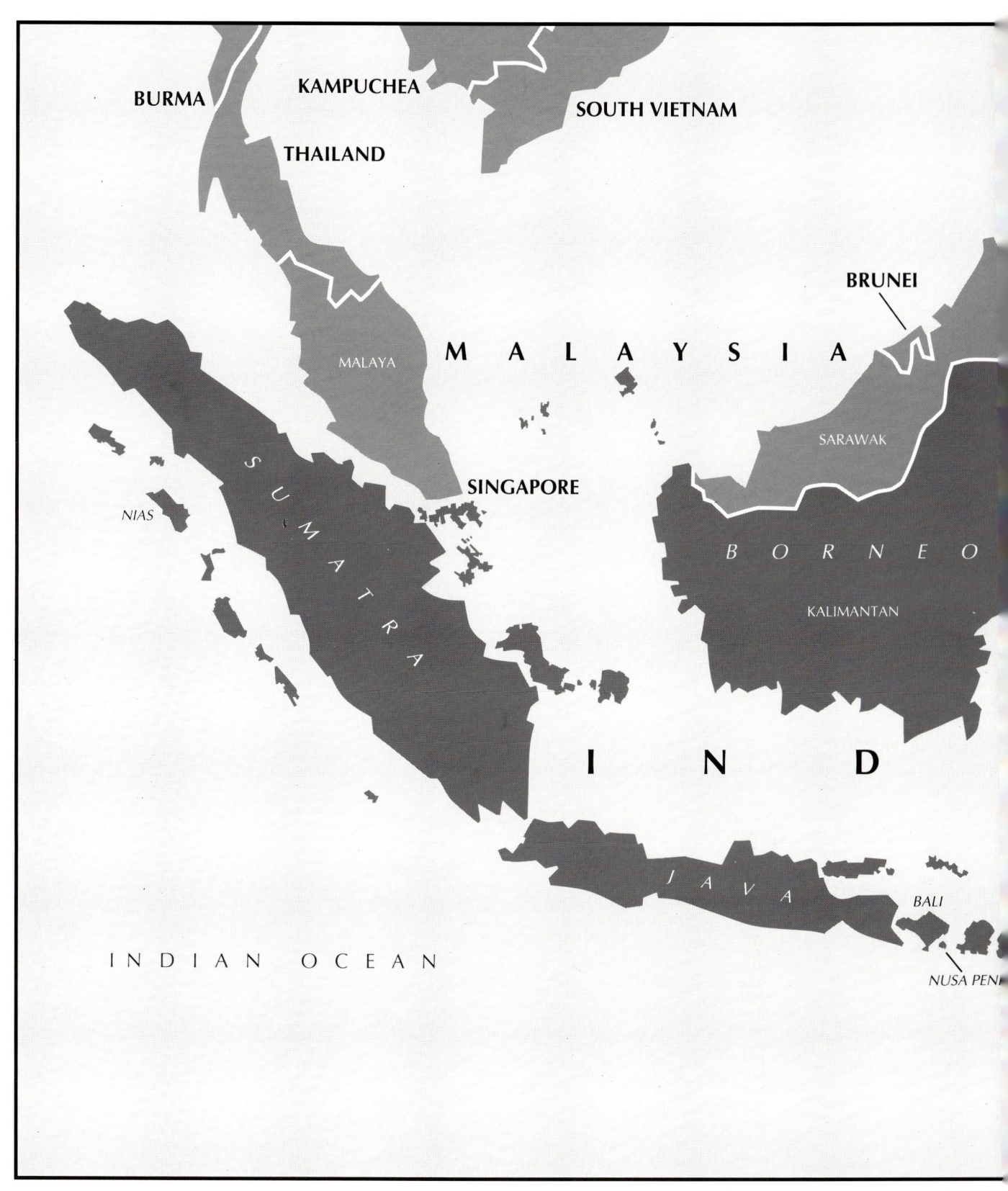

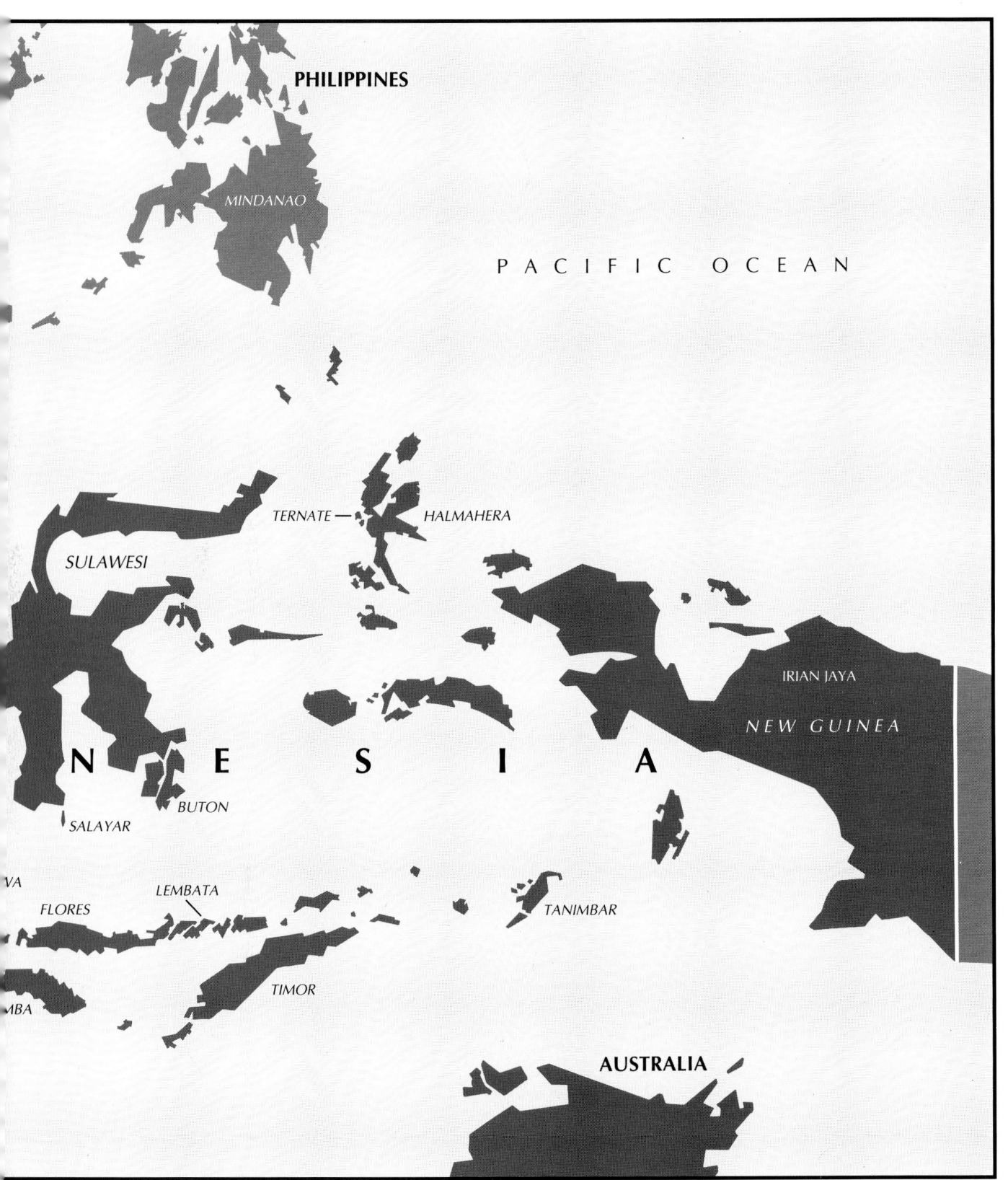

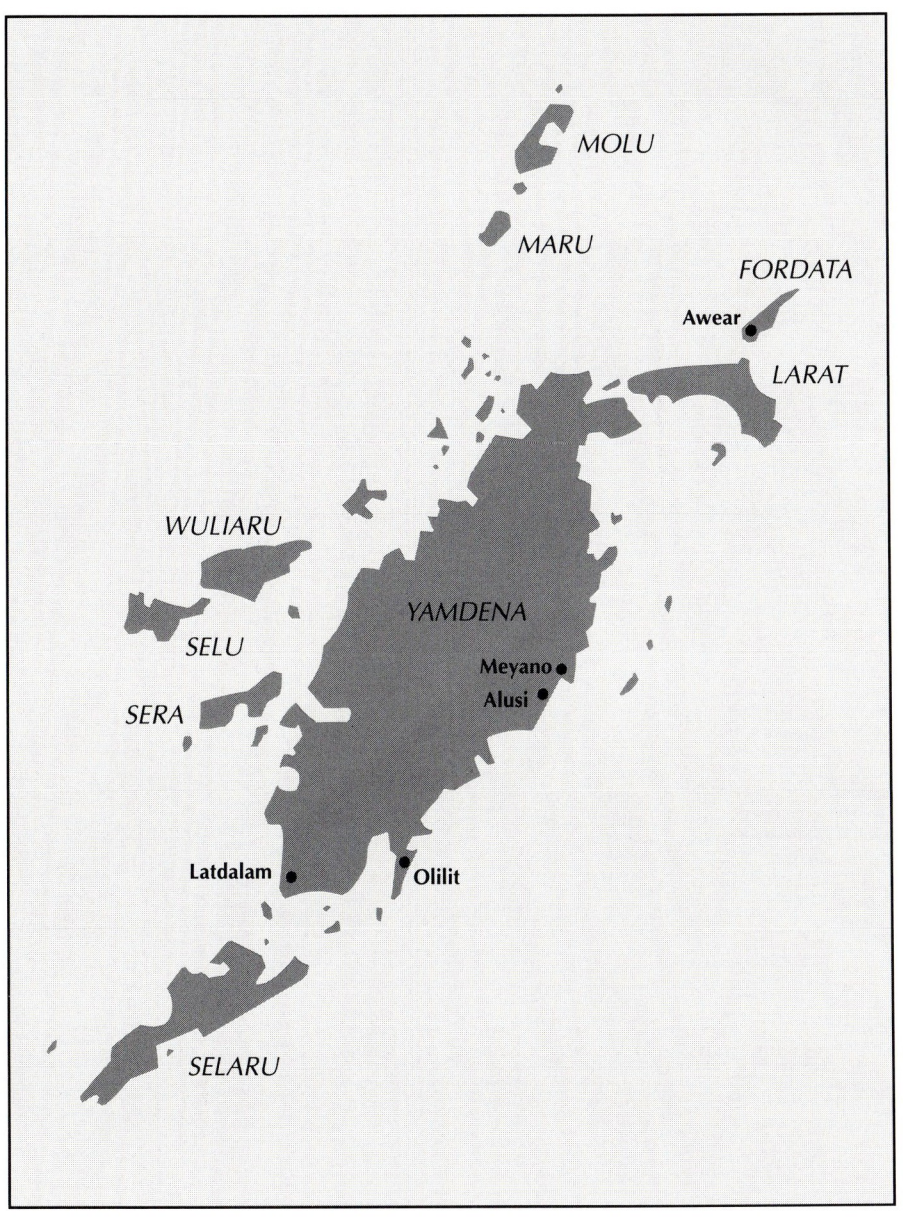

The Tanimbar Islands.

Flags and Half-Moons
Tanimbarese Textiles in an "Engendered" System of Valuables

Susan McKinnon

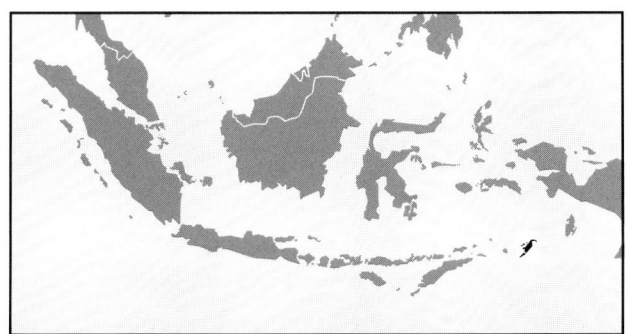

The Tanimbar Islands lie just beyond the great arc that forms the Lesser Sunda Islands—beyond the point where it veers northward into the central Moluccas.[1] One might also say that Tanimbar forms the furthermost extension, and last bastion, of the great textile traditions found in the Lesser Sundas; the islands further to the east and north—Aru, Kei, and of course New Guinea—have never produced woven textiles. It would even seem that Tanimbar is located at the point where the impetus to a cultural complexity involving cloth begins to wane. There are no myths about textiles; weavers observe no taboos or rituals when producing their cloth; and knowledge of the various processes involved in weaving is not the secret or privileged knowledge of any social group or class. Moreover, the different types of textiles, as well as the motifs they display, are not used—as they are in many parts of Lesser Sundas—to differentiate class, rank or status.[2] Nor have they ever been used as an insignia of membership in a particular house or village.[3] Given this initial rather negative characterization of textiles in Tanimbar, one might well wonder what is left for an anthropologist to write about, especially one whose expertise does not extend to the technical side of weaving.

As a way of posing the question of the significance of textiles—and, more broadly, of all valuables classified as "female"—I would begin by considering certain types of death payments. There are two points at which, in the past, Tanimbarese paid what might be called bloodwealth: firstly, when a man murdered another man or woman (outside of warfare); and secondly, when a noble woman married a slave (in which case her family considered her as good as murdered). In such cases, the relatives of the murderer, or the masters of the slave, were required to make a prestation for each part of the body of the slain person or the ex-noble (now, technically dead) woman: an imported Chinese earthenware water jug for the head; an antique gold breast pendant for the breast; an

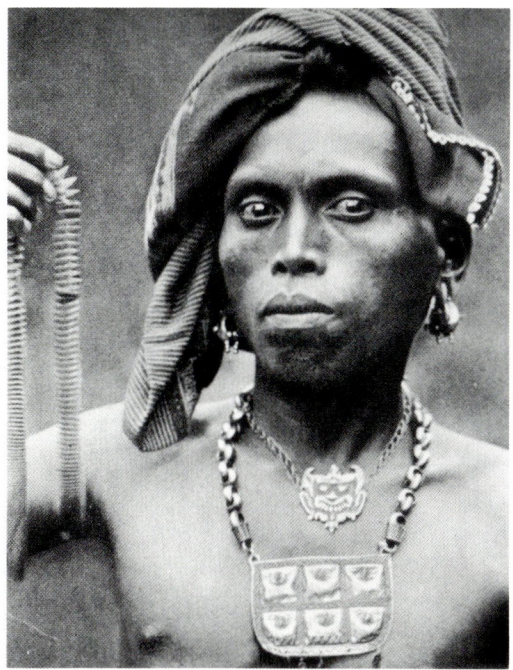

Figure 1. A man wearing a pair of male earrings, two gold breast pendants, and an antique sarong (bakan mnanat) *as a headdress. From Drabbe 1940: between pages 320,321.*

elephant's tusk for the spine; an antique sword for the ribs; gold earrings for the eyes, the hair, the hands and the feet; and so on (Drabbe 1940:197-98,208). What is remarkable about these payments is that they are comprised of valuables that are all classified as "male." Absent are all "female" valuables—including woven textiles.

Why, then, when Tanimbarese represent the body of a dead person under such circumstances, do they do so exclusively with "male" valuables? Every other exchange in Tanimbar—no matter what the occasion—includes both "male" and "female" valuables: the party that gives male valuables can always expect to receive female valuables in return. This is true even in the exchanges that are carried out in the event of an ordinary death, in which case, moreover, female valuables of all types play an especially important role (Drabbe 1925:35-42). So why do female valuables fail to make their appearance in the bloodwealth exchange? The provisional and obvious answer is because it is not an exchange. It is a one-sided affair, a kind of one-hand-clapping. It represents not only the death of a person, but also, and more importantly, the death of a relationship. There will be no continuity of life, no continuity of relationship, and no further exchange between the relatives of the murderer and the murdered, or those of the noble woman and the slave.

But there is a deeper connection between male valuables and death which I would like to explore: that is, why male valuables, in themselves, are such an apt representation of death. To the extent that they are, the further question arises as to whether female valuables are then a representation of life. The answer, however, is not simple.

Consequently, this essay has a number of aims: to place textiles within the broader system of the male and female valuables that are used in the exchanges that mark every phase of Tanimbarese life; to investigate the different qualities of these valuables—what they are saying about what it means to be male or female; and, ultimately, to explore how these qualities are associated with the forces of death and those of life. I do this in the belief that it is impossible to understand what textiles mean without seeing them in a much larger context of meanings. In this paper I hope to provide something of that larger context within which the very special qualities of Tanimbarese textiles can be appreciated.

A World "Engendered"

From early on, observers of Indonesian societies have noted the pervasiveness with which gender has been used to differentiate activities, social groups, and the goods and valuables used in exchanges between social groups. In this regard Tanimbar is no exception: here everything, or practically everything, has a gender.

There are very few unisex activities in Tanimbar: most activities are either male (*brana*) or female (*vata*). Men hunt and do the deep sea fishing; they clear and burn off the gardens; and they make palmwine. Men build houses and boats; they negotiate marriage exchanges; hunt heads (or used to) and, on occasion, still engage in warfare. Women, on the other hand, fish on the reef, and do the planting, weeding, and harvesting of gardens. Women carry food and water, cook, and take care of children. Finally, women plait baskets and weave textiles.

Social groups, like activities, also have a gender—although, here, the gender is relative. The main social unit in Tanimbar is the "house" (*rahan*) to which members may be affiliated patrilaterally or matrilaterally, depending on the relative completion of a complex series of affinal exchanges. The men in any house have wife-givers who are considered "male" and wife-takers who are considered "female." This characterization makes sense from the perspective of a brother and a sister: the house of the brother (the wife-giver) is male, while the house into which the sister marries (the wife-taker) is female. The position is obviously relative, since the same brother will be the wife-taker (and therefore female) to his own wife-givers. In the end, wife-giving and wife-taking houses are linked along extended pathways of exchange that follow the course of female blood lines (McKinnon 1983:64-77).

Finally, the objects that pass between wife-takers and wife-givers in marriage exchanges (which continue throughout the lifetime of the couple, their children and grandchildren) also have a gender. Male goods and valuables move from wife-taker to wife-giver, while female goods and valuables move in the opposite direction, following the women who move in marriage. In everyday life and on festive occasions, wife-takers give the products of male activity—meat, fish, and palmwine—to their wife-givers, while the latter reciprocate with the products of female activity—garden produce and betel nut. Similarly, in the more formal marriage prestations, the gifts of the wife-takers consist of male valuables, which include a particular kind of earring, gold breast pendants, elephant tusks and swords. These are reciprocated by the gifts of the wife-givers, which consist of female valuables and include another type of earring, bead necklaces, shell armbands and textiles.

The Relative Values of Valuables

Each particular type of valuable can be said to have an opposite sex counterpart. By examining what differentiates each set of male and female valuables, it will be possible to understand something of the qualities the Tanimbarese see as essential to entities considered male and female.

Several comments should be made, however, regarding the nature of this analysis. First, it is primarily concerned with the contrast between male and female valuables, not with the differences in various grades of any particular type of male or female valuable—a topic that would require a paper in itself. Secondly, this is an analysis of valuables that in the context of affinal exchanges are categorized as male and female. It is not an examination of what men and women wear. Not only is there a whole range of other decorations that were formerly worn by men and women (Drabbe 1940:20-33); but some male valuables (breast pendants and, formerly, earrings) are occasionally worn by women, just as some female valuables (primarily cloth) are worn by men. The ways in which male and female identities are constructed through dress is far too complex a topic to discuss in the context of this paper.

Perhaps the most easily contrasted set of male and female valuables is that of earrings: *loran*, which are thought of as male earrings; and *kmena*, which are thought of as female earrings. As with all valuables, there are many different grades of both *loran* and *kmena*. Some are very fine, antique pieces with names and histories; others are newer, nameless, and rather coarse in their construction. The male *loran* (Figs. 1,2) may be made of silver or gold, but they are all of one basic form: pear-shaped, with an opening slit through the center that is sometimes filled with a swatch of red

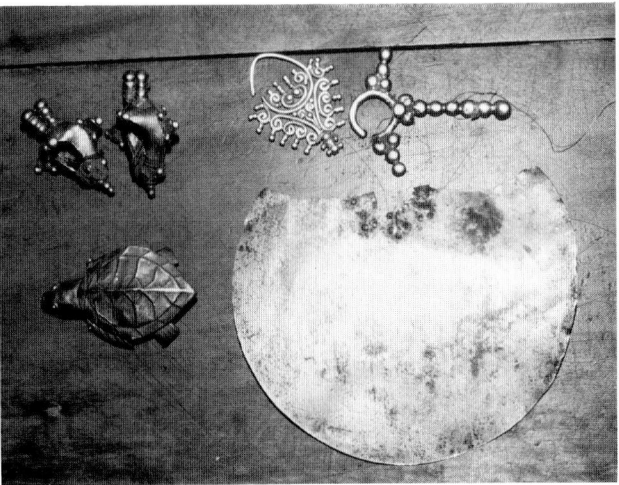

*Figure 2. Clockwise from the top left: a pair of male earrings (*loran*); an odd-matched pair of female earrings (*kmena*) including a "shield" *kmena* and a "pebble" *kmena*; a gold piece in the shape of a disc or "moon"; and a turtle-shaped gold piece. Private Collection.*

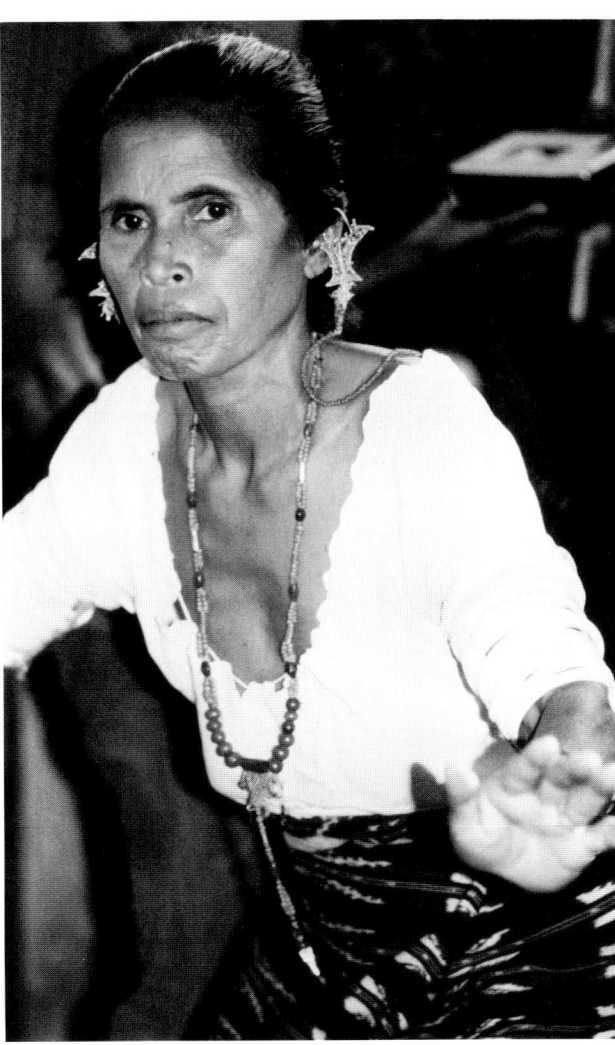

*Figure 3. A woman wearing a pair of female earrings ("shield" *kmena*) linked by a strand of beads, a female necklace, a pair of shell armbands, and a sarong of the* bakan inelak *type with flag and half-moon motifs. Tanimbar, 1979.*

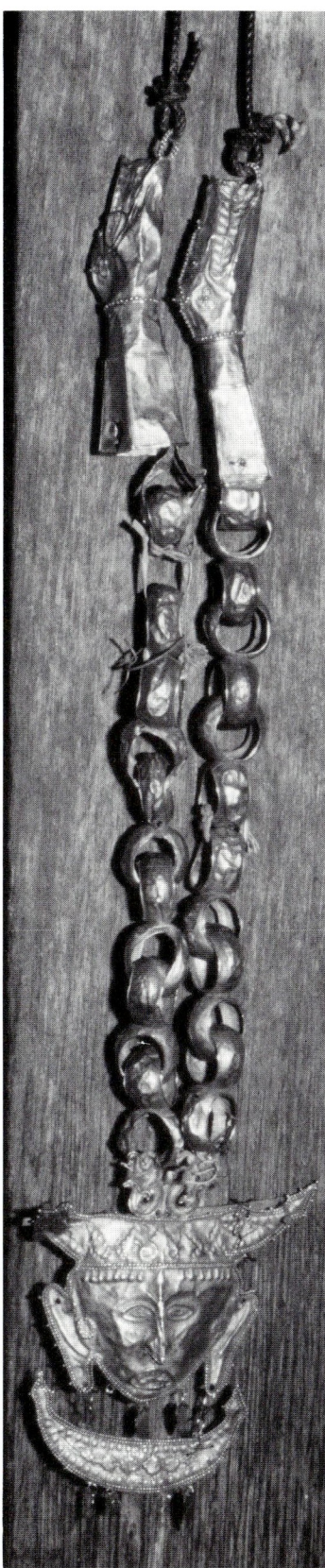

Figure 4. A breast pendant showing a boat form suspended from the face of a man. The piece boasts a gold link chain and a clasp with "shrimp" figures. Private Collection.

European cloth, which is said to make the metal "flash like lightening" (nfitik). They also have small appendages or "eruptions" (kamoa) that protrude from the top, the base, and the sides—in the latter case called "wings" (manin). While loran may appear to us to take an essentially female form, what is important here is not graphics, but rather tactile qualities. The significant characteristics of loran include their solidity, their density, and their weight. This becomes evident when they are contrasted with female earrings, kmena—especially the most valuable type, the "shield" earring (kmena ngelya)—which is a dance of fillagreed curvilinear forms composed of thin gold or silver wires (Figs. 2,3). The airy, light and open qualities of the "shield" kmena are only slightly muted in the second type—the "stone" or "pebble" earring (kmena vatu), which is formed by a graceful clustering of small dots of gold or silver around an open circle of wire (Fig. 2). In addition, some highly prized kmena have a string of beads (kmena ni lean) that connects the two earrings of the pair and is worn across the woman's back (Fig. 3). In place of the solid density of the male earrings, here there is a composition of light, swirling small bits of metal which dovetail into and around one another. The composite and fluid qualities of female earrings are further accentuated by the addition of the connecting string of beads.

Necklaces also come in two basic forms: male breast pendants, which are made of solid, hammered or cast gold—and, in fact, are simply called "gold" (masa); and female bead necklaces (marumat). The breast pendants most often represent a human face (or full human figure), alone or in conjunction with horn, boat or moon motifs (Figs. 1,4). But they are also sometimes found in the form of a simple, flat round gold disk, a golden kris handle, or in the shape of some animal, such as a turtle (Fig. 2). The most valuable gold pendants boast a large gold link chain (wika sitana) and clasps, which are thought to represent "shrimps," or snguran (Fig. 4). Female necklaces, or marumat, are made of imported Venetian glass beads or, most often, of beads made from sard, a variety of reddish-orange chalcedony, known in Indonesia as muti-salah. Marumat proper should be distinguished from the simple, single strand bead necklace, called a "tie for the neck" (kakeat rela), formerly worn by both men and women (Fig. 5). Marumat, which are far more valuable, are composed of double or triple strands of beads, joined together at regular intervals by a larger bead or thin tube of gold. From the center of the necklace there hangs a triangular mass (laun) of beads and fragments of gold that have been woven together (Fig. 3). The most valuable of marumat are those known as ungrela, which have an additional long strand of beads—called a "tail" (kikurn)—that hangs down the back of the woman. While male necklaces are of solid gold, often of a single integral piece, or at least all of the same material, female necklaces are made up of tiny pieces of heterogeneous materials—beads and gold—which are strung together into two or three strands that are alternately united and separated.

The third pair of contrasted valuables include elephant's tusks (*lela*), which are considered male, and shell armbands (*sislau*), which are considered female. Obviously, an elephant's tusk is long and hard—a heavy, dense, penetrating sort of object. Tusks are valued in accordance with their length: the longest ones, which measure a full double arm span of a man (or more) are most highly prized [cf. Maxwell's comments (1981) on the role of elephant's tusks in Flores]. Unlike the tusks, the female shell armbands come in pairs, each consisting of ten shell rings that have been cut by Tanimbarese women from a variety of *Conus* shell, rounded and polished, and then lashed together along a thin bamboo lath (Fig. 3). Again, there are various grades of armbands. The most valuable fit on the upper arms of a woman and have a dark ring made from coconut shell or thick Venetian glass added at the top. Other less valuable sets have no black rings or fit only on the lower forearms, or on the arms of young girls. The contrast between elephant's tusks and shell armbands is evident. The tusks are single, whole, uncut pieces, while the armbands are a composite of numerous rings, each cut from a different shell. The tusks are hard and penetrating, while the armbands are open, encircling, and encompassing.

The characteristics implicit in the contrast between tusks and armbands become even more evident in considering the next pair of valuables, swords (*suruk*) and cloth (*eman-bakan*, "loincloth-sarong"). Even if Tanimbarese may not know what a tusk is to an elephant, they do know what a sword is to a man (Fig. 5). Tanimbarese say the swords were of "Portugis" origin, although there were never any Portuguese in Tanimbar. What this means is that they are extremely old and, indeed, the few swords left in Tanimbar are such antique pieces that they are no longer used in exchange, but rather kept as heirloom valuables. A sword is a long, hard, sharp metal weapon. It is used to kill people and sever heads from bodies: it is, in short, an instrument of death. While swords are the epitome of fierce inflexibility, cloth is the epitome of softness and pliability. While swords are meant to

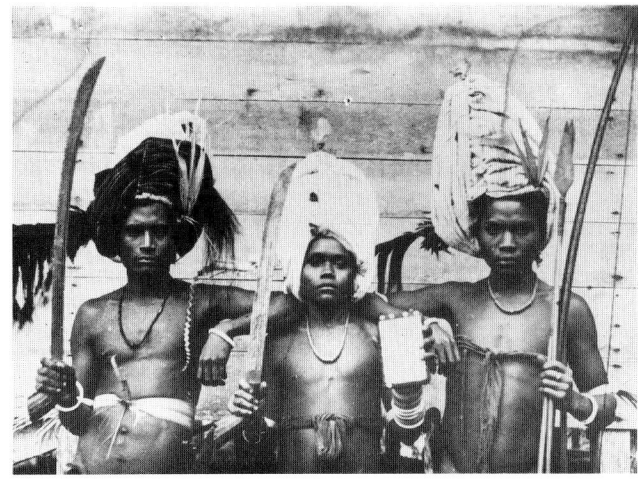

Figure 5. Men with swords. They are wearing male earrings and single strands of beads. The two men on the right are also wearing chestcloths. Early 20th century. Photographer unknown.

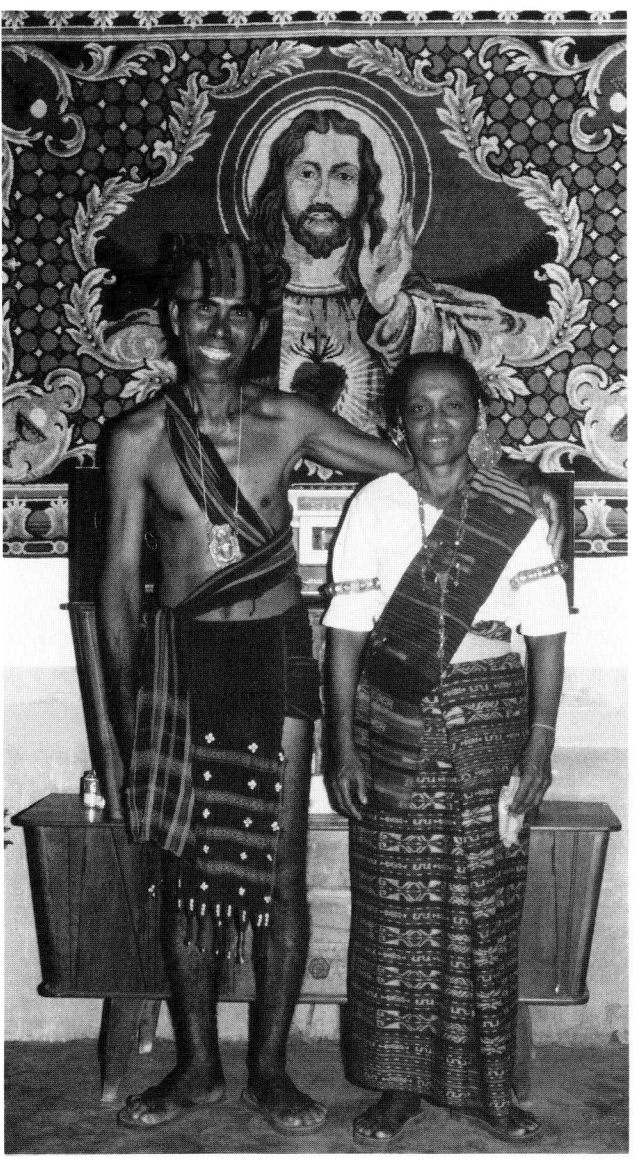

Figure 6. A Tanimbarese couple in full dress, 1979. The man wears a gold breast pendant, two loincloths (one tied in the traditional manner, the other in an innovative fashion around his chest), and a sarong as a headdress. The woman wears a bakan inelak *(with flag and half-moon motifs) as a skirt and has a* bakan maran *draped across her shoulders. She is also adorned with a female necklace and two unique heirloom gold pieces—a pair of armbands and a pair of disc earrings.*

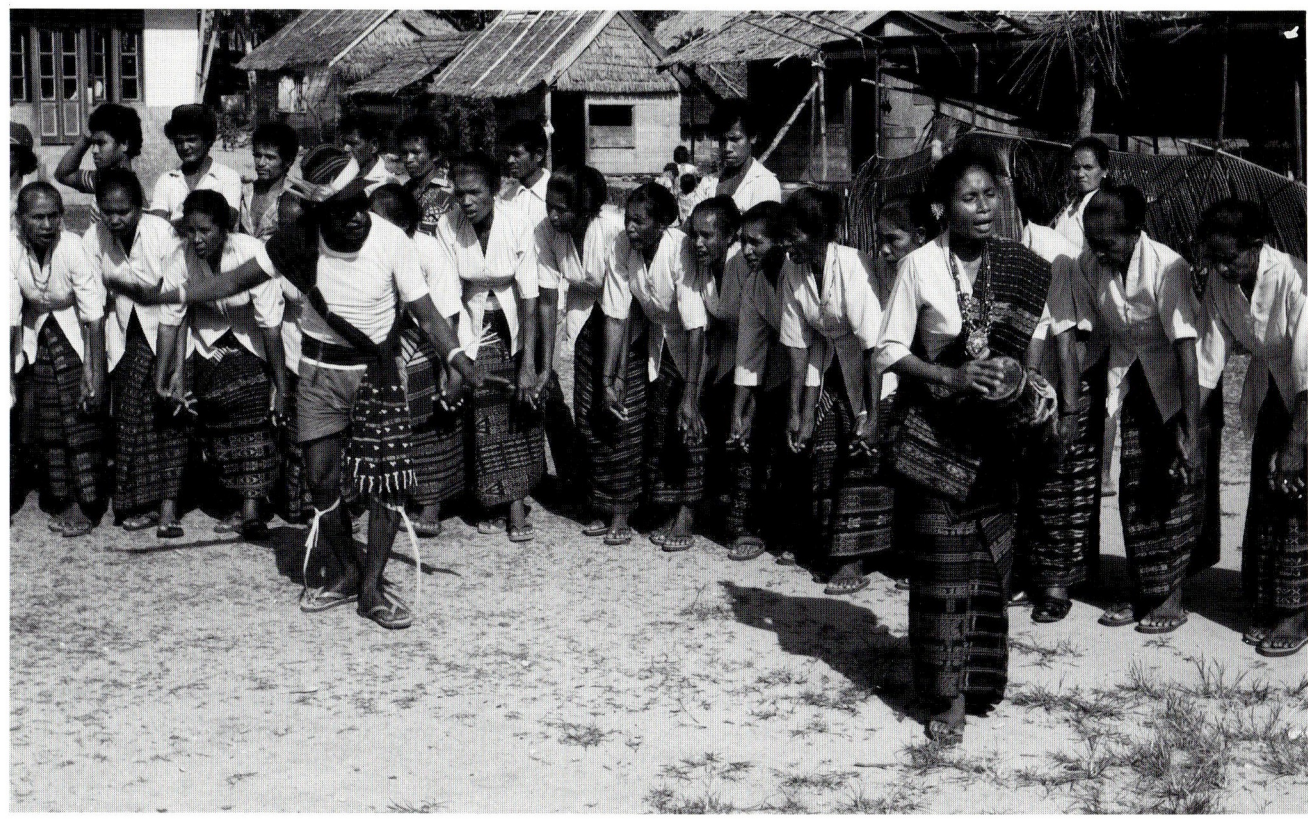

Figure 7. People from the villages of Temin and Weratan (on Sera) dancing in the village of Latdalam, on the southwest coast of Yamdena, in 1980. The man in the center is wearing a loincloth tied around his chest with two gold pieces hanging from it. The woman is wearing "shield" earrings, both a male and a female necklace, and two striped sarongs (bakan maran).

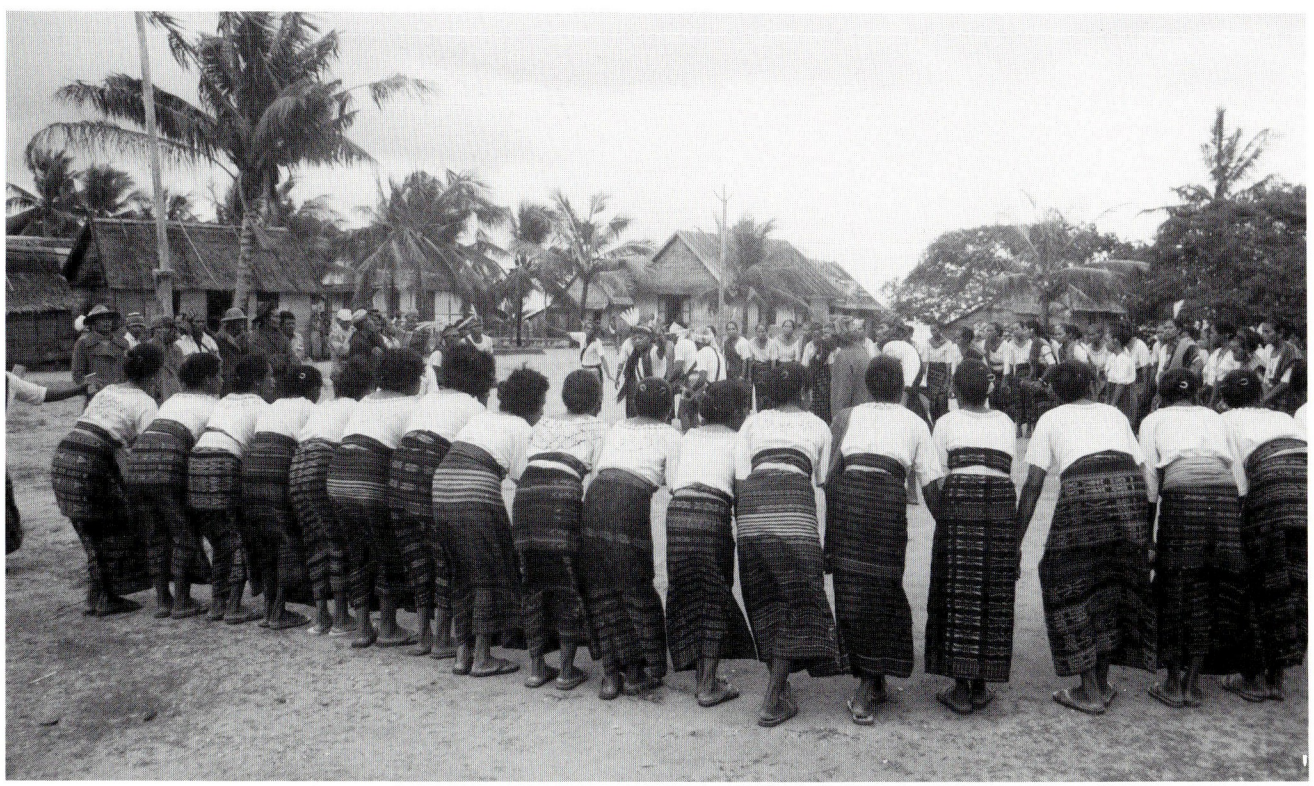

Figure 8. A circle of women from the villages of Temin and Weratan (on Sera) dancing in the village of Latdalam, on the southwest coast of Yamdena, in 1980. The picture shows a variety of Tanimbarese sarongs.

penetrate and sever, cloth is meant to encompass, encircle, and bind.

All indigenous textiles in Tanimbar are woven by women and are considered to be female valuables—despite the fact that some kinds are worn by men.[4] Of those worn by women there are presently two major types. The first is a sarong (*bakan*) made from two tubes of cloth joined together at the selvedges. The resulting cylindrical form is from four to six feet long. There are three main kinds of *bakan*, differentiated by the relative distribution of the warp ikat and colored bands that run through the indigo-blue or soot-black ground. The second type of textile worn by women is a latter-day invention—a small piece of cloth known as a *shal*, which is worn over the shoulder. In contrast to the *bakan*, which are predominantly dark, the *shal* is woven in "living color"—the brighter and more fluorescent, the better. Sarongs are still worn today, primarily on ritual and festive occasions. In full dress, a woman will wear one *bakan* as a skirt (folded over at the waist, and secured with a cloth tie), one or two *bakan* draped diagonally across the shoulders, and sometimes another wrapped around the hips (Pl. 1, Figs. 6-8). Often, the modern-day *shal* replaces the sarong draped across the shoulders.

The two forms of textiles traditionally worn by men include a loincloth (*eman*) and a chestcloth (*sinuun*). The *eman* is a narrow, nine-foot-long strip of plain indigo-dyed cloth embellished with ikat designs—and often red cloth appliqué work and small shells—at the very end (Figs. 6,7). Loincloths were woven by Tanimbarese women and also imported from the southwestern islands of Babar and Luang (Drabbe 1940:21). They are sometimes still worn today on ritual occasions, but rarely in the traditional manner. The chestcloths, which have practically disappeared, are composed of two woven panels joined together along their selvedges; they are both considerably shorter and broader than the loincloths (Drabbe 1940:22). It is unclear how the overall designs of chestcloths were patterned (Fig. 5).

Since these types of men's textiles are no longer woven by Tanimbarese women, nor imported, the few that still exist are kept in houses as heirloom valuables, and are not circulated in exchanges. However, the women's sarongs of all three types (as well as the shoulderclothcloth, *shal*) are still being woven. In fact, the textile production is quite active, partially because cloth is an important valuable used in marriage exchanges, but also because it is the only valuable—of any type—for which there is still an on-going supply.

In sum, the contrast between what Tanimbarese characterize as male and female valuables can be drawn along a number of dimensions. First of all, male valuables are hard metal and ivory objects: they are solid, dense and heavy. Female valuables—even when they are made of hard substances—deny that hardness, solidity and density. They are, on the contrary, light, fillagreed and open forms. Secondly, male valuables are of one piece, the epitome of singleness and permanence, but also of inflexibility and immobility. Female valuables, however, are pieced together from a myriad of elements. They speak more of multiplicity, flexibility, mobility and, perhaps, impermanence. The density and weight of male earrings contrast with the light, delicate and open fillagree patterns of female earrings. The unity of a man's gold breast pendant finds its counterpart in the multiplicity of beads and small bits of gold which are strung together into a woman's necklace, just as the unique solidity of an elephant's tusk or a sword contrasts with the numerous open rings that are lashed together to form shell armbands, not to mention the multiplicity of yarns which must be woven together to form a finished textile. Finally, the long, pointed and cutting qualities of male valuables such as tusks and swords complement the encircling, receptive and binding qualities of women's necklaces, armbands and tubes of woven cloth.[5]

In looking at the contrast between swords and cloth—or any pair of male and female valuables—we can understand the ways in which they can be seen to epitomize the most essential characteristics of what it means to be male and female in Tanimbar. The outright sexual symbolism is evident enough. But there are at least two other sets of values that are expressed through these valuables. One is the relation between life and death, which will be dealt with later. The other is the relationship between permanent, enduring entities on the one hand, and those things that relate them—that make the ties that bind—on the other.

Like the valuables that speak of their qualities, men occupy single, permanent and fixed places in the world: they remain in the houses to which they are born. The place of women in their natal house, however, is impermanent—for they are destined to move to the house of their husband upon marriage. Thus, when people are asked the sex of a newborn infant, they answer either "house master" (*rahan duan*) if it is a boy, or "stranger" (*mangun*) if it is a girl. The identification of males with a permanent, fixed position, and females with an impermanence born of mobility, is also evident in the fact that men who are "lifted" or adopted out of their natal house to become the head of another house, are considered (from the vantage point of the members of their natal house) to be "female" (*vata*) or "like a woman." In contrast with males, then, the place of females is always shifting and composite: their role—like the lashings of armshells, the threads of a necklace, or the yarns of a textile—is to bind together a multiplicity of discrete houses through the encircling flow of the life-blood they bear.[6]

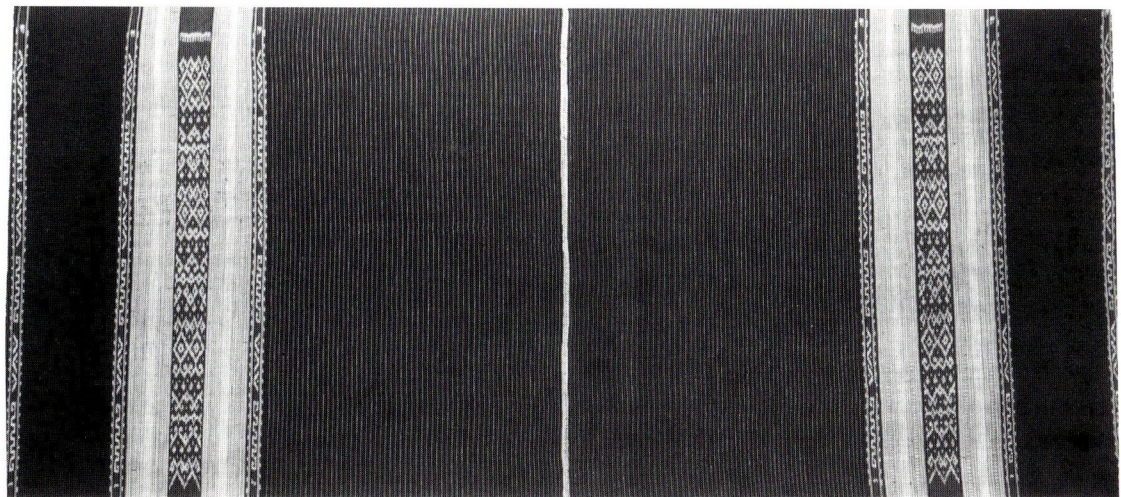

Figure 9. Antique sarong (bakan mnanat) *from the village of Meyano on the east coast of Yamdena. Collection of author.*

Figure 10. Antique sarong (bakan mnanat) *from the village of Alusi on the east coast of Yamdena. Collection of author.*

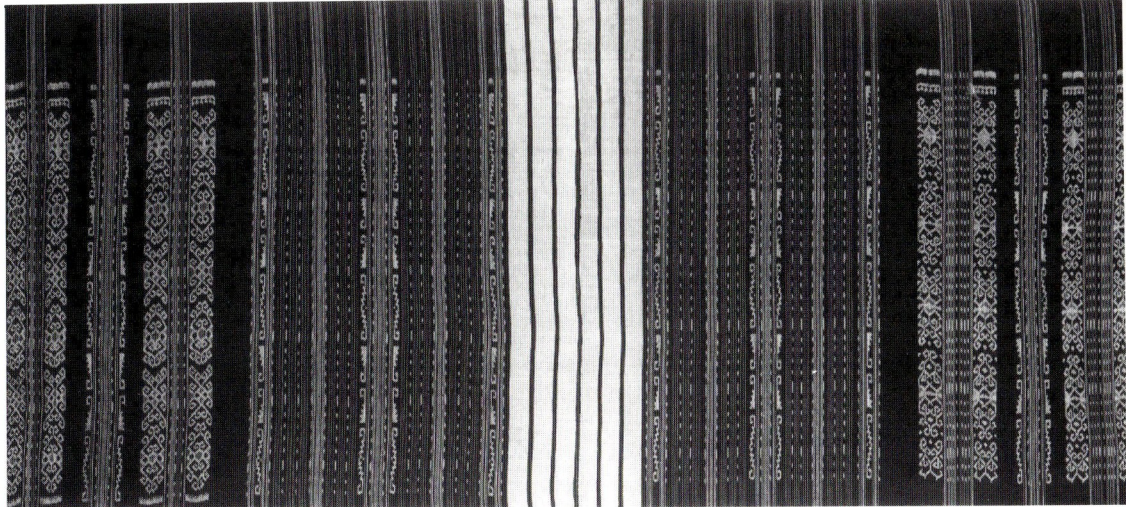

Figure 11. Striped sarong (bakan maran) *with a "half rainbow" pattern from the village of Latdalam on the southwest coast of Yamdena. Collection of author.*

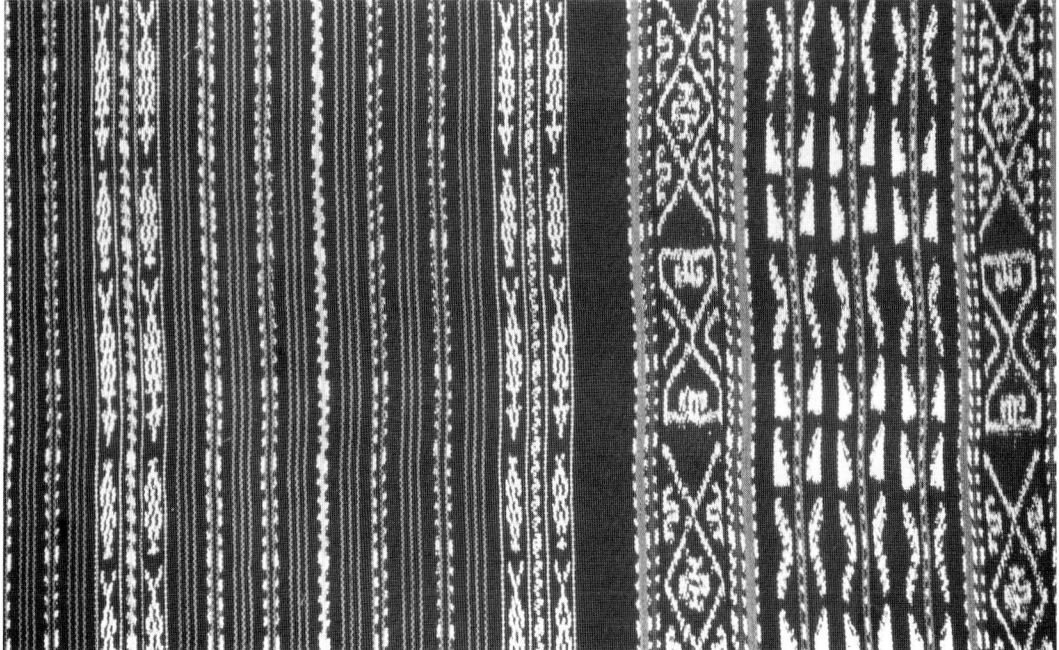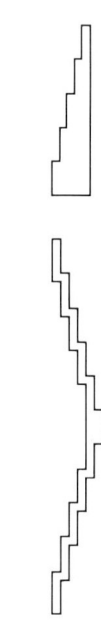

Figure 12. Part of one side of a sarong, bakan maran faduur, *with a "full rainbow" pattern and a "flock" of flags and half-moons between the two "rainbows" from the village of Awear on Fordata. Collection of author.*

Figure 13. Flag and half-moon.

Flags and Half-Moons in "Female" Textiles

The composite and binding qualities characteristic of females have been noted in connection with all the female valuables looked at so far. But this tying together, this binding of heterogeneous, complementary elements is also very much at play in textiles. This is true, not simply in the obvious way that one must weave together a great number of yarns to make a textile, but also in a less obvious way: that is, in the way that Tanimbarese women construct the ikat motifs with which they decorate their sarongs. However, before investigating the significance of the ikat motifs, themselves, I would like to clarify what features differentiate the overall designs of the three main types of Tanimbarese sarongs.

The most valuable sarongs are those called, in the Fordatan language, *bakan mnanat* ("antique sarongs") or, in the Yamdenan language, *tais matin*.[7] These are characterized by a large black center section that is graced with subtle brown pinstripes. Toward each end, there is a broad band of ikat designs which is framed on either side by a section of alternating beige, blue and brown colored bands that are themselves bordered by a thin band of small ikat patterns. The ends of the cloth are finished off with a wide plain black or brown section which is sometimes set off by a thin band of ikat patterns at the extreme edge (Figs. 9,10).

Bakan maran (or *tais marin* in Yamdenan) can be easily identified by the bold black and white stripes—the *maran* proper—in the center of the piece, on what is otherwise known as the "sitting place," *dakdok waan* (Pl. 2, Fig. 11). The middle section on each side is characterized by three medium-sized bands of ikat and colored stripes and—spaced equidistant between these three bands—two additional, narrower bands of colored stripes and (usually) ikat patterns. The space between these five middle bands is filled with row after row of ikat stippling that either frame, or are framed by, fine lines of colored yarns. The end section on either side is set off from the middle section by an unadorned black band, and distinguished by the "rainbows" (*ler mida*) whose number and placement differentiate the two main types of *bakan maran*. In the first, which is called a "full rainbow" (*ler mid tinemun*), each of the two double, mirror-image bands of ikat are framed on either side by two bands of color (usually red and blue), which comprise the "rainbow," and an outer row of stippling and colored lines (Pl. 2). In the second type, called a "half rainbow" (*ler mid lihir*), the two double, mirror-image bands of ikat each frame a single "rainbow"—which consists of two bands of color, often adorned with further ikat stippling (Fig. 11). In between the two "rainbow" sections there is usually yet another section of ikat patterns, thin colored lines and stippling. A third type of *bakan maran* is distinguished by its elaboration of the section in between the two "rainbows." This type is called a *bakan maran faduur*, where *faduur* means to "cause to flock together," and refers to the clustering of three or more single or double bands of ikat patterns—often carrying patterns of alternating flags and half-moons (Figs. 12,13).[8]

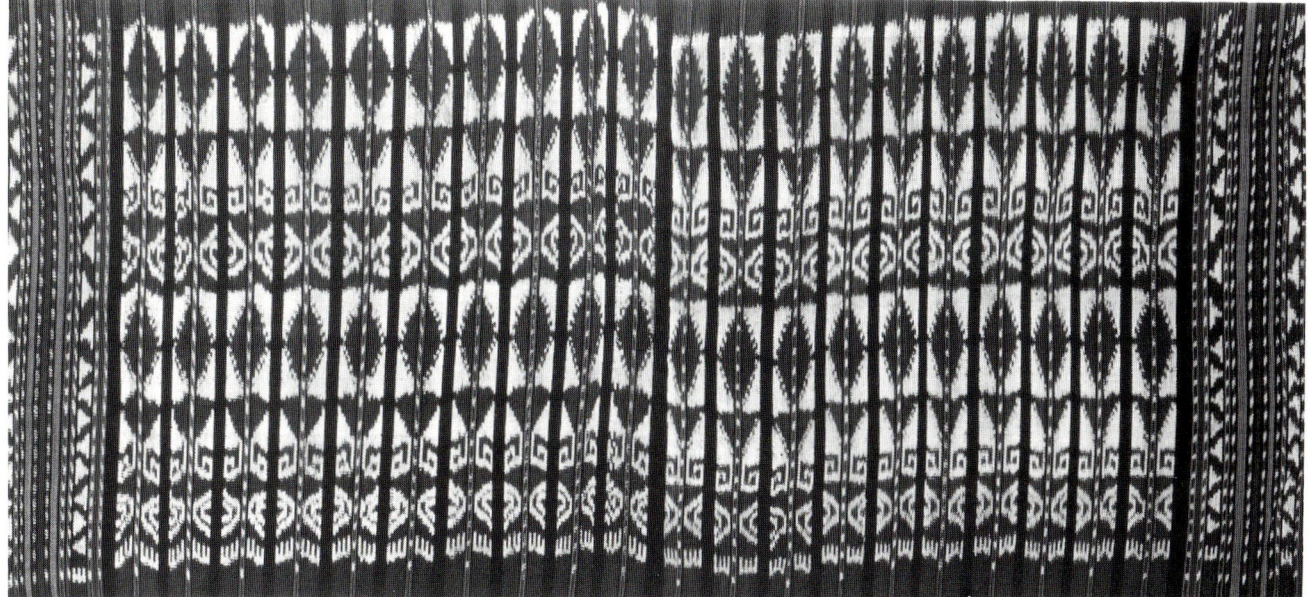

Figure 14. A bold sarong, bakan inelak, *with a repetitive flag and half-moon pattern, from the village of Awear on Fordata. Collection of author.*

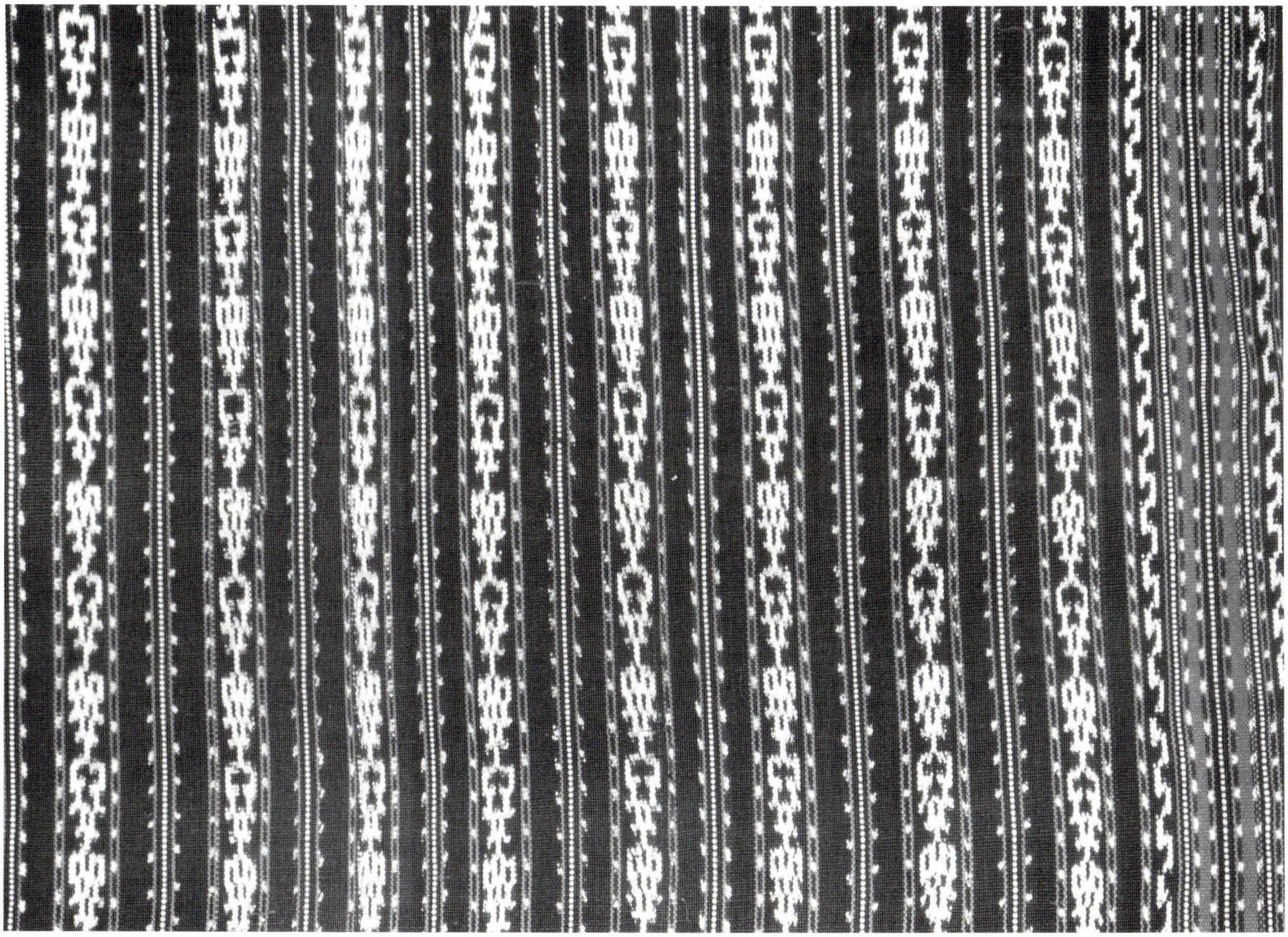

Figure 15. One half of a sarong, bakan inelak, *with a repetitive pattern of headless and tailless animal body motifs, from the village of Awear on Fordata. Collection of author.*

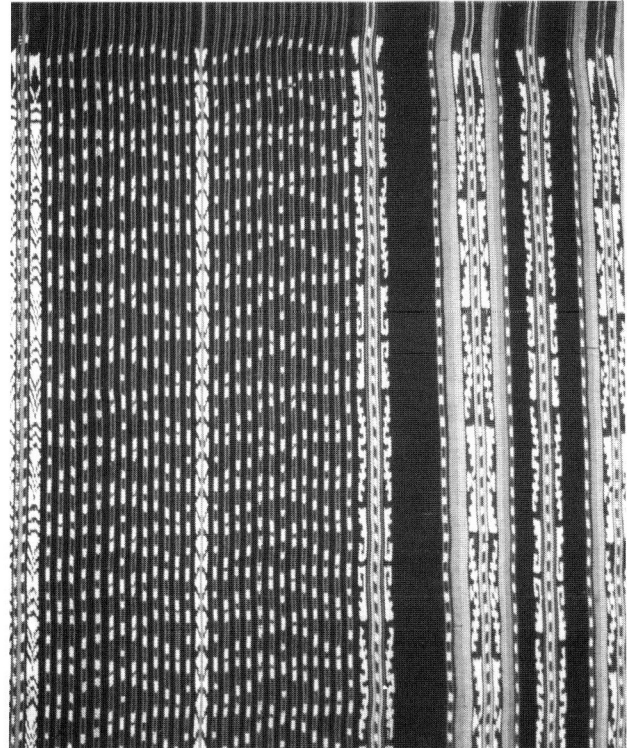

Figure 16. A detail of the bakan maran *in Plate 2, showing the flags and half-moons in the "rainbow" section and the "fishnet" of ikat stippling which ties together the entire piece. Collection of author.*

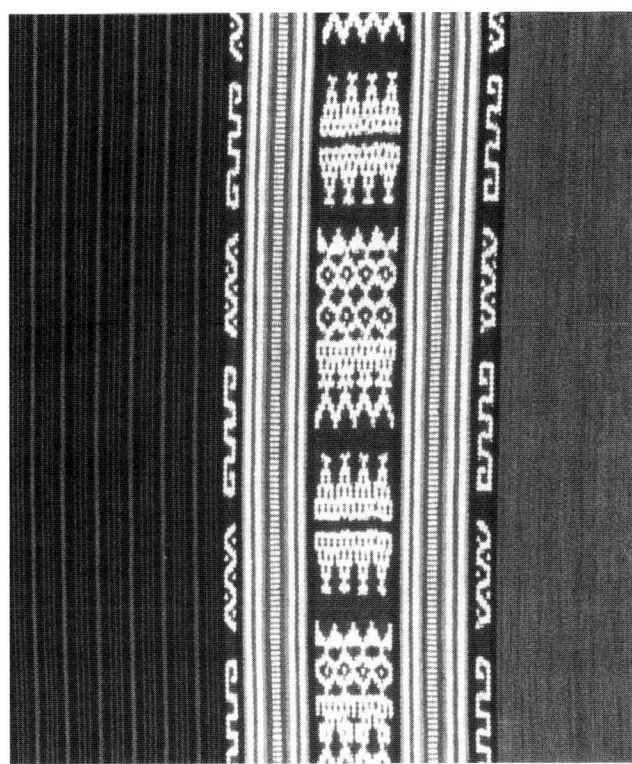

Figure 17. A detail of the bakan mnanat *in Figure 10, showing a composite motif of double-headed fish with flags on their heads in between headless, tailless animal body motifs. Collection of author.*

The least valued sarongs are those known as *bakan inelak* (*tais sikatim* in Yamdenan, *sikatim* meaning to "clip" or "catch"). These are characterized by bands of identical ikat patterns which are repeated throughout the length of the piece. In *bakan inelak*, either two mirror-image bands of ikat patterns frame (i.e., "catch") stripes of color and ikat stippling between them (Fig. 14); or each ikat band is itself framed (or "caught") between stripes of color and ikat stippling (Fig. 15). In the latter case, between each of these bands, there run additional bands consisting of three or four colored stripes that are set off by a row of stippling on either side. The edges of a *bakan inelak* are finished off with a cluster of broader colored stripes with or without two narrow bands of ikat patterns and several rows of ikat stippling. Tanimbarese distinguish a "straight" *inelak* sarong (*bakan inelak malolan*) from a "fern leaf" one (*bakan inelak ngeng roan*). While Drabbe suggests that these different terms refer to different types of borders (1932:33), I was told those of the latter always consisted of "flag" (*sa'ir*) and "half-moon" (*vulan lihir*) motifs only. Whether or not this is the case, it is nevertheless true that *bakan inelak* with ikat patterns consisting of flags and half-moons are extremely common (Figs. 3,6,12,14).

Returning to the question of how Tanimbarese ikat motifs are constructed, it is clear they are built up from a mulititude of tiny dots which are strung together, or spaced out, as if they were beads on a necklace. If one thinks, for instance, of Sumbanese ikat motifs—comprised of large, integral figures of humans, plants, and animals—and contrasts these with Tanimbarese ones, the particular logic of the latter becomes clearer. Tanimbarese women string together a number of bead-like dots to create fairly simple and abstract forms—flags, half-moons, fish, lizards, and such (Figs. 12,16). These simple forms are then often strung together into larger, composite images: a double-headed fish, for instance, with a flag on its head (Fig. 17). This stringing together of dots sometimes dominates the piece, so that it is overcome in a mesh (actually called a *fuat*, or "fishnet") of dots, which, while difficult to read from close up, presents a striking image from a distance (Pl. 2, Fig. 16). The point is that in constructing their ikat patterns, women create an image which epitomizes their own actions in the world. They string together many discrete bits, form the relationships between one thing and another, and tie them into an enduring pattern of relations.

There is yet another aspect of this composite quality of Tanimbarese textile designs. That is, an overall design is often comprised of heterogeneous and often complementary motifs. Just as the female earrings and necklaces are composed of both beads and gold, so too the designs of Tanimbarese sarongs are composed of qualitatively different motifs, which are

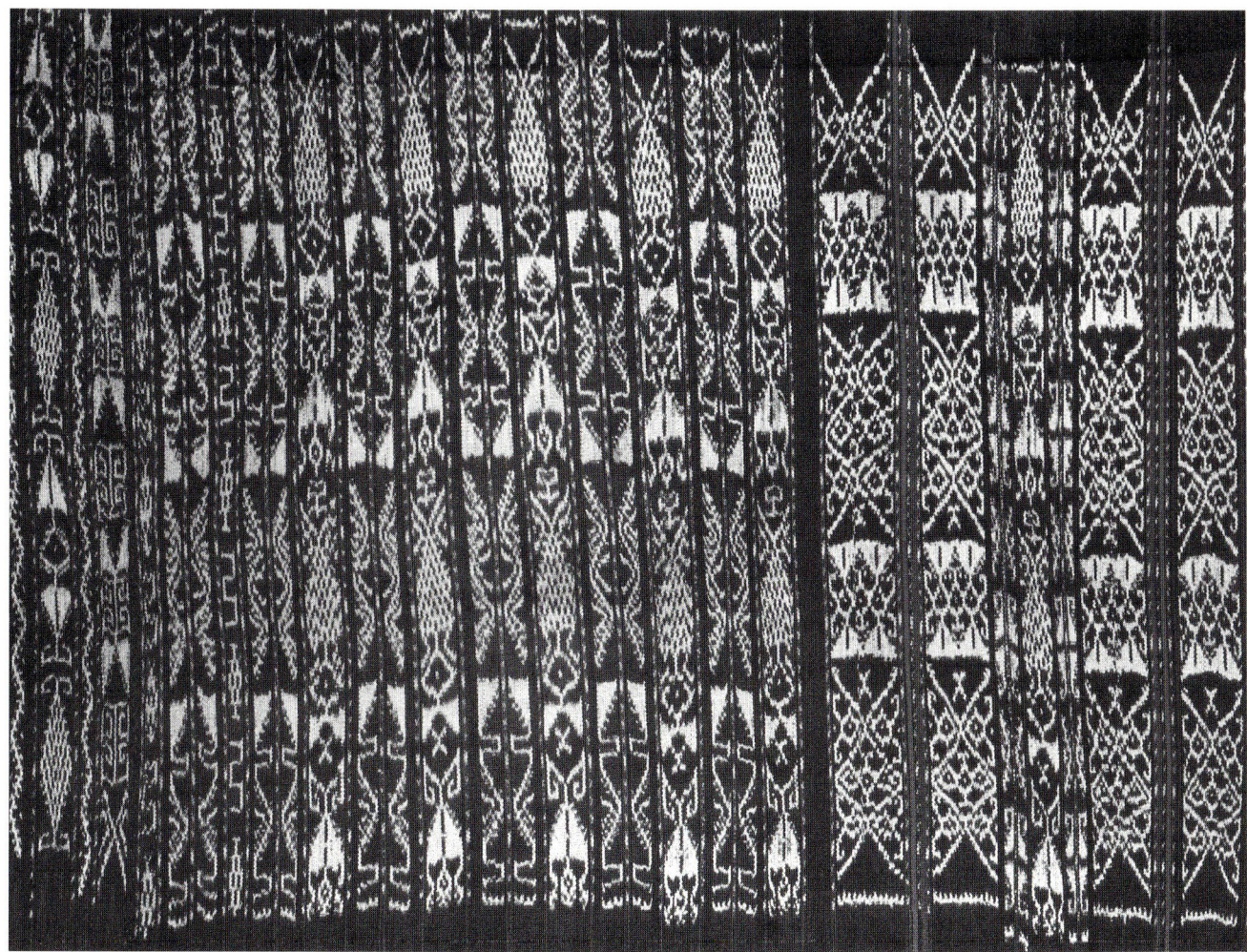

Figure 18. Two thirds of a particularly complex "morning-evening" sarong (the two sides of which have different overall design patterns) from the village of Awear on Fordata. Most of the composite images here can be disassembled into flags and half-moons. Private Collection.

often explicitly male and female symbols. Thus, not only does the female category of textiles ("loincloth-sarong") include both male and female cloths, but within the female cloths themselves, one finds a replication of both male and female elements.

Perhaps the most prevalent images in Tanimbarese textiles are those of flags and half-moons. If not every textile, then every other textile produced in Tanimbar will be embellished with images of flags and half-moons (Pl. 2, Figs. 3,6,9,11-14). Moreover, a great many of the more complex images can ultimately be reduced to an intricate pattern of flags and half-moons. I once asked an old woman to tell me the names of the designs on a particular complex textile she herself had woven (Fig. 18). What was surprising to me was that, instead of seeing the larger images as integral pieces, she disassembled almost every one into a series of intertwined flags and half-moons.

Flags are a male symbol of victory in war, in exchange and in marriage. Flags are hoisted on boats when men return from a war or an intervillage alliance renewal ritual and have taken a head, killed an enemy in battle, received an important named valuable (which is equated with a head taken in battle), or taken a woman in marriage and brought her back home with them. By contrast, the moon is a female symbol (unlike the sun). The half-moon recalls the fact that there is a full moon and that there are cycles to the moon's phases, just as there are cycles in women's bodies. Tanimbarese women explicitly equate these cycles, such that the coming of their menses is referred to as the coming of the moon (*vulan nmaa*). The connection between women and half-moons is also evident in the fact that, formerly, women adorned the outer rim of their ears with a multitude of small rings of four different types, at least two of which were thought of as half-moons (Drabbe 1940:30).

In the conjunction of flags and half-moons, there is an explicit coming together—within a female valuable itself—of both male and female images. A similar conjoining of male and female motifs can be found in the bold design of a *bakan inelak* which is comprised entirely of images of the diamond-shaped point of a headhunting spear (*dubil*) juxtaposed with images of the breast beam (*katkatan*) of a back-tension loom (Fig. 19). In this, the contrast is even more explicit as a piercing, death-dealing head-hunting spear used by men takes its place beside the instrument used by women in weaving textiles.

In sum, on the one hand there are "male" valuables, which are unabashedly and unambiguously male—hard, penetrating kinds of objects, including weapons. On the other hand, there are "female" valuables which are just as unabashedly and unambiguously female; but which, at the same time, seem to contain both male and female elements—both images of war (flags and spear points) and images of female productivity (half-moons and looms). What is the significance of this difference: why is it that male valuables do not include images of both male and female elements, whereas female valuables do?[9]

Heat, Death, and Male Production

In order to make sense of this asymmetry, it is necessary to relate, in a much more direct way, Tanimbarese concepts of male and female with ideas about death and life, heat and coolness. This can be done by considering the differences between male and female productive activity.

Aside from warfare, hunting and fishing are considered quintessential male activities. Moreover, pig meat and fish are the male goods given in exchange for the female products of the garden. Hunting takes place in an isolated, all-male world that is permeated with heat, danger, and death. It is considered a "hot" (*ngnea*) activity, not only because the men use hot magical "roots and leaves" (*aa wa'ar-aa roan*) to ensure their effectiveness, but also, and primarily, because it involves the death of a living creature, as well as encounters with dangerous spirits of the forest and souls of dead and dying people, which often transform themselves into pigs. After a successful hunt, a feast called "the feeding of the dead" (*nitu ni fafa'an*) is held for the ancestors. In this, men cook and eat the hot, "tabooed parts of the pig" (*vavu ni malmoli*), give thanks to the ancestors for their success in the hunt and, in the process, ensure the success of future hunts. This offering feast (like the one given when a sea turtle is caught) is one of the few activities in which women are strictly forbidden to take part. In short, the productivity of men depends upon their isolation from women, the effectiveness of the "hot" roots, and their entrance into a world that is, by definition, hot and deadly. Male productivity works through the agency of death: for the object that is produced always involves the death of a living being.

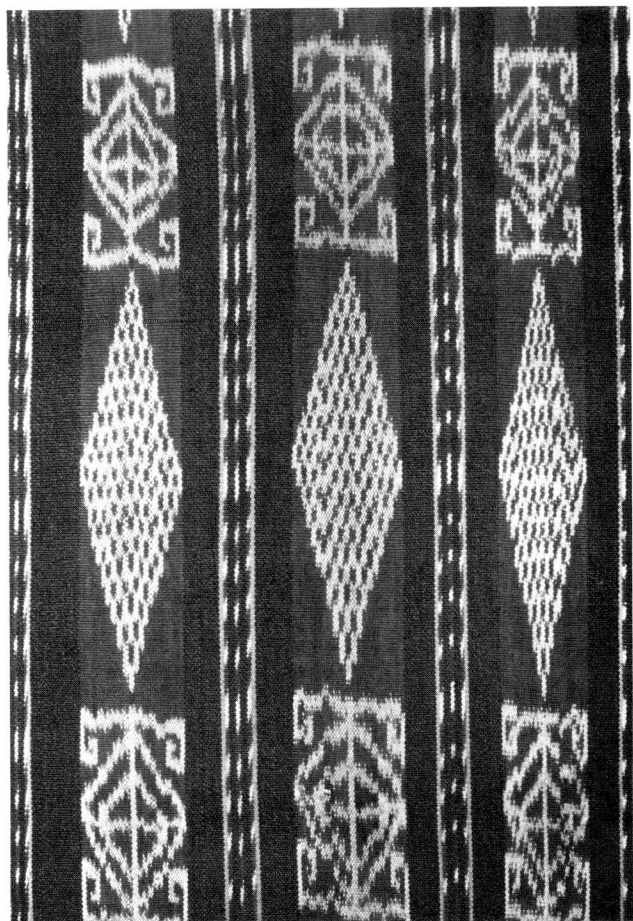

Figure 19. Section of a sarong, bakan inelak, *with spear points and loom motifs, from the village of Awear on Fordata. Collection of author.*

This can also be seen from the manner in which Tanimbarese conceive of the production of male earrings (*loran*). The only type of male valuable ever actually produced in Tanimbar was a particular form of male earring known as "our" *loran*. While male earrings were, on the whole, imported from outside Tanimbar, this inferior model was formerly manufactured in Tanimbar—from imported coins—by men who possessed the inherited right to practice metal work. In this work, small ancestor images (called *kukuwe* in Yamdenan and *walut* in Fordatan) were used to invoke the ancestors—both in order to produce the required heat for smelting, and to protect the producer from the heat of the object once it had been made (Drabbe 1940:112). Not only did the production of earrings involve a situation of intense heat, it also involved the "killing" of the gold:

> Just as in the working of an elephant's tusk, one speaks of killing, *rfen mase* [they kill the gold], and if one kills something, one says, one must take care that the ancestors help so that the heat of the object killed does you no harm (Drabbe 1940:112; translation mine).

The production of male earrings is clearly seen to involve a process in which the heat of the fire "kills the gold," and creates an object whose heat—but for the protection rendered by the ancestors—is dangerous for the person who has caused the death of the gold.

The mention of elephant's tusks is of interest, for tusks were occasionally sawed into armrings and bracelets by men, and the process was conducted in a very different manner from the cutting of the *Conus* shell by women in the production of female shell armbands. Although tusks are no longer cut into rings, and although the resulting ivory rings were never used as exchange valuables, still the production of these rings provides a good example of the way men work in the world. Drabbe states that the tusk itself is known as *fenreu*—which is the ritual language word for a noble man—and that the process of cutting the tusk into rings is called, literally, "they kill the tusk," *rfen lela* (1940:135). Furthermore, when they cut off the wide end of the tusk—which is too thin to make rings—it is said: "they sever the head" [of the tusk/man], *rtetak ulun* (1940:135). Offerings are made to Ubila'a (the supreme deity) and the ancestors, who are invoked in the following manner:

> ...if I now go to kill this man, make it so that he bewitches neither me nor also the owners of the tusk, cool us off with coconut and candlenut and also the owners of the tusk, so that we may not become sick and that we may finish the work, you my ancestors there (Drabbe 1940:136; translation mine).

Here again, it is evident that the killing of the tusk involves a process characterized by intense heat and danger, from which the workers can only be protected by the use of cooling substances and the intercession of the ancestors. During the entire process, the workmen are accompanied by the beat of a drum and a gong, and by the singing and dancing of a group of men; and it is not unreasonable to draw the comparison between this dance and the one which follows the taking of heads in warfare. At the time of the final offering made to Ubila'a and the ancestors, the man who has cut the tusk also makes an offering to the sawdust, not unlike the way men make an offering to the heads captured in war. Moreover, like a captured head, the sawdust of the beheaded tusk is fed and then thrown outside the village wall, where it is asked to remain contentedly, and not to seek vengeance for its death (Drabbe 1940:138).

Thus it could be said that the prototype of male activity is warfare, or more specifically, headhunting. Killing, death, and heat are essential to male productivity.

Coolness, Life, and Female Production

While male goods and valuables are produced in an atmosphere of heat, the opposite is the case with female goods and valuables. Consider, for example, the production of female shell armbands (*sislau*). Although they are no longer made in Tanimbar, it is obvious from Drabbe's notes (1940:134 35) that the process was not thought to involve the killing of the shell, and did not create or take place in a condition permeated by heat and danger. In fact, Drabbe's commentary appears to indicate that no ritual mediation whatsoever was involved in the production of shell armbands.

The situation is similar in the production of textiles. In the past, a woman might have given the ancestors an offering of rice, a knife and an armband when she undertook to weave her first sarong, and thereafter might have offered them a betel quid upon the completion of each piece, or during the weaving of one, if the yarns became sticky (Drabbe 1940:126-7). But these offerings were meant to facilitate the ease and smoothness with which the weaving was carried out. They had nothing to do with the creation of a hot condition or, conversely, with the cooling of an object permeated with heat. Weaving is an activity which, in itself, is thought to be "cool" (*radridin*).

The conditions of male production are hot and dangerous, for they involve the killing of an object. On account of its death, the object produced is itself considered hot, and this heat can only be neutralized through the ritual mediation of cooling substances and the protective intercession of the ancestors and Ubila'a.

By contrast, because the productive activity of women does not require the killing of the object concerned, both their work and the resulting object are considered inherently "cool."

Yet, while the heat that is productive of death is strictly associated with males, and coolness is clearly connected with females, it can nevertheless not be said that life itself is associated with females alone. Rather, what is productive of life requires the union of both male and female. The difference between processes which result in death and those which result in life can be seen most clearly in connection with the activities of hunting and gardening.

In contrast to the conditions for effectiveness in the hunt, effectiveness in gardening depends not upon a condition of heat, but rather upon that of a coolness which fosters the growth of plants. The objective of gardening—the generation of living things—is (or at least was) ritually achieved at planting time through the medium of cooling substances, the application of which required both male and female actors (Drabbe 1940:75-76). Garden rituals, moreover, always include a hunt as an intregal part. But the first-fruit harvest rituals, which take place at the opening of the large communal yam gardens, and celebrate the successful growth and fruition of a garden crop by a communal feast and offering to the ancestors, contrast quite sharply with the feasts that celebrate the conclusion of a successful hunt. In the hunting rituals male food (that is, the hot, tabooed portions of the animal) is consumed exclusively by men; however, in the gardening rituals, both male food (meat obtained in the hunt) and female food (yams and taro from the garden) are consumed together by both men and women.

What I am suggesting here is that death involves the denial or absence of sexual complementarity, while growth and life explicitly require the complementarity of male and female. The process that is productive of death always turns in on itself: it pits heat against heat, man against man. The process that is productive of life always turns toward an other, which is complementary in nature: it requires the union of male and female, the union of objects generated out of heat and death with objects generated through coolness and growth.

The Asymmetry of Life and Death

Male valuables, as representations of male activity, are associated with ideas about death, heat, isolation, singleness and the differentiation of discrete entities. Female valuables, as representations of female activities, are associated with ideas about life, coolness, multiplicity and the continuity of relationships. As a representation of life, female valuables must themselves contain the conditions of life: the creation of relations between heterogeneous and complementary entities—the union of male and female. It is not surprising, then, that female valuables are constructed in the way they are. Just as the female products of the garden require the union of male and female action, so too the quintessential female valuables—textiles—encompass both male and female images. Male valuables, in themselves, can never represent the continuity of life, for they are associated with that which negates life, and defines the bounded fixity of isolated entities. It is only when they are brought into relationship with female valuables through exchange that they can speak of the dynamics of life and the fluidity of relationship.

Coming full circle, then, it becomes obvious why blood-wealth prestations consist exclusively of male valuables, why there is no exchange, and why female valuables are noticeably absent. Firstly, in normal death exchanges, the presence of female valuables signifies the conditions for the continuity of life and relation. But in the bloodwealth prestations, the sole presence of male valuables is uniquely appropriate as a statement not only about death—and a violent death at that—but also, and more importantly, about the severing of all further relationship. Secondly, female valuables (and textiles in particular) are uniquely inappropriate in a representation of discrete bodies (alive or dead), because what they express is the connection between bodies: that is, what moves between fixed entities, what relates and encompasses numerous discrete entities, ties them into enduring patterns, and gives them their lifeblood.

NOTES

1. Doctoral research was carried out in the Tanimbar Islands during the years 1978 through 1980, and was assisted in part by a Grant for Doctoral Dissertation Research for Anthropology from the National Science Foundation. Both doctoral (1978-80) and postdoctoral research (1983-84) in the Tanimbar Islands were assisted by grants from the Joint Committee on Southeast Asia of the American Council of Learned Societies and the the Social Science Research Council with funds provided by the National Endowment for the Humanities and the Ford Foundation. My research in Tanimbar was focused primarily on the islands of Fordata, Larat, and Sera. Although I visited the main island of Yamdena many times, I have never set foot on Selaru, the southernmost island of the archipelago, nor Molu and Maru, the two northernmost islands of the group. My perspective on Tanimbarese life is, therefore, primarily Fordatan. Unless otherwise specified, the terms used in this paper are all of the Fordatan language—one of four distinct languages spoken in the islands and the ritual language for the entire archipelago.

2. A few people I spoke with suggested that, in the past, the three major types of sarong found in Tanimbar—*bakan mnanat*, *bakan maran*, and *bakan inelak*—were worn by women who belonged, respectively, to the class of nobles, commoners, and slaves. There was, however, no general agreement on this point. Moreover, while this may have once been practice, it certainly is not so today.

3. In general, however, it is quite easy to distinguish a textile woven on the islands of Sera, Larat and Fordata from those woven on Yamdena or Selaru. Textiles from the former islands tend to be much coarser, and their ikat designs much larger and bolder, than those from the latter. It is also true that certain villages may have a recognizable style which everyone acknowledges, but over which no one has any particular rights. As a whole, the differences from area to area, or from village to village, are not fixed, but rather very fluid. This derives, in part, from the fact that women often move from one village to another, or from one island to another, in marriage. The exception to this general stylistic fluidity is the rare case where a particular house claims sole rights over the production of a certain ikat design. The house Balak in the village of Awear, for instance, claims sole rights to produce a certain bird motif which no one else produces.

4. Using the Yamdenan language, Drabbe (1940:187) notes that the wife-takers are obliged to "cut palmwine" (*raflait*) while the wife-givers are obliged to "give loincloths-sarongs" (*ral umbin-tais*). In this, it is evident that textiles worn by both men and women were traditionally included within the general category of "female" goods given by the wife-givers. Today, as Western store-bought clothes increasingly replace indigenous woven textiles in at least some exchanges, the prestation of cloth is occasionally referred to, in the Fordatan language, as "pants-shirts" (*kadar-ravit*). Again, despite the fact that it includes both men's and women's clothing, it remains a category of female valuables.

5. Speaking of the Atoni of Timor, Schulte Nordholt (1980:239-40) comments: "Hard, sharp, and pointed objects are symbols of manliness. Like the horned buffalo and the metal gifts that wife-taking houses give, they are classified as male objects. Similarly a woman offers a betel and areca nut to the warriors. In this offering of *puah manus*, the areca nuts (*puah*) are female and the tapering betel leaves (*manus*) are male."

6. Note Adams's reflection (1980:220) that the "... Sumbanese consider textiles, as they do women in a clan household, impermanent. Thus, cloths provide the feminine counterpart to masculine metal goods, which are regarded as permanent." Similarly, Traube (1980:98-99) suggests that as "a social metaphor, the opposition of hard bone to soft blood and flesh associates forms of relatedness with a duality of immutable and alterable elements, expressing a crucial distinction between the lasting, perduring, "hard" character of agnatic connections and the more perishable, "soft" connections established through women....Overall, bone plays a noticeably muted role in Mambai symbolism....Descent groups look elsewhere for representations of their enduring nature; they find them, significantly enough, in metal objects which mythological traditions trace back to the bones of Father Heaven."

7. In the Fordatan language, there is no separate term to distinguish antique, heirloom sarongs (which in the Yamdenan language are called *tais wangim*), from sarongs of this particular design (which in Yamdenan are called *tais matin*). The reason for this may be that this particular pattern of sarong is less commonly woven in Fordata, Larat, and Sera; and those that are found there not only often originate from Yamdena and Selaru (or even from the Babar archipelago to the west), but also are frequently older or antique pieces.

8. Drabbe (1940:125-26) refers to a number of other variations of the *bakan maran*, which I have never seen. Using the Yamdenan language, he mentions the following types. In the *tais marin sa'irlili* (and also the *tais lar tameru*), the bold black and white stripes in the middle of the piece are replaced by red and white stripes. In the *tais marin motik* or *marin toke*, the black and white stripes are omitted altogether. The *tais lar mid mafuti* is characterized by a red and white "rainbow" in place of a red and blue "rainbow." It should be said, however, that with the introduction of the many colors of store-bought threads, nowadays one may find "rainbows" of almost any color combination, although red and blue ones are still the most common. The interested reader should refer to Drabbe's notes (1940:125-26) in which he describes still other sarong designs that are now rarely to be seen in Tanimbar and probably, even in his time, were far less common than the three main types I have outlined here.

9. There are some possible exceptions to this contrast. First of all, as already mentioned, red European cloth is sometimes tucked into the center of male earrings. However, here, it is significant that it is not indigenous cloth that is used, and that its purpose is to make the earrings flash like lightening, which is associated with male action. Secondly, gold breast pendants not only have gold link chains, but sometimes also contain images of half-moons—although these latter are often indistinguishable from horn and boat images, which are clearly male. Furthermore, the round gold discs are referred to as "gold moons" (*mas vulan*). Nevertheless, while certain of the images on gold breast pendants appear to be female, most gold breast pendants—which portray faces, horns, boats, turtles, and kris handles—are male images. Even if one takes these ambiguous cases into account, I think the broad contrast I am drawing between male and female valuables is still significant and valid.

The Bridewealth Cloth of Lamalera, Lembata

Ruth Barnes

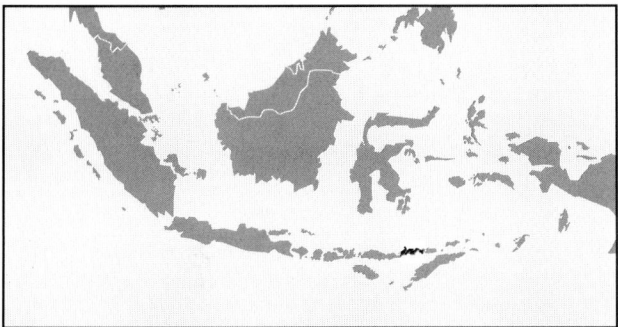

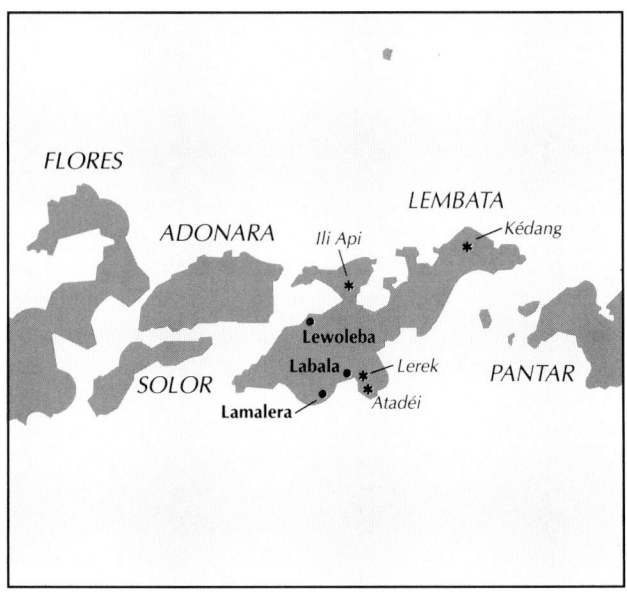

The Lamaholot Islands.

Until recently there has been little serious scholarship on the textiles of the Lamaholot islands, which include East Flores, Adonara, Solor, and Lembata. Now politically united as the Kabupaten Flores Timur, these islands are culturally and linguistically unified with the exception of the district of Kédang at the eastern tip of Lembata, where a separate language is spoken. Political unity, however, is a recent imposition, first implemented by the Dutch colonial power. Certain of the textiles woven here have become known as particularly fine examples of Indonesian ikat cloths, and they are included, if sparingly, in many collections. Since the area of production is limited, a relatively small number has reached museums and collections outside Indonesia.

The ethnographer Ernst Vatter was the first to write at some length about Lamaholot textiles, in particular about those showing ikat (1932:217-26). In 1928-29 he spent eight months traveling from Flores to Alor, and commented:

> The textiles produced on East Flores, on Solor and on Lomblen (Lembata) lose out in a first comparison to the cloths of Sumba, with their vivid animal ornaments, or to the decorative products of the small islands Savu and Roti, with their brilliant colors, but in the long run, they exert the stronger artistic effect. One never grows tired of them (1932:217).

Vatter's book contained some useful information on the textiles, although he barely began to address the topic in sufficient detail. It took thirty years for another scholar to notice that the ikat cloths of the Lamaholot might be of historical interest: Alfred Bühler was the first to point out the particular importance the textiles of the area, and especially those from Lembata, might have for a study of patola influences on Indonesian ikat (1959:8). More recently Robyn Maxwell has published

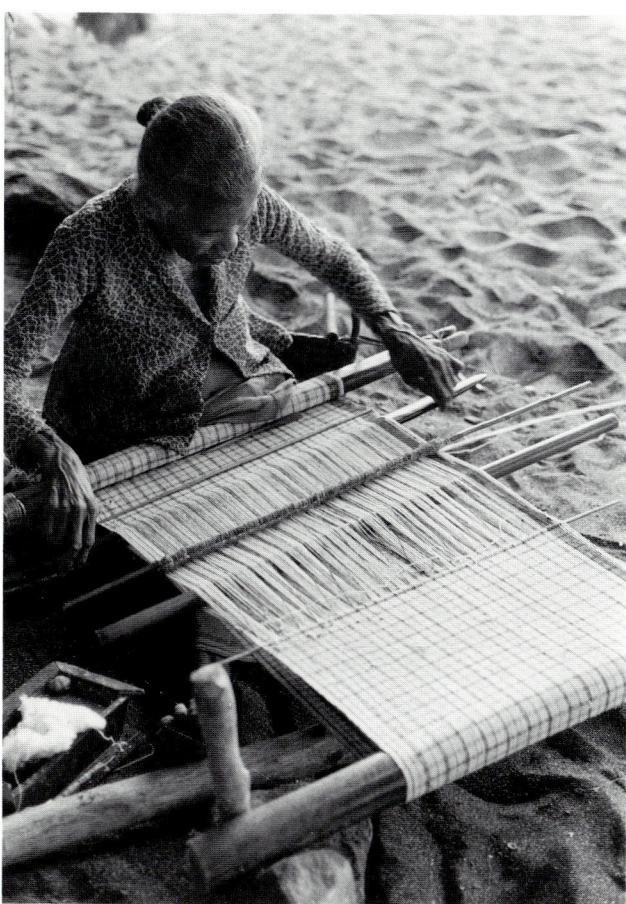

Figure 1. A woman weaving a man's sarong (nofi). *Lamalera, 1979.*

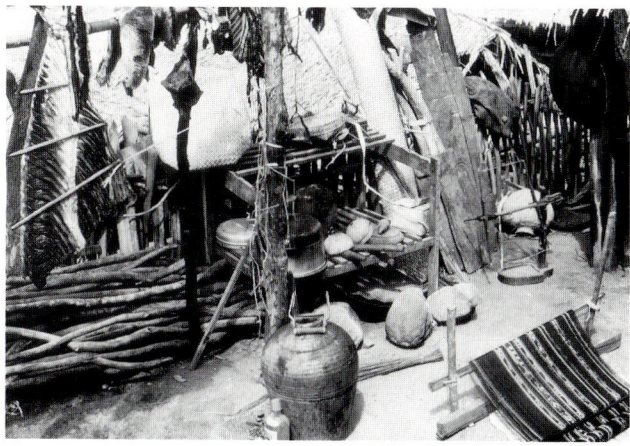

Figure 2. A kitchen yard showing manta ray (belelā) *drying on the left and a loom set up, lower right, for the weaving of a festive sarong* (kewatek menikil). *Lamalera, 1982.*

material based on her extensive travels through Flores and the Lamaholot area (1980,1981). She gives the first published account of the use of Lamaholot textiles in their social context. My own research has focused on the ikat cloth of one community, Lamalera on Lembata (R. Barnes 1984,1989).[1]

It is tempting but often misleading to come to generalizations about Lamaholot textiles. Maxwell mentions that the Lamaholot language consists of approximately seventeen different dialects (1980:148),[2] and the linguistic differences often go hand in hand with local variations on general concepts of social structure, traditional religion, and material culture. This is also reflected in the design and use of textiles. For example, it has been said that Lamaholot patterns or their arrangements display evidence of clan membership (Gittinger 1979a:169; Khan Majlis 1984:86). This implies a strictly followed prescription. Yet the visual evidence can vary greatly.

The use of particular patterns to show clan membership can have a surprisingly vague meaning. In Lamalera, where I have done most of my research, certain patterns are associated with specific clans (see R. Barnes 1984:152-54). Furthermore, there exists a definite prohibition on using patterns inconsistent with a woman's clan affiliation. Patterns are acquired through clan membership, in particular through the clan a woman is born into, rather than her husband's clan, which she enters at marriage. This apparently rational, clearly defined position is in complete contrast to what the observer finds in reality. In fact, a woman may know how to tie not only the pattern of her native clan, but also that of her mother's or grandmother's (which differ from her own). She may wear any of these, and will justify it by pointing out the relationship, which may be very distant indeed. So, in effect, a woman has the right to use the patterns associated with numerous clans, without violating the prohibition. The textile she herself makes is not primarily a 'calling card', but rather, a reflection of her personal preference from among a variety of patterns available to her. While the cloths women make may be similar, I have yet to see two that are identical. The ideology of correct patterns is certainly familiar to the weavers of Lamaholot; but this may allow a wide choice.[3] Finally, we must remember that only a very small fraction of all the cloths woven by Lamaholot women are decorated with elaborate ikat designs or are intended as ceremonial cloths. As is no doubt true for most textile-producing areas of Indonesia, much of the cloth made is primarily mundane and functional.

Already in the seventeenth century Wouter Schouten observed (1676) that only certain of the islanders showed an interest in fabrics and clothing, while others went virtually without dress. Against this background it must be noted that while the Lamaholot islands have a variety of weaving and ikat-producing traditions, there are also areas where little or no weaving is done, or where it may actually be prohibited to weave. Any discussion of a particular tradition must be seen in this context. One approach needed at the moment is a detailed description and interpretation of a specific Lamaholot cloth; I will attempt that task here. It is only one of many possibilities—the one I am most familiar with (see R. Barnes 1987). What I say about this cloth does not necessarily apply to similar textiles from other parts of the region. While the textile may have only a very general message for all of Lamaholot, it certainly has a specific meaning in the place where it is produced.

Weaving in Lamalera

As my example I take the bridewealth cloth made and used in the village of Lamalera, a fishing village traditionally dependent on the hunting of large sea animals—whale, dolphin, and manta ray. The community has few fields, and the women trade the dried meat and fish for staple goods in the mountain villages of the island's interior.[4] They also produce and export cloths to the same communities, both for daily wear and for special occasions. Lamalera is one of three areas on Lembata where ikat of exceptional quality is produced. The others are Ili Api on the north coast and Atadéi in the south (see Map).[5] In contrast to these other two centers, which encompass an entire district each, Lamalera's cloth production occurs only in one village. If a woman in the mountain hamlets weaves a cloth in the style of Lamalera, one will almost certainly discover that she, or at least her mother, came from Lamalera. All Lamalera women can supposedly weave and produce ikat (*mofa*): a woman in her twenties who cannot do so is very likely not of Lamalera descent in the female line.[6]

Both men's and women's sarongs are produced in the village, but only women's cloths are differentiated in type and value; certainly this is related to the amount of ikat worked into a woman's sarong and to the use of certain female cloths as bridewealth. There is only one name for men's cloth, *nofi* (Fig. 1); it includes no ikat. But there are three types of women's cloth, or *kewatek*. The first, "ordinary sarong" or *kewatek biasa*, is worn daily, while working. In Lamalera it is usually not decorated with ikat but only different-colored stripes; in neighboring Atadéi this category of textile may include ikat bands dyed with indigo only. The second type of women's cloth, "fine sarong" or *kewatek menikil*, must include a border decoration of ikat (Fig. 2). Traditionally, the ikat would be dyed with indigo and morinda, the red dye derived from *Morinda citrifolia*; when the two are used together in one pattern the result is called *belapit*. In Lamalera, commercial dyes and

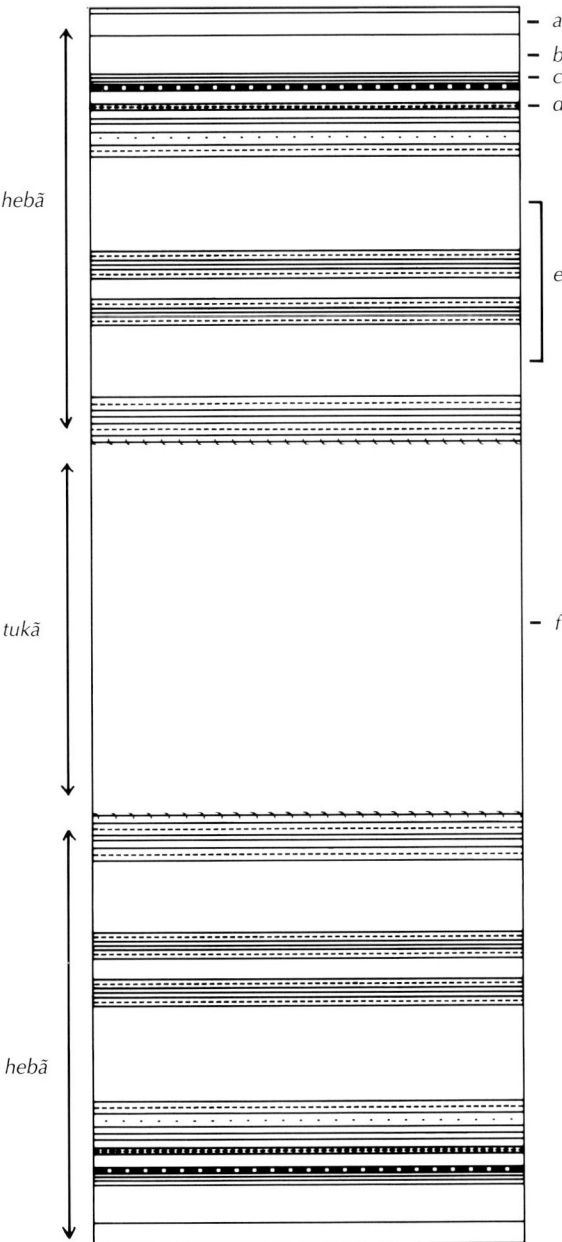

Figure 3. The three-panel bridewealth cloth (kewatek nai telo).
 a. patterns aran, kelulus, ka'u belapit
 b. no ikat
 c. stripes of a single color (nulur)
 d. belikung
 e. wide ikat bands with specifically appropriate patterns
 f. ikat bands that visually link to create a continuous design

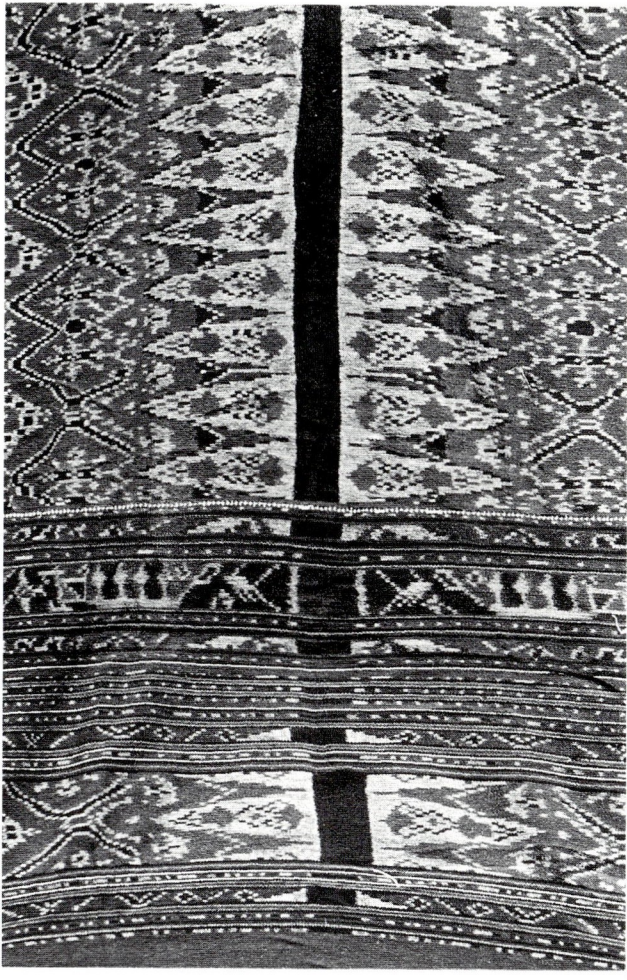

Figure 4. Detail of a three-panel bridewealth cloth (kewatek nai telo). The patterns of the lower panel (hebā) show the boat motif (téna), the manta ray (moku), and the shark (iu), as well as a single width of the linked pattern beléré, which appears again in the central panel (tukā) here above. Approximate size, outer panels: weft, 60 cm. Central panel: weft, 40 cm., warp, 125 cm. (circular; only half visible). Lamalera, 1979. Also shown in Plate 3.

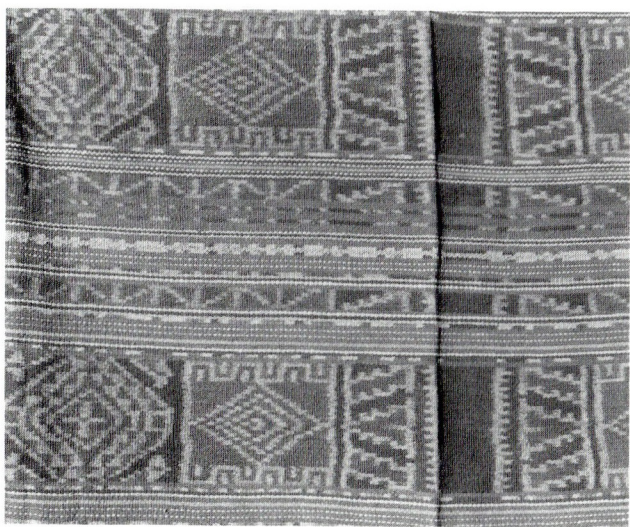

Figure 5. Detail of one of the two outer panels of a three-panel bridewealth cloth. Lamalera, 1979.

machine-spun threads are now most frequently used. In other areas, as in Atadéi, west Solor, and east Flores, indigenous dyes are still common. The third and most elaborate women's textile is the bridewealth cloth, called *kewatek nai ruā* or *kewatek nai telo* (Figs. 3-5, Pl. 3). This cloth is part of the prestations offered by the bride's clan at, or following, a marriage. The return gift from the groom's side is an elephant tusk.[7]

Although Lamalera has excelled during this century in adopting foreign—particularly European—designs for personal, festive sarongs, its bridewealth cloth must be made entirely from indigenous material: it is not acceptable to use thread, dye, or patterns that are not "given by the ancestors." The cotton is locally grown and handspun, and the dyes are locally obtained. The numerous ikat bands must be of the *belapit* type. *Kewatek nai ruā* is made up from two panels (*ruā*: "two"), sewn together to form the tubular sarong. The *kewatek nai telo* has three panels (*telo*: "three") and is the more highly valued. As the three-panel bridewealth cloth is the most complex in design and manufacture, I will describe it here in detail. Much that can be said about it also applies, in moderation, to the other types of cloth. Some of its peculiarities, such as the central panel, illuminate the particular role cloth can play in the Lamaholot context.

Kewatek Nai Telo, Three-Panel Bridewealth Cloth

The three-panel cloth, *kewatek nai telo*, consists of a central panel, *tukā*, and two outer panels, or *hebā*, which are mirror-symmetrically identical with each other (Figs. 3,4, Pl. 3). In all two-panel cloths the term *hebā* (*heban* in other Lamaholot dialects) refers to the border which is decorated either with bands of ikat, or at least with colored stripes. In its least flamboyant appearance, the Lamaholot *heban* refers to a single-colored, thin stripe that forms the border of a man's sarong. Here, however, it designates the entire panel, which is then further divided into wide and narrow ikat bands, interspersed with unicolored areas. These are dyed with *Morinda citrifolia*, creating a dark brownish red tone which accounts for the generic term used for the bridewealth cloth throughout Lamaholot: *kewatek méan*, "red woman's cloth." In Lamalera, the bridewealth cloth is always specifically named *kewatek nai ruā* or *nai telo*, depending on the number of panels. Another term used in formal bridewealth discussions is *tukā-hebā*, or "center-border," a reference to the panels that distinguish the three-panel cloth.

Moving inward from the border, there is a thin stripe of red warp, followed by the first band of ikat. The design of all Lamaholot ikat is made up of narrow skeins of cotton into which the reserve knots are tied. These form the units from which the patterns are

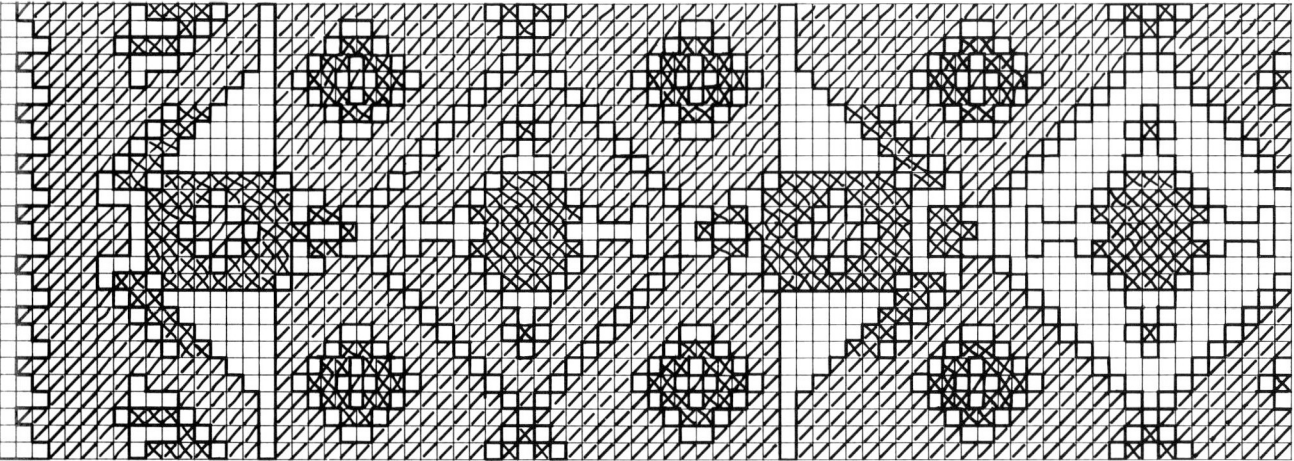

Figure 6. Example of a pattern appropriate to the central panel. This one is called moku bela.

built up. The yarns making one unit are called *kulu*, "seed," and the combined "seeds" are *kenumak*. In Lamalera, the *kulu* must contain an even number of yarns—six each; but the number of units per pattern width must be uneven.[8] There is never any deviation from this prescription. The first ikat pattern is narrow: no more than five ikat knots wide, *kenumak léma*. All patterns are named; only certain patterns are suitable for certain widths.[9] Every ikat band has to be surrounded by a thin colored stripe, *nulur*, which separates it from the red. On either side of a wide ikat a thin ikat skein, called *belikung* ("protector"), must be added. The use of stripes dyed a color other than red (by using indigo, turmeric, and certain leaves) is unique to southern Lembata. In other parts of Lamaholot, the "red" cloth includes only yarn that has been dyed with morinda and indigo.

Following the narrow ikat strips close to the border and the wide red area, there are two wide bands of ikat decoration (Fig. 5), whose patterns occupy the entire width and are frequently recognizable representations of specific objects; the number of ikat units is between fifteen and thirty-three. Between the two wide design bands, narrow patterns and the "protective" *belikung* are set in. Narrow lines of morinda-dyed yarn establish the continuity of the red appearance. When one counts all the ikat bands of a panel, wide and narrow, their number is always uneven.

The central panel has a different appearance altogether: rather than being divided into bands, it shows a continuous design (Figs. 6,7). The patterns found here are usually directly linked to patola cloths (see R. Barnes 1984 and In Press a). They are tied to a width of no more than thirty-three units, but then linked to each other to create a continuous design. The orientation of designs into bands is here ignored, rather than emphasized as in the border; for this reason, only patterns that can be successfully linked to each other

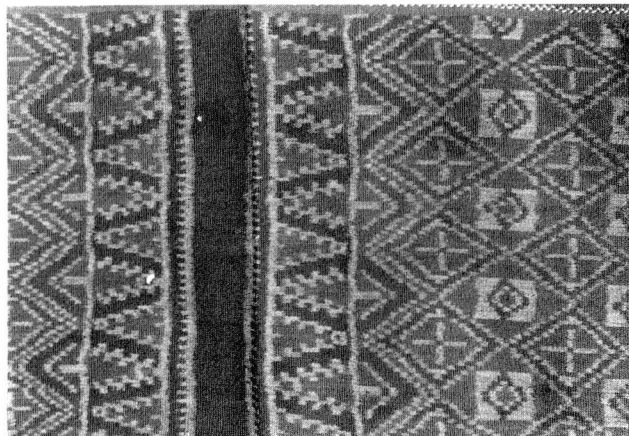

Figure 7. Detail of the central panel of a three-panel bridewealth cloth. Lamalera, 1979.

are suitable. Neither the colored stripes nor the *belikung* are used in this panel. All ikat in Lamalera's bridewealth cloth *must* include both red and black— that is, morinda and indigo: pattern bands dyed with red only, such as occur on the bridewealth cloth of Ili Api, are not permitted.

Narrow Designs

The above description suggests that the position of patterns on the cloth is prescribed. The concept of the three-panel textile, which allows little variation in the overall structure, makes only certain patterns suitable for certain places on the cloth (R. Barnes 1984:135-37). The narrow pattern band most commonly has a width of five ikat units. Motifs that fit into this width are the plank (*arã*) and the small boat (*kelulus*). The minimum used is a width of three units; the pattern created thereby is called *ka'u belapit*, or "folding coconut leaves, ikat dyed with indigo and morinda," the

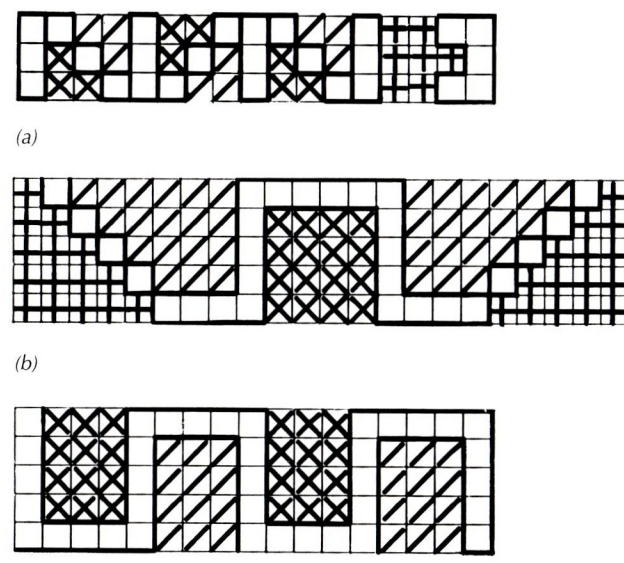

Figure 8. Examples of patterns appropriate to the narrow ikat bands of bridewealth cloth: (a) "folding coconut leaves, ikat dyed with indigo and morinda," or ka'u belapit (b) "small boat," or kelulus, and (c) "plank" (of a boat), or arã.

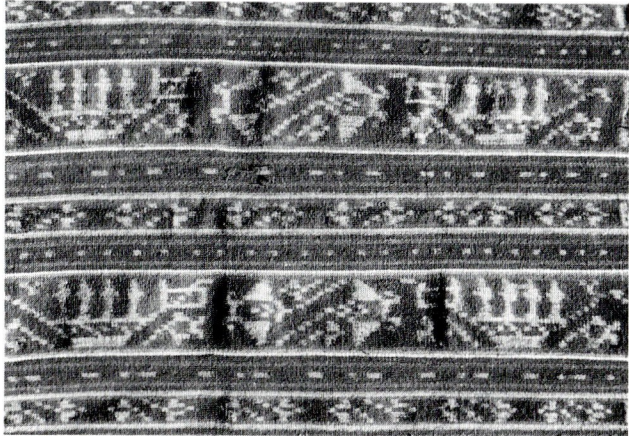

Figure 9. Detail of a shouldercloth (senai) with boat (téna) and manta ray (moku) patterns. Lamalera, 1982. Also shown in Plate 4.

narrowest named pattern (Fig. 8a). Anything less appears as a single beaded pattern rather than as a figural design; however, this narrow design may be the section of a larger pattern found elsewhere on the cloth. Any of these designs smaller than five units wide are called *belikung*, "protect." If a wider pattern is divided to provide the *belikung*, an even number of skeins may be used: it is the complete pattern width that must have an uneven number. The figural patterns, starting with *kelulus* and *arã* (Fig. 8b,c), are called *kojang*.[10] The majority of those restricted to use in the band-type design of *hebã* are closely related to other Lamaholot patterns, or even to a wider area of ornamental design. Some are related to pottery finds in maritime Southeast Asia, which show their presence prior to the introduction of bronze into the archipelago (see R. Barnes 1984:291-92, fig.43).

Certain designs are peculiar to Lamalera. One of these is the boat, *téna*, a representation of the village whaling vessels showing the harpooner's platform and the oars (Figs. 9,10, Pl. 4). The latter have sometimes been mistaken for people (Khan Majlis 1984:93). However, the representation of the human figure is confined to the abstract image of the "linked-ancestor" type. Two fish appear on Lamalera cloth: a type of manta ray, *moku*, and the shark, *iu*. The whale is never represented in traditional cloth.[11] Vatter (1932:223) and Khan Majlis (1984:93), who claim it is, are incorrect. Moreover the boat which Vatter identifies as a *pledang* (local dialect for the boat used in Lamalera) is actually called *jõ*, and represents a junk rather than the indigenous boat. A similar version of the *jõ* also appears in Atadéi cloth, where it is called *téna* or *jon*, and is identified with trading vessels of Chinese or Portuguese origin. The *moku* pattern (Fig. 10) might seem particularly suitable for Lamalera, as the manta ray, next to the whale, is a primary subject for the hunt. The fish most sought after, however, is a much larger variety of ray, the *belélã*. Curiously enough, the *moku* is the one representative pattern found in all three ikat-producing areas of Lembata—in Lamalera, Atadéi, and Ili Api (Pls. 3,5). It is unique to Lembata.

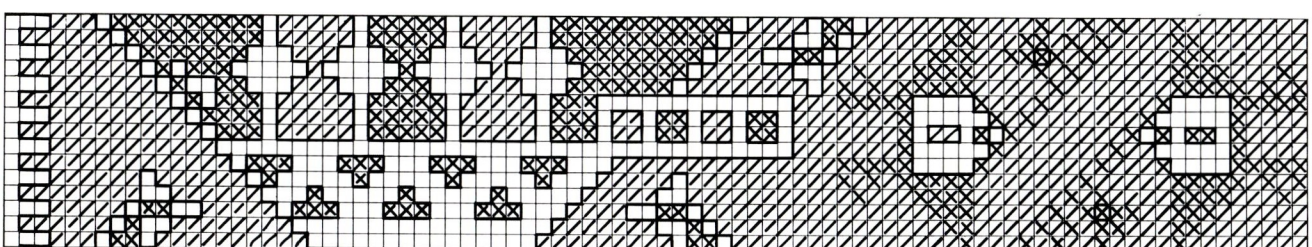

Figure 10. Examples of patterns appropriate to the wide ikat bands of bridewealth cloth: left, "boat" (téna), and right, "manta ray" (moku).

Central Design

It seems that patterns associated with specific clans are either copied from, or inspired by, patola cloths that were brought into the community prior to living memory and have become clan treasures (for a full description and analysis of the origin of central panels of bridewealth cloth see R. Barnes 1984:151-57 and 1989). As such they are associated with the group's well-being, prosperity, and fertility. Other Lamaholot clan treasures are silver chains, tusks, and objects brought in by outside trade connections, or by contrast (or complement) objects "found," typically emerging from the earth: Chinese pots or plates, strange stones, or pieces of metal.

The patola and the chains in particular are said either to be alive or to change their appearance (see also Maxwell 1981:61). The patola are believed to change with the moon: when it is full they are complete, and they unravel as it wanes. At new moon, when the night sky is black, the cloths are merely shreds, only to restore themselves as the moon returns. As long as the cloth stays in the clan house, its power is harnessed and brings fortune to all members of the group. However, if it is allowed to leave the clan it destroys all fortune. It is remarkably close, in the way it is described, to the snake that is represented by the silver chain. A detailed description of the latter is available from Kédang (see R.H.Barnes 1974:105-7). There it is benevolent, even representative of all wealth, as long as it is not treated incautiously. In fact, as the guardian spirit of the clan or the village, it may take on the appearance of a rainbow, whose multicolored luminous appearance, I would suggest, may be most adequately captured in and associated with the silk cloths from India.

The Use of Color

Lamaholot bridewealth cloths are nowhere as brightly colored as the patola from which certain of their patterns are adopted. This seems to be mainly by preference. For example, though brazilwood (*sapan*) is known as a dye, it is disliked for its bright red color. Bright green and yellow from natural dyes are often used in festive sarongs, together with or in place of commercial ones. They are not, however, suitable for bridewealth cloth.

Here it may be appropriate to consider the importance attached to the colors used in Lamaholot textiles generally. The basic color scheme is red, black, and white. This is not to say, though, that the local color code does not make further distinctions. Precise hues and shades of dyes can be identified without difficulties (see R. Barnes 1984:194). Yet despite the linguistic ability to distinguish between slight variations in color, the categorical color classification of traditional cloth is the triad of white (*burã*), red (*meã*), and black (*mitã*). White refers to the undyed yarn, some of which is reserved to become a part of the design. *Meã*, further explained below, means "red," but it does *not* refer specifically to the brownish-red color of the morinda-dyed yarn; that is called *nubar*. *Mitã*, black, in textiles only refers to a deep blue color achieved with repeated indigo dye baths, never to the true black which is the result of overdying indigo with morinda. That color is called *fangẽ*.

From East Flores to the Lamaholot-speaking area of Lembata (in other words, excluding Kédang), the predominant color in all bridewealth cloth is red (Pl. 3). Coastal Adonara and east Solor are exceptions; there the bride's parents formerly gave imported patola in exchange for tusks. Nowadays the cloths given are locally woven, but made from commercial dyes in bright colors, none of which are specifically prescribed. In Kédang, however, the cloth has to be black. Schulte Nordholt mentions the same division into red or black (blue) cloths from Timor. He says, "The extraordinary fact remains that red and dark blue (black) as the main colors of cloths are spread in an extremely irregular pattern across Indonesian Timor. They are at the same time the colors which play an important, though rather vague part in the classificatory system" (1971:45).

Gittinger has suggested that the process of dyeing with morinda—comparatively more complex than with indigo—was a foreign one which may have come into the area with the Indian trade (1979a:169). This must be considered independently from the patola trade, however, as red cloths showing few patola influences are also used in some parts of Lamaholot. For the Flores-Solor region, a historical explanation of the use of red, that is to say its possible arrival only some centuries ago, might partly explain the differences in the color of bridewealth cloth between Kédang (black) and Lamaholot (red).

Kédang is in many respects more conservative and seems to preserve some features that have disappeared elsewhere. However, this explanation is only relevant from an outsider's point of view. The people of Kédang know of red sarongs used as bridewealth, through their trade ties with Ili Api and other Lamaholot regions. To them, however, a red bridewealth cloth would not be acceptable. Red is a color of ambiguous meaning, frequently associated with moral wickedness (R.H. Barnes 1974:167). Black cotton cloth is instead more appropriate for bridewealth. The use of black cloth at other times, during offerings and as part of the burial, suggests that the color is associated with physical aspects of the community. It is remarkable that at ritual offerings in Kédang, such as the harvest ceremony, cotton pellets—that is, the not yet transformed source of textiles—and pieces of black cloth are juxtaposed. R.H. Barnes says, "One gains the overall impression, then, that the cotton (which is white) stands often for the spirit as opposed to body, represented by the black cloth; in other cases the cotton seems to stand for pure spirit (the wind, God) as opposed to spirit which has undergone the transformations connected with embodiment (the living and the ancestors together)" (1974:222).

This interpretation of black is not alien to Lamaholot, either: traditionally, a person is not considered mature enough to marry until his or her teeth are blackened. Pots, coconut cups, and wooden or clay plates are not strong enough for use until they have been stained black with charcoal. Thus the Lamaholot and Kédang may interpret certain colors similarly. But the choice made is different. At this point it is, in my opinion, not possible to say more than Schulte Nordholt (cited above): colors play an important but vague role. Apparently, these colors can change their meaning, depending on circumstances. Although red is an ambiguous color in Kédang, frequently associated with uncontrolled anger, bits of red cloth are needed in the ceremony for the "renewal" of a person's navel cord, a ritual which may be essential to his or her well-being. In Lamaholot, where *méan*, red, has generally a positive association, it is nevertheless the color of witches.

On Timor color may be associated with the cardinal points and with male or female (Schulte Nordholt 1971:413). This cannot be reported for the Lamaholot. Although the woman's clan offers the red cloth, the color itself is not in particular affiliated with the female. It is more likely that other, superlative associations with the word *méã*, or *méan*, make it the preferred cloth. Although always directly translated as "red," the word seems to refer to extraordinary powers or wealth. Vroklage, writing about the Belu of Timor, translates their term *mean* as "golden, red, strong, healthy; God himself may be called *mean*" (1953 I:576). Closer to the Lamaholot, among the Ngada of Central Flores, *mean* means "extraordinary (Arndt 1933). And to compare to the Kédang once more: there the term *matan-méan* refers to "all forms of extraordinary wealth of which golden objects are particularly representative" (R.H. Barnes 1974:106). It also describes the manifestation of the snake guardian spirit of the village.

The red cloth or *kewatek méan* of the Lamaholot, in its Lamalera version, may possess certain powers of healing. A man in the village who was known for his ability to cure illnesses told me that he once achieved a most spectacular recovery when a woman was accidentally hit by a *parang*, the long-bladed bush-knife used throughout eastern Indonesia. He dressed the gaping wound with herbs and chanted over it, but ascribed the real power of healing to a bridewealth

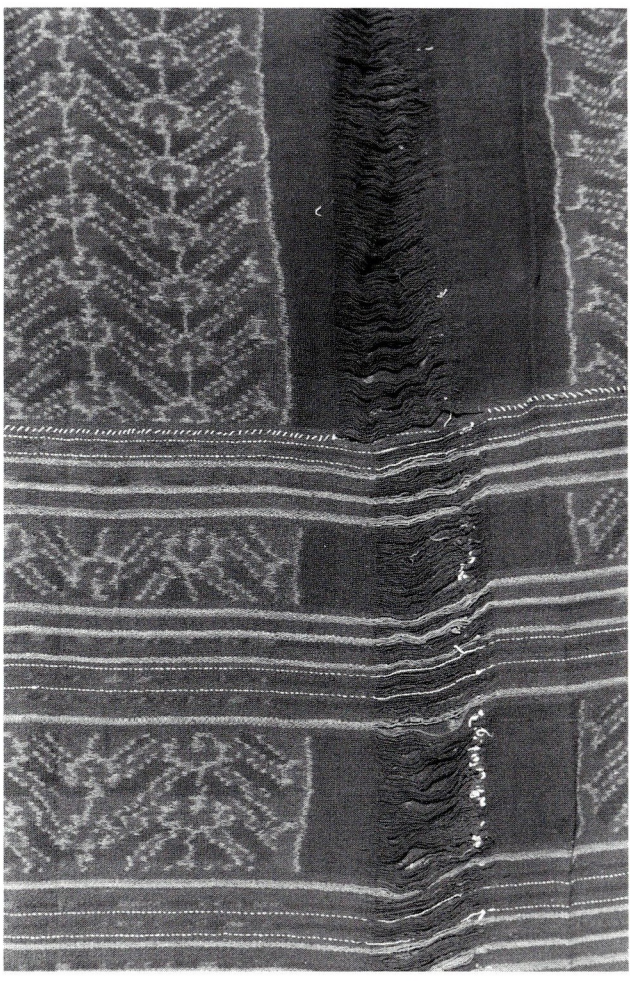

Figure 11. The "hair" (ratā) of a three-panel bridewealth cloth. Lamalera, 1979.

cloth which he put onto the cut "to soak up the blood." It was a specific part of the textile, he said, which could close the wound: the *ratã*. All cloths are woven with a continuous warp, and when they come off the loom, they have an open section of warp left; this is the *ratã*, or "hair." If a cloth is intended for wear, it is cut and then sewn together at this point, to close the tubular shape. However, if the cloth is to be used as a bridewealth gift, these warp threads may not be cut (Fig. 11). This is a clear proscription in Lamalera which also applies to other (though not all) parts of Lamaholot. For the purpose of bridewealth, a cloth with a cut warp is worthless. In East Flores it was once explained to me that the continuous warp thus preserved in the *ratã* (there called *ratan*) represented the threads of kinship and descent. This interpretation may not be articulated in the same way everywhere, but the context in which the cloth is exchanged makes the explanation important. It is reinforced by the use described above, where the open warp, the "hair" of the red cloth, is used to soak up blood and close a wound. Kinship and descent are for the community the "flow of life" (R.H. Barnes 1974:306), just as blood is for the individual. The cloth can be the essential mediator.

Odd and Even Numbers

A combination of odd and even numbers is an essential aspect of Lamalera women's cloths. It should be recalled that the number of ikat skeins making up the width of one pattern has to be uneven. The individual skein contains six yarns—thus an even number. The number six, however, is made up of a combination of two times three or three times two: it combines the odd with the even. The separate warp yarns that make up the single ikat skein are called *kulu*, "seeds." Once combined, they form a *kenumak*. An uneven number of *kenumak* make up each pattern. When a pattern (*kenirak*) is tied on the ikat frame (Fig. 12), for technical reasons each knot will actually cover four times the same design (R. Barnes 1984:94-95). The complete ikat section to be tied with knots will therefore produce four times the same pattern. This section on the ikat frame, then, contains four times the uneven amount of ikat skeins which make up each pattern, thus an even number is achieved. The section on the frame is called *matã* (Fig. 13). *Matã* is of course the Proto-Austronesian *maCa (Dempwolff 1938). It has a variety of meanings, among others "eye, source, origin."[12] We have encountered it above in the Kédang expression *matan-méan* which might be translated as "the source of wealth." The *matã* on the ikat frame refers to all the ikat yarns which are tied into one design. It is only used for the warp on the ikat frame, not for the woven pattern. If translated as "source," it is to imply the source of the ikat patterns.[13]

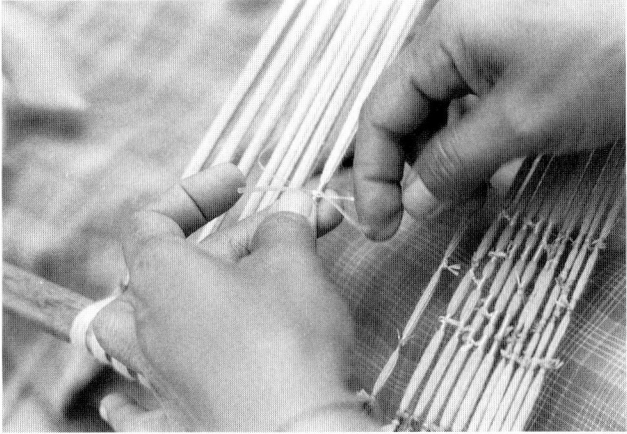

Figure 12. The pattern is tied into the warp: one knot holds four times six threads. Lamalera, 1982.

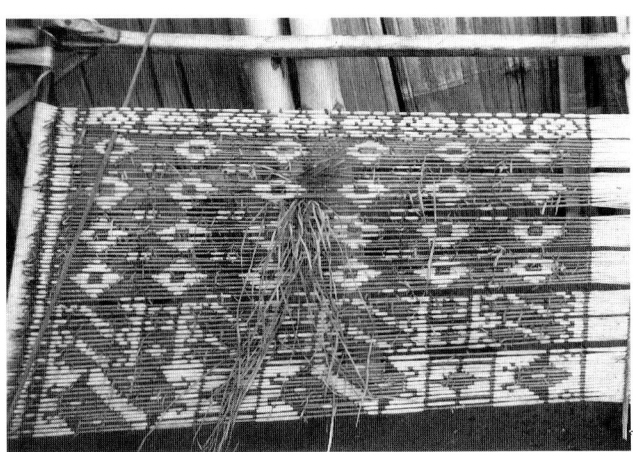

Figure 13. The ikat frame with eight pattern sections (matã), each with an uneven number of ikat skeins (kenumak). Lamalera, 1979.

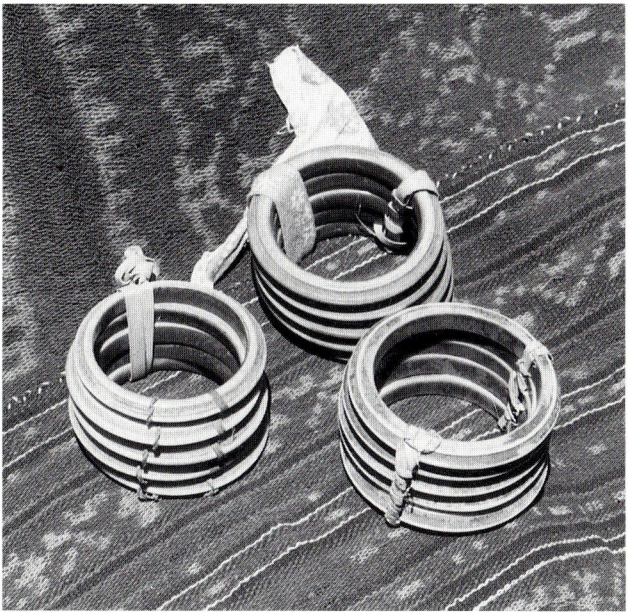

Figure 14. The cloth and ivory bracelets, part of the exchange at marriage, are given by the bride's family. Lamalera, 1979.

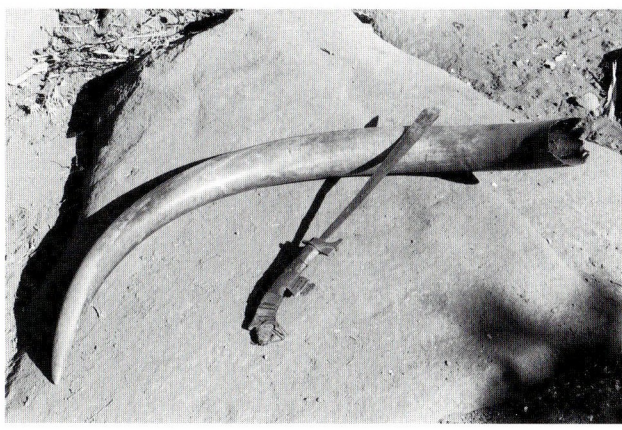

Figure 15. A tusk (approx. 180 cm.) typical of those given by the groom's family to the bride's, here shown with a sword which is a clan treasure. Lamalera, 1979.

The total number of warp stripes and ikat bands decorating the two-panel women's cloths is always uneven. The three-panel bridewealth cloth is made up of two symmetrical outer panels, which makes the combined number of ikat bands even. However, with the addition of the central panel, the uneven number is again established.

The contrast between odd and even is also found strongly expressed in the building of the village's boats. They are divided into eleven sections, called *uak*. Some boats, though, being slightly shorter, do not have the correct number of compartments, but only ten. Such boats are *téna uak nalã*, "boats with a section lacking." Keraf, a linguist from Lamalera, gives the following interpretation based on his detailed knowledge of the structure of the boats and of the terminology and attitudes associated with them:

> Odd numbers express a form of life, a continuous dynamic. This situation represents an important factor in the attitude of life of the people of Lamalera. Even numbers indicate that everything has been finished, is complete. Thus there is no living dynamic, there is no life. Because of that, whenever a boat of the form *uak nalã* (i.e., "section missing") does not possess an odd number of sections, it is nevertheless still thought to possess an odd number, through the description as a *boat lacking a section*. In other words, it is "a boat whose sections are not complete," i.e. odd in number. By this method, thus no violation of the prevailing norm occurs (1983:6).

The bridewealth cloth, which in itself is made up from yarns and designs defined in terms of even and odd, should also be seen in the context of the complete gift exchange. The goods to be exchanged are clearly defined. From the woman's side they consist always of cloth called *tukã-hebã* in the formal language used during the discussion of the required prestations, and of several sets of ivory bracelets, *kala* (Fig. 14). The man's family will have to find the necessary tusks, *bala* (Fig. 15). Ideally, there are two parts to the exchange: one directly between the bride's and the groom's clan and the other, a smaller set of prestations between the latter and the bride's mother's brother, her *opu-pukã*. All exchanges of tusks, cloths, and bracelets are measured in terms of a unit called *kesebõ*, used exclusively in the context of the marriage exchange.[14]

One set of prestations is always measured in an uneven number of units. The tusk requires the equivalent units in the form of cloth and bracelets. For a tusk that measures, for example, seven *kesebõ*, seven units have to be returned. These are made up of two gifts: the textile and the ivory bracelets. The complete exchange, then, involves an uneven set of gifts: the tusk, the cloth, and the bracelets. Odd signifies incomplete, but also continuing (R.H. Barnes 1982:17).

The three-panel bridewealth cloth of Lamalera bears comparison with another Lamaholot ikat tradition, that of Atadéi (Fig. 16, Pl. 5). The two cloths are obviously closely related. Both use the central pattern with a continuous design; the Atadéi cloth also shows strong patola influences in this panel. Certain patterns seem to be common to both weaving centers. Lamalera's oral history can help to shed some light on the relationship between both areas. I have said elsewhere that Lamalera is a village of outsiders who managed to use their new locale to great advantage (R. Barnes 1984:242-66, and 1989). The original settlers of the community traced their origin back to Sulawesi, to a place called Luwuk-Belu. A Lamalera teacher who recorded the local history identified Luwuk with the town of that name in eastern central Sulawesi. Perhaps at least as much to the point would be a connection to the ancient state of Luwu, once situated in southeastern Sulawesi, at the Bay of Bone. The area has iron-nickel deposits, and Luwu may have had the early control of metal export to Java and elsewhere. The *Nagarakertagama*, a fourteenth century Javanese document dealing with the Majapahit reign, mentions Luwu as a dependency of the latter (Andaya 1981:18). The iron export from Luwu would have been important in the development of trade. In any case, Lamalera's ancestors claimed Majapahit dependency and were supposedly sent out from Sulawesi as emissaries for the Javanese kingdom.

When they settled first on Lembata, they lived at Mulan, just inland from Labala. However, a fight broke out between the host community and the new arrivals when (according to Lamalera's story) a chick was crushed by a falling rice mortar. Lamalera's ancestors left and eventually settled at the present site. The entire history, which is too elaborate to describe here, has one major theme: how a small group of outsiders gains influence over an indigenous population, almost entirely through their superior knowledge. It also tells how power and positions of superiority changed within the small group of immigrants, and how one clan emerged as the leader of the community. The success, implicitly, shows adaptability to new situations: this is still the major strength of Lamalera today.[15]

It is not clear whether the women of Lamalera knew how to weave before they came to the island. Vatter says that they brought that knowledge with them (1932:205); I could not find confirmation of his report. But the textiles they produce today fit stylistically into the general type of Lamaholot cloth, and they are specifically close to their neighbors in Atadéi, the area in which they first settled. Yet traditionally the village and the region it governed were not friendly with the

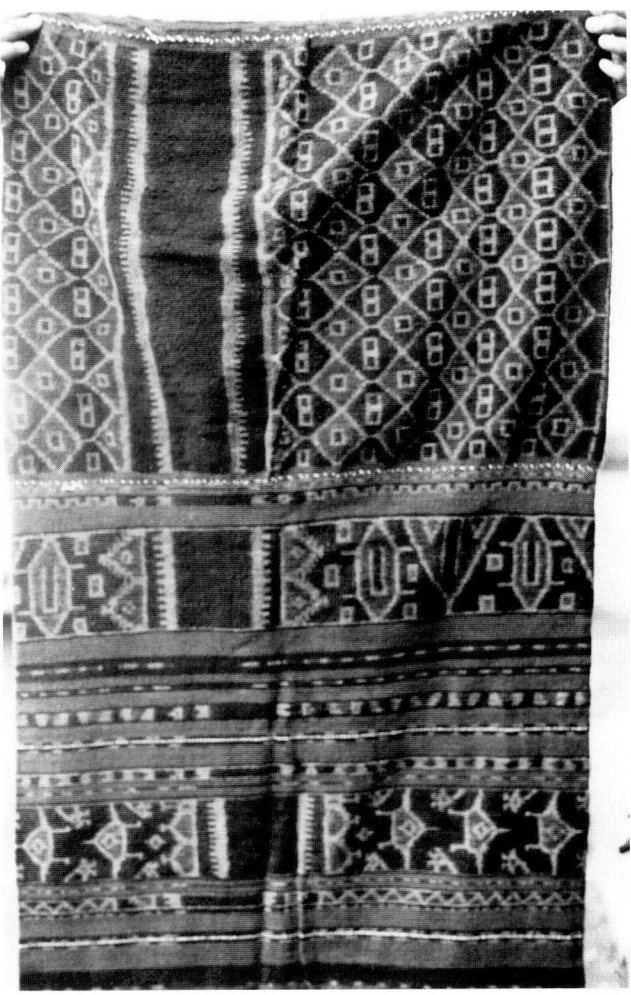

Figure 16. A three-panel bridewealth cloth of Atadéi, photographed in 1982.

neighboring peninsula and its local ruling settlement, Labala. Into this century warfare was frequent between the two areas, and the animosity was explained in traditional Lamaholot terms: Labala and its dependents are "Paji," while Lamalera and the villages further inland consider themselves "Demon." These terms signal a division found in Lamaholot culture, based on political and mythological animosity between regions. Frequently the opposition is supposed to be between original inhabitants and later arrivals (R. Barnes 1987). The division seems to have a long history in the area; it was first mentioned by Europeans in 1636 (Basilio de Sá 1956:486). It has been suggested by Maxwell (1981:53) that there might be a connection between weaving and non-weaving, especially non-ikat-producing areas, and the ancient Demon/Paji division. For Lembata there is no consistent correlation. In particular Labala/Atadéi and Ili Api (both Paji) contradict the suggested association of Paji with non-ikat-producing, non-weaving communities.

The evidence in southern Lembata points to a strong ikat tradition in Atadéi that influenced the new arrivals who ultimately settled in Lamalera. The patterns found on the Atadéi peninsula almost all also appear on Lamalera cloth (Pl. 5); in addition, the Lamalera weavers have added their own designs. The central panel showing patola influences is a prominent link between the two regions. Again, Lamalera women have included additional motifs. While Atadéi ikat takes up many of the geometric designs of the Indian cloths, the stars and lozenge shapes, Lamalera uses patola floral designs as well. It could be, of course, that both Atadéi and Lamalera reacted in similar ways to an outside influence, in particular to the patola trade. My own inclination is to accept that Lamalera's ancestors were first introduced to Lamaholot culture and adopted many aspects of it when they settled at Mulan, near Labala. There is a certain amount of linguistic evidence for this: Keraf classifies Lamalera's dialect, together with that of Mulan, as an eastern branch of West Lamaholot, unlike the village's immediate neighbors, which he identifies as High Lamaholot (Keraf 1978: app. VI). Written documents which give us dates about the Lamaholot go back to the Portuguese arrival on Solor in 1515 (Jacobs 1974 I:301). Lembata is first described in a Portuguese document of 1624, which also refers to the hunting of whales and the presence of ambergris on the island: undoubtedly a reference to Lamalera, the only community in all of Indonesia known to hunt the sperm whale (Basilio de Sá 1956:486-87). A few years earlier the name of Lamalera had been mentioned directly in an account of the martyrdom of two Catholic priests on Solor. Apparently, they had managed briefly to find refuge on the south coast of Lembata, but were returned to be tortured and killed in 1618 (R. Barnes 1984:280).

Conclusion

Two aspects of Lamalera's bridewealth cloth have emerged in particular. First, the cloth reveals much about the society, not only in the display of patterns, but also in some of the technical aspects of making the cloth. The ritual and conceptual value of the red cloths has to be seen in combination with the elephant tusk for which it is exchanged. The two complement each other, although they are opposites in many respects. The tusk is most definitely non-indigenous, while the cloth must be indigenous, made entirely from local material. Although outside influences may be acknowledged by some weavers (who know of the link between patola and their own patterns), this is insignificant to them. Designs that were once foreign have become an essential aspect of their indigenous textile art. When using such patterns, the weaver takes as her model the cloth she has seen her mother or aunt use, not the patola the clan may have as a treasure. These cloths, in fact, are hardly ever viewed.

The tusk's material solidity stands in contrast to the fragility of the cloth. The very nature of textile production is evidence of a changing state: from raw cotton to yarn, from white yarn to colored fabric. It has been mentioned that patola cloths, as clan treasures, are said to change with the moon. A similar explanation is sometimes given for the unraveled appearance of an old bridewealth cloth.[16] Textiles are obviously created through change. It is only women who can manipulate the transformation, and to a certain degree they may be vulnerable while doing so. The tools they use—that is, all parts of the loom, the ikat frame and the threads used for ikat tying—must never be burnt: that would bring mental confusion to the women. Writing about West Sumba in this volume, Danielle Geirnaert comments on proscriptions connected with spinning and yarn-winding in Laboya (see also Geirnaert In Press a). I have not been able to discover similarly explicit information in Lamalera, but the theme of creating through transforming, and the danger involved with it, is nevertheless an interpretation that makes sense in this context as well. Although younger women in Lamalera learn how to ikat from their mothers or other female relatives (not from those in their husband's clan), they will not attempt to make their own red cloth until they are past the age of child-bearing. The process is gradual rather than clearly defined, and young women will be partially involved for years. But occasionally an illness, especially if it involves mental confusion, is said to be caused by a women's attempt to make a bridewealth cloth although her children are still young.

Finally, I want to remark on the use of textiles as historical sources. In a society where a permanent record of motifs is not clearly datable, and where such a record is more often than not expressed on non-permanent material—cloth, wood, basketry, or the human body, in the form of tattooes—the art historian faces great problems. We depend on the cooperation of other disciplines, in particular on that of linguists, anthropologists, and archaeologists. That joint effort is necessary if we are to shed light on the history that predates the arrival of Europeans in eastern Indonesia.

NOTES

1. My first stay on Lembata was from 1969 to 1971, when I accompanied my husband on his anthropological fieldwork in Kédang. I returned to the island in 1979 and again in 1982, when I spent altogether nine months in the village of Lamalera. All visits were carried out under the auspices of the Lembaga Ilmu Pengetahuan Indonesia (LIPI). My research in 1979 was funded by a postgraduate studentship from the English Department of Education and Science; in 1982 I was supported by the Social Science Research Council of Great Britain.

2. Gregorius Keraf has analyzed the linguistic variations among the Lamaholot (1977; 1978).

3. Here it may be useful to compare the attitude to prescription and choice in textile patterns to the marriage prescriptions of the region, which are of the asymmetric type and call for the alliance with a clearly defined category of persons, yet often in fact make room for a wide choice of partners (see R.H. Barnes 1974:295-304).

4. For a more complete description of the village setting, see R. Barnes (1984 & In Press a).

5. The name Atadéi refers to the peninsula east of Labala Bay. Ikat textiles of the same type are also produced in the mountain region called Lerek, which is to the north of Atadéi, and in Labala, the trading center and former seat of the Rajah of Labala.

6. She may, however, claim to belong to an established Lamalera group: it was common into this century for prominent people in the village to adopt outsiders into their clan.

7. Both cloths and tusks are measured in standardized units, *kesebō* (R. Barnes 1984:183-91).

8. Vatter erroneously says that two warp yarns make up one skein, *kenuman* (1932:223). In some parts of Lamaholot the minimum number of yarns is four, rather than the six of Lamalera.

9. Vatter (1932) says that usually the weaver only identifies the number of ikat units, i.e. the width of the pattern, when giving its name. In Lamalera I found that especially narrow patterns, which are therefore limited in design possibilities, are referred to by number of ikat units, but that eventually a specific name can be discovered even for these patterns. This name may not be common knowledge, though.

10. A list of patterns known and used at the moment appears in R. Barnes (1984:132-35, figs. 13-38).

11. In 1982, however, two weaver friends made me a farewell present of a shouldercloth which included a depiction of a whale. They had probably been prompted to invent this totally new design by the comments of an Indonesian marine biologist, a Toba Batak who participated with my husband in a World Wildlife Fund project in the village in 1979. He had suggested that "for the tourist trade" the women should try to show the spectacular whale hunt. It is prohibited for women to go out to sea with the men, and so they could not depend on firsthand experience: perhaps it is for that reason that the boat was shown to approach the whale under full sail; in reality the sails are always lowered when going after whale.

12. See R.H. Barnes (1977) for a discussion of *maCa in Indonesia and the Pacific.

13. The combination of *kulu*, "seed," and *matā*, "eye source," is found in Kédang *mato uluq*, "pupil of the eye," literally "eye, seed."

14. In his account of Labala merchandise and trading in market goods Beckering refers to *kaseboeng* as a unit of payment (1911:193). In Lamalera, the *kesebō* is no longer used when measuring market goods, but only in discussing the value of marriage prestations.

15. While retaining many of their traditional customs, the villagers have been unusually successful in taking advantage of modern schooling (see R.H. Barnes 1987).

16. More often, however, the tattered appearance is blamed—realistically—on the presence of mice in the house.

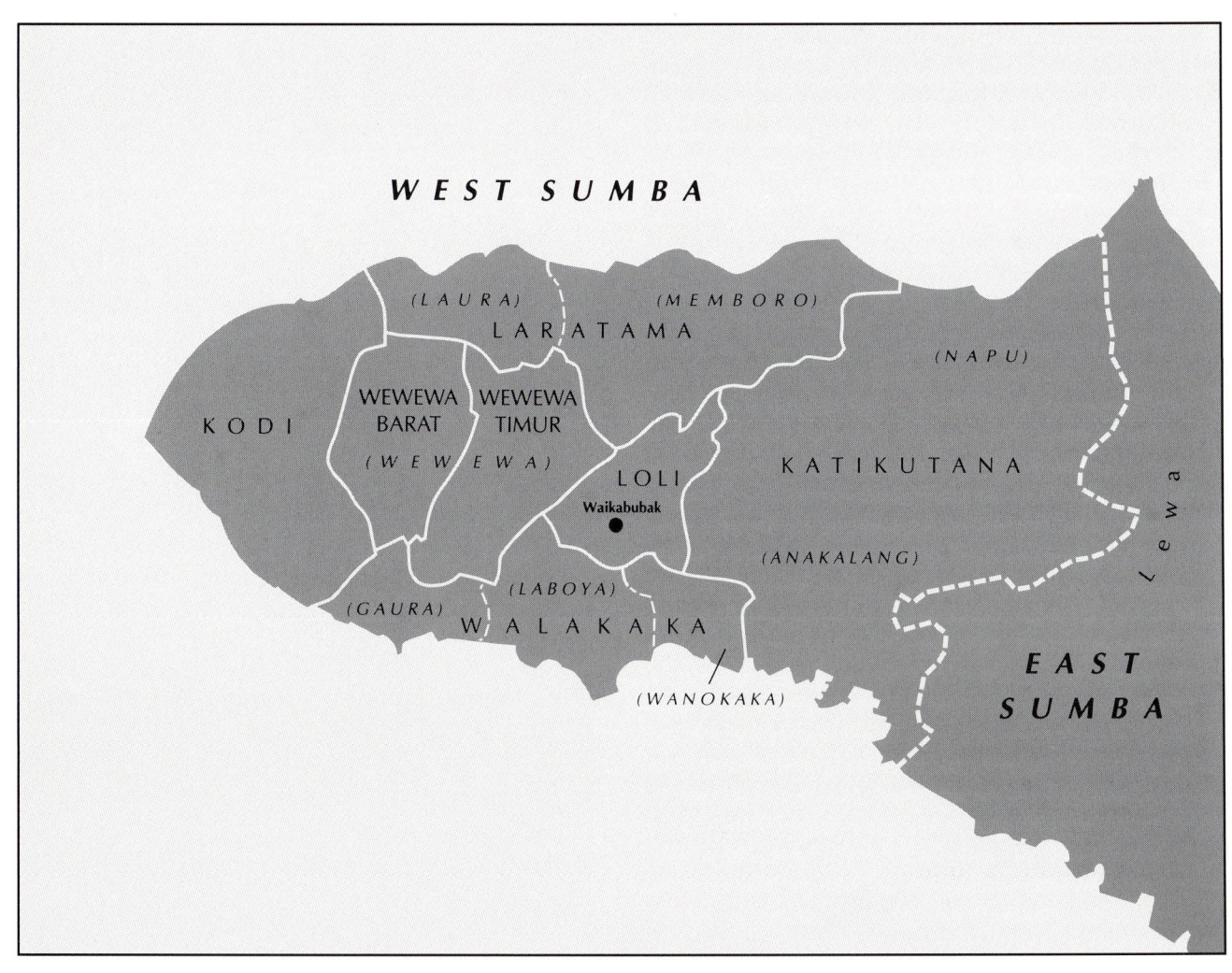

West Sumba, showing modern administrative units (kecamatan).
Names of former regencies are indicated in parentheses.

Textiles of West Sumba
Lively Renaissance of an Old Tradition

Danielle Geirnaert

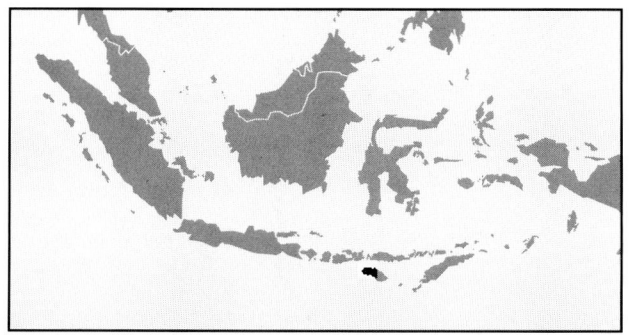

...slechts witte en zwarte doeken mogen door U gedragen worden, of Mijn slangen zullen komen.

...only white and black cloths you may wear, or else My snakes will come.

The snake spirit of Memboro in "De Heilige Paarden" (Fabricius 1960)

Within the renowned Indonesian textile tradition the cloths of West Sumba might be considered respectable but unobtrusive. Some can rightfully claim great ancestry. Others are the newborn children of modern trade relationships. All share the common fate of being overshadowed by their sumptuous eastern cousins. Yet it is largely thanks to weavers from the western part of the island that the Sumbanese textile family is growing. While one may wonder whether such high-quality production will last, West Sumbanese textile creativity deserves recognition.

The great majority of West Sumbanese women still weave their own daily and ceremonial cloths as well as those for the men of their family. On busy market days in early morning, the fast-moving crowds along the roads are silhouetted in bright colors. A closer look reveals a great variety of techniques and patterns that can be traced back to sharp regional differences.

The image of West Sumba has not always been so colorful. Administrators and missionaries who traveled in this region before World War II recall that the women wore full black sarongs, and this is confirmed in the collections and photographs brought back by Alfred Bühler in the 1950s.[1] Thus changes have taken place in the last two decades. The purpose of this paper is to document the major types of West Sumbanese textiles, both in the past (as far as possible) and now. It includes a description of the way cloths are woven, sewn, and worn; a survey of regional style differences; some speculation on the historical and geographic origins of certain textiles; and finally, a brief discussion of the esoteric properties of textiles in West Sumba, as well as suggestions for further research.

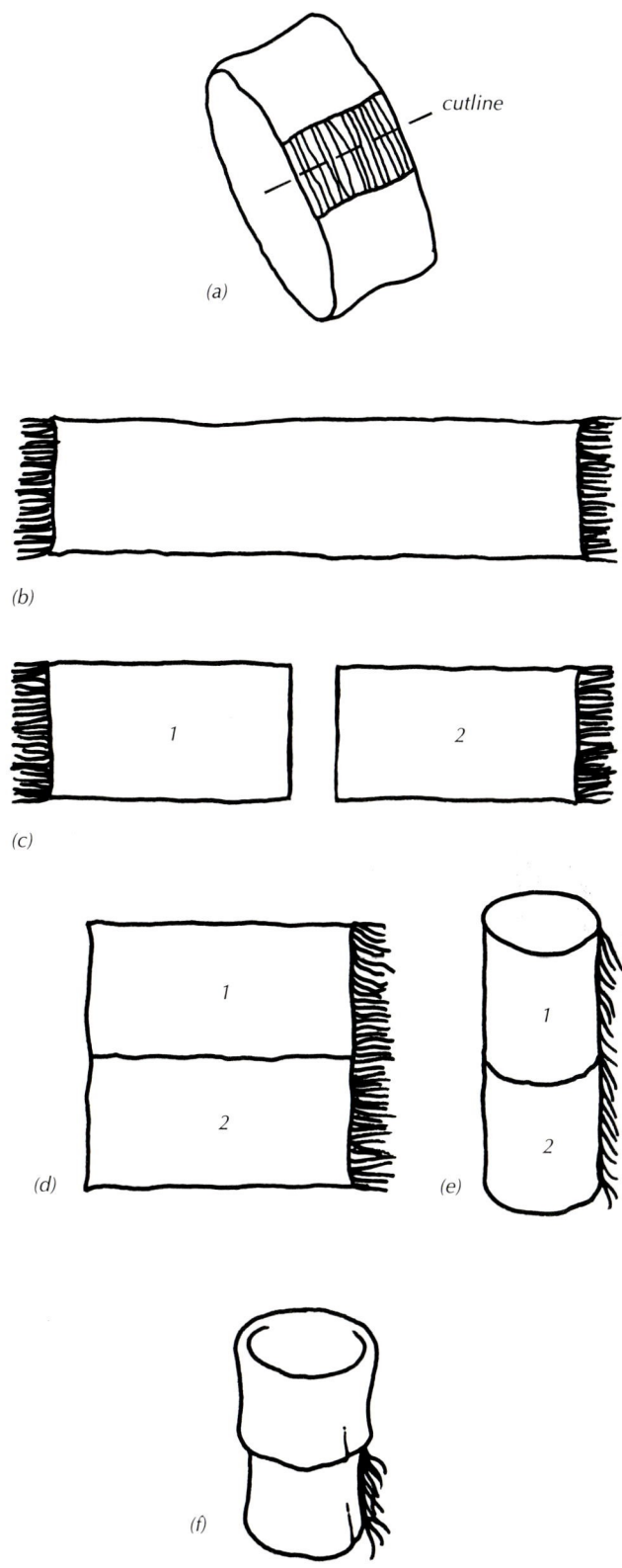

Figure 1a-f. Woman's cloth, from loom to skirt. Just off the loom, the cloth is circular (a). It is cut across the unwoven part (b) and cut in half (c). The halves are joined at one of their selvages (d). Finally, the short ends are sewn together to make a ready-to-wear, tubular skirt with a fringe (e). About two-thirds of the top half is folded back over the outside, allowing for adjustment to the desired length (f).

West Sumba is far more divided linguistically than East Sumba. It was Dutch colonial policy to grant the status of regency to each linguistically and culturally distinctive group. So-called rajas, usually recruited among the traditional nobility, were appointed and put in charge of local affairs. After Independence the rajas lost their official power there, as elsewhere in Indonesia. In West Sumba, however, their descendants still exercize considerable authority, although this is never formally recognized. Wives and daughters of the former authorities play a leading role in introducing new dress styles.

Modern Indonesian administrators have created new, larger administrative units, called *kecamatan*, by regrouping several former regencies together (see Map). Now that all children receive basic schooling, the new generation is learning to communicate across ancient territorial boundaries, using the Indonesian language as a lingua franca. Enmities that date from headhunting days are fading. Nevertheless old ties remain strong and at times matters of dress provide a way of expressing pride in one's own group. Indeed in some respects it appears that new styles have been created for that very purpose.

The Making and Wearing of Cloth

All Sumbanese cloths, east and west, are woven in plain weave with a weftwise rib (Burnham 1980:111) on a backstrap loom without a comb (type A in Gittinger 1979a:230). Because the warp is continuous, the completed cloth, when taken off the loom, is circular. Part of the warp, once the heddle sticks and rod have been removed, remains unwoven, hanging loosely (Fig. 1a).

On the basis of patterning technique, West Sumbanese cloths fall into four main categories. Easily recognizable are the ikats and the plain cloths. The other two, slightly more difficult to identify, are patterned either with selected warp floats or with supplementary wefts. Additional twining and tufted embroidery may embellish any of the four types. Differentiating these techniques is essential for the identification of a textile's regional origin.

The Female Costume. A woman's cloth, called *ye* (*lau* or *lawu* in the Kodi region), is woven in one circular piece. When finished, it is taken off the loom and cut open transversally across the unwoven part of the warp (Fig. 1b). The cloth, now flat, is cut into two equal halves (Fig. 1c) which are sewn along one of their selvages to form another flat piece of material (Fig. 1d). Then the short sides of the cloth are sewn together, face to face. The end product is a tubular skirt, ready to wear, averaging 120-150 centimeters in circumference and 120-180 centimeters long (Fig. 1e). This is the standard method of making a skirt in West Sumba except in Memboro (see below), where tubular skirts are made of three panels instead of two.

In traditional skirts the loose hanging warp threads along the vertical seam were not removed. Instead, they were plied and twisted to form a fairly stiff fringe. In some regions, this fringe was dip-dyed in indigo. Traditionally the cloth was worn with the fringe hanging at the back. Noblewomen had the privilege of decorating it: the twisted fringe bundles were inserted into long tubular brass beads and knotted at the ends to keep the beads from slipping off.[2] People still remember how pleasant it was to hear the beads tinkle as women danced.

Traditional *ye* were blackened in a special kind of mud. But not all were dyed as soon as they came off the loom: only those made of coarsely-spun second-rate cotton were treated in this fashion. Finer cloths were carefully kept white for festive occasions,[3] until they had grown soiled and worn; then were they dyed black for daily wear. The white or black *ye*, with its twisted fringe, was worn throughout West Sumba, except perhaps in Kodi and Memboro, until the early nineteen-sixties.

Plates and drinking bowls made of wood or coconut shells are still mud-dyed; however this method is rarely applied to cloths any longer, and certainly not to the extent that has been recorded in East Sumba (Adams 1971:323). Now West Sumbanese women would rather purchase a plain, factory-woven piece of material sold by the meter in the local shops: black but also dark green and blue are the most popular colors. In modern woven tubular skirts, the fringe is cut off before the sewing is done. The vertical seam is worn in front instead of at the back.

Otherwise, the way of wearing a *ye* or *lau* has not changed. About two-thirds of the top half is folded back on the bottom part, allowing proper adjustment to any desired length. Also, in this way, the horizontal seam is concealed (Fig. 1f). In the width, the extra material is folded into a front pleat, the top end of which is tucked in at the waist. Because of the depth of the front pleat, the vertical seam is invisible as well. With some patterning techniques that use either warp floats or supplementary wefts, designs do not appear in exactly the same way on both sides of the cloth. In that case, before the two panels are sewn together, one of them is turned over. This is the case of the Lolinese skirts called *lambelekko* (see below).

The Male Costume. A man's cloth, or *hanggi*, is also made up of two pieces, but it is flat instead of tubular. Its average size is about 240-260 centimeters long and 120-160 centimeters wide. The procedure for making a *hanggi* shows essential differences from that used for the *ye*. The weaver must set up her warp not

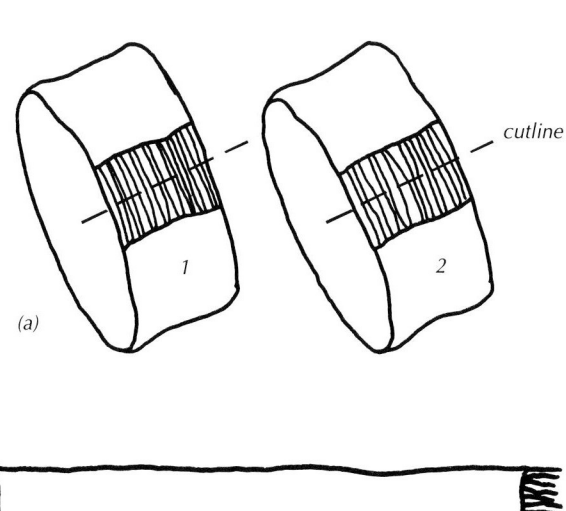

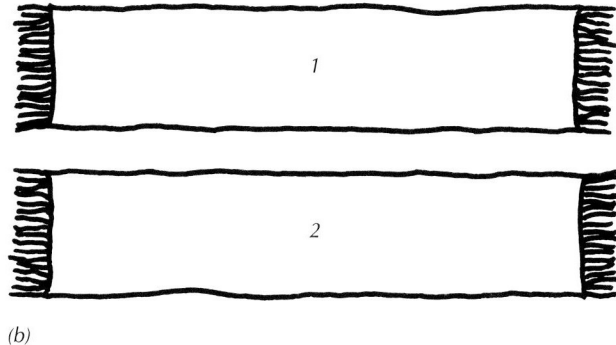

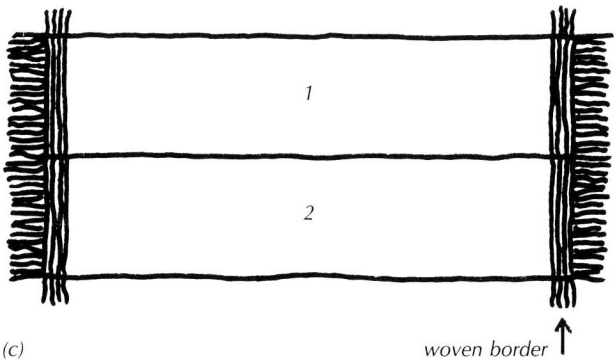

Figure 2. Man's cloth with woven border. Two circular pieces are woven independently of one another (a). Once off the loom they are each cut across the unwoven part (b). The two flat pieces are sewn together at one of their selvages. Finally, using the fringe of warp yarns as weft, a narrow border is woven at either end (c).

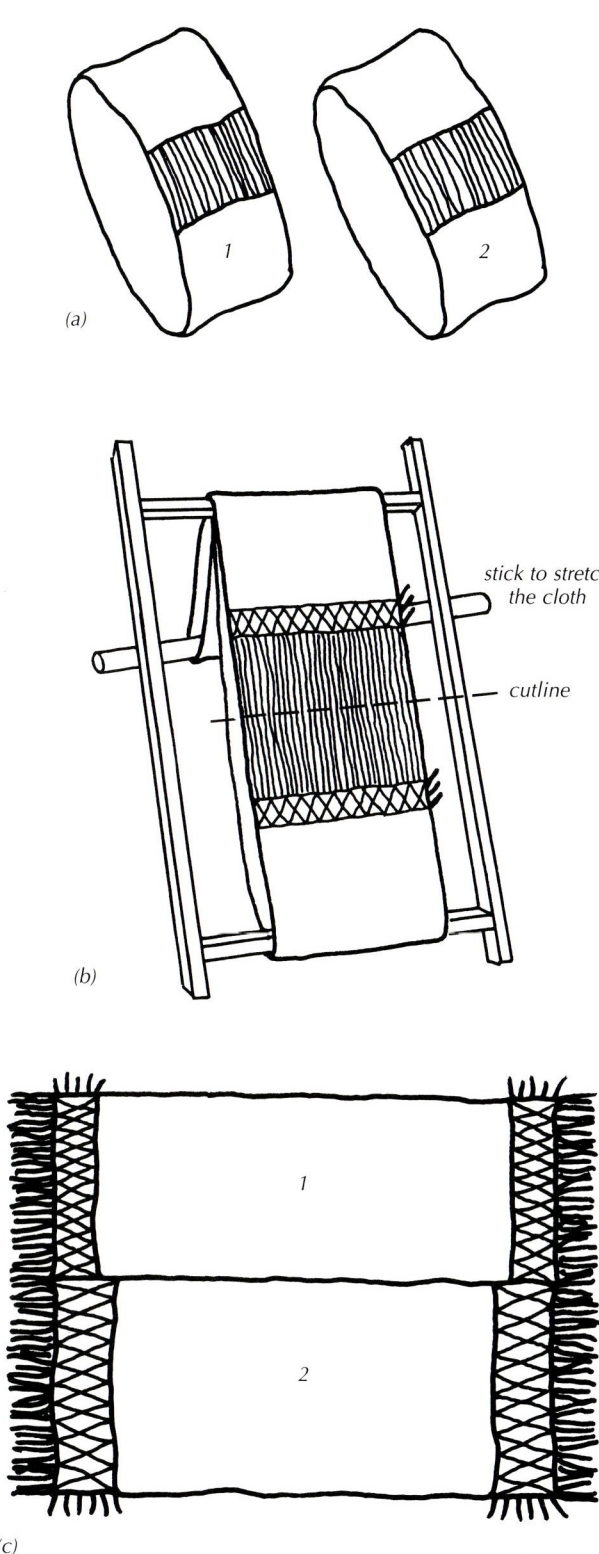

Figure 3. Man's cloth with twined border. Two woven panels just off the loom are circular (a). Each panel is stretched and prepared for twining (b). The twined panels are joined along one of their selvages (c). In the Laboya type, the halves are uneven.

once but twice, and weave each piece separately. When finished, she is left with two circular cloths instead of one (Fig. 2a).

At this stage, she must choose between two different finishing techniques. She may follow the East Sumbanese method for men's cloths (called *hinggi* there). In that case, the circular cloths, once off the loom, are cut open across the unwoven part of the warp. The resulting two flat pieces of material are sewn together along one of their selvages (Fig. 2b,c). Then a continuous narrow warp of colored yarns, about three to five centimeters wide, is set up on a small loom whose length slightly exceeds the width of the sewn material. The cut yarns of the warp from the woven textile are divided into bundles. Now part of each bundle is used as a weft and woven into the new colored warp. The remaining yarns of each bundle form the fringe of the cloth. When the weaving is finished, the small warp is cut at both ends. The result is a woven border in weftwise ribs perpendicular to the ribs of the cloth (Fig. 2c) and bearing the color of the narrow warp. At both ends of the border the yarns hang loosely. The whole process is repeated on the other side of the cloth.

A second technique, looked down upon in East Sumba but far more popular in West Sumba, consists of twining instead of weaving the final border (for technical details cf. Khan Majlis 1984:365). The circular finished cloths are stretched over a wooden frame (Fig. 3b). Paired colored threads are twined around the uncut warp yarns (Fig. 4), a process repeated on both ends of the woven cloth. Finally the twining threads are cut on the right side and bound in little bundles. Only then is the cloth cut open. When both pieces of material are complete, they are sewn together. The result is a twined border at each end. One of the commonest motifs is diamond-shaped.

In either case, whether the border is woven or twined, the fringe may or may not be plied and twisted, depending on local custom, in the same way as for a women's *ye*. While twining is a job for either men or women, plying and twisting are done exclusively by men. In some regions, the fringe is dipped in an indigo bath, as for the female skirt. Beads, however, are never used for men's cloth.

Formerly, for a twined border, two or more handspun and naturally dyed threads were plied together. Nowadays, a thick, machine-spun cotton embroidery thread is available in the market. Thinner cotton or rayon embroidery threads, also machine-made, are used for the woven border. In Kodi one still occasionally finds textiles with handspun and indigo woven borders; however they are becoming very rare.

Throughout West Sumba, the borders on a man's cloth, whether woven or twined, are of crucial importance. They testify that the weaver has been circumcised and thus that he has reached adulthood with all its social implications. I was assured that no man who had been brought up according to traditional values would be willing to wear a cloth with borders missing. Such a cloth would be considered childlike, unfinished, and would bring shame upon its owner (Geirnaert, In Press b).

When a *hanggi* is worn, one end hangs loosely in the front while the rest is tucked in at the waist. Some West Sumbanese men have adopted an East Sumbanese, or at least an Anakalang habit, by which the length of the front flap indicates the wearer's status. For the high nobility it nearly sweeps the ground, whereas for commoners it should not hang below the calf. Formerly, slaves were not allowed to let it fall below the knees. For working in the field or horseback riding, the flap is pulled up between the legs and tucked in at the back.

Proper dress and status. Competitive feasting is a major feature of West Sumbanese society and on such occasions, matters of dress are just as revealing as verbal behavior for the study of social hierarchy. Traditional and modern apparel is imaginatively combined for the purpose of making social prerogatives explicit, and one is certainly expected to do so. In Laboya, claims for higher status, for instance, may be expressed by folding a headdress so that the end of the cloth stands upright in the middle of the forehead, instead of to the side, above the temple. Perhaps ostentatious dressing is a modern habit. Some say that noblemen should dress in an ordinary fashion so as to avoid the jealousy of both the living and the dead. In the old days, it seems that it was not uncommon for a slave to wear his master's beautiful clothes while the latter went humbly dressed (of course one may argue that people would know exactly to whom the luxurious cloths belonged). A similar custom has been recorded in East Sumba as well (Adams 1965:27 and 1974:273).

Such behavior may have been more specific of Loli than of other regions. In Laboya, if the costume is deemed congruent with the status of the wearer, it will later be recalled with words of praise. Unwarranted claims, however, are punished, at least verbally. When women are working in the fields they have a way of singing short couplets to mock their enemies or their husbands' enemies if they happen to be passing by. This is a socially acceptable way for women to express grievances publicly. The songs are composed spontaneously, but their message is no less clear. The following example, sung by an elder woman, was meant for the ears of a girl whose father had refused to give her to the woman's son in marriage, because he had more ambitious plans for his daughter.

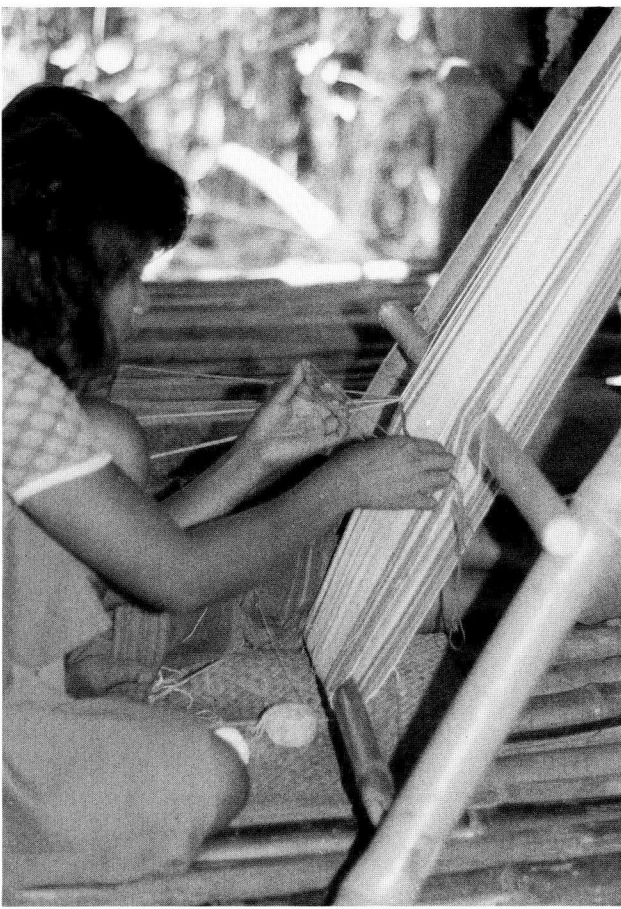

Figure 4. A woman twines a border or kalib'ra; *yarns are still on warping frame. Laboya, 1984.*

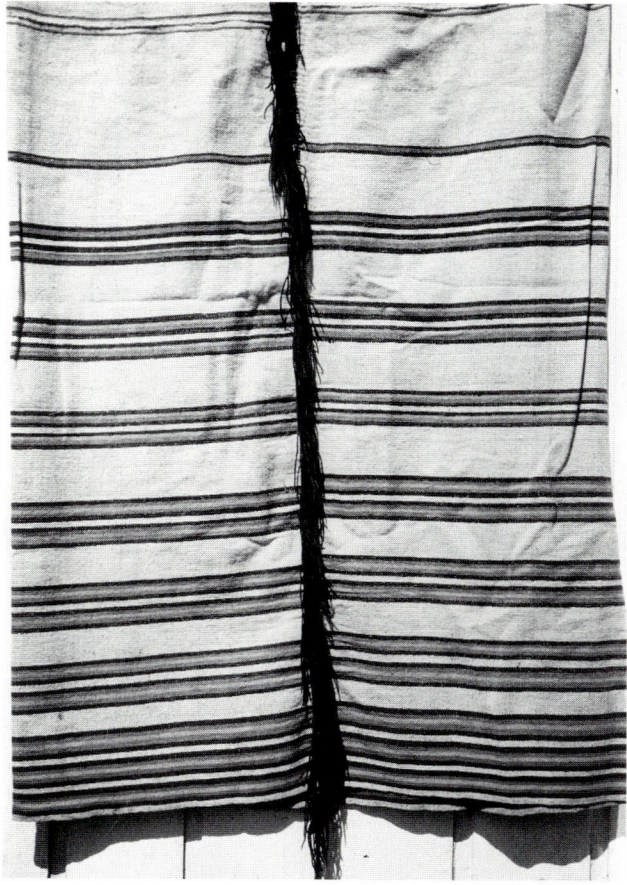

Figure 5. Traditional Laboyan ye made with handspun yarns, natural dyes (red, yellow, and black stripes); indigo fringe hangs at the back. Also shown in Figure 6, below.

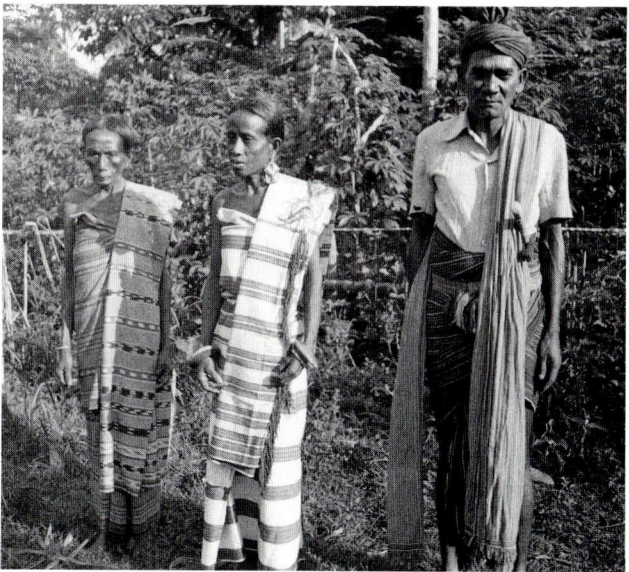

Figure 6. Laboyans in full ceremonial dress, 1984. The skirt is tied under the armpits instead of at the waist as for daily wear. Mrs. E. Doki Ledi, center, wears a mamuli, or golden ear pendant, and costly ivory bracelets on both wrists. Her shouldercloth is also seen in Figure 5. Her aunt, left, wears a modern costume of light blue cloths dyed with commercial dyes and patterned with simple ikat stripes (formerly forbidden in Laboya). Her husband Mr. Ledi, right, wears a Kodinese gundu *wrapper and Laboyan* gudu *shouldercloth.*

You who go to Waikabubak,
you stand so upright in the front of the truck,

(a relatively comfortable place to which, in the eyes of the singer, the young girl has no right)

You who wear a white, white skirt,
your family has no land,

(the skirt described is like that in Figure 5. Allusion to its whiteness—unsuitable for field work—suggests that the girl is lazy; allusion to her parent's landlessness suggests that they are of slave origin)

You look so proud,
but you have nothing to eat.[4]

Underlying rivalries, to which such couplets obviously refer, must sometimes be settled by the appropriate ritual, during which a pig is sacrificed.

Full traditional ceremonial dress for both men and women requires a second cloth, identical to the first one, worn as a shouldercloth (Fig. 6). For daily wear, West Sumbanese men are clad in a Western shirt and shorts, over which they wrap a cloth. Often this is a checked Kodinese *gundu*, acquired by barter, or a simple green or blue piece of material purchased in the local Chinese shops of Waikabubak. A knife, variant of the Indonesian *parang*, is tucked into the cloth, at the front (Fig. 7). A plaited pandanus or palm leaf bag for betel nut and lime completes the traditional costume for both men and women.

In the *desa* or villages, when attending a ceremony or when going to an urban center, women wear a traditional blouse (*kebaya*), or, if they have attended secondary high school, preferably a white blouse. As elsewhere in Indonesia, urban educated people wear Western clothes, but when they are invited to a ceremony in the *desa*, they take care to wear either a *hanggi* or a *ye* over the Western clothing. This is a sign of respect towards the hosts.

Local differences in dress will now be considered in more detail on a geographical basis, following the territorial boundaries of the former regencies. These correspond to ethnolinguistic communities, though not to modern administrative realities. Within former regencies there is remarkable homogeneity: different clans wear the same patterns.

Regional Differences

Loli

Travelers to Loli inevitably stop in Waikabubak, the small[5] regional capital in the heart of Loli country to which all public transport leads. But they will no longer see the rather disappointing traditional *ye*. Instead they will be charmed by the newest fashion, the *lambelekko* cloths worn by women as skirts and named for the technique used in the border panel (Pls. 11,12, Figs. 8-10). On important occasions, small versions of this cloth are worn by both men and women as shouldercloths, in imitation of the Indonesian *slendang*.

Visually, *lambelekko* is reminiscent of the East Sumbanese supplementary warp technique used for women's skirts or *lau pahodu*. From a technical point of view, however, *lambelekko* is entirely different. It is a pick-up technique, and more precisely a "*sélection par baguette*," because sticks instead of the finger are used when choosing the picks. The resulting structure is a warp-faced alternating floating weave, not the supplementary warp structure used in East Sumbanese skirts (Burnham 1980:59,99; Bolland, pers.comm.; Viallet 1971:45).

In Loli, people say *lambelekko* is an entirely new technique that dates back to the mid-1960s. As we shall see when considering trade relationships, this is only partly true. Since the end of the 1960s, Lolinese women, taking advantage of massive imports into West Sumba of Javanese thread (*benang jawa*), seem to have blown new life into a technique which was rarely used in earlier days, and most probably only in Kodi. They have adopted this form of weaving with such enthusiasm and perseverance that one may truly speak of a renaissance of West Sumbanese textile art. In Waikabubak's Chinese shops they can choose from various brands of embroidery thread (generically, *benang borduur* in Indonesian) such as *Cap Delima Manggis* or *Kiyang*. It is said to be silk thread (*benang sutera*) but is probably artificial silk or rayon, imported into Java from other South East Asian countries (pers. comm., Heringa). It is appreciated for the brightness of its colors and the fact that it does not run in the wash.

A woman's particular choice of tints, however, is dictated by a code related to color symbolism. If the cloth is meant for a mature woman, the preferred colors for the plain part of the skirt will be either dark green, dark blue, or dark red (as in Pls. 11,12). Bright blue befits a young girl. For the *lambelekko* panel itself, two contrasting colors will be chosen, both different from the plain part of the skirt: one for the background and the other for the patterns. In 1982, green for the background of the *lambelekko* and yellow for the patterns was the most common combination. A year later, white patterns standing out on a black *lambelekko* background had become equally popular. As elsewhere in West Sumba, what really matters is that designs should contrast strongly with the background in order to produce a light-dark impression which is considered to be like "life" (*hidup*) and not like "death" (*mati*), that is to say, dull. The same principles and associations apply to the indigo ikat process in Kodi for

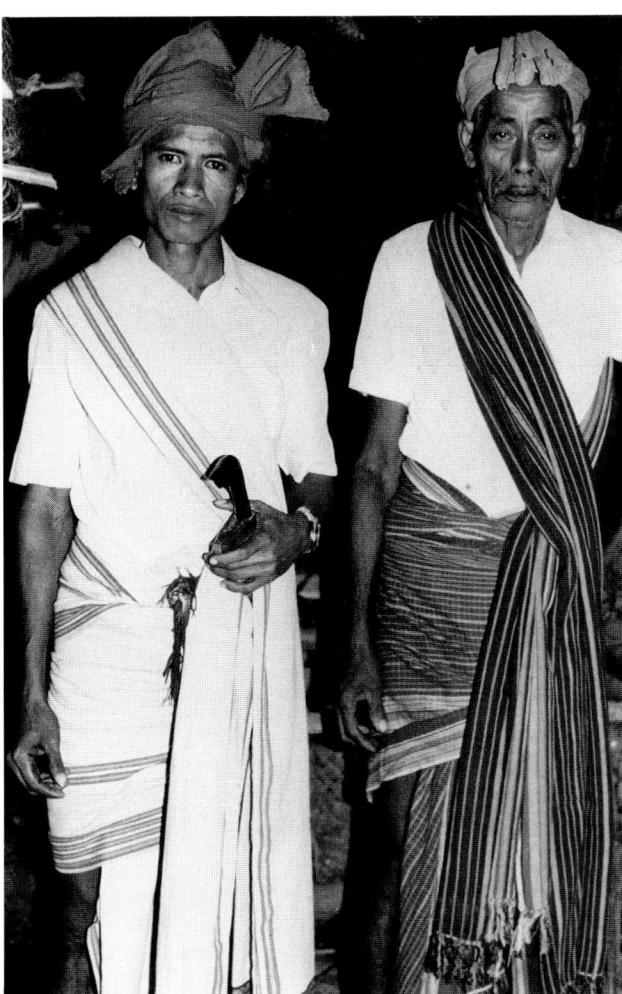

Figure 7. Laboyan men in full ceremonial dress, 1983. The man on the left wears a set of identical Laboyan hanggi *of handspun yarn. The man on the right wears a Kodinese* gundu *wrapper and a Laboyan* gudu *shouldercloth of handspun indigo-dyed yarn. The Kodinese* gundu *has horizontal as well as vertical lines; a Laboyan* gudu *has only vertical ones of light indigo.*

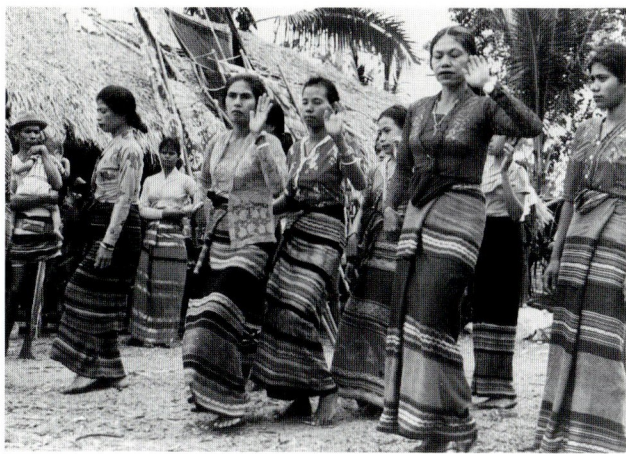

Figure 8. Women dancing at a feast in Loli in 1982. The dancer on the far left wears a modern Kodinese gundu. The lady behind her, right, wears a skirt with shiny horizontal stripes in plain weave with gold threads, the latest fashion that autumn. The rest of the dancers wear lambelekko cloths from Loli. On the roof are textiles from both East and West Sumba brought by the host bride-givers.

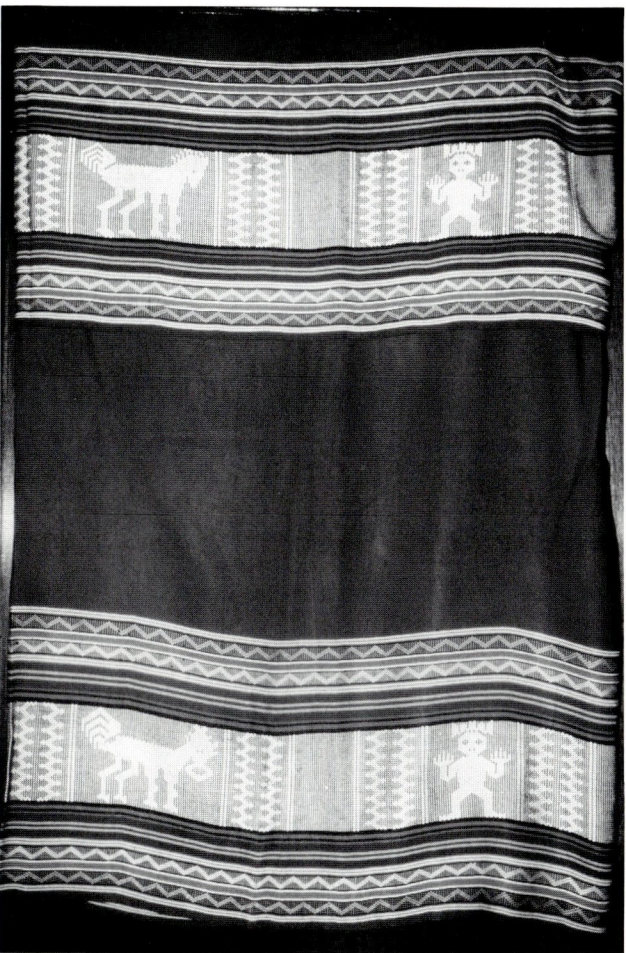

Figure 9. Lolinese lambelekko skirt seen in 1982. Note difference between horses in bottom and top borders. The weaver worked without patterns, from memory. She commented while weaving that she did not like the wide mouth of the first horse (bottom, left) and decided to represent it in profile (top, left). The human figure is a pattern borrowed from East Sumbanese textiles.

instance (Geirnaert, In Press b). Implicit is the idea that a person's life cycle is bright in the beginning and dark at the end. Throughout Indonesia this is a well-known theme, often related to the solar and lunar cycles (Geirnaert 1983, and Heringa in this volume).

The weavers are not entirely free in their choice of colors because they are dependent upon the available supplies. Towards the end of 1983, the shelves of Waikabubak's shops were laden with unusually bright orange and red skeins. About three months later, one could observe these two colors combined in *lambelekko* skirts on the streets. Similarly, in the autumn of 1982, some girls experimented with golden stripes in their skirts (Fig. 8). About a year and a half later, golden *lambelekko* were highly popular. This fashion was probably the result of a Jakarta-born interest in Indian silver and gold thread. Around 1980, there were special expositions in Jakarta showing such ordinary Javanese cloths as *lurik* into which metallic threads had been woven (Heringa, pers. comm.; Kartiwa 1982,1983[6]). Another source of inspiration is the golden *songket*-clad ladies seen on Indonesian calendars in the shops where thread is bought.

It has been noted elsewhere that West Sumbanese like thick cloths because they provide extra protection from destructive powers and thus insure longevity (Geirnaert, In Press b). Apparently this idea applies to the Lolinese *lambelekko* as well. In a good one, the warp yarn is double instead of single, and the weft triple instead of double. There is no particular technical reason for this. Weavers from other regions (such as Kodi, see below) deliberately choose the thinner version because they do not want to imitate Lolinese exuberance which they judge as being pure arrogance. Moreover to the naked eye it makes no difference because in both thick and thin versions, the pick to make the pattern always consists of two yarns. But the barter value of a good *lambelekko* is relatively high because it requires not only the purchase of more skeins than usual, but also the added labor of winding these additional skeins into usable balls. The number of warp yarns per centimeter is remarkably constant, if one considers the fact that no reed is used when setting up the warp. It is nearly always forty.

The *lambelekko* border itself is delimited above and below by narrow stripes, either plain or in the *lambelekko* technique. The latter uses motifs representing the cassava liana, called *lua* (or *loluga* in other regions), the ubiquitous motif in all West Sumbanese cloths (Geirnaert, In Press b). When women start to practice *lambelekko*, they choose a simple motif, usually the *lua*. Golden ear pendants (*mamuli*) are popular designs among the Lolinese, as are those replicating the typical peaked-roof houses of Sumba (Pl. 11). Many *lambelekko* patterns, such as the human figures with hands upwards, are borrowed from

East Sumbanese cloths (Figs. 9,10). However, for the large *lambelekko* borders, about seventy centimeters wide, floral designs of European origin are favored (Pl. 12). At the beginning of 1984, Lolinèse *lambelekko* borders were tending to become wider and wider and to represent flowers, birds and fountains (Fig. 11). In the autumn of 1986, this was no longer the case with the skirts meant for daily wear. By then, the *ye* with the largest borders were kept for special, festive occasions only. Another feature of interest relates to a difference in layout between the *lambelekko* of 1984 and those of 1986. The former show a great variety of patterns within a single cloth. Lately, however, weavers tend to repeat the same motif along the whole border of a skirt. In 1986, floral designs borrowed either from Timor or from Western decorative art were on the increase, to the detriment of the more characteristically Sumbanese motifs such as the peaked-roof houses, horses, and ear pendants.

Old and new cross-stitch pattern books are as eagerly sought as they are reluctantly lent. New patterns are jealously guarded until the day a daughter or a sister-in-law asks to borrow a skirt so that she can copy its design. Because of strong affinal obligations, such a request cannot easily be turned down. Incidentally, it is one of the reasons why designs are not bound to clans. Educated women may have more facility reading pattern books, and the fact that they know how to count may initially help them set up the more intricate designs. Yet the commonest way for experienced but illiterate weavers to increase their pattern repertoire is by copying directly from a *lambelekko* skirt. Also, they practice patiently, making corrections as they weave (see again Fig. 9). It is not unusual for a woman who comes from another region to settle for a while in Loli, if she has any family there, in order to learn *lambelekko*. Widows who no longer have to care for small children hope to improve their financial position in this way.

People from other regions consider the Lolinese well off and have ambivalent feelings towards them. The central position of their capital, Waikabubak, has probably favored economic conditions in Loli over those of more remote areas. In any case Lolinese have a reputation of being loud and ill-behaved. The very width of Lolinese *lambelekko* is commented upon as a manifestation of arrogance. This antagonism is strongest in Kodi, whose traditional enemies are the people from the central highlands, that is, the Wewewa and the Lolinese.

Laboya and Wanokaka

Laboya is a quiet, strongly traditional area, although its frontier with Loli is only about ten kilometers south of Waikabubak. It still produces the

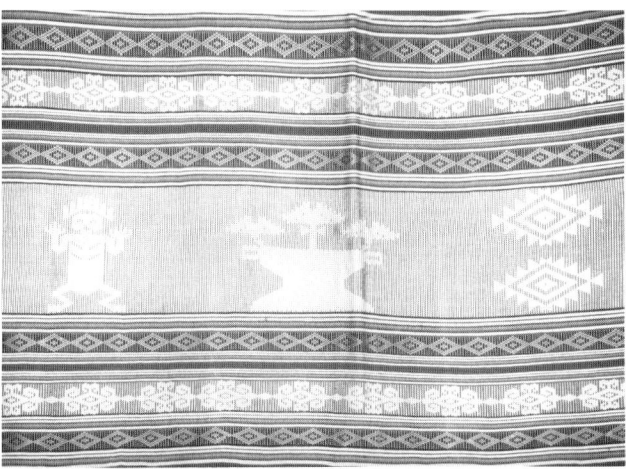

Figure 10. Detail of a Lolinese cloth seen in 1983, with lambelekko *border. From left to right: human figure (an East Sumbanese motif), flower decoration, and buffalo eye (variant of the Indonesian* mata kerbau*), a well-known West Sumbanese pattern.*

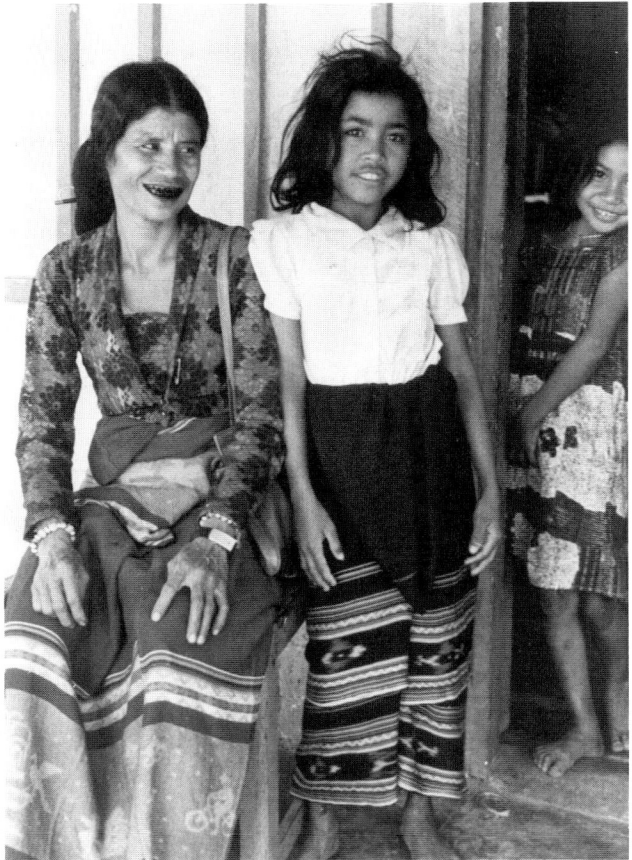

Figure 11. The seated lady is the hostess of a feast given in 1982 by her husband, a village headman (kepala desa) for the Indonesian administration in Loli. Honoring her husband's ambition, she wears her best cloth with a wide lambelekko *border. Patterns include, left to right: an elegant "flower bowl with a resting bird," (most likely a fountain with pigeon, typically copied from a European cross-stitch pattern book); two golden ear-pendants; little stars; and a unique man on a motorcycle. One daughter wears a modern ikat skirt from Wewewa, and a white schoolgirl's blouse. The youngest wears a modern batik dress. When older, she will be allowed to wear a traditional skirt.*

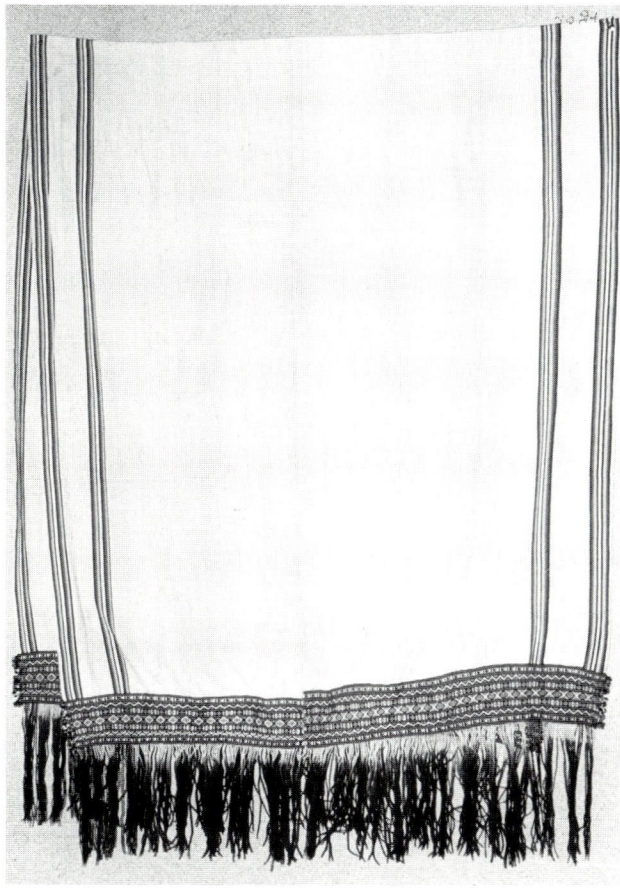

Figure 12. A traditional Laboyan man's cloth (hanggi or hang'), seen in 1984. It is made of handspun yarns, except for the machine-made yarns of the twined borders or kalib'ra, purchased in Waikabubak, and those of the stripes along the selvages. The fringe is twisted and dyed in natural indigo.

old type of cloth, handspun and with a fringe at the back of the women's skirt [7] (Figs. 5,6). Laboyan textiles are almost entirely white. A *ye* may have narrow yellow, red, and black stripes; perhaps this is a fairly recent addition. The fringe is dipped in indigo.

A man's cloth, *hanggi* or *hang'* is white with narrow yellow and red stripes along its selvages (see Warming and Gaworski 1981:139), and twined borders called *kalib'ra* (Fig. 12). The spinning and the weaving is done by women. Twining may be carried out by either sex: it is not uncommon to see a man sitting on a veranda, laboriously twining a *kalib'ra*. The plying and twisting (*pote*) of the fringe, however, is always a man's work (Fig. 13). It is done in the same way as the plying of lianas to make rope, also a man's chore. Several yarns are vigorously rolled on the thigh, their ends are tucked back a little, and a sharp roll in the opposite direction fastens the twist of the yarn bundle. The fringe-tips are given a fine point. When it has been plied and twisted, the fringe is dipped in a bath of indigo, either synthetic or natural; dye solutions here are much lighter than in Kodi. Throughout the operation, the cloth is protected by a mat of pandanus leaves, and the fringe, called *wu* (which also means "hair") is treated with great care. The same type of textiles are made in Wanokaka, although the twined border patterns differ slightly; there men's cloths do not have colored lines along the selvages. It is Laboyan textiles that have the widest and most beautiful twined *kalib'ra*, and the Laboya people are very proud of this work, which takes a great deal of time.

A Laboyan man's cloth has one essential and interesting peculiarity: the two halves of the textile are deliberately unequal in size. One panel is always slightly longer and wider than the other. This is only possible, of course, because each warp has been set up separately (as explained above). The difference is also apparent in the *kalib'ra*. Although the patterns are exactly the same for both parts, the threads tend to be tamped more firmly in one panel than in the other; hence the height of the twined border is greater on one side (Figs. 3c,14).[8]

Last but not least, before the two panels of the *hanggi* are sewn together, one of them is turned over. As a result one side of the twined border is the inverse image of the other: white diamonds, for instance, become black, while black crosses become white (Fig. 14). This is a fine example of a reversal of symmetries, a procedure which has been observed many times in so-called "traditional" or "primitive" art (Boeren, In Press; Gerbrands 1983; Lévi-Strauss 1958,1979). In addition, this decorative method is applied, with many variations, elsewhere in Indonesian textile art, and often carries a symbolic significance (Geirnaert 1983). In the case of the Laboyan *hang'*, it is explicitly stated that the largest panel with the widest *kalib'ra* represents a man while the smaller one is a woman.

A Laboyan *ye* carries no special information by itself, and is always less valuable than a man's cloth. There is no difference between the two panels of a *ye*; this would not be technically possible since it is woven in one piece. The once strict taboo against ikat is being slowly abandoned. Some women claim that they have been able to learn how to do it because they have Kodinese ancestors. Apparently, Kodinese kinship ties legitimatize ikat in Laboya. Esoteric knowledge concerning textile production taboos lies in the hands of men. Curiously, women were particularly ignorant about these matters. When asked why the *kalib'ra* is higher on one side than the other, the women believed that it had been a mistake and they were prepared to unsew the cloth and make it again. Similarly, women do not usually know the names of the patterns in the twined border. Men always do.

Laboyan ikat skirts are usually dark, dyed either with synthetic or natural indigo. Flower motifs dominate in the better ones (Pls. 13,16); otherwise, triangles, squares, and other simple geometric designs are chosen for the ikat. Laboyan women themselves say that they have just learned the art of ikat and are not yet very good. They are very conscious of the fact that their ikat skirts are dark blue and not red like the modern Wewewa examples.

Another type of indigo-dyed skirt in Laboya is called *gudu*. Though very similar to the Kodinese indigo cloth known as *gundu* (discussed below), the Laboyan *gudu* has no colored ikat border. Said to be traditional, it is a plain woven cloth used by men and women, with alternating light and dark blue, and sometimes red or yellow stripes in the warp. At the top and bottom of *gudu* skirts Laboyan women are starting to make *lambelekko* borders which they call *labelekko* or *labalekko*. Again, they say that they are just beginners in this craft. Lolinese women who have married Laboyan men are regularly asked to act as teachers; however they prefer to weave for themselves without too many witnesses. Laboya has not yet developed a *lambelekko* style of its own, in contrast to Kodi for instance. As for Wanokaka, the situation is very similar.

Memboro

In the former north coast kingdom of Memboro, people traditionally wore plain cloths, white as well as black. During ceremonies these are still very popular, although women like to wear Endenese sarongs as well. One can see the coast of Flores from Memboro, and boats from Ende arrive daily.

The usual Memboro man's cloth is entirely white with a woven white border and fringes that are plied

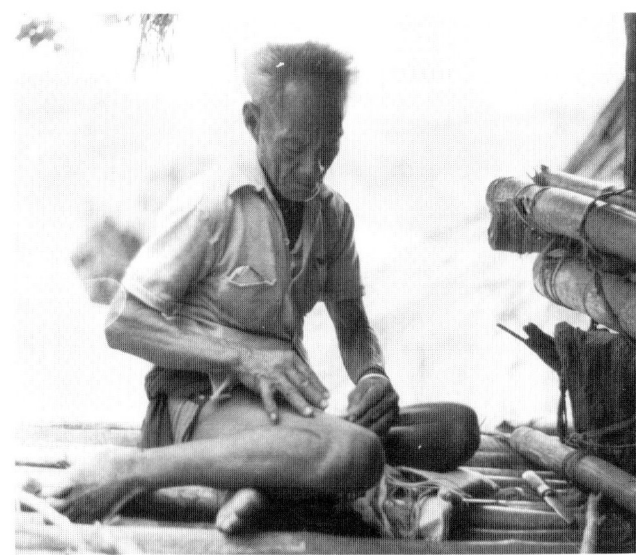

Figure 13. Plying of the fringe, or pote *(a man's task). Laboya, 1984.*

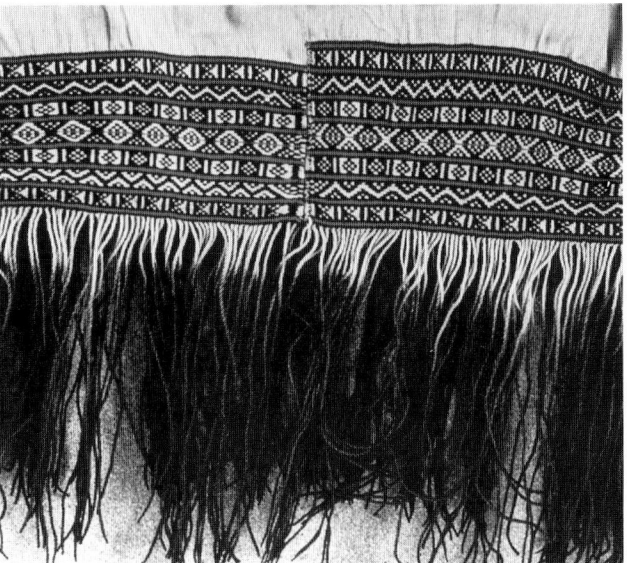

Figure 14. Detail of the twined border (kalib'ra) *on the Laboyan man's* hang' *shown in Figure 12; its colors are yellow, red, white, and black. Note the difference between the "male" and "female" halves of the twined border.*

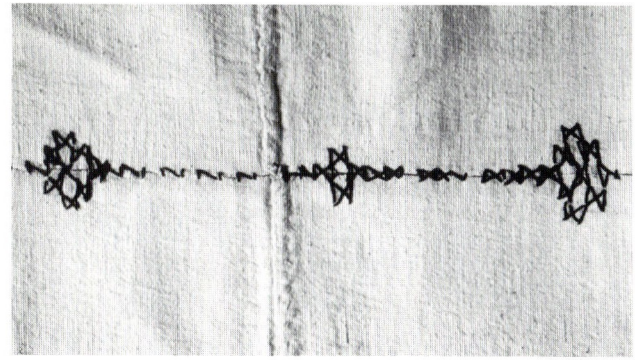

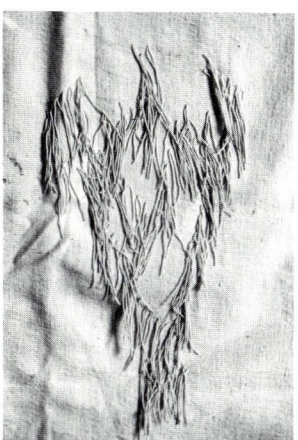

Figure 15 (above). Seams embroidered in red or black are characteristic of skirtcloths from Memboro. This one, done in black, was photographed in 1984.

Figure 16 (left). A shrimp pattern worked in tufted embroidery (pote) appears on the same Memboro skirtcloth seen in Figure 15, above.

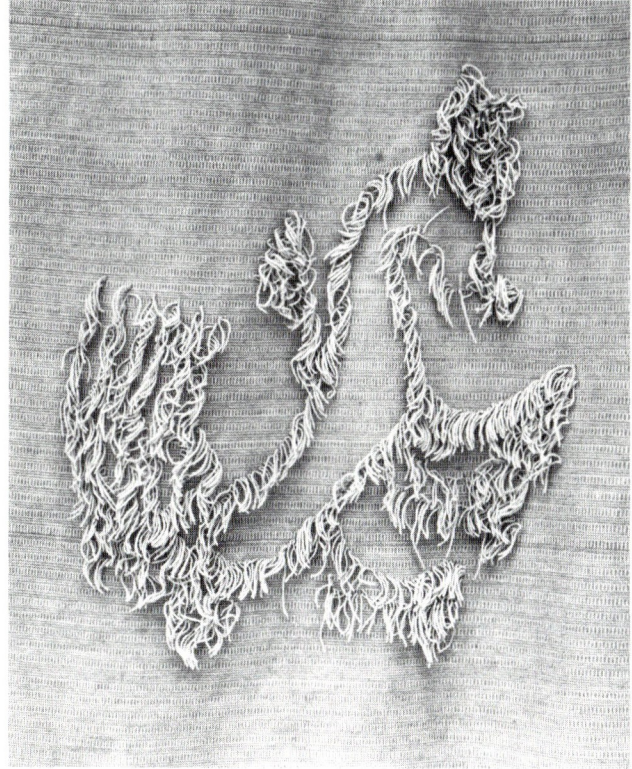

Figure 17. A horse in tufted embroidery appears on a cloth from the north coast of West Sumba (Memboro or possibly Napu), photographed in 1982. The man who embroidered the horse lived near Cape Sasar. Private collection, East Sumba.

and twisted, but not dyed. Formerly, only the nobility had the right to a twined border, the patterns of which were borrowed from East Sumba. The preferred twining thread was red. If a slave or commoner put on such a garment without the authorization of the nobleman who was its owner, he was liable to be killed (so I was told by the Raja of Memboro, who witnessed such an event about fifty years ago).

Like all Sumbanese skirts the Memboro women's skirt is tubular, but it is made of three panels instead of two, following Endenese fashion. As in the rest of Sumba, it is worn with one- to two-thirds of the top folded over, but because the lower panel is small—only a third of the whole skirt—the horizontal seams are visible. However, they are preferably embroidered over to make the cloth look more attractive (Fig. 15).

The unique characteristic of Memboro skirts is their tufted embroidery. Shrimps (Fig. 16) and horses (Fig. 17) constitute the most spectacular design motifs; human figures, however, are proscribed. While women do the weaving, the tufted embroidery, called *pote*, (the same word as for the plying and twisting of the fringe) is done by men. A thread is inserted into the cloth, and a second one, of equal length, is placed on top of it. Then both ends are twisted separately on the thigh, and the whole process is repeated until the pattern is complete. Although tufted embroidery designs are usually white, certain simpler motifs, like small triangles, are sometimes done with colored threads. This is said to be a fashion of recent origin. Women of the high nobility add a beaded border at the bottom of their dress. Amsterdam beads were imported into Memboro until at least the 1920s, and perhaps even later (Fig. 18). Neither ikat nor *lambelekko* are practiced in Memboro; its textiles are similar to those of Napu, a domain that is now part of East Sumba.

Kodi

Textiles from Kodi exhibit the greatest textile variety in all of West Sumba, particularly in female dress. The Kodinese wear dark, mostly ikat cloths, in contrast to plain, essentially white traditional textiles of the regions heretofore considered. The men's *hanggi wola remba*, the only relatively well-known cloth from West Sumba (described elsewhere) represents a snake, usually a python, and it is a highly sacred textile[9] (Geirnaert, In Press b).

Gundu. Kodinese men's *gundu*, called *hanggi gundu*, is a far more mundane textile. It is a dark indigo cloth with both vertical and horizontal lines in a lighter shade of blue, which has become very popular in West Sumba; Laboyan men, for example, can be seen wearing Kodinese *gundu* (Figs. 6,7). In the 1950s *hanggi gundu* were handwoven and dyed a natural indigo with only one or two yellowish or reddish stripes running parallel to the selvages. Today, very few are still handspun. The better quality *gundu*, however, are dyed with natural indigo. Modern ones show several narrow multicolored stripes along the selvages, instead of the single color of three decades ago. Yellow, red, light blue, and white stripes are usual; lately green ones have become fashionable as well. Increasingly, imported rayon or cotton threads, or *benang jawa*, are used for the cheaper *gundu*. In that case, they are much lighter in weight and in color than the more luxurious ones.

Both woven and twined borders (*kalidir* in Kodinese) are found in Kodi, the twined ones being small—one or two rows only. Fringes are never plied. Kodinese men like to complete their costume with bright orange headdresses and betel nut bags. Handspun and indigo-dyed yarn is still made for embroidering betel nut bags, which are worn by women as well as by men.

It is female dress that is remarkable in its variety. First there is the female counterpart of the *hanggi gundu*, called *lau gundu* (Pl. 14, Fig. 19). It is a dark blue cloth with a single set of light blue stripes in its warp which appear to be horizontal when the skirt is worn. The top and bottom borders of the female *gundu* are ikatted with bright colors. This seems to be a fairly recent style which has spread in the last five to six years; indeed, it is not very common among the *gundu* in museum collections acquired during the 1950s.[10] In those days the light and dark blue stripes or checks filled the total surface of the cloth; there was no ikat border, there were no colored stripes, particularly in men's *gundu*. The border patterns of the female *gundu* are the same as those found on the ikat skirts described in the following section.

The Ikats. The fully ikatted traditional skirt is known as *wola*, from the verb *wolo*, to ikat (Fig. 20). Synthetic dyes have considerably brightened the colors of this cloth. Nowadays, patterns stand out in bright red, yellow, or white on a background which is nearly black. This is because the cloths are dipped into two different baths. The first, either red or yellow, is synthetic. The second is indigo, either a synthetic or natural. Interestingly, the natural dye process imparts to the cloth a very different smell; it is also far more expensive because it requires the sacrifice of a piglet.

Whereas the men's ikat cloths, *hanggi wola remba*, have shown great consistency of design for at least the last hundred years, the decorations on women's skirts have manifested great variation in shape if not in theme. To remember how women were dressed a few decades ago required a genuine effort from both men and women who were asked about it. Ikat skirts were the exclusive prerogative of noblewomen. Patterns were small and the whole textile was indigo and white only. Some people recalled a kind of white skirt

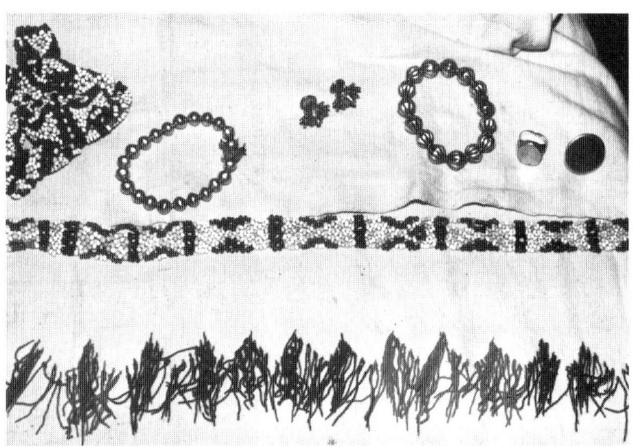

Figure 18. A modern Memboro skirt, woven from machine-spun yarns and decorated with colored tufted embroidery. The pair of borders created from Amsterdam beads can be seen at the bottom of the skirt. Beaded borders and jewelry are worn only by noblewomen. Photographed in 1983.

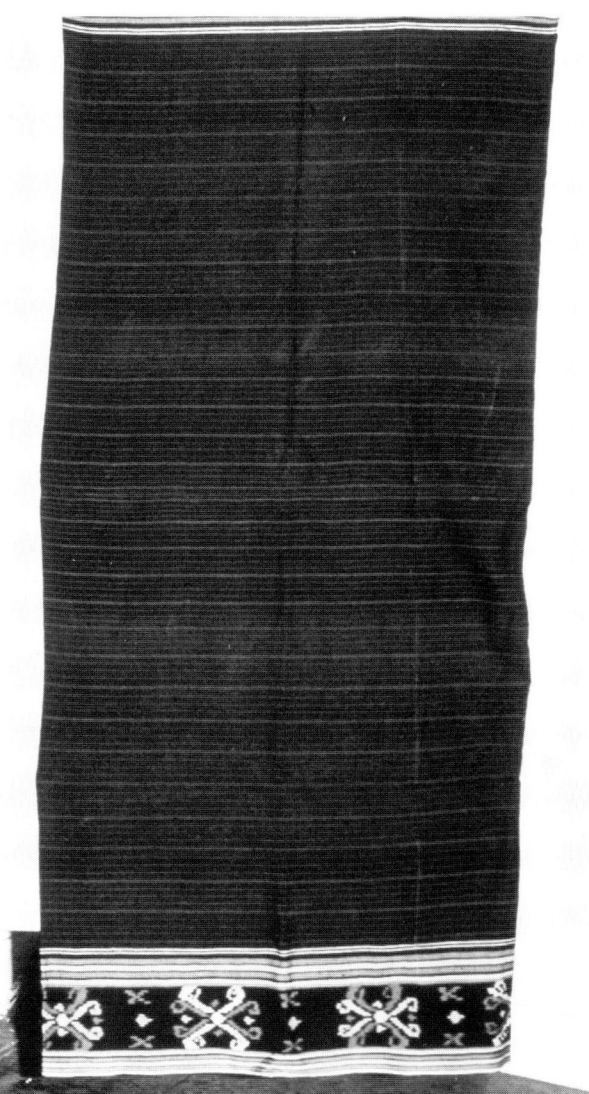

Figure 19. A modern Kodinese woman's cloth, lau gundu, *with a crab motif in bright red, yellow, and white. Photographed in 1983.*

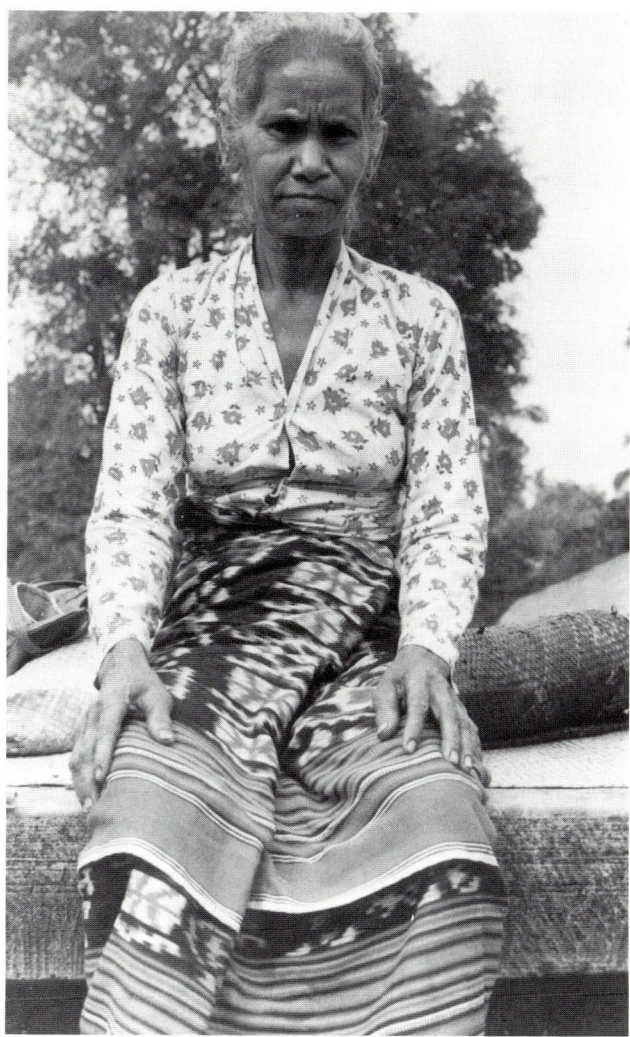

Figure 20. A Kodinese lady in 1983, wearing a modern indigo dyed ikat skirt (wola) with a combination of the rose and cross motifs. The border, unusually wide, is made of red and yellow aniline-dyed stripes. The patterns and colors were admired.

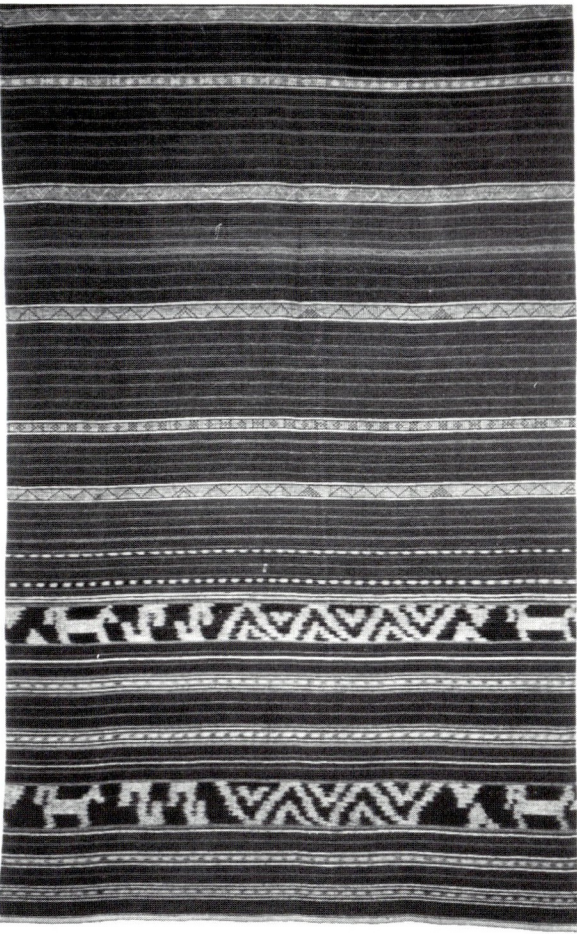

Figure 21. A Kodinese lau in the Alfred Bühler collection. Bühler recorded it as "Lau nggoko Lambalekko" [sic], that is, " lambelekko snake skirt." This cloth is unusual for two reasons. First, it combines lambalekko (the Kodinese term for lambelekko) with a gundu-like skirt, characterized by dark blue and light blue stripes with an ikat border. Second, this is the only Kodinese cloth that I have ever seen with a horse pattern. Museum für Völkerkunde, Basel, II c 8784.

White and blue women's cloths are no longer made in Kodi and I never saw one, not even an old specimen. This gives some indication of the age of the textiles which many Kodinese present to art collectors as being old ones. With rare exceptions, they are ten years old at the most.

It is particularly interesting to consider the vast collection of Kodinese skirts brought back from Kodi by Alfred Bühler in the 1950s. Indeed, they match the people's recollections. Skirts in the Bühler collection do not and never did have a twisted fringe at the back. The most common motif on the skirts in the Bühler collection is the cassava liana (loluga) which is definitely a female pattern in Kodi. The absence of ear pendant motifs (mamuli) seems to confirm the people's claim that in former days women were forbidden to wear them as a pattern on skirtcloths (they did wear them in their ears). The majority of cloths in the collection are handspun, and dark indigo with white motifs, without any of the red or yellow modern designs. However white skirts with narrow stripes and blue indigo motifs, or "negative ikat" as it has been called before, were also fashionable.[11] The white skirts remembered by the people in Kodi were probably of this fashion.

Bühler's information confirms my hypothesis that all textiles in Kodi, both male and female, are considered to be snake's skins, including the gundu and the lambalekko[12] (Fig. 21). Female textiles and gundu types of cloth always bear the names of either minor or imaginary snakes, such as the "white snake" or the "lambalekko snake." In myth, all serpents are subordinated to the largest one of all, the python. Only powerful ancestors appear as pythons to the living. In the realm of textiles, the python is represented by the hanggi ngokko karaha kaboko or "man's cloth with the shape of a python," which is the most sacred cloth of all Kodinese textiles. This is most likely the reason it has undergone only minor changes up to now.

All the other textiles are less laden with supernatural power than the "python's skin." Until recently, the ikat cloths were more awesome than plain ones. Because of their supernatural power only men and women of high birth were able to wear them without the risk of becoming ill. Nowadays, with the exception of the sacred "python's cloth," the association between snakes, ancestors, and the power of cloths is no longer of importance. Indeed, modern female skirts are just called *lau lambelekko,* and the *gundu* cloths, *hanggi gundu,* without apparent mention of specific snakes.

Apart from bright, synthetic dye colors, the greatest change since the fifties is, of course, the weavers' slow surrender from handspun to machine-made thread. This is particularly noticeable in women's skirts. The *lambalekko,* which was already being made in the 1950s to adorn skirts' borders and men's small shouldercloths or headdresses, has become very popular. It requires no handspinning. Interestingly, *lambalekko* has long been forbidden for the "python's cloth," which ideally still has to be handspun. Narrow *lambalekko* stripes do adorn the selvages of some modern versions of it. According to *adat* or customary law, spinning was a skill which all nubile girls had to master before marrying (Fig. 22). In other parts of Sumba, spinning is a metaphor for a major female task, that of "glueing together" the components of the human soul for the newborn (Geirnaert, In Press a). In West Sumba, much of the intrinsic power of textiles is derived from such conceptions. However, for the younger generation who attend school, such beliefs belong to the past. Most young boys and girls are unaware of them, just as they would have been in the old days because such knowledge is potentially dangerous. But when they are old enough to learn such esoteric secrets, the latter will have disappeared for the most part, since the elders who could transmit them will have passed away.

Lambalekko. The modern Kodinese women's skirt, called *lambalekko,* is a conscious reaction to the Lolinese *lambelekko.* The warp is set up with only a single yarn instead of the two used in Loli, and the weft consists of a double yarn instead of three as in Loli. It is decorated with rows of equal width, bearing such motifs as the cassava liana, *loluga,* and or butterflies, *kabebo* (Pl. 15). Kodinese ladies readily laugh at the "pretentious" Lolinese *lambalekko* and find their own far more exquisite. The difference between background and pattern is the result of contrasting shades rather than the effect of a sharp opposition between two bright colors as in Loli. The imperative of combining "light

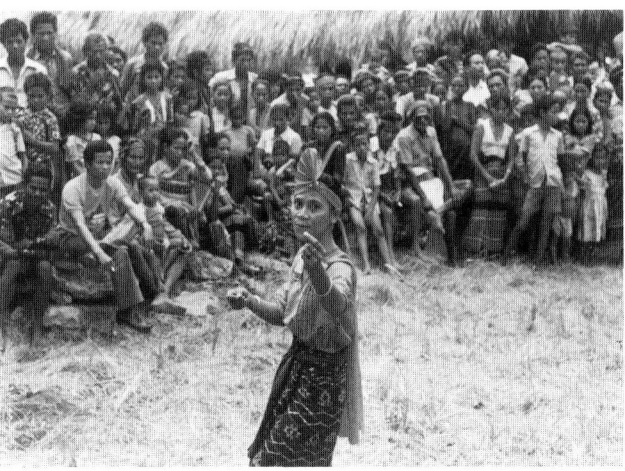

Figure 22. *A young Kodinese dancer in the "Dance of the Spinner," 1983. Her mime is a perfect reproduction of a spinner's movements. In her right hand she holds a fluff of cotton. With her left hand she spins, holding the thread between her left thumb and forefinger, and supporting an imaginary spindle that hangs downward. She wears a modern Kodinese ikat skirt with intertwining red and yellow cassava lianas, yellow stars, and ear pendants—formerly, in Kodi, a male motif forbidden to women (see Geirnaert, In Press b).*

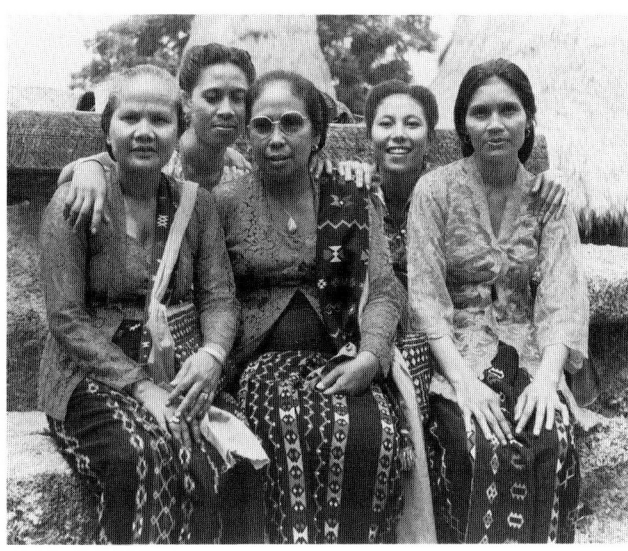

Figure 23. *Kodinese ladies of high nobility wearing* humbi *skirts—the latest, most expensive fashion in 1983. In the center is Nyonya Mace, youngest wife of the late Raja of Kodi. Her* humbi *is decorated with butterfly and cassava liana motifs. Her friends'* humbi *show variations of stars, buffalo eye, and cassava liana. Their costumes are completed with* humbi *shouldercloths, lace blouses (*kebaya*), and the traditional Kodinese bag for betel nut, embroidered with handspun and indigo dyed yarns.*

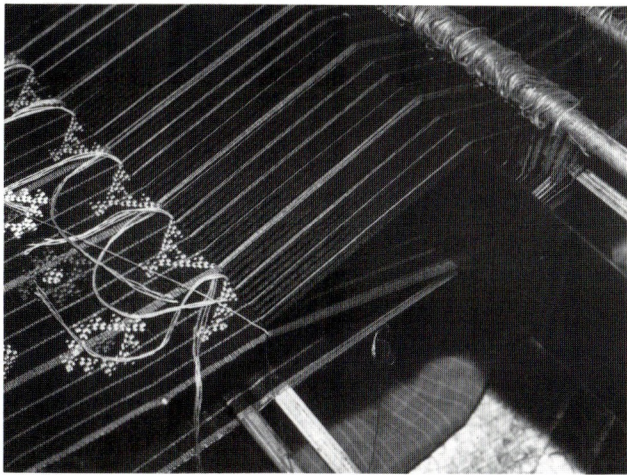

Figure 24. Detail of a cloth seen on a loom in Kodi in 1984, showing the Kodinese humbi technique. It is done with the fingers rather than with a small instrument, as is usual elsewhere (pers. comm., R. Bolland).

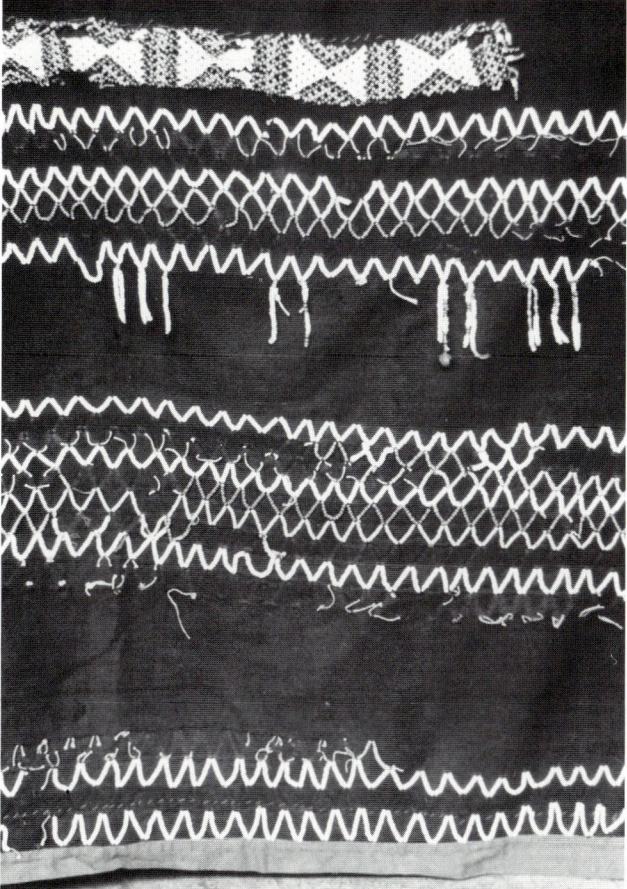

Figure 25. An old Kodinese ceremonial skirt, dating from approximately 1900, was decorated exclusively with beads, in butterfly and liana patterns. Photographed in 1983.

and dark" elements, symbolically important because of their "life-giving" property, is often obtained in Kodi by alternating lighter rows of *lambalekko* with slightly darker ones. Kodinese weavers explain that they do not find it beautiful to combine two "loud" colors the way the Lolinese do, preferring a much more subdued appearance. *Lambelekko* skirts are increasingly popular in Kodi, particularly among the younger generation; nearly all Kodinese women know how to weave them.

Humbi. This is certainly not the case with the *humbi* type of skirt, which is said to have appeared in Kodi only recently, in the early 1980s (Fig. 23). *Humbi* is a supplementary weft technique. More precisely, it is done with the fingers, using a discontinuous supplementary yarn, or *songket* in Indonesian (Maxwell 1980:144). Other denominations (per Burnham 1980:18) are "brocade," or "brocading weft" (Fig. 24). The yarns used for the *humbi* are the same as for the *lambalekko*. The background is black. The discontinuous wefts chosen for the patterns, or *humbi* proper, are light blue, white, yellow, and red. For collectors who expect to find ikat, the *humbi* may be puzzling, and perhaps even disillusioning. And yet the *humbi* is the highest fashion, a costly one which so far only mature and wellborn ladies dare to wear. The novelty is spreading. In 1984 in Waikabubak, wives of government employees were coveting a Kodinese *humbi*. In the Central Highlands of West Sumba no one yet knew how to make one. In 1986, a few Kodinese men's cloths, adorned exclusively with patterns made in the *humbi* technique, could be seen in market places—a novelty.

In Kodi, only a few younger women have mastered this new technique, from which they draw a fair amount of prestige. When discussing the several Kodinese textile techniques, women agreed that *humbi* was the most time-consuming of all, which justified its costliness. Their argument reflects the fact that weavers are still unfamiliar with this technique.

The beaded skirt. If a new set of techniques has readily been adopted in Kodi, an old one has definitely been abandoned. Skirts decorated with glass beads are no longer made (Fig. 25). Most of the glass beads found in Sumba came from Europe between roughly 1880 and 1939. After Independence, they were no longer imported to Sumba. Throughout the island, to wear beads is the exclusive privilege of women of high birth. Relatively few skirts seem to have been decorated with glass beads in West Sumba, and if so, apparently in Kodi and Memboro only.

Continuity in Kodinese design. If Kodinese weaving exhibits the greatest versatility in West Sumbanese textile decorative technique, the continuity of its patterns is all the more remarkable. The patterns on the glass beaded skirt—the liana, *loluga,* and the

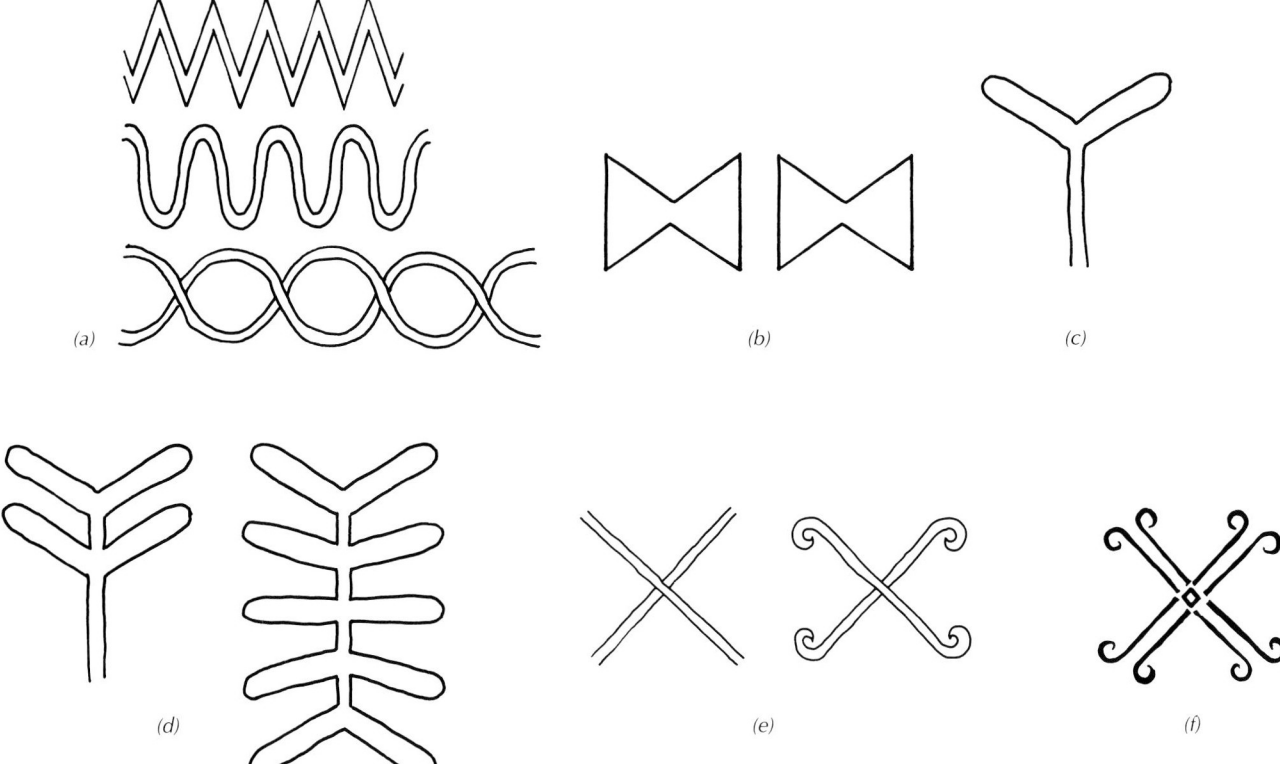

Figure 26. Popular motifs on women's skirts in Kodi: (a) cassava liana, or loluga *(b) butterfly, or* kabebo *(c) rose motif designed by Nyonya Lien, cut out of transparent paper (d) compositions inspired by the rose motif (e) old and new shapes of* kadango kadoro, *instrument used for winding rope (f) crab pattern or* karapako, *adapted by Nyonya Mace from* kadango kadoro. *See Figures 19,20,23,25.*

butterfly, *kabebo* (Fig. 26a,b)—are found in ikat and *lambalekko* skirts (Fig. 22, Pl. 15) as well as in *humbi* (Fig. 23). Unfortunately, museum collections seldom give information about the names of patterns. Hence it is almost impossible to know whether the names are the same now as fifty years ago, or whether old motifs have new designations. For instance, the design called *kabebo* is said to be new, but this is questionable: compared with *loluga*, it may be new, but it is at least eighty years old, as the beaded skirt demonstrates.

It is easier to assess the approximate age of motifs which have been designed more recently. Thus the wife of the late Raja Horo of Kodi, Nyonya Lien (seen in Pl. 15), claims that she first created the rose pattern (Fig. 26c). She says that the Dutch introduced the rose (which the Kodinese pronounce in the Dutch way, *roos*) both as a plant and as a motif sometime around the 1920s or 1930s; under colonial rule it became a popular motif throughout Indonesia (Kartiwa 1983:25). Before ikatting a rose, she cuts a paper pattern of the flower, which she then uses as an element for more intricate designs (Fig. 26d).

In a similar fashion Nyonya Mace (seen in Fig. 23) has created a wholly new pattern by transforming the traditional cross motif known as *kadango kadoro*, which depicts the instrument used for making balls of rope, into a crab motif called *karapako* (Fig. 26e,f). So far, however, these new designs are kept for ikat skirts only. In 1984, no one yet had tried out these patterns either in *lambalekko* or in *humbi* technique.

Wewewa and other regions of West Sumba

Wewewa, Laura, and other former smaller kingdoms are areas where ikat used to be forbidden. In modern times, like Kodi and Loli, Wewewa has acquired a style of its own. The borders of its skirts, which are sometimes as wide as Lolinese *lambelekko*, are ikatted. Since indigo does not thrive in the cool highlands of Wewewa, it is commonly replaced with the black dye mud (*habbu*) formerly used for the dying of white skirts. The ikat motifs can be elaborate (Fig. 27); they are partly borrowed from European cross-stitch designs or inspired by Lolinese *lambelekko* motifs. Apart from the black ikat border, the skirt proper is predominantly bright red, with yellow and white stripes. In 1986, however, Wewewa women were increasingly adopting the *lambelekko* technique to decorate the borders of their skirts. Ikat borders were becoming rarer. Red still dominated in Wewewa *ye*.

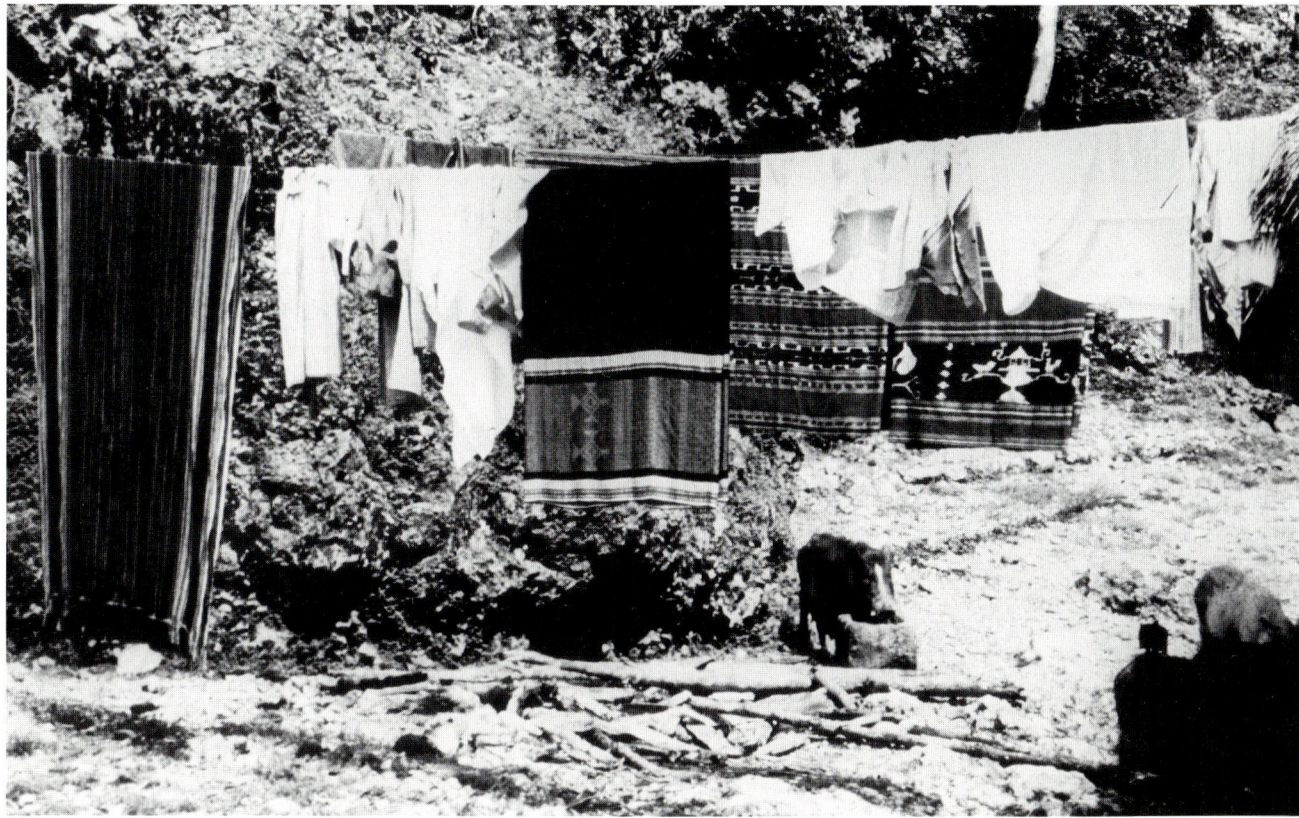

Figure 27. Wash drying on a line in West Sumba in 1982 includes (left to right): a Kodinese man's gundu, a Lolinese lambelekko skirt, and two Wewewa ikat skirts, (predominantly red, except for the black and white ikat borders). The elaborate ikat motif of the last cloth was one of the most popular patterns in Wewewa, 1982-84.

Trade and Textiles
Historical and Geographical Links

In cultures lacking written tradition, there is perhaps nothing so mysterious as the advent of apparently new techniques and motifs, even if, as it is the case in West Sumba, it all seems to happen under one's very eyes. My on-the-spot inquiries as to who had taught the women *lambelekko* or *humbi* proved to be either unfruitful or totally misleading.

One of these encounters illustrates how powerful matters of hierarchy can be in all Sumbanese social relationships, including those that play a part in the teaching and learning processes. An East Sumbanese lady of noble descent who was a renowned weaver claimed that she had introduced the use of the supplementary warp technique of East Sumba into West Sumba by teaching a few women in Loli how to set it up. However, her pupils had not been able to master the technique properly, and it had degenerated into *lambelekko*. It happened that one of her pupils was herself a well-known weaver in West Sumba, long before the advent of the East Sumbanese teacher. Recalling the visit of the noble lady and her demonstration, she explained that she herself was able to make a cloth with a supplementary warp, but that it was not the custom to do so in West Sumba, because that technique was the speciality of noblewomen, "and she was just a commoner." She was willing to accept the East Sumbanese contempt for *lambelekko* and to consider it inferior. Curiously, even though she had known the technique long before the noblewomen's visit, she did not refute the noblewoman's claim to have introduced it as a result of attempting to teach how to set up a supplementary warp in the East Sumbanese way. This illustrates a general unwillingness among West Sumbanese women to dispute a noble person's statements. But like a cloth I saw at the Rijksmuseum voor Volkenkunde in Leiden,[13] the Bühler cloth shown in Figure 21 attests to the fact that *lambelekko* existed, in Kodi at least, long before the East Sumbanese teacher made her way to Loli in 1975 or 1976.

Another explanation for the difference between the techniques used in the eastern and western parts of the island was advanced by an East Sumbanese noblewoman, who attributed it to the fact that the "people who came to inhabit West Sumba came originally from Western Indonesia, whereas the people who settled in the eastern part came from Eastern Indonesia." Vague and at first unverifiable as this statement may seem, it proves in the end to be more helpful as far as West Sumba is concerned, for reasons which we will now put forward.

Fortunately the extensive studies on Indonesian textiles that have been done particularly in the last decade allow us to suggest plausible historical connections between West Sumbanese cloths and textiles from another part of Indonesia. In Kodi, for example, the word *gundu* means "from the mountains" and by extension "from outside, foreign." Weavers in Kodi say that *gundu* patterns came originally from the *gundu* people, that is, from foreigners. People added more precise information, namely, that *gundu* cloths were introduced by Ende people. And indeed, there is a small Endenese community in Kodi.

According to Maxwell (1980:144), "Manggarai textile forms include the stripes and plaids from the Todo area [West Flores] where some myths claim Minangkabau (West Sumatra) ancestry but probably reveal South Sulawesi influence" (my underlining). This remark suggests that *gundu* textiles might be connected to Todo cloth, and perhaps more remotely, to South Sulawesi textiles. Elsewhere in Eastern Indonesia, plaid ornaments seem to be related to Buginese cloths—that is, again, South Sulawesi (R. Barnes 1986). Maxwell's article, while lacking photographs of the Todo textiles, illustrates a discontinuous supplementary weft cloth from the Central Northern Districts of West Flores (1980:150, fig. 1). It shows great similarity with the Kodinese *humbi*. Technically, the Flores and the West Sumbanese cloths are made in exactly the same way— by *songket* or discontinuous supplementary weft. It is striking that in her books on Central and South Sulawesi, S. Kartiwa mentions that these are indigenous *songket* cloths, called *subi*. She also recalls how Buginese trade has had a considerable influence since the seventeenth century on the Lesser Sunda islands.

It is worthwhile recording the linguistic transformations that occur in Sumbanese languages. Thus the sound "s" is commonly replaced by the sound "h," and "Sumba" becomes "Humba." In Laboya language, all words starting elsewhere in West Sumba with an "s" are changed to begin with an "h." Another common linguistic Sumbanese habit consists of dropping the "m" before the consonants "b," "p," and "d." Thus *lambelekko* becomes *labelekko* and *gundu* changes into *gudu*.

Therefore, it is not improbable that the *humbi* technique is originally a South Sulawesi technique known there as *subi*, which has come to West Sumba through West Flores, by means of Endenese merchants, or perhaps, directly through Buginese trade. Of course, one should not underestimate the influence of Sumbawa, and more precisely of Bima, upon Kodi. Intermarriages and trade have regularly taken place between Kodi and Bima. However, there is no Bimanese community in Kodi. From a textile point of view, it is significant that the Bimanese predilection for metallic, silver and golden threads has had no influence on Kodinese cloths. As far as patterns are concerned, the Kodinese *humbi* are indeed much closer to the designs of the northern districts of West Flores than to Sumbawa decorative textile art.

Regarding the term *lambelekko*, several suggestions could be presented, but none is so far satisfactory. However, R. Bolland has pointed out that the same technique—that is, a pick up with a floating warp—can be seen in an old South Sulawesi cloth which came into the collections of the Tropenmuseum, Amsterdam, in 1880.[14] Nowadays, *lambelekko*-type cloths are common in Timor. Textiles brought back from Flores and Timor at the end of the last century, in 1892 and 1893, under the auspices of the Louis Lapicque research expedition (Mission Louis Lapicque, Musée de l'Homme, Paris), are very similar to *gundu*, but there are none of the *lambelekko* type (Lapicque n.d., cloths 96.16.1 and 96.16.16). Perhaps *lambelekko* came to West Sumba by the same route as the more modern *humbi*.

The fact that Kodi is the only region in West Sumba acquainted with all types of textile decorative techniques is significant. Kodi appears to be the gateway for innovations, which apparently come from Flores, and more remotely from South Sulawesi. The statement that novelties "come from the West" seems to contain much truth indeed. It would be erroneous to end this paragraph on trade without mentioning one important aspect of the exchanges of textiles on the island of Sumba itself. In matters of textiles, there is no doubt that the East Sumbanese feel immensely superior. I have never seen a woman from East Sumba wear West Sumbanese cloth[15]; in fact women of high status openly discredit the weaving done in the west. But their contempt obscures the fact that if West Sumbanese have copied motifs from the eastern part of the island, exchanges in the opposite direction do occur, particularly on such occasions as intermarriages. Thus an East Sumbanese man's cloth may have West Sumbanese elements. A *hinggi* collected by Langewis and Wagner is decorated with a border that is unmistakenly Laboyan (Fig. 28).

Finally, one should not forget to take into consideration the influence of a few Timorese women who have settled in West Sumba after their marriage. As independent weavers, they may be a source of new inspiration. They themselves borrow some typically West Sumbanese elements of decoration. So far, their art is very localized and their products attract government officials' wives only. Nevertheless, they make the odd cloth whose origin one cannot immediately identify. Clearly these special textiles are beyond the scope of the present paper.

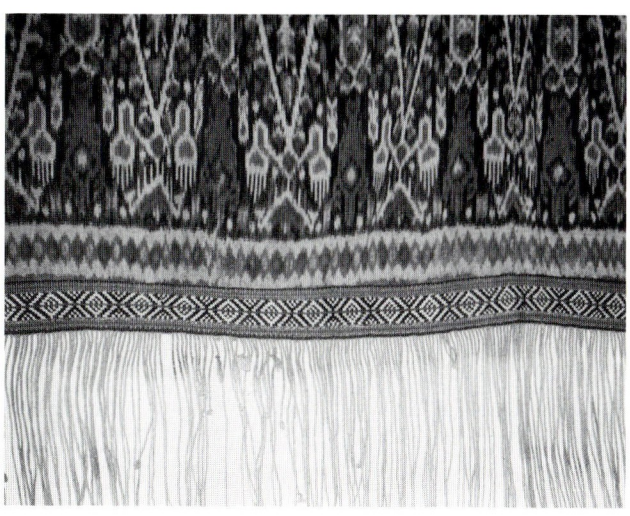

Figure 28. An East Sumba man's ikat cloth collected by Langewis and Wagner, and depicted by them without its border (1964: pl. 24), is unmistakably of Laboyan origin. The cloth is now at the Museum für Völkerkunde, Basel II c 15961.

However there is one very special and fairly rare type of textile that should be considered. A red and blue ikat of unusual size, and definitely East Sumbanese, is increasingly being sold as a West Sumbanese item. Textiles of this kind are only about three-quarters of a meter in width, but they may reach more than twelve meters in length. Recent collectors have been told that they are "*pasola* cloths," worn as "headdresses," and "typical of West Sumba."[16] Of good quality and quite attractive, they do not deserve this erroneous information. *Pasola* is indeed a West Sumbanese word. It designates the horse-mounted combats held for ritual purposes among the populations who live along the southwestern coasts of Sumba. These kinds of combats do not occur anywhere else on the island of Sumba. But the fact is that no specific "*pasola* cloth" is ever used during those ceremonies; and the long, narrow textiles sold by that name are completely unknown to the West Sumbanese. In color and design, they are unmistakably from the eastern part. This is confirmed by earlier literature on Indonesian textiles, which mentions such a specimen in Tabundung, East Sumba, where it is called "Rohu Banggi"[17] (Warming and Gaworski 1981:79). Roughly a hundred years ago, according to Warming and Gaworski, the king used to wrap this narrow material around his waist for protection before going into battle. But by the time of my visit to East Sumba, it was no longer made or worn.

Most of the specimens I have seen are, I suspect, modern ones, woven in East Sumba for the tourist industry. They represent particularly large scale human and animal figures such as shrimps and horses. But so far, I have no information as to exactly where and how they are made. Their very length suggests that, most probably, they are not woven on a traditional Sumbanese loom. The average continuous warp of such a loom does not exceed four meters' circumference at most. This raises the question of whether the Dutch introduction of Western looms to Sumba at the turn of the century inspired or encouraged the production of such long cloths. So far no further information is available.

Suggestions:
Textile Puzzles and Symbols

The explosion of new textile forms in West Sumba leads us to revise or modify the generally accepted assumption that craft industries decline as traditional values disappear (Graburn 1976:12). A loss in quality and in quantity is a common result of such changes, but obviously it is not necessarily so in all cases. For the textile renaissance in West Sumba, some tentative explanations might be suggested, even if more specific investigations are necessary.

First, there seems to be a longstanding tradition, or route, by which textile innovations brought to Kodi slowly penetrate in the Central Highlands. Above and beyond the profusion of textile decorative techniques in Kodi, it is significant that weaving implements, for instance, are most elaborate in that same region.[18] Loli's importance as a center of modern trade is being challenged by developing urban centers in Western Wewewa which are nearer to the seaports. Hence Kodi may keep its leading role in the future.

Secondly, dress plays a prominent part in expressing identity, both ethnically and in the social hierarchy. In a region that used to be intensely divided into small rival kingdoms, textile production may be a mild reaction to the necessity of complying with the norms of modern Indonesia whose goal is unification. Cultural identity is maintained in dress behavior. The development of a market economy and the increasing demand for cash to pay taxes and school fees have encouraged men and women to look at textile production as a slight contribution to the family's economy. But so far, this economic aspect is underdeveloped, perhaps because West Sumba has not become yet a place of large scale tourism. As we have seen, textile production is meant largely for local consumption.

There is a third reason why textile production has not decreased. Women's dress has taken remarkable advantage of new possibilities such as the introduction of new types of yarn. It is worth mentioning a peculiar feature of West Sumbanese societies that may have contributed more specifically to new modes of expression in the realm of female textiles. As I collected information about textiles, I noted a pattern emerging: men and women's answers seemed to reflect a sexual "division of knowledge," so much so that one could speak of a cleavage between two separate domains—one male, the other female. Most of the practical work of weaving and dyeing is done by women, and they alone were able to describe precisely the various stages involved in the production of a cloth. Also they knew which taboos men and women had to obey at which stage, and could explain them to some extent, mostly in practical terms. However, no matter how old they were, women were unable to tackle the topic of the symbolic significance of textiles. This particular subject could be discussed with men only. As we shall briefly see, symbolic associations between textiles and other social contexts are closely related to cosmological ideas, and more specifically to ancestor worship. Such conceptual relationships constitute the core of religious esoteric knowledge on which much of ritual life is based. This is a male-dominated sphere, for the following reasons.

In West Sumba, renown is very highly valued. In former days, to be a warrior of great repute was a way of acquiring a name (*ngara* in Laboya) that would be remembered by a male's descendants long after death. Warfare and headhunting therefore enabled an individual, and far more important, by extension, his lineage, to transcend death. Yet killing, which leads to renown, contradicts the idea of life and fertility; men are associated with the former, while women are primarily responsible for the latter. There is no warfare anymore, at least openly. But to "search for a name" (in Indonesian, *cari nama*) is still of the utmost importance.

Competitive feasting has in many ways replaced headhunting, as has the ritual slaughter of large quantities of cattle. But in West Sumba people still hold to old conceptions about the incompatibility between the need to kill (for renown's sake) and the need to promote communal well-being through the fertility of men, animals, and crops. Remembered ancestors are often just "names" that relate to powerful war leaders in former times. As such, in their aspect of "death-giving," they are dangerous to the life-giving properties of women. They should be protected from such contamination because it would destroy their life-giving capacities. This is the reason why, ideally, women are excluded from matters concerning the afterlife and the ancestors.

The taboos men and women have to follow when spinning, weaving, and dyeing refer to this basic contradiction between killing and giving birth (Geirnaert 1987). On many occasions, women are mere "executors"—that is, spinners and weavers who know how to count the threads, but ignore the esoteric symbolic meaning of the pattern they make, because they must protect their own fertility. While life and death are experienced as being complementary, and ritual devices do exist to cross over from the realm of the dead to that of the living, the ceremonies and esoteric knowledge they presuppose are handled essentially by older men.

As traditional beliefs about ancestor worship and its connection with headhunting disappear, men are less eager to control female behavior in this respect. Hence women will be freer to experiment with new expressive forms. Furthermore, the rules forbidding men to approach women during certain stages of weaving are no longer respected by the younger men. Spinning and spinning instruments were the most closely connected to headhunting (Geirnaert, In Press a). Nowadays, only the elder religious practitioners still remember the hidden meaning of the spinning implements. Headhunting no longer occurs and the necessity of spinning is decreasing for practical, economic and perhaps religious reasons as well. Nevertheless, in West Sumba, the most sacred and ritually powerful cloths are incontestably those for men. Female textiles are less related to cosmological themes. This may be one reason why female textiles have undergone a renewal which was thought to be too dangerous for male cloths.

The cosmological well-being of the island is conceived of in terms which are borrowed entirely from the realm of textiles. For instance, in Lewa it is altogether forbidden to weave. Lewa is the region of high plateaus in Central Sumba at the geographical heart of the island. Crossing it, there is said to be a bunch of invisible threads, attached at one end to the bottom of the sea, and at the other to the highest layer of the sky. It is said that weaving in Lewa would destroy this bunch of threads: as a result, the island would fall into the sea and disappear. The textile analogy is obvious. The action of weaving requires a continuous shuffling between sword and heddles, along the warp. It weakens the warp-threads which tend to break. Clearly, the "bunch of threads" that holds the island of Sumba on the surface of the sea is a continuous warp. The theme of cutting the warp as a metaphor for death has been recorded many times in Indonesian textiles. Generally associated with ancestor worship and ideas of descent, it is a dangerous and crucial enterprise (Adams 1965; Geirnaert 1983: note 29; Niessen 1984:196; see also Barnes in the present volume). This is also the case in West Sumba, but more specific data is beyond the scope of this article.

Ikat is allowed only at the eastern and western tips of Sumba (see Geirnaert, In Press b). It is necessary to tie (ikat) both ends of the island in order to keep the "vital fluids" from flowing out. In between, no ikat should be done, so that these fluids can circulate freely. This taboo applies to the regions situated west of Lewa, that is Napu, Anakalang, Memboro, Wanokaka, Laura, Loli, and Wewewa. In other words it corresponds to the areas where only white cloths are made. Similar analogies between cloth and the human life cycle have already been mentioned; they are found elsewhere in Indonesia as well as in Sumba (Adams 1971,1974; Geirnaert 1983; Gittinger 1979a; Niessen 1984).

West Sumbanese cloths help to make concepts about life and death explicit, both at individual and cosmological levels. Cloths derive their intrinsic power from such mental representations. It is understandable why only the members of the society who score the highest in the social hierarchy may wear, literally, such power without risks. Any disobedience to taboos and to the social order endanger the well-being of the whole society. Formerly, trespassers of the taboos were severely punished, sometimes with immediate death, sometimes indirectly by ancestors who would take on the shape of a snake and bite the culprits.

It has been observed that "the expression of religious belief throughout the Lesser Sundas seems to depend to a considerable extent on cloth," (Fischer 1979:64). This all-embracing capacity points to a major conclusion. The cloths of Sumba, in analogy to the cosmological system they reflect, should be considered as part of a textile system in which color, design, and technique may carry specific symbolic meaning. The differentiation between male and female textile activities and the mirror imaging in certain patterns are features of the utmost importance for the understanding of textile symbolism. In Laboyan *hanggi*, for example, as noted earlier, white becomes black in a reversal of symmetries that represents the contrast between male and female, and at another level between life and death. Thus textiles, with their visual inversions, convey information about the nature of relationships between different social groups (men and women, the living and the dead), which must be decoded to be understood (Geirnaert, Forthcoming). It is only in the context of such relationships that the role of textiles in gift exchanges can be understood.

NOTES

Fieldwork between August 1982 and April 1984 was sponsored financially by the Netherlands Institute for Pure Research (ZWO). My visits to the Museum für Völkerkunde, Basel, and to the Pitt Rivers Museum, Oxford, have been partly financed by the Institute of Cultural Studies, Leiden State University. In autumn 1986 I spent five weeks in West Sumba.

1. The collection purchased in 1950 by Alfred Bühler for the Museum für Völkerkunde, Basel, proved an invaluable source of information for comparative purpose. To my knowledge, it is the only extensive and well-documented collection of West Sumbanese textiles in Europe. I wish to thank Dr. M.L. Nabholz-Kartaschoff and Dr. Urs Ramseyer for all their help and cooperation during my visit to the Museum in April 1986.

2. The Bühler-Sutter expedition purchased some *ye* in Anakalang in 1950 (Museum für Völkerkunde, Basel, IIc 8800, with a plain fringe, and IIc 8801, with a brass-beaded fringe, from Wewewa). They correspond to the descriptions given by Lolinese and Wewewa women, aged forty to fifty. Black *ye* have seldom been collected because they were thought to be uninterestingly plain.

3. White cloths are still worn ceremonially in Memboro, Laboya, and sometimes Wanokaka.

4. Translated and explained to me by Mrs. E. Doki Ledi.

5. In 1984 the population was approximately 6,000.

6. I am particularly grateful to Mrs. R. Heringa for lending me Kartiwa's books, which are unavailable in usual Dutch libraries.

7. So far, the only Laboyan textile I have seen in Dutch collections is in the Tropenmuseum, Amsterdam (109/5). It has a handspun and naturally dyed twined border. The Wielenga collection in the Museum voor Land- and Volkenkunde, Rotterdam, has several West Sumbanese cloths, but I do not have up-to-date information on them. Unfortunately the museum has only recently reopened after three years of renovation and I have not been able to visit since then. A. Veldhuisen-Djajasoebrata kindly offered her help on my past visits there.

8. Bühler's observations in 1950 confirm that the panels of white cloths with a broad plaited border differ in width (5 to 7 cm. difference).

9. In 1955, Jeanne Cuisinier visited Kodi on a collecting trip for the Musée de l'Homme in Paris. In one of her field notes concerning a Kodinese *hanggi* (55.68.8) she mentioned that the cloth is said to represent a python (*kaboko*). This information confirms my own findings (Geirnaert In Press b). I am particularly grateful to Dr. C. Pelras and to Dr. M. Bataille, of the Musée de l'Homme, Paris, for allowing me to see the museum's textile collection and to consult unpublished material, such as Cuisinier's field notes and the Lapicque report, 1893-95, during my visit in June 1986.

10. For example, R. Needham's collection at the Pitt Rivers Museum, Oxford, which was acquired in the fifties. In March 1986, not only did Dr. R. Barnes and her family offer their hospitality, but she also kindly introduced me to the museum's Indonesian collections.

11. See Adams 1965:5 regarding the *lau ngokko kaka* or "white snake skirt" in the Museum für Völkerkunde IIc 8972.

12. In the Museum für Völkerkunde collection see numbers IIc 8786 (*lau ngoko pangilung*) and IIc 8784 (*lau ngoko lambalekko* or "lambalekko snake skirt").

13. Mrs. M. Lahman showed me a West Sumbanese *lambelekko* purchased by the Rijksmuseum voor Volkenkunde, Leiden, in 1972. It has simple motifs and it is poorly made, an indication that the weaver had not yet fully mastered the technique.

14. I am greatly indebted to Rita Bolland, former curator of the Textile Department of the Tropenmuseum, Amsterdam, for pointing out this South Sulawesi textile, number 40C6Z, and for patiently explaining technical resemblances between it and *lambelekko*.

15. Nowadays, rather than weave their own skirts for daily wear, East Sumbanese women prefer to buy ready-made material in local shops.

16. Mrs. Annette Berra first introduced me to the so-called "*pasola* cloths" in April 1984, in Jakarta. Since then, I have seen another four pieces, acquired by tourists or by private collectors outside Sumba. The only one collected by a museum is a "Rohu Banggi" at the National Museum of Singapore to which the museum's curator, Dr. Lee Chor Lin, first drew my attention in a letter (November 1986). During a visit at the National Museum in December 1986, I was able to see the cloth and consult the references to Warming and Gaworski's book, through the help of Mr. Prithiui Raj. Adorned with delicate designs, the cloth may be an original one. The color scheme of its woven borders at the top and bottom edges, a simple alternation of yellow and blue lines, accentuates its East Sumbanese origin.

17. As far as I can make out, it translates in Indonesian as *ikat pinggang*, meaning "belt" (literally, something to tie your waist with). See the dictionary by Kapita (1982).

18. The names of the West Sumbanese loom and its parts do not correspond to Sulawesi terminology (Kartiwa 1983:41-42).

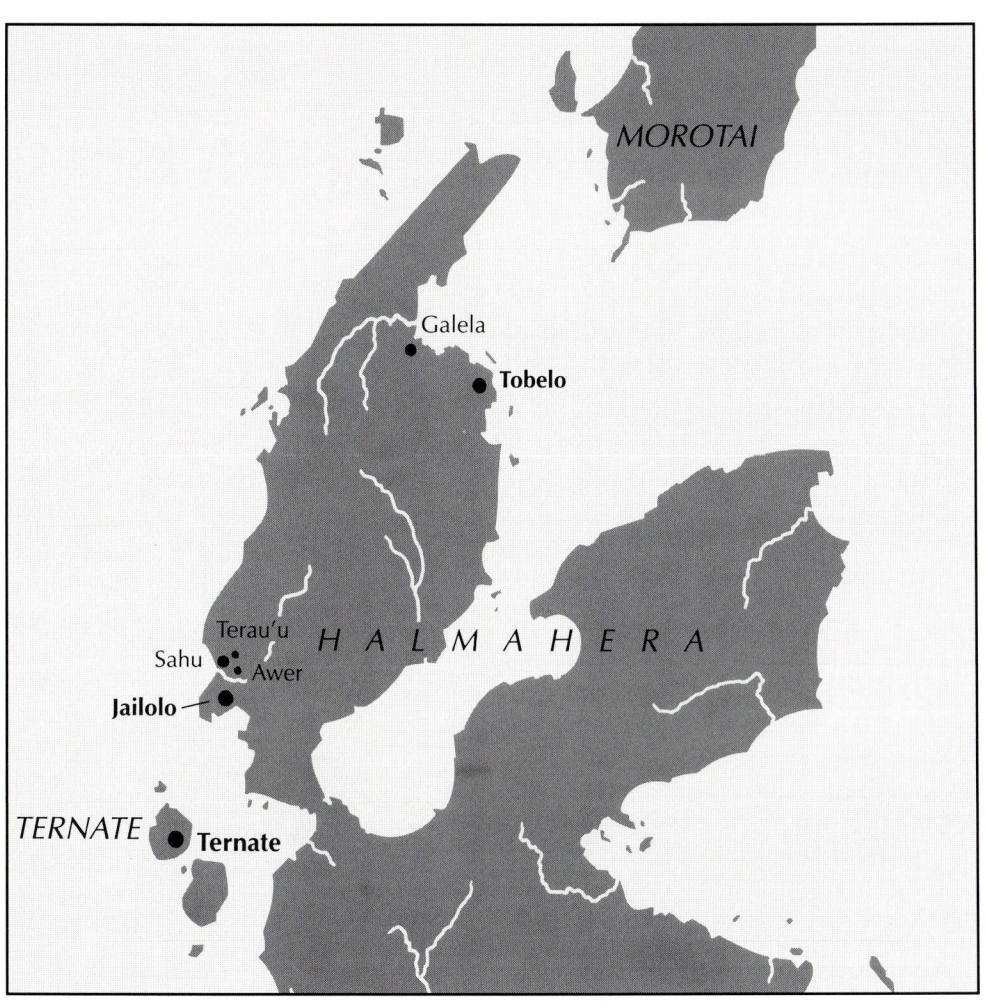

North Halmahera and Ternate.

Foreign Textiles in Sahu Culture

Leontine E. Visser

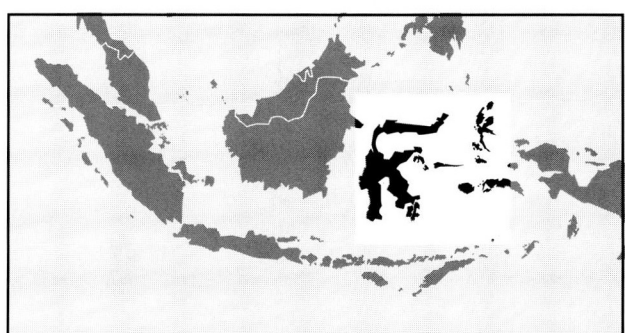

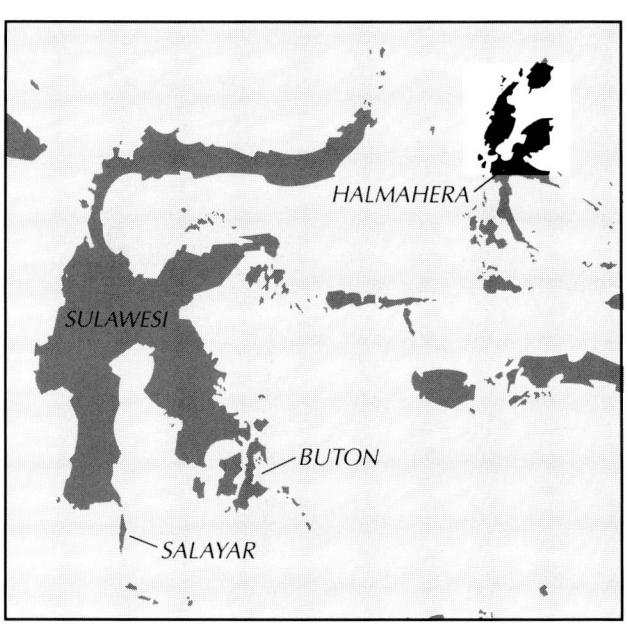

Halmahera in relation to the islands of Buton and Salayar, once part of the Ternate Sultanate.

Anthropologists are frequently able to study textiles within their culture of origin or use, and can interpret their symbolic colors, motifs, and meaning accordingly. In my own research[1] I have had to take a different point of departure because the textiles used by the Sahu people, imported from elsewhere, originate in a culture that is foreign to them. Moreover the textiles that are the subject of this paper were imported one or more generations ago. Studies on textile trade usually focus on the material object; but I am interested in the selection criteria of the importing culture. Textiles are chosen not at random but rather, as I hope to show, deliberately, for their colors and motifs or patterns, in order to fit the value system of the receiving culture. The Sahu people live on the northwest coast of the island of Halmahera in the Northern Moluccas. Numbering about 8,000 people, they inhabit a fertile river basin where they grow rice as a staple crop by means of swidden cultivation. Culturally and linguistically Sahu is closely related to other North Halmahera societies, like Tobelo and Galela, and distantly to the peoples in the western part of the Bird's Head, the northwestern section of Irian Jaya. Until the end of the last century Halmahera was subordinate to the sultanate of Ternate, which ruled over most of eastern Indonesia, including southeast Sulawesi (Buton), Minahasa, and even Mindanao (Philippines) and parts of western Irian Jaya. Ternate was, and in many respects still is, the economic and political heart of the Northern Moluccas.

Weaving Tradition in Ternate

The Halmahera cultures do not have a weaving tradition. Mat plaiting is very important among the northeastern peoples, but much less so in Sahu. The same is true with regard to barkcloth, more significant (historically) on the northeast coast than in Sahu. Our museums store beautiful pieces of red and yellow ornamented barkcloth and jackets, but all from Tobelo, Galela, and Tobaru societies (Chijs 1885:175; Loebèr 1921-22:264,266). There are hardly any objects from Sahu and the northwest coast in museum collections; literature about these areas is very scarce and nothing is known about their textiles.

In the middle of the last century, Tobias, the Dutch administrator at Ternate, reported (1857 [1980]:29) that the inland people of Sahu were "naked, except for a *cidako*" (man's loincloth in Moluccan Malay, called *pisa* in Galelarese). Almost thirty years later, Campen, a high military officer in Ternate, writing about the northeast coast of Halmahera, described this as a strip of barkcloth fifty centimeters broad and about four meters long and painted at both ends when used for ritual purposes, whose decoration was made by women and consisted of squares and arabesques (1884: 172-74). For their daily dress, however, the Sahu people used the same white cotton from which Moslem turbans were made. Women's barkcloth jackets, called *kotanga*, were decorated with arabesques, tassels, mica, and embroidery (Campen 1884:172-74; also Baarda 1895:56,137). However, Campen also noted that this traditional clothing was already almost completely replaced by imported cotton sarongs, jackets, and trousers. The natural scientist Kükenthal, another early visitor to the northeast coast of Halmahera, described patterns and designs of plaited mats comparable to those on Tobelo and Galela barkcloth (Kükenthal 1896:162, pls. VI:38, VII:41).

Most of what we know about Sahu textiles is from a publication by the Dutch missionary Fortgens, who lived on the west coast south of Sahu during the first decade of this century (Fortgens 1913:508-20). He describes the annual harvest festival, a major Sahu ritual which is still performed today. Even in his time, most textiles were imported; moreover we know they have not been imported since early this century. However, the textiles used today by the men performing the *legu* dance still appear to be quite similar to those shown in Fortgens's photographs of 1913; and they are part of a much vaster corpus of imported textiles used during the harvest festival. In this article I shall focus on three categories of textiles worn during the ritual: woven textiles, embroidered cloths, and batiks.

"Kulincucu Cloth": *Ba'a Boba* and *Ba'a Suje*

Woven textiles known collectively by the Moluccan Malay name of *kain Kulincucu*[2] play an important role in the Sahu harvest ritual. There are two types of "Kulincucu cloth": *ba'a boba* and *ba'a suje*. They constitute part of family heirlooms that are at least fifty to eighty years old, but their origin is no longer known to the present population. Indeed it presents a

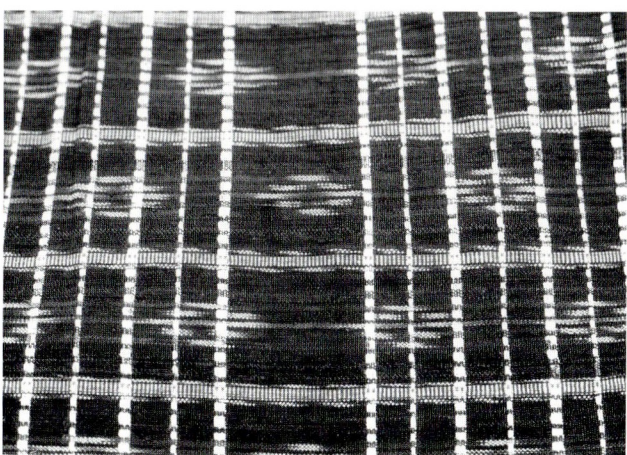

Figure 1. Detail of the central design portion ("head") of a two-paneled indigo sarong (ba'a boba) *with supplementary weft lines in the head. Full cloth shown in Plate 6. Awer, 1982.*

special challenge to the researcher, for reasons that will will be discussed below.

Ba'a boba. Ba'a boba is an indigo blue ikat sarong with a red central design portion or "head," and white ikat motifs both there and in the "body" (Pl. 6, Fig. 1). It consists of two panels sewn together along the selvages, measuring about 120 by 176 centimeters, with a head of 40-45 centimeters. Except for the small selvage rim of white commercial yarn, the cloth is made of coarse handspun cotton in warp-faced plain weave. In the blue body, white warp ikat creates diamond-shaped or six-pointed stars (or inverse diamonds). Rows of ikat motifs alternate with narrow bands, each consisting of alternating red and white lines. The head consists of a blue warp and a red weft, and shows the same white ikat pattern as the body. Moreover, the head is symmetrically divided into two groups of ten supplementary weft white lines which are alternately one and three millimeters broad. It should be noted that the two panels are somewhat discontinuous or asymmetric as far as the head is concerned, a characteristic of all two-panel sarongs worn by Sahu women. A beautiful example of this is seen in a cloth with a supplementary-weft diamond pattern (Pl. 7). The asymmetry is explained by analogy with a house: the centers of the upper and lower parts of the textile, as with a house and its roof, should never be precisely aligned, lest the person using it fall ill. The upper and lower red borders of the ba'a boba are about three centimeters, the white selvages about a half centimeter. It is worn as a sarong (ba'a) or, folded diagonally, as a complementary shouldercloth (sangkola) loosely hanging over the left shoulder, in the manner of the kain mandar from Sulawesi worn by the woman in Figure 2. Whether worn as sarong or as shouldercloth, the red head should always be visible.

Ba'a suje. Ba'a suje is a woven red two-paneled sarong, with continuous supplementary wefts creating geometric patterns (Pl. 8, Fig. 3). These are yellow in the body, which gives it a predominantly yellow hue except in the head, where a red supplementary weft pattern barely contrasts with the red ground. The cloth measures approximately 120 by 184 centimeters; the head is about 40 centimeters wide. It is made of commercial red cotton yarns, in balanced plain weave. The various diamond shapes or zigzag lines are transformed into a smaller checker-block design of about three centimeters along the red selvage rim of a half-centimeter. As in ba'a boba, the head of ba'a suje is symmetrically divided into two groups of ten supplementary weft white lines which are alternatively smaller and broader. It is worn by women as a sarong or as a complementary shouldercloth. Sometimes, too, it is sewn into a man's jacket of Moslem style.

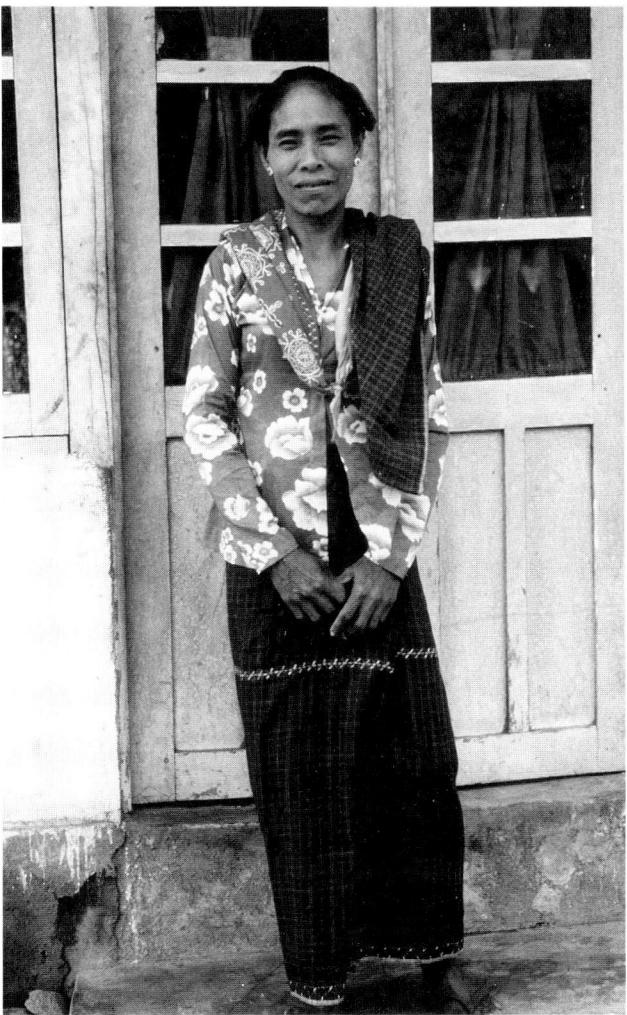

Figure 2. Embroidered sarong from Sulawesi known as kain mandar, worn with complementary shouldercloth (sangkola). Tarau'u, 1980.

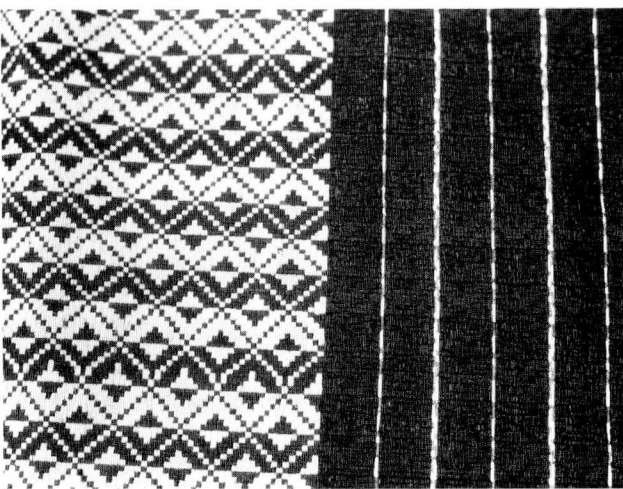

Figure 3. Detail of a red two-paneled sarong (ba'a suje) with supplementary weft patterns throughout (only visible in "body," left) and white lines in "head." Awer, 1982. Full cloth shown in Plate 8.

The Origins of *Kain Kulincucu*

Kulincucu, the general term used to describe *ba'a boba* and *ba'a suje*, is the name of a part of the Wolio realm of Buton, the island southeast of Sulawesi which was conquered and became part of the Ternate sultanate in 1580. Because of its strategic geographical position, Buton served as a major stopping place for military and merchant vessels, whence it got the name of "market" after the Ternate word *butu* for market place. Some years later the southern island of Salayar (Saleyer) also became subordinate to Ternate (see Map).

As the personal domain of the crown prince of Wolio, Kulincucu had considerable status in local politics and trade. By custom every crown prince spent his childhood and adolescence there before being crowned ruler, and it was said that the queen of Wolio should give birth to the prince in Kulincucu (Abdurachman 1983:24). It also was the center of the Butonese weaving tradition—a fact related to its importance for royalty. In the seventeenth century a group of Kulincucu weavers were transferred to Ternate, where they were allotted a piece of land on the periphery of the palace grounds.[3] But they were allowed to weave only for the Ternate court, the district chiefs as far as the interior of Halmahera, and all those connected with the court. Color, pattern, and motif were prescribed by the court (Abdurachman 1983:26). The so-called Kulincucu cloths used by the Sahu people for their harvest festival may have been brought to Sahu by men who served in the households of the Ternate nobility, where they appear to have been good servants (Clercq 1890:108); or they may have been exchanged for rice with Sahu-based court officials and Arab merchants.

A problem arises, however, when we compare the Kulincucu weaving tradition observed in Ternate in 1985 with Butonese textiles and loom documented in the literature in museum collections (Jasper and Pirngadie 1912:160). The loom used by the last family in Ternate who continues the Kulincucu weaving tradition sheds more light on textile trade relationships in Eastern Indonesia. A Butonese loom, according to Jasper and Pirngadie, has no reed. The Ternate Kulincucu loom, on the other hand, does have a reed; but its warp, although actually discontinuous, appears to be circular and continuous. The Kulincucu loom is of the heddle and shed stick type.[4] The only function of its bamboo reed is the spacing of the warp yarns, as it is not strong enough to act as a beater. The sword, placed behind the reed, serves to beat in each weft and to enlarge the shed. Finally, apart from the string heddle, an extra heddle is used to create the pattern.

These characteristics make it most likely that the Ternate Kulincucu loom is a new example of Type C as described by Gittinger (1979a:230-31): "...in the warping the yarns pass about a common stick which acts like a linchpin to hold the great loops of yarn. When on the loom, this allows the warp to have a circular structure."[5] This type of loom is already known from Minahasa, Sangihe-Talaud, and Mindanao, and it is quite possible that it was introduced from one of these areas to Ternate, which was the political and economic center of the region.

The terms used by the Ternate Kulincucu weavers do not coincide with those used in Buton. Jasper and Pirngadie give a list of words for the different parts of the Butonese loom, of which only those of the warp beam, *tetera* (which might be a Ternate word) and the sword, *balida*, are comparable to the words used by my Ternate informants, *tetera* and *wali'da*. The bamboo shuttle in which the weft yarns are inserted, having been wound on bobbins, is called *balone kusoli* in Jasper and Pirngadie, and *mbalo-mbalo* by the Kulincucu women. Further comparison between the Ternate Kulincucu terms and the Butonese ones given by the authors shows the heterogeneous origin of the first. For instance, the Kulincucu words for reed (*yangka*), clothbeam (*fakanga*), and backstrap (*bubungkua*) closely resemble the Bare'e Toraja words *jangga*, *wakanga*, and *boko-boko*.[6] According to Kruyt (1922:403-25), in the language of the Tae Toraja, reed is *jaka*, and warp, *sa'u*, which resembles the Kulincucu term *sawu*. I cannot trace the origin of other Kulincucu terms such as those designating the additional sword (*pedunsi*), string heddle (*punci*), pattern heddle (*lailoa*), cross sticks (*panata*), bobbin (*potongwule*), and sword support (*petambeaha*). Finally, Kulincucu women call the woven textile *arimo*, and the weaver herself, *pohuru*.

The Sahu names for the textiles, *ba'a boba* and *ba'a suje*, are basically Kulincucu terms. The Kulincucu word *bomba*[7] transforms to *boba*, and means "to tie up with yarn"—that is, to ikat. The Sahu people themselves have no explanation for the term *suje*, although they also apply it to an embroidered cloth used during the harvest festival. Kulincucu women today use the word *suje* for the supplementary weft technique or, as they say, the technique in which "your hand takes the yarn up and down." My senior informant could recall orders made from Sahu for *suje* textiles; however, the yarns, colors, and designs of their work have now changed to follow the taste of today's clients, such as government officials and Chinese businessmen. Ikat is not practiced anymore but supplementary weft still is.

Comparison with Butonese textiles from museum collections does not convince me of the Buton/Kulincucu origin of the *ba'a boba* and *ba'a suje*. It is more likely that they came to be called "Kulincucu cloth" only because they were made by women originating from Buton, but living in Ternate. In the early nineteenth century, as we know from Dutch administrator Tobias, the specific claims of the Ternate sultanate on the people from Kulincucu were abolished and they were free to go home or to settle outside the palace grounds. At the same time, it seems likely that court restrictions on weaving were gradually done away with. This created a new market where, in addition to court officials, local dignitaries from Halmahera and even commoners could order textiles from Ternate's Kulincucu weaving community.

Nevertheless we have not answered the question of where the Sahu textiles originate, if not from Buton. At first sight they look like Sulawesi textiles from different parts of the island, because of their geometric patterns and colors. But a study of some of the Dutch museum collections[8] reveals that none of the Sulawesi textiles clearly resemble the Sahu ones either in texture or color combination. Because of their supplementary weft technique and floating yarns,[9] certain specimens from the island of Salayar come closest to the Sahu *ba'a suje* although it is a much coarser handspun cotton, and differs in color from the Salayar cloth. In 1672 the sultan of Buton was entitled by Ternate to collect revenues from three villages on Salayar, but nothing is known about the nature of the goods imported from that island. Yet it is very likely that a great number of textiles has been traded from Salayar through Buton to Ternate.

The red-bordered *ba'a boba* can be traced not only to southern Sulawesi but also to other parts of the island. It is characterized by a head with supplementary weft white threads, similar to the Gorontalese textiles described in Jasper and Pirngadie. These textiles were mostly exported to other parts of Sulawesi and to the Moluccas (Jasper and Pirngadie 1912:230). This makes it quite likely that they were known to Kulincucu women on Ternate. Moreover it is interesting to see that the head of the Donggala double ikat *bomba kota* (Kartiwa 1983:23) compares very well with the Sahu *ba'a boba*, as they both show two groups of ten or eleven supplementary weft lines, and a dark border of about three centimeters.

I conclude, therefore, that the so-called Kulincucu cloths in Sahu were made on Sahu command by Ternate women originating from Buton/Kulincucu, and that they are an assemblage of characteristics borrowed primarily from Salayar and Gorontalese textiles which were traded to Ternate. In this context it is very interesting that the loom is of the Sangihe-Talaud type, whereas the terms for the parts of the loom and the patterns of the textiles were taken instead from other parts of the Ternate realm, such as Central Sulawesi.

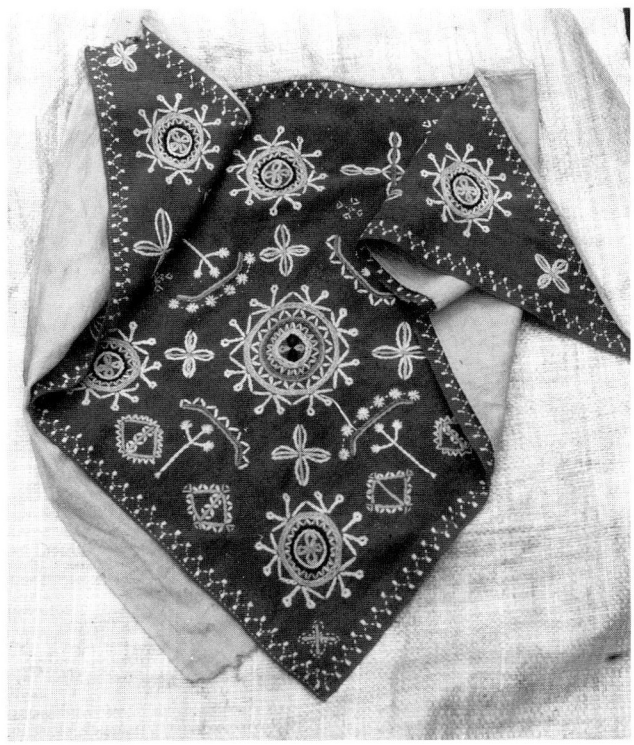

Figure 4. Embroidered cloth with non-geometrical motifs known as tuala suje. *Awer, 1980.*

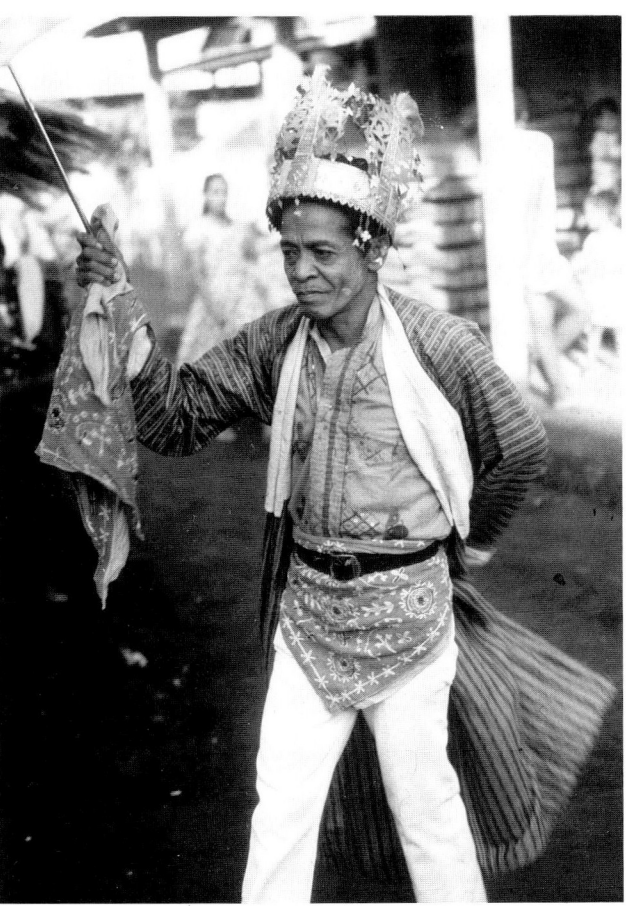

Figure 5. Man dressed for legu *dance with* tuala suje. *Awer, 1980.*

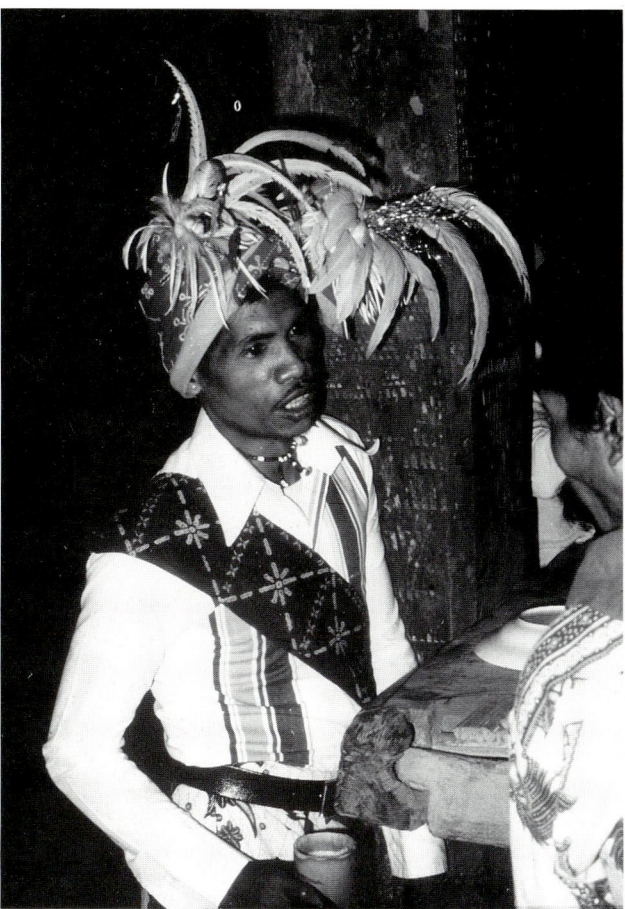

Figure 6. Young man wearing a headdress of tuala suje *and a shouldercloth,* salempa geritoroa. *Tarau'u, 1980.*

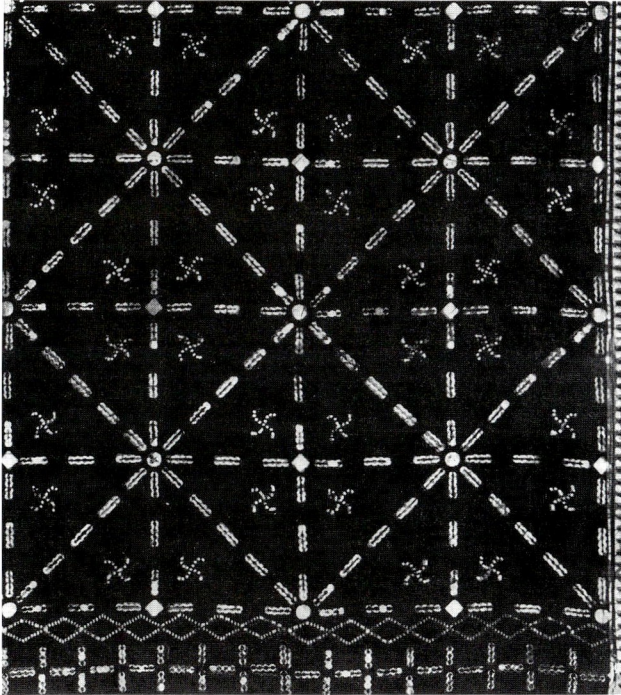

Figure 7. Indigo batik shouldercloth, salempa geritoroa, *with triangle motif* (tumpal) *along the selvage. Awer, 1982.*

Embroidered Textiles

Textiles that have been imported and then locally embroidered form a second category of cloth used in the Sahu harvest festival. Cloths with embroidery are well known in Indonesia despite Loebèr's assertion that they are rarely encountered (1914:10-12); he cited Java, Sumatra, and Kalimantan, but apparently knew of no examples from the eastern part of the archipelago. In Sahu we find several kinds. First, there is *kain mandar,* a sarong with embroidery applied along the join, at the selvages between the two panels (Fig. 2). Embroidery may also decorate a woman's jacket, and sometimes mica spangles are incorporated into the work as further embellishment (Pl. 9); a rare example of this appears on the indigo jacket seen in Plate10. A related technique known as *jongoto* is practiced in Sahu in the fabrication of small betel nut boxes.

Another locally embroidered textile is the cloth called *tuala suje,* an almost square cotton cloth of about 55 by 66 centimeters, diagonally divided into two triangles, one yellow and one red (Fig. 4). The *tuala suje* is always folded into its triangular shape and used as a kind of kerchief (*lenso* in Moluccan Malay) and may be worn by either men or women in three different ways. Women wear two, one over each shoulder, knotted together in one corner over the breast (Pl. 10). It is then called *kalaotala* which means something like "brought together." Men who are classified as elders wear the *tuala* in an inverted way, as a kind of *tumpal,* wrapped around their waist (Fig. 5), whereas men classified as younger wear the same cloth wrapped around their heads with a knot on top (Fig. 6). If both red and yellow parts are plain the cloth is called *tuala dale,* but for ritual occasions the *tuala suje* cloth with an embroidered red part is preferred. When it is worn, the red embroidered section should appear as the upper part, but a rim of the yellow part should always be visible as well. Either commercial cotton or silk yarn is used in the embroidery. Yellow, black, and white are the principal colors; bluish-grey is sometimes used instead of black or in addition to it. Other supplementary colors are beige and violet. Running stitch and chain stitch are most commonly used, but we also find flat stitch. The designs are manifold, and include rosettes, tendrils, a four-leafed motif, six-pointed stars, diamonds, and bows. Although it is claimed that these kerchiefs were once made in Sahu, no one could tell me whether any living women still know the art. Neither could anyone tell me the names of the embroidered symbols.

Imported Batik

Two types of imported batik are used in the Sahu harvest festival. The first is called *salempa geritoroa*, a Galelarese word meaning the "shawl for the affine," a one-sided hand block-printed indigo batik with a geometric pattern (Fig. 7). It measures 210 by 50 centimeters, which is actually half of a small *kain panjang* cut in two lengthwise after the dyeing process. This is evident from the stitching of the long side of the textile which is not dyed, and therefore of a more recent date than the colored stitching of the shorter sides. The cloth is folded lengthwise to form a kind of shouldercloth (*selempang*) about twenty-five centimeters wide, and is worn diagonally across the body from the right shoulder to the left hip, its ends loosely fastened on the hip (Fig. 6). There is a remarkable uniformity in the geometric design of the various cloths observed. It is composed of lines built up of small figures which are not unlike embroidered chain stitches. In the field are dotted motifs similar to what Jasper and Pirngadie term tetrasquetrum.[10] Along the selvage run small *tumpal* motifs.

However, although the indigo color and block printing resemble Javanese batik, the characteristics of the *salempa geritoroa* rather suggest Javanese fabrication on Sahu command. This textile is part of the family heirloom, but as far as I know is not transferred in marriage. The textiles were imported before the 1940s. Both men and women who are classified as genealogically younger wear the cloth during rituals.

A second type of imported Javanese batik used during the festival is a headcloth known as *lipa* or *tuala jawa*. It is about 155 centimeters square, and has predominantly non-geometric motifs; often there is a square, *modang* (Loebèr 1914:30), in its center (Fig. 8). Its colors may be red, blue, or brown. To wear this kind of headdress is the prerogative of classificatory elder men. The cloth first has to be starched and folded in its particular way, an art which only a few Sahu men still master (Fig. 9).

Social Significance of Sahu Textiles

It is evident that not just every textile traded to Ternate was also imported into Sahu, but that a deliberate choice was made as to what colors and motifs were considered to fit Sahu cultural values. We cannot properly understand the social meaning of the textiles without some knowledge of the wider context of Sahu social organization and of the way textiles are used as material expressions of the values governing it.

Sahu, like other North Halmahera societies, had to pay tribute to the sultans of Ternate, but whereas those other regions provided Ternate with warriors, Sahu

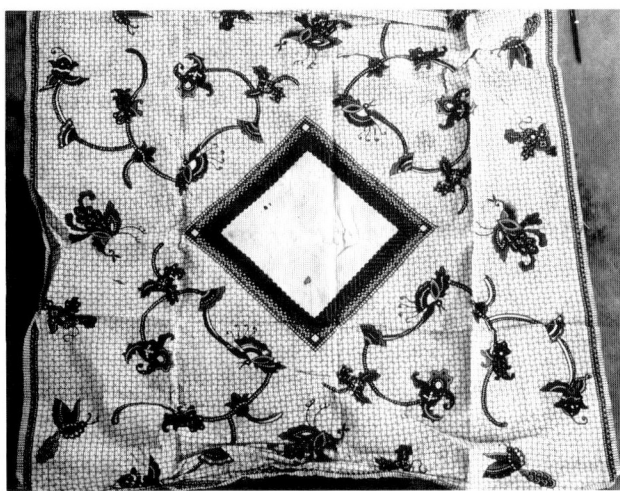

Figure 8. Javanese headcloth, known as lipa *or* tuala jawa. *Awer, 1982.*

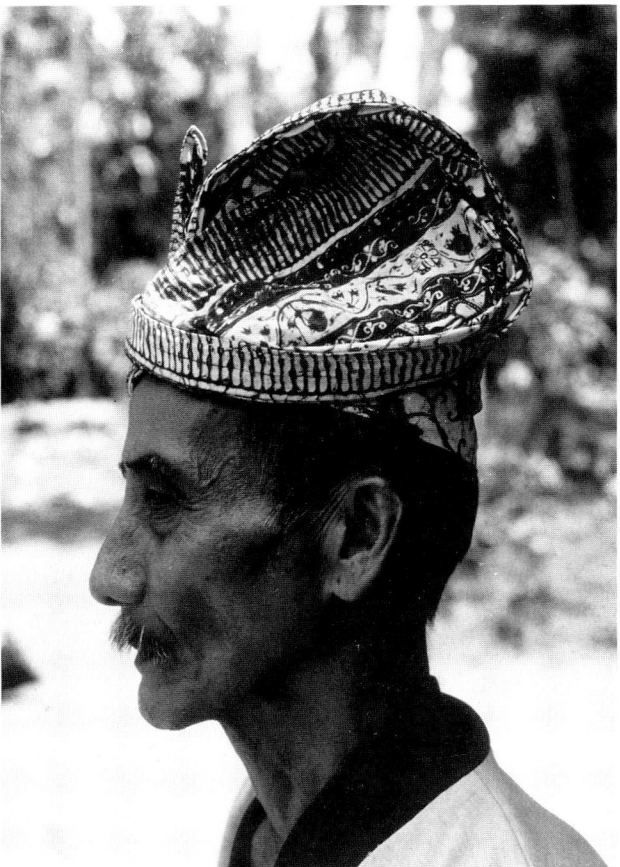

Figure 9. A headcloth folded in its particular way. Awer, 1982.

became the granary of the court. Dry rice cultivation became the basis not only of their physical existence, but also of their ideology: the Sahu identify themselves metaphorically with the rice stalks which grow from the earth. Because of this historically and politically based preoccupation with rice cultivation, the Sahu highly value their claims to the land. Social organization in many ways is dominated by a concern about the permanence of the specific rights to the land of the different social groups.

This territorial interest is clearly expressed during the yearly harvest ritual that takes place in the ceremonial house in the center of the village. The representatives of the different social groups are seated according to genealogical rank at long tables during three nights and two days. On the tables there is a display of food, of which only small amounts are eaten, because the ritual is intended to be a thanksgiving to the ancestors—or nowadays to God—who bestowed fertility upon the land and its people. Rights to the land are clearly related to the positions at the tables for those who represent the social groups in the village. Inheritance of land titles goes in the male line according to a hierarchical order based on genealogical relationships.

Like the rights to land, textiles also belong to a man's inheritance. In contrast to other Indonesian societies where women weave their own textiles, Sahu textiles, whether worn by men or women, belong to the domain of men. A married woman borrows the cloths from her father-in-law, not from her father. Some men may be classified as elder and dressed accordingly (Figs. 5,9), not because of individual age, but because of social rank. Others may be classified as younger and dress differently, like the man in Figure 6. Married women follow their husbands' classification and, if unmarried, their fathers'. Yet one cannot tell from their clothing whether women are classified as elder or younger because in both cases women wear a blue indigo sarong, as in Plate 10 and Figure 2.

In connection with the value of land the idea of a circle is very important in Sahu. It stands for protection and preservation. In agricultural practice planting as well as harvesting activities proceed in circles upon the field, and there are many rituals to ward off negative influences and to safeguard fertility of the soil and growth of the grain. Likewise, during the first day of the harvest festival the *legu* or *ciawa* is danced by elder men (Fig. 5) who surround young marriageable women. In the words of the accompanying song: "Fertile she shall be, but let us surround her, that her offspring shall settle within the boundaries of our land." The sarongs of the participating women symbolize the idea of enclosure no less than the harvest ritual itself.

During the first night's dancing and festivities and also during the following day and night the women wear a closed cloth or sarong. The dark blue colors of *kain mandar* and *ba'a boba* are congruous with the idea that the agricultural or yearly cycle is closed on the first night of the harvest festival.[11] The next day, a new cycle starts like the red and yellow sun which rises at dawn, and like a woman who creates new life in marriage by giving birth. This is symbolized in the *legu* dance where red and yellow are the colors of the *ba'a suje* (Pl. 8) and the other women's textiles, as well as of the *tuala suje* worn by women and young men. These colors dominate the dresses of the dancers with their crowns of birds of paradise feathers and long kaftans. During the last day, however, imported commercial batik wraparounds replace the sarongs. The harvest ritual which marks the end of the agricultural year is now coming to its final stage, and a new cycle will soon be opened up: the heavy circular woven cloths of the previous days are now replaced by light and bright open batik textiles.

Apart from fabrication, texture and design have a distinct social meaning. However, we should know something about the social history of the textiles in order to be able to interpret these properly. The Sahu people reportedly used barkcloth until late last century, which was then replaced by foreign textiles, like the Kulincucu sarong and the Javanese batik headcloth (Campen 1884:172-74). Also, men's loincloths (*sabeba*, as they are called in Sahu) were replaced by the embroidered *tuala suje*. The blue indigo jacket with its mica embroidery might well be a substitute for the *kotanga* jacket mentioned by Campen (1884:173). The textiles worn during the modern harvest festival show two contrasting patterns and designs: a geometric one, either woven (*ba'a boba* and *ba'a suje*) or batik (*salempa geritoroa*), and a non-geometric one full of arabesque motifs, again either batik (*lipa jawa*) or embroidered (*tuala suje*).

Sahu orientation is based on a dichotomy of land and sea, instead of the more familiar quadripartite south-west-north-east orientation. The land/sea dichotomy is both geographical and cosmological, and therefore vital to every part of Sahu culture. The upper part of the human body is associated with land, the lower part with the sea. In agricultural practice and in ritual, circular movements and movements in the direction of the land are thought to have a positive influence on the preservation and permanence of fertility of land as well as people. Thus ritual textiles with circular and non-geometric designs worn around the head and upper part of the body, and the use of closed or tied cloths, are a material expression of the Sahu concern for land and progeny.

Woven cloths are never worn around the head. Their geometric pattern seems to continue the image of the squares on the barkcloth of the men's loincloths and the women's jackets of earlier times. Although it is

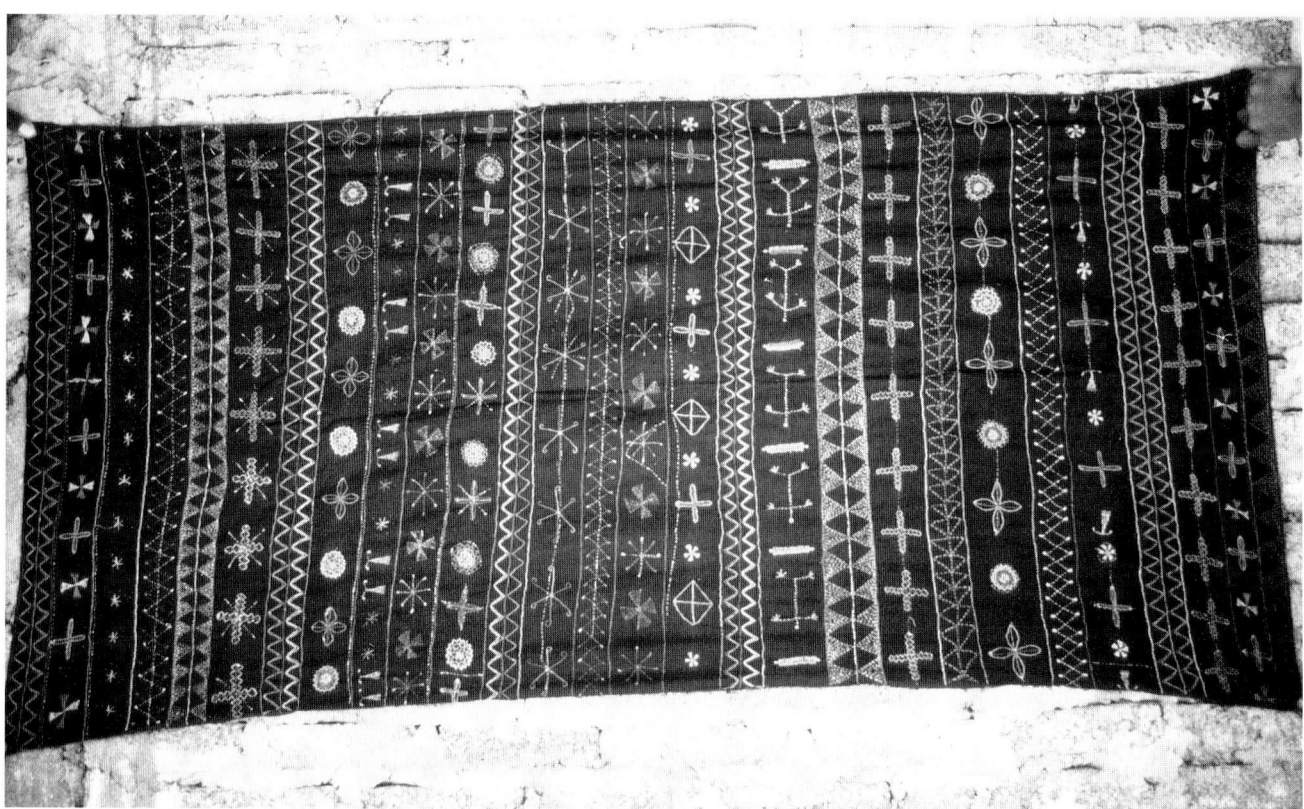

Figure 10. Embroidered ceremonial cloth with tortoise motif and other elements. Awer, 1982.

difficult to prove from what is known today about Sahu, the geometric pattern seems to be related to the idea of descent lines. Women wear the sarongs with the supplementary weft which are owned by and passed on within the descent group to which they belong, and young men show their descent in their shouldercloth, *selempang*. These men also demonstrate their ties to the land in the red and yellow headdress of *tuala suje*. Yet the way the *tuala suje* is worn differs according to a man's classificatory status. Young men wear it as a headdress with a knot on their forehead, whereas elders wear the cloth as a waist-scarf, but tied at their backs, thus emphasizing its design and color. Its triangle thus points downward, like an upside down *tumpal*. Campen shows us an example of a decorated *tuala suje* with downward pointing *tumpal*s (1884: pl. III). Apparently, changes in material and technique are irrelevant to the continuity of the representation of certain ideas. Formerly it was a loincloth with arabesques and *tumpal* motifs that classified a man as genealogically elder; today he wears an embroidered cotton cloth in the shape of a *tumpal*, with comparable colors and motifs.

Although we now may have an impression of the social meaning of *tuala suje*, it is difficult to explain the symbolic meaning of the motifs themselves. The Sahu do not have an explanation (anymore?) and hardly know any names for them. The trident-like motif in Figure 4 is worth special note: it strongly resembles the designs on a richly embroidered indigo cloth I was shown in Sahu (Fig. 10). The man to whose heirloom it belonged called this motif a tortoise (*tuturuga*). It was not thought to represent a human being, although the resemblance is rather close if we compare it with human motifs on barkcloth from Northeast Halmahera (Kooijman 1963: pl. XV, fig. 2). Moreover, the extremities of both figures are depicted like the kind of tendrils comparable to the motifs on the *tuala suje*. Since we know very little about the symbolic value of these motifs, it is not very convincing to declare that "these ornamental patterns belonged to the sphere of head-hunting," (Kooijman 1963:51). Headhunting as an explanation for designs on barkcloth and headdress has been rather popular, although the activity as such has never been attested in Halmahera (Hueting 1922:207-12; Ellen 1942:72). It is more likely that the motifs are connected with warfare, not only in Northeast Halmahera but also elsewhere in eastern Indonesia. For instance, the colors red, yellow, and black, and comparable designs are found on Toraja headcloths, Ceramese pubic belts, and barkcloth garments from the coastal area of western Irian Jaya (Jasper and Pirngadie 1916:248; Adriani and Kruyt 1912/14 II:323 and 1950 I:366-67; Kooijman 1963:111,123, pls. XII,XIV). So the Sahu *tuala suje* motifs resemble those of surrounding cultures, a fact which adds to our understanding of the Sahu cloth only if we recognize the differences as well. Unlike other North Halmahera societies Sahu did not engage in warfare on behalf of the Ternate sultanate, so the *tuala suje* motifs express Sahu identification with the permanence of the fertility of the land and the claims upon it, rather than superiority over other people through warfare.

Certainly no simple conclusion can be drawn about the origin of the Sahu textiles. Pattern and color of textiles should be interpreted primarily in the context of the culture in which they are used, whether this is their culture of origin or the society into which the cloths have been imported. Secondly, our understanding may be improved by comparison with related cultures. Finally, symbolic value does not depend upon the material used in its expression; on the contrary, there is a remarkable continuity in the representation of cultural ideas irrespective of changing material expression.

NOTES

1. I carried out anthropological research on shifting cultivation in Northwest Halmahera (Sahu) in 1979-80 and 1982, with grants from the Stichting voor Wetenschappelijk Onderzoek van de Tropen (WOTRO).

2. In other sources, also: Koloncucu, Kalencusa, Kulincusu.

3. In the nineteenth century most of the Kulincucu population then living in Ternate returned to Buton, and the remaining families were allowed to settle on government land (Tobias 1857:21). Today there are a few families living in what is locally known as Kampung Makassar, near the palace grounds. Only the women of the Bonso family today still weave what is called in Ternatan *rapi dino*. These textiles are red or green with small gold thread figures. Recently the *rapi dino* are mentioned in a survey of Indonesian *songket* by Kartiwa (1982:74) who uses information from Joseph (1982).

4. This classification is that of Rita Bolland, who kindly helped me with all technical terminology.

5. Burnham (1980:133) calls it an open spiral warp.

6. See also the terms for different parts of the Donggala loom, as described by Kartiwa (1983:27): *yangga* (reed), *tanyanga* (clothbeam), and *boko-boko* (backstrap).

7. This word is also found in the name of a Rongkong Toraja ikat cloth, called *bomba bula* (Adriani and Kruyt 1912/14 III:275). It is also known in the Donggala area where ikat textiles are called *buya bomba*. Here, *bomba* means "flower" or "flower like motif" (Kartiwa 1983:13). I am grateful to Rens Heringa who drew my attention to this fact and to this publication.

8. Rita Bolland was so kind as to show me the collection of the Tropenmuseum, Amsterdam, and Ms. Maria Laman allowed me to visit the Leiden ethnographic collection.

9. Especially Nos. A 5169 and 15/58 of the Amsterdam collection and Nos. 2429/10 and 2429/15 in Leiden.

10. Jasper and Pirngadie present such ornaments from Toraja (1916:247, fig. 343).

11. A parallel can be drawn here with Sahu marriage, when the bride is abducted from her parents' house and taken during the night to the house or village of her parents-in-law, and covered with a blue cloth (Visser 1984:142).

Batik Patterns of the Early Nineteenth Century

Anthony Forge

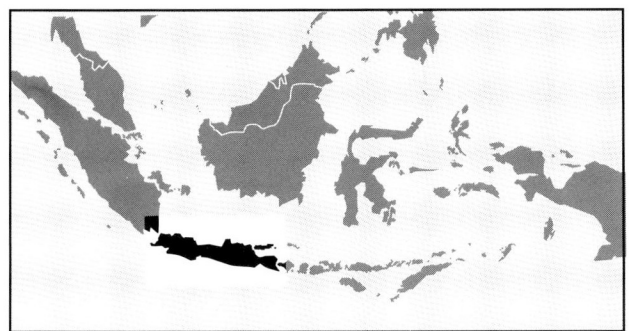

Sir Thomas Stamford Raffles, during his period as Lieutenant Governor of Java (1811-16), made an extensive collection of Javanese material, both contemporary and antique. Part at least seems to have been made for the purpose of illustrating his monumental *The History of Java*, published in 1817. There is some published documentation of portions of it, but so far no overall account of the surviving collection has been undertaken (Barrett 1953, Scott-Kemball 1970). Raffles seems to have gathered diverse material during the whole of his period in Java. Most of the collection whose remains eventually reached the British Museum was certainly made before Raffles left Java in 1816 and part at least went with him in the *Ganges* to London. In 1824 he bought Highwood House and installed all his scattered property. He lived there with his wife until his death in 1826. The collection stayed at the house until the death of Lady Raffles in 1858. Her nephew and executor, the Rev. Raffles Flint, at first offered to sell the entire collection to the British Museum for one thousand pounds, but the Museum declined to purchase. Nevertheless it was deposited there on September 3, 1859, and was entered in the register in December of that year.[1]

Eighty years later, in 1939, the Raffles descendants presented to the Museum some further objects that had been retained or overlooked in 1859. This much smaller group is known as the Drake collection. Included in it were two pieces of batik, presumably the last survivors of the "22 pieces of Java cloths intended as specimens for the English Manufactures," recorded as released from excise in the London Dock Minute Book on October 10, 1816.[2] The existence of these batiks, with an indisputable early date, has of course been known for some time. They are, however, of very coarse cloth and not particularly distinguished in workmanship or design (one is illustrated in Elliott 1984). They have therefore tended to confirm the impression given by the Gresik designs of 1822,

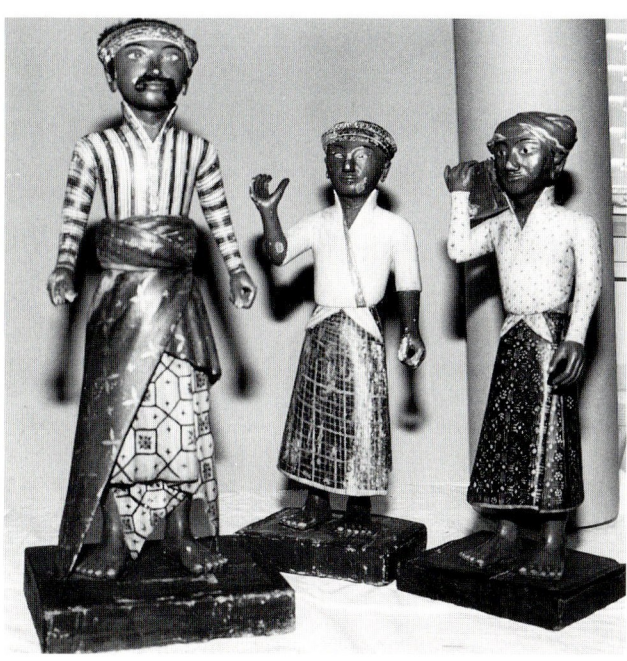

Figure 1. Front view of three models from the Raffles collection. These three were used for the plate "A Madurese of the Rank of Mantri" (Raffles 1817 I: opp. 94). The height of the Mantri, left, is 16". Left to right, British Museum 1859.12.28.188, 185, 187.

published in Rouffaer and Juynboll (1914), that batik in the early nineteenth century was not refined in technique or very developed in design.

Raffles was something of a polymath. He was interested in everything—economics and linguistics, history and contemporary culture, plants and animals (he was a founder of the Royal Zoological Society)—and he made systematic collections to document all his interests. He assembled a wide range of factual data and statistics for his projected book, but also collected animals as well as the objects that eventually reached the British Museum. The Raffles collection is very large and diverse: there are a great number of sculptures in stone, wood, and a range of metals; antique and contemporary vessels; *lontar* (palm leaf manuscripts); parts of at least two *gamelan* (bronze metalophone orchestra); a very fine set of masks; weapons; and many everyday objects. Included as well—the part with which this paper is concerned—are at least one superb and large set of *wayang kulit* (flat leather shadow puppets) and other sets of *wayang* (wooden puppets), covering all the types of puppets used in the Java of Raffles's day.[3] There is evidence, from the remaining labels on some pieces, that he also listed and numbered with considerable care most of the objects and sets that make up his collection, but none of these inventories survive. Of the various lists of the collection dating from the nineteenth century, none are complete or precise in their descriptions. None are the original ones made in Java.

In *The History of Java* many of the monochrome plates are line engravings obviously made from objects brought back by Raffles. However the source of the tinted plates, illustrating types and costumes of the Java of Raffles's day, is more complex. These hand-colored aquatints are by William Daniell (1769-1837), who with his uncle had paid three visits to the Indonesian area between 1785 and 1794. Daniell and Daniell published some of their own aquatints of Java (1810), as well as their more famous huge six-volume series on India (1795-1808). Bastin and Rohatgi (1979) list the drawings on which Raffles's plates were based as "anon" without further details. There are indeed five pen drawings in the Department of Oriental Antiquities, British Museum, that relate to five of the ten plates, and they presumably had these in mind. These authorities, however, do not seem to be aware that in the library of the Department of Ethnography of the British Museum (Museum of Mankind), there are seven small oils attributed to Daniell, painted on cardboard and about the same size as the finished aquatints in Raffles. Six of these are very close to the published plates, except that one, captioned "Bridegroom," is reversed. I presume them to be trials made for Raffles's approval before Daniell started working on the copper. In some cases changes were made. For instance, the painting captioned "A Javan in the War Drefs" shows him wearing a *kain* with a vague *ceplok* (lattice and star) pattern. In the corresponding aquatint (Raffles 1817 I: opp. 90) it has been changed to a strong *parang rusak* ("broken knife"—diagonal lines of looped figures), which is of higher status.[4] While he was in England, including the time spent writing and publishing *The History of Java*, Raffles was accompanied by Raden Rana Dipura. This Javanese prince, whose portrait forms the frontispiece, was consulted for both the text and the plates, so we may take what is shown to be authoritative. Whether there were other original drawings is uncertain, but in one case it is evident that no drawing ever existed.[5]

The Models

As part of his documentation Raffles commissioned a group of carvings referred to in the customs documents and an early list as "models." These were apparently made to show the costumes of the day. One painting and the plate made from it, captioned "A Madurese of the rank of Mantri" (Raffles 1817 I: opp. 94), has clearly been made directly from three of the commissioned models. The correspondence between these models and the plate is so exact in costume, pose, and color, that Daniell must have had the specific models in front of him as he worked. Since he could only show one aspect of each figure, the models contain much more information than he could include. The painting and the plate show the Mantri (junior minister) with a headcloth, a jacket of *lurik* (a striped, densely woven, typically Javanese fabric), and a cloth round his waist with a black *kawung* pattern (a subclass of *ceplok* in which the grid element is developed and the flowers decrease in importance); it is of the straight line type on a white ground. Tied over the whole is a green cloth with a simple four-pointed motif in gold—presumably a *dodot*, the large double cloth used in court circles. The carved model shows exactly the same from the front (Fig. 1), but the back reveals that the green cloth is a *kain kembangan*— a cloth whose center color differs from that of the main body, and usually produced by *tritik*, a sewn-resist process; moreover it has a much more elaborate *prada* (gold-leaf) motif over its white center (Fig. 2). The two servants also disclose more interesting details from the back: for instance on the one carrying the *sirih* box (used for betel-chewing accoutrements), the headcloth is also a *kembangan*. In this case there obviously never was an original drawing; the painting was produced directly from the models.

There are now thirteen of these models in the Raffles collection, but none of the other ten correspond so precisely in pose and costume to any of the published plates. Daniell used the five "anonymous"

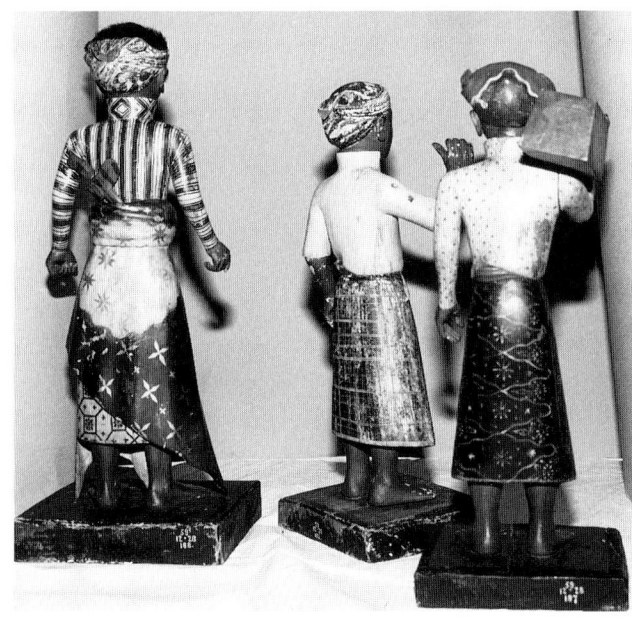

Figure 2. Back view of the three models seen in Figure 1.

Forge

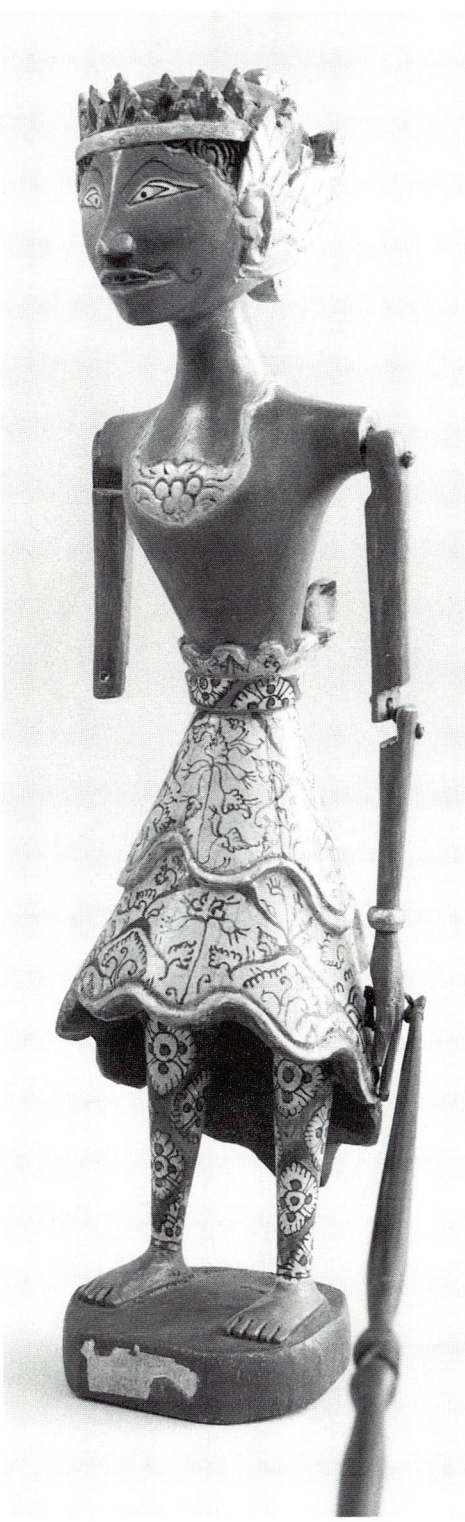

Figure 3. Puppet No. 407 from the Raffles collection. It is recorded in the register as "Manak Joyo Prulong Depati Problu," although the label is now largely illegible; the last word reads, in my opinion, "Prabhu." He wears leggings, a belt of patola, and a cloth of alas-alasan. Note the remains of a label, possibly in Javanese, on the front of the base. This is one of the most complete puppets that remain, having one of the buffalo horn sticks and missing only the lower right arm. He stands 11.5" high. British Museum 1859.12.28.407.

drawings, the models, the cloths, and the puppets that Raffles brought back to produce the plates; and Raffles corrected them. Certainly the *tumpal* (chevron) leggings and the *dodot* with *alas-alasan* (stylized wild forest) seen in "A Javan in the Court Drefs" (Raffles 1817 I: opp. 92) could have been taken from the set of puppets that is the main subject of this paper.

The models stand on bases and range from fourteen to seventeen inches in height,[6] including the base. They are not in any sort of Javanese style, but are definitely "naturalistic" in a European manner, designed to show the costumes and the cloths that compose them with total visual accuracy. Yet they were certainly made by Javanese, since two have labels with Javanese numbers and a third bears a long inscription in Javanese characters. The models are in good condition; but for the historian of batik there is little joy to be found among them. Most of the characters portrayed are wearing sarongs (sewn-up cylinders of cloth). They either have vague patterns in indigo with *kepala* (a differentiated panel, at that era always worn— at least by men—at the back), similar to the surviving Raffles batik, or are woven with simple checked patterns. Apart from the Mantri, there is just one other figure wearing an elaborate flowered *kain panjang*, a longer piece of cloth not sewn into a cylinder but worn tied from the whole open cloth. Presumably it is of batik. While many of the *kain kepala* seem to have interesting batik designs, they are so realistically rendered that no complete design element shows.

An Unusual Set of Carved Wooden Puppets

However among the sets catalogued by the British Museum as "puppets," there is a group of carvings of very considerable interest. They are carved from wood, with extra pieces used for the more extravagant clothing and for the heads, which are immovably joined to the body. Each has been painted with very great care. They all have a base of flat painted wood and look at first sight as if they were intended to be placed upright on that base (Fig. 3). However even in their present condition, some will not stand on their base at all, while others will balance on it but not stand upright. In one case, the back of the *kain* is actually so long that it projects below the level of the base (Fig. 7, left). Inspection reveals that the carver has made no attempt to obtain a flat underside. Furthermore it is obvious that at least in the majority of cases the figures originally had a peg projecting from the center of the base. All that can now be seen of these pegs is their roughly square root on the underside, as they have all been cut away by a coarse-toothed saw. This must have been done after the acquisition of the puppets by the British Museum. In several cases some of the original label was cut away at the same time as the peg so that only part of the text can now be read. However in the 1859 register the full text is recorded, evidently from an intact label (Fig. 4). All the puppets had moveable arms of wood jointed at the shoulder and elbow, with tied string joints typical of *wayang*. The arms were controlled by sticks of buffalo horn, another typical *wayang* feature. Most of their arms are now missing but there is a plentiful supply of loose arms and sticks that clearly belong to them.[7]

There are now forty-seven of these figures, forty-six deposited in 1859 and one added in 1939.[8] The remnants of the original numbers suggest there were once at least fifty-five: the number "55" appears on the puppet labeled "A Waiting Maid," which is likely to have been towards the end of the set if not the last. Each figure seems to have had three labels before the addition of the museum numbers; all are of paper and stuck on. The first is on the front of the base and in all cases is very rubbed and eroded. Some examples appear to show traces of a script which could be Javanese, but the ink is so faded it is impossible to read even under ultra-violet light. Of the forty-three figures that still have bases, twenty-two show traces of such a label. The other two labels are found on the underside of the base and were presumably added after collection by Raffles. Both are written with a European pen on laid paper, in a clerkly hand, in ink now faded to pale brown. The second set of labels are numbers on very small squares of paper; only eight survive (ranging from "4" to "55"). In one case there is a number in ink written directly on the wood in the same style. There are also a variety of numbers written in pencil, which I have ignored. The third label, though variable in size, is much bigger. This label records the names and titles of the figure in English, for example "Dewi Wahito, Queen of Menak Jinggo." Twenty-two such labels are recorded in the register of 1859, although not all were then complete. Only seventeen survive and some of these are more extensively damaged than they were at the time of registration.[9]

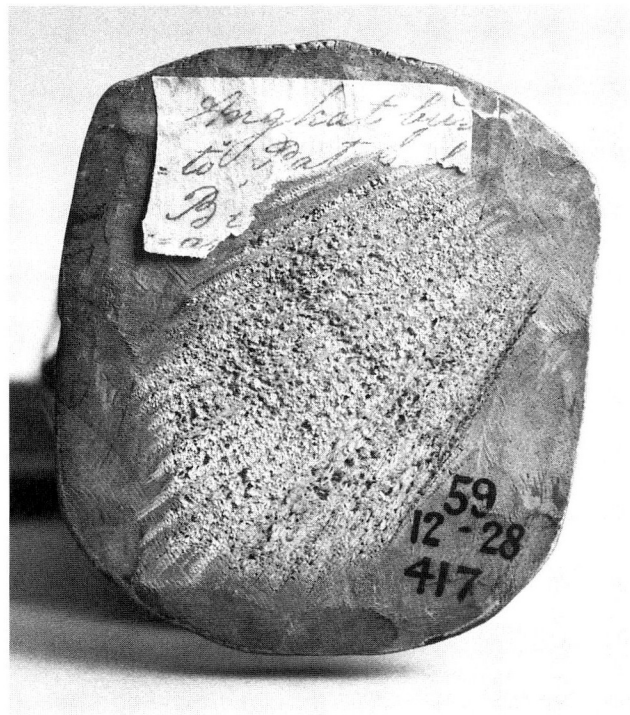

Figure 4. The base of Puppet No. 417 from the Raffles collection, showing that the label was cut away along with the peg. The full text in the register reads "Angkat-buto Patih of Blambangan." British Museum 1859.12.28.417.

Damar Wulan Stories

From the names in the register it is obvious that this set of puppets was concerned with a Damar Wulan story. Damar Wulan is the protagonist of a set of stories known to have been very popular in the nineteenth century, particularly in Central Java for the *wayang golek*, the three-dimensional puppets discussed below.[10] Damar Wulan, a refined character, defends the reigning Queen of Majapahit, Dewi Kencana, from the sexual and political advances of the revolting King of Blambangan. Marrying her himself, Damar Wulan becomes ruler of the Majapahit empire. "Raden Damar Wulan," No. 443, is identified in the register, but the label is now lost. "Menak Jinggo, King of Blambangan,"

Forge

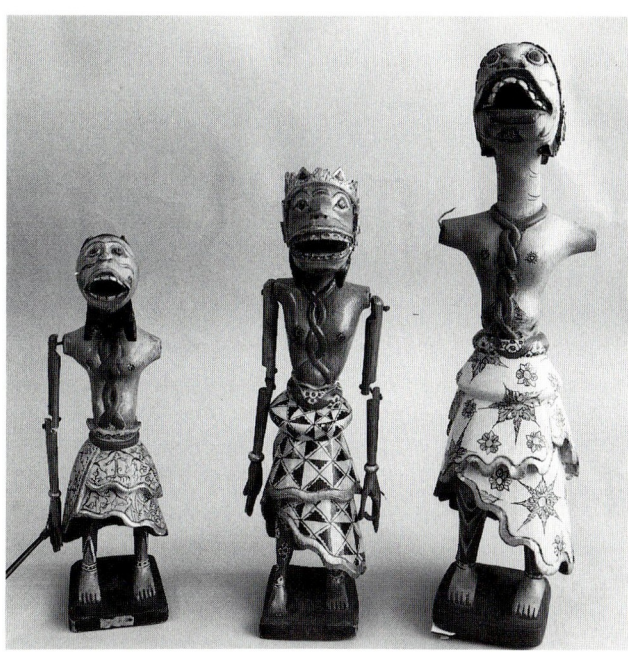

Figure 5. Puppets Nos. 449, 448, and 447 (left to right) from the Raffles collection, probably depicting the royal family of Blambangan. Left, "Menak Pangsing." Center, King "Menak Jinggo." Right, unnamed figure. All have bright blue skin with a red twist of cloth round their necks; left and right wear leggings patterned with triangles (tumpal), while the king has patola leggings and belt. Left, nearly the shortest of the set, stands 10.75". Right, by far the tallest, stands 15.25". British Museum 1859.12.28.449, 448, 447.

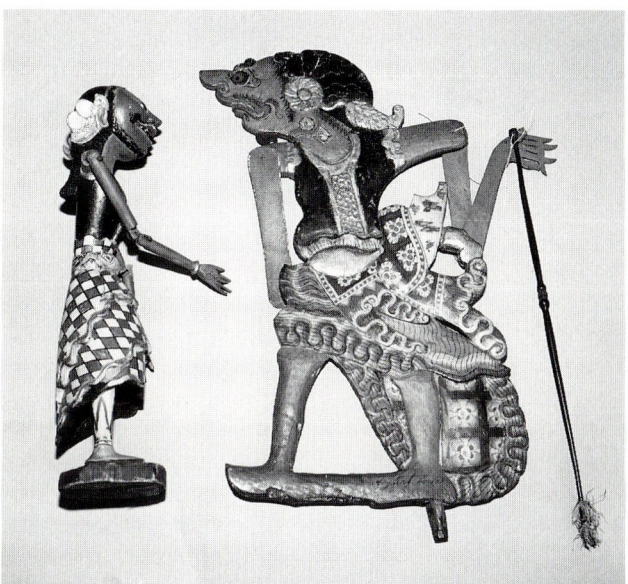

Figure 6. Puppets Nos. 417 and 479 (left to right) from the Raffles collection, depicting two versions of "Angkat-buto." Left, from the first set, wears a jacket and red and white poleng and stands 13.25" high. Right, from the second set, shows the remains of the peg and stands 16.25". The skin color of the two is very similar but their style and clothing differ, although both wear sleeveless jackets. British Museum 1859.12.28.417, 479.

No. 448, is identified by a surviving label, as are his two wives "Dewi Payengan," No. 436, and "Dewi Wahito," No. 446. His majesty is painted with a bright blue body, coarse features, and a gaping mouth full of rough teeth (Fig. 5, Pl. 17). There are two further figures with this coloring, whose features are even more coarse (Fig. 5). I take these to be his sons. The smaller, No. 449, is labeled "Menak Pangsing," while the larger, No. 447, has no extant label. He is described by the writer of the register as "monstrous" and is by far the largest in the set, standing fifteen and a half inches high. There are also two "Patih" (senior ministers) of Blambangan with labels: "Kot-buto," No. 418 (not shown here), and "Angkat-buto," No. 417 (Fig. 6, Pl. 18). The hero and his side are less well identified: in particular no indication remains as to which of the many high-status ladies present is Dewi Kencana, Damar Wulan's love and the Queen of Majapahit; but I suspect it may be No. 437 (Fig. 14).

To sum up so far, we have forty-seven figures very carefully carved and painted, probably the remains of a coherent set of at least fifty-five, representing characters from a Damar Wulan story.[11] The style of carving and painting suggest *wayang* but they do not correspond to any type recorded in the literature. What are they? This question must be faced, at least in a preliminary manner, since I wish to argue that they are a representative part of Javanese culture of the first decades of the nineteenth century. My first thought was that they were, like the models, commissioned by Raffles and showed, perhaps, a troop of *wayang wong* (human dancers who, with or without masks, perform stories from the same repertoire as the *wayang* puppets). Such a view is untenable. Apart from the apparently much older labels on the front of the bases, the form of the bases precludes any comparison with the models. The figures now appear as if designed to stand flat; but while the bases are flat and smooth on top, underneath, they are not. With the pegs intact none of the figures could have stood on a flat surface. They must have been displayed or employed by being stuck into some yielding medium, such as a banana trunk. I thus decided that they were not made specially for Raffles but were, rather, a form of *wayang* produced and used within Javanese culture of the time.

The closest analogy from the *wayang* world known to us seemed to be *wayang golek*, which are carved in the round but have moveable heads, which the Raffles set lacks, as well as moveable arms. *Wayang golek* are dressed in real cloth—often batik—which forms another analogy with the Raffles puppets and their painted cloths. In *The History of Java* Raffles discusses the forms of *wayang*, but he never mentions *wayang golek*, although he covers all other now-known types. However, there does occur the following paragraph:

In the *wayang klitik* the figures exhibited are more properly puppets than shadows: they are of wood, about ten inches high, and made to perform their parts without the intervention of a curtain. In these are represented that portion of the history commencing with the establishment of the western empire of *Pajajaran* and ending with the destruction of the eastern empire of *Majapahit*. Of this, by far the most favourite scenes are found in the popular story of the adventures between the *Menak Jing'ga*, a chief of *Balambang'an*, and *Damar Wulan* (the light of the moon), on account of the Princess of *Majapahit* (Raffles 1817 I:339).

This description fits the set under consideration perfectly, and particularly significant is the height mentioned by Raffles, "about ten inches." Of the forty-seven figures, 76% stand between ten and a quarter and twelve inches, while only three are more than thirteen inches tall.

A second set of puppets

The Raffles collection also contains a set of forty-three puppets that we would now instantly identify as *wayang klitik*, that is, with flat carved wood bodies. These are well carved and painted but their pegs have obviously been shortened with a saw to about one inch, so it is impossible to say how long they originally were. In this case there is no definite evidence that the cutting was done at the British Museum. However some of the cut pegs have been drilled with a small hole in their center, presumably so that they could be stood up for display. This set is also for a Damar Wulan story, and most have names written directly on them between their feet. Many are now very difficult to read. Otherwise, they do not appear to have been documented at any stage with the care Raffles took with the first set. Even without the central peg, all are considerably more than ten inches in height. The males range between fifteen and more than twenty inches, and even the smallest, the females of high status, start at eleven and a half inches. A comparison of the same character in the two sets makes their totally different nature clear (Fig. 6). Since Raffles's description clearly fits the first set better, while the second set looks like what we now associate with *wayang klitik*, it seems possible that there were two different types of *wayang klitik* at the time. Whether the first set was an ancestor of the *wayang golek*, nowhere mentioned by Raffles, is an intriguing possibility that further research may determine.[12]

It seems therefore that the first set was made for Javanese purposes and probably originally had names in Javanese script on the front labels. They were not made specially for Raffles but were collected by him and documented with considerable care. Although this is also true of the collections of *wayang kulit* (leather puppets) and the *wayang* masks, more of the documentation of these has survived. Raffles obviously regarded these puppets as an important part of his documentation of Javanese culture. They must have been a set for some performance purpose, "without the intervention of a curtain." Whether they should be classed as *klitik* or *golek*, their particular form obviously did not survive until the later nineteenth century when Dutch scholarship began. It seems probable then that they were actually used in Javanese court circles in the late eighteenth or early nineteenth centuries.[13] It is known that this was a time of considerable cultural ferment and creativity, before Javanese culture was finally colonized, controlled, and codified by the returning Dutch, more especially after the wars of the eighteen-thirties.

Two Types of Realism

In terms of the present discussion the status of this set of carvings is not of paramount importance. It is appropriate, however, to speculate about whether it was a genuine part of Javanese culture of the time, before considering its relevance to the study of batik. The puppets are certainly in a *wayang* style: most necks crane forward, most chins are lifted, and skin colors are gold, red, and blue as well as various shades of buff and yellow. Faces are sometimes in a contrasting color to the body, usually white, and the eye and face conventions of *wayang* are observed in all cases. Yet the exaggerated stylization of the body associated with flat *wayang* in wood or leather is reduced by the carving in the round. In many cases the carver went to great trouble to portray facial expression and in every one the fall of cloth was obviously a major concern. Almost all the cloths shown have a gold border, which is usually wavy. This wavy edge at the bottom of garments remains typical of leather *wayang kulit* characters to the present day, and also occurs in the flat wooden *klitik*. Some figures, like No. 439, have engraved lines clearly intended to indicate the folds of a tied *kain*, which always fit with the wavy bottom border (Fig. 7). The borders of tailored coats, on the other hand, are always shown straight. I believe the wavy border to be a representation of the fall of a real cloth; as such it is a conventionalization of the *wayang* genre, not an indication of a real scallop-edged cloth.[14]

With the exception of two priests in long tailored coats down to their ankles, all the characters wear tied cloth. Of the forty-five tied cloths, thirty-five are undoubtedly batik; their patterns are shown in full color and painted with great precision (although some of greens and blues seem to have faded). The designs are

Forge

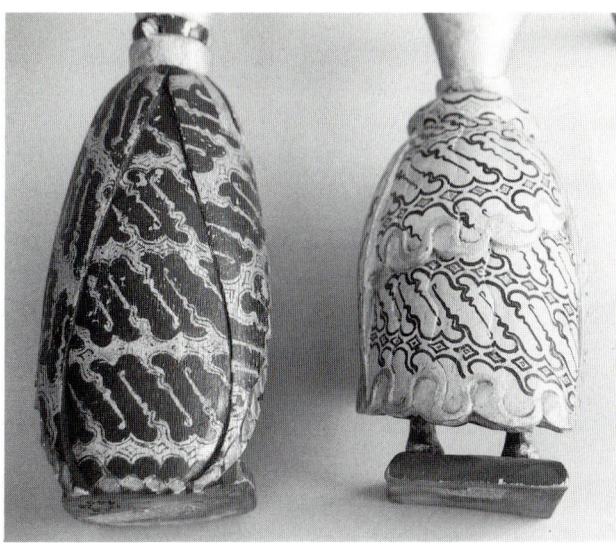

Figure 7. Puppets Nos. 440 and 439 (left to right) from the Raffles collection. Parang rusak appears in different media. Left, in prada on dark indigo, is "Menak Kindah" according to the register (label now missing). He shows the most complex kain *tying style, with slanting "wings" coming down each side. Right wears a* dodot *in batik, black on white with gold border.*
British Museum 1859.12.28.440, 439.

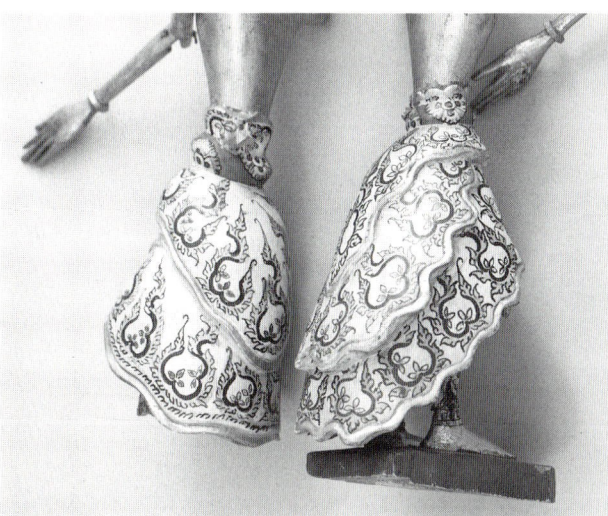

Figure 8. Puppets Nos. 445 and 444 (left to right) from the Raffles collection. These are the only two dressed in virtually identical batik, of developed parang *design.*
British Museum 1859.12.28.445, 444.

too large in proportion to the size of the figures for "true realism" in the European sense; but they are right for another sort of realism, where it is important that the patterns should be accurate and recognizable. In the finest *wayang kulit* the patterns of the cloth are shown in great detail and clarity, but seem to be some ideal cloth of great richness, difficult to relate to actual cloth. The same is true to some extent with the second set of *wayang klitik* in the Raffles collection, although they do have some real cloth too. In the first set, however, the craftsmen who painted them were determined to communicate the actual pattern of real cloths. So while both the figures are scaled down to fifteen and twenty percent of living reality and so are the cloths themselves as totalities, the patterns on them are painted on a much larger scale and are clearly identifiable. An obvious hero such as No. 444 (Fig. 8), with his gold body and his magnificent *kain*, showing a developed sword or *parang* pattern of the type now associated with the north-coast city of Cirebon, looks as if he were dressed by the modern designer, Iwan Tirta. But this is an illusion produced by European dominant visual conceptions.

The point is that the models Raffles had made in order to show contemporary clothing are realistic in our sense, and were indeed used to engrave at least one realistic illustration for his book. But while their *kain kepala* look interesting, the realistic folding prevents any identifiable batik pattern being discerned. In contrast, the *wayang* figures under consideration are "realistic" in a contemporary Javanese sense: that is, their bodies are *wayang* in style, but their clothing is realistically shown as cloth with clear and recognizable patterns. The distinction is that between the European concept of realism concerned with the look of a clothed person, and that of the Javanese concerned with the pattern of the actual cloth, which tells much about the wearer. In this set the cloth patterns and colors are shown with the same attention to detail as the other indicators of status--headdresses, breast ornaments, and so on. Of course the same applies in *wayang golek*: the carved figures are in *wayang* style but they wear real batik, so that they inevitably appear to have unrealistically large patterns. What we have, then, is a set of puppets carved with the ancient *wayang* conventions about status and ornamentation and dressed in clearly represented cloth suitable for court use at the end of the eighteenth century.

The Puppets' Clothing

To turn at last to the actual clothing, I shall start at the bottom. One of the priests wears shoes; otherwise all characters have bare feet. Many of the males wear leggings, which are of three main patterns. The simplest is of solid color with a decorative band (of embroidery?) just above the ankle. The second type has a *tumpal* pattern with chevrons usually stretching all the way up the visible leg. The *tumpal* are in red, blue, and white, except for a small group including Damar Wulan, where they are in gold. *Tumpal* leggings are shown in Figure 5 and in the Raffles plate mentioned earlier, "A Javan in the Court Drefs." The third type of legging is made with cloth I have tentatively identified as patola. The pattern is always the same, the regularly placed floral motif constant. Only the color of the field varies: red is the most common but green, blue, and yellow also occur (Fig. 3). Exactly the same form and range of colors are used for many waist wrappers and belts. The same conventionalization for patola is used on the waist wrappers of some puppets in the second set of *wayang klitik*. In two cases, both high-status and desirable women—Nos. 437 and 438—a patola is worn with a batik *kain* (Fig. 14). The presence of such cloths with a yellow background suggests very strongly that the representational convention is intended to indicate a patola, or an Indian patola imitation, since no other cloth with a yellow field would have been available at that time.

Thirty-five of the tied *kain* are clearly batik. I include in this class various *poleng* designs of black-and-white and red-and-white checks, as well as triangles of the same colors within squares. I have excluded from the batik category one superb *parang rusak*, No. 440, because it is all in gold on dark indigo, with no visible use of batik, and is likely to have been a *kain prada*—glue-work with gold-leaf (Fig. 7). The other non-batik cloths worn are either *kain kembangan*, much used by women as breastcloth, or plain red cloth, sometimes with a simple *prada* design. There are also examples of *dodot* with layered bands of related colors, presumably made by a *tritik* process. In addition there are three further figures whose cloth seems unlikely to be batik (Fig. 9). Each has a strong background color—blue on No. 441, lavender now patchily faded on No. 442, and deep indigo-black on No. 421—with widely spaced, large multicolored star or flower motifs. These cloths have the feel of Indian prints rather than batiks: their dark fields and their use of many colors is not a feature of the other undoubted batiks, which tend to use at most shades of two colors—usually on white.[15]

Various ways of tying a *kain* are represented, and a number of figures have a great roll of cloth in front and sometimes all round that very strongly suggests a *dodot*. At least ten puppets fall into this group. One of the undoubted *dodot* wearers, No. 429, is identified in the register as "Kennoko Bentar, daughter to Depati of Lumajang" although the label has been lost (Fig. 10). She wears a breastcloth of *kain kembangan*, a gold belt, and a very large *dodot* with an *alas-alasan* motif. At the back are two large wing forms that meet with a large

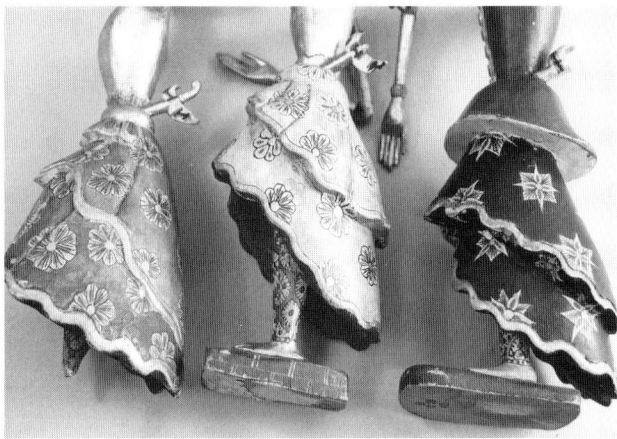

Figure 9. Puppets Nos. 441, 442, and 421 (left to right) from the Raffles collection. The cloths depicted on these figures may be Indian. Left is in blue. Center is in faded lavender (the fading reveals that some of the "flowers" have been moved further apart by over-painting, which indicates the importance of wide spacing in the reproduction of this design); the remainder of its label reads "...ing Setro son to Patih Lugin...." Right is in black. British Museum 1859.12.28.441, 442, 421.

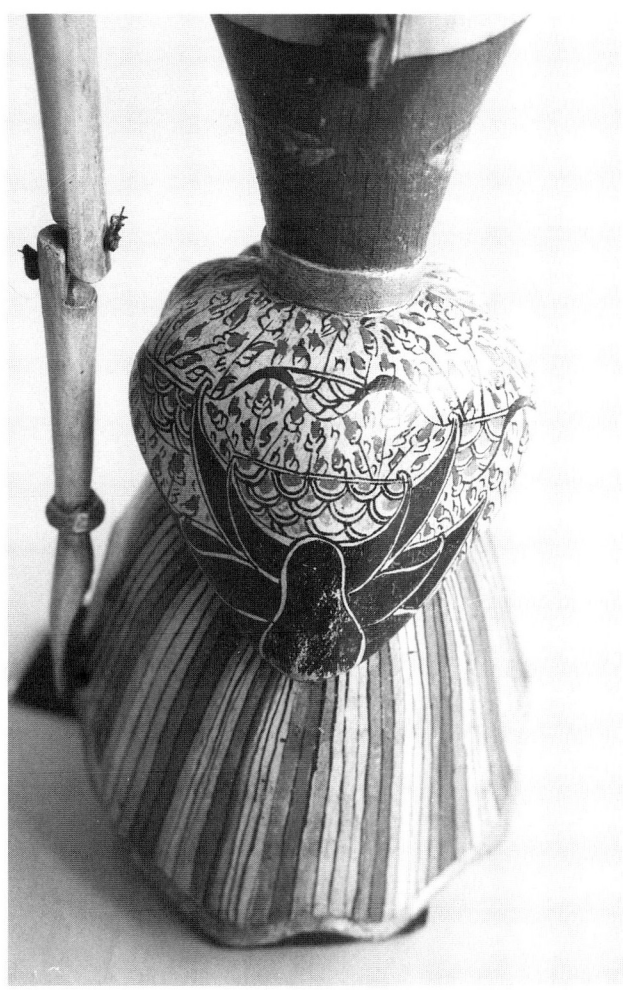

Figure 10. Puppet No. 429 from the Raffles collection. Kennoko Bentar, daughter to Depati of Lumajang, wears a dodot alas-alasan with "buffalo head" and six color rays in tritik. British Museum 1859.12.28.429.

Forge

PATTERN CLASSIFICATION

Basic Classification of Patterns on Tied Batik *Kain* of Puppets in Raffles Collection BM 1859.12.28.
(listed by last three digits of collection number)

Alas-alasan	Stripes	*Ceplok*	Kawung	*Parang*	*Poleng* triangle	*Poleng*
405	408	409	410	438+	418-red	417-red
406	428	412	411	patola	422-red	450-blk
407	432	413	414	439	424-blk	423-red
429+		420	426	444	448-blk	
tritik		427	430	445		
436		447	434			
443			437+			
446			patola			
449						
8	3	6	7	4	4	3 = 35

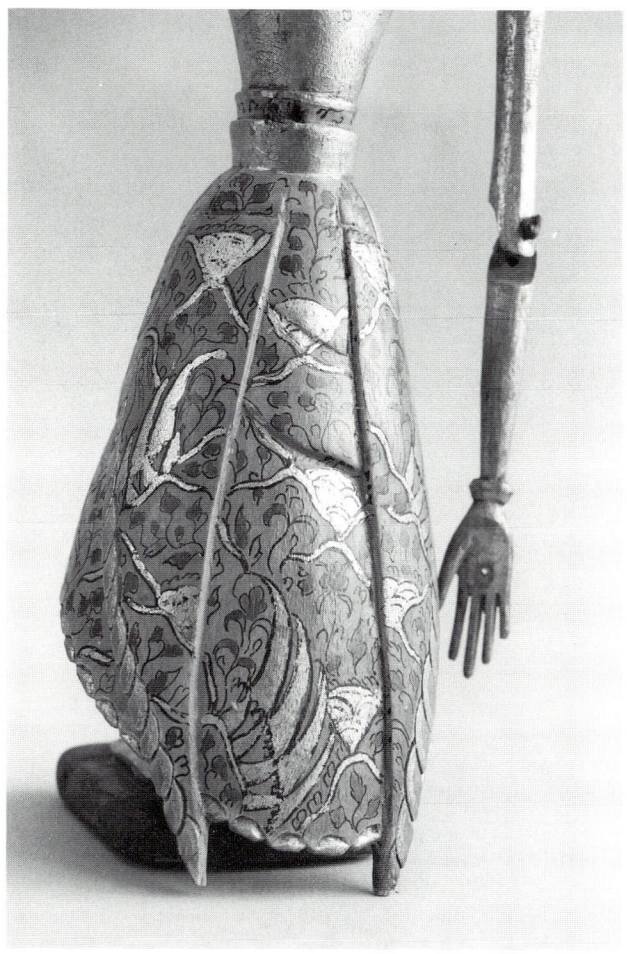

Figure 11. Puppet No. 443 from the Raffles collection. "Raden Damar Wulan" wears a pale brick-red cloth with drawing in black and green, and added gold. On it are mountains and pools (some obscured by gold), and wings, but no trees. Although tied in the most elaborate form, it is not a dodot.
British Museum 1859.12.28.443.

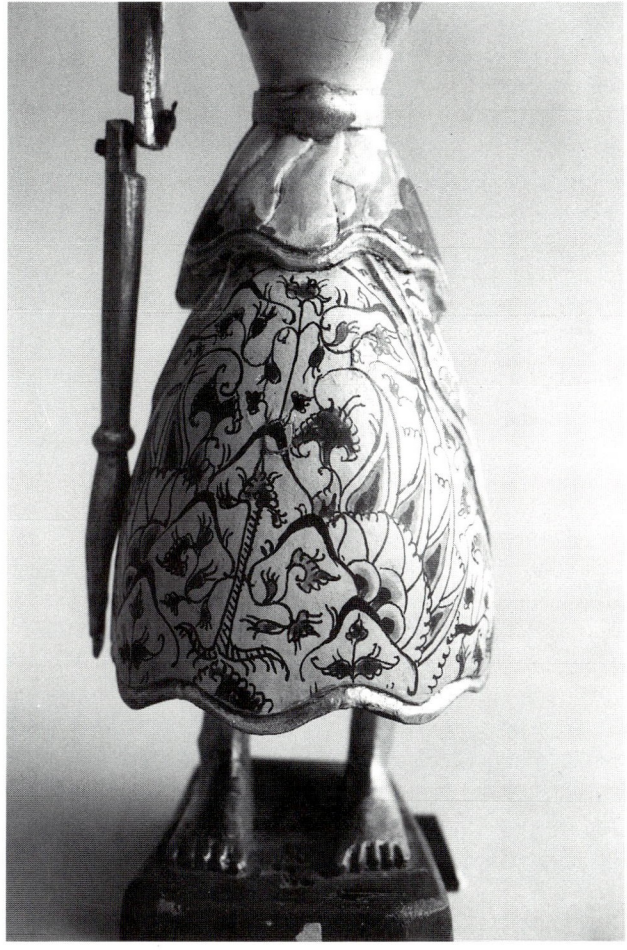

Figure 12. Puppet No. 446 from the Raffles collection. "Dewi Wahito, Queen of Menak Jinggo," wears a cloth of alas-alasan in black, blue, and pale blue-green on white, with big trees and fine "wings," and no explicit pools although the same motif forms part of the wings. Note the fine breastcloth in white, gold, and blue, that falls well over the batik. Note also the gold belt with a heavy buckle. British Museum 1859.12.28.446.

gourd-like form between them, producing a totality remarkably similar to a buffalo head. This effect is emphasized by the carver's treatment of the *dodot*, which gives it the effect of a bustle at the rear with a downward pointing peak, of which the painter has taken full advantage. Below this heaviest of all the *dodot* emerges a lower pattern of polychrome rays in six different colors: red, blue, pale blue, yellow, white, and pink. At first sight this looks like an unrelated cloth, but presumably it is part of the border of the *dodot*, elaborately dyed in *tritik*, the batik portion forming the center.

The table on page 100, opposite, classifies the thirty-five batik worn round the waist in terms of large categories now in use. There are of course problems: the distinction between *ceplok* and *kawung* is to a large extent arbitrary, and *parang* also includes what I regard as *parang*-derived designs. I have chosen to call the biggest class of designs *alas-alasan*. It consists of mountains, trees, other plants, but no animals or birds, except some "wing" motifs; it could perhaps have been called *semen*, but it does not exactly match any now known design class. *Poleng* triangles have a network of squares each divided diagonally, the resulting triangles being white and either black or red. In the case of the King of Blambangan (Pl. 17), the long edge of the black triangle is scalloped, producing a design for which Jasper and Pirngadie (1912) recorded the name *slobok djamang*.

The *alas-alasan* are mainly in black, green, and blue on a white field. There is one, No. 406, with a deep brown field, presumably *soga*—the rich reddish brown dye distinctive to central Javanese batik—with lines in white and pale yellow, possibly very pale *soga*, and details in black (Fig. 13). Damar Wulan, No. 443, has a sort of pale brick red field, with black lines, green details, and *prada* (Fig. 11). The gold seems to have been very carelessly done: it is by far the worst *prada* from among all the puppets, and may have been added later. Six of this group have "wings" as part of the design. These are very open, stretching out into the surrounding design. They are drawn with layered color and the tips of the "feathers" spiral round (Fig. 12). They differ considerably from the much tighter and self-bounded *lar* today, nor do they appear to have any body or tail, except in the "buffalo head" case (Fig. 10). The basic elements of *alas-alasan* design are stacked mountain forms surrounded by leaves and branches; substantial trees with a three-branched top are common, sometimes rising from what appears to be a pool in blue, as in No. 405 (Fig. 13). A similar motif occurs at the base of some of the "wings" and above the buffalo head in what Steinmann (1958) would no doubt have identified as a "ship of the dead."

The classical type of *parang rusak* design occurs once each in batik and in *prada*, Nos. 439 and 440

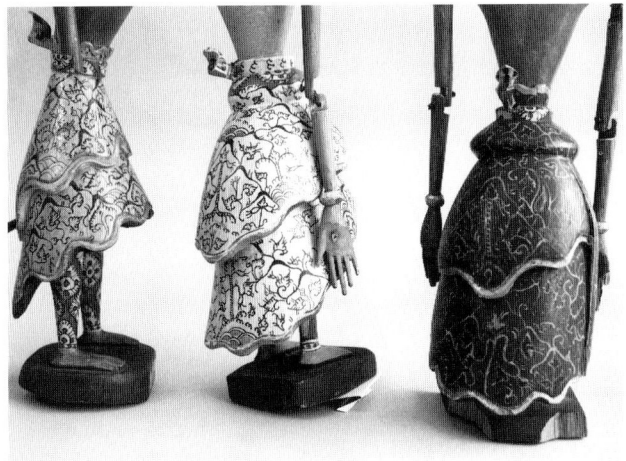

Figure 13. Puppets Nos. 407, 405, and 406 (left to right) from the Raffles collection. The cloth shows a range of alas-alasan. Left is in black on white with "pools" but no big trees (see also Fig. 3). Center is a dodot with big trees and pools in blue, neither with "wings." Right shows a soga field, with black, white, and pale yellowish-brown designs, big trees, and wings but no pools. British Museum 1859.12.28.407, 405, 406.

Forge

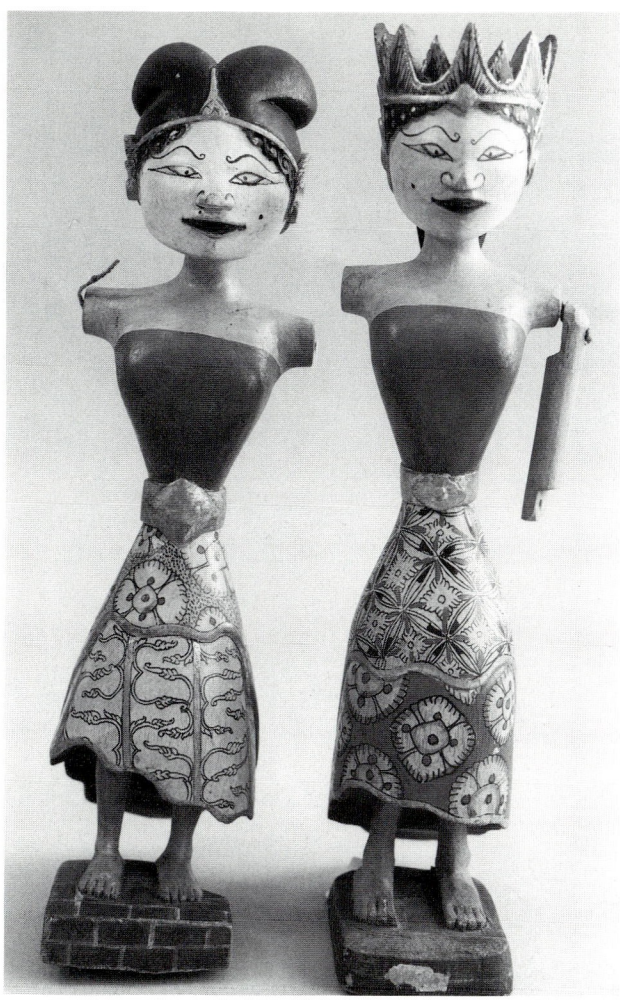

Figure 14. Puppets Nos. 438 and 437 (left to right) from the Raffles collection. Left is "Dawi (sic) Sekati, daughter to Rongga Lawe," according to a label now on the bottom, but it is recorded in the register with a different label. She wears a patola with yellow field speckled in black; a second cloth with a parang-related design in black on white with a prada stripe; a plain red breastcloth; and a heavy gold belt. The hair style is interesting and unique in this set. Right, possibly Dewi Kencana (?), wears a patola with red field, a second cloth with a kawung pattern in black and red on white, and a plain red breastcloth. Both stand on a brick pavement. British Museum 1859.12.28.438, 437.

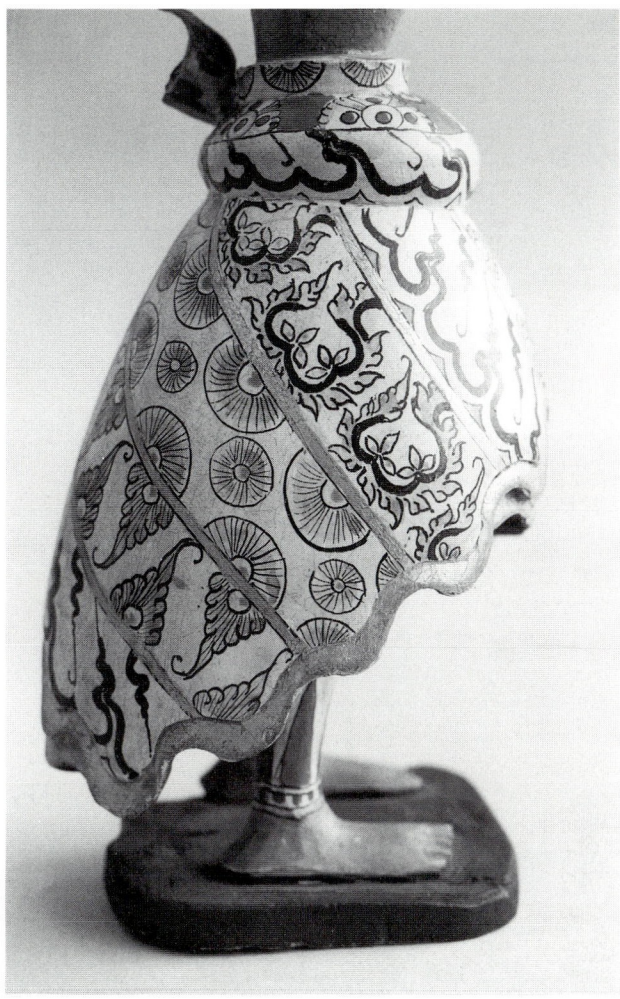

Figure 15. Puppet No. 408 from the Raffles collection. This figure wears a dodot with a striped pattern in black on white, four designs on the diagonal, and thin gold bands between. British Museum 1859.12.28.408.

(Fig. 7), although it occurs again in the best of the striped cloth, No. 408 (Fig. 15). While the various examples of developed *parang* design provide the only case of two figures, Nos. 445 and 444, wearing identical cloth (Fig. 8), the same design also occurs on the best striped textile. Perhaps it was the height of fashion at the time. A further *parang*-related design is worn with a patola, No. 438, whose yellow field is speckled in black (Fig. 14). The best of the multi-stripe designs, No. 408, is apparently meant to be a *dodot*, with four stripes each separated by a thin gold band, producing a most elegant effect (Fig. 15). The other stripes include a rather crude four-band version worn by a maid, and a six-band cloth in white and red on a dark indigo field, with vine motifs and *kawung* varieties

in the stripes. The more hard-edged black-and-white *kawung* stand out strong and clean (Fig. 16 and the Mantri in Fig. 1), but this group tends to merge with *ceplok* as the design elaborates and the number of colors increase (Fig. 14, right, and Fig. 17). The *ceplok* tend to be rather small designs. But there is one very fine large variant on an individual, No. 447, who is of high status, albeit extremely coarse (*kasar*). His stars all have gold centers; the effect is dramatic (Fig. 18).

Social Status and Cloth

Although many labels are lost or damaged, making some of the figures impossible to identify, the conventions of *wayang* enable a rough classification by

Early Batik Patterns

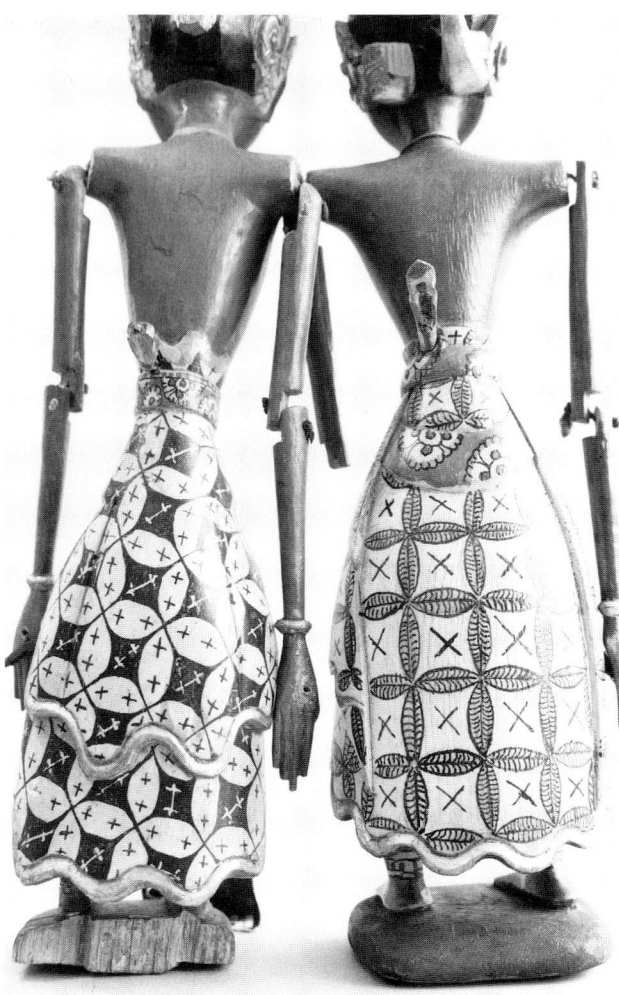

Figure 16. Puppets Nos. 410 and 411 (left to right) from the Raffles collection, wearing cloth with clear kawung designs. Left is "Pu Lambang." Right is "Rongga Jayang Sakar...of Limping" according to the register. Both labels are now more damaged, so these readings cannot be confirmed. The patola sash of No. 411 loops down at the back. British Museum 1859.12.28.410, 411.

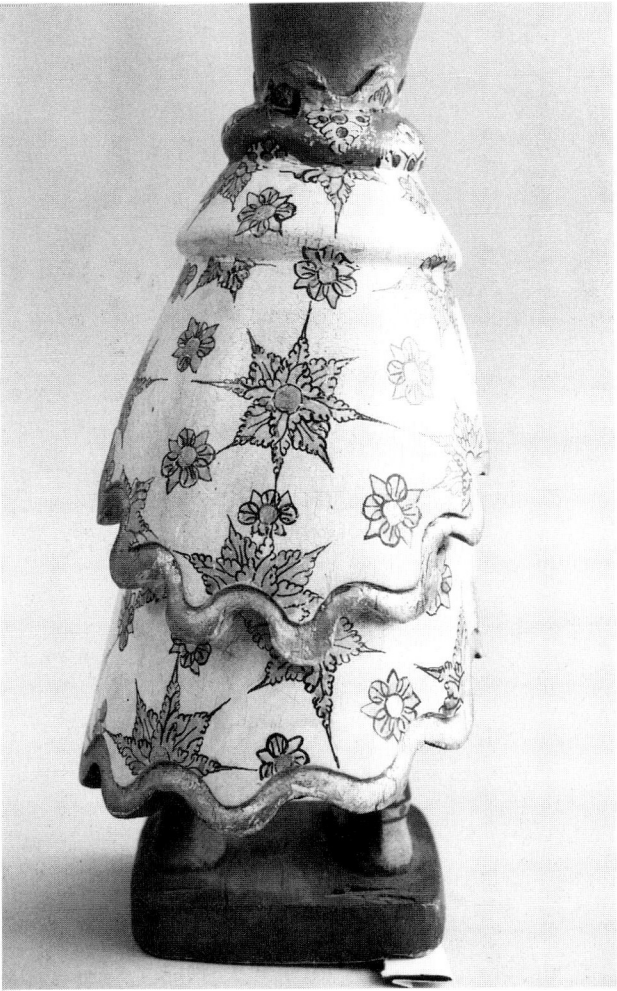

Figure 18. Puppet No. 447 from the Raffles collection. Possibly the Prince of Blambangan, this figure is dressed in a dodot with a ceplok pattern in black and red, and prada centers. British Museum 1859.12.28.447.

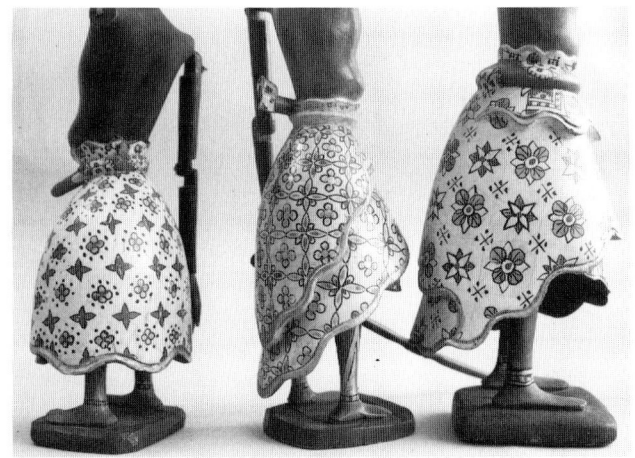

Figure 17. Puppets Nos. 420, 414, and 413 from the Raffles collection. These figures wear examples of ceplok and kawung. Left has ceplok with green flowers and red stars. Center, "Menaki, Lumping" according to the register (label now lost), has a design here classified as kawung, using black, red, and blue; the flowers have gold centers. Right wears ceplok, mainly black on white; the flowers have red centers. The end of the patola sash, showing a simple border, is visible. British Museum 1859.12.28.420, 414, 413.

social status to be attempted and correlated with the cloth worn. To start with the most refined (*halus*) and powerful, "Prabhu mahisa wulan" (No. 433, not shown here) has a copious *dodot* in red with a simple *prada* design all over, and he wears a close-fitting cap with a similar gold design on it. His hair is thus confined and he looks slightly down, both signs of a mature man of controlled power. Two others have similar caps and poses: one wears a plain red *dodot* and the other a *tritik dodot* of layered color. All three have faces of the most refined type. One male and one female also wear *dodot* of layered *tritik*, and both have crowns. It seems therefore that the people of the highest status do not wear batik at all. The two priests have cloths with fringes over their shoulders that look very much like the narrow north-coast silk batik with tree motifs, known in the later nineteenth century as *lokcan*. Apart from these two characters, no one wears anything like batik above the waist.

Batik with the *alas-alasan* pattern is worn by younger men and women of high status—basically princes and princesses. *Parang*, too, is very high status but it is worn only by men, the sole exception being the *parang*-related pattern worn with a patola by No. 438, one of the ladies in Figure 14. *Poleng*, triangular or square, is exclusive to men. It is much lower in social status, and in the classic black-and-white form it is worn of course by the Semar-like servant figure. Otherwise it is mainly the "Patih" who wear *poleng*, and a jacket as well. Designs of the *poleng* group only get an entrée into the aristocracy with the extremely coarse King of Blambangan, who wears *slobok djamang*. *Kawung*, especially if clear, is mid-range as in Nos. 410 and 411 (Fig. 16), even high if setting off a patola as in No. 437 (Fig. 14). But basically *kawung* and *ceplok* rapidly tail off towards the lower orders and servants. The probable Prince of Blambangan, No. 447, wears a *ceplok*, but it has a very large and fine pattern, and he is anyway the coarsest of coarse, and so excluded from the refined court culture (Fig. 18).

Striped cloth seems variable according to the fineness of design and workmanship. These generalizations have validity within this set of puppets. What they are able to tell us about the courts of Central Java at the start of the nineteenth century will need much more research.

Although this is only a preliminary paper, I believe these puppets to be very important because they present the earliest set of batik designs known; furthermore they are in color. Possibly because they do not obviously correspond to any class of "genuine" Javanese object documented in the literature, they have been overlooked both as *wayang* and as a record of batik design. I trust that I have managed, at least, to establish them as genuine and Javanese, and very possibly unique.

It seems to me that some of the elaboration of designs, among which the development of the basic *parang* stands out, previously believed to have taken place in the nineteenth century, will now have to be pushed back into the eighteenth century. The set of *alas-alasan* also raises a whole host of questions. Why are there no animals? The general impression is not one of strict Islamic orthodoxy. The mountain, tree, and pool complex, shown unmistakably in these patterns, may help to unravel some of the iconography of later cloth, both *alas-alasan* and *semen*. They also pose questions about the relationship to much earlier religious ideas involving forests, three-branched objects, and water. It is probable that the "wings" are ancestors of the *lar*, but it also seems likely that they had a much wider range of meaning and reference in the form they had when these puppets were made. There are many other problems and, I hope, answers, suggested by the cloth on this set of puppets, and indeed by the Raffles collection as a whole. Much more work will be necessary before its potential is exhausted. To make this resource generally available for batik and textile studies, it is to be hoped that all forty-seven puppets can soon be published in color.

NOTES

1. It was entered under the general number 1859.12.28.

2. The details of the release of Raffles's collection from excise are drawn from a manuscript by the late Jeune Scott-Kemball held at the Museum of Mankind.

3. The Museum of Mankind kindly allowed me repeated access to their stores. I am grateful to the keeper, Mr. M. D. McLeod, and to Dr. B. Durrans for permission and general benevolence; and to Louise Schuller, Mike O'Hanlon, and Harry Persaud for practical aid and for drawing my attention to parts of the collection I might otherwise have overlooked.

4. There are no paintings in this group for three of the colored aquatints, "A Javan Chief," "A Javan in the Court Drefs" and "Ronggeng." On the other hand there is a very vigorous painting, "A soldier exercising in front of his chieftain," that was not used.

5. The generation of the plates for *The History of Java* is discussed in detail in Forge (In Press).

6. That is, between 35.6 and 43.2 centimeters. The British Museum lists the height of the puppets in inches rather than centimeters. For that reason and because Raffles's own description of collection—a central point of reference for the present discussion—likewise mentions their height in inches, the usual conversion to metric measurement is not appropriate within the body of this essay.

7. Storage during the second World War obviously caused much damage. Jaap Kunst photographed five of these figures in September 1938; all were then complete, but none is now.

8. The numbers on the first forty-six run from 1859.12.28.405 to 1859.12.28.450. From now on I shall use only the final three digits to refer to them. The single figure added in the Drake collection is numbered 1949.As.4.107. on the bottom; it also has a round cardboard label with the number 1939.3.13. and the remains of a Raffles label that cannot be deciphered. The 1949 number does not lead to enlightenment in the register but the entry for 1939.As.4.108. does appear to refer to this figure.

9. On the other hand, a label in the Raffles style not recorded in the register has appeared; it is now on a figure (No. 438) that was originally recorded with a different label, which itself now appears on yet another figure (No. 419). There is also a label fragment reading "A Wa..Ma.." which was not in the register; from the figure it is certain that it originally read "A Waiting Maid."

10. *Wayang golek* are now associated mainly with the Sundanese culture of West Java, but in the nineteenth century they were considered especially suitable for such stories as Damar Wulan in Central Java.

11. Pigeaud (1967-70) gives as fifty-seven the largest number of puppets in a *wayang klitik* set for the Damar Wulan cycle.

12. Scott-Kemball (1970) mentions this set but says only that they are "of a type that appears to be unique."

13. From further research it seems virtually certain that Raffles obtained this set at the sack of the Jogyakarta *kraton* in 1812. A paper on this set as *wayang* is in preparation.

14. My views on this matter were formed in discussion with Dr. Mattiebelle Gittinger and I am most grateful for her assistance on this point.

15. One further textile may be Indian. A somewhat grotesque but obviously prosperous commoner (No. 419) wears a long-sleeved, tailored jacket with a very open and continuous vine pattern in blue and green on white. This seems likely to represent imported piece-goods and I do not consider it further.

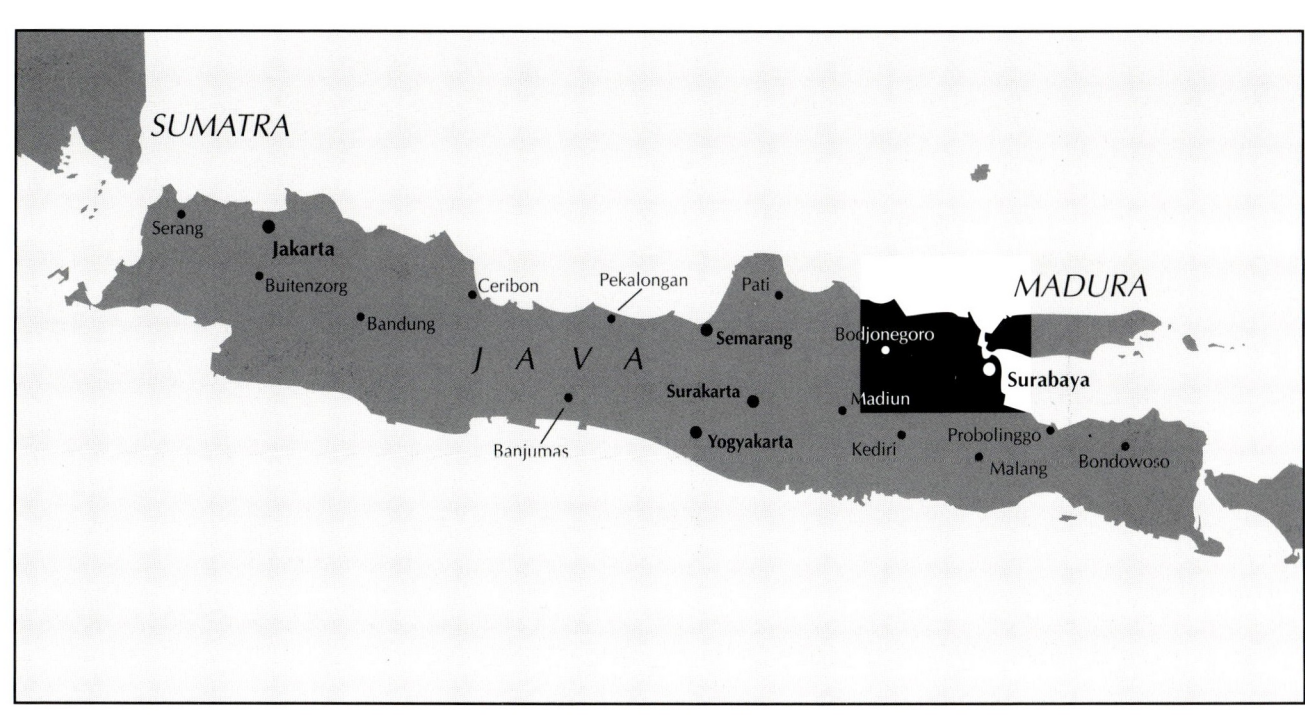

Dye Process and Life Sequence
The Coloring of Textiles in an East Javanese Village

Rens Heringa

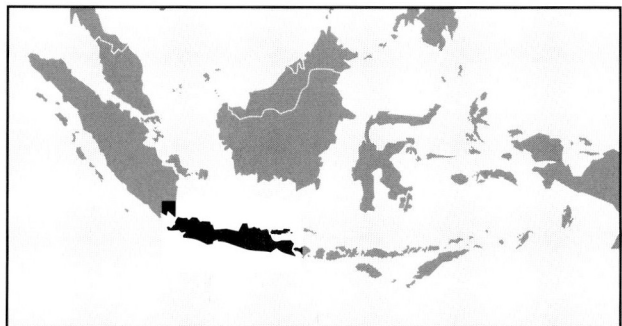

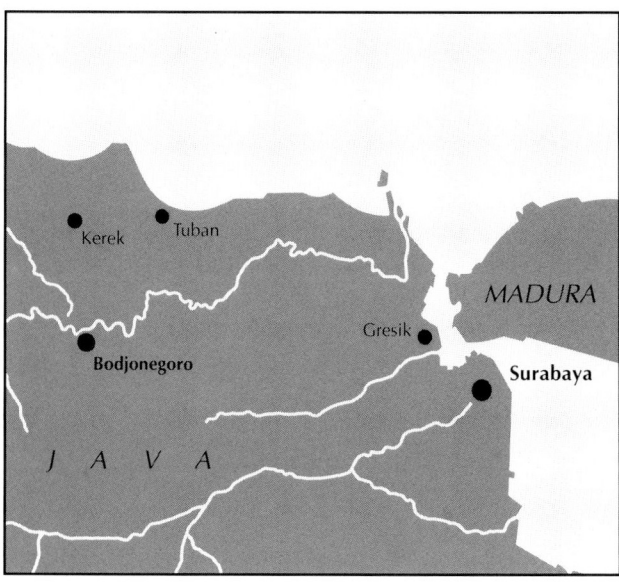

Northeast coast of Java, highlighted on map at left.

*The Goddess Uma glanced around
And everywhere her feet had touched
There was whiteness, there was redness   (...ana putih, ana abang
There was yellowness and blackness   ana kuning, ana ireng)
(Hooykaas 1974:64)*

In traditional Indonesian communities the physical form of crafted objects has been found to be closely related to cosmological concepts. Generally, although scholars have considered outward form, they have paid little attention to the possible meaning of the raw materials chosen and the technical process—that is, to what I propose to call the "inward" form. Traditional textiles in particular, fashioned of meaningful materials through a process of detailed—and to the Western observer, seemingly endless—effort, may offer possibilities to the study of this inward form.

The relationship between phases of textile work and symbolic structures in a traditional community on East Sumba has been demonstrated by Adams (1971). Details from the early descriptions of the Javanese batik process suggest similar connections, but the considerable upheaval of traditional process over the past half-century has narrowed the research possibilities.[1] Scholars have consequently preferred to study the batik cloth related to the courts of Central Java. Geirnaert-Martin (1981), analyzing the color and pattern of ritual batik and *lurik* textiles, has interpreted the cloths as a visual expression of the relationships between man, society, and cosmos. Others have discussed the symbolic significance of color in ritual textiles or as a social marker (see Veldhuisen-Djajasoebrata 1984; Heringa 1985). Abdurachman (1982:18) mentions the ritual significance of materials and *modus operandi* in the Javanese manufacture of artifacts in pre-Hindu times, but from her description of various art forms in the Ceribon area (northwest coastal Java) it is not clear if this continues today.

This article focuses on the materials and techniques employed by the hereditary female cloth-dyers in the traditional community of Kerek, on the northeastern coast of Java, where repeated visits have enabled me to record continuity and change.[2] The blue and red batik cloths made in this group of villages are the last survivals of the old littoral or *pesisir* style (Fig. 1) previously worn with slight variation of pattern and color all along the north coast of Java (Geirnaert and Heringa, In Press). Since only the women of the community still wear the cloths and little could be recorded on traditional male dress forms, my analysis is necessarily one-sided.

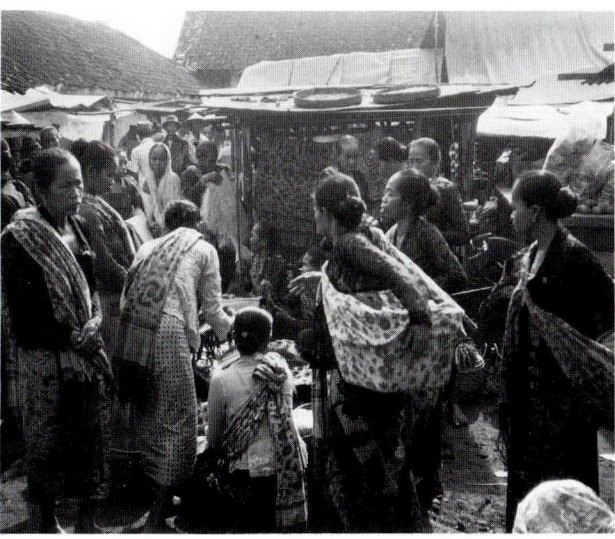

Figure 1. The market in Kerek, circa 1980. Some women wear the traditional jarit, *local term for the* kain panjang. *All carry their marketwares in shouldercloths* (slendang), *which indicate through their colors the women's social status.*

Three aspects of the dye process are to be considered here: first, the dye-materials and their classificatory values; then, the different phases of the dye process and the seven distinctive batik color types that result; and finally, the function of each of these textiles in relation to their color values. The core of my structural analysis is based on Javanese classification concepts endowing the four main colors—white, red, yellow and blue-black—with relative and interrelated values which appear to underlie use of color on the textiles. For the most part the dyers themselves do not state these concepts explicitly. Though deeply aware of how the process should be ideally executed, they rarely articulate why it should be so. Still, when my suggestions ran counter to their sense of logic, they responded with surprise or straight-out disapproval. It must be kept in mind that expression in Indonesia is often nonverbal, and that certain sacred concepts should not be disclosed to outsiders.

Javanese Color Concepts

On Java, colors, like so many other categories of things, both concrete and abstract, are never felt to exist as separate entities: each forms part of a series. There are binary, triadic, and quadripartite series, and a single color may belong to more than one. Each color is seen as complementary to the others. The effort to maintain a balance between elements of a series is of major importance in Javanese action. It should be realized, however, that this balance does not imply equality. Nor are all elements always visible to the eye. The fact that they can only be felt or imagined does not make them less real: for outer and inner knowledge, outward and inward form are intrinsic to Javanese thought.

The Javanese distinguish four main colors: white (*putih*), red (*abang*), yellow (*kuning*) and blue-black (*ireng*).[3] Together these form a quadripartite series in which each color is associated with a cardinal direction and at the same time with the stages of day and night and the stages of the life cycle (Pigeaud 1977:67). Thus for the Javanese, colors, directions, and the stages of life are all closely linked. On a spatial and temporal plane, life can be envisioned as a circular continuum. This code, or cosmological system, is depicted in Diagram One. White corresponds with origin, and with the east. Life starts in the east with white, and runs clockwise towards youth or adolescence, passing the south in gradually darkening shades of red. Maturity is reached in the west with yellow, which changes into green and gradually darkening shades of blue, and ends in the north with blue-black and death. At the intermediary points, the main colors combine and gradually change shades (Swellengrebel 1977:90); the center of this life-circle, being the sum of all parts, is conceived as multicolored (Pigeaud 1977:67). In accordance with the old Indonesian concept of reincarnation, there is an "invisible" period between death and rebirth, connected to shades of greyish blue, and located conceptually between north and east.

While the directional code can be depicted on a horizontal plane, the spiritual realm of life is conceived to be a vertical axis (Zenith-Nadir), and associated with a triadic series of colors (Diagram 2). The Upper World, connected to the Gods and ancestors, is white; the Lower World, abode of chthonic creatures and demons, is black. In the center between them, the world of human life is red. A comparison of the horizontal and vertical series shows that a single color may belong to both, expressing two different concepts according to its context.

Whereas the quadripartite and triadic series of colors combine into relatively static sets, a varied and shifting range of binary sets shows an infinitely more dynamic picture. The horizontal color-circle, for instance, is also divided in a binary series of blues and

Diagram One

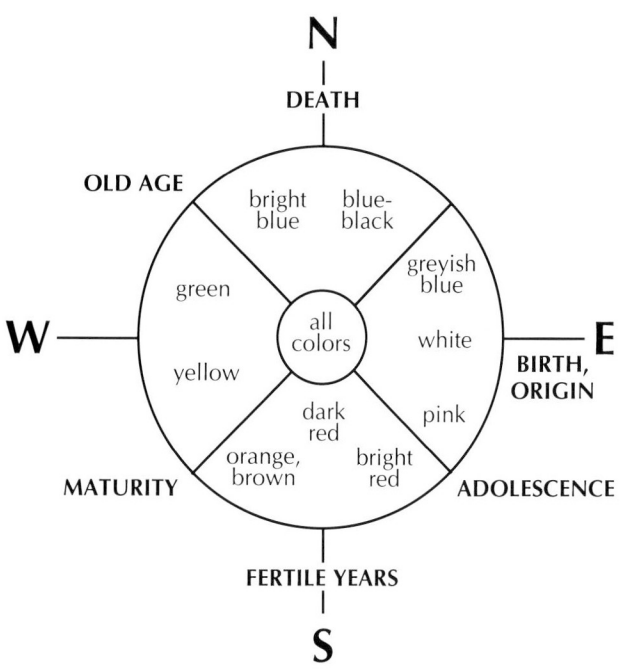

Diagram Two

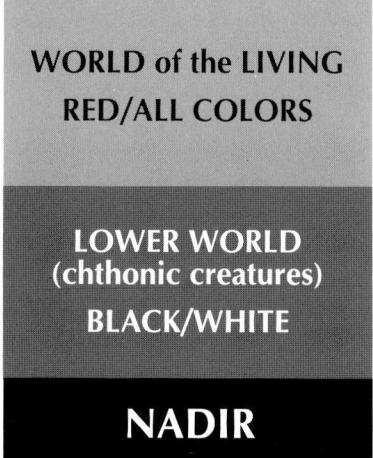

reds. The northern half of the circle is considered to consist of blue shades, including green, blue-gray, bright blue, and blue-black. The southern half ranges from light red (pink) to scarlet to brownish red, including shades that a Western eye might consider to be brown (Rouffaer 1900:10). This dichotomy is also linked with gender. The blue shades are generally thought of as female with connotations of dark, cool, old, and death; the red shades are mostly known as male with images of bright, hot, young, and fertile life. However, different sets of opposing categories may be formed which are then connected to the abstract binary notions mentioned above, in a variety of contexts; for instance, red and blue can each consist of dark and light shades, and therefore each may stand for young and old. A combination of red and blue should consist of one light, and one dark shade. Two dark or two light tones do not go together. Moreover red, blue, and also black may each be opposed to white in sets of more contrasting dark and light shades.

Village Textiles, the Historical Perspective

Javanese village batiks have never been seriously studied, because general interest has favored finely-worked cloth such as the court-related batik of Central Java or the high-quality products of Indo-European and Indo-Chinese entrepreneurs on the north coast recently described by Veldhuisen (1980,1985) and McCabe Elliott (1984). Yet in motif and color, the latter commercial types show only distant similarity to the north-coastal village cloth. During the early nineteenth century each village woman made the cloths needed for her family (Raffles 1978 I:86,168). Homegrown cotton was spun and made into strong pattern weaves or into plain weave, which served as a base for batik (see plates in Cornets de Groot 1822). Natural dyes provided shades of blue and red (Raffles 1978 I:170). Ironically, European interest in Javanese textile craft directly set into motion the sequence of events leading to its gradual disappearance (Raffles 1812). Cheap low-quality European imitation batiks and the locally produced stamp-batiks (*cap-capan*) gradually became the accepted dress for the village women (Koloniaal Verslag 1892). Time-honored motifs and colors to a large extent lost their meaning as social and regional markers.

The Persistence of Village Traditions

The last area where the old traditions still largely persist is an isolated group of villages in the subdistrict of Kerek on the north coast between Tuban and Lasem. Oral tradition on west-coastal Java traces the textile patterns and techniques used there to this area (Abdurachman 1982:130). Bounded by the Java sea to

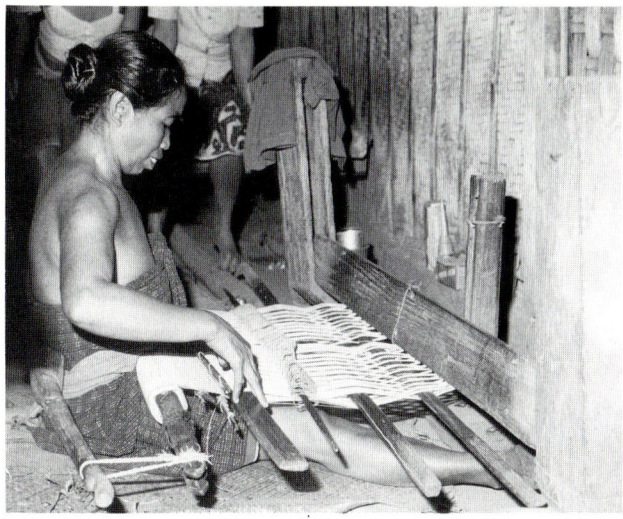

Figure 2. The weaving of lawon, *the basecloth for batik. Kerek, circa 1980.*

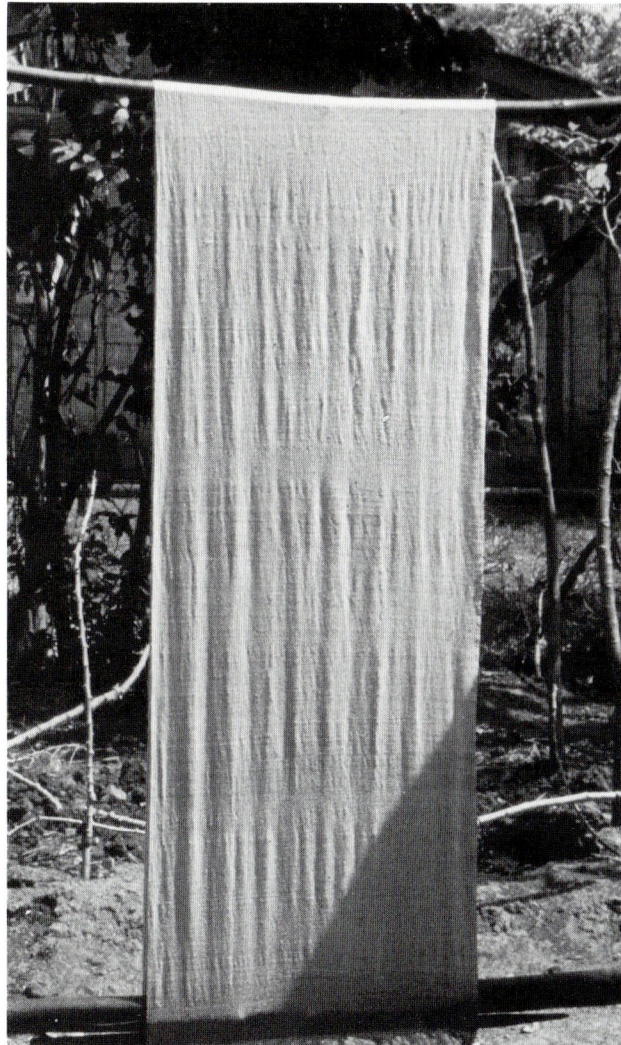

Figure 3. The drying process (getek): *a finished cloth, sewn together along the short ends, washed, and sized with rice-starch, is hung to dry* (digetek), *stretched between two ends of bamboo. At the lower end a weaving sword* (lira) *has been inserted. Kerek, circa 1980.*

the north, and the limestone mountains to the south and southwest, the settlements lie among teakforests and dry fields that stretch eastward along the hilly road toward the regional administrative center of Tuban. Sandtracks connect the villages, where small local markets are held on rotating days. A larger market on the main road provides the few necessities not produced in the fields. Agriculture is the main activity of men and women. Crops of maize and rice, which together make up the staple food (eaten mixed, in the typical east-Javanese way) are harvested from the calciferous soil. The dryer areas yield the tuberous rootcrops that form an addition to the diet. Secondary crops include peanuts—a cashcrop—and cotton. Recent government programs have tried to encourage cotton as a second cashcrop, but with poor results. The villagers have shown remarkably little interest in new developments, mostly keeping to their old ways.

Between the eleventh and the seventeenth centuries, however, the area was a center of international contact, an important emporium in the spice trade. Chinese, Persian, and Indian mechants came to trade Indian textiles for the pepper, cloves, mace, and sandalwood that Javanese seafarers had brought from the Moluccas and Timor. Local textile manufacture is mentioned as early as 1599 by the first Dutch who came to Tuban (Keuning 1938/49 III:34,36).

Phases and Divisions of Textile Work

Textile work is strictly the domain of women, keeping pace with the yearly agricultural cycle. Little activity takes place during the planting and harvest seasons, when all women except the very old and the very young are busy on the fields. But for three months after the harvest, during the dry season, from September through November, all attention is turned towards the intricate phases of textile work—the various types of pattern weave, and most important, the batik cloths that are the subject of this paper.

The production of cloth is a long and painstaking process. First, the raw cotton must be cleaned by hand or run through the ginning mill (nowadays a rare method) and dried in the sun. Then the fibers are fluffed and rolled into sausagelike shapes (*pusuh*), and spun. Finally they are woven on a body-tension loom with a discontinuous warp and a reed into the plain, natural-colored cloth (*lawon*) which is the basecloth for batik (Fig. 2). *Lawon* is woven in two different widths—one narrow, one wide. The first measures three handspans (*kilan*) and is destined for use on the upper part of the body, either as a breastcloth (*kemben*) or as a shouldercloth (*slendang*) for carrying babies or marketwares. The wider cloth, measuring five handspans, is worn as a skirt—either the rectangular wraparound kind (*kain panjang*), or the tubular *sarung*.

All cloths are approximately two and a half to three meters long (Fig. 3).

The three generations of women—grandmother, mother and daughter, ideally residing under one roof[4]—are each assigned particular phases of the task. Only the oldest generation is considered experienced enough to take care of spinning and warping. Weaving and the waxing of the batik motifs is done by the second generation. The daughters help with the easier preparatory phases like cotton-cleaning or yarn-winding, and are allowed to weave their first cloth only when they are of marriageable age.

A second division of labor exists on the intervillage level. Each village is considered expert in one specific process. In some cases this is a matter of preference, but in others the precepts are rather more strongly imposed. Batik in particular is the acknowledged specialty of the centrally-located village. Although in recent years the rule has been less strictly observed, the batik made by women of the other villages is considered to be of inferior quality and will be sold outside the area or sewn up into Western-style blouses and skirts.

In the centrally-located village only traditional motifs are used. They are waxed freehand on the cloth and retraced on the back (Fig. 4). The format and motifs of the cloths clearly evoke the centuries-old foreign contacts that once supplied Indian tradecloths like the "Javanese tapi(h)"—cotton substitutes for the silk patola (Gittinger 1982:153). In the typical village cloth, a centerfield, (termed *badan* or "body" in Javanese) is enclosed by a double decorative border (*pinggir*, or *sikilan*, "extremities"), and by a row of triangular motifs (*tumpal*) on a rectangular base (*papan* or *umpak*) at each narrow end in the cloth's head (*kepala*).

Like the trade textiles (Rouffaer and Juynboll 1914:155), the village cloths manifest two main motif types. In the first, the centerfield is covered with flowers and birds, surrounded by a wealth of free-flowing vegetative patterns. Although identified by the village women as local species and related to local symbolism, these motifs are similar to Persian and Chinese ones found on embroidered altarcloths and imported porcelains (Abdurachman 1977:3). The second motif type can be directly related to patola, (or in Javanese terminology, *cinde*) motifs. Two kinds of stylized flowers with four or sometimes eight leaves alternate to cover the centerfield in a geometric whole. The flower-and-bird patterns serve for daily wear; the geometrical motif is reserved for ceremonial purposes.

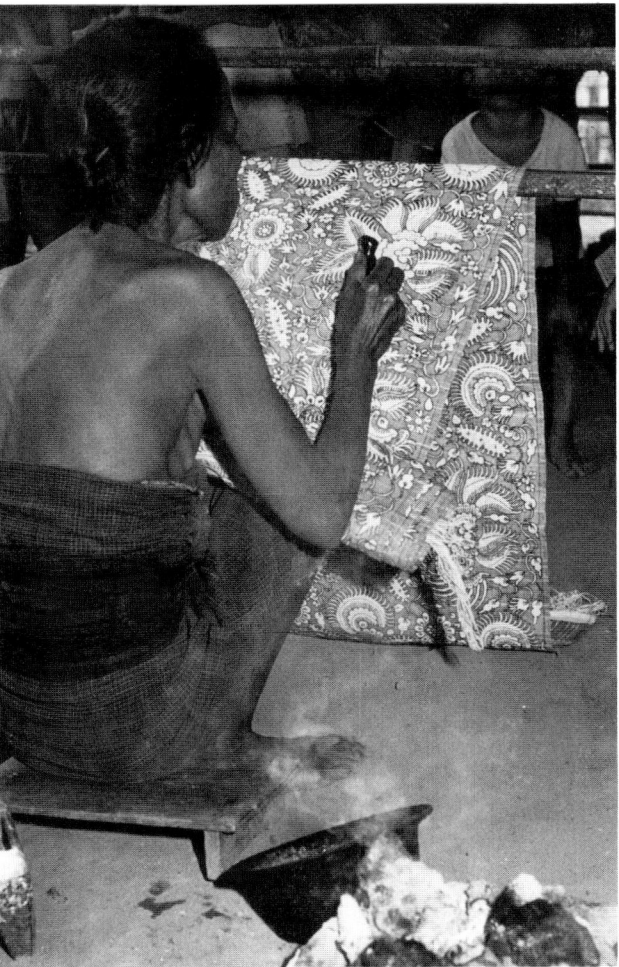

Figure 4. The waxing of cloth. The outline of the motifs and the background have been finished first. As a last step the inner motifs (isen) *are drawn and the pinpricks* (coblosan) *pierced into the background. Kerek, circa 1980.*

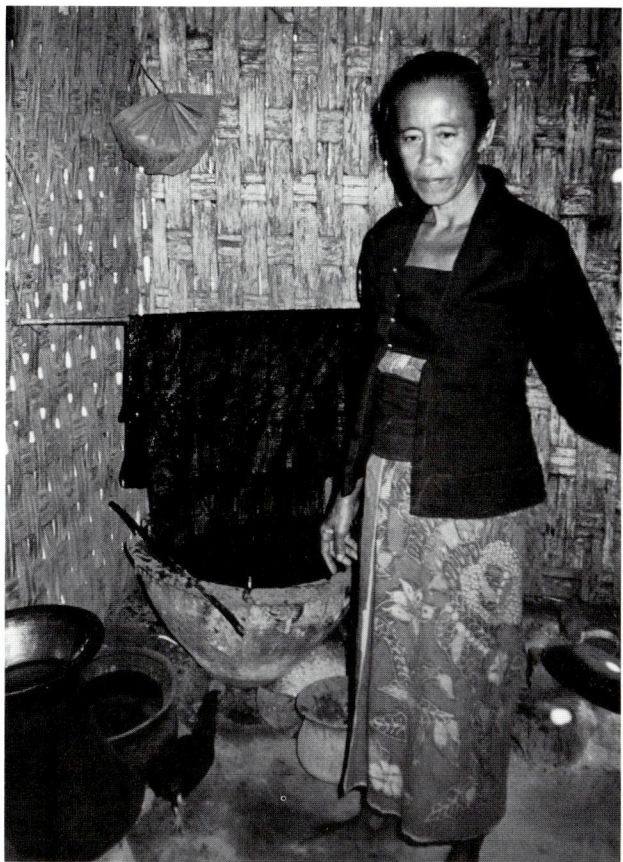

Figure 5. Mak Modin, the dyer. In the corner stands the ancient mother vat with a cloth hanging to drip over the nila; to the left, the cooking fire with a copper rice-steamer. The same material is used for the red-dye container. Kerek, circa 1980.

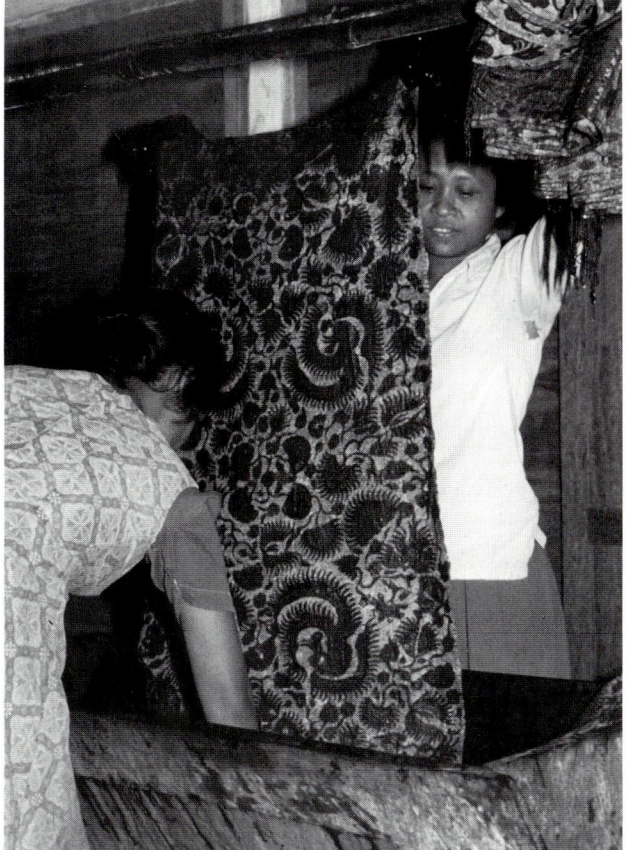

Figure 6. Kasmi (left) and Rugayah (right), dyeing with synthetic dye on the premises of the village-head. The rubber gloves and the tubs have been provided by the Department of Industries. Kerek, 1979.

Dyeing traditions in Kerek[5]

On Java, textile dyeing and dyers have been known for centuries. Inscriptions in Old Javanese from East Java dating back to the tenth century mention *nila* or *nula*, the Sanskrit word for indigo dye, and *wungkudu* or *mengkudu*, the traditional red dye derived from the rootbark of a species of Morinda. They also mention the dyers of blue and red, called *mangulawungkudu*[6] (always a single expression). Contemporary ethnographic evidence suggests that throughout Indonesia, dyeing is a female activity (cf. Maxwell 1981:49; Niessen 1982; Bühler, Ramseyer et al. 1975:61-62). It is not clear whether this has also always been the case on Java. While the female dyers of Kerek are keeping to the precept, nineteenth-century descriptions of indigo dyeing on Java mention male dyers (*tukang medel*). However this was only in connection with commercial batik operations, where men worked as hired labor.[7] Furthermore traditional textile dyeing is generally a more or less sacred activity all over Indonesia, as it is in Kerek. Even though the dyers show a willingness to share information about their work methods with other village women and with outsiders, there is considerable circumspection about the preparation of the annual supply of indigo and those activities related to the "mother vat."

While the villages of Kerek each have a dyer who is allowed to dye the hanks of yarn to be used for weaving, the dyeing of batik cloths is reserved for one older woman (Fig. 5), whose husband is the central village's Islamic *modin*, or summoner to prayer. Known as Mak Modin ("Granny Modin"), she is aided by her daughter, Rugayah, to whom she gradually passes on the secrets of her art.[8] None of the other women will venture to dye their own batik; once in a while they may catch the drops from cloth hanging over the indigo vat after a dip in the dye. This liquid is then used for dyeing a hank of yarn or sometimes for medicinal purposes.

Respect for the skill of the dyer extends even to the much simpler procedure of dyeing with synthetic naphthol (*naptol*), which has been potentially within the reach of all women for some years now. In 1976, the Ministry of Small Industries provided free of charge a quantity of dyes and modern dyebasins. All women were allowed to take part in a free course taught by men (*sic!*) from the Tuban office. Simplified work methods offered the possibility of earning some income from the cloth. Initially the wife of the village head organized twice-weekly dyeing sessions in a small shed specially built on her premises. But the actual work was carried out by Mak Modin's daughter Rugayah, with the assistance of Kasmi, a niece of the village head (Fig. 6). Women from all the villages of Kerek brought their waxed cloths and paid a small sum to have them dyed. But this typical Javanese solution to a delicate problem still did not satisfy the villagers. After seven years it was decided "for the sake of convenience" to move the entire process back to the premises of the traditional dyers.

Now the work in Kerek is organized as follows: Mak Modin continues to occupy herself with the indigo dyeing in a separate space near the cooking fire in the back of her house. Rugayah is already allowed to take care of the overdyeing (*nyoga*) of the indigo-dyed cloths with brownish red. In a newly built lean-to she also oversees the synthetic blue and red dyeing, assisted by several of her own female relatives. Only the synthetically dyed cloths are sold outside the villages, while the traditional indigo cloths remain for the use of the village women themselves. Thus it appears the acceptance of new procedures should preferably be fitted to the logic of the old concepts (Heringa 1988).

Dye Materials and Preparation Processes

Traditionally the batik dyers of Kerek used four kinds of natural dyes which enabled them to produce a range of blues, dark red, bright red, and yellow. Now, however, only two types of natural dyes are still in use. *Nila*, extracted from the leaves of a species of indigo cultivated in the dyer's yard, yields various shades of blue. *Soga*, made from the rootbark of a species of mangrove available in the village shop, is the source of a dark brownish red. The dye called *mengkudu*, derived from the bark of a species of Morinda, and once used to achieve a natural bright red, is no longer available: it has been replaced for several decades by synthetic naphthol dyes bought in faraway Surabaya. In contrast to synthetic blue, which the local people reject, synthetic red has become an accepted element of the traditional dress. In view of the villagers' inclination to keep to old traditions, this seems at first surprising. The dyers and some older village women still have a clear memory of the traditional *mengkudu* process, but explain that it was abandoned as the Morinda dyebark disappeared from the market. The traditional yellow dye has also fallen out of use. Ethnobotanical classification of the natural dyes is difficult at present, partly because details and fine distinctions have blurred in the local memory. The testimony of field informants has been supplemented and clarified by information from early European sources, the most rewarding of which proved to be Rumphius (1750/55), who was said to have "imbibed the native ideas on the relationship of plants" (Merrill 1917:14, citing Robinson). This apparently meant that Rumphius took note of properties that at present would be considered as belonging to the ethnobotanical field. Table One catalogues the organic dyes and the plants from which they derive. The nature of the materials and processes used to obtain and apply each of the dyes is explained below and in Tables Two and Three.

The Blue Dye

The indigo species used for dyeing in Kerek is called *tom gresi* or *presi* by the dyers. It is probably *Indigofera guatimalensis* (Heyne 1927:774), which was introduced on Java by the Colonial Government only in the late nineteenth century during a period of forced indigo cultivation (Gorkom 1881:36).[9] In the villages, according to Heyne (1927:773), indigo was commonly propagated by seed rather than by cuttings, as on most Dutch plantations. *Indigo guatimalensis*, which was grown from seed, could therefore have easily been accepted by the village women as a substitute for the original *Indigo arrecta*, the native indigo species. Mak Modin sows the *tom presi* annually at the beginning of the rainy season, in her yard (Fig. 7). In other villages it is grown on the dikes between the rice fields. The single yearly cutting can be taken after approximately six months. It is best cut early in the morning and leaves should have a dark-green, almost bluish sheen. Because it is the leaves that are used, the plant is considered a species with "hanging fruits," *pala gumantang* (Fig. 8).

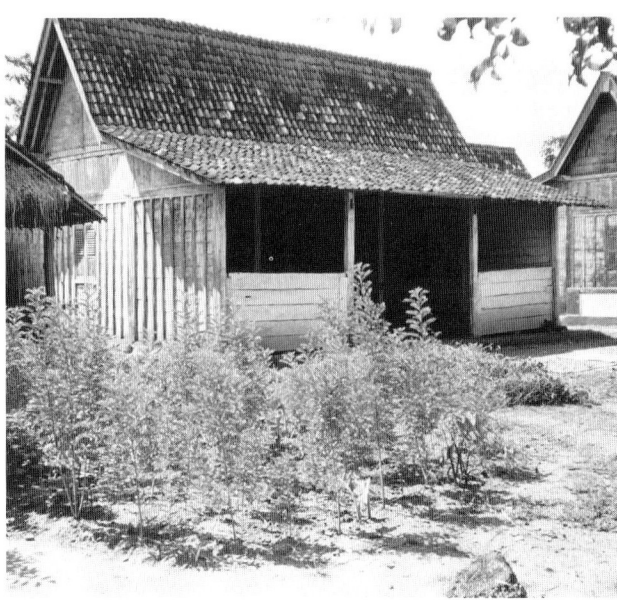

Figure 7. Indigo cultivation in the dyer's yard. The tom *has almost reached maturity. Kerek, circa 1980.*

Table One: THE ORGANIC DYES

COLOR YIELDED	SPECIES (Latin)	PLANT NAME (Local)	NAME of MATERIAL	DYE YIELDED	PROCESS
Blue to Black	*Indigofera guatimalensis* or *Indigofera tinctoria*	*tarum* (Indonesian) *tom* (Javanese)	*daun tom*	*nila*	long, difficult
Dark Red	*Bruguiera*	*mangi tongki* (Javanese, 18th c.)	*kayu tingi*	*soga tingi*	easy
Bright Red	*Morinda bracteata* and *Symplocos fasciculata*	*bangkudu laki-laki* (Malay, 18th c.) *jirek* (Javanese)	*mengkudu* or *kudu* *jirek*	*kudu-* *jirek*	easy
Yellow	*Cudranus javanensis*	*tegerang* (Javanese)	*tegerang*	*tegerang* (?)	difficult

Table Two: NATURE OF DYE

DYE MATERIAL	GENDER	KIND OF PLANT	PART USED (VISIBILITY)	WHERE FOUND	HOW OBTAINED
TOM (blue)	female	annual shrub	leaves (visible)	cultivated dyer's yard	home-grown
KAYU TINGI (dark red)	male	tree (medium)	bark (visible)	wild, from coast	bought or gathered (young dyer)
MENGKUDU (bright red)	male	tree (high)	rootbark, below ground (not visible)	wild, across sea	bought
NAPHTHOL (Synthetic bright red)	—	—	—	across sea	bought
TEGERANG	ancestral	old tree	trunk, inner part, above ground (not visible)	wild, mountains	gathered (grandmother)

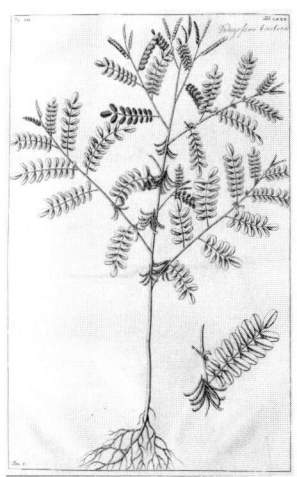 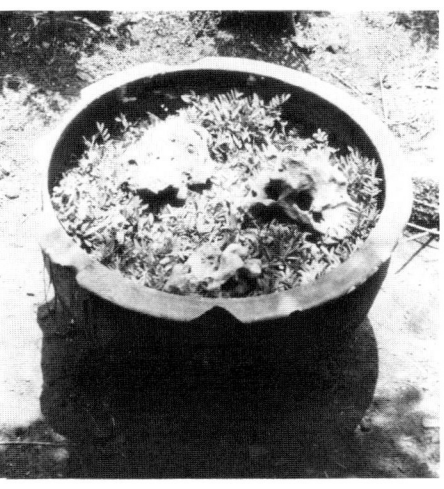 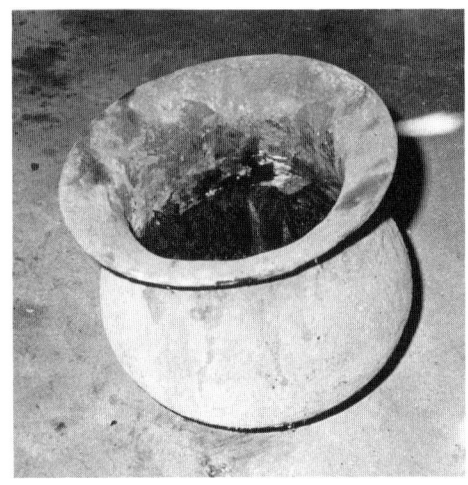

Figure 8. Indigo tinctoria. As the leaves of the plant are used, it is considered a pala gumantang, *species with "hanging fruits." From Rumphius 1750/55 V:225.*

Figure 9. The indigo leaves are left outside in an earthen pot (jembangan) *for fermentation. In the background, bundles of extracted indigo, thrown between the* tom *plants, act as fertilizer. Kerek, circa 1980.*

Figure 10. The annual supply of "seed" (bibit nila) *is kept in a small earthen pot with a narrow opening, as protection against the light. Kerek, circa 1980.*

According to Rumphius indigo never grows wild, but is always cultivated; he describes the smell of the soaking leaves as sickening, which he says explains why blue-dyeing was considered a difficult and revolting activity (1750/55:221). The mixing of the yearly supply of *nila*, the indigo leaf extract, is in fact shrouded in the highest secrecy. This is true of all activities related to the "mother vat," which is kept out of sight near the cooking fire in the back of the dyer's house (in my seven years in the area I have not been allowed actually to see the complete sequence of *nila* preparation).

First, the cut leaves and upper parts of the leafstalks are bound into small bunches and left to soak in an earthen pot (*jembangan*) outside the house, completely covered with water (*dilep*), and weighted down with stones (Fig. 9). After some time the water starts to bubble and, as the dyers express it, "the heat comes out," starting the process of transforming the *tom* into a "cool" dye. The next day the dye fluid is strained into another earthen pot. The pressed-out plant matter is removed and used as fertilizer on the indigo plants in the yard. Now quicklime (*kapur*) is added to the fluid and vigorously stirred in (*dikebur* or *diganting*) until the resulting froth settles, after which the *nila* is left to settle or rest (*disirep*) overnight. After the first "natural" cooling of the dye through fermentation with water, there is a second "cultural" cooling, accomplished through the addition of the quicklime, a hot element whose effect is literally beaten out. The next morning the clear fluid on top is strained off (*disaring*) and the sediment is stored in a smaller pot with a narrow opening. The less it is exposed to the light (and the heat), the better it keeps (Fig. 10). In contrast to indigo previously made for commercial purposes, which was boiled for preservation (Heyne 1927:772, citing de Bie and Mayer), this indigo is never boiled, the dyers insisted. Only the red dyes are boiled.

At each dye-session a quantity of *nila* is added to the mother vat with some quicklime and brown palm sugar (*gula Jawa*). This process is called *makanni* (to feed) or *nglabuhi* (literally, "to set to float offerings"). After all the ingredients have been stirred together (*diremed*) the vat is once more left to rest overnight. The slow and gradual process of blue-dyeing (*wedelan*) begins early in the morning. The folded cloth is alternately immersed for short periods in the dye (*dikom*) and then hung for a while (*diatuskan* or *disirep*) in the shade outside the house, to be exposed to the light for oxidizing. After intermittent rinsing in clear water the same sequence is repeated over and over again. Three days of dyeing through countless dippings result in a bright blue; five days will give a deep blue shade[10] (Fig. 11). Seven-day steepings are needed to produce a dark blue-black, achieved in combination with the rootbark of mangrove extract, *kayu tingi* (see below). Only clear weather is suitable for indigo-dyeing; during the rainy season it is altogether forbidden. In the literature, reports on indigo cultivation, preparation and dye process do not differ much from those given by the village women. According to most, cloths are left overnight in the dye vat and exposed to the light in the morning, taking many more days to reach the intended shade.

There is much evidence suggesting that the indigo vat is understood metaphorically as a womb. Cornets de Groot mentions certain ingredients used to "feed" or "offer" to the *nila* vat: fermented sticky rice (*tape*

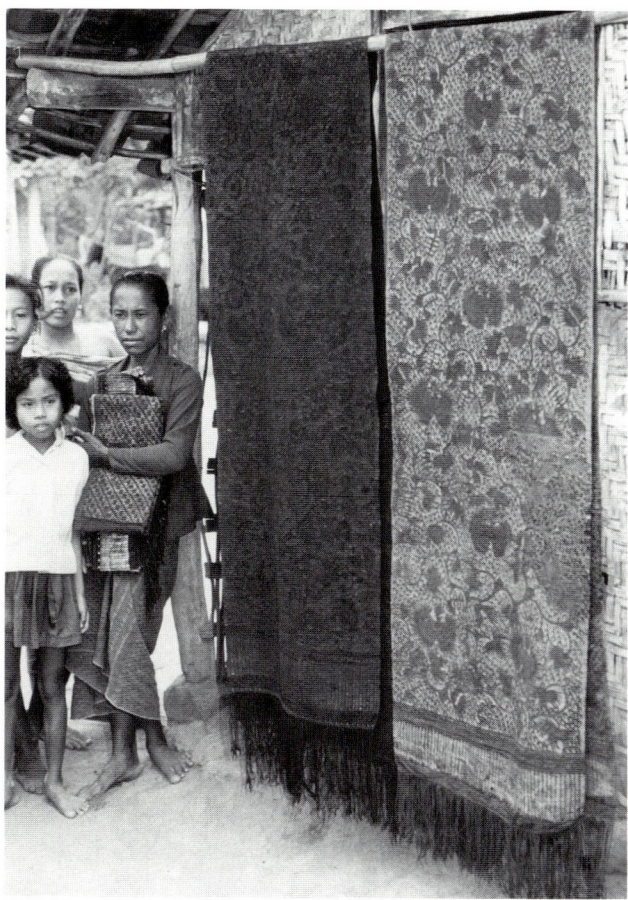

Figure 11. Stages of indigo dyeing: three- and five-day dippings give gradually darker shades of blue. Kerek, circa 1980.

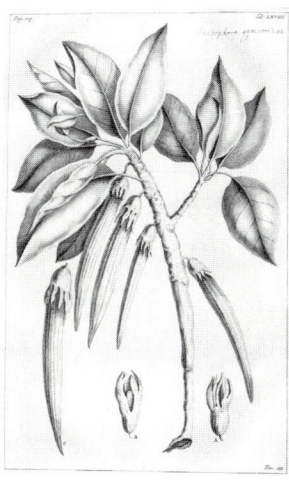

Figure 12. Mangium celsum or mangi tongki, the Bruguiera. The phallus-shaped fruit may suggest why the plant was considered male. From Rumphius 1750/55 III: plate LXVIII.

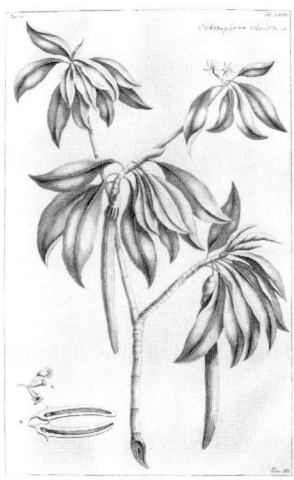

Figure 13. Mangium minus or palun, the Ceriops Candolleana. From Rumphius 1750/55 III: plate LXIX.

ketan), pineapple, and other fruits (1822:584). Traditionally these are the fruits that are made into a fruit salad and covered with a hot spicy sugar syrup called *rujak*, which is "sold" by prospective grandparents to guests at the seven-months-pregnancy ceremony and the proceeds of which are meant "to buy medicine for the baby" (Geertz 1960:44; Does 1893:44,47). When the dye vat actually refuses to foam or take the yellow sheen, it is said to be "sulking" (*mlengkek*); this is blamed on a quarrel between the dyer and her husband. The situation can be remedied by more offerings, or *labuhan* (Does 1893:44,47). Obviously the harmony of husband and wife and the welfare of their offspring are related to the indigo vat, more particularly during pregnancy. The term for blue-dyeing, *wedel*, is also used in the expression "*tunggal wedel*," literally "from a single vat," brothers and sisters from one womb.

The Dark Red Dye

While all shades of blue, whether dark or light, come from a single plant, dark red and bright red are made from different materials and by different processes. Dark, or brownish red, the easier of the two, results from the use of the bark of a species of mangrove or rhizophore known as *kayu tingi*, and found in coastal swamps all over Indonesia. The exact botanical determination of this plant presents some difficulties. Apparently several different species of dye tanning-bark go under this name, locally also referred to as *kayu tengar*, *kayu katia* and *bakau* (Heyne 1927:1165). Among several samples bought in the village shop, most were heavy with a coarse texture and a dark, almost blackish-brown color. Others had a lighter texture and color. Possibly all species, growing in tidal swamps along the coast, are gathered indiscriminately, as they are sold for the same purpose (Heyne 1927:1165). Most likely *kayu tingi* used in the village is a species of *Bruguiera* (Figs. 12,13), which according to ethnobotanical concepts used to be considered "male" in earlier times (Rumphius 1750/55 III:106).[11] But as far as the Kerek dyers are concerned, its outstanding properties are its dark red color and the fact that the rough bark chips can be purchased in the market at Gresik, sixty kilometers to the east, where it is imported either from Sulawesi or from areas on Java. (At present it is even available in the village shop, which suggests a possible increase in its use, or a better infrastructure.)

During the late nineteenth century *kayu tingi* was still being sold as a product of the Tuban region (Koloniaal Verslag 1892:4). The fishermen along the coast use it as a tanning agent to protect their nets against the sea water. Another type of tanning agent, *kayu pilang* (*Acacia leucophlea*), also used in the

Dye Process and Life Sequence

Table Three: NATURE OF DYE PROCESSING

	TOM (indigo)	**KAYU-TINGI** (dark red)	**MENGKUDU** (bright red)	**NAPHTHOL** (bright red)	**TEGERANG** (yellow)
STARTING MATERIAL	complete leaves	powdered bark	1) 2 parts powdered rootbark (=coloring agent)	1 part powder #1 (mordant)	whole chips (trunk)
RENDERING PROCESS	a) natural heating	boiling	boiling together 1 and 2	consecutive a) hot water +caustic soda b) cold water	boiling
ADDITIVE	quicklime *(kapur)*	------	2) 1 part *jirek* powder (=mordant)	2 parts powder #2 (coloring agent)	alum (mordant)
SECOND PROCESS	b) beating out heat	------	------	------	
NATURE OF RENDERED DYE	sediment	fluid sediment	fluid/ solved	2 different fluids	?extract
HOW APPLIED	cloth soaked	dye rubbed in (by hand)	dye rubbed in (by hand)	dye rubbed in (roller)	dye rubbed in or boiled
HOW STORED	earthen pot	copper vessel	copper vessel?	wooden tub	?
LENGTH/ DIFFICULTY OF PROCESS	difficult	'quick'?	difficult	quick	difficult
HOW USED (WHETHER COMBINED)	separately and with all others	only with indigo	separately and with indigo	separately and with indigo	separately? and with indigo
NAME OF PREPARED DYE	*NILA*	*SOGA TINGI*	*KUDU-JIREK*	*"NAPTOL"*	*?TEGERANG*

Gresik leather industry (Heyne 1927:714), is mentioned by the dyers as a low-quality substitute, which they seek in the woods if their yearly supply of *kayu tingi* is late. But the cloths dyed with *kayu pilang* quickly fade.

To prepare the dark red dye, or *soga tingi,* the bark is finely pounded (*diceplok*) after an overnight soaking in clear water (*dikom*). The powdered bark (*pispisan*) is boiled for an hour (*digodog*) in a pot with fresh water, and then strained (*disaring*). In this case it is the fluid that is kept instead of the sediment, as with the indigo. A quantity of the *soga* is left to cool (*diademi*) in a large shallow copper dish (*kenceng*). The cloth is not dipped or left in the dye, but carefully rubbed and patted with the flat hand so as to spread the color evenly into the textile. For each consecutive bath a fresh amount of dye is added.

The Bright Red Dye

Nowadays bright red is obtained from synthetic naphthol dyes bought in Surabaya, and consisting of two different powdered substances—one a mordant, the other a color-salt. This dye type is an Azo dye, developed for the batik industry and imported from Germany. For the first bath a quantity of naphthol (in this case AS or ASD) is mixed with caustic soda and boiling hot water, to which cold water is immediately added. The second bath, which produces the actual color, consists of a quantity of the salt Red B, carefully made into a paste with cold water and filled up to the amount needed. The cloth is switched through the first bath five times, hung out to drip (*diatuskan*) over the dye tub for a short period, and almost immediately given a similar treatment in the second bath.

Though the naphthol process has time-saving advantages over the traditional one, the village women still praise the depth and beauty of the red achieved with the dye root called *mengkudu* in Malay or *kudhu* in Javanese, which was used for the traditional bright red dye. So-called Moluccan *mengkudu*, said to be the best quality, was always imported from Macassar, having originated in the Moluccas, and particularly Ambon, where it grows uncultivated (Heyne 1927:1408). Although *mengkudu* was cultivated in certain areas of West Java as a dyewood during the late nineteenth century (see Reports for the Ceribon, Karanganyar, and Priangan regions in Koloniaal Verslag 1892), in East and Central Java it was only cultivated for medicinal purposes. Rumphius distinguished between two types: a "male" tree of medium height growing wild in the woods near the sea coast (Fig. 14), whose roots provided the bright red dye; and a shorter, "female" species which grew near inhabited places and was used for medicinal purposes (Fig. 15).[12]

It can be hypothesized that the finer distinctions regarding the classification of *mengkudu* (similar to those regarding *kayu tingi*) not only appeared increasingly unimportant to Western botanists in the course of time, but also grew blurred in the minds of the people. However, combining the dyers' information and the supplementary descriptions from earlier sources it appears both *kayu tingi* and *mengkudu* were classified more precisely at one time. Both *mengkudu* and *kayu tingi* originally came from a "male" tree. At present people emphasize only that they are "bought in the market" in contrast to indigo,

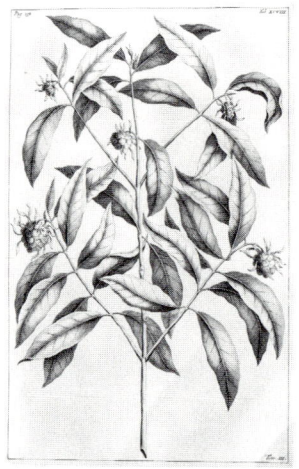 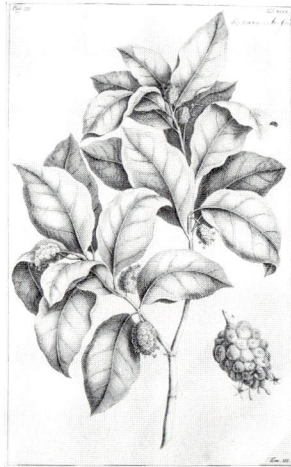

Figure 14. Bangkudu laki-laki or male mengkudu *from overseas, the* Morinda bracteata. *From Rumphius 1750/55 III: plate XCVIII.*

Figure 15. Bangkudu latifolia *or* female mengkudu *used medicinally, the* Morinda citrifolia. *From Rumphius 1750/55 III: plate XCIX.*

which is cultivated. This distinction also applies to the synthetic dyes. Thus the red dyes might be designated as coming from "outside" in contrast to indigo, which derives from "within." Between the two red dyes another fine distinction seems still relevant. Whereas the dark red dyebark, *kayu tingi*, came to local markets from nearby swampy coasts, the *mengkudu* was always described as coming from outside (just like the modern substitute naphthol dyes). This point, though not explicitly stressed by the village women, is invariably mentioned in the written sources (Rumphius 1750/55 VI:158; Kiliaan 1892:5; Musschenbroek 1878:8). *Kayu tingi*, then, is conceptually more "in" than *mengkudu*, and the substitution of locally found *kayu pilang* for *kayu tingi* reinforces this interpretation; possibly during the last century even *kayu tingi* came from the local coasts. It is the bright reds, whether naphthol or *mengkudu* based, that are the most "out."

The description of the preparation of the traditional bright red dye, which was known as *kudu-jirek*, is pieced together from the scattered memories of Mak Modin, sometimes added to by other older women. The *mengkudu* rootbark was pounded (*ditumbuk*) in a

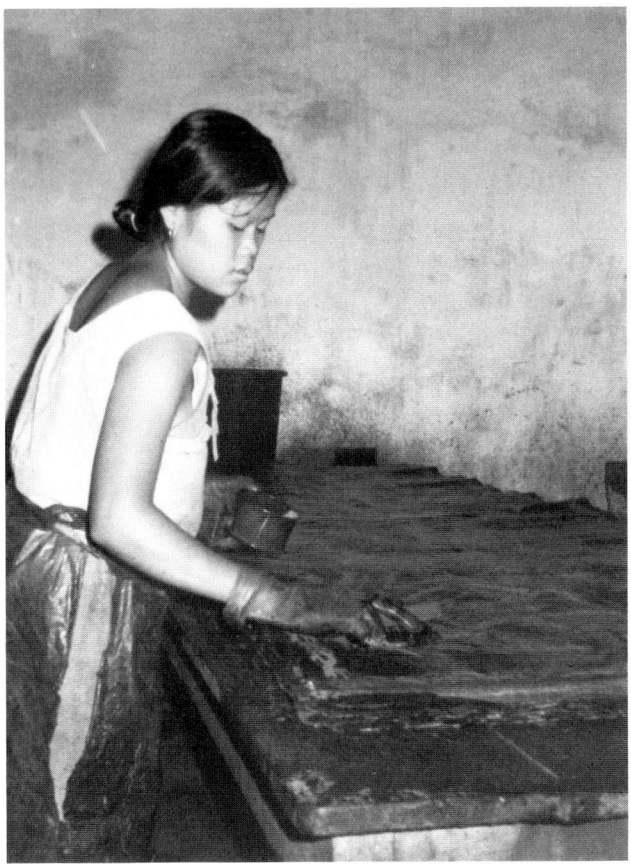

Figure 16. Dyeing with synthetic bright red in a Lasem batik enterprise, circa 1980. The cloth is spread on a flat surface and the dye is rubbed on little by little. This method is exactly similar to the method used in dyeing with the traditional bright red (kudu-jirek).

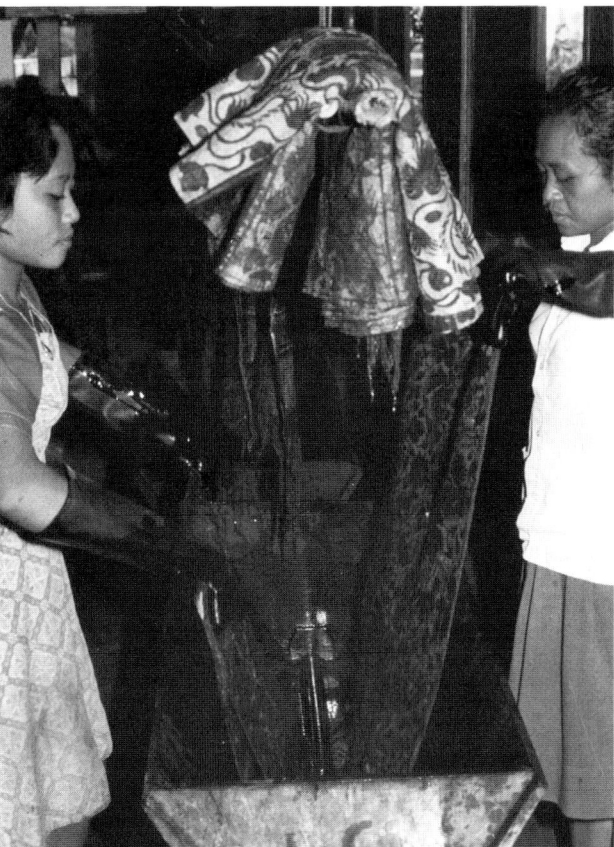

Figure 17. Kasmi (left) and Rugayah (right) with the tub used for synthetic dye. The wooden roller is clearly visible on the bottom. Kerek, 1979.

mortar, or ground (*dipipis*) on a flat stone. This powder was mixed in a proportion of two to one with the bark of *Symplocos fasciculata*, called *jirek*, which was also bought in the market, but already finely ground (*pispisan*), and which served as a mixed-in mordant because of its alum content. The mixture of *mengkudu* and *jirek*, made into a paste and diluted with water, was ready for use without boiling, as my informant noted, "just like the synthetic red dye."

With the bright red *kudu-jirek*, as with the dark red *soga*, the cloth was not dipped or left in the dye. Rather, the dye was poured over the cloth in small quantities and rubbed in with a flat hand. In a Lasem batik enterprise I saw this method still being used with naphthol red dyes (Fig. 16). In Kerek, however, the dyers utilize the wooden tubs donated by the Department of Industries (Fig. 17). The cloth is pulled under a wooden roller fixed in the V-shaped bottom of the tub. Two women then draw it back and forth through the dye, letting the roller take over the task of rubbing the dye in. It has not been possible to get more precise information on dyeing with *kudu-jirek*. All women consider the dyeing of red a difficult and time-consuming process, while its preparation is described as relatively easy. This is the reverse for the preparation and dyeing of indigo: the women maintain the latter is the more difficult. Obviously, these concepts are unrelated to the actual time and effort spent.

Yellow Dyes

Yellow was once but is no longer in use as a separate dye. Mak Modin vaguely remembers how her mother would search the mountain forest, a trip fraught with danger at the time, to obtain the precious dye wood called *tegerang* (*Cudranus javanensis*, Fig. 18), a species of wild, thorny citrus growing in stony, mountainous areas (Rumphius 1750/55 V:22). Mak Modin has never handled it herself and does not recall details about its preparation or use, except that it was very difficult. Rumphius mentions its use as a separate dye for yellow as well as an overdye on blue to obtain green. The part of the tree used for dyeing was the trunk or the roots of old trees. The woodchips had to be soaked in water overnight. The next day the mixture was boiled over high heat until the fluid became brown "like beer or honey," and strained through a piece of cloth. The addition of pulverised white alum (*tawas*

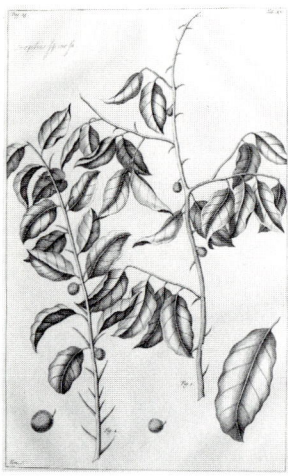

Figure 18. Tegerang, the Cudranus javanensis. Its long sharp thorns were probably those originally used to make the pinpricks (coblosan). From Rumphius 1750/55 V: plate XV.

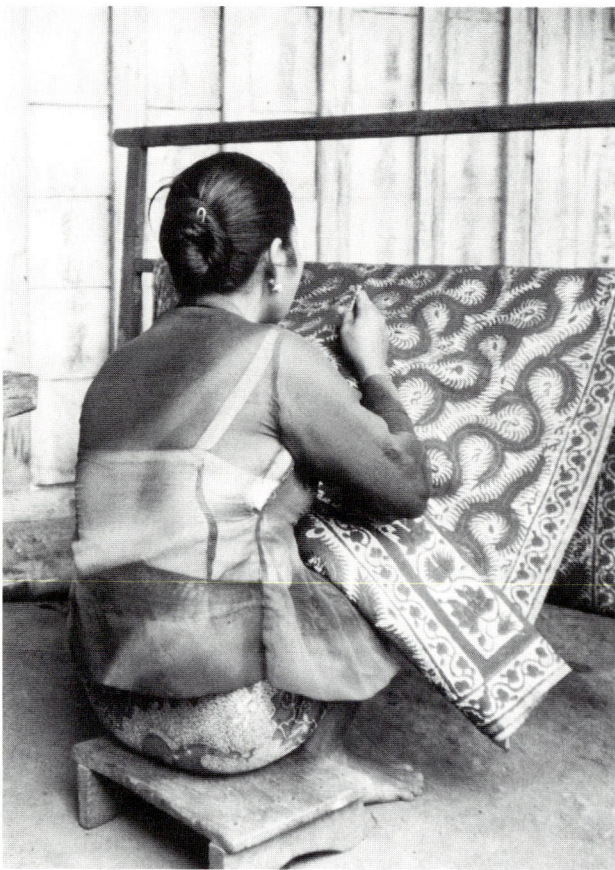

Figure 19. The red-dyed cloth undergoes a second waxing: inner motifs are covered in resist on the red; and coblosan are pierced into the already waxed (thus white) background. Kerek, circa 1980.

cudrangan) made it turn yellow. White cloth had to be boiled in the fluid, with a few grains of unhusked rice. When the husks came off this was the sign the dye process was completed. As an overdye on blue to obtain green, the dye was kneaded into the cloth instead of being boiled (Rumphius 1750/55 V:24). Depending upon the relative strength of the blue the yellow overdye may possibly also have produced a darker greenish blue shade such as I have seen on several heirloom cloths, whose motifs were outlined with a yellow tinge.

Interestingly *tegerang* is still used in the dye process on Madura, and is therefore easily available in the markets of Gresik and Surabaya. Nevertheless the Kerek dyers do not buy it there. To them because yellow is conceptually related to regeneration and fertility, the dye wood had to come from the mountains, which according to village myths of origin are the abode of gods and ancestors, the originators of regeneration. There at the mountainous cave *Goa Terus*, near a large altarstone entirely rubbed with a yellow substance, a yearly ritual is held in honor of Batari Uma, the mythical ancestress, and Dewi Sri, the goddess of rice and cotton. The use of rice grains to indicate the completion of the yellow dye process suggests a relationship to Dewi Sri as well.

At present the only way Mak Modin still produces yellow, however fleetingly, is in the initial indigo bath. When the cloth is taken out of the vat it appears yellow, but as it is exposed to the light, the yellow gradually turns green. In this case, too, a connection to fertility is found: the first indigo bath is called *bayèni*, "to lie in." A *bayi* is a child that has to be carried; the term is also used for a child still in the womb (Jansz 1932:39). The "invisibility" of this yellow is in keeping with village concepts regarding fertility which I have extensively discussed elsewhere. Fertility as life-perpetuating power is generally kept hidden or secret, to be protected from negative infuences. Only during appropriate rituals or among insiders is it allowed to come to the light (Heringa In Press a).

It is remarkable how "ideal" concepts regarding dyes and processes are the common property of the dyers and the other women, though only the dyers know all details of the actual execution. The nature of the various dye materials and their preparation suggest certain concepts and contrasting sets that have significance in the Javanese context (see Tables 2,3). Moreover similar concepts are found in other Indonesian cultures. Thus the idea of the trunk of a tree as a metaphor for the ancestors, with roots, bark, and leaves or tip for the descending generations is one that recurs frequently (Fox 1980:117, Platenkamp 1984:171). The opposition soft/hard is encountered in terms of the material contained (leaves/bark) and again, likewise, in terms of the container: an earthen pot is used for the leaf extract, whereas bark extract is kept in a copper vessel. This set can be related among other things to the division of work between men and women. Men make the implements out of hard materials—wood, bamboo, and metal—while women manufacture pots out of soft clay. A third dichotomy is contained in opposition between the cultivated annual shrub, and two different types of wild-growing tree— a contrast also linked to the contrasting set: inside/outside. The indigo cultivated each new season by the dyers refers to women in their regenerative role, which is made even more explicit in the connection of the indigo vat with the womb. To the dyers, guardians of the generations-old indigo vat, hidden in the innermost part of their house, the man of the house has come from outside the village like the dye woods they search for or buy in distant places.

The Color Categories as Seen in Batik

Seven different categories of batik cloth can be distinguished on the basis of color. All but one have a white background and colored motifs; the seventh is a reversal of this—white motifs on a colored ground. Three use a single color, while the other four are overdyes of red and blue. In two of the latter there is an asymmetric bright/dark opposition: dark blue is matched with bright red, while dark red covers one of the light indigo shades. In some cases, not all elements are visible to the eye. All combinations of blue and red result in black in the areas where no intermediate waxing has been carried out. Before being waxed each cloth is sewn together along the short ends, washed, and sized with rice starch. A length of bamboo keeps the cloth stretched while it dries, *digetek* (see Fig. 3). The dye process involved in producing each of the seven cloth types, summarized in Table 4, is described below, starting with the cloths with white backgrounds.

(l) ***Bangrod.*** Nowadays synthetically dyed, *bangrod* is a cloth with bright red motifs worn as a shouldercloth by the youngest generation of women, girls of marriageable age. Its name is a contraction of the words *diabang* ("reddened") and *dilorod* ("being stripped"); thus *bangrod* means reddened and stripped (of the wax) by boiling. Traditionally it had to undergo a preparatory treatment before the bright red *kudu-jirek* could be applied, for without this protracted first step the dye would not "take" (*'ndak mandi,* "to be ineffectual," said specifically of poison or a magic potion). In Kerek exact details of that process are not remembered, but Jasper and Pirngadie mention that it took forty days (1916:16)—a length of time reminiscent of ritual periods before or after childbirth and other life-ceremonies.[13] In village terminology the cloth had to be oiled or "dirtied" (*dibolot,* or in Central Javanese terminology, *diketel*), a term especially applied to human "skin dirt." The village women remember this included repeated sessions of kneading the cloth with oil pressed from the seeds of *Ricinus communis* (*lenga jarak*), thorough washing (*nglungsur*), pressing, and drying in the sun. When all this was finished the cloth could be batiked. At present the use of synthetic red has made the oiling technically obsolete. After the motifs have been drawn and the background covered thoroughly with wax, the latter is pierced all over with a long needle or (ideally) the large thorn of a citrus tree (Fig. 19). This piercing is called *nyoblosi* and also *nyocohi;* the second term is used as well for the planting out of rice seedlings on the wet rice field. When it has been dyed, the cloth is boiled in water to remove the wax (*dilungsur*) and dried in the shade.

(2) ***Putihan.*** This cloth has bright blue motifs on white, usually flowers and creatures of the sky and earth co-mingled; and it is generally worn as a shoulder cloth. The name *putihan,* however, actually means "whitened" as well as "whitening," and as such can be understood in terms of its function as a protection against illness or bad influences. The process is relatively simple. After the waxing of the outlines, fillings, background, and pinpricks (*coblosan*), three sessions of indigo dyeing result in a deep but bright blue. According to the dyers this is the whole process; but an early nineteenth century report on village dyeing in Gresik maintains that for a fine and brilliant bright shade of blue, the cloth should be put in peanut or coconut oil before dyeing (Cornets de Groot 1822:584). Such a preparatory oiling makes sense in connection with the function and "place" of the *putihan.* The dyers seem to have forgotten about the oiling process, but did admit the difficulty of making the blue "smile" (*ngguyu*). Recent results do in fact seem rather flat in comparison with heirloom *putihan* cloths.

(3) ***Biron.*** This cloth is covered with deep blue motifs. In Kerek, *biron* means [cloth] covered in wax to dye the uncovered parts blue. In color, it could almost be mistaken for *putihan,* as the blue is only slightly darker. However, unlike *putihan,* it is a skirtcloth, not a shouldercloth. Its motifs are different, too: instead of sky and earth creatures, it is covered with flowered creepers (*lung-lungan*). Furthermore its name stresses the dark element in the cloth instead of the bright one.[14] I have never been able to see the exact dye sequence, since *biron* is rarely made anymore. The dyers mention a five-day series of dippings in the indigo vat. Here, too, as in the case of *putihan,* I presume an initial oiling was originally part of the process. The few remaining examples still function as part of the gift called *paningset,* which literally means "girdle," given by the bride-takers to the bride-givers to bind the two families.

(4) ***Pipitan.*** A skirt or shouldercloth with motifs in bright red, dark blue and blue-black, *pipitan* is worn by

Table Four
THE SEVEN CLOTH TYPES: Dying Processes

CLOTH TYPE	PRELIMINARY STEPS			COLOR	FINAL STEPS		
layers of color	*bolot*(a)	rice starch	application of batik	application of dyes	*lanasi bolot*(b)	*nglungsur*	shade drying
BANGROD one layer	yes	yes	once	*kudu-jirek* or *naptol*	no	yes	yes
PUTIHAN one layer	yes	yes	once	*nila*-3x	no	yes	yes
BIRON one layer	yes	yes	once	*nila*-5x	no	yes	yes
PIPITAN two layers	yes	yes	twice 1) *kotong* 2) *isen*	a) *kudu-jirek* or *naptol* b) *nila*-5x	no no	yes yes	yes yes
IRENGAN three layers	no	yes	once	a) *gadung* b) *soga tingi* c) *nila*-5x	*lanasi bolot*	yes	no
RITUAL IRENGAN three layers?	no	yes	once	a,b) as above c) *nila* 7x	*lanasi? bolot?*	yes	no
RITUAL PUTIHAN three layers?	no	yes	once	a,b) as above c) *nila* 7x	*lanasi? bolot?*	yes	yes

GLOSSARY OF DYES:

nila, indigo
kudu-jirek, organic bright red
naptol, synthetic bright red
soga tingi, organic dark red-brown
gadung, fleeting green,
    result of quick dip in *nila*

GLOSSARY OF PROCESSES:

bolot/a, preliminary oiling
bolot/b, final mud bath
lanasi, final sun bath
nglungsur, removal of wax by boiling

the middle generation, married women with children. Its name, when read as modern Javanese *pipit-an*, means "close together" and refers to the bond between wife and husband, parents and child. In Old Javanese, moreover, *pita* means "yellow." The contracted form *pipitan* (from *pi-pita-an*) then means "yellowed" or "yellowish."[15] Although this second, secret meaning is no longer recognized in the village, the designation of this cloth as "yellowish" fits in with its conceptual place in the west. *Pipitan* may be considered to combine aspects of the red *bangrod* and the blue *biron*. Here again, traditionally, an oiling had to precede the waxing. Now that process is left out, although older women still remember it. The first waxing of the cloth is only partial: the motifs are outlined (*dikotongi*, meaning the motifs are left empty) and the background is solidly waxed, after which the red dye is applied. Only then, during a second waxing, are the fillings or inner motifs (*isèn*) and the pinpricks (*coblosan*) added. Apart from the *isèn* the motifs are left uncovered. Then a five-day indigo process follows, resulting in black motifs (where the indigo has "touched" the red) with bright red fillings. The blue-marbled background is due to the repeated steepings of the carefully folded cloth in the indigo vat, when the indigo gradually seeps through the wax.[16] In modern cloths dyed with synthetic blue this does not happen, because the dyes take much faster. The result is a clear white background on which the black and red motifs contrast strongly (see Fig. 20). The last step consists once more of the removal of the wax by boiling and drying in the shade.

(5) Irengan. *Irengan*, a black cloth dyed in three layers, is a shouldercloth worn by the eldest generation of women, the grandmothers. Its name, meaning both "black" and "lying fallow after the last harvest," alludes to its function. *Irengan* has blue-black motifs with white fillings on a marbled blue background dotted with black *cocohan*. Although indigo and the dark red *soga* dye are combined to yield this cloth, the dark red is invisible. The cloth ends up seemingly blue-black with white fillings; there is no indication of red. The process is as follows: After being washed and starched, the cloth is waxed. Here *isèn* and *coblosan* are immediately applied in a single move. The first dye-step, called *gadung* (green), is a very brief indigo bath resulting in a greenish blue which darkens as the cloth is exposed to the light. After the cloth has dried, the dark red *soga* is kneaded and rubbed into the "light blue" without intermediate waxing or boiling.

A second dip in the indigo vat follows. This third step is called *mbironi* (to dye blue); its purpose is said to "*nyarèni*"—to apply the essence or pollen, known as *sari*, to the cloth (Rouffaer and Juynboll 1914:365). Now the cloth must be left to rest or recover (*disirep*). The same process should be repeated five times.

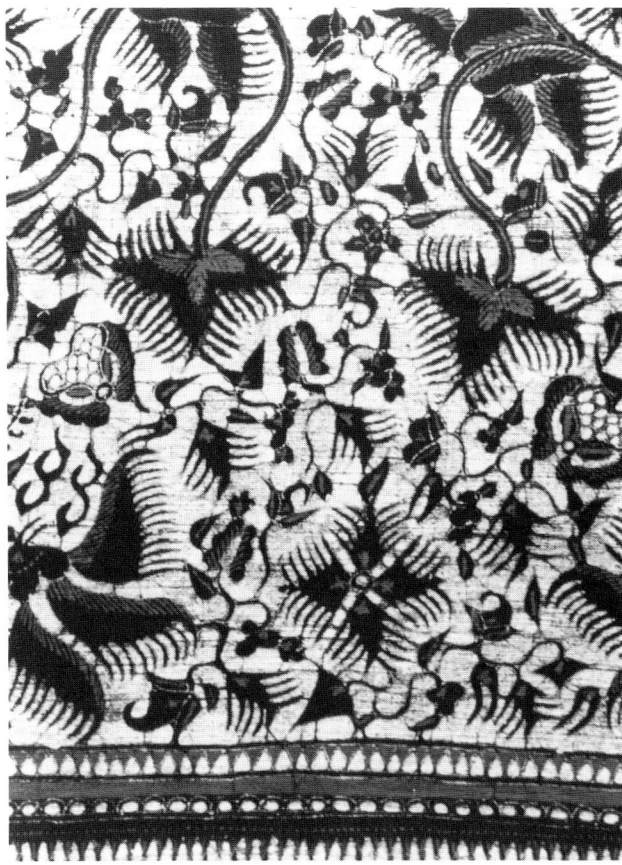

Figure 20. Synthetically-dyed pipitan. *The practically clear white background and the omission of the pinpricks* (coblosan) *indicates the textile is meant for use outside the villages. Kerek, circa 1980.*

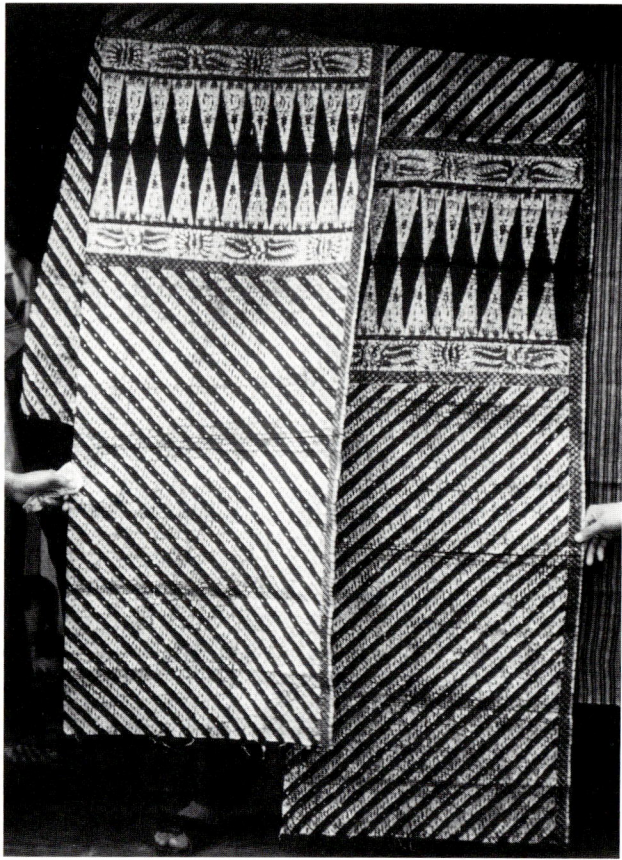

Figure 21. Putihan simpenan, *the two-part ritual cloth connected to the Upper World. The sarong format with two sets of triangles (papan/tumpal) in the middle contains an exceptional type of* parang *motif on the centerfield (badan). It is a much simpler version than those known from Central Java. Kerek, circa 1980.*

While I received conflicting information regarding the time spent on the consecutive indigo dippings, I had the impression this is a relatively fast process. Although five was mentioned as the ideal number of dippings the dyers may use short-cuts. Dutch sources have explained the use of *soga tingi* as an overdye on indigo as being merely a speeding-up or fixation of the indigo process (Jasper and Pirngadie 1916:34). It may well have been used as such in commercial batik enterprises, because of its relative low cost in comparison to elaborate blue-dyeing processes. Along the north coast, as in Kerek nowadays, the process was termed *nyoga*, a term that means overdying of indigo with *soga*,—proof that the color of the second dye, the dark brownish-red, is an important element (Cornets de Groot 1822:583). Either before or after the removal of the wax—the information remains unclear—the cloth is hung in the sun, in contrast to all other categories which are dried in the shade. This sun bath is called *lanasi* and is meant to make the red "flare up" (*lanas* or *ganas*, also said of irascible old women). Originally the final step consisted of a half day's steeping in mud from the riverbank (*ndut becekan*) to achieve a deep shiny black. The verb *mbecek* also means to make *sambal*, the spicy chili paste used at all meals as a condiment. The mud may be considered as the agent to "spice" the black, a step which can be considered a complement to the flaring up (*lanas*) of the red. It was however also an analog to the preparatory oiling of *bangrod* and *pipitan*. Interestingly the same term, *dibolot* ("to be made dirty") is used for both processes. Here it forms a final closing step against the initial, opening step of the oiling.

(6 and 7) *Putihan* **and** *Irengan*. Two special categories of cloth, also called *putihan* and *irengan*, are seldom encountered anymore. Both have ritual and ceremonial functions and are not actually in use as dress cloths. The remaining examples are mostly carefully kept heirlooms. The ritual *irengan* is used primarily as a shroud in the form of a wraparound. It also appears in a second format which is similar to that of the ceremonial *putihan*: as a two-piece set consisting of two *sarung* halves. They have been woven in the archaic half-width, which was intended to be cut in half and sewn together lengthwise, to yield the length appropriate for a waist to ankle skirtcloth. But in spite of having known long and extensive use, the available examples have never been made into tubular cloths. They are designated in the village as *simpenan*, objects kept in a secret place, and they appear only on ritual occasions, neatly folded, as part of the *pusaka* inherited from the ancestors (Fig. 21).

The ceremonial *putihan* should be completely covered in black geometrical motifs on its white base; the ceremonial *irengan* is its opposite, with white motifs covering a black background. They are distinguished from their nonceremonial counterparts of the same name by differences in motif and in color contrast, and are generally of high workmanship (though a few *irengan* of obvious lower quality have lately been made). The dye sequence for both is said to be similar to that of ordinary *irengan*, but entails seven repetitions of the three-step dye-bath resulting in a deep even black. The dyers insist the process needs patience but is not particularly difficult. The real problem lies in the waxing of the geometrical motifs, the intricate details of which few women remember. Even more important are the requirements of a steady hand and attention to the right temperature of the wax as it is applied on the heavy cloth. Repeated steepings in the indigo vat and particularly the rubbing-in of the *soga* will scale off large areas of wax if it has not been applied correctly. The cloth will then end up partially blank—either white or black.

Together, three of the cloth types—*bangrod*, *pipitan*, and *irengan* (the first, fourth, and fifth described)—form a significant triad: they are worn, respectively, by the daughters, the mothers, and the grandmothers. The youngest generation receives, as it were, one layer of color; the middle, two layers; and the eldest, three. We have already established the importance of the dyer's position in the village. Now it can be seen that she plays a crucial role in presenting the village women with the colors appropriate to their life stage. The term *nglungsur*, "removing the wax," which designates a final step in each of the seven cloth types, means in a deeper sense the act of revealing these colors, and emphasizes the dyer's high responsibility (Fig. 22). *Nglungsur* also refers to the act of offering clothing to family members who are less highly placed than the donor. The functions and appearance of each of the seven kinds of cloth are seen in Table Five.

The Sequence of Cloths as a Life Journey

The sequence of cloths can be understood metaphorically as a life journey in which each color type has its proper place, spatially, temporally, and spiritually, in accordance with Diagrams One and Two. I would like to emphasize that the following analysis has not been detailed by my informants but is the result of my own deductions, based on the materials provided by the village women, and supplemented by information from published sources.

Life starts in the east, the point of origin, with a plain white cloth. According to Javanese concepts, a baby "exists" after the mother has been pregnant for seven months (Mayer 1897:264). The woman then wears a five-meter-long piece of white *lawon* (called *bengkung*) tightly wound about her abdomen, to protect the baby in utero. At delivery, her own mother presents her with the first colored cloth, a *slendang*

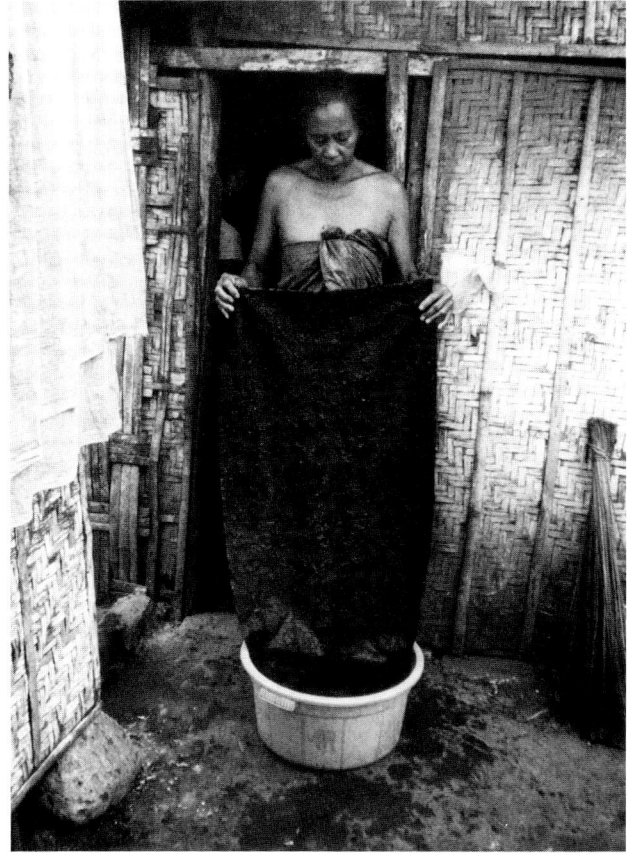

Figure 22. Mak Modin busies herself with boiling the wax off the cloths (nglungsur). She is clad in ritual attire–a multicolored cloth worn pinjungan style. Kerek, circa 1980.

Table Five
THE SEVEN CLOTH TYPES: Function/Appearance

	WEARER/ FORMAT, FUNCTION	BACKGROUND COLOR	DESIGN COLOR	MOTIF
BANGROD	maidens/ daily wear shouldercloth (young husband) wraparound	white	bright red	'seedlings' flowers, birds floral creepers
PUTIHAN	pregnant women, babies/ shouldercloth/ protective (ritual) wraparound	white	bright blue	flowers, birds floral creepers
BIRON	new wives/ wraparound bridal gift (ritual)	white	deep blue	floral creepers
PIPITAN	mothers/ shouldercloth or wraparound daily wear	white	bright red blue & black	'seedlings'(blue) birds, flowers
IRENGAN	grandmothers/ shouldercloth daily wear	white	blue-black dark red (invisible) & green (invisible)	birds flowers
RITUAL IRENGAN	a) shroud/wraparound b) *simpenan*/2 half-*sarung* not worn (ritual)	black	white	geometric
RITUAL PUTIHAN	*simpenan*/2 half-*sarung* not worn (ritual)	white	black	geometric
RITUAL CINDE (previously)	bridal couple wraparound wedding cloth	red	multicolored	geometric

putihan. The baby, considered "not yet human," is held close to its mother's body, wrapped in the *putihan* sling and thereby safeguarded from evil influences. It may be clad in a protective girdle of homespun cotton thread, *lawai*. As long it has to be carried around it is felt to belong still partially to the period between life and death, in the northeastern quarter.

Immediately after birth the newborn baby is rubbed and massaged with oil by the midwife (*dukun bayi*) to ease its entry into this world (Poensen 1876-77:21). This can be compared to the oiling of the cloth, *bolot*, and adds credibility to the idea that the *putihan* was in fact originally oiled. The function of the *putihan*, as a cloth that protects one at the boundary between life and death, offers a second reason for oiling. The *putihan* is preferably never washed to keep its accumulated magic power intact. Once the child is able to walk, it is used in case of illness or to carry valuable marketwares. The action of *bolot*—whether with oil or with mud—occurs on this boundary for the other cloths as well.

As a girl moves from birth into puberty, and is considered marriageable, she gets her first proper cloth, the *bangrod*. Against its pure white base the bright red motifs stand out, expressing the life-force of youth. Small seedlings, *coblosan*, have been "planted," but the fillings are still white, neutral, and pure. Many have classified red as "male," and blue as "female." But in this context that is not the case. As a potential bride, the girl belongs to the bride-giver's side—classified as younger—and thus wears bright red (Josselin de Jong 1977:169). The groom belongs to the "older" bride-takers, and as such is expected to wear blue. This actually correlates with the suitcaseful of blue *biron* cloths carried as *paningset* gift from the bride-taker's side which cloths serve to bind the ties between the two families; the groom does not actually wear them.

The oiling of both cloths, *biron* and *bangrod*, can be compared to the rubbing of bride and groom with *boreh*. The yellow paste is meant to give their skin a brilliant luster, just as the oil will make the red and the blue "smile." The forceful rubbing-in of the red dye can be seen as a metaphor for the period of initiation young people must undergo before they are considered ready to serve as full members of the community. The girl undergoes her learning period before marriage, when in fact she wears the red cloth.

After marriage the context changes. For the young husband, the period called *magang*, during which he serves his father-in-law, is in effect his initiation. It is now he who takes to wearing a red cloth; and it is his relationship not with his wife, but rather with his father-in-law, that determines the color of his "younger" cloth. Once married, the young wife wears the blue *biron*, gift from her husband's family. Through this cloth she symbolically comes into possession of the yellow, invisibly contained in the dye sequence, which is the essence of regeneration.[17] The linking of regeneration with an invisible yellow is suggested in the Javanese myth of origin known as the *Manikmaya*. According to the myth, Maya, the dark one, "whose colour is like indigo and whose task is to keep the cosmos in balance" (Winter 1843:3-4) gives "the Luminous Golden Jewel" (*Retna Jumilah*) to his younger brother Batara Guru. This younger brother proves to be the only one capable (as the mythical ancestor and creator) of forcing the gift open. The jewel brings forth a beautiful child, Tisnawati, from whose body all useful plants grow. She is later identified with Dewi Sri, Goddess of Fertility (Winter 1843:46,54). Similarly the bride-takers give the dark cloth incorporating the yellow to the bride; only she is able to bear a child. This is the secret of *kain biron*, invisibly contained in the dye-sequence. Thus the exchange of *bangrod* and *biron* effects the union of husband and wife and at the same time implicitly hints at the progeny that will result. The cloth names also insist on opposing qualities that are seen as crucial to each separate process. *Bangrod* stresses the act of stripping or uncovering, as *lorod* means "to strip." In *biron*, which means "to cover in wax before dyeing blue," the act of covering is emphasized. The resemblance of *biron* to *putihan*, as it were in a stronger version, also suggests that it serves as a protection around the lower part of the young wife's body, in particular her womb. These three cloths then—*putihan*, *bangrod*, and *biron*—are the single-layered cloths associated with the early stages of life.

In the overdyed categories the visible and invisible layers become more intricate. When the young wife becomes a mother, she is allowed to wear the *pipitan* cloth. Blue and red have now mingled to become black, symbolizing the union of husband and wife. As in the *bangrod*, the bright red fillings symbolize the younger generation, this time the new child. The second stage of waxing, which in effect keeps the red from being touched by the blue, may possibly be compared to the incest prohibition between parent and child. The blue *coblosan* promise further offspring, while the marbled indigo seepings predict the gradual move towards the end of life. In the secret or ritual meaning of *pipitan*, the yellow is now emphasized in connection with the western position of maturity the woman has now reached. In this life stage she personifies the mythical ancestress, Batari Uma, living in the west (Hooykaas 1974:11,15). The *pipitan*, though it looks blue and black with red, can also be considered to be multicolored—incorporating all possible colors and thus positioned in the center. It is here that Earthmother Batari Uma and Skyfather Batara Guru are joined in their role of parents, fullfledged members of the community. Thus it should be pointed out that like white, yellow, too, can "move" along the central axis towards the center (Swellengrebel 1977:90). Now the mountain connection of yellow becomes clear: it is on the mountain that the old tree-trunk was found, the core of which provided the yellow dye connected to fertility. The mountain is the center of the world, the abode of kings and the contact point with ancestors and gods, often viewed as one. Thus the old heirloom cloths including the yellow *tegerang* were probably used in connection with ceremonies relating to the center, symbolizing the total community or the village head as its representation.

The next stage of life is attained when the woman has become a grandmother. She wears the dark *irengan*, blackened and "fallow," as she has left behind the fertile stage of life. The fillings of her cloth are white again as when she was a girl. However, there is more than the eye can see. The seemingly single color black, connected to the end of life in the north, consists of three invisible components. First is *gadung*, the green belonging to the northwest; it can be considered a dark yellow, a second fleeting phase connected to procreation. This dark yellow is followed by *soga*, the dark red, representing a woman's lost fertility as opposed to her daughter's and granddaugher's bright red. Through *nila*, which is the third component, the first two—the greenish yellow and the dark brownish-red—are covered up. But at the same time the *nila* serves to add the (invisible) *sari*, the essence or pollen (Rouffaer and Juynboll 1914:365), which may be meant to ensure the continuation of life beyond death. Therefore it can be considered the element that will enable her to be reborn in a following generation, for on Java it is believed a grandparent will be reincarnated in a grandchild.[18] The last two steps, the "sun" (*lanasi*) and mud (*bolot*) baths, together uniting a sky and an earth element, form the ritual purification preparing the woman to enter the Realm of Death. Thus the cycle is closed. From *bangrod* and *biron* through *pipitan* to *irengan*, continually protected by *putihan*, the colors of a woman's cloth indicate her appropriate position and social status; this cloth-cycle is visualized in Plate 19.

A comparison of the three generational cloths (*bangrod, putihan, irengan*) and their functions indicates more precisely why it is not only red that may be classified as both male and female, but blue as well. The dark red of *irengan* is the "male" red, belonging to the "older" bride-taker. Therefore it is the grandmother who wears the dark red, as bride-taker for her sons. However the relatively "lighter" blue (which covers the dark red) expresses her relationship as "younger" bride-giver of her daughter. The woman of the middle generation wears *pipitan*, which contains the bright "female" red appropriate to her role as a childbearing wife, while it also stands for her role as bride-giver for her daughter. Moreover it is combined with the "male" dark blue, which denotes her role as bride-taker for her son. The bright red in the young girl's *bangrod* stands for her role as the prospective bride and expresses her fertility. As she has no partner as yet, the red is not combined with blue but only stands against the white of beginnings.

In sum, both red and blue are therefore seen to contain male as well as female elements in patterns of recursive complementarity: anything categorized according to one component of a complementary pair can contain elements of its complement (Fox, In Press: 23). When linked with the set young/old, the complementary pairing of a light and a dark shade, combined in the overdyed cloths, serves to denote the wearer's relationship to her own, older generation and to the following, younger one. Moreover the three sets of light and dark shades which are found in the three generational cloths together express a scale of hierarchical relationships in which the dark shade in each case stands for the older group and the light shade denotes the younger one, here alluding to the shifting of generations and also to the varying order of precedence between wife-takers and wife-givers. This hierarchical use of dual categories depends upon the conjunction of recursive complementarity and categorical asymmetry (Fox, In Press: 33). Although these features have been analyzed for Eastern Indonesia in connection to linguistic phenomena and descent, it appears the concepts related to the use of color on Java conform to similar basic ideas.

In all overdyed cloths the indigo functions as a cover, a means to disguise the other colors. This is in accordance with the myth of origin, the *Manikmaya*, in which indigo is said to be the symbol of the night that "serves to disguise" (Winter 1843:4). In this respect the ritual *putihan* and *irengan* resemble the other overdyed cloths, though in other aspects they are dissimilar.

While the five nonritual cloth categories can be understood in the horizontal (spatial and temporal) map, earlier seen in Plate 19, the ritual *putihan* and *irengan* can be imagined on the vertical one as arranged in Plate 20. They are related to the "vertical" or spiritual moments in life, the liminal periods of ceremony and ritual, at particular times when the people of this world are in communion with the Upper and Lower Worlds. Thus they belong to the whole community, male as well as female. As already noted, two aspects serve to distinguish the daily *putihan* and *irengan* from the ritual cloths: the difference in motifs and the contrast in color. The flowers and birds of the daily cloths belong to this world and are depicted on a two-dimensional plane. The geometric motifs of their ritual counterparts are abstract expressions, blueprints, of three-dimensional concepts, mountains or temples reaching up into the sky and connecting this world to other worlds. The color contrast of daily and ritual *putihan* is a matter of shade: bright blue becomes deep black through the fusion with *soga tingi*, thus combining opposite (male and female) elements, as a metaphor for the totality. The ritual *irengan* is the exact opposite (dark background and white motifs) of daily *irengan* as well as of the ritual *putihan*, both of which have black motifs on a white background. It would be impossible to mistake the former for the latter, however, as the black of the ritual *putihan* is darker than that of the daily *irengan*, since its dye sequence is repeated seven times instead of five. Through these extra layers of dye, the color also has an increased height, as it were, reaching up in analogy to the motifs.

Oppositional values are also expressed in the function of the ritual cloths. As a shroud, the *irengan* is connected to the Lower World, dark like its background. It covers the body of the deceased, through motifs and colors reaching out into the nether world. The *putihan*, now merely displayed at ritual occasions, originally visualized the Upper World connection even more explicitly: in times past, the two identical half-*sarung* were attached to bamboo poles as banners, and paraded during life-ceremonies. That practice has died out. Nevertheless all village people are still aware that the *putihan* are the male and female cosmic trees, emblems of the relationship between macro- and micro-cosmos. These *putihan* should also accumulate magic power by never being washed.

A third difference between daily and ritual cloth is contained in the terminology. The ritual cloth takes its name from the background color. Ritual *putihan* has a white background (*putih*=white) whereas ritual *irengan* has a black background (*ireng*=black). By contrast, the daily cloth types mostly take their names not from the color of their backgrounds, but from the color of their motifs; for example *bangrod*, which shows red motifs and *biron*, the cloth with blue motifs, cloths exchanged in the human context, derive their names from the color of their motifs. *Pipitan* is the exception: meaning both "joined" and "yellowed," its name refers not to its visible motifs, but rather to its invisible quality, that which perpetuates life in the context of the human world.[19]

One other life-cloth should be mentioned, although it has not been used in the village for almost a century and does not actually belong to the village dyers' domain. It is, however, the connecting cloth in the ritual center, where the horizontal and the vertical axes cross, the ritual cloth used originally during all rites of passage. I encountered one threadbare but jealously kept example in Kerek (Pl. 20b): it was a *cinde* or patola, the silk double-ikat once imported from Gujarat. On this precious red cloth, which came, like the red dyes, from overseas, geometric motifs reach up into higher spheres as in *putihan* and *irengan*. But here each separate color is clearly visible: white, dark red, yellow, green, bright blue and black on the bright red life-giving base, as fits the center, the sum of all parts.

In conclusion, it can be said that the outward and inward form of the batik cloths of Kerek together visualize a detailed and intricately consistent language. The consistency does not merely relate to general Javanese cultural concepts but also connects with those adhered to elsewhere in Indonesia.

NOTES

1. Nineteenth and early twentieth century literature on batik (Kiliaan 1892; Does 1893; and in particular Rouffaer and Juynboll 1914; Jasper and Pirngadie 1916). The final draft of this article has benefited considerably from comments by Dr. Reimar Schefold and members of the Indonesia Circle at the Vrije Universiteit of Amsterdam. Dr. Leontine Visser has helped me sort out the (ethno)botanical lore and Dr. Jim Fox provided the Eastern Indonesian connection. To all of them I express my gratitude.

2. Regular field research was undertaken between 1977 and 1984. My age and status as a grandmother allowed me access to knowledge denied younger women.

3. The terms used here are the Ngoko or Low-Javanese versions. The Krama or High-Javanese terms *petak, abrit, jene, cemeng* are rarely used in the village setting.

4. Both uxorilocal and virilocal residence occur.

5. Part of the following section has appeared in a slightly different form (and in Dutch) in Heringa 1985.

6. See Wahyono (1979:32), Barrett Jones (1984:49). The second author, however, translates the term *mangulawungkudu* as "fishing with Morinda," which to me seems improbable.

7. Jasper and Pirngadie (1916:31) and Rouffaer and Juynboll (1914:317) mention female blue-dyers.

8. The dyers are uxorilocal.

9. Around 1890 a commercial indigo plantation operated in the subdistrict (Koloniaal Verslag 1892); this may have been the origin of this imported *indigofera* variety.

10. Wahyono mentions that the blue can be lightened by adding *kapur* (1979:9).

11. In the twentieth century descriptions, *Ceriops Candolleana* is generally given as the Latin name for *kayu tingi* (Jasper and Pirngadie 1916:34; Heyne 1927:1167). During the nineteenth century it is described as a *Bruguiera* species (Musschenbroek 1878:18, Note 4). Both belong to the family Rhizophoreacae (Heyne 1927:164, note 1). Still earlier Rumphius (1750/55)

distinguishes between three different *mangi* species: the large *mangi* tree, *mangi tongki*, or, in his Latinized terminology *Mangium celsus* (vol. 3, p.107), the *toncke parampoean*, the "female" *tongki* or *Mangium digitatum* (vol. 3, p. 107) and the *palun*, or small *mangi* tree, *Mangium minus* (vol. 3, p.106; vol. 4, pp. 104-7). The first was a tree growing in coastal areas "where the salt water covers and uncovers the roots." Its rootbark was coarsely textured and used by the Chinese in the dyeing of black (vol. 4, p. 104). There seems to have been some debate at the time whether the *mangi tongki* should be considered "female." Rumphius, however, insists on the determination "male" (vol. 4, p. 103) and designates the second variety as the "*tongke parempoean*," or the female *tongki*, as it was generally smoother and had fragrant roots. The *palun* was used on Ambon as a fixative for red dyeing (vol. 4, p. 58). We therefore see two unconnected oppositions: (a) "male/female," with the connotation "rough-smooth"; and (b) "fixative for black dyeing/fixative for red dyeing." During the early twentieth century the three species were determined as *Bruguiera conjugata, Bruguiera sexangula,* and *Bruguiera cylindrica* (Merrill 1917:388-89). A decade later the *Mangium celsum* is mentioned as the equivalent of *Bruguiera gymnorhiza* under the Javanese name *tanjang*, while the *Mangium minus* has become *Ceriops Candolleana* and is called *kayu tingi* on Java (Heyne 1927:1167,1171). The *Bruguiera sexangula* was later called *Bruguiera eriopetala* and no note is taken of the female-male connection. The *kayu tingi* mentioned as one of the many ingredients in Central-Javanese *soga* dyeing seems to conform to the second species (Jasper and Pirngadie 1916:40; Musschenbroek 1878:19,22). To summarize, it can be stated that, even though the village people of Kerek use the term *kayu tingi* instead of *tanjang*, the dyebark used by them is probably a *Bruguiera* species, conforming to the nomenclature used by Musschenbroek during the last quarter of the nineteenth century and consistent with Rumphius's findings.

12. Bühler's conclusion that *mengkudu* dyeing did not yet exist during the eighteenth century was obviously an oversight (1941:1423). Rumphius does indeed mention two types of *bangkudu*, which is the Moluccan Malay spelling for *mengkudu*. The first is the *Bangkudus angustifolia*, in Malay called *bangkudu laki-laki* or the "male" *mengkudu*, which grows wild in woods near the sea coast; it is a tree of medium height with narrow leaves. Roots from this tree provide the bright red dye and were imported into Java in large quantities for this purpose (Rumphius 1750/55 V:157). The other type, *Bangkudus latifolia* or *bangkudu daun bezaar* (with large leaves), is designated as the "female." It is not as tall as the first species and has broader leaves. It grows near inhabited places and is only used for medicinal purposes (Rumphius 1750/55 V:159). According to nineteenth century Western botanical identification Rumphius's *Bangkudus angustifolia*, renamed *Morinda bracteata*, was the wild species of his *Bangkudus latifolia*, which was now designated as *Morinda citrifolia* (Gresshoff 1894:169). In twentieth century descriptions the two types are mentioned as one and the same botanical species, equally suitable as dye-wood although the best quality for dyeing was still said to come from Sulawesi or the Moluccas (Heyne 1927:1408). The rootbark of young trees which yet have to bear fruit were giving the best results (Daubanton 1922:40).

13. A ritual period of thirty-five (5 x 7) or sometimes, in later usage, forty (5 x 8) days, called *selapanan* ("a number of thirty-five days"). It occurs when a particular day of the five-day week and a particular day of the seven-day week (or also an eight-day week), which are used concurrently in Java, coincide. This occurs every thirty-fifth day and is a propitious occasion used for various types of ritual, for instance *selamatan*, or ceremonial meals (Hien 1912-13 I:224). The *labuhan* can be considered as a ceremonial meal for the indigo vat.

14. It should be noted that in Central Java *mbironi* means: to cover the already blue-dyed parts in wax, before the cloth receives its second brownish red or *soga* dyebath (Jasper and Pirngadie 1916:61).

15. I would like to express my gratitude to Dr. I. Kuntara Wiryamartana of Yogyakarta for filling in this part of the riddle.

16. Probably a better quality wax would prevent the marbling effect to a large extent. Older cloths are slightly brighter.

17. While the young bride's cloth was a *slendang*, the husband's cloth is a wraparound consisting of two *slendang* widths sewn together along the length and—as it is invariably in *sarung* format—also along the short sides. It is thus both "long and wide," according to my informants, and called *kampuhan*. This *kampuhan* is, like the *biron*, extremely rare at present. Few families nowadays can afford to prepare a full complement of new cloths for the betrothal or *paningset* gift, while the village men only may wear a borrowed cloth during the wedding ceremonials. A few affluent families own a series of heirloom cloths to be borrowed or rented for such occasions. It is hoped that at least some of these beautiful textiles will not be sold outside the village and disappear without a trace.

18. According to Balinese views however, reincarnation occurs in the generation of the great grandchildren (Hien 1912-13 I:164).

19. Elsewhere I have analyzed the function of the various Kerek pattern-woven and batik cloth types in relation to the social system (Heringa In Press b); the spatial implications of the role of the dyer have been elaborated in Heringa 1988.

Political Motives
The Batiks of Mohamad Hadi of Solo

Robyn J. and John R. Maxwell

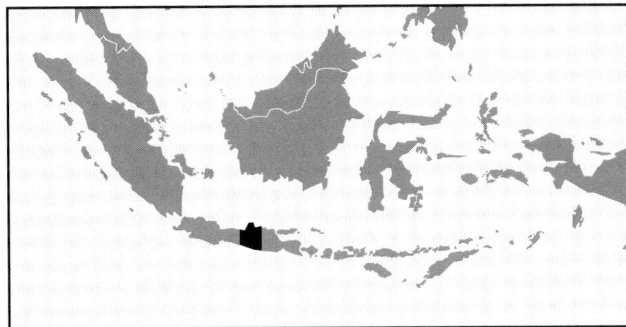

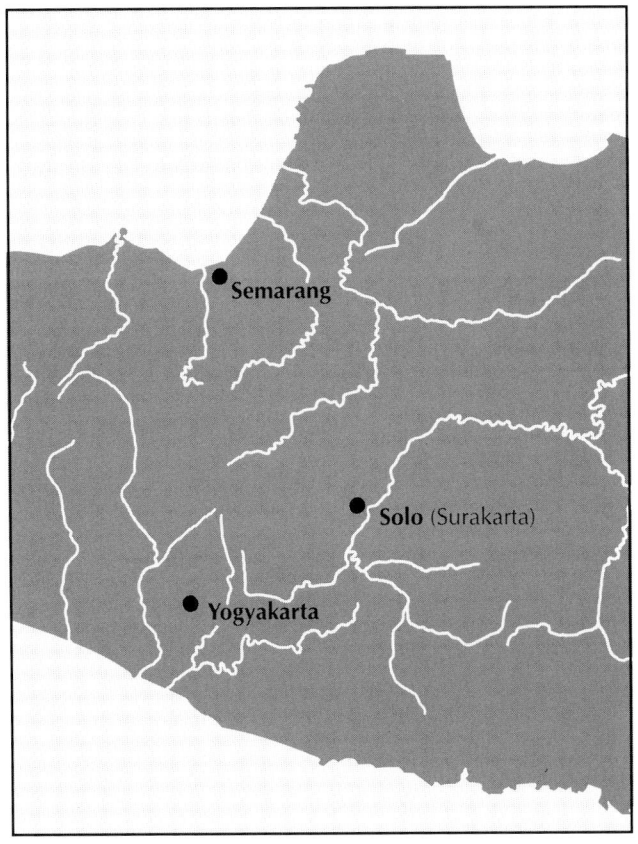

Central Java.

While it might appear surprising to discuss traditional textiles in the context of contemporary politics, the textiles of Southeast Asia have often reflected the social and political divisions of the communities that make and use them. Frequently containing designs and patterns symbolic of power and authority, traditional textiles have often served to indicate rank and status, particularly membership of a ruling elite.

Batik, textiles patterned by the wax-resist technique, over the centuries have reflected the history and politics of Java, as ancient indigenous patterns have been supplemented by designs derived from exotic foreign sources. Changes in motif have often reflected new or changing political influences. Indian motifs on batik illustrate both the divine statecraft of the Hindu-Buddhist world and the value of imported luxury trade goods. Islamic motifs indicate the growing importance of another religion and ideology, and European and Chinese designs reflect the dominant role these groups played in colonial times. Hence batik cloths display many of the historic divisions within Javanese society. Style, color, and design distinguish the various regions of Java from one another, in particular marking off the Central Javanese kingdoms from the coastal towns. In the traditional royal principalities of Central Java certain designs have been associated in the past with the Javanese aristocracy, and until the effective power and authority of those domains declined in late colonial times, such designs were forbidden to commoners outside court circles.

Mohamad Hadi and His Times

The relationship between politics and art is clearly evident in the life and work of a little-known Javanese artist, Mohamad Hadi, who for a short period during the early 1960s created some remarkable batiks. Hadi succeeded in combining a number of traditional design elements, certain original technical innovations and, on some of his batiks, a powerful political message.

Usually nothing is known about the individual textile artisans who made the objects that find their way into gallery and museum collections; consequently it is the textiles themselves, often in isolation, that are the object of scrutiny and explanation. However, to understand their real meaning and purpose it can help to have biographical data about those who made them. Batik is better served than other textiles in this regard, as at least a little is known about a handful of twentieth century batik artisans; and while fragmentary, the little we are able to record about the life and work of Mohamad Hadi provides valuable insights not only into his own work but also into a chapter of Indonesian artistic experience that remains clouded with ambiguity and controversy.[1]

Mohamad Hadi was born in Solo in 1916. It is evident from his name that his family were devout Moslems and their home was located in the *kauman* district near one of the principal mosques of Solo. His family appear to have had good connections with both the Susuhunanate and the Mangkunegårån, the two royal houses that maintain courts within the precincts of the city. Hadi's uncle, K.R.T. Hardipaningrat, was the senior Islamic official (*penghulu*) at the *kraton* of the Susuhunan from 1960 until his death in 1975, and also the administrative head of the palace's Radya Pustaka Museum. While we cannot relate anything of Hadi's early formative experiences or his activities during World War II and the subsequent revolution, we know that he began his working life as an elementary school teacher. It appears that, despite his apparently Islamic family background, like his uncle he was attracted to traditional forms of Javanese culture, in particular the Javanese theater (*wayang*) and mysticism (*kabatinan*). As a young man Hadi became interested in the arts and turned his attention especially to the medium of painting. Although it is doubtful that he ever received any formal training, he soon became well known in the Solo area as a painter. Active in the Surakarta Cultural Association (Himpunan Budaya Surakarta[2]), he established himself as a prominent identity in the city's cultural and artistic elite.

During the 1950s Hadi, like many Indonesian painters, was drawn into radical and left-wing artistic circles through his involvement with the Institute of People's Culture (Lembaga Kebudayaan Rakyat, or Lekra). Lekra had been founded in August 1950 in the wake of radical nationalist opposition to the cultural exchange accord which was a part of the Round Table Conference agreement between the Netherlands and Indonesia in 1949 at the conclusion of the struggle for independence.[3] During the 1950s Lekra developed into an important broadly-based forum of writers, artists, musicians, and performers who espoused a radical-nationalist cultural position. This group rejected the domination of Western cultural and artistic influences and sought to establish the grounds for an independent national culture based upon the interests and shared experiences of the Indonesian people. While the organization was never formally attached to the Indonesian Communist Party (Partai Komunis Indonesia, or PKI), and few Lekra artists were actually members of that political party, PKI activists were evident in both its leadership and membership. Although the relationship between Lekra and the PKI remains unclear,[4] throughout the 1950s Lekra displayed its radical and nationalist character in the way it supported the strengthening and revitalization of Indonesian folk and popular art traditions and actively promoted a class-based radical ideology to achieve a "people's culture."

Solo had one of the largest and most active Lekra branches in the country. Hadi became one of its leading members and by the late 1950s had been appointed the head of its Central Java provincial branch (Holt 1967:246). In January 1959 Solo played host to the First Lekra National Congress, an important event that brought about significant structural reforms and a new assertive cultural offensive by the organization (Foulcher 1986:105-7). The National Congress was preceded by a painting exhibition in Jakarta, sponsored by Lekra, which represented more than sixty Indonesian artists and included two of Mohamad Hadi's own paintings.[5] The Congress proceedings were held at the Sriwedari Park, headquarters of the famous Solo *wayang wong* dance-drama troupe, and were accompanied by a week of cultural exhibits and performances. Hadi himself, in his capacity as deputy chairman of the Congress organizing committee, formally opened the proceedings with a short speech[6] and during the week's deliberations he represented Central Java on the Congress presidium.[7]

Perhaps it was through their mutual involvement with Lekra that Hadi became a close friend of Utomo Ramelan, a prominent member of a well-known Solo family.[8] He and his wife shared Hadi's interest in painting and the arts, and were particularly active in left-wing artistic circles. Utomo Ramelan was also originally a school teacher but by the late 1950s was launched into a career in local politics, and with the active support of the PKI had assumed the important position of mayor (*wali kota*) of the city of Solo.

By this time Hadi had also become a senior government official and had been appointed head of the cultural section of the Solo office of the Department of Education and Culture. As a painter he was himself involved in the task of preparing some of the large decorative political banners which were used at mass meetings, ceremonies and official functions. He was also commissioned to paint sets and backdrops for the

Sriwedari *wayang wong* theater on the occasion of the All Indonesia Festival of *Wayang Wong*, which was held in Solo in 1962 and opened by the Minister of Education and Culture, Professor Prijono. These sets are still in use today.

It was not until the 1960s, however, that Hadi turned his attention to the possibilities of batik as a means of artistic expression. Although it appears that he had no background as a batik maker, some time after 1960 Hadi and his wife Sutrisni[9] established a batik workshop in Solo as a means of supplementing their income. We do not know how many batiks were produced during the short time that it operated under Hadi's direction; it seems likely that the output was quite small and only a few examples of his batiks have been positively identified. Although some of these appear to have been based on floral and aquatic designs in a typically Central Javanese and Surakarta style,[10] he was also responsible for producing a number of batiks with an overt political message.

Batik in its classical Central Javanese form has become, like *wayang*, closely identified in its history and development with the Javanese aristocracy and the royal court centers of Yogyakarta and Surakarta. This presented a particular problem for Lekra and its supporters, for although it was an important plank of the organization's radical nationalist policy during the 1950s to support national "folk" art forms (Foulcher 1986:30-31,112-13), the association of batik and *wayang* with what were regarded to be the "feudal" traditions of Javanese society and the conservative court circles, placed the organization and its supporters in an ambiguous position. It became important for Lekra artists to find a way of fusing these art forms with the artistic expression of the common people as part of the search for a "people's art."

In his own exploration of batik as an art form, Hadi attempted to grapple with this dilemma. While he used materials, techniques, and even certain motifs that were traditional, he also set out to inject many of his designs with a contemporary political theme in line with the pro-*rakyat*, or pro-people's, perspective espoused by Lekra and its supporters and by the radical nationalist politics of the Indonesian government during the early nineteen-sixties.

Hadi's batiks were not only all designed while he was an active member of Lekra; they were also completed during the Guided Democracy period when politics in Indonesia were moving steadily to the left under the direction of President Sukarno's radical nationalist ideology, based on the Political Manifesto he had announced on August 17, 1959. This was the period in external affairs when Indonesia embarked upon the campaign to reclaim West Irian from the Dutch, and then later opposed the formation of Malaysia by its policy of Confrontation. The President declared Indonesia to be aligned with what he termed the New Emerging Forces of world politics and to be in opposition to the Old Established Forces represented by Western imperial and colonial powers. And just as Western-style parliamentary democracy—"free-fight liberalism"—was rejected, so too were Western-inspired artistic endeavors (including films, literature, and painting). Sukarno, himself a staunch patron of the arts, was known to favor the promotion of Indonesian popular national art forms, including the use of batik as national dress. He also encouraged art that promoted the notion of an Indonesian cultural identity and depicted the domestic and international political aspirations of the Guided Democracy regime.[11]

This period of Indonesian politics was effectively ended by the attempted coup in Jakarta of September 30, 1965, since this event gave the armed forces the opportunity to crush their political opponents. Although this was merely the beginning of a slow, protracted political struggle to replace the old political order of President Sukarno with a new regime led by Major General Suharto, the PKI in particular and the left in general were quickly destroyed.

In late October 1965 as the Indonesian army began its sweep across Java against the PKI, the region around Solo was one of the few places to offer some resistance (Crouch 1978:149-50). However this was shortlived; the city of Solo was quickly occupied and its mayor, Utomo Ramelan, arrested.[12] In the weeks and months that followed hundreds of thousands of Indonesians were killed and tens of thousands arrested as the anti-communist campaign ran its course. The PKI was banned, along with many other organizations accused by the army of harboring communists. This included Lekra, and Hadi himself was one of many members to be arrested. Although never formally charged or put on trial, he was held in a detention center for political prisoners near Salatiga in Central Java until 1976. After his detention, his wife Sutrisni remarried and continued to produce batiks under her own name using many of Hadi's non-political designs. Hadi himself resumed painting while in detention. Upon his release he also remarried and he and his new wife, a village batik maker, began making batik again in a small way. Hadi lived quietly outside Solo until his death in 1983, as one who knew him describes it, "a victim of the times."

Mohamad Hadi's Batiks

Hadi's designs for hand-drawn (*tulis*) batik were worked on cotton cloth (*mori*) of the finest quality (*primissima*). Despite his background as a painter, there was a deliberate decision to work within the established classical medium and all his designs were intended for the standard Central Javanese skirt (*kain panjang*) of approximately one by two and a half

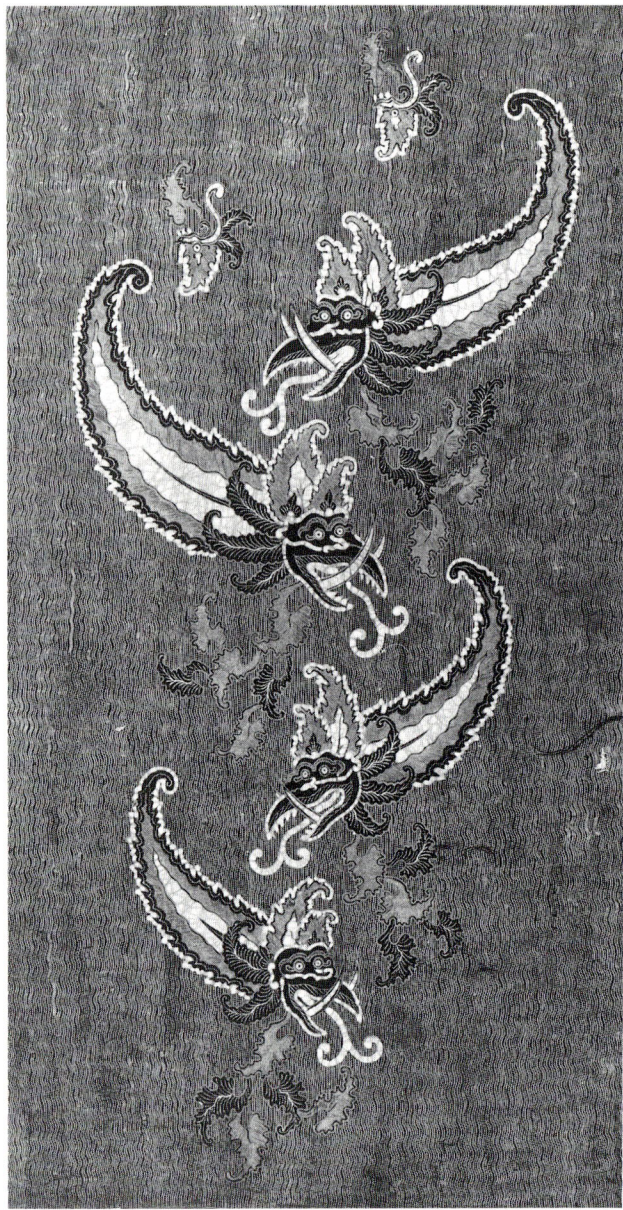

Figure 1 (detail of Figure 13). "Galar Sumping Dåråwati" (The Ceremonial Ear Ornament Pattern). Batik skirtcloth (kain panjang) designed by Mohamad Hadi (Trishadi workshop). Solo, Java, 1966. Cotton, natural dyes, 104.0 x 251.0 cm. Purchased from Gallery Shop Funds, 1984. Australian National Gallery, Canberra, 1984.3066.

meters.[13] The modern style of free batik painting on cloth sizes akin to actual paintings, which became popular in the homes of the urban, Westernized Indonesian elite, particularly during the late 1960s and 1970s, had no attraction for Hadi. Instead, he was attempting to use the structure of traditional Javanese batik as a vehicle for his own purpose. His batiks were very carefully executed with the waxing pen (canting), and not with the faster, cruder, and more common block waxing process (cap).

Hadi's batiks are greatly enhanced by his use of rich traditional dyes: blue-black indigo (tarum or tom, or the Sanskrit-derived nila or nula) from the leaves of Indigo tinctoria or Marsdenia tinctoria and the distinctive brown (soga) from the bark of Pelthophorum ferrugineum for which the Central Javanese batiks are famous. At a time when a number of the prominent batik designers of Surakarta, such as K.R.T. Hardjonagoro, were experimenting with naphthol dyes in an attempt to marry north coast and central Javanese batik styles to achieve a new aesthetic,[14] it is ironic that a painter accustomed to a wide palette of colors accepted the restrictions imposed by traditional dyestuffs.

Like many of the most beautiful Surakarta traditional batik textiles of the 1960s and 1970s, his remarkable brown dyes (babaran soga) can be credited to the skills of Ibu Kangjeng Wonogiri, the wife of a former Regent (Bupati) of Wonogiri, a district within the suzerainty of the Mangkunegårån principality. Ibu Kangjeng Wonogiri was renowned for the quality of her soga dyes, although this was attributed by some to phenomena such as the chemical composition of Wonogiri water. On retirement and the death of her husband, she was granted for her lifetime a home within the precincts of the palace, the Mangkunegårån kraton in Solo, where she established a workshop (pers. comm., N. Tirtaamidjaja, Canberra, 1984). The batiks, which glowed with the wonderful brown color of her dyes, became generally known as batik kanjengan wonogiri, batik kanjengan or batik wonogiren. Although Ibu Kangjeng Wonogiri died in the mid-1970s, her daughter, Raden Ajeng Praptini Hardjowiratmo, had already assumed a leading role in continuing her soga dyeing skills.[15] Mohamad Hadi was sufficiently well-connected to gain access to Praptini's limited and strictly monitored workshop, circumstances he shared with the royal family and the best known batik makers of the Mangkunegårån, including Nyai Bei Mardusari.[16]

Hadi made one important contribution to batik technical procedures. His interest in the craft of waxing and soga dyeing led to experimentation; he and his wife are credited with the introduction of a new decorative technique, wax crackling (remukan?).[17] Hadi discovered that by modifying the pure waxes

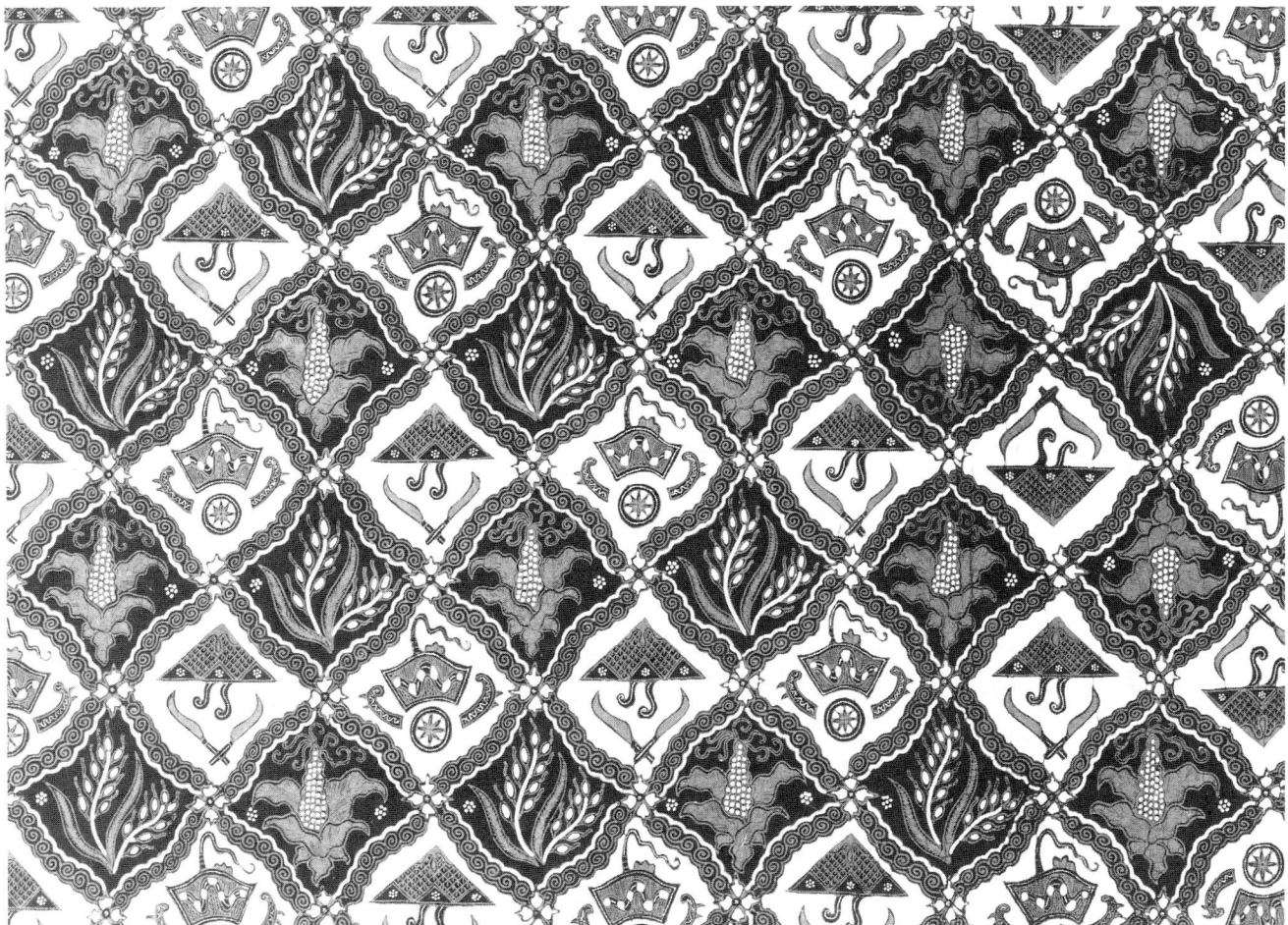

Figure 2. "Ceplok Tani" (The Peasants' Grid Pattern). Batik skirtcloth (kain panjang) *designed by Mohamad Hadi. Solo, Java, 1965. Cotton, natural dyes. 251.2 x 105.4 cm. Purchased from Gallery Shop Funds, 1984. Australian National Gallery, Canberra, 1984.3063.*

applied to the surface of the cotton cloth which is to remain cream, a gentle crumpling and cracking of the wax results in the *soga* dye seeping through to create a subtle brown marbling on the light fawn background area, against which the main motifs and designs appear superimposed (Fig. 1). The crackled effect provided a faster and perhaps cheaper method of achieving the background patterning on a batik, since the more painstaking and detailed filling patterns (*isen-isen*) are, by this method, rendered unnecessary. Whether Hadi's motivation was primarily aesthetic or economic is not known, but the "crackled" style pioneered in their workshop quickly became popular and was widely known as *wonogiren*.

However it was Hadi's batik designs (*seratan*) which were especially significant. He drafted his ideas into sketchbooks, and local women were employed to wax the designs onto the cloth. (As far as we are aware, Hadi's role in the actual batik process was restricted to the drafting of designs and the overseeing of the business.) Elements of his experience as a painter are evident in his designs: the patterns are conceived in a bold, clear, linear style and unlike the customary etiquette of classical Central Javanese artisans, his batiks, though in the *kain panjang* skirt form, are signed, dated, and often named.[18] But Hadi usually worked within accepted and classical Solo pattern categories, such as *semèn*, *garis miring*, *truntum*, and *ceplokan*.[19] His distinctive contribution can be seen in the way he harnessed and transformed the motifs that are a normal part of these designs into symbols of contemporary political and social issues.

"Ceplok Tani" The Peasants' Grid Pattern

Although the name of the batik in Figure 2 is not inscribed on the textile there seems to be general agreement that *"Ceplok Tani"* was Hadi's title. The batik is signed in the upper corner MD.HADI SOLO 12.65.[20] The design adapts one of the best known and most distinctive of the Mangkunegårån patterns, *sidå mukti* (Fig. 3). This pattern falls within one of the major Central Javanese batik design categories, *ceplok* or

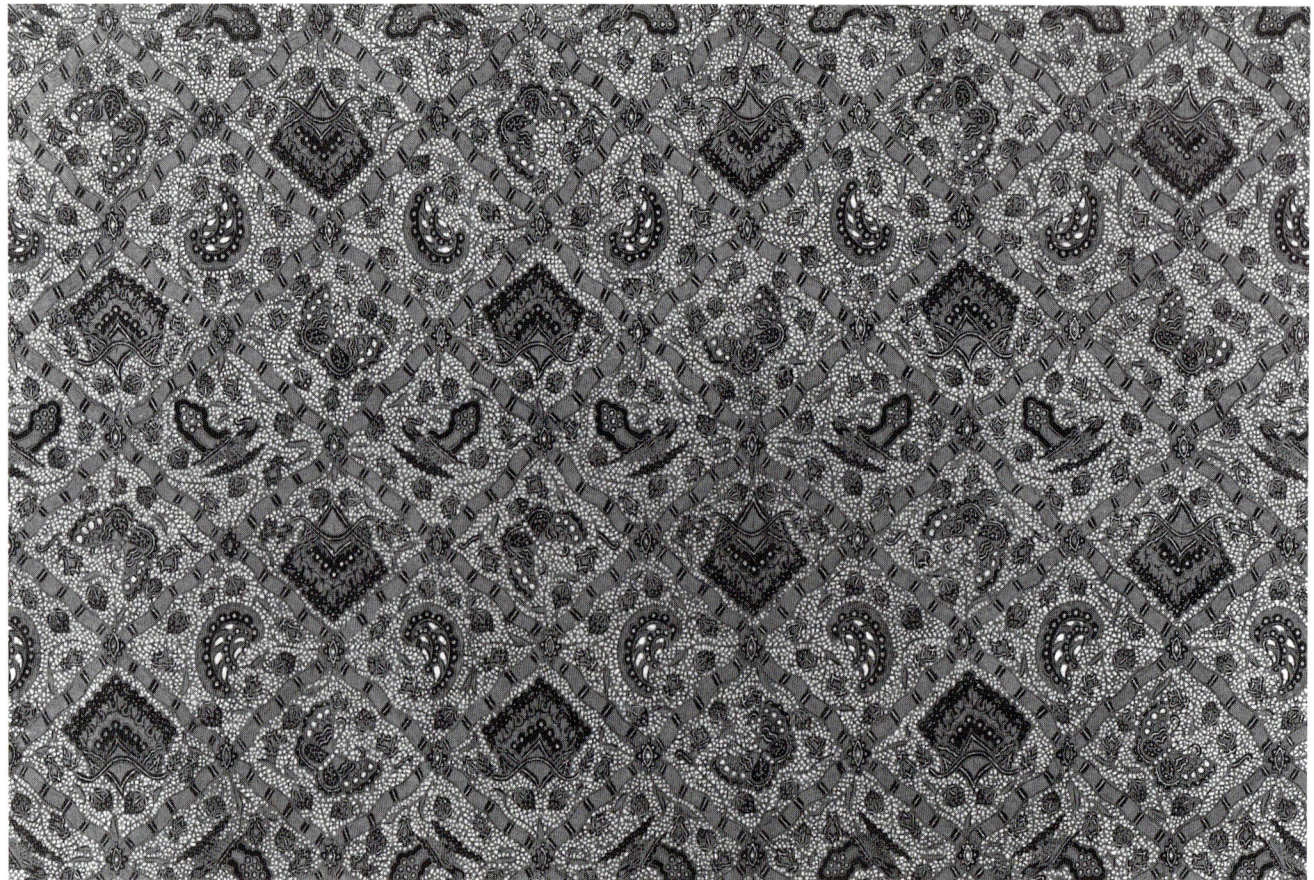

Figure 3. *Good fortune and prosperity pattern known as* sidå mukti. *Batik skirtcloth* (kain panjang). *Solo, Java, circa 1965. Cotton, natural dyes. 257.0 x 104.0 cm. Purchased from Gallery Shop Funds, 1984. Australian National Gallery, Canberra, 1984.3076.*

ceplokan. These consist of geometric patterns often forming a diagonal lattice or grid, within which realistic motifs may be found (Tirtaamidjaja et al. 1966:11-12, 25). On the classical *sidå mukti* and the closely related *sidå luhur* and *sidå mulya*, the lattice is filled with propitious symbols promising good fortune to the wearer, and today batiks of these patterns are particularly popular throughout Java with bridal couples and with young men at circumcisions. The titles of these patterns convey messages of good fortune and wishes for a glorious and noble future (Jasper and Pirngadie 1916:225-26; Haake 1984:58-59).

Each of these traditional batiks features a similar design format, although slightly different objects fill the grids, and the backgrounds differ significantly. In fact the plain, light, unfilled ground of the *sidå luhur* is closer to Hadi's "Ceplok Tani" design than the filling of tiny hooks (*ukel*) characteristic of the *sidå mukti* pattern. The plain grounds of Hadi's batik, alternating between black and cream, enhance the clarity of the motifs in a way that is not possible with the conventional intricate filling (*isen-isen*) found on many Surakarta designs. In Hadi's design the spiral shapes of the *ukel* have been incorporated into the interlocking grid. Another change to the classical *sidå mukti*, and a feature of a number of Hadi's designs, is the division of the surface pattern into two halves and the subtle reversal of the pattern to form the style known as *pagi-soré* (morning and evening), which permits the skirt to be turned around and worn on different occasions with either end of the design revealed.

Among the fine foliage of leaves and flowers on the traditional *sidå mukti* wedding cloth a number of familiar motifs appear. The symbol of the Garuda, the mighty bird of the Hindu-Buddhist Ramayana legend, is usually depicted by the *lar* (the single ornate wing), although some versions of the *sidå* patterns show the *lar* with the truncated body of the Garuda or the mythical winged serpent (*någå*), also a propitious symbol. Another stylized bird, sometimes with an elaborate down-sweeping tail, suggests a peacock, while in some versions of the *sidå mukti* designs it resembles the phoenix. The butterfly is clear and unmistakable, a feature most commonly associated with north coast batik designs, especially on cloth intended for use at the weddings of Indonesian-born Chinese (*peranakan*), where it signifies happiness and joy. In contrast, the triangular motif has Hindu-Buddhist origins and represents a stylized cosmic mountain, the Mahameru, or its earthly replica, the temple-pavilion shape.[21] Although schematically drawn, the shrine often rests on a curving line which appears to be a stylized relic of an ancient serpent-boat motif.[22]

The inclusion of auspicious symbols of ancient and foreign origin has been a source of rich iconographic invention on many Indonesian textiles, including batik. Old Indian trade cloths with similar lattice designs are part of the heirlooms of the aristocracy and an ancient magical painted cloth (*kain kumudåwati*, meaning "rich in white lotus blossom") is used in Solo's Kraton Hadiningrat as a seat for royal brides. This type of cloth may have been an important source of inspiration for the bridal *sidå mukti* design, since the *kain kumudåwati* itself displays a diagonal lattice grid containing motifs such as a stylized lotus star, semi-realistic animals, and insects.[23] The custom of elevating a bridal couple to "king and queen for the day" which has spread throughout Southeast Asia may have contributed to the widespread use in Java of a batik pattern originating from within the Mangkunegåran court.

Hadi's choice of one of the best known and recognized batik patterns was clearly intentional. He has taken the familiar *sidå mukti* motifs that appear within the lattice and has subtly adapted their shapes into new symbols. In an evocation of future blessings, good fortune and noble ideals, he has transformed the well-known—though not always understood—auspicious elements of the wedding cloth into symbols of a new social order and the glorification of the Javanese peasant farmer (*wong tani*).

One Utopian agricultural image is the two-wheeled ox cart (*grobag*), here transformed into the fine chariot of classical art with a floating banner which will carry the peasant to a bright victorious future. Hadi's rendition of this motif draws upon many sources. The sun-wheel (*cåkrå*), the ancient Indian symbol of the wheel of law, is widely used in classical Javanese art and literature as the wheel of fortune and the cycle of life. Here it is flanked with upward curving hooks that evoke the *någå* serpent, the bows of the ship, or the paired Garuda wings (*lar mirong*) of some *sidå mukti* patterns.

Both the body of the chariot and the peasant's sunhat—another striking motif in the *"Ceplok Tani"* design—draw upon the *sidå mukti* temple-cosmic mountain triangular shape and the sinuous roots of the cosmic tree that are often part of this symbol.[24] Below the hat the upward curving lines are repeated, this time in the form of crossed sickles (*arit*), an attempt to promote the position of the ordinary people of rural Java by displaying one of the tools of their hard physical labor (just as the well-known hammer and sickle is used to symbolize the struggle of workers and peasants).

While he retained the basic shapes of certain traditional symbols, Hadi also introduced new elements into his design which were evocative of fertility and well-being appropriate to a wedding cloth. Instead of birds and insects Hadi substituted robust ears of corn and stalks of rice. Like the sunhat and the crossed sickles, these were to be recurring motifs on many of his batik designs, which were committed to elevating the status of the peasantry as the most important social class in Indonesian society.

"Srikandi Gerwani": Srikandi as Goddess of the Indonesian Women's Movement

Other social and political aspects of peasant life are evident in a Hadi design to which two different titles have been attributed (Pl. 21). This batik, which reinterprets another well-known classical pattern, is also signed in one corner IX MD.HADI SOLO 1964. A name suggested for the design is *"Berdikari,"* one of the many acronyms made popular by President Sukarno during Guided Democracy. *Berdikari* literally means "to stand on own's own feet" (*berdiri di atas kaki sendiri*) and evokes the notion of national self-reliance. However, the other suggested name for the design, *"Srikandi Gerwani,"* is more specific and in view of the content of the batik's design seems even more appropriate. Srikandi is the name of a prominent female character from the great Hindu Mahabharata legends which are a major source of themes for Javanese theater and art, while Gerwani is an acronym for Gerakan Wanita Indonesia, the Indonesian Women's Movement, an organization led and directed by the PKI. Gerwani was very active in social development and rural reform in the Javanese countryside throughout the 1950s and early 1960s when Hadi was creating his batiks.[25]

For the design of *"Srikandi Gerwani,"* Hadi relied on a number of classical Javanese sources and conventions. In particular, the figures on the batik are depicted in the flat, two-dimensional, stylized form of Javanese leather shadow puppets (*wayang kulit*). Traditional theater, especially the shadow puppet play, has been used in Javanese society to provide role models of appropriate behavior. The personalities and behavior of its well-known characters, and their experiences and adventures, have been studied to see what lessons can be applied to the real world. Moreover, *wayang* theater performances have often been used to explore contemporary political themes, present political propaganda and comment critically on current events. In particular, the jesting of the clown retainers (*pånåkawan*) of the aristocracy has often been used as a vehicle for the expression of contemporary

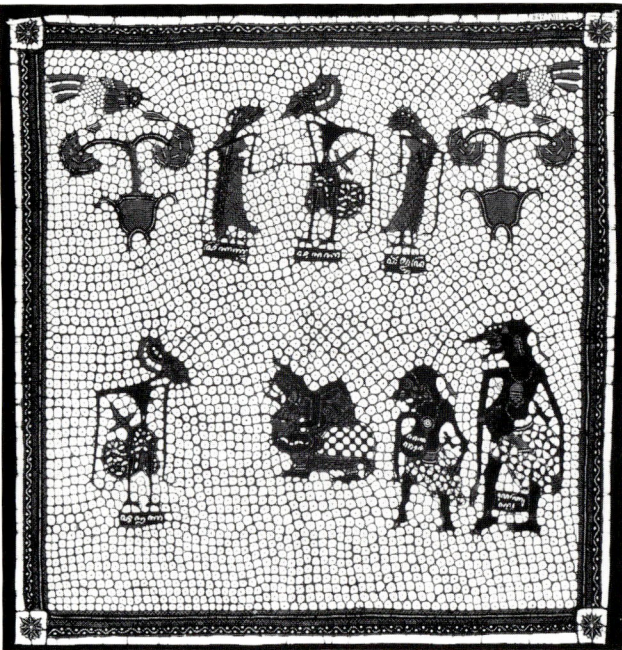

Figure 4. Classical design known as gringsing wayang *appearing on a small batik pattern sampler. Yogyakarta, Java, circa 1890. Cotton, natural dyes. Rijksmuseum voor Volkenkunde, Leiden, 847.114.*

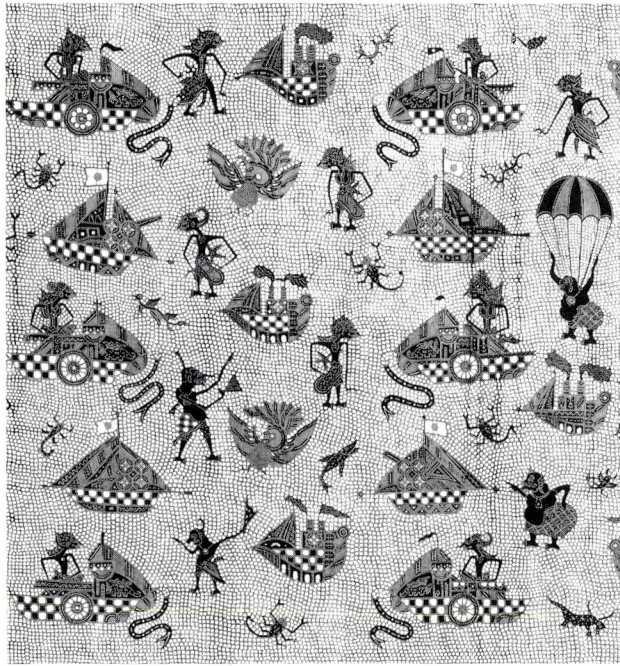

Figure 5. Detail of a classical gringsing wayang *design appearing on a batik skirtcloth* (kain panjang). *Yogyakarta, Java, circa 1942. Cotton, natural dyes, 240.0 x 106.0 cm. Purchased from Gallery Shop Funds, 1984. Australian National Gallery, Canberra, 1984.3110.*

social views, a custom that continued into the 1960s despite isolated attempts at official censorship.[26] Thus *wayang* characters provided Hadi with an ideal batik pattern to use as a vehicle for his own social and political ideas.

Figures in the style of *wayang* characters appear against a scaly background (*gringsing*) on one of the classical batik designs, *gringsing wayang*. An early set of batik samplers which came into the collection of the Rijksmuseum voor Volkenkunde, Leiden, from Dr. I. Groneman in 1891-92, includes an example of the *gringsing wayang* pattern with Javanese script on the base of the puppet figures' feet (Fig. 4).[27] Just as the *wayang* theater provided a medium for political and social comment, so too did certain batik designs displaying *wayang* figures. This is illustrated by a *kain panjang* cloth with a *gringsing wayang* design, made during World War II in Yogyakarta (Fig. 5). Noble figures of the warrior class (*satriya*) are depicted in battle on foot and in multi-patterned and checkered tanks or amphibious vehicles. Their weapons are the arrows, the traditional daggers (*keris*) and the razor sharp fingernails (*pancanakha*) used by characters in the *wayang kulit* legends. The clown figures (*pånåkawan*) accompany their noble masters and, as usual, the rotund shape of Semar dominates the scene as he falls from an open parachute. Since the enemy's sailing and steam ships appear to fly the Japanese flag, this batik was probably made during the Japanese occupation of Indonesia (1942-45).[28] Minor motifs include crustaceans and birds, and the filling pattern (*isen-isen*) is the scaly *gringsing* design that usually appears on the classical *wayang* batiks of Yogyakarta. This is a particularly appropriate background for a battle scene, since early Javanese chronicles record that the wearing of *gringsing* cloths rendered warriors invulnerable to harm.[29]

Although it may have been influenced by the well-known Yogyakarta *gringsing wayang* pattern, Mohamad Hadi's design is dramatically different. By again adopting the reversible *pagi-soré* structure Hadi was able to present two different *wayang* patterns on one cloth. The change in the background pattern between each half of the cloth is inconspicuous; the subdued *soga* brown clouds or rock shapes become leafy tendrils on a blue-black ground, only occasionally highlighted with cream detail. Two related but distinctively different main patterns are found on each side of the textile. In contrast to the central ground, these major motifs are depicted in shadow form against a light fawn ground, a technique usually associated with the batiks of the Cirebon courts. There is no evidence of tightly pressed pleats at either end of this elaborately decorated *kain panjang*, which indicates that the cloth has never been used. Such figurative cloths are rarely worn, especially in Surakarta.

As his main focus, Hadi chose to use the aristocratic Srikandi, wife of Arjuna, one of the Påndåwa brothers (Fig. 6).[30] The selection of Srikandi was not random and should be seen as a deliberate attempt to depict a certain style of female personality and behavior. Observers steeped in the Hindu legends would not be surprised that Hadi selected Srikandi and not the reserved and dignified Sumbadra, Arjuna's other main wife. As Benedict Anderson points out: "For the Javanese, Srikandi is the honored type of the active, energetic, disputatious, generous, go-getting woman."[31] She has often been used as a model for modern women in recent Indonesian history although her image as the warrior wife has been emphasized above her other characteristics.[32]

Hadi appears to have taken the shadow puppet depiction of Srikandi and transformed it into several versions of the same character, displayed by the three main female figures that appear together in groups across one side of the fabric (see again Pl. 21). Srikandi is portrayed in the first figure as an aristocrat in the classical formal attire of the courts. She wears a wrap skirtcloth of the diagonal *parang* pattern reserved for royalty in Central Java, and the breastcloth (*kemben*) still worn on ceremonial occasions in the Javanese courts. This royal costume is combined with costly jewelry.[33] Her head is uncovered, her hair is elegantly arranged, and she wears a large aristocratic earring. The next figure of Srikandi wears the headcloth of a devout Moslem woman and a modest, long-sleeved, floral blouse (*kebaya*), while the third figure is depicted wearing a striped, short-sleeved jacket of Javanese woven *lurik* and a peasant's sunhat.

We are not certain what Hadi's depiction of these three *wayang* images was intended to mean. It may have been an attempt to represent the principle of Nasakom enunciated by President Sukarno in the early 1960s to symbolize the unity of three major forces in Indonesian society (*nasionalisme, agama, komunisme*—nationalism, religion and Marxism).[34] As a political slogan, Nasakom was taken up and actively promoted by left-wing organizations such as Lekra, Gerwani and the PKI to justify and defend the active role they were playing in government and public affairs.[35]

Whatever the exact meaning of the three Srikandi figures, their depiction is a clear attempt to identify with the cause of peasant women which was being actively promoted under the banner of Gerwani. Throughout the 1950s this organization had been responsible for defending and extending the rights of women in both urban and rural Indonesia, but during the early 1960s Gerwani began to pay special attention to the problems of peasant women and its organizational program was directed at the social and economic concerns of women in village Indonesia as a part of the widespread

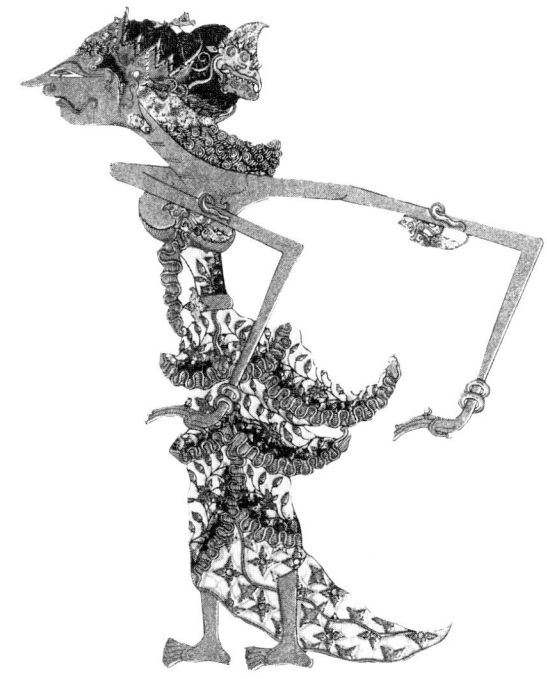

Figure 6. A drawing of Srikandi as a Javanese shadow puppet character. From Kats 1923: opposite 328.

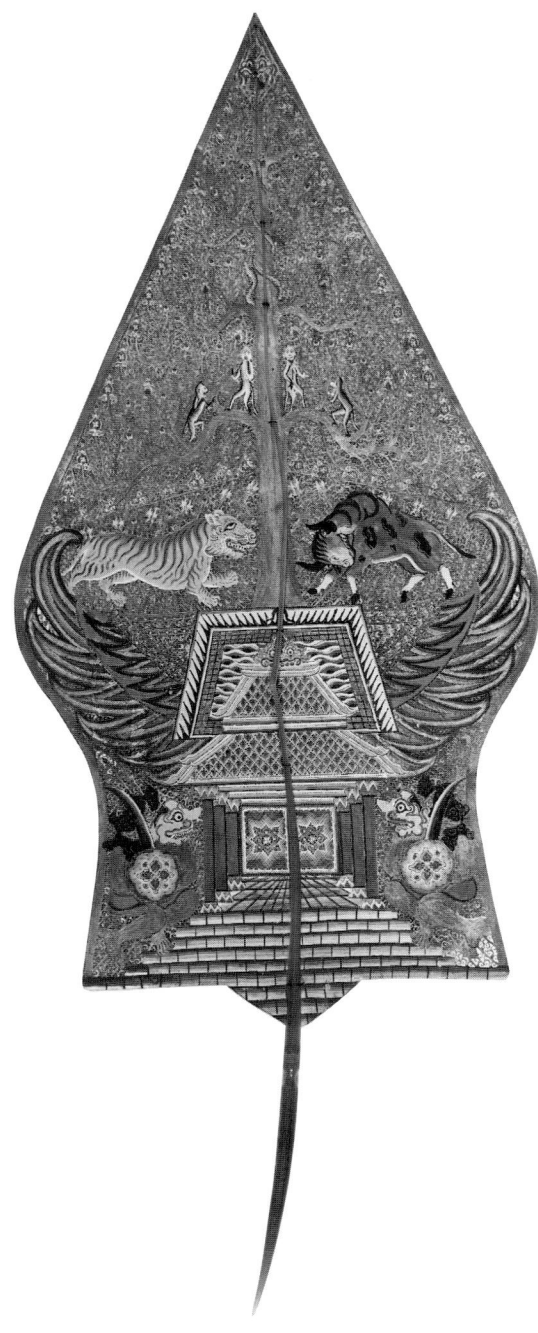

Figure 7. A kekayon or gunungan shadow puppet, Central Java. Collection of David Stuart-Fox, Canberra.

left-wing "go-down-to-the-people" (turun ke bawah) campaign.[36] Gerwani was particularly active in the organization of small scale self-help and credit schemes, literacy courses and campaigns for women's legal and marital rights.

Hadi's three figures carry a floating banner, a book (suggestive of Gerwani literacy campaigns), and an obscure item—perhaps, judging from the deliberately crooked finger, a rice knife (ani-ani). Other peasant women, also wearing striped woven lurik and simple batik, are shown at one end of the cloth carrying the wooden clapper (klonthong) used to sound the alarm or frighten off birds from the ricefields. Hadi has ignored the usual wayang distinction between the profiles of commoners and aristocrats by showing all figures with the fine-pointed features of the rulers and deities. They are depicted as part of an idyll of lush foliage, butterflies, chickens, and ducks.

Along the reverse side of the kain panjang, Hadi has designed a series of cosmic tree-of-life or mountain images, based on the shadow puppet device (Fig. 7) central to every wayang performance and known as kekayon (from kayu = tree, wood) or gunungan (from gunung = mountain). Like the flags above the figures of Srikandi these images follow the pagi-soré convention by increasing in size across the cloth towards the edge displayed when the skirt is correctly wrapped. The smaller kekayon depict various fragments of the cosmic totality: the watery Lower World of fish, crabs, frogs, and snakes below the sacred lotus with entangled roots; the Upper World of birds, flowering trees, and the sun; and the symbolic cosmic axis of the flowering tree entwined by the serpent-snake, its branches filled with animals and birds, and flanked by noble beasts such as the elephant and tiger. The tree rises out of a temple-pavilion, which also represents Mount Meru, the cosmic mountain at the center of the universe.[37] The largest kekayon motif combines many of these symbolic elements of the Upper and Lower Worlds.

In wayang performances, the kekayon or gunungan is used to indicate changes in scene and the passing of time. When fluttered vigorously by the puppeteer (dalang), it is also an indication of tumultuous events. Hadi has used these allusions to the traditional role of the kekayon to direct attention to the far-reaching social and political changes that seemed to him about to occur during the early 1960s in Indonesia.[38]

"NEFO": The New Emerging Forces

The batik seen in Figures 8a,b and c is signed MD.HADI SOLO 1964 in the upper left corner; but its title is contained in the inscriptions in the upper right and lower left-hand corners of the cloth, "NEFO" MD.HADI SOLO 1964 (Fig. 8c). NEFO was an abbreviation of the term New Emerging Forces, one of

Batiks of Mohamad Hadi

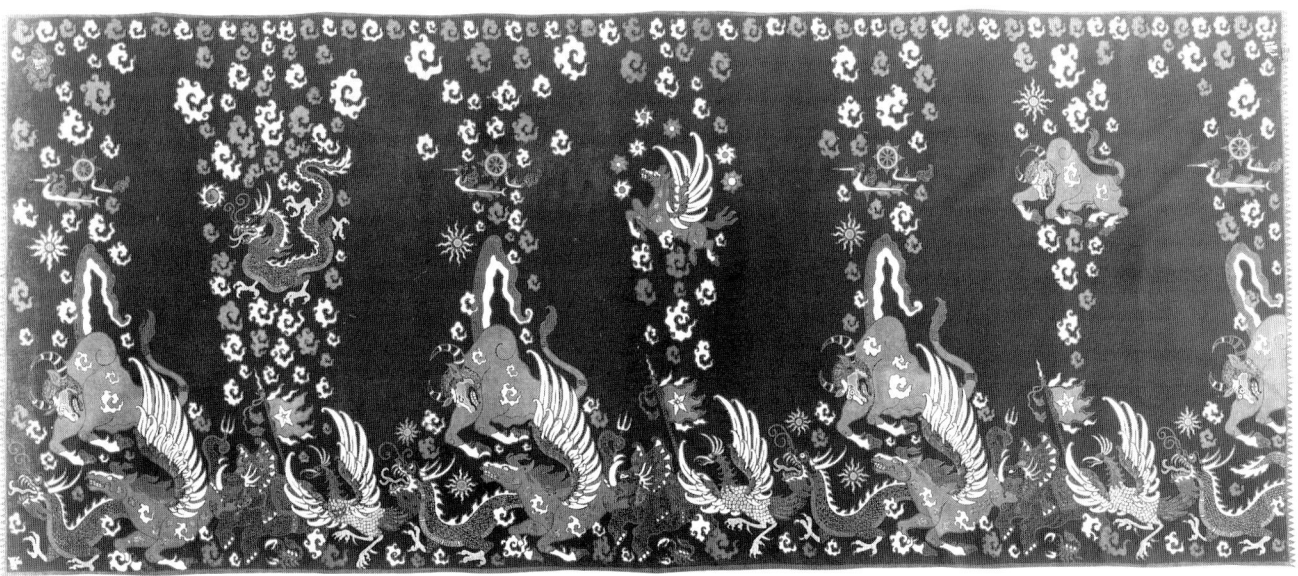

Figures 8a, (above), b, c, (details, below left and right). "NEFO" (The New Emerging Forces). Batik skirtcloth (kain panjang) designed by Mohamad Hadi. Solo, Java, Indonesia, 1964. Cotton, natural dyes. 105.0 x 250.0 cm. Purchased from Gallery Shop Funds, 1984. Australian National Gallery, Canberra, 1984.3064.

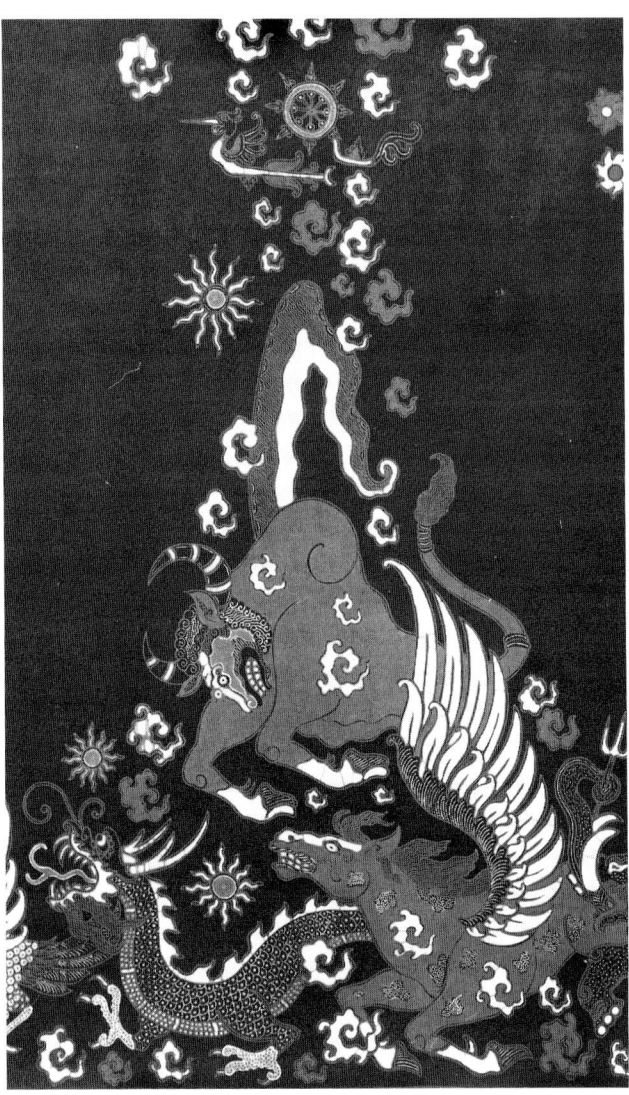
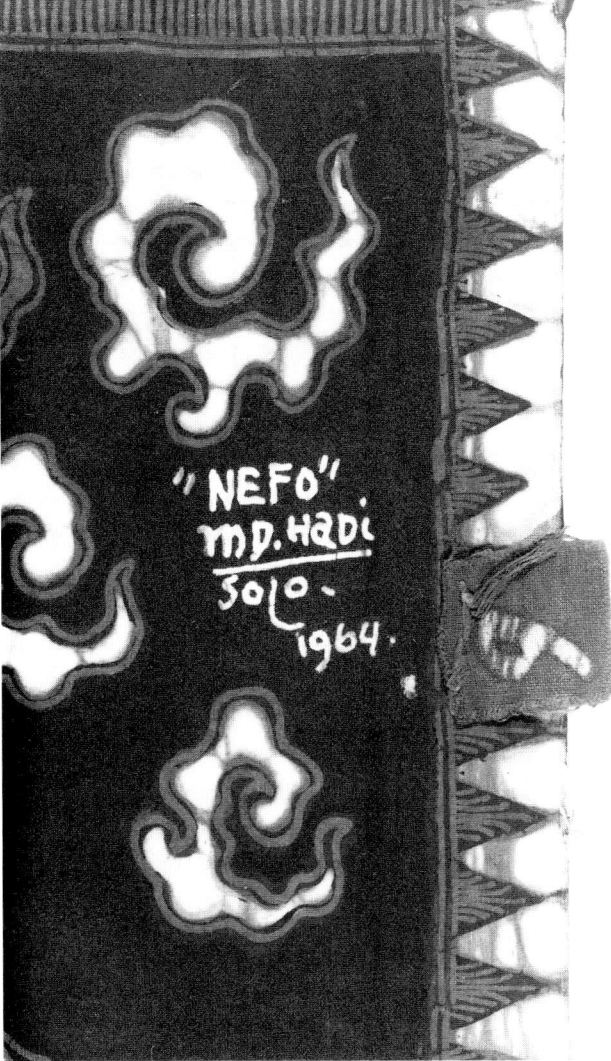

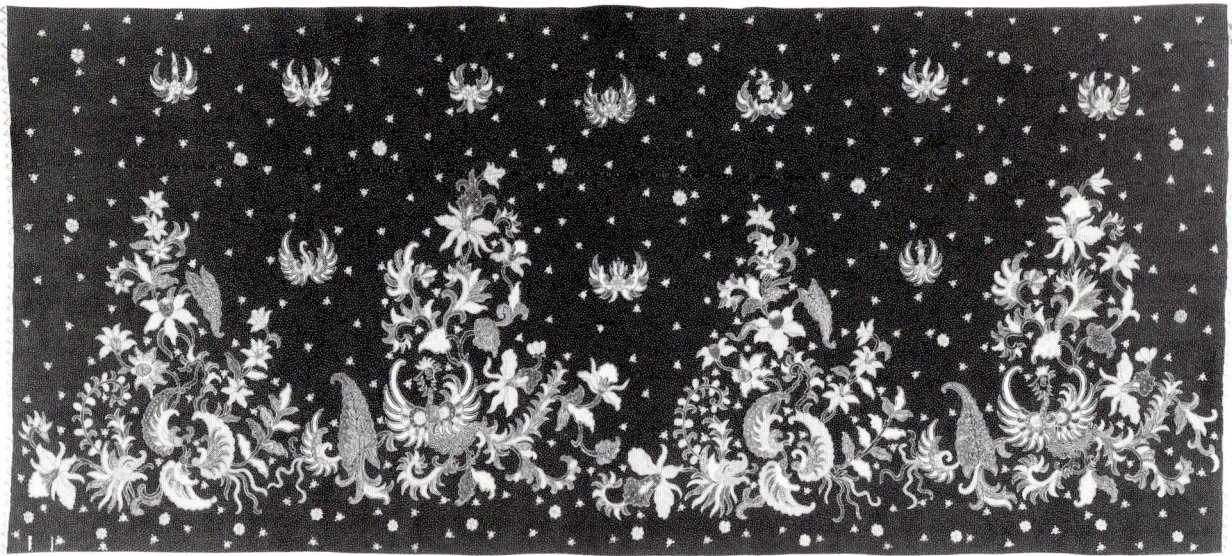

Figure 9. Batik skirtcloth (kain panjang), Cipta Karya workshop. Pekalongan, Java, circa 1970. Cotton, dyes. 104.5 x 240.0 cm. Gift of John and Robyn Maxwell. Australian National Gallery, Canberra, 1988.641.

the ideological constructs coined by President Sukarno during the early 1960s as a part of his dramatic attempt to locate Indonesia's place in the world order and distinguish between its foreign political friends and enemies. Its ideological opposite was Sukarno's notion of Oldefos, the Old Established Forces, and although neither of these slogans was ever rigorously applied or defined by Sukarno, the thrust of his intent was clear.

Sukarno's attitude towards the West in the 1960s was formed against the background of his experience of Dutch colonialism and, more recently, his anger at Western sympathy and support for the regional rebellions in Indonesia of the late 1950s. He saw the affluent Western nations as committed to the continued economic and political oppression of the poor, struggling, and exploited people of Third World countries like Indonesia.[39] The threat posed by these Old Established Forces required Indonesia to align herself with nations who shared the same political interest and experiences. These New Emerging Forces were to be found among the excolonial nations of the Third World, especially in the Afro-Asian,[40] nonaligned and socialist blocs, although exactly which countries were intended to be included under this label was never made explicit.[41]

Although Hadi's batik is executed in traditional Surakarta dyes, he has chosen a design structure influenced by the north-coast batik-producing center of Pekalongan. This style of *kain panjang* skirt design (many characteristic Pekalongan designs favor the cylindrical *kain sarong* form) features a wide, ornate, patterned border along the lower half of the cloth with flame or tendril motifs (*cemukiran*) thrusting into the plainer top section (Fig. 9). This design format

apparently developed during the 1960s as a variation on long-established north coast Chinese and Indo-European styles. The motifs were executed in the most detailed hand-drawn batik penwork on super fine cotton fabric and usually show intertwined flowers and birds although specifically Javanese elements sometimes appear. The example illustrated is signed along the border with the name of the workshop, CIPTA KARYA, and exhibits the bright naphthol dyes of contemporary Pekalongan cloth.[42] Set among the leaves, orchids, and other flowers in the main pattern is a mythical creature, possibly the winged Garuda (shown here in the form of the head and ear ornaments worn by the Javanese aristocracy) or the *makara* (legendary aquatic monsters in the shape of gargoyles). Floating on the finely spotted field[43] are pairs of *sawat* wings with a central spiral body, possibly stylized versions of a phoenix or Garuda or even a winged *någå*-serpent.

Since Hadi's own NEFO design was intended to convey a message of cooperation and solidarity, it is appropriate that he has chosen a style readily recognizable as a favorite of the descendants of Chinese immigrants in Indonesia rather than one of his customary central Javanese designs. But what do the individual design elements represent? Given the vagueness of the New Emerging Forces concept it is not possible to identify all the motifs with certainty although some of the major elements are obvious. The powerful, charging bull, depicted with bold mid-brown hide and bearing an unfurled pennant (suggesting the red and white national flag) clearly represents Indonesia. The creature is the *banteng*, the Javanese wild bull adopted in the late colonial period as a

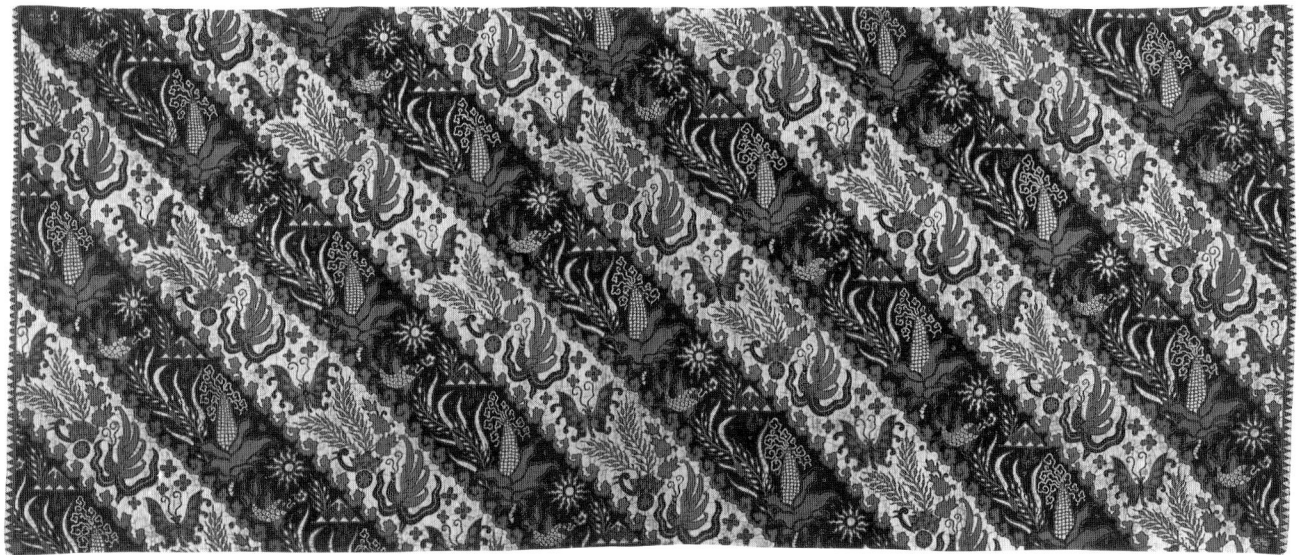

Figure 10. "Jembatan Mas" (The Golden Bridge). Batik skirtcloth (kain panjang) designed by Mohamad Hadi. Solo, Java, 1965. Cotton, natural dyes. 105.5 x 256.0 cm. Australian National Gallery, Canberra, 1987.1056. Also shown in Plate 22.

symbol of Indonesian nationalism.[44] During the 1950s and 1960s the *banteng*, in the same threatening stance, was also used as a political campaign symbol by the Indonesian Nationalist Party (Partai Nasional Indonesia, PNI) which sought to identify itself closely with President Sukarno and his policies, especially in foreign affairs, and which attempted to project itself as the party of the common people (*massa marhaèn*). Here, however, the *banteng* seems intended to represent the Indonesian nation under President Sukarno's leadership and his independent, aggressive style of foreign policy, which had seen the country distance itself from the West during the campaign to claim West Irian in the late 1950s and then the Confrontation policy with Malaysia after 1963. These policies culminated in Indonesia's dramatic withdrawal from the United Nations in late 1964 and Sukarno's repudiation of Western, especially American, foreign aid.

The New Emerging Forces with whom President Sukarno sought to align Indonesia are represented by some of the other creatures on Hadi's batik. A second prominent creature is the dragon, depicted in conventional Chinese style as a symbol of the People's Republic of China with whom Indonesia had forged closer ties under Guided Democracy. A third major motif is the galloping winged horse. Although it appears more like the mythical Greek Pegasus, the *borak* (also *burak, bouraq*)—the legendary winged creature with the body of a horse and a human head, which transported the Prophet Mohammed on his journey to Heaven—is often used in the art of the Islamic peoples of Indonesia, and is closely identified with the Middle East. It is probably intended as a symbol of that region or a particular country within,

perhaps Egypt with whom Indonesia had close relations. (President Nasser and Sukarno were both charismatic nationalist leaders and had much in common. Nasser, like Chou En-lai of China, had attended the 1955 Bandung Conference and Sukarno had paid several official visits to both their countries.) Other animals appear along the lower frieze, including an elephant (a convenient symbol for Afro-Asian solidarity), a small lobster, and a bird or fowl beside a star-decorated flag.[45]

The three main motifs—buffalo, dragon, and horse—appear separately and intertwined amid a cloud or rock pattern, a popular north-coast motif that often appears on Hadi's batik. Another commonly used motif included here in various styles is the flaming sun, a sign of enlightenment. The rendition of the sun motif adjacent to the dragon incorporates the *yin-yang* cosmic unity symbol of the Chinese, who by the mid-1960s were considered one of Jakarta's strongest political allies. A number of other minor images evoke classical Javanese notions of power and military might. The Buddhist wheel of law (*cåkrå*) is best known in Javanese iconography and legend as the magical weapon of Kresna, a legendary Javanese king who is an incarnation of the god Wisnu. It is depicted in Javanese art as an arrow tipped with a blazing wheel of fire.[46] A symbol of the wheel of fortune, the *cåkrå* conveys for the Javanese the notion that things will change and that life proceeds through cycles. The magical arrow (*pasopati*), also depicted in art and *wayang* as a bird or winged *någå*, is the legendary divine but dangerous gift of the gods to favored heroes such as Arjuna.[47] Another weapon of the gods, the trident (*trisula*), is depicted held in the elephant's trunk. The potent weapons and

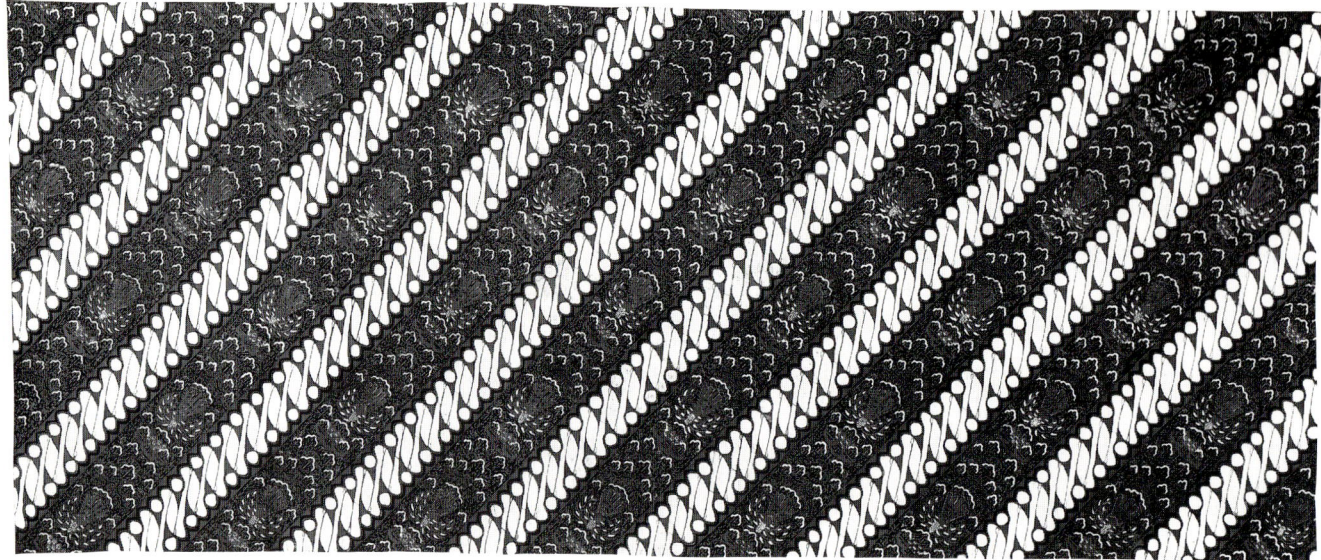

Figure 11. Large broken sword pattern alternating with large plant and landscape pattern (parang rusak barong seling semèn gedé). Batik skirtcloth (kain panjang). Yogyakarta, Java, circa 1930. Cotton, natural dyes. 106.5 x 262.0 cm. Purchased from Gallery Shop Funds, 1984. Australian National Gallery, Canberra, 1984.3113.

the bold aggressive depiction of the animal figures have been combined by Hadi in a strong fluid design which conveys the defiant notion of the NEFO concept.

"Jembatan Mas": The Golden Bridge

As we have noted it was Hadi's practice to select a well-established batik type to explore and expose his ideas. For his batik "Jembatan Mas," the Golden Bridge (Fig. 10, Pl. 22), he chose the ancient *garis miring* (sloping line) style of diagonal design arrangement as a vehicle for Utopian rural symbolism. Although the particular pattern upon which he has based his design is clearly not the noble *parang rusak* (broken sword), which is reserved for members of the Javanese aristocracy, the meander of clouds placed between Hadi's bands is reminiscent of the flame or broken spiral motif on that aristocratic pattern (Fig. 11).

Within the basic *garis miring* design structure, Hadi has adapted elements of the well-known *semèn* (*semi* = shoots, sprouts) pattern. In alternating diagonal rows of crackled cream and indigo-black ground, Hadi has placed the sun, ears of corn, sheaves of rice with the sickle, the fish, and the butterfly. The foliage, presented in a crisp clear style, is the element that holds all *semèn* designs together. The ambiguous winged *någå* serpent-bird suggests the paired wings (*mirong* or *sawat*) and the peacock, all of which are familiar motifs in classical *semèn* iconography. The peaked peasant hat and the chariot-ox cart (*grobag*), from which sprout the basic necessities of life (*sandang pangan*) symbolized by stalks of rice and cotton, form triangular lines similar to the mountains and pavilions of many *semèn* designs (Fig. 11).

Rather than creating an entirely original batik pattern, Hadi seems to have intended those who saw his batiks to identify them as traditional styles which he had endowed with another dimension of meaning. The classical *semèn* patterns are associated in the courts of Central Java with growth and fertility, particularly appropriate at ceremonial occasions such as weddings.[48] Hadi, however, has drawn these symbols of life and prosperity into a contemporary social context, suggesting the prospect of a better future for the peasant farmers of rural Java. The batik's title, "Jembatan Mas," and the golden ripeness of the sun, rice, and corn, are reminders of the popular vision, common throughout Javanese history and literature, of the coming Golden Age. This batik is signed 115-65 MD. HADI SOLO in the upper left corner, and, upside-down, in the lower right corner, although the design is not in *pagi-soré* style.[49]

Other Mohamad Hadi Batik Designs

Many of the themes and motifs already discussed were repeated in other batiks Mohamad Hadi designed. A concern with the place of the peasant (*wong tani*) and an emphasis upon agricultural themes also appear in a design entitled "Sandang Pangan" (The Basic Necessities of Life, literally food and clothing).[50] Hadi has again adapted the well-known *semèn* or *alas-alasan* (*alas* = forest) batik design, and filled it with rural imagery, emphasizing his political and social concerns. The classical Central Javanese *semèn* patterns permit a rather loose combination of plant images, and Hadi's corn, rice, sun, flowers, and leaves stand out strongly against a dark indigo ground. Cloud-like white shapes

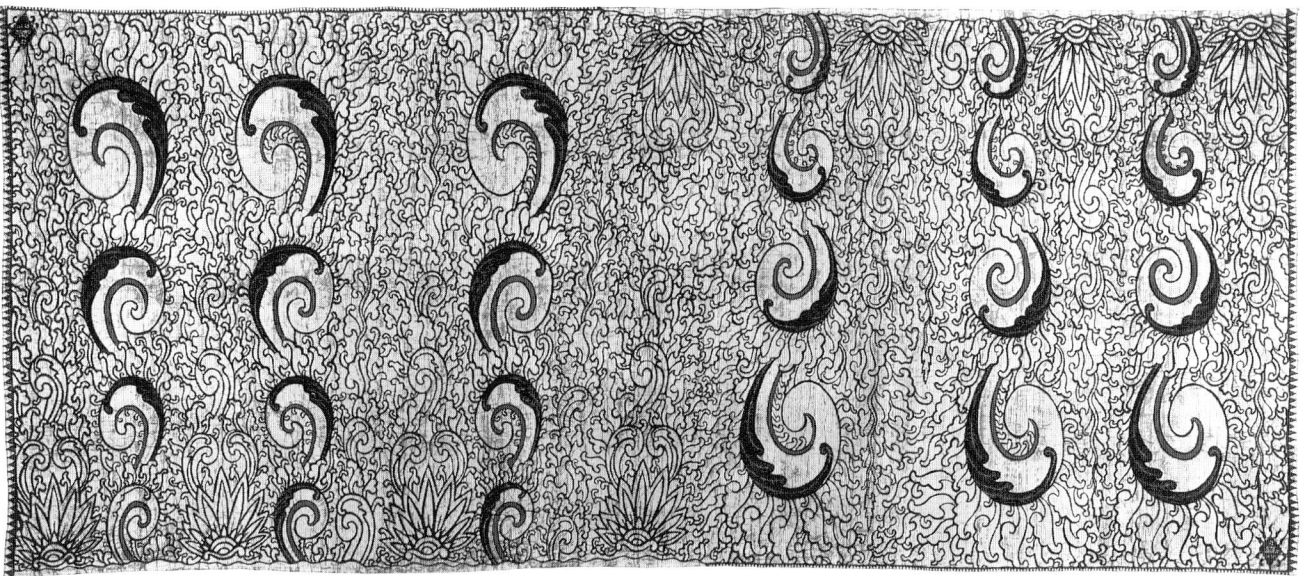

Figure 12. Batik skirtcloth (kain panjang) with curling fern motif (paku), designed by Mohamad Hadi. Solo, Java,1965. Cotton, natural dyes. 106.5 x 250.5 cm. Australian National Gallery, Canberra, 1987.1057.

appearing on this batik are stylized cotton bolls, depicted with rice stalks as a symbol of the basic necessities of food and clothing. The same motifs have been used to convey the notion of social justice (*keadilan sosial*) in the pictorial representation of the *Panca Sila*, the Five Principles of State first enunciated by Sukarno in a speech in 1945.[51]

However, not all Mohamad Hadi's designs carried overt political messages or social themes. He also designed purely decorative cloths with classical Javanese allusions. He seems to have given these batiks esoteric Javanese titles, unlike the more widely understood contemporary Indonesian names he gave to many of his politically motivated designs. This is the case with the pattern called *"Cohung Kraton,"* which he created with his daughter Ida Hadi.[52] Their batik design is easily recognizable as a variation on the classical *semèn* type with tiered *sawat* wings. Although the term *cohung* means literally "the cry of the peacock," the Hadis' rendition of this motif is based upon several other images: the phoenix bird, the winged *någå*-serpent and the mythical Garuda. Between the wings is the characteristic Hadi sun motif.

The other part of the batik's title, *kraton* (palace, court),[53] suggests that like many fine batik patterns, this is a noble design intended for royal or at least court use.[54] The double wing (*sawat*) motif on which the *"Cohung Kraton"* pattern is based is one of the reserved designs of Central Java, including Surakarta (Veldhuisen-Djajasoebrata 1980:201-2), and it appears likely that this batik was made at the request of Gusti Kangjeng or one of the Mangkunegårån royal family. This is one instance of a Hadi design that seems to move away from the classical style of Surakarta batik colors; although it contains Hadi's deliberate crackled effect, the ground appears to be white rather than cream, and it is not clear whether the *soga* dyes are from R.A. Praptini Hardjowiratmo's workshop.[55]

Hadi also reworked other traditional patterns in purely decorative designs based on naturalistic flora and fauna. He favored aquatic creatures such as fish, crabs, lobsters, and shells, while his decorative floral and leafy patterns moved away from the agricultural motifs of his politically inspired batik designs and included the frangipani, the peony, bamboo shoots, and vineleaves. Many of these designs incorporated the crackled wax ground, and irrespective of design differences, all these batiks appear to have been dyed in the Kanjengan Wonigiri workshop.

The curling fern (*paku*) was a favorite and recurring form. On one striking and unusual textile (Fig. 12) signed 156.65 MD. HADI SOLO in the upper left and lower right corners, the wax has been applied in a sinuous linear outline of dark brown and indigo on a pale crackled ground, an effect more akin to drawing. In reversible *pagi-soré* form, the large bold fern spirals grow larger as they rise up the cloth while the shadowy curls emanating from the star-like foliage diminish in size. The fern coil is a popular motif in many parts of the Indonesian archipelago and is a form of the ancient Southeast Asian spiral and hook design. It is also featured within a *ceplok* diagonal grid on other Hadi batik patterns.

After Hadi's imprisonment his wife Sutrisni remarried. She and her new husband continued to operate a workshop in Solo that made fine batiks, including some that reproduced Hadi's non-political designs. Despite the classical Javanese origin of many

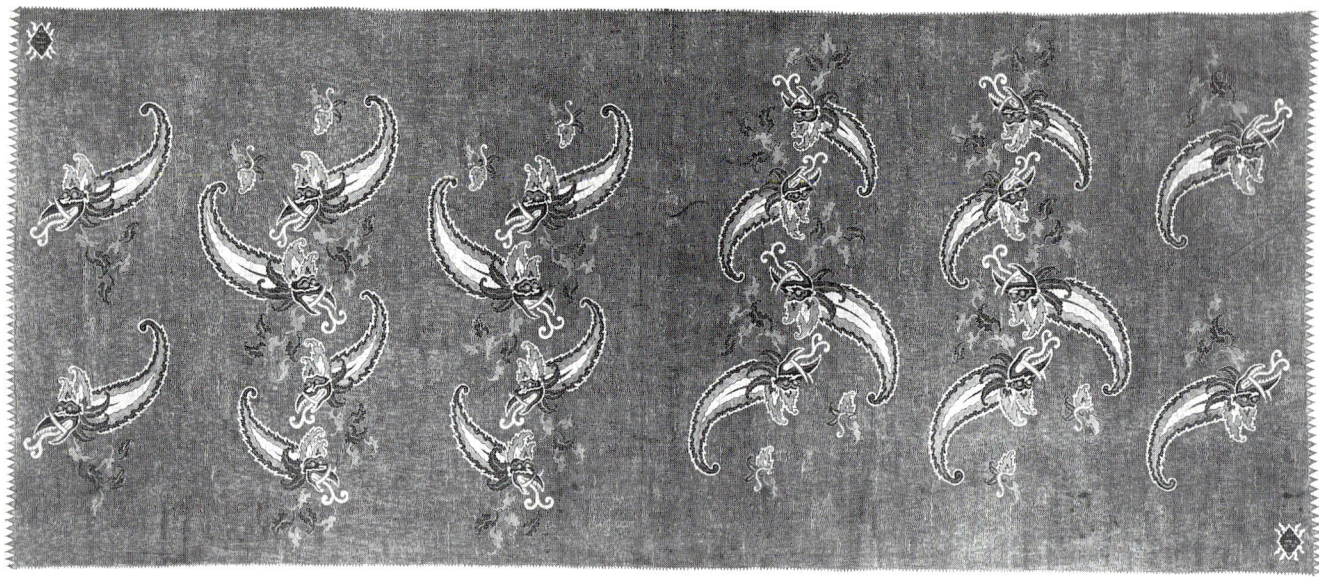

Figure 13. "Galar Sumping Dåråwati" (The Ceremonial Ear Ornament Pattern). Batik skirtcloth (kain panjang) *designed by Mohamad Hadi (Trishadi workshop). Solo, Java, 1966. Cotton, natural dyes. 104.0 x 251.0 cm. Purchased from Gallery Shop Funds. Australian National Gallery, Canberra, 1984.3066.*

of these, she continued Hadi's custom of signing each batik. One 1966 example is signed 58-66 Trishdi [*sic*], SOLO in the upper corner (Figs. 1,13).[56]

The full title of this design seems to have been "*Galar Sumping Dåråwati.*" The traditional central filling pattern (*isen-isen*) consists of a ground of wavy parallel stripes. This is known generally as *galar* or *galaran* (from *galer*, a line or path)[57] and appears over the Hadis' innovative crackled wax marbling effect, of which this elegant batik is an excellent example. Against this complex background, the major design element is arranged as a subtle *pagi-soré*, the reversible format that Hadi often used. The design motif is based on an ear ornament (*sumping*) worn with formal court and dance costume and also displayed by noble *wayang* characters. Dåråwati is the name of one of the legendary kingdoms in the Mahabharata epics upon which many of the *wayang* stories are based.[58] On this batik the *sumping* depicts a mythical creature with a sweeping wing or tail closely resembling the Garuda headdress worn with the refined hairstyle (*gelung*) on *wayang* aristocrats and gods (Ulbricht 1972:43). The *Garuda jaksa* image integrates many of the features of other mighty legendary figures with its strong beak, sharp teeth, fangs, and viper's tongue. In this synthesis it shares many characteristics with the classical *makara*, a mythical creature that incorporates features of the elephant, lion, bull, and crocodile.[59] Similar images have been recorded on antique Javanese jewelry from the Majapahit period.[60]

There are similarities between Mohamad Hadi's purely decorative designs and those that appear on his politically inspired batik. Agricultural motifs such as the ear of corn or the goldfish also appear in Hadi's ornamental patterns, and his political designs often contain universal symbols such as the sun and the butterfly, which he clearly favored. However, he depicted both types of symbols in a classical style.[61]

Hadi's Contributions

Mohamad Hadi's period as a batik designer was brought prematurely to an end by the political upheaval of the mid-1960s and in the field of batik he remains a minor and obscure figure. If he is remembered at all in Indonesian artistic circles, it is probably for his work as a painter. And yet, although it was too brief to make any impression on the direction of Javanese batik (which has in fact been devastated by dramatic economic changes in the industry in the last twenty years), Hadi's small contribution to the history of batik is nevertheless important. His workshop's cloths were of a consistently high technical standard and his discovery of the wax crackling effect was an important innovation soon taken up by others. His much longer experience as a painter obviously contributed to his sense of good design when he turned to batik, and although he chose to work within the parameters of traditional Central Javanese batik patterns, his creative imagination enabled him to produce a range of bold and dramatic designs, distinctive for their clear, clean lines and enhanced by the finest traditional dyes obtainable in the Surakarta region of Central Java.

Any assessment of his work, however, must take account of his conscious attempt to imbue his batiks with his political and social concerns, and in particular, his determination to draw attention to the central place of the peasant farmer within Indonesian society. At a time when other painters and designers in Central Java were moving towards free batik painting, creating new patterns or transforming north-coast batik styles, Hadi's batik largely adhered to the classical design formats of Central Java where position in the social order traditionally dictates who may wear certain restricted aristocratic designs. Even though the Mangkunegårån court—a relatively late principality in Central Java—did not develop the same rigid system of forbidden patterns as those found in the other courts of Surakarta and Yogyakarta,[62] Hadi's designs were based on traditional patterns. An understanding of the social and political message of his designs depended upon an intimate knowledge of Javanese culture, and in particular an understanding of the meaning of these classical batik patterns, and the symbols and images of the Javanese world view they contained.

How successful was Hadi's attempt to stand these traditional elements on their head and inject them with a fundamentally radical, even revolutionary political and social perspective? To some extent this remained an uneasy ideological marriage. Although a concern for the place of the Javanese peasantry was central to Hadi's work, this was not *batik rakyat*. Hadi himself, by culture and social background, was an urban bourgeois, a position he shared with many of his fellow Lekra writers and artists, who like him were nevertheless committed to finding a way to link their radical ideological beliefs with their pursuit of artistic excellence. But with batik it remained difficult for a radical nationalist to overcome the "feudal residue" successfully. The influence of the Mangkunegårån court connections remained powerfully strong in Hadi's work, and although his batiks may have promoted a pro-peasant (*kerakyatan*) ideology, Hadi was unable to avoid the problem that his batik was essentially an expensive elite commodity. It is an irony that despite Hadi's radical pro-*rakyat* sympathies, his batiks were beyond the reach of the ordinary Javanese. In fact, the only published examples of his batiks are the three that appear in *Puspita Warni*, the Jakarta Textile Museum's catalogue of the private batik collection of Gusti Kangjeng Putri Mangkunegårån VIII, the late wife of the Mangkunegårån prince (Museum Tekstil 1980:21,31,33).

It is impossible to say whether Hadi or other politically radical batik designers might eventually have been able to overcome this dilemma and find a way to integrate fully their socially-oriented and nationalist ideological vision, and their technical and artistic achievements with the peasants who were the subjects of much of their art.

Most of Hadi's batiks, especially those that displayed overtly political themes, were probably lost or destroyed during the political turmoil of 1966. In any case, the total output of his workshop was probably quite small. However, some of Hadi's batiks had been collected by the traditional elite of Surakarta and by his friends and acquaintances in radical artistic circles. A few of his textiles found their way to Jakarta, brought there by admirers of fine Surakarta batik, and collected, among others, by the wives of both Indonesian Presidents, Hartini Sukarno[63] and Tien Suharto. In fact, Tien Suharto herself has family connections with the Mangkunegårån and spent her childhood in Wonogiri as the daughter of the *wedana*, the district officer below the rank of *bupati* or regent.[64] It is ironic that one of the most enthusiastic supporters of *batik wonogiren*, and one who helped establish the style as contemporary Jakarta fashion in the 1960s, was so politically distant from Hadi's vision of the new society in Indonesia.[65]

Batik has moved in different directions over the past twenty years. While modern Indonesian artists have begun to use free batik techniques as a form of artistic expression, mass-produced batik has appeared bearing the political symbols of the New Order government of President Suharto, particularly designs representing the *Panca Sila*[66] and the ruling government political party Golongan Karya (Golkar).[67] However, unlike Hadi's finely executed batik designs, these motifs have been produced on cheap fabric intended for items of modern clothing such as shirts and jackets. This mass-produced cloth has been printed either by the use of the metal block wax-resist batik technique, *cap*, or more recently by a non-batik mechanical printing process which has condemned much of the wax-resist batik industry in Java to extinction.[68]

Hadi's work, however, was an example of one man's attempt to find a continuing vital role for batik in the culture of modern Java as part of Indonesia's national heritage. Although his designs were unique, they were firmly located within a Javanese tradition. If it is true that batiks and their designs reflect the batik designer's own innermost wishes, thoughts, and feelings,[69] then Mohamad Hadi's work reveals a man steeped in Javanese traditional culture and possessed of a strong social and political concern for the plight of the people, particularly the peasant farmers of rural Java.

NOTES

1. Our account of the life and work of Mohamad Hadi is based upon interviews with several Indonesians during 1984 and 1985. While they must remain anonymous, we wish to thank them for their assistance. We are also indebted to Philip Kitley for his help during the writing of this article.

2. This association had been formed by a group of Solo painters in 1949 under the leadership of Dr. R. Moerdowo. It also functioned as an art school (see Holt 1967:254, fn. 23).

3. For an account of Lekra's development, see Foulcher 1986.

4. The relationship between Lekra and the PKI is a complex one, and the political upheavals of the mid-1960s have further clouded this issue. There is no clear evidence that in its formation or development Lekra was actually controlled by the party, although some PKI members were active in it, and the two organizations were in agreement over many political issues. Nevertheless, many writers have created the impression that Lekra was a PKI "front organization." For example, see Hindley 1966:184-86 and Kroef 1965:217-19. For an account seeking to balance this view by giving at least equal emphasis to the non-communist but radical nationalist elements within the organization, see Foulcher 1986, especially chap. 7, "Epilogue, Interpreting LEKRA."

5. The painting exhibition was held January 16-21, 1959 at the Wisma Nusantara (formerly Harmoni), Jakarta. For a critical review of the exhibition see Sibarani, "Pameran lekra," *Bintang Timur*, Jan. 23 & 24, 1959.

6. See "Kongres LEKRA pagi ini dibuka," *Harian Rakjat*, January 24, 1959, and "Kongres nasional Lekra dimulai," *Kedaulatan Rakjat* (Yogyakarta), January 23, 1959.

7. "Hari ini Komisi² bersidang," *Harian Rakjat*, January 26, 1959.

8. Utomo Ramelan's sister, Mrs. Suryadarma, was a powerful left-wing figure in Jakarta political elite circles, who led the campaign against American films in Indonesia in 1964. Her husband, the leftist air force chief of staff, Air Marshal Suryadarma, was close to President Sukarno (see Feith 1962:447-48, Legge 1972:335 and Crouch 1978:84).

9. Sutrisni appears to have been Hadi's second wife. Although she was an active partner in the batik business, she was a nurse with no artistic background or talents.

10. Both before and after independence Surakarta has been used as the name for this region of Central Java. Since independence the city within its territory has been known as Solo.

11. Sukarno and his Minister for Education and Culture, Prijono, attended both the 1959 Lekra art exhibition in Jakarta and the closing ceremony of the Lekra National Congress which took place at the Mangkunegåran palace in Solo. See the reports in *Harian Rakjat*, January 16 & 31, 1959.

12. Although Utomo Ramelan was charged and convicted as a member of the PKI there remains some doubt about his exact political affiliations.

13. Skirtcloths of these dimensions are known by a number of Javanese terms such as *kain jarik*, *nyamping*, *sinjang*, and *tapih*.

14. Gittinger 1979a:25. Hardjonagoro himself sees his naphthol phase as a temporary one. Examples of his work in the 1960s appear in Gittinger 1979a:26, and in Museum Tekstil 1980:18-19.

15. For a brief summary of the significance of R.A. Praptini's *soga* dyeing on recent Surakarta batik, see Veldhuisen-Djajasoebrata 1984:148-49.

16. All the examples of Mohamad Hadi's batiks illustrated here and also those illustrated in Museum Tekstil (1980:21,31,33) were dyed at the workshop of R.A. Praptini. The *sidå mukti* batik illustrated in Figure 3 is also *batik kanjengan wonogiri*, though not from the Hadis' workshop.

17. This crackled effect is described as *remukan* ("crushed" or "shattered") in Museum Tekstil 1980:21. Only special quality waxes can be used to achieve such results and these are not always available to batik makers.

18. The signing of batiks is unusual in Central Java, although it became the established practice in European and Chinese batik ateliers elsewhere in Java during the late nineteenth century. Although contemporary connoisseurs must have recognized the distinctive batiks of the most highly respected batik makers in Central Java, this information was never recorded on the fabric for posterity.

19. For an analysis of the major types of batik patterns, see Tirtaamidjaja et al. 1966.

20. While Hadi apparently named and numbered his patterns there are certain discrepancies in the information we have been able to gather about some of his batiks. In particular, those batiks of a clearly political nature have been difficult to discuss with some informants. The numbers that appear on Hadi's batiks refer to both the year they were made and also the design number. Bearing in mind the political upheaval in Java in late 1965, it is highly improbable that this batik was made in the December of that year.

21. For discussion of the sanctuary, temple (*candi*) or cosmic mountain shapes as they appear particularly on *semèn* and *alas-alasan* patterns, see Adams 1970:25-40 and Solyom and Solyom 1980a:248-74.

22. Adams 1970 explores the use of this widespread Southeast Asian symbolism in Javanese batik designs.

23. The *kain kumudåwati* is illustrated in Solyom and Solyom (1980b:279) and Veldhuisen-Djajasoebrata (1980:116-17). A recent study of Javanese batik suggests that the *sidå* pattern always contains the lotus. Symbolizing the stages of the lotus, it represents growth, purity, and spiritual realization (see Boow 1986:24, 214).

24. In Hadi's design these dark brown and blue-black motifs on a cream ground resemble the pavilions found in the fragrant garden (*taman arum*) patterns of the courts of Cirebon in northwest Java. For an illustration of another classical batik motif, the *pusaka* (sacred heirloom), which closely resembles an upside-down sunhat with numerous streamers, see Haake 1984:50-51.

25. On Gerwani see Hindley 1966:203-8, Kroef 1965:214-16, and Fallick 1983. While the PKI played a dominant role in this organization's development, it seems clear that the movement's success in attracting a large mass membership was due to its very active support for women's rights and social welfare, especially in rural Java, rather than its ideological campaigns on behalf of the political objectives of the PKI and Guided Democracy (see Hindley 1966:206-8).

26. Anderson notes that a Sriwedari *wayang wong* clown actor was arrested in 1963 for jokes critical of the government (1965:28).

27. This cloth appears in Rouffaer and Juynboll (1914: pl. 55) and (with photograph reversed) in Steinmann (1947:2112). Other nineteenth- and early twentieth-century textiles containing scenes from the *wayang* were made elsewhere in Java. One Cirebon example in the Australian National Gallery collection (1984.3101), depicts the *Balé Si Gala-gala* episode from the Mahabharata in which the Pandåwå are threatened with being burnt alive. This cloth, illustrated in Elliot (1984:67,206), is also interesting because it is signed along one edge with an aristocratic name in Romanized script. In the twentieth century the *wayang* motif on batik has often appeared on cloth made for export or for tourist souvenirs.

28. The Japanese were received as liberators from Dutch colonialism by most Indonesian nationalists. However, the harsh and brutal treatment of the local population by the

Japanese occupation army made them extremely unpopular with many Indonesians. Moreover, a strong alliance had been established between the local Indonesian aristocracies and the Dutch colonial administration and this was probably a batik from the courts.

Batiks depicting ships of various types, often with the scaly *gringsing* background pattern, were popular in many parts of Java and Madura. Other well-known batiks containing soldiers and battles include the north coast Indo-European type generally known as the Lombok wars (*perang Lombok*) design, which invariably appears on *kain sarong* cylindrical cloths with a contrasting head-panel (*kepala*) of floral bouquets and lacy borders. Unlike the *gringsing wayang* designs, this kind also contains stylized Dutch soldiers.

29. It is not known whether the *gringsing* of the chronicles was a cloth decorated with the scale pattern or whether the designs were wrought by the double ikat resist dye process like the Balinese cloths which also take the name *gringsing*.

30. The Leiden Rijksmuseum *wayang gringsing* batik (Fig. 4) also contains Arjuna and two of his wives.

31. Anderson 1965:22. For a description of Srikandi and Sumbadra as characters in the Javanese versions of the Mahabharata, see Anderson 1965:21-22.

32. Anderson notes that women's military units in the Indonesian army took Srikandi as their model, and that Sukarno referred to the first Indonesian woman guerrilla to land in West Irian in 1962 as "our Srikandi" (1965:26).

33. The jewelry includes the crescent-shaped neckpiece (*kalung bulan sabit*), ear ornaments (*sumping*), upper arm bangles (*kelatbau*) and bracelet (*gelang*). For an outline of these items of clothing and jewelry see Ulbricht 1972: chap. 7. Specific examples of the jewelry are illustrated in Jasper and Pirngadie 1927:124,147,161,169,179.

34. The division of Javanese society into three streams of belief and behavior—the bureaucratic gentry (*priyayi*), the devout followers of Islam (*santri*) and the peasantry with syncretic religious and philosophical beliefs (*abangan*) —was also a focus of Western scholarship on Indonesia (in particular, see Geertz 1960).

35. In fact, the choice of the *wayang* drama symbolism to display political and social doctrines was in keeping with the style of Sukarno's government, described by Clifford Geertz as a "theatre state," in which the inner meaning of the ruler's "court," conceived as the center of the cosmos, "the exemplary centre," was presented to the people in clear symbols (Geertz 1968:36,38,107).

36. In January 1961 Gerwani had organized a special seminar in Jakarta on the problems of peasant women. The conference was attended by women from rural areas, especially from throughout Java (see Hindley 1966:207 and Kroef 1965:215). After the Lekra 1959 Congress in Solo, *turun ke bawah* also became an important part of that organization's policy and activity (see Foulcher 1986:107-11).

37. The mountain-tree patterns are also closely related to the *alas-alasan* designs found on batik, *pradå* gold-leaf gluework and other art forms such as the sheaths of the ceremonial dagger (*keris*). "Male" and "female" versions of the *gunungan* have been distinguished: the "male" type exhibits an asymmetrical arrangement of animals and a preponderance of Upper World tree patterns above the temple-palace; the "female" counterpart displays Lower World images in a stylized pond (see Bondan et al. 1984:10).

38. Peasant land reform campaigns under the leadership of the Indonesian Peasants' Front (Barisan Tani Indonesia) had resulted in the seizure and redistribution of land in Central and East Java during the early 1960s. In national politics this period saw the domestic political pendulum swinging to the left as President Sukarno appeared to be relying more closely on the support of the PKI.

39. Sukarno's application of another acronym, Nekolim (neo-colonialism, colonialism and imperialism), was a further example of his antagonism towards the forces of the Western world he saw ranged against Indonesia.

40. This batik had also been referred to as *Solidaritas Asia-Afrika* (Afro-Asian Solidarity).

41. Sukarno's ideas were outlined in a series of major speeches delivered to various international forums from 1960 onwards, such as the United Nations General Assembly and the conferences of nonaligned nations. For a useful account of his foreign policy, see Legge 1972 (chaps. 13,14, esp. pp. 343-45), Weatherbee 1966, and Modelski (ed.) 1963.

42. Hadi's batik is dyed by total immersion in the solutions. Most of the brightly colored Pekalongan batiks are waxed in such a manner that certain sections of the pattern are dammed off and hand-painted with various colors.

43. This decorative technique is the opposite of the classical Indramayu style, in which an area covered with wax is pricked before dyeing to give dark spots on a light or undyed ground. The Pekalongan batiks were worked with waxed dots applied with the *canting* so that white spots appear on a dark black ground.

44. Hadi's batik design appears also to have been known by the title *Banteng Ketaton*, the raging and potentially dangerous bull (*ketaton* = wounded). The *banteng* has continued to be used as a symbol of nationalism and the sovereignty of the people by the New Order government of President Suharto.

45. This flag may also be symbolic of the People's Republic of China.

46. Anderson 1965:76. An illustration of a shadow puppet version of Kresna holding aloft the *cåkrå* appears on p. 14. Two early examples from the East Java period, now in the collection of the Museum Pusat in Jakarta, are illustrated in Fontein et al. (1971:108-9).

47. *Wayang kulit* versions of these magical arrows depicted as *någå*-serpents and winged *någå* shapes are illustrated in Solyom and Solyom 1978:51.

48. For detailed analysis of *semèn* see Solyom and Solyom 1980a.

49. Another version of this design, on a plain black ground, is illustrated in Museum Tekstil 1980:31. The text attributes the design named *Jembatan Mas* to the artist Md. Hadi and his ideals of social justice (*cita-cita keadilan sosial*), although it is not clear how that batik was signed.

50. This batik appears in Museum Tekstil 1980:31. Signed 190-65 MD. HADI SOLO, it is now in the collection of the Australian National Gallery, Canberra, 1987.1822.

51. The Five Principles of State of the *Panca Sila* cover belief in God, humanitarianism, democracy, social justice, and nationalism (Zainu'ddin 1980:236-39).

52. This batik appears in Museum Tekstil 1980:21,33. The cloth is signed at the edge, Ida Hadi and Md. Hadi.

53. Tirtaamidjaja et al. (1966: pl. 66) shows a similar design known as *srikaton*. This is a Javanese musical term that alludes to the majestic royal appearance.

54. The Solo batik designer, Hardjonagoro, uses the term *kain kraton* to indicate complex court-inspired designs, which contrast with *batik rakyat* (folk batik). See Gittinger 1979b:26.

55. A white background (*bledak*) is a feature of Yogyakarta batik. In Solo when a light background is required for a batik design, it is always a pale fawn or cream. However, the color of the textile may have been inaccurately reproduced in the photograph.

56. According to one informant, even after Hadi's arrest, batiks bearing the signature Md. Hadi continued to appear. Since Mohamad Hadi was entirely responsible for the creation of all

the designs, it is possible that some of his other batik designs may have survived in this way or under his wife's signature, Trishadi. After her remarriage she eventually changed the signature on batiks produced in her workshops from Trishadi to Trisni.

57. *Galar* is also the term for a mat made of flat bamboo strips. Tirtaamidjaja et al (1966: pls. 80,81) show examples of patterns on a *galaran* ground. The *galaran* background is probably best known as a feature of the *terang wulan* (moonlight) pattern.

58. We are grateful to Mr. M. Slamet, Melbourne, for this information.

59. For *makara* gargoyle images at the majestic Borododur temple complex, see Bondan 1982:60,64.

60. See Fontein 1971:142 for photographs of ear ornaments from the Majapahit period in the form of monster heads.

61. For example, the gold fish and mythical creatures such as *makara* or *gangga-mina* and Garuda are all depicted in similar ways. The *gangga-mina* is a mythical elephant-fish creature that also appears on classical batik and may have inspired Hadi's fish images. The depiction of the fish motif on batik also owes much to Chinese popular culture and art.

62. These restricted patterns are discussed in Veldhuisen-Djajasoebrata 1980:201-21. She suggests (p. 202) that the rules on forbidden patterns are less well-defined in Surakarta than in the principalities of Yogyakarta.

63. The textiles illustrated in Figures 10 and 12 were formerly in the collection of Hartini.

64. See the popular biography by Suripto n.d. (chap. 1).

65. Suripto n.d. (p. 98). Suripto comments: "It is interesting to note the fact that Ibu Tien Soeharto made *kain batik* 'Wonogiren' both popular and fashionable. She liked wearing *kain batik* 'Wonogiren' so much that other women noticed and also began to wear it. Consequently, in women's circles generally, *kain batik* 'Wonogiren' became the fashion" (our translation). She is said to have learned batik in Wonogiri as a young girl and continued it later as a hobby (p. 100). See also Veldhuisen Djajasoebrata 1980:149. According to a reliable informant, Tien Suharto favored Hadi's batik with a *pring cendani* (slender bamboo) design, which she often wore on public appearances long after its designer had already been placed in detention.

66. A crudely worked *Panca Sila* batik is illustrated in Warming and Gaworski (1981:187). It is in the *semèn* style with four of the five symbols of the *Panca Sila* filling the diamond grid: the *banteng* (horned head), the giant *waringin* or banyan fig tree, the star, and the wreath of rice and cotton. (For an explanation of these symbols see Zainu'ddin 1980:238). A *ceplok* lattice version with the same *Panca Sila* design also appears as a *cap* wax imprint in Balai Penilitian Batik dan Keradjinan (n.d.: pl. 22).

67. An Indramayu hand-drawn batik with the Golkar symbol (*lambang Golkar*) is illustrated in Djoemena 1986:50.

68. Ironically one of Hadi's own decorative bamboo designs, *pring cendani*, has recently been reproduced as a "batik" print by one of the large textile companies of Central Java.

69. This is the view of the batik designer, K.R.T. Hardjonagoro, in Gittinger (1979b:26). Batik making has historically been viewed as a spiritual and philosophical activity, and a vehicle for meditation (Hardjonagoro 1980:223-42).

Batiks in the Central Javanese Wedding Ceremony

Judi Achjadi

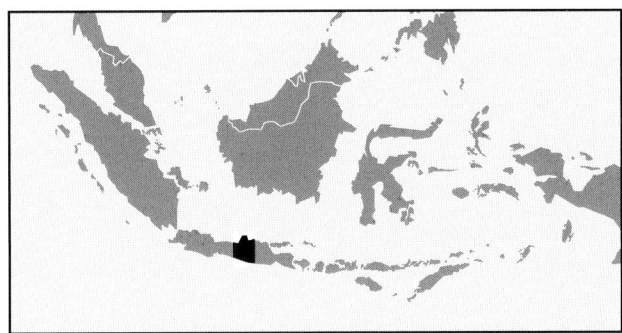

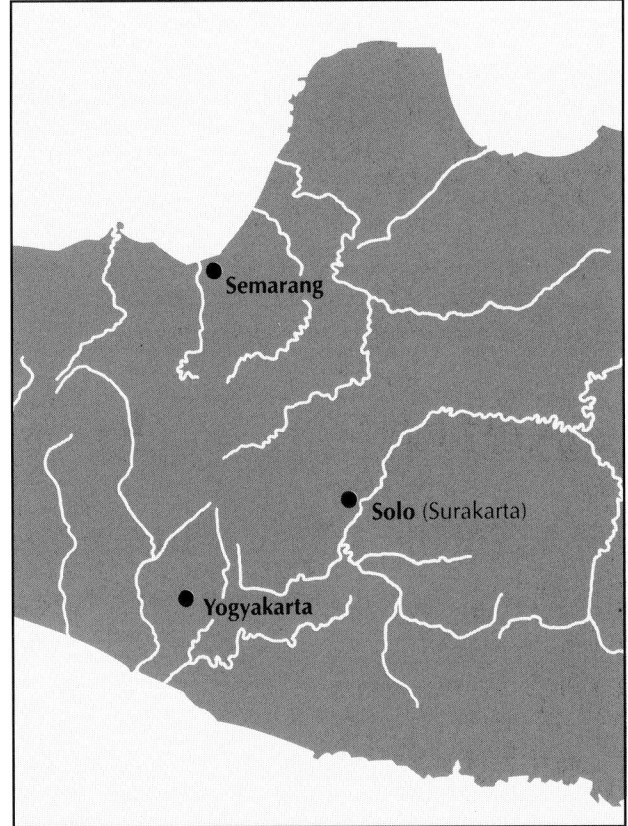

Central Java.

In Indonesia, getting married is the most important event in traditional community life. Marriage joins not only a man and a woman, but also their families and villages. A good marriage brings peace and contentment to the parties thereby united and allows them to concentrate on prospering; it ensures continuity. A negative union brings unhappiness and drains energies; it can bring ruin as well, particularly when one party feels abused. This upsets the universal balance of things which the traditional Indonesian works so hard to maintain. The wedding ceremony is therefore replete with ritual and symbolism to guarantee that all goes well. It also marks the rebirth of the core participants, the bride and groom, into another more advanced stage in the life cycle. The wedding is a reenactment of the original creation of the universe; thus much of its symbolism relates to the cosmos and fecundity. This is superbly exemplified by the wedding dress and ceremony of Central Java.

The ideal dress for both bride and groom is considered to be the *dodot ageng*, sometimes also referred to as *kampuhan*, a voluminous cloth wrapped in generous folds around the torso (Figs. 1,2, Pls. 23, 26a). Traditionally, this costume was the most formal court attire; in recent times it has been adopted by commoners for weddings, although under normal circumstances it is still reserved exclusively for the royal family. The *dodot* is wrapped layer upon layer around the bodies of the bride and groom, surrounding them with cosmic and fertility symbols, and making them metaphorically the center of the universe. Within the micro-cosmos of their own bodies, there is another center, precisely rendered in a knob, *nyamat*, on the man's cap and a dot, *cithak*, painted in the middle of the woman's forehead (pers. comm., Ibu Maktal[1] 1984). This concept, suggested in the wedding costume, is explicit in the titles of the Central Javanese rulers and their consorts, for whom the *dodot ageng* was originally designed: the kings are called the "axis around which the world revolves" or "lap of the universe"; their consorts are *garwa padmi*, literally "lotus womb,"[2] "container of the universe" (Snodgrass 1985:207). Since bride and groom are commonly referred to as "king and queen for a day," the message is clear.

The Rites of the Central Javanese Wedding

Before examining the role of textiles in the traditional Central Javanese wedding ceremony, one must understand, at least in broad outline, its ritual organization. The central rites take place over the course of at least three days. At the core of the wedding are the series of events surrounding the ritual meeting of the bride and groom, called *panggih* or *temon*[3]; these conclude with a ritual exchange of wealth known as *kacar-kucur* or *tampa kaya*, followed by a ritual feeding and blessings. The final rite, *kirapan*, takes place about five days later, when the bride is officially welcomed into her new husband's home. Before these rites can take place, however, the bride must undergo a ritual confinement—traditionally forty days, but now more typically a week—which is a period of dietary restriction and meditation. Near the end of this period, about two days before the central rites, a temporary guest pavillion (*tarub*) is raised.

The Eve of the Wedding

The cocoon-like seclusion of the bride-to-be culminates in prayer and ritual bathing on the eve of the *panggih*. The young woman is in transition from a single state to a newly married one; thus she is prepared for rebirth much as an unborn child in the womb prepares for its thrust into the world, and the room of her seclusion is a replica of the womb. By popular custom the room chosen for this is the bedroom in which the bridal couple will spend their first five nights (palace custom is slightly different[4]). At its center is a richly decorated bed, *kerobongan* (Fig. 3), the inner and outer perimeters of which are richly decorated with textiles,[5] and under which a tray of prescribed offerings has been placed[6]. Other designations for this bed are *petanen*, "place of agricultural activity," and *pedaringan*, "rice granary."

That evening before twilight the bride-to-be is given a ritual shower with water taken from seven sources, and she is scented with seven kinds of flowers and leaves, *air kembang setaman*; the water, contained in a coconut shell, is poured over her head first by the ritual expert, and then by her mother, father, and up to seven other respected elderly female relatives. These, like the ritual expert, are preferably grandmothers who have experienced the bittersweetness of long and fruitful married lives; they fill her with advice throughout the long evening.

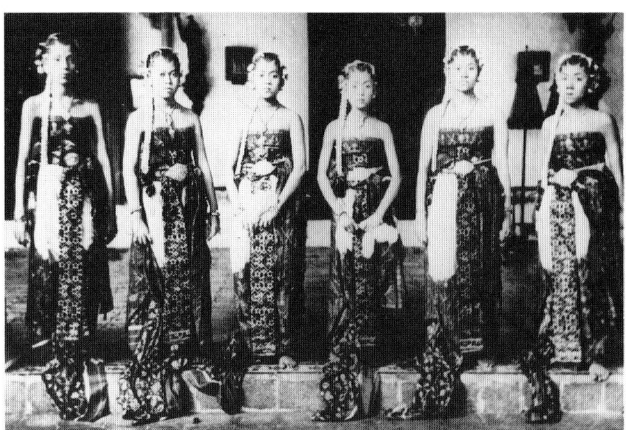

Figure 1. Royal brides in Surakarta, 1927. It was not unusual practice for several princes and princesses to marry at the same time. On this memorable occasion a total of five princesses and one prince of Surakarta were wed. Their dress, known collectively as the dodot ageng (dodot ngumbar konco *for brides and* dodotan bhuweng *for bridegrooms), is considered the correct bridal dress for all Central Javanese whether royal or not. All brides and bridegrooms go bare-shouldered, except the ruler himself who would wear a simple black jacket over his dodot.*

The brides include, from left to right: BRA Surjohamidjojo, granddaughter of Sultan Hamengku Buwono VII; GRA Sugondo; GRA Adipati Judonagoro; GRA Sosrodiningrat; GRA Wirjodiningrat; and GRA Surjonagoro. (The initials before the names stand for honorific titles. Adipati is a titled earned through merit and not a prerogative inherited by one's wife. Princess Judonagoro was the official hostess of the Surakarta Palace and, as such, was given the title of Adipati.) The royal grooms are seen in Figure 2, below. Photographer unknown.

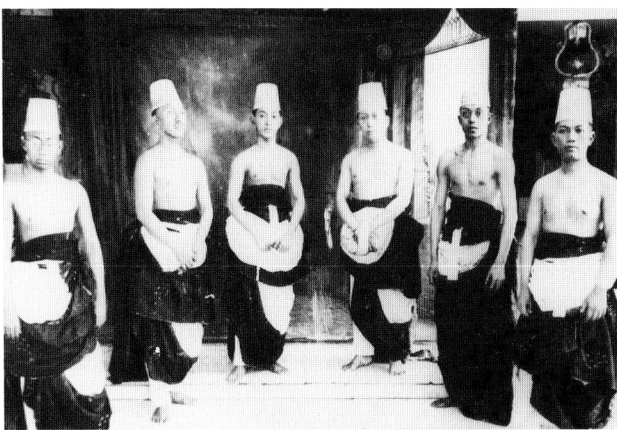

Figure 2. Royal grooms in Surakarta, 1927. The grooms include, from left to right: KRM Adipati Ario Judonagoro (father of Ibu Maktal); KRM Ario Wirjodiningrat; GPH Surjohamidjojo, Prince of Surakarta; RM Adipati Ario Sugondo; KRM Ario Surjonagoro; and KRM Adipati Ario Sosrodiningrat. Photographer unknown.

After her bath she is led to the bedroom to be prepared for the long night's vigil and the meeting with her husband on the morrow. All mirrors are covered so that the bride's quadruplet guardian spirits (who are the amnios of her own birth, her afterbirth, placenta, and umbilical cord) will not be confused by the changed appearance of her reflection due to bridal makeup. Such confusion might cause them to wander about aimlessly searching for her—a disaster that could result in the miscarriage of her first pregnancy (pers. comm., Ibu Maktal 1984).

In the bedroom she sits on a special protective pad or cushion (*klasa bangka*) while the hair on the nape of her neck is clipped first by her mother, then by her father, and lastly by the ritual expert.[7] The hair framing the bride's face is neatly trimmed and redesigned with pigments to conform to lines of traditional beauty. This is the test of the ritual expert's skill: it has to be perfect. The new hairline, called *paes*, is applied in three stages which mark the bride's passage from her liminal state in the "womb" to her new, well-defined status as an inseparable part of a marital union. First the fine strands of short hair are trimmed in the scalloped lines of the *paes* (Fig. 9b). This is outlined and filled in with a light application of green pomade, *lilin dandang gula/kendhis*. A small mark known as *cithak* is painted between the bride's eyes. A tiny lock of hair, *centung*, has already been braided over each temple.[8] Dressed in a simple costume, without jewelry, the bride-to-be must now sit as still as possible by the bed (Geertz 1969:55), which has been adorned with coconut leaves (*janur*). The leaves are arranged in a pair of ornaments called *kembar mayang*, supposed to have been "sent especially" by Dewi Sri for this wedding. They are said to represent the tree of life or cosmic tree, as well as the sacred mountain.

At midnight the young woman is permitted a very light meal of plain food; then she is admonished to get some sleep before her dawn awakening. This night is known as *malam midadareni*, the night in which an angel, *widadari*, descends to bless the bride with her perfect beauty. The angelic being is variously referred to as Sembadra, beautiful wife of Arjuna in the Mahabharata epic, Dewi Ratih (Kamaratih), wife of Kamajaya of Javanese legend, and Dewi Sri, the goddess of fertility.

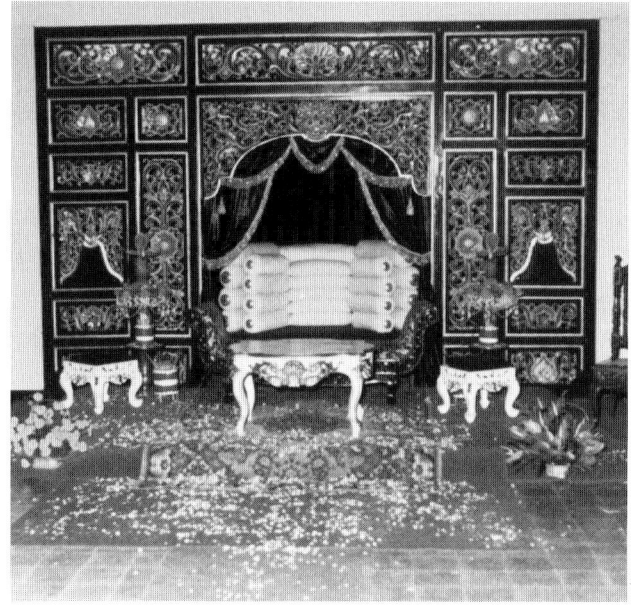

*Figure 3. The nuptial bed (*kerobongan* or *petanen*) marks the center of the house and is the "resting place of Dewi Sri, Mother Earth." This one was photographed in Solo in the mid-1980s.*

The Wedding Day

At dawn, before the sun rises, the bride is awakened to begin preparations for the *panggih*. The *paes* is darkened by an additional application of protective green paste (explained below), the lock of hair (*centung*) is coated with gold leaf, and the *dodot ageng* is draped around her body. (Later, when the union has been consummated, the *paes* is blackened and the bride changes into a long velvet blouse and pleated batik skirt, once also royal attire.)

At the prescribed moment, bride and groom are brought face to face at the threshold of the sacred bedroom, the bride inside, and the groom waiting to enter. This is the start of the events comprising the *panggih* ceremony. First the bride and groom throw bundles of betel leaf (*sirih*) at one another. Then the bridegroom stamps on a chicken's egg, crushing it, and the bride stoops to wash and dry his foot. The egg is crushed to expose the red yolk and white fluid that make up the whole; the contents are mixed so as to be inextricably blended. From the name of the egg, *wijidadi*, it is inferred that the couple should be mature in their approach to the marriage (*wiji* = seed; *dadi* = grown). The mixing of female-associated red and male-associated white elements is clear in its significance.

Now they are ready for their symbolic "journey." Bride and groom are turned to stand side by side and the bride's father anoints the tops of their heads or their foreheads with scented oil. To sustain them on the journey, the bride's mother gives them one glass from which they each take a sip of greenish coconut liquor, said to have the power to remove all bad luck (pers. comm., Ibu Maktal 1986). Then, led by the bride's father and symbolically "carried in a sling" by her mother, they cross the threshold and enter the room (Pl. 24)—just as, shortly after birth, a baby is carried in a naming rite by its maternal grandmother. The wedding sling is a sacred red-and-white scarf that expresses the two-in-one life-giving theme: red stands for female and blood, white for male and plasma, and therefore the "beginning of all life, *purwaning dumadi*" (Kuswadji 1984b). Placing this sling across the shoulders of the couple, and stationing herself behind them, the mother appears to hold the cloth there as the procession makes its way across the room. The bride and groom, meanwhile, have linked their little fingers and their free hands are hooked into the bride's father's waistband. The path they travel represents life and the journey from rebirth to maturity in their new existence. Upon reaching the bedside, the couple are "weighed"[9] symbolically and then, like a coconut tree, "planted" firmly (into the ground) by the bride's father, who presses on their shoulders as they sit on their haunches at the foot of the marital bed (*kerobongan*). They are facing south, the direction where "capacities are at the highest peak" (Veldhuisen-Djajasoebrata 1980:208). There they sit side by side for the first time.

Concluding Rites

Now comes the final series of rituals in the *panggih*. Once seated, the bridegroom pours "all his wealth" into the bride's lap in the rite called *kacar-kucur* or *tampa kaya* (Pl. 25). His wealth is represented by yellowed rice grains, soya and other beans, seeds, flower petals (rose, kenanga, and jasmine), metal coins of various denominations, and perhaps some candies. The container is usually a small square of pandanus matting lined with a piece of black-and-white tie-dyed cloth. The bridegroom may stand up or remain seated by his bride, as the ritual expert helps him pour these symbols of worldly wealth into a red-and-white cloth that the bride holds in her lap. The bride in turn hands the bundle for safekeeping to her mother, who accepts it and passes it on to the ritual expert or someone else pre-designated to take it away for safekeeping. Each of the two mothers feeds her child a ball of yellow rice for the last time; then the bride and groom feed each other and are offered a glass of water from which they each take a sip. They are now relinquished to each other's care and the central part of the ceremony is complete. The bridegroom's parents are invited to join the party and the couple kneels to ask their blessings. So ends the *panggih*. Guests are invited to offer congratulations at a formal reception shortly thereafter.[10]

Sometime during the five days that follow, the wedding is consummated. On the fifth day, before the husband takes his bride home, they enact the final rite of the wedding. The ritual, known as *kirapan*, shows the public the two persons just united. In this ceremony the bride and groom circumambulate the bride's home, turning to the right as they exit and keeping the center of the house always on their right side as they traverse the outer perimeter (pers. comm., Ibu Maktal 1986).

The Role of Textiles in the Wedding

The multiple meanings of a Central Javanese wedding ceremony are given full expression in the language of its textiles, starting with the apparel worn by the bride's parents. Most of the rites take place in the bride's home, without the bridegroom's parents and, indeed, once upon a time without any male other than the bridegroom and his prospective father-in-law or an appointed substitute.[11] The bride's parents, therefore, have a primary responsibility that is symbolized in the batik pattern known as *teruntum* (Fig. 4). The word *teruntum* is given various interpretations. It is said to be rooted in the word *tuntun*, to lead: the bridal couple should, hand in hand, follow the good example set by their elders. This idea finds ritual expression in the part of the ceremony described above, in which the bride and groom are led (*dituntun*) to the bridal seat by the bride's father, at the same time being "carried" by her mother in a red-and-white scarf. For this occasion, both parents are clad in *teruntum*-patterned batik skirts.

The *teruntum* motif is that of a small flower with eight petals. This configuration—eight petals radiating from a central dot—expresses an ancient Javanese, and even Indonesian, concept of the cosmos, wherein power is understood as radiating from a central force in the compass directions, referred to as *mancalima* or the Sacred Nine (Ossenbruggen 1983:32-81). Originally, each petal was a small *stupa*, or Buddhist shrine mound, whose shape has become distorted with time (pers. comm., Ibu Maktal 1984). Just as the *stupa* represents the path a person must follow to enlightenment, the ideal of Buddhism, so the *teruntum* flower depicts the ultimate social responsibility of a Javanese person: the harmonious marriage of one's children resulting in the subsequent birth of grandchildren. In this context, the *teruntum* batik pattern is not generally considered suitable for a young person to wear (pers. comm., Ibu Maktal 1984). Other meanings attributed to the word *teruntum* (and hence to the motif) are prosperity, growth, reunion as a whole, and love reawakened.

Special red-and-white scarves, *sindur* or *gula klapa*, intensify the solemnity of the *panggih* ceremony. They appear at several points: wrapped around the waists of the bride's and the groom's parents (even though the latter remain in their own home and do not attend the nuptials); as part of the offerings placed about the house and decorating the marital bed; held in the bride's lap to catch her new husband's symbolic wealth (Pl. 25); and laid across the bridal couple's shoulders at the start of the symbolic journey, signifying the moment at which they are actually united (Pranata 1984:104). Beyond the color symbolism of red and white, there is meaning in the word sindur, derived from the Javanese *isin*, ashamed, and *ndur*, to retreat. Together with the egg, *wijidadi*, the scarves teach the bride and groom that they should have thought carefully about marriage and be determined to make it last.

Even the cushions used in the ceremony hold symbolic meaning. The bride sits upon a small, protective cushion, *klasa bangka*, composed of efficacious leaves and various colored cloths which are sandwiched between a pandanus mat and a small black-and-white cloth, the two being bound together[12] with a scarlet edging (pers. comm., Ibu Maktal 1984).[13] The black and white of the cushion cover, called *bangun tulak*, reiterates the color scheme of the batik that forms the basis of the bridal *dodot ageng*.

The *Dodot*

The wedding cloth itself, properly titled *dodot bangun tulak alas-alasan*[14], is a highly significant textile in all aspects: color, format, and ornamentation. A huge cloth measuring approximately three-and-a-half to four meters in length and two to two-and-a-half meters in width, the *dodot* encodes the Javanese propensity to classify everything in antithetical but

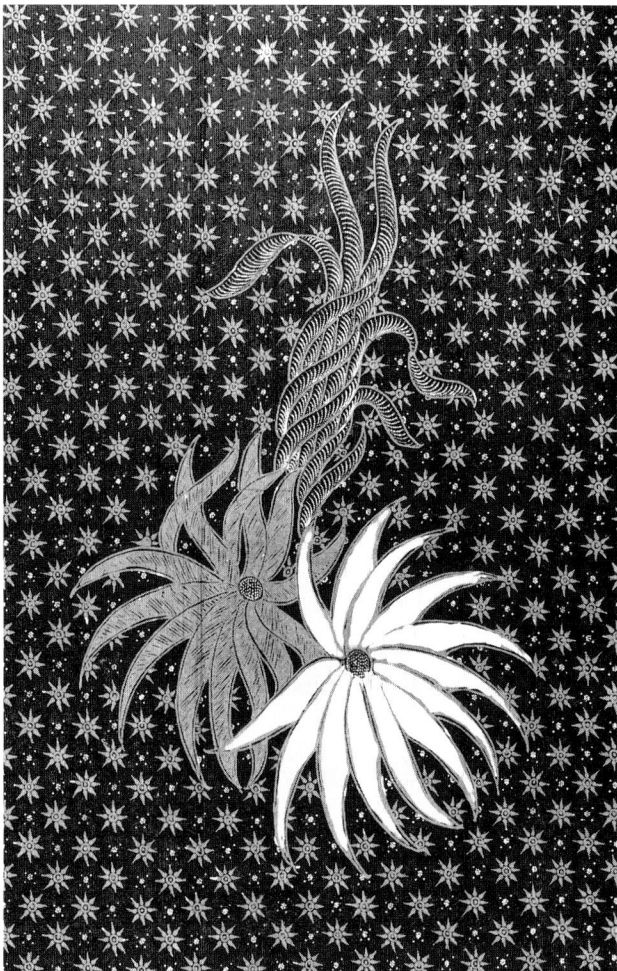

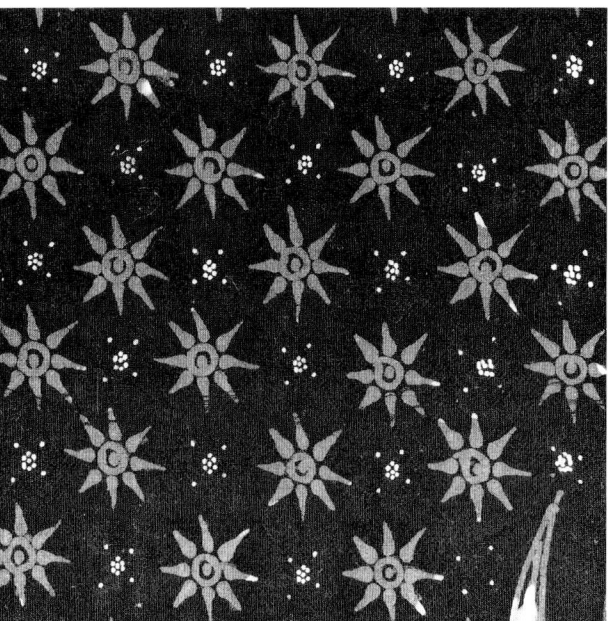

Figure 4a,b. The flower pattern, teruntum, *worn by the bride's parents. Each petal of the* teruntum *flower is a distorted* stupa, *symbol of the ultimate obligation of Javanese parents: the successful marriage of their children, enabling the birth of grandchildren and thus ensuring the continuity of mankind. These batiks are considered unsuitable for young people. Jakarta, 1987.*

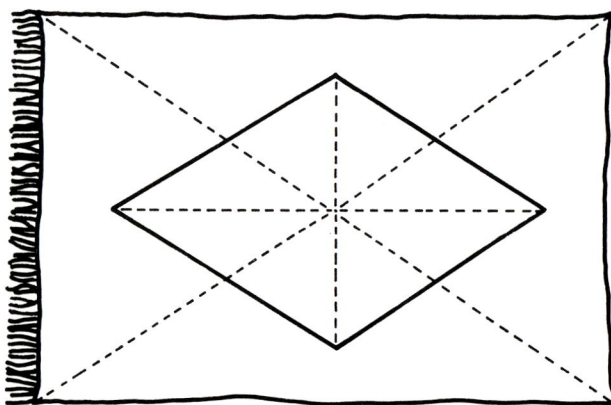

Figure 5. In the diamond centerfield format of the dodot bangun tulak, *the extremities of the four cardinal compass points are drawn out of the center and joined to form a lozenge; then a line is drawn joining up the extremities of the intermediate compass points to form an outer rectangle.*

complementary opposites. It is dominated by a large, plain white diamond set in the middle of a midnight-blue field (Pl. 26a). The surface of the blue-black ground is filled with gold-leafed tracings of mythical and actual forms from nature in the pattern known as *alas-alasan*, which means forest-like (Pl. 26b). The black-and-white combination represents life and death, beginning and end, male and female, negative and positive. It is a supernaturally powerful medium able to contravene malevolent forces; only a "king" is considered strong enough to carry its potency. Thus its color, format, and ornamentation all designate the *dodot bangun tulak* as a royal prerogative.

The concept of the Sacred Nine, or *mancalima*, is reiterated once again in the diamond centerfield. The blue-black field represents land, while the white centerfield, known as *blumbang*, is a pool of water (pers. comm., Ibu Maktal 1984). A *blumbang* is defined by Javanese as a pool fed by a spring located in its exact center (*Selera* magazine, September 1984:20). On the *dodot*, the extremities of the *blumbang* equate with four cardinal compass points radiating from this "spring" nucleus; the resultant shape is a diamond. The outer margins of the *dodot* form a frame for this central diamond. The corners of the frame are determined by intermediate compass points using the same center (Fig. 5). Thus eight imaginary lines radiate out from the spring nucleus which feeds the "pool": the central "power" is dispersed outwards to give life to all around it. By wrapping their bodies in the *dodot bangun tulak*, bride and groom become the nucleus of the world or universe that is represented by the images on the cloth (Solyom and Solyom 1980a:260).

Birds, trees, and animals both real and mythical create the universe in the *alas-alasan* pattern (Pl. 26b). For the Javanese, the lushness of the forest as represented in the *alas-alasan* connotes fertility and procreation. One of the main design elements is a scraggly tree. It may have three or five branches, the two outer ones bending down on left and right to create a mountain effect. The sacred mountain, which symbolizes the cosmos, and the numbers three, five, seven, and nine are important in Javanese mental imagery and inevitably present in ritual life.

Accessories to the Wedding Costume

Beyond the wedding cloth, each detail of the nuptial costume has meaning. Wrapped around the body and underclothing of bride and groom, the sumptuous *dodot* leaves shoulders and arms bare. These exposed parts of the torso are dusted with yellow powder, *boreh*, which is composed of seven elements.[15] Sashes and belts hold the *dodot* in place. They and the undercloths—a long skirt for the bride and trousers for the groom—are made of patola or *cinde*.[16] Despite the fact that they may be cheap imitations of the original silk patola from India, the *cinde* cloths emphasize the great stature of the participants (since the original patola was so precious as to be a prerogative of royalty) and the solemnity of the event (pers. comm., R. Soegito 1978, Ibu Maktal 1984). The belts, delicately woven from gold metallic yarns, are called *janur*, the same name given to young coconut leaves.[17] The yellow of the yarn represents fertility and noblesse; the young coconut leaf is deemed to have the mystical power to divert misfortune. When these leaves are used to decorate the bride's house,[18] their spines are removed and they fall limply into a curl, *sulur*, which is thought to symbolize everlasting life, *hidup sempulur*, and to intimate that all obstacles will be overcome and misfortune will be averted (Kuswadji 1984b).

Hair accessories are equally important. With his *dodot*, the bridegroom wears a white fez-like cap, *kuluk matak*, which today is usually made of light blue cardboard covered in plastic (Pl. 27).[19] The *kuluk* is topped by a small, unobtrusive, five-petaled knob (*nyamat*), which is made of gold for festive wear, or even surmounted with a diamond when worn by a prince.[20] From the nucleus of the *nyamat*, ten narrow lines radiate outwards. All but one of these go halfway down the sides of the cap to an enclosing, horizontal boundary line. The tenth ray runs down the back center of the cap, all the way to the edge, marking the spot behind which the force of life is located (pers. comm., Ibu Maktal 1984). This force of life is in the center of the skull at a spot determined by the intersection of three lines drawn from three vulnerable accesses to the skull's interior: the foramen at the base of the skull, the fontanel or former soft spot on the top of the head, and the depression between the eyebrows. The lines on the cap radiating outwards from the knob represent the life-giving rays of the sun; while barely visible on the pale-colored *kuluk matak* of the king-bridegroom, they are eminently visible, indeed marked by gold ribbon on the black *kuluk kanigaran* (see again Pl. 27) worn by lesser princes on other occasions (pers. comm., Ibu and Bapak Maktal 1986).

The bride's hair is knotted high on the back of the head in the style known as upturned-bowl (*bokor mengkurep*), and covered in a net of fragrant jasmine flower buds (*wiji timun*), with a golden Garuda-bird protruding from the center (Fig. 6). Around the top of the hairknot are inserted nine pins (*cunduk alas-alasan*) with ornamentation that continues the themes from nature. The number nine, according to some, invokes the blessings of the nine prophets of Islam; however the nine pins are arranged as four symmetrical pairs placed on the left and right of the ninth, which is set in the center—all of which again suggests the concept of the Sacred Nine.

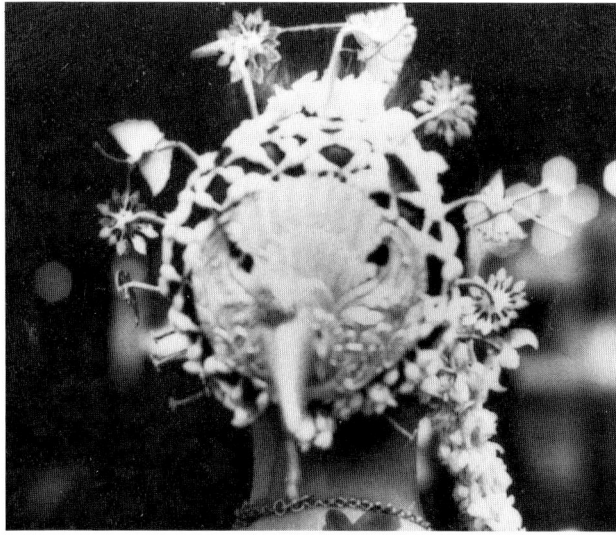

Figure 6. A bridal hairdo, seen from the back. The bride's "upturned bowl" hairknot is encased in a net of fragrant jasmine buds and surrounded by a halo of decorative stickpins continuing the wildlife theme. A golden Garuda pin juts from the center of the knot. The young lady was dancing the sacred bedaya ketawang *dance at the palace of Surakarta, Central Java, at the beginning of the reign of the present Susuhunan, circa 1959. Photographer unknown.*

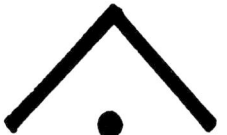

Figure 7. A small, right-angled mark harboring a dot, called cithak, *is drawn in between the bride's eyebrows.*

Achjadi

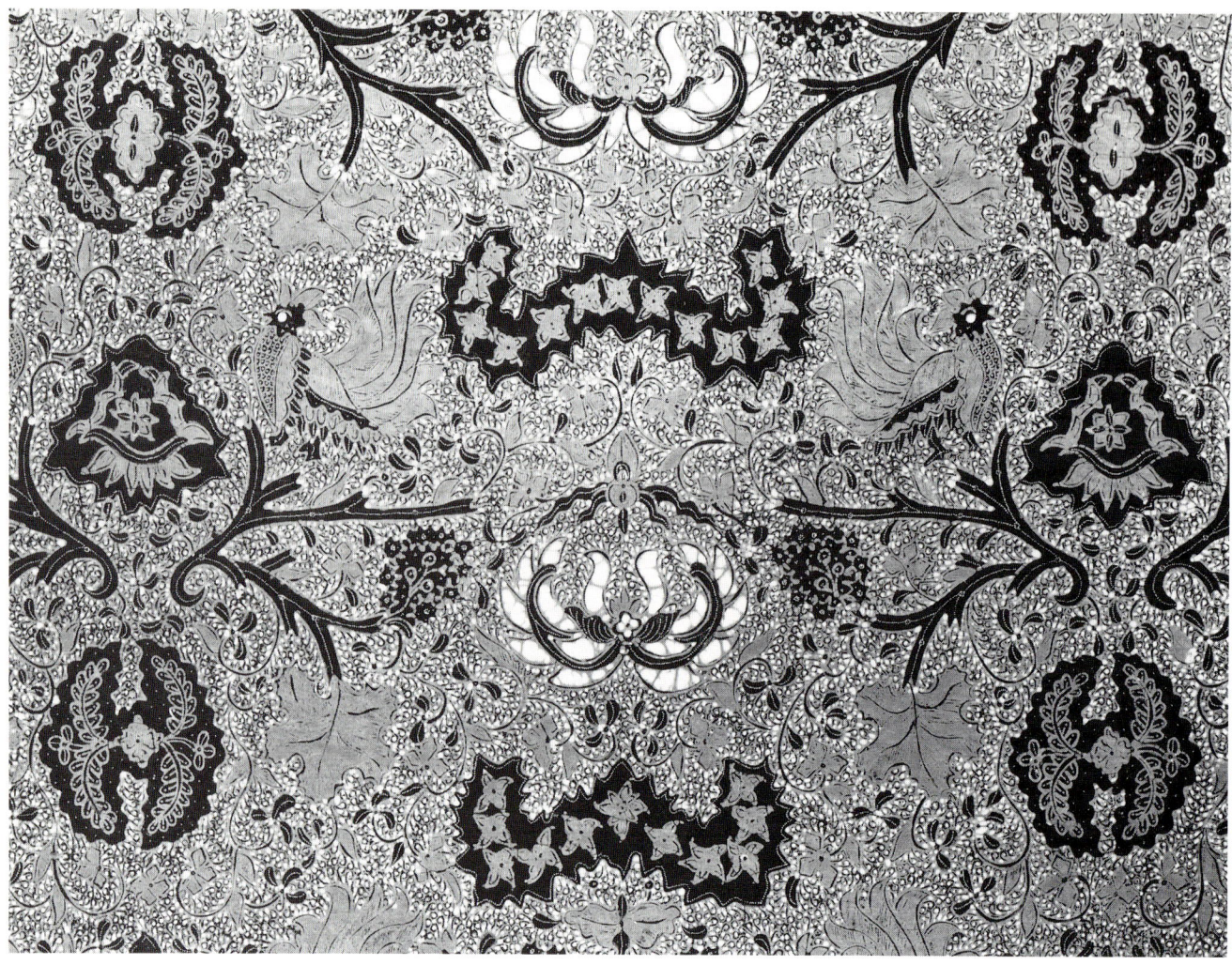

Figure 8. Detail of a batik patterned with the wahyu temurun *motif, representing the trinity of water, earth, and fire* (trimurti). *Originally worn by the bride's father in the* tarub-*raising ceremony which started off the wedding rites, this batik is now an accepted bridal batik. Jakarta, 1987.*

Over the bride's forehead is a gold-and-diamond, semi-circular, fine-toothed comb, *cunduk jungkat*[21], symbol of royalty and virginity. To the left and right over the temple is a pair of smaller semi-circular combs, *centung*, worn only by brides. Apparently the combs are a recent replacement for the tiny braids plaited from the bride's own hair that was cut short especially for the purpose on the day before the wedding (pers. comm., Moeryati Soedibyo-P. Hadiningrat 1982). These combs enhance her hairline, which has been redesigned with dark green pomade in the *paes* fashion described earlier.

The pomade used to create the *paes* is made of the meat of a small coconut (pers. comm., Ibu Maktal, 1984) or candlenut (pers. comm., Moeryati Soedibyo-P. Hadiningrat 1982) burnt crisp over a charcoal fire and ground to a paste, to which are added beeswax and the crushed leaf of *dandang kendhis* or *dandang gula*. The two leaves are interchangeable and related; the latter, which Jasper and Pirngadie identify as

Telanthera strigosa Moq. (1916:48), is in turn linked to a piece of *gamelan* music of the same name whose lyrics contain words and phrases to avert danger (pers. comm., Ibu Maktal 1984). Before the addition of this leaf, the pomade is black. The green color of the leaf signifies protection. It is only when the marriage has been consummated, when the bride is "safe" and danger past, when the drama of Creation is safely concluded, that this protective green coloring is no longer needed. Then the dress is changed as a mark of the wearer's reborn status.

There are many explanations given for the odd shape of the *paes*. The most common is that the scallops are the petals of a lotus, the flower of the godhead, and as such are a direct communication seeking His blessings (pers. comm., Ibu Maktal 1984). The lotus represents ideal beauty and its whiteness connotes purity (pers. comm., Moeryati Soedibyo-P. Hadiningrat 1982). The *paes* completes the image of the bride as a lotus within the metaphor of cosmic

Central Javanese Wedding Ceremony

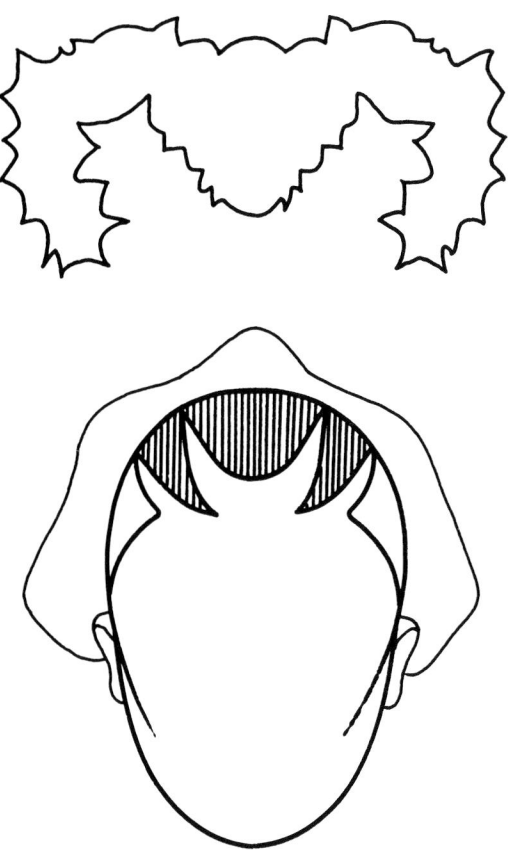

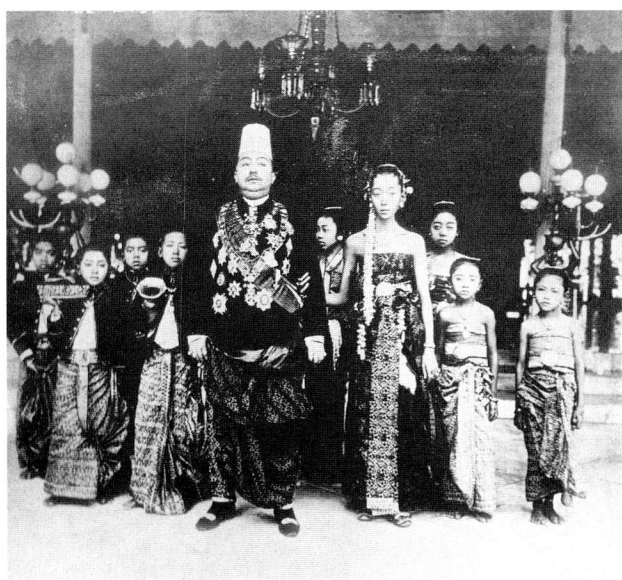

Figure 9. (a) The wahyu temurun *motif (seen in Fig. 8) looks like this when inverted. (b) The outline of the* paes *mirrors the outline of the inverted* wahyu temurun *motif. Both represent the fire, water, and earth trinity (*trimurti*).*

Figure 10. Wedding photograph of Sri Susuhunan Paku Buwana X, Surakarta, circa 1918. The king wears the exclusive dodot ngumbar konco *with a plain* sikepan cekak *jacket. This dress remains the prerogative of the Susuhunan and its intricacies are known to a very few. Although the Central Javanese bridegroom is "king" for a day, he is certainly not the ruler, and his dress, albeit princely, is not exactly the same as that worn by the king. In fact the jacket of the Susuhunan is unadorned because his great personage needs no fancy trappings to mark his status. His bride and second official consort or* permaisuri, *Kanjeng Ratu Emas, the 17-year-old daughter of Sri Sultan Hamengku Buwana VII, however, wears the same* dodot ngumbar konco, *more commonly referred to as* dodot ageng, *worn by today's brides. The attendants are the Susuhunan's children and grandchildren dressed in costume indicative of rank, age, and duties in attending the royal couple. It was not unusual for a ruler to have two official consorts, usually because the first had been unable to bear an heir. As it turned out, Kanjeng Ratu Emas produced only daughters. The eventual heir to the throne, selected when still in the womb by his father, who had some sort of mystical prevision, was, oddly enough, the child of the only concubine not to have been given official status. Photographer unknown.*

creation. This sees the axis of the universe arising from the lotus at the moment of re-creation of the ultimate Creation. Another explanation is that the central arc of the *paes* is the sacred Mahameru mountain, *maha* meaning great and *meru* translating from Sanskrit into mother (**me**me) and father (g**uru**). This interpretation accommodates not only the godhead theme, but also the male-female, red-white classification. The central arc is also said to stand for God, the projections on left and right, *lingga* (male genitalia), while the sections over the ears are *yoni* (female genitalia), and the curls down the cheeks represent *cucu*, grandchildren (pers. comm., Ibu Maktal 1984). Again, there is the intimation of male and female, and divinity.

It has been suggested as well that the central semicircle is a manifestation of the fire-water-earth trinity known as *trimurti* (Kuswadji 1984a; pers. comm., Ibu Maktal 1984). This concept, which complements the themes of godhead and Mahameru, is evident, too, in the mark in between the eyes, the *cithak*. In Surakarta,

this mark is a right-angled arch harboring a dot (Fig. 7). The dot is *bumi*, firmament or earth; the core of a person's entire being is behind this point, deep within. The left leg of the arch is water; fire is on the right (pers. comm., Ibu Maktal 1984).[22] Early in the prewedding rites this fire-water-earth theme is evoked by the batik called *wahyu temurun* (Fig. 8), which the bride's father wears during the ceremony to celebrate the raising of the roof of the guest pavillion or *tarub* (pers. comm., Ibu Maktal 1984). When inverted, the major design element of his batik pattern mirrors in form the outline of the *paes* (Fig. 9). The central scallop symbolizes the firmament or earth, *bumi*, and the arches to the left and right, water and fire. (This pattern is now included in the list of batiks acceptable for a bride to wear with a knee-length velvet blouse.)

The design, color, and configuration of textiles in the Central Javanese wedding all lend credence to the proposition that the ceremony is a reenactment of the preeminent Creation of the Universe. It is manifest in the profusion of cosmic symbols and the implied identification of bride and groom as micro-versions of the cosmos. Costumed in royal attire, the bridal couple become for that day the symbolic king and his consort, who are the axis of the world and the lotus womb. (Although dressed regally, their costumes are not quite like those of actual rulers, as seen in Fig. 10.) The enactment of core rituals in the exact center of the house, in the presence of Dewi Sri/Ibu Pertiwi/Mother Earth (in the bed, in the red-and-white scarf, in the coconut leaf) is intended to bring to the newly wedded couple all the power of the earth's fecundity in this most sacred of all events.

Today, fashions have changed. For Islamic, Christian, and even traditional rites, the formal *dodot ageng* has become reception attire and the velvet jacket with pleated batik skirt has been elevated to wedding dress.[23] But certain things never change. Bedroom and bed, though no longer marking the exact center of the Javanese house, are still the scene of the *malam midadareni*; and the spirit of Dewi Sri is still manifest in the inevitable coconut leaf decorations and the red-and-white scarves, although they may no longer feature in the *panggih* or *tampa kaya* ceremonies. The light green pomaded *paes* is still applied during the *malam midadareni*; and the medium green *paes* must still be worn with the *dodot ageng*, even when the *dodot* is only reception wear. (The black *paes* is reserved for the velvet-jacket-and-batik-skirt costume.) The green *paes* is thus inseparable from the diamond-centered *dodot ageng*, and a reiteration of its statement. Though Islamic or Christian rites prevail and even take precedence over traditional ways, they are still commonly preceded by a ritual bathing and followed by traditional rites whose interpretations have been adapted to fit the tenets of the religion concerned.[24] The more overt references to the sexual relationship and the marital duties and obligations of the bridal couple, which are recognized by all religions, have tended to overlay and perhaps obscure the philosophical mysteries of the Central Javanese wedding ceremony. But the mysteries are still encoded in batik cloth and ritual, and they will reward those with the patience and inclination to explore them.

NOTES

1. Ibu Maktal, whose full name is Raden Ajeng Maktal Dirjokusumo, is a ritual expert and costumier well known in Jakarta and Central Javanese court circles. She has an avid interest in the history and significance of these traditions. I finally met her in 1984 when she was supervising my niece's wedding, and we are now fast friends. I am indebted to her for sharing her knowledge and for making available the photos in Figures 1,2,6, and 10. Ibu Maktal's father, son of a prince, married three times (see Fig. 2). From his first two wives, he had two daughters, of which Ibu Maktal was the younger. When she was about ten, her father fell in love with the daughter of the ruler of Surakarta, Sri Susuhunan Paku Buwana X, by his royal consort. Although Islam allows four wives at one time, by Javanese custom such an illustrious person could only be first wife, so Ibu Maktal's mother and stepmother were released from their marriage vows and the two girls came under the care of their princess step-mother. The princess, known then as Gusti Raden Ajeng Judonagoro, was an intelligent, lively lady, versed in court tradition. She was entrusted with the care of her father's guests-of-state. By custom, a mother would pass such expertise down to her eldest daughter, but in this case the younger girl, Ibu Maktal, showed early promise and became the recipient of all the princess's lore. Of Gusti Raden Ajeng Judonagoro's children, only a son survived birth.

2. *Padmi* means lotus; *garwa/garbha* is translated by Snodgrass as womb or container, since the embryo of the universe is believed to be contained in the womb, making it a container. The word *garwa/garbha* is Sanskrit, and also Javanese. It can most likely be compared to Indonesian, wherein the word *kandungan*, referring to "womb," actually means "container." The verb *mengandung* may mean either "to be pregnant" or "to contain."

3. There are four levels of speaking in the Javanese language. On one level (High Javanese), these events are called *panggih*; on another (daily Javanese), *temon*. They both mean "meeting."

4. A royal bride spends the night before her wedding in her own room and only enters the ceremonial bedroom after she has ritually met the bridegroom in the adjacent hallway (pers. comm., Ibu Maktal 1986). Palace wedding custom differs in several respects from that of the common people; in this essay, some differences shall be pointed out in notes.

5. Batiks, plain cotton *lurik* weavings, red-and-white and black-and-white and other magic-endowed textiles decorate the inner perimeters of the bed (Kuswadji 1984b). The outer perimeter is enclosed in curtains, either mosquito netting in the villages or red *cinde* in the palace, held back by a pair of curtain holders in the shape of the mythical Garuda (Kuswadji 1984b). At the head of the bed hangs a pair of intertwined cloths belonging to the bride and groom, signifying total unity (pers. comm., Ibu Maktal 1986).

6. In the royal palaces this would equate with the *senthong tengah*, the sanctified center of the house which is marked by a great tester-bed said to be the resting place of Dewi Sri, who is synonymous with Ibu Pertiwi, Mother Earth (Departemen Pendidikan dan Kebudayaan 1977-78:50).

7. The clippings are carefully gathered up and put in a small bowl of the scented water, later to be thrown into the current of a river—probably by the bride's mother—using the left hand and facing downstream—to dispose of any misfortune, so it is said.

8. In recent times this has been replaced by a comb.

9. Father sits and "weighs" the couple. If he is on a mat, they "sit" on his feet; if on a chair, they each "sit" on a knee. Mother asks which is heaviest; father replies that they weigh the same.

10. During the royal wedding, after the *panggih* rites, bride and groom retire to a private room to rest and change clothing. They come out again in the velvet jacket (long for a woman, short for a man), and tightly wrapped batik skirt.

11. The bride's father, when he is the Susuhunan of Surakarta, only needs to be present when the bride asks his formal permission to marry before the ritual bathing, and when she and the groom have to "kiss" his foot in homage after the *panggih* is over. Otherwise, he is represented by his *patih*, a high palace official.

12. The pandanus mat is laid on the floor, varicolored cloth and leaves are laid on top, the black-and-white cloth on top of all, and the mat and black-and-white cloth are stitched together along the edges with red thread or bound with red tape. This makes a much neater, flatter mat than stuffing a sewn pocket with leaves and cloth.

13. A royal bride sits upon a *kumudawati*, a rectangular, stole-like textile bearing motifs and geometrical structure with the same qualities as the *klasa bangka* pad and the bridal *dodot* attire. These include protection, fecundity and cosmic references (Solyom and Solyom 1980a). *Kumuda* is Sanskrit for a ripe lotus bud; *wati*, also Sanskrit, means female (pers. comm., Ibu Maktal 1986). In other words, the bride sitting upon this textile is a budding lotus, *padmi*.

14. The full name translates roughly as "black and white dodot carrying a pattern of forest life." *Bangun*=heron; *tulak*=taking off and also warding off. The heron, which is white with some black feathers, takes off in flight when it senses a threat, thus warning others of pending danger. Thus *bangun tulak* refers to the black-and-white color scheme and to the function of the cloth; it also serves as the name by which the cloth is referred, whether it is a black cloth with white centralized diamond, or a black cloth with resist stitching.

15. Turmeric is one of the ingredients. The powder is rubbed into the skin to give it a soft yellowish tinge, called *kuning langsat*. This is considered to be a most desirable skin color.

16. *Cinde* or *chindai/cindai* is the Javanese name for patola. It is used today for the original patola as well as for local copies. In fact, the copy should be called *cinden*, which means "like cinde"; but few people are aware of this grammatical technicality, which was brought to my attention by Rens Heringa. The word denotes a distinctive pattern and color combination. Each variation of pattern has a name, as well, the name being preceded by the word *cinde*.

17. A rare few were once woven from human hair, I have read, but these would not be called *janur* because *janur* must be yellow. *Cinde* scarves may be trimmed with gold fringe.

18. When it is raised, around two days before the ritual bath, the roof structure of the guest pavillion is trimmed around the edge with plain hanging coconut leaves. During preliminary decoration activities, coconut leaves, either plain or plaited into decorative mobiles, may be hung/placed. There are, in addition, two pairs of coconut leaf spheres bearing other ornaments (birds, *keris*, etc.) that are required in the Central Javanese wedding ceremony. On the night before the wedding, one pair is "loaned" to the bride by Dewi Sri (Kamaratih). These are removed on the wedding day and replaced with a pair sent by the bridegroom, which are placed by the bridal seat (mat, carpet, etc.) just before the bridegroom arrives for the core events.

19. At least one in a private collection in Surakarta is made of the dried and stretched embryonic sac (*widungan*) of an unborn goat, once the material for all *kuluk matak* (pers. comm, Ibu Maktal 1986). When dried, the sac is bluish white and transparent. In the 1960s it was replaced on the *kuluk* with blue cardboard covered with the celluloid paper. Now the *kuluk* is being made of a light blue plastic.

20. The Sultan of Yogyakarta wears a knot of real cloves rather than metal for certain religious rites (Kuswadji 1984a). Cloves are not only recognized for magic and medicinal power, but the dried flower bud carries the cosmic symbolism in its calyx of four sepals placed like the points of the compass around a central sphere, or a corolla of five petals (Kuswadji 1984a).

21. *Jungkat* is a plain fine-toothed comb; *cunduk jungkat* is a fine-toothed bomb with a metal cap. Both are semi-circular. *Cunduk* is a stick-pin—the kind one puts in the hair; it is about 8" long and has a flower on the end, attached to the main pin with a spring.

22. In the principality of Yogyakarta, the *cithak* is a small lozenge of betel leaf (*sirih*) pasted to the forehead.

23. As people began to lose knowledge of traditional ways, they turned more and more to the velvet and batik dress. In 1958, when I first came to Indonesia, this had become the usual wedding dress worn by commoners. In the early 1970s, based upon remembered knowledge that the *dodot ageng* was the proper wedding dress, President Soeharto reintroduced it when his daughter married. It is becoming more and more popular, but only for the traditional ritual—not for Islamic/Christian rites. Nowadays there are two ways of observing traditional ritual: either immediately after the Islamic/Christian rites, or at the evening reception. In the first case, the bride and groom have no time to change from the velvet and batik dress; in the second case, they are more and more frequently wearing the *dodot ageng*.

24. Today most Christians and Moslems are unaware of the cosmic interpretation of the ceremony and see everything from a Moslem or Christian point of view. Thus, while the core events are standard, other items may be left out. To them, the *paes*, for example, is a sign of beauty. This is what is meant when one talks about the layers of meaning to everything Javanese, or even Indonesian. There is the sexual interpretation, which elders are all aware of. There is the male-female complementation theme of marriage, which everyone understands. There are Moslem and Christian parallels; and there is the cosmic interpretation which only some people know, almost all of whom are at least middle-aged or related to the royal families.

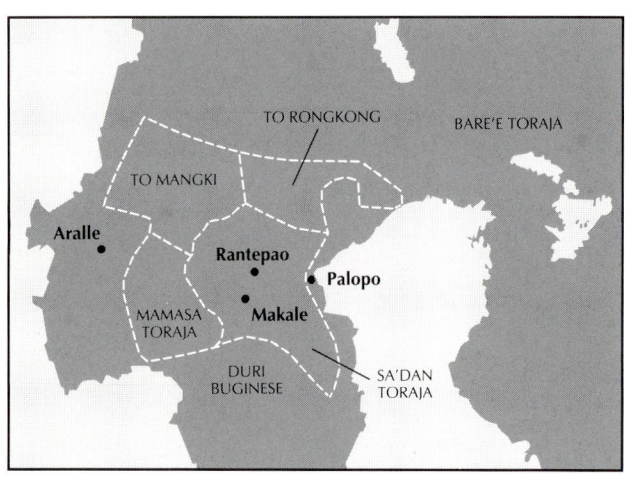

Ethnic groups in southwest and central Sulawesi. After a map by E.J. Brill, Leiden.

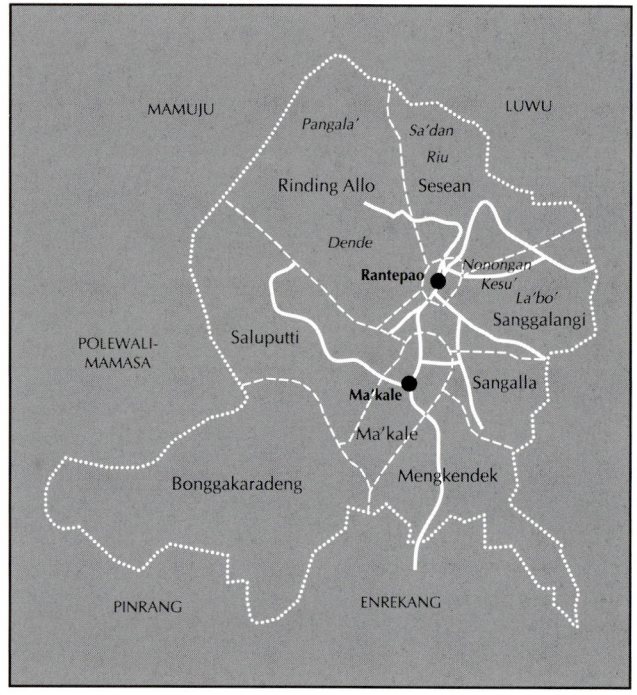

The Regency (Kabupaten) of Tana Toraja, home of the Sa'dan Toraja people, divided into districts. The names of sub-districts are indicated here in italics.

.... Boundary of the regency.

-------------- Boundary of the district.

———————— Main road.

The Sacred Cloths of the Toraja
Unanswered Questions

Hetty Nooy-Palm

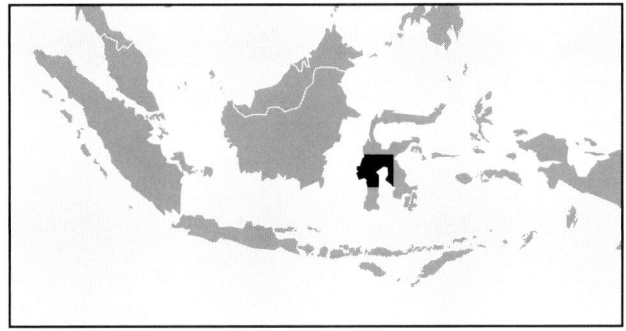

The Toraja live in the mountainous areas of central Sulawesi (formerly Celebes). Toraja is a contraction of *to-ri-aja*, "Men of the mountains"; the name was given them by the Buginese, a group to the south who in previous centuries traded their goods to the mountain dwellers. The Toraja themselves were composed of several tribes (see Map).

The sacred cloths called *maa'* and *sarita* have played an enormous role in the traditional ritual life of the Toraja people. These ancient cloths—some of indigenous make, and others imported from from Asia and the Netherlands—are still highly valued. However they are no longer either made or imported, and the role they play in the life of the Toraja people is diminishing. This is partly because so many have converted to Christianity; also, new teaching systems are undermining the belief in the holiness and magical power of these fabrics.[1] Furthermore, sacred textiles are victims of wear and tear, destruction in times of political unrest, and so forth. In rituals nowadays, the Toraja are apt to decorate with imported Sumba cloths, batiks, and cheap towels, to compensate for the lack of old *maa'* and *sarita*. Moreover, the sacred cloths sell so well on the antique market that fake ones are being fabricated.

As the authentic sacred cloths diminish in number, so do those people who can give us information about them: the last generation that could do so is dying out. Thus the ancient cloths remain shrouded in mystery, and questions we have about them are increasingly difficult to answer. When were they imported into Sulawesi? What sorts of cloth came from India, what was their special appeal, and how were they incorporated into Toraja culture? What was the source of inspiration for the indigenous *maa'* and *sarita*, who made them, and in which regions? And what was the technical process of fabrication? This paper, while it does not pretend to solve all these puzzles, will address some of them. Sacred cloths are owned by several

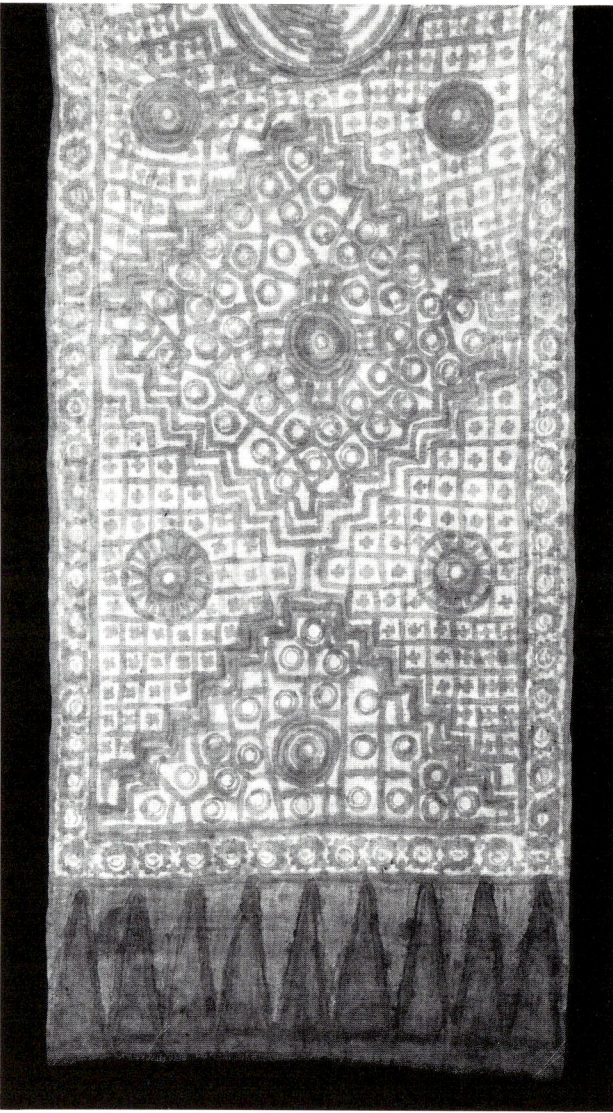

Figure 1. Early 20th century maa' *with triangles* (tumpal), *or in terms of the Toraja language, arrowheads* (pa'sora'). *The figure at center is Tulangdidi', spinning in the moon. Painted, woven, handspun cotton. 68.5 x 274 cm. UCLA Museum of Cultural History X86.2064.*

ethnic groups including the To Mangki, the To Rongkong, and the Bare'e-speaking people[2] as well as the Sa'dan and Mamasa Toraja. This paper will focus on the latter two groups, except when the cultural heritage of the others can shed light on the subject.

The Sa'dan Toraja, numbering about 340,000, live in Tana Toraja, a regency in the northern part of the southwestern peninsula of south Sulawesi (see Map). Closely related to them, the Mamasa Toraja, numbering about 84,000, live in the regency of Polewali Mamasa, situated west of Tana Toraja. The principal means of subsistence of both groups is agriculture. Rice, maize, cassava, and tubers are staples. Coffee and cloves are the principal cash crops in Tana Toraja, coffee alone in Mamasa. Animal husbandry is practiced on a large scale by both peoples; only the breeding of pigs, however, is of importance. The water buffalo, rarely used for work in the fields, is a primary status symbol. It has to be as fat as possible, with large horns and a beautiful hue, jet-black or dappled—a real show animal. After being shown at rituals, it is sacrificed; at death feasts of a high order dozens of buffaloes are killed. The pig is also a sacrificial animal. Buffalo hides and pigs, however, are exported: the value of these animals is not only ritual, but also economic.

Though traditional values are still important, social change was initiated in the last century with the introduction of coffee growing and coffee trade. The subjugation of the Sa'dan and Mamasa country by the Dutch in 1906, the period of Japanese occupation (1942-45), and the declaration of Indonesian independence in 1945 accelerated the process. In 1913 the region inhabited by the Sa'dan and Mamasa Toraja became the missionary field of the Reformed Alliance of the Dutch Reformed Church.[3] Today half of the population has been converted to Christianity. The school system introduced by the Netherlands Indies government and the missionaries opened a new world to these peoples, who had known only oral tradition. Tourism, a recent development (since about 1975) has brought further changes.

Despite social changes, rank is still a value in Toraja society. There are several classes: the nobility, the common people, and those who were formerly bondsmen—slaves and serfs. Even after slavery was abolished by the Dutch in 1906, slaves stayed with their former masters, and until very recent times performed several duties at rituals.

In the three southern districts of Tana Toraja (Ma'kale, Mengkendek, and Sangalla'), a fourth class, consisting of the princes (*puang*) and their families, was superimposed on the other three. Genealogies count much, being closely related to rank. Noblemen and priests can be genealogical experts; reciting and consulting genealogical trees is the task of the *to minaa*, a priest versed in tribal lore. Other priests are the

Sacred Cloths of the Toraja

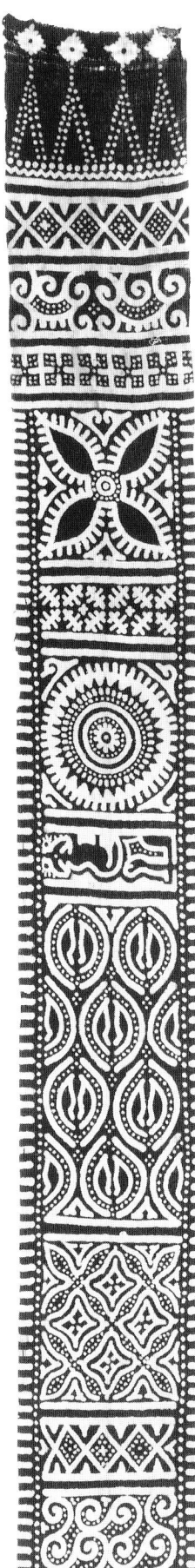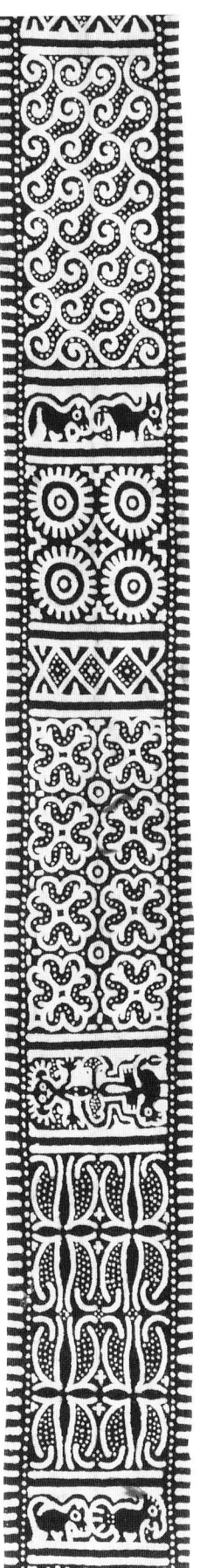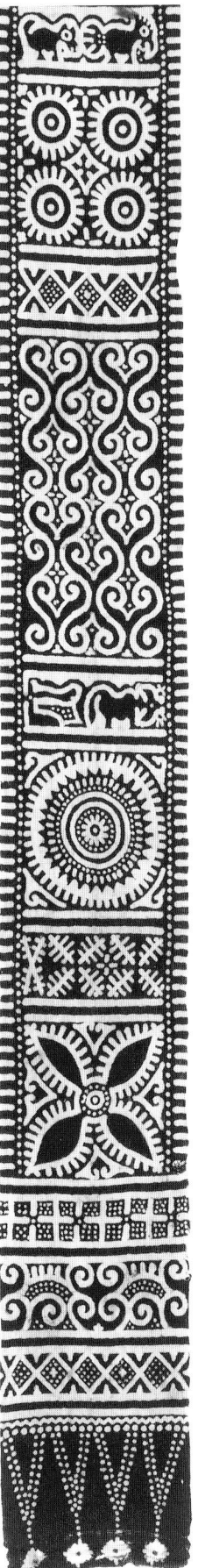

Figure 2. Late 19th or early 20th century sarita *made in Tana Toraja, depicting a buffalo drawing a plough and motifs like those on the woodcarving of the* tongkonan *and rice-barn, such as the* radiating sun *(*barre allo*) and* tadpole *(*pa'bulintong siteba'*). The names of the leaf-like motifs are unknown. Indigo-dyed handspun cotton. 19 x 419 cm. UCLA Museum of Cultural History X86.2065.*

burake, who used to preside in the *bua'* ritual (discussed below), the medicine man, the rice priest, and the death priest. All experts, including the priests, are held in high esteem (although the death priest is more or less shunned because of his connection with death). Men may excel in smithing, carpentry, and woodcarving, women in singing or weaving (although that art is deteriorating). Most of the experts, priests included, belong to the class of commoners; a noblewoman, however, may be an expert weaver.

The nuclear family is the smallest unit among the Toraja kin groups. More often than not, it consists of three generations. The largest family group, composed of numerous small nuclear and three-generation families, is called a *rapu* (or *pa'rapuan*); its members cooperate at big rituals. The *rapu* is neither patrilineal nor matrilineal, but traces its origin to an ancestor who founded a house, *tongkonan*, which is the visible material symbol of the kin group as well as its social and religious center. At family feasts, the gable of the *tongkonan*, which always faces north, is decorated with beaded ornaments, sacred cloths, and weapons. Cardinal points are important in the cosmic order. North is the realm of the deified ancestors and of the gods and ghosts of the firmament, known collectively as *deata*, the deities of the North or the Northeast. It is the sphere of heaven and light, as opposed to South, the region of darkness and the world below. Likewise West, the region of the setting sun, is opposed to East, where the sun rises. Each region has its set of rituals. The rituals of the West are associated with death; they deal with funeral ceremonies. The rituals of the East are connected with life, with the well-being of man, his animals, and his principal food, rice. Exorcistic rituals and those concerned with the healing of the sick fall also in this domain.

The Uses of Sacred Cloth

Every family group has set of sacred cloths that are displayed at ceremonies or worn as scarves or headdress[4] by ritual officials. *Maa'* are usually wide rectangles of cloth in varying sizes[5] (Fig. 1). *Sarita*, by contrast, are long, narrow fabrics (Fig. 2). Imported *maa'* come from India via Java; those of indigenous make can be traced to one of three regions: Pangala', Riu, or La'bo', a complex of villages in Kesu' (see Map). Imported *sarita* are of Dutch origin and can be as long as 492 centimeters. Those made locally are generally shorter than the imported ones. According to Toraja informants, *maa'* are considered holier than *sarita* and command a higher price. *Maa'* bless their owners and make them rich, so that after death their families are able to organize a superior funeral (Nooy-Palm 1980: sec. 5). Some cloths, considered very holy, fall outside the categories of either *maa'* or *sarita*, and therefore constitute a third type; but since they differ substantially one from another, they have no group name.

Sarita are used at festivals of both the East and the West (Nooy-Palm 1980: secs. 6.4.1, 6.4.2, and 1986: chap. 2). The same is true of *maa'*, but those preferred for Eastern ceremonies bear the cow-in-corral design, which is probably a fertility motif (feminine in contrast to the stylized buffalo head, *pa'tedong*, with its horns).

Celebrations of the Eastern sphere include feasts connected with the renewal of the ancestral house, the *tongkonan*. Even the re-roofing of this building is a big ceremony: many *rapu* members attend, bringing fat pigs in decorated litters. The decoration consists of holy plants and sacral cloths. As is usual with big feasts, the front of the *tongkonan* is adorned with sacred objects, cloths among them, which are heirlooms of the *rapu*. Another ritual of the East is the *merok*, a feast of thanksgiving, in which the *deata* are asked to bless the *tongkonan* and the *rapu*. Many members of the family group attend the ceremony. A sandalwood tree is set up in the yard, in front of the *tongkonan*. By means of two lianas and a long, narrow *sarita*, the tree is connected with the *tongkonan*. Like the latter, the sandalwood tree is a symbol of the *rapu*. If it grows, the *rapu* will prosper. The highlight of the ceremony is the killing of a water buffalo by means of "stabbing" (*rok*, hence the name of the feast, *merok*, to stab). The sacrificial animal is tied to the tree; after the priest (*to minaa*) has recited the tribal myth, the buffalo is slaughtered.

The most impressive feast of the Eastern sphere is the *bua'* ritual. A *bua'* is a territory encompassing one, two, or more villages; all the *rapu* in this territorial community participate in the feast. One of the *tongkonan* in the *bua'* territory is chosen for the fetish, called *anak dara*, "virgin." While it may seem odd to Westerners, the "virgin" is considered the symbol of potential fertility of the entire *bua'*. The fetish is a complex structure of eight bamboos, connected and tied together by means of a *sarita*, and decorated with objects that allude to fertility. The *anak dara* is guarded by the *tumbang*, a maiden or woman of high rank belonging to one of the important *rapu* in the *bua'* (though she does not have the status of priestess; that woman is the *burake*, who presides over the *bua'* ritual). For at least one "rice-year" (a rice-cycle), the *tumbang* stays near the *anak dara* and is not allowed to leave the *tongkonan*. When her guardianship is over, she is carried out of the house, entirely covered with sacred *maa'* cloths (which she later removes). During the *bua'* ceremony, she is escorted by seven other women or girls who take part with her in several rites. In one, the eight women sit in a circle, connected by a *sarita* that is draped around their shoulders, and they handle a winnowing fan; thus the rite is called *mangria barang*, "handling the winnowing fan." Another rite

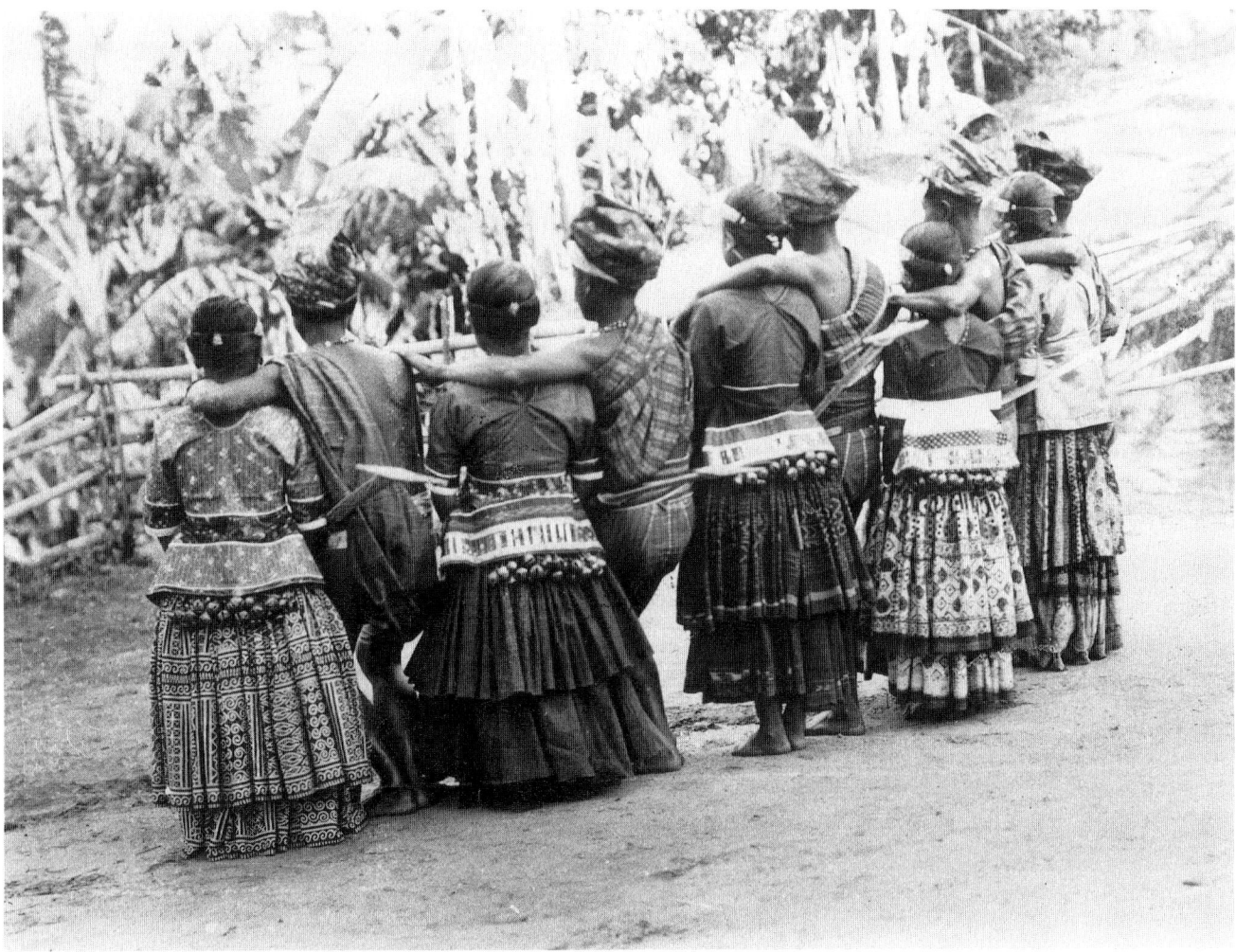

Figure 3. A rare early photograph shows men and women doing the raigo, *a round dance of the To Kulawi people. The dancer at far left wears a skirt of imported* sarita. *Late 19th or early 20th century. Photographer unknown.*

involves bamboo sticks (*piong*) filled with sticky rice; the women stand in a row, again linked by a *sarita* that is wrapped around the left hand (over the pulse) of each. This rite is called *ma' tekken piong*, "the *piong* stand there like sticks."

The rituals of the West, dealing with death, are too elaborate to describe here in detail. The corpse is laid in state in the central room of the *tongkonan* and swathed in layers of cotton cloth. Over these are spread a covering of red flannel and, finally, a sacred *maa'*. Sacred cloths adorn the room; the gable of the *tongkonan* is also decorated with *maa'*, and the effigy that is supposed to house the soul of the deceased is often adorned with a *sarita* as its headdress. The To Kulawi, distant cousins of the Sa'dan and Mamasa Toraja who live on the upper reaches of the Palu River, use imported *sarita* as part of their festive dress.[6] Young men wear them as sashes around their waists. Young women sew several together to make a rather voluminous skirt (Fig. 3).

Problems of Classification

Maa' are particularly difficult to classify because there are so many kinds, and because Toraja names for them can be confusing. Of the *maa'* imported from India there are a great variety. They include the large block-printed cotton cloth, *palampore*, from the Coromandel Coast; silk double-ikat *patola* from Gujerat; and the large cotton cloth known as *kalamkari*, either block-printed or hand-penned. All three terms are Indian, but the term "patola" (*patolu*, sing.; *patola*, plu.) is used in Toraja and indeed throughout Indonesia. Other commoner types are also imported from India. But for the Toraja, the rarer they are, the holier; and the larger, the better. The patola depicting elephants are extremely valued. In 1970 I saw one in a village near the Sangalla' Kesu' border, whose red background represented the color of life, strength, and magical power, and whose great size added to its holiness. Its value at the time (about 1970) was an odd

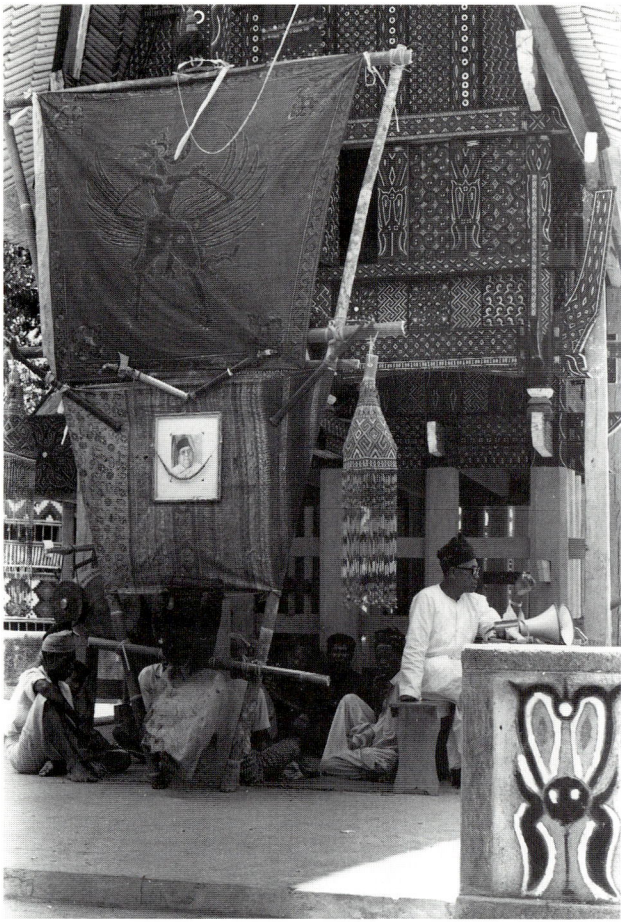

Figure 4. The Bate Manurun of Sangalla', displayed with other heirlooms at the first part of the death ritual of the prince (puang) *Lasok Rinding of Sangalla' in 1970. A portrait of the deceased is hung on a* maa'. *The Bate Manurun is displayed on a bamboo frame decorated with kris and* kandaure, *the beaded ornament, mounted in front of the* tongkonan *Buntu Kalando, where the bodily remains of the* puang *rest. The sacred cloth depicts a shadow-puppet-like figure with wings—a kind of bird-man. Sangalla', 1970.*

twenty buffaloes—approximately US $2,000. The large *kalamkari* with scenes from the Ramayana are held in high esteem also.[7] Even though the tale is unknown to the Toraja, the monkey-kings with their many heads appeal to them, for creatures having a number of heads must be very powerful. Hence these cloths are named *rangga ulu,* "split heads" or "many heads." Other kinds of *maa'* include *patola gayang,* a patola with kris-like motifs; *bulu lembang* or *bulu toli,* the name of an old *maa'* in Riu (*bulu* = hair, *lembang* = ship); *balang bai,* "the piebald pig"; *maa' tedong lambang,* the *maa'* which is fastened on the back of the *parepe',* the buffalo which carries the deceased to the Land of the Souls (see Nooy-Palm 1980: sec. 6.4.1). *Tedong lambang* means "the buffalo which crosses" (i.e., which takes the path to Puya, the Hereafter). A more complete survey of the names of these textiles can be found Nooy-Palm (1979: sec. 4). Certain indigenous *maa'* play a special part in Eastern feasts; this is the case with those *maa'* depicting buffalo cows with their calves in a corral (discussed below).

Classification of sacred cloths is further confused by the fact that, to the common name of the *maa'* or *sarita,* the Toraja add a "personal" name if it concerns an important cloth. Thus while the *rangga ulu* mentioned above designates a genre of *maa'* of the *kalamkari* type depicting the many-headed monkey kings from the Ramanyana, "Rangga Ulu" is the personal name of a precious patola of an altogether different design, which is in the possession of the princely (*puang*) family of Sangalla'; but in this case it is a personal, not a generic, name. Sometimes these old fabrics are not very spectacular from our point of view, as was the case with the *maa'* I acquired in 1972 for the Museum of the Koninklijk Instituut voor de Tropen (Royal Tropical Institute). The family that owned it had become Christian, so the function of the textile, once sacred, was obsolete. The cloth's personal name was Telo-telo Langi', or "Summit of Heaven." Originating from Dende, it had once had the power to increase the family's wealth and its herd of buffalo and flocks of chicken. It was used only in Eastern ceremonies.

Cloths with personal names tend to be especially sacred and powerful, having the magic capacity to bring their owners prosperity. Many fall outside the strict categories of *maa'* and *sarita,* and into the third, unnameable class of sacred textile. Among these is the sacred Bate Manurun of Sangalla' (Fig. 4), an heirloom of the *puang* (prince) of the princedom of Sangalla'. Bate Manurun means "The Banner which Descended." It is supposed to be of heavenly origin and was once the property of Lakipadada, the famous ancestor of the *puang* families of Tana Toraja. Thirty generations ago Lakipadada gave this banner to his son, who inherited the princedom of Sangalla' (Nooy-Palm 1979:151).

The cloth, which is rectangular, depicts an anthropomorphic figure with a bird's head and wings on a red background. It is in fact a bird-man, a creature that does not play a role in Toraja mythology. What intrigues me is the origin of this heirloom, which in style resembles the holy flags and banners to be found among the heirlooms of south Sulawesi (Buginese and Macassarese) kings and princes. Where was this cloth actually made, and when and how did it come to Sulawesi? Most probably it was Javanese, made in Batavia (Jakarta) in the last quarter of the seventeenth century and imported into Sulawesi by the Dutch. It closely resembles a flag given in 1679 by the Dutch governor-general Rycklof van Goens in Batavia to the Buginese prince Aru Palakka (Arung Palaka); the prince was an ally of the Vereenigde Oost Indische Compagnie or V.O.C., the Dutch East India Company (Le Roux 1930:258-65, and the color plate between 258-59). According to Le Roux, the flag was made in Batavia by a Javanese artist. Another flag of Bone (the princedom of Aru Palakka) resembles the Bate Manurun even more closely, depicting the same type of Garuda (Le Roux 1930: pl. III, fig. 7). The Garudas are late Hindu-Javanese in style: we find the same figure on South Sulawesi krises. The Bate Manurun is displayed on ceremonial occasions whether of the East or of the West. It has a tear which has been mended, and which is supposed to disappear when the cloth is shown. According to the princes of Sangalla' it also changes its color, becoming green on the second day of display.

Another in this category is the intriguing Tannuntangmangka of Nonongan (Nooy-Palm 1980: sec. 5) which is stored in the famous *tongkonan* of Nonongan. Tannuntangmangka, "The Unfinished Cloth," is said to have been woven by Manaek, the famous female ancestor of Nonongan, who lived approximately thirty generations ago. She is believed to have woven the cloth on her large loom, which spanned the Sa'dan River. The cloth appeared to be of Chinese origin, a kind of *shantung* or coarsely woven silk. Extremely holy, it is displayed only in Eastern rituals, such as *merok*, or other rituals in which the house is the center of ceremonies (Nooy-Palm 1980: sec. 6.4.2; 1986: chap. 3). If the family agrees, it can be shown on special request, together with the other heirlooms of *tongkonan* Nonongan. This requires the sacrifice of a special type of pig, *bai ballang sanduk*, a black piglet with a white back and an upturned white snout (like a spoon, *sanduk*, according to my Toraja host who spent an entire day procuring this animal). In 1983 the family of Nonongan met my request with utmost graciousness. However, the elderly couple in charge of the heirlooms still clung to the old faith (Aluk to Dolo, "The Belief of the Forefathers"). Unlike the other members of the family, who had been Christian for a long time, they did object. At first the old nobleman, guardian of the heirlooms, refused to show Tannuntangmangka, and it was only with difficulty that I finally managed to see the cloth. It turned out to be a greenish-yellow piece of silk, very long indeed. I could not photograph it or take its measurements, however, because of its holiness. Its color, light and bright, is associated with the realm of life in ritual, which is the Eastern sphere. Because it is extremely sacred, Tannuntangmangka can cause the wearer to have a headache. Such a thing happened before World War Two, when one of the members of the family had to use Tannuntangmangka as a turban during the *merok* ceremony.

These sacred cloths are stored in the southwestern part of the rear chamber of the *tongkonan*, in a basket called *baka' bua*, or in trunks and wooden chests. The house is a cosmic symbol, and the southern (also southwestern) part of the dwelling is associated with the ancestors (*to dolo*), who live in the southwest. When the textiles are displayed in ritual, and the house is the center of the ceremony, they are hung on the northern gable, the holy part of the house associated with the gods of the northeast, the *deata*. Although the textiles are likely to be worn out and not altogether very clean, they are handled with care and kissed (or, rather, "sniffed") when they are taken out of their hiding places.

As on the islands of Sumba, Flores, Roti, Babar, Bali, and Lombok, the job of guarding textiles is given to women, for they belong to the realm of the weaker sex. Often it is a woman of the family, "she in whose lap the cloths are thrown," "she who is handling the cloth" (*to mangria sampin*), who is in charge of these textiles. The leading women in the family know exactly how old the *maa'* and *sarita* are. Mrs. Indo' Lai' Rante of Ba'tan, Kesu' informed me in 1978 that her *maa'*, with a "spots of heaven" (*doti langi'*) motif, was seven generations old, which meant that the cloth had been in the family for that period. A cloth with the *alli barra'* ("to buy husked rice") motif had been in the possession of the family four generations, as had one with a betel leaf motif (*daun bolu*). According to myth and tradition, the holy textiles became heirlooms of the family in different ways. Some, like the Bate Manurun, came from heaven; some were brought to Tana Toraja by the ancestors; or they appeared "all of a sudden" in the house. But the Toraja are also aware that many came from elsewhere, even from overseas: *sarita to lambang* means *sarita* brought by people fording a river (*lambang* also translates as "floating"), which should be interpreted as *sarita* coming from outside Tana Toraja. Another called *maa' to norrong*, means *maa'* brought by people swimming. Waters had to be crossed before the textiles came to the interior of Sulawesi!

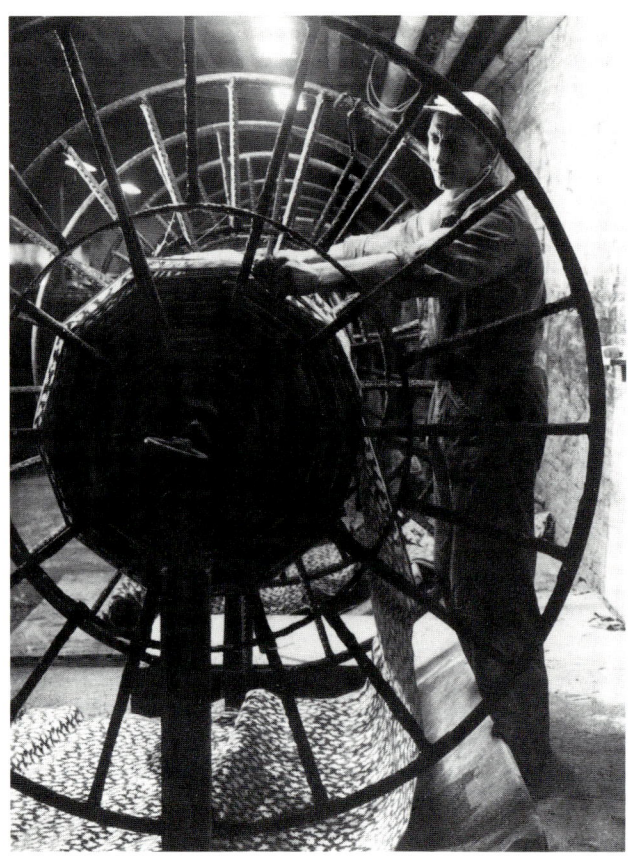
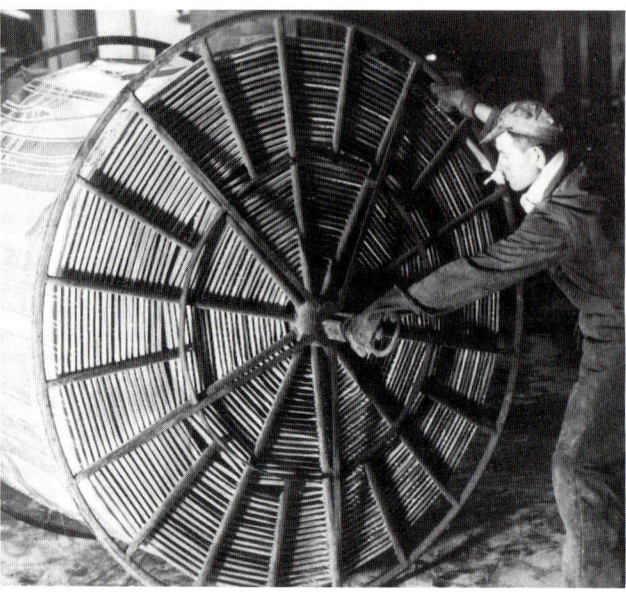

Figure 5a-e (left to right). Photographs from the Vlisco B.V. archives show sarita *cloth being dyed in the Vlisco factories, probably in the 1920s. After being block-printed with a special paste, the cloths were wound on the special rack (reep) which was then rolled and finally dipped into the dye-vat.*

How Trade Brought Textiles to Sulawesi

Originally, the cloths came from overseas. For centuries, the vessels of south Sulawesi have played a great part in the trade of Indonesia. A *bas relief* of the famous stupa of Borobudur in Central Java depicts a ship sailing in full seas.[8] In spite of its outrigger—a feature absent from today's larger sailing ships of Sulawesi—the tripoid masts make it clear that this beautiful boat is the prototype of a Buginese or Macassarese trading vessel called *paduwakang*.[9] As the Borobudur dates approximately from the eighth century A.D. (the exact date of its foundation being unknown—see Bernet Kempers n.d.:45), we may assume that ships from south Sulawesi were trading with Java at that time. What was traded remains unknown. Was it rattan, resin, or other forest products? Nickel and iron for fabricating krises with *pamor*[10]? Old daggers from the fourteenth-century kingdom of Majapahit, however, do not show this elaborate pattern-welding technique. Perhaps ceramics were traded already, but (importantly, from our point of view) we do not know if cloth was part of the cargo.

In the following centuries the seafarers from south Sulawesi expanded their trading activities, visiting many ports in Southeast Asia.[11] Not only Javanese and Malaysian ports, but Indian towns as well were included in the trade. With Arabian and Chinese they exchanged spices, cloths, forest products, weapons, ceramics, beads, and other goods. To Tana Toraja, the Buginese and Macassarese traded Chinese ceramics; examples there date from the fifteenth and seventeenth century, though, curiously, sixteenth-century earthenware and porcelain are absent from all of south Sulawesi (Orsoy de Flines 1939).

The Europeans found their way to Asia at the end of the fifteenth century. Their main objective was to monopolize the spice trade; to that end, they sold spices, textiles and other goods in the Moluccas. First came the Portuguese; the Dutch followed about a century later, when Cornelis Houtman and Pieter Dirksz de Keyzer landed in Bantam in 1596. The Dutch ousted the Portuguese from the East Indian waters, and even curtailed the age-old trade of the Buginese and Macassarese. Nevertheless, the Sulawesian seafarers continued their trading, and from Macassar they reached Pare-pare and Palopo on the west and east coasts, bearing articles brought by the Dutch. Textiles from India, Dutch coins of the V.O.C., beads, and so forth, were traded from Macassar to the interior. The trade continued from the 1602, when the company was founded, until the very end of the eighteenth century, when it ceased to exist (see De Graaf 1949:169-71; Louwerse 1894:270; Stapel 1930:180-95).

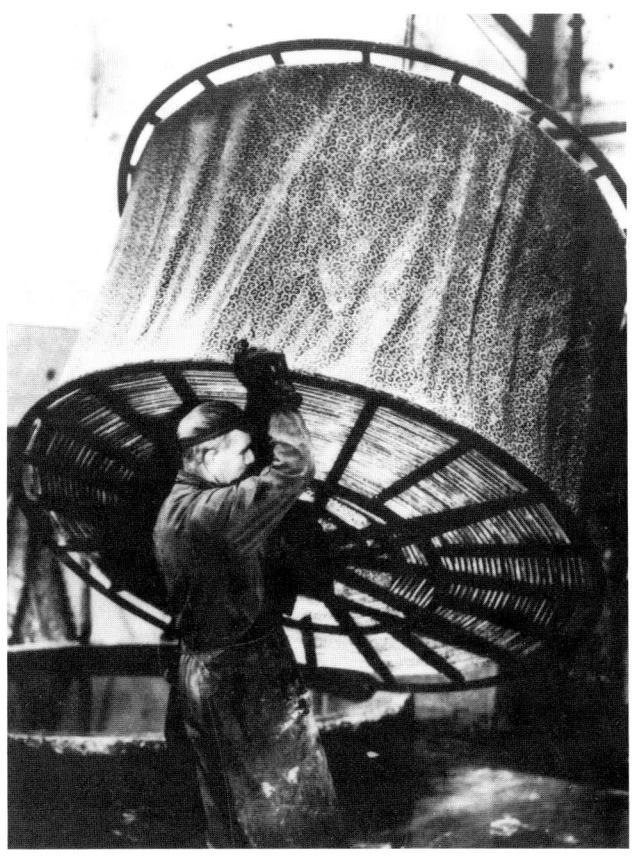
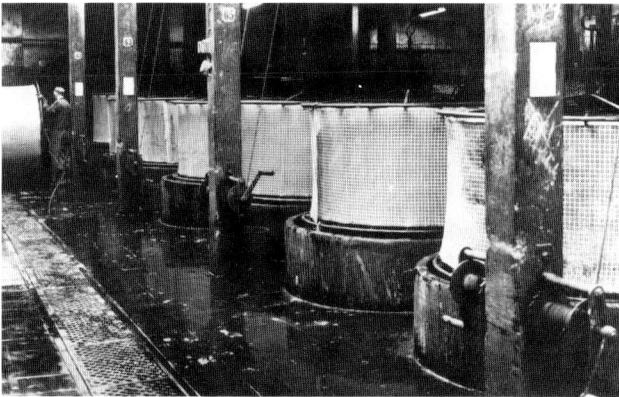
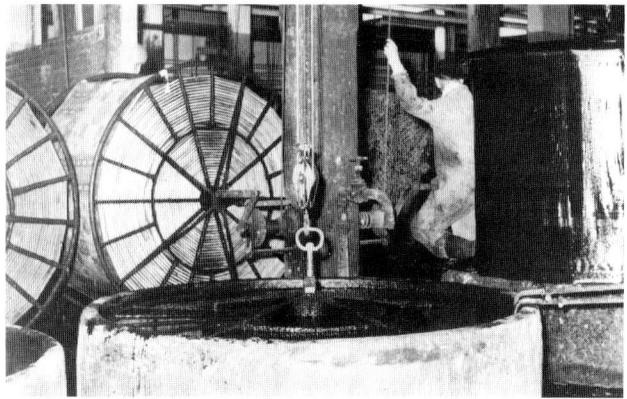

Dutch-made *Sarita*

Imported *sarita*, made in Holland, holds a special challenge for the investigator (see Nooy-Palm 1980: sec. 2). How and when did it reach the interior of Sulawesi? Was it the prototype of the locally made *sarita*, or vice versa? The problem intrigued J.W. van Nouhuys, who mentioned in his article a printed *sarita* in the collection of Dr. P.A. Driessen in Leiden, with an attached note (in Buginese) making it clear that such cloths were much sought after in Sulawesi (Nouhuys 1925-26:110-22). Nouhuys further established that the cotton mills of Van Vlissingen and Co., Ltd., had made these fabrics since 1880, which meant that they had probably reached Tana Toraja in the same year—twenty-six years before the Toraja were subjugated by the Dutch. Contact between the Dutch sellers and the Buginese dealers was made by a Mr. Bienfait, who lived alternately in Batavia and Macassar[12]. The factory-made *sarita* were exported to Indonesia until approximately 1930, when the world was in economic crisis; from then on the Dutch East India government did not allow the importation of European (Dutch) printed batik or other cloth in order to protect Indonesian-made textiles.

Nouhuys stated, probably rightly, that a Toraja *sarita* must have been the prototype of the Dutch printed *sarita*.[13] He tried to find these cloths in the stock of Dutch factories between 1924 and 1926, but did not succeed. Nor did I, sixty years later, when looking for information in the Vlisco archives in Helmond. Nouhuys, however, published a picture of a *sarita*-like indigenous cloth, made in the upper Karama region north of Tana Toraja, which showed some resemblance to the Dutch-made textile, and which, according to him, was batiked (Nouhuys 1925-26: figs. 12,13). Perhaps a cloth like this one was the prototype for the Dutch-made *sarita*.[14]

The imported *sarita* were block printed. How this was done has kindly been explained to me by Mr. C.H. Krantz of the Vlisco firm. Motifs were cut out of felt and these then pasted on wooden blocks (*viltvulder*). A pad was soaked in a paste called *mastiek* which, the subsequent procedure makes clear, acted as a resist in the dye process. As the wooden block was pressed on the soaked pad, the felt absorbed the *mastiek*; the printer then carefully pressed the block on the cotton cloth by hand. This was repeated many times; several blocks, each with a different design, could be used on a single cloth. After the paste dried the cloth was placed on a special rack called a *reep*[15] that may be described as two carriage wheels connected by an axle the width of the cloth to be dyed (not all *sarita* are the same size). The cloth printed with the *mastiek* paste was then stretched between the two wheels, its edges secured with little wooden pins fastened to the spokes of each

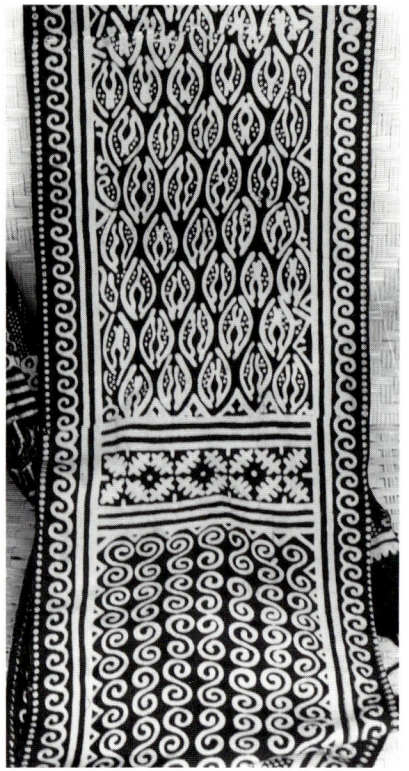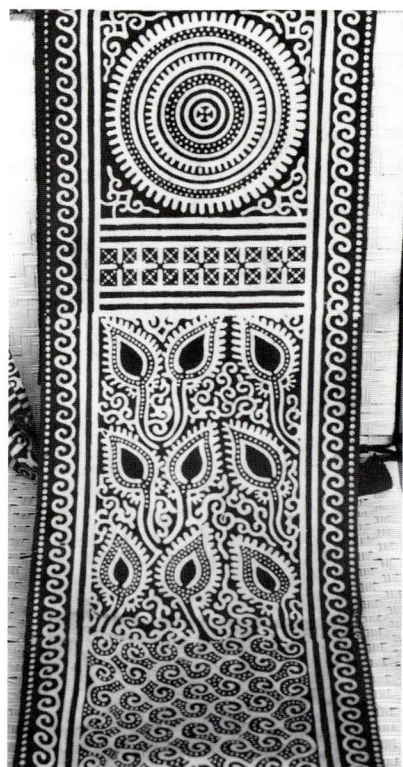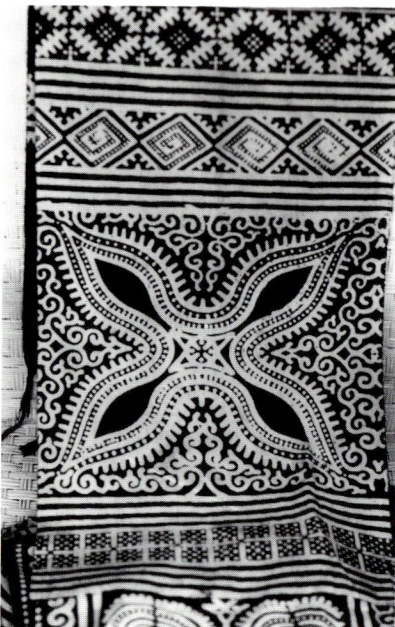

Figure 6a,b,c. Parts of a sarita *printed at Vlisco B.V. in Holland now in the possession of Mrs. M. Pasaka in Rantepao where it was photographed in 1978. From left to right: (a) The "cowrie-shell" motif at the top is used as a* vulder *(block), to fill in empty space; near the top edge is exactly the same line of "misprints" as the one depicted in the article by Nouhuys (1925-26: figs. 11,12); along the side may be seen tooth-like dots caused by fastening the* sarita *to the rotating wheels of the* reep *(Fig. 5a-e) preparatory to dyeing. (b) The tadpole motif (pa'bulintong siteba'), the betel leaf (daun bolu), perhaps inspired by the paisley motif, and the sun with rays (barre allo), in the customary dark blue and white. These Toraja motifs must have reached Vlisco B.V. in Helmond in some way. (c) Two pairs of buffalo ears (talinga tedong) as well as hook motifs and patola-inspired designs. The full cloth measures 36 x 630 cm.*

wheel. Beginning at the axle, the cloth was rolled onto the *reep* in such a way that no two of its surfaces could touch one another. A large pin or standard was then passed through the axle to permit handling without soiling the cloth. The whole was moved to the indigo vat and dipped into the solution eight or nine times (Figs. 5a-e). The intervals of exposure to the air allowed the dye to oxidize onto the cloth. After this it was unrolled, washed, and dried. Where the *mastiek* had been printed, the white of the cloth remained. Unprotected areas came out indigo blue.

There are six *sarita* in the Van Vlissingen Vlisco collection (housed in the Vlisco Archives, and in the process of being transferred to a museum): one narrow and five broader examples.[16] The quality of the thread and weave of the cloths varies from coarse to fine; the finer cloths were originally broad enough to permit the printing of double *sarita*. After dyeing, the cloth was divided in two, but this step was not always done carefully and sometimes resulted in damaged *sarita*. Other errors could be incorporated by overlapping the blocks when printing the *mastiek*. A Helmond cloth displays such an "error"; so does an example in the collection of the Museum voor Land- en Volkenkunde in Rotterdam. How surprised I was, when looking at Mrs. Pasaka's collection of old *maa'* and *sarita* in Rantepao, to see the very same type of "misprint" again (Fig. 6)! It was like meeting an old acquaintance.

Sacred Cloth Made by the Toraja

In addition to these imported textiles, the Toraja have *maa'* and *sarita* that are obviously of local make and decorated with a kind of printing process in alternation with freehand designs (Figs. 7-12). Bamboo, which has the advantage of being hollow, was probably used for stamping (Fig. 7). Some examples look as if they had been stamped with wooden blocks. I suspect that this is the case, because the Toraja are very familiar with the art of woodcarving.

What kinds of colors were used to print or paint the textiles? We know that Morinda, or *bangkudu* (*Morinda citrifolia*) was used for red. Black was obtained from the leaves of the *bilante* (*Homalanthus populnea*), which were cooked. Afterwards the color could be fixed by dipping the cloths in a mud bath. We do not know if the Toraja used mineral pigments,

Sacred Cloths of the Toraja

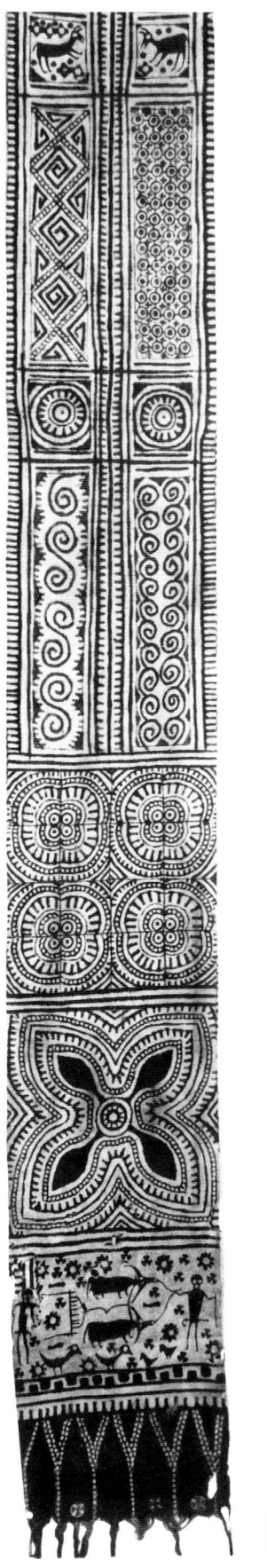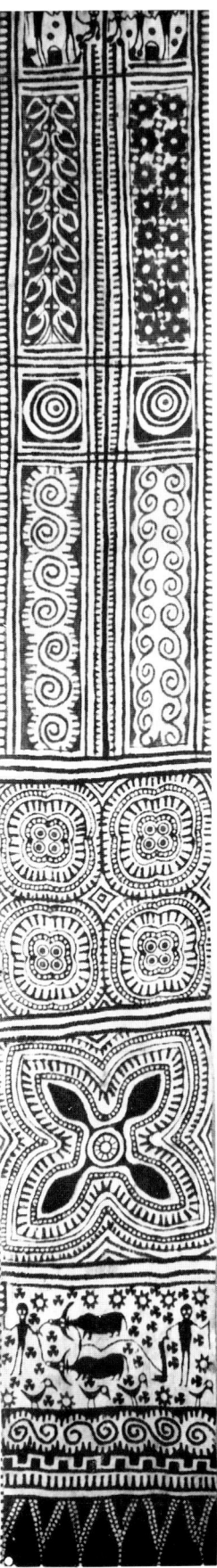

Figure 7. An indigenous *sarita* shows a great similarity to the imported one (Figs. 2-6), both in individual motifs and layout. The end, however, is done in the same manner as on the indigenous *sarita in Nouhuys* (1925-26: figs. 12-14). The designs consist of buffalo ears (talinga tedong), the sun with rays (barre allo), spirals, and hook motifs. The scenes portray a team of buffalo pulling a harrow, deer, houses, people pounding rice, buffalo, a man with a dog, and four ducks. Leaf ornaments and flowers are also depicted. The crosses are a variation on the spots of heaven (doti langi') or the spotted buffalo (pa'doti siluang), the symbol of a very expensive carabao which is a token of wealth. The concentric crosses are inspired by those on the Indian patola. The light, tooth-like dots along the sides replicate those on the imported one. The circles are stamped, probably with bamboo, while the rest of the textile is painted. Of handspun and hand-woven cotton yarn. Approximately 660 cm. long (small portions of the textile are omitted in the photographs). Collection of Mrs. Anne Summerfield, Los Angeles.

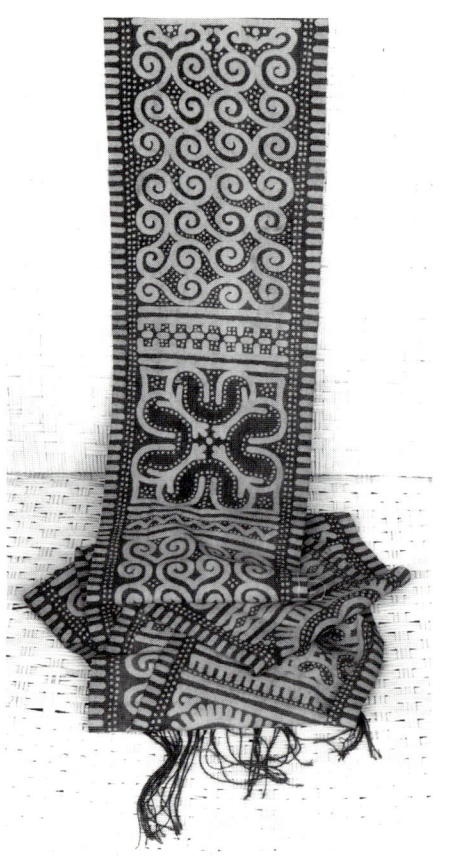
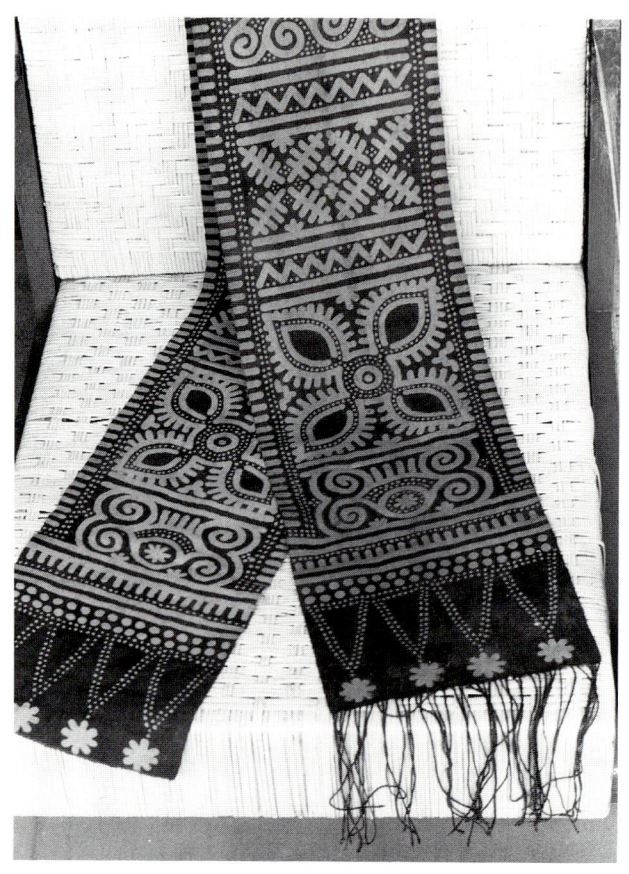
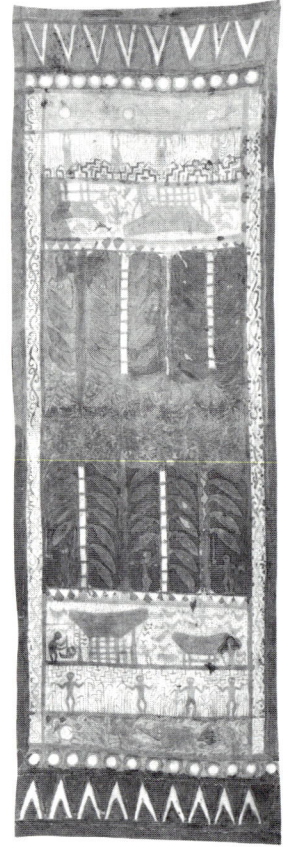
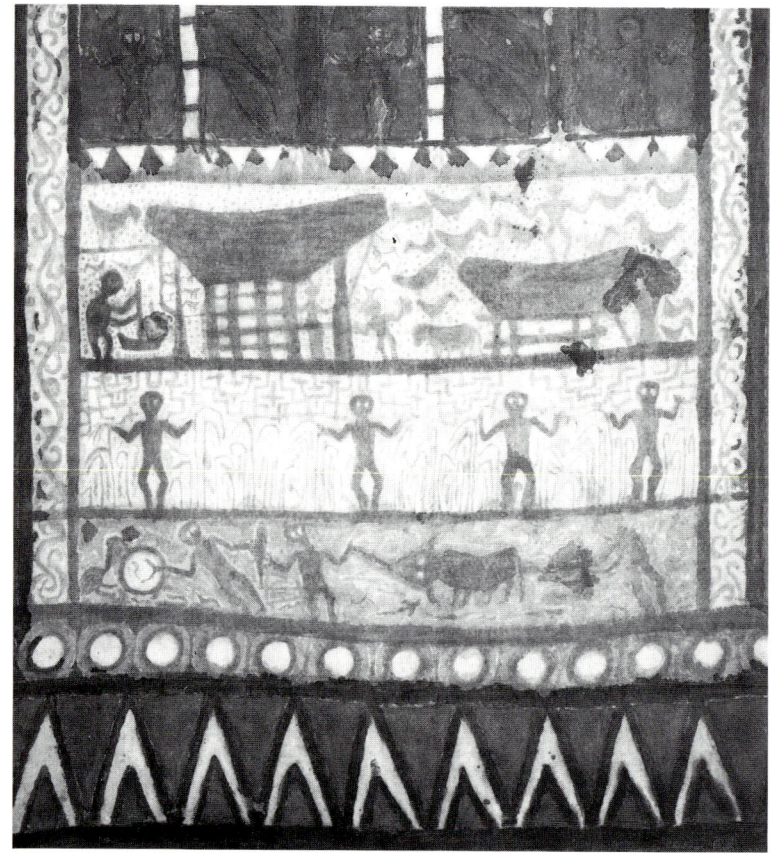

Sacred Cloths of the Toraja

Figure 8a,b, (left). An indigenous sarita *seen in 1978 shows the tadpole (pa'bulintong siteba') and horned banana (pisang tanduk) motifs. At its end, the same toothed or comb-like figures appear in combination with spirals as on the imported* sarita *(see Nouhuys 1925-26: fig. 7a). Like those, this* sarita *has fringes. It is ochre/copper and dark blue. Collection of Mrs. M. Pasaka, Rantepao.*

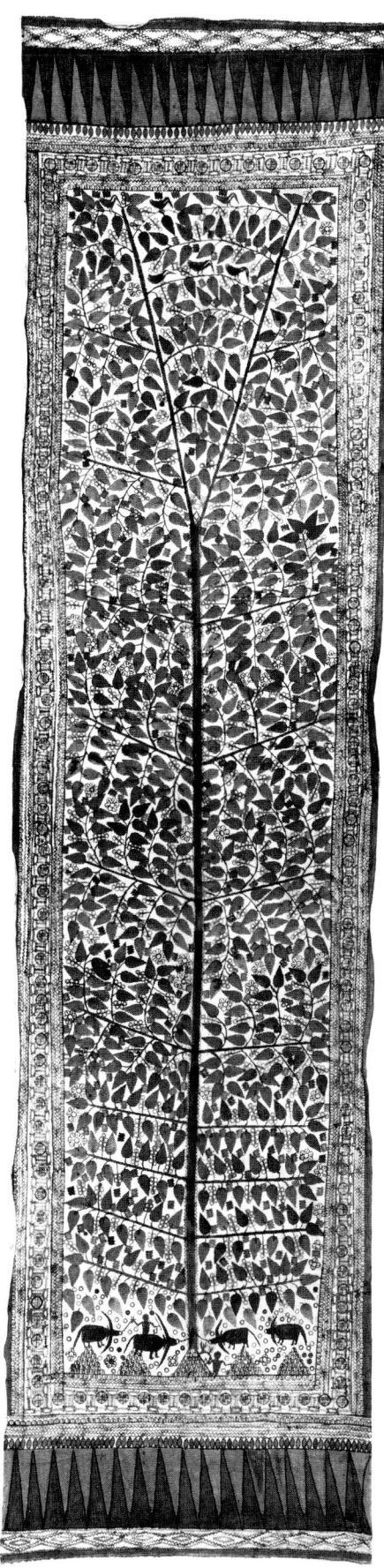

Figure 9a,b, (left). This indigenous maa' *shows* patola *influences in the layout, and in the row of triangles at each end; the scenes, however, are typical Toraja. The tendrils lining the sides may derive from Indian motifs or from older elements that also appear in some Dayak ornamentation. The circles framing the scenes derive from the shell discs (kara-kara) decorating a headhunter's or war dancer's jacket. Detail at right shows a* tongkonan *and a rice barn, pigs, ducks, and people, one of whom is pounding rice. In another register men dance between stalks on a background filled with crosses, a symbol of abundance; below, more men and buffalo. Red, grey, and brown are the main colors. Origin unknown. Approximately 73 x111 cm. Collection of Mary Hunt Kahlenberg. Textile Arts. Santa Fe, New Mexico.*

Figure 10, (right). A beautiful indigenous maa' *shows strong Indian influence in composition and layout, with the tree of life growing from a mound and reaching to the heavens. Tied to its base are two buffaloes, one mounted by a herdsman. Two other carabaos form part of the small herd. The depiction of buffaloes with turned heads is typically Toraja. The tree bears flowers and fruits; at its top are birds, a symbol of heaven. The main color is green. Origin unknown. Size 69.5 x 276.5 cm. Victoria and Albert Museum I.S.35.1980.*

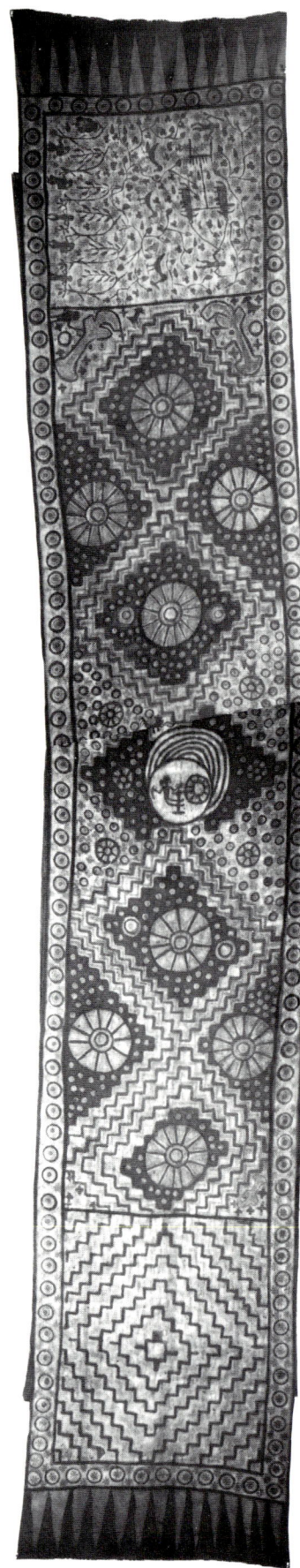
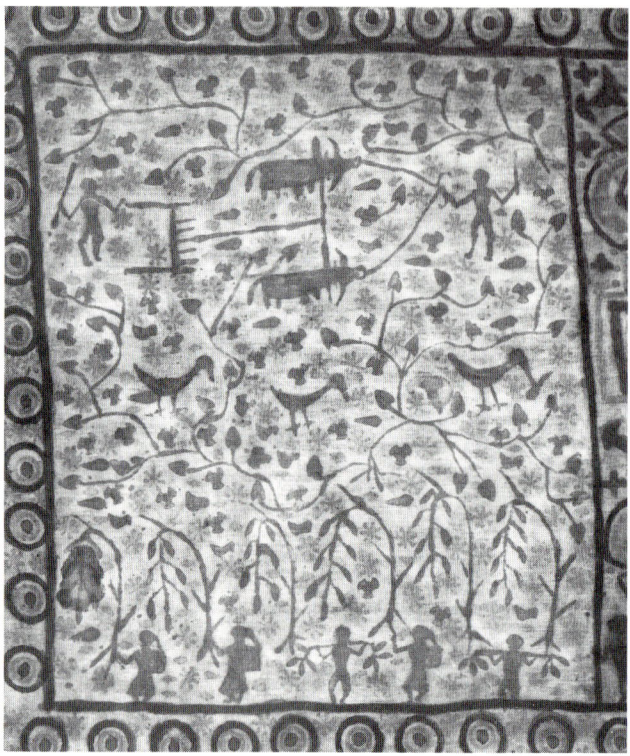

Figure 11a (left), b (above). An indigenous maa' with layout showing Indian influence in the cross motif and the triangles at the ends, but outlined in circles deriving from the shell (kara-kara) ornaments of the headhunter's outfit. One scene shows two men with a team of buffalo drawing a harrow. Other details include ducks, herons, creepers, and three men and two women going to market. Near the center is Tulangdidi' spinning in the moon. Her activities as well as the phases of the moon, also shown, are symbols of the rice cycle. To the left and right of the moon are spinning wheels and dots or stars in a constellation, consulted in former times by the rice priest to establish the proper time for rice planting. The Pleiades is called Cock of Tulangdidi' (Manukna Tulangdidi'), after the rooster that brought her good fortune. This cock is depicted twice: sitting on a spinning wheel above and to her right, and next to the constellation above her, left. Size approximately 350 x 62 cm. Private Collection.

Figure 12, (facing page). A maa' of indigenous make. It is of the buffalo-corral type which is inspired by the central medallion on the imported Indian cloths. These imports may have also inspired the row of triangles at the ends, but the circles that represent kara-kara (shell) ornaments are Toraja. At the corral are two men, two buffalo, and a calf on a ground of stars. Pairs of buffalo ears and buffalo hair are used as a decorative element. The whole is framed by two rows of stars. As a rule, this type of maa' is used in Eastern ceremonies; sometimes, however, it is also used in ceremonies of the West, in the death ritual of a nobleman or woman (a deceased of high rank is supposed to promote fertility, hence the use of the buffalo-corral-type maa'). It is wrapped around the horns or serves as a saddle on the buffalo who carries the soul of the deceased to Puya, the Land of the Hereafter. Origin unknown. Size approximately 68 x 221 cm. Private Collection.

which could have been made wear-resistant just like the paints used on the woodcarving of the houses. At a relatively early time even aniline coloring was used to pattern the textiles, as can be seen in some examples dating from before World War Two in the collection of the Rijksmuseum voor Volkenkunde in Leiden. Many of these locally-made sacred cloths are painted or block-printed on imported machine-made cotton fabric; sometimes the design was worked on silk and locally-woven cotton. Even old imported *maa'* coming from India were used as a canvas.

Maa' with Scenes. The indigenous *maa'* show a great variety of technical skill, composition, and color. How artistic most of these local textiles are! The vivid scenes (as well as more static ones with geometric ornamentation or floral patterns) make it clear these are made locally. The houses pictured are typical Toraja dwellings. Often there are people pounding rice (Figs. 7b, 9b). Buffalo and herdsmen appear frequently (Figs. 7, 9-12). On one, a team of water buffalo draws a harrow with one man leading the animals and a second manipulating the harrow, as is the practice in Tana Toraja and Mamasa (Fig. 11). Ducks, creepers, women carrying baskets on their back, and men carrying loads (maize) on a pole enliven the scene. On another part of this cloth appears Tulangdidi', the legendary woman who weaves or spins in the moon, and who is associated with the rice cycle (Nooy-Palm 1979:166-68). Segments of the moon represent her various stages.

Maa' depicting buffalo are used in ceremonies of the East and sometimes in those of the West.[17] One of the aims of the feasts of the Eastern sphere is to promote the multiplication of buffalo; hence the use of this type of *maa'*. The corral of buffalo cows—symbol of an increasing herd—is an image of wealth (Fig. 12). Typically it is guarded by men or boys. Frequently a tree, creeper, or other plant appears in the design. In other instances the corral is surrounded by paired buffalo ear motifs. The small lines near these "ears" probably represent buffalo hairs; this combination of hairs and ears is inspired by the patterning of a common type of imported Indian *maa'* (Fig. 13). For the ceremony, the textiles are mounted in front of the beautifully decorated pig litters that form part of the festive processions.

The Influence of Indian Textiles. There is no doubt that *maa'* made in Sulawesi have been influenced by Indian imports. Like the latter, they demonstrate a preference for red as the main color. Their layout, too, often shows Indian influence—as in the row of triangles at one or both ends. As far as I know, however, *sarita* and *maa'* lack the typical layout of Indian patola, which consists of two horizontal and two vertical framing elements. But the central medallion of many Indian *palampore* may have inspired the circular corral as the

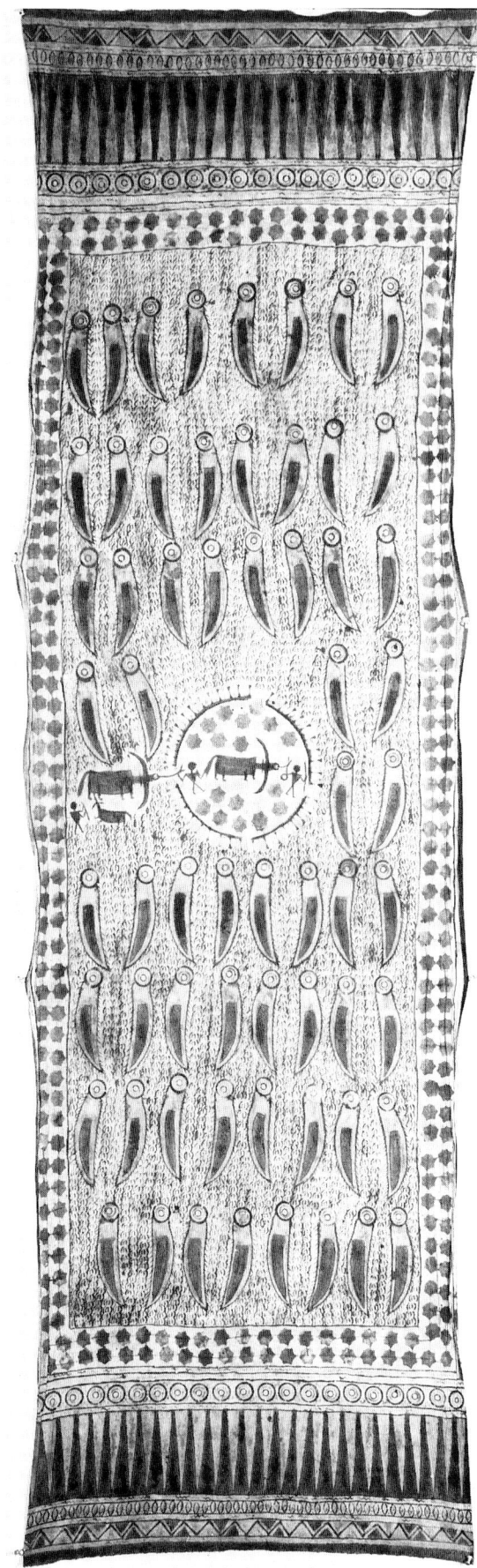

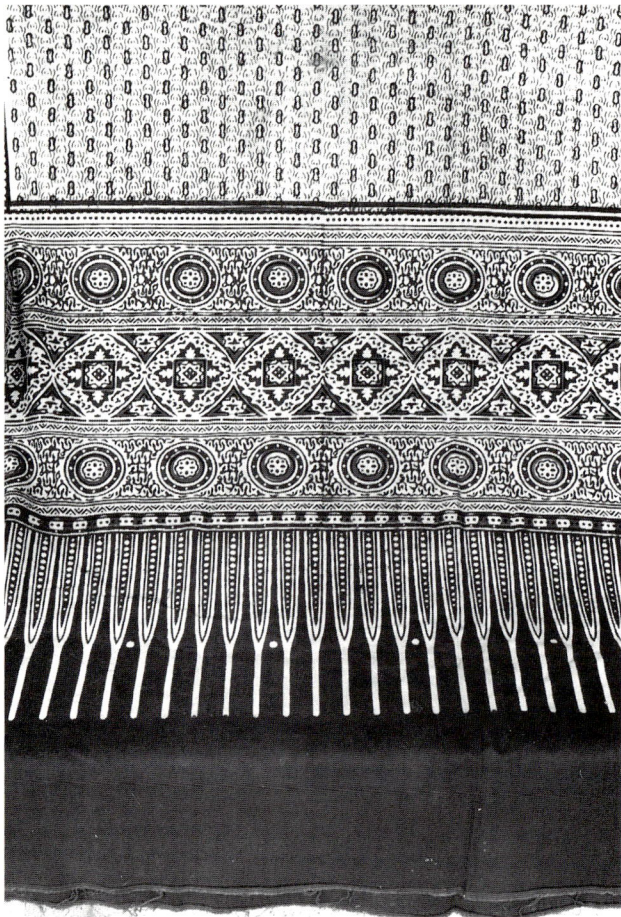

Figure 13. A rather common type of imported Indian maa' *called "black back" (*lotong boko*), probably the inspiration for the rendering of buffalo hairs and ears in Figure 12. Red and grey-green predominate. Photographed in Rantepao in 1978. Collection of Mrs. M. Pasaka, Rantepao.*

central design element in some *maa'*. Indeed an Indian textile in the Anne Summerfield collection in Los Angeles has the central medallion painted over with a Toraja buffalo-corral motif. A cloth similar to this was collected by Robert Holmgren and Anita Spertus in the Batuisi region of the To Mangki. The abundance of tendrils, leaves, and flowers, a feature common to the Indian cloths, has also been copied (and transformed) by the Toraja people.

On locally-made *maa'*, the corral with calves, cows and herdsmen is often placed in the center either of a plant or of a tree trunk standing on a mound of earth. This representation is no doubt inspired by a type of imported Indian cloth that depicts a tree or plant growing from a mound or a pot, a beautiful example of which, obtained from Limbong (north of Tana Toraja) in the To Rongkong area, is now in the Holmgren-Spertus collection. In these imported cloths, the representation consists of two parts: a mountain and a tree. This motif, well known in Hinduism, became part of the Hindu-inspired art motifs of Java and Bali as seen in the stylized mountain motif (*gunungan* or *kekayon, kakayon*) used in Javanese and Balinese shadow puppet performances, or *wayang kulit purwa* (Bosch 1948:202-218). Although Hinduism was only a minor influence in the Toraja Aluk to Dolo religion (for example the Hindu word *deata* is adopted in Toraja for deities or ghosts), the symbolism of the earth mound and the tree of life are well-known in indigenous culture. The Toraja say that the Round Mound or Small Hill (Pongko' or Kalebu) was the first dwelling place of the Toraja on earth (Nooy-Palm 1980:112-13). The tree of life plays a very important part in the two major Eastern rituals, the *bua'* and the *merok* feasts. Both the *barana'* (*Ficus religiosa*) and the *sendana* (sandalwood tree) are cosmic symbols with their roots and branches connecting earth and heaven. In *The Merok-Feast of the Sa'dan-Toradja,* H. van der Veen demonstrates the importance of the heavenly *sendana*, which is glorified in beautiful poetry—part of the long litany spoken by the priest when he consecrates the buffalo, the principal sacrificial animal in this feast (Veen 1965).

Some motifs originating in Indian textiles became extremely popular in Toraja, for example the cross ornament called "spots" (*doti*) or "spots from heaven" (*doti langi'*)—stars. These are a token of abundance, wealth (Fig. 7). The motif of quail's eyes (*mata puyo*) is perhaps of Indian origin, as is that depicting water spirits (*bombo uai*). The popular betel leaf motif (*daun bolu*) may be inspired by the palmette or paisley motif (Fig. 5b). Like the quail's eye and water spirit motifs, it is used in woodcarving[18]; and it is applied in painting techniques of the indigenous textiles as well.

Original Toraja Motifs. There are several patterns of Toraja origin. A *sarita* in the collection of Robert Holmgren and Anita Spertus (see Gittinger 1979a:202) depicts a headhunting motif (*snelmotief* in Dutch). An ancient one in Indonesia and Melanesia, it would have been part of an original design vocabulary. For other indigenous textile motifs we have to look at the old coffins that are no longer used. The art of carving them precedes the woodcarving of the well-known Toraja *tongkonan*. These ancestral houses, which are approximately 200-300 years old according to the genealogies of the families who inhabit them, were decorated sparsely or not at all. The application of woodcarving to *tongkonan* is a rather recent convention, so the motifs of this form of decoration often derive from imported *maa'*; however some traditional indigenous ornamentation is also applied to them.

A number of designs appear on the ancient wooden coffins. They include paired cosmic snakes (*ula'*); cock's feathers (*pa'bulu londong*); outstretched horns (*pa'tanduk ra'pe*); the stylized buffalo head (*pa'tedong*), symbolizing strength and bravery; the tied basket or Gordian knot motif (*pa'kapu' baka*); the sun with rays motif (*barre allo*, seen in Fig. 6c); double spirals (*pa'barana'*)[19]; the shell-disc motif (*kara-kara*)[20]; and various hook motifs and combinations of meander, such as *pa'kadang pao*[21], *pa'sepu' to Rongkong*[22], and *pa'sekong kandaure*[23] (cf. Kadang 1960:18,19,24 and Pakan 1961:28,43,45). Cock's feathers, outstretched horns, and the stylized buffalo head, three of these traditional designs which also occur on the wood carving of the traditional house, were never used on indigenous cloths. Their absence on the textiles is difficult to explain. In the case of the buffalo head (*pa'tedong*), perhaps it is a male motif which has the function of sealing off something of the outer world. The design is applied on window shutters, and on the small doors that close a rock tomb. Sometimes it is difficult to make out whether an ornament is indigenous or Indian, as in the case of plant motifs, and tendrils, which occur both on coffins and on Indian *maa'*. Some motifs are derived from Javanese batik, long imported into the Sulawesi area.

Why did the Toraja not depict elephants or monkeys on their *maa'*? Elephants are unknown on Sulawesi; but they are also absent in the Lesser Sunda Islands, and yet some ikats in that region depict elephants copied from Indian patola. There is a species of black baboon (or baboon-like monkey, *Cynopithecus nigrescens*) in the forests of Sulawesi, but neither it nor the popular *rangga ulu* textile served as a source of inspiration for the Toraja artists. In trying to solve the mysteries that surround *maa'* and *sarita* we often get stuck in them. We need the cooperation of art dealers, anthropologists, and the Toraja themselves before we can truly make progress.[24]

NOTES

1. People need money for the education of their children and for newly valued commodities such as education and articles not available before World War II—motorbikes, radios, cameras.

2. The Bare'e differ linguistically and in other aspects of their culture from the other tribes mentioned.

3. Missionaries of the Gereformeerde Zendingsbond in de Nederlandse Hervormde Kerk (Mission League of the Dutch Reformed Church) came to Tana Toraja in 1913. A mass conversion took place during the time of political turbulence between 1950 and 1966.

4. Both *maa'* and *sarita* are used as headgear, folded. A *maa'* is worn by the *tumbang*, tied by a strap around the head and chin. A *sarita* is put on a frame, made up like a bonnet.

5. One imported *maa'* I measured recently was 492 x 21.5 cm. Another was 444 x 26 cm.

6. A pair of To Kulawi *raigo* dancers appears in a photograph in Kruyt; the young man is wearing an imported *sarita* around his waist (Kruyt 1938: photo 42). Kaudern (1940) reproduces an oil painting of his own representing a young man similarly dressed dressed for the "morego" (=*raigo*) round dance.

7. There are two *kalamkari*, one very damaged, in a shop in the conservation village of Ke'te Kesu'. The photograph I took of the undamaged one turned out very badly, so the information on it is scanty. Both fabrics depicted scenes from the Ramayana. For the *kalamkari* we refer to Lotika Varadarajan 1978:18-21.

8. This ship in particular is an eye catcher, being reproduced often in works on Indonesian art or in treatises that deal with the stupa. See Bernet Kemper (n.d.: fig. 27). It is also depicted in van Erp's work on the ships of Borobudur (1923: fig. 6). Besides this ship, Erp depicts other vessels from South Sulawesi (1923:18-35).

9. Once—in the remote past—the Toraja, Buginese, Luwunese, Macassarese, Mandarese and some other tribes belonged to the same linguistic stock, and probably also shared other culture traits. This linguistic group, referred to by Mills as the Proto-South-Sulawesi, inhabited the northern part of the southwest isthmus. In the course of time, the groups separated. The Macassarese and Buginese settled in the south, becoming not only agricultural, but seafaring people as well. The Toraja remained inland people. Linguistic investigations make it clear that the Macassarese were the first to split off. The Buginese came to the south at a much later time (Mills 1975: 205-25). So the ships depicted on the Borobudur may be Macassarese ones.

10. *Pamor* is a Javanese word referring not only to nickelous iron, but also to the laminated patterns found on the kris. For the forging of Toraja swords see Zerner 1981:87-112.

11. In the last century Buginese vessels even went to the northern part of Australia in search of sea-slugs (*trepang* in Indonesian, or *bêche-de-mer* in French).

12. The Bienfaits were a large family of weavers who settled and worked in Leiden and Antwerp.

13. According to Dr. H. van der Veen it was the other way round; see Nooy-Palm 1979: sec. 2.

14. Ms. Rita Bolland, who accompanied me on the trip to Helmond in 1976, observed that the plain cloth was machine-made and Indian in origin.

15. This complicated construction is still in the possession of Van Vlissingen en Co. Ltd. (Vlisco) in Helmond, The Netherlands.

16. The narrow one is No. 176/1; the others are Nos. 176/2-6.

17. Langewis and Wagner also illustrate such a cloth—a *maa'*, not a *sarita* (1964: pl. 206).

18. The row of triangles is another Indian motif used in woodcarving. Older woodcarving motifs not derived from *patola* or other Indian cloths include the hook, the double spiral, the sun with rays, the stylized buffalo head, the swastika-like *pa'bungkang tasik*, and the kris (or *gayang*) motif.

19. Spiral motifs abound in Toraja art, as do meander motifs; thus it is impossible to give all the names. *Pa'barana'*, leaves of the *Ficus religiosa*, is one name.

20. The shell-disc motif—always shown in a row—is derived from the shells, made into discs by grinding, which decorate the headhunter's jacket and cap (headhunting was abolished by the Dutch in 1906).

21. This motif is named after the hook that is used to fetch mangoes off a tree.

22. This translates as "that which looks like a betel bag of the Rongkong people."

23. The *kandaure* is a beaded ornament; this is a hooked figure which is a motif of the *kandaure*.

24. For their kind help and advice regarding this article I would like to thank Mrs. Rita Bolland, Mr. C.H. Krantz, Mr. F.G.L. van Rood of Vlisco B.V., Helmond, Ms. Mary Hunt Kahlenberg, Ms. Anne Summerfield, Ms. Anita Spertus, and Mr. Robert Holmgren.

A Sacred Cloth of Rangda
Kamben Cepuk of Bali and Nusa Penida

Marie-Louise Nabholz-Kartaschoff

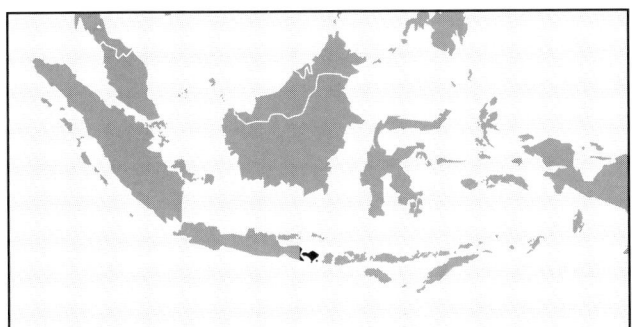

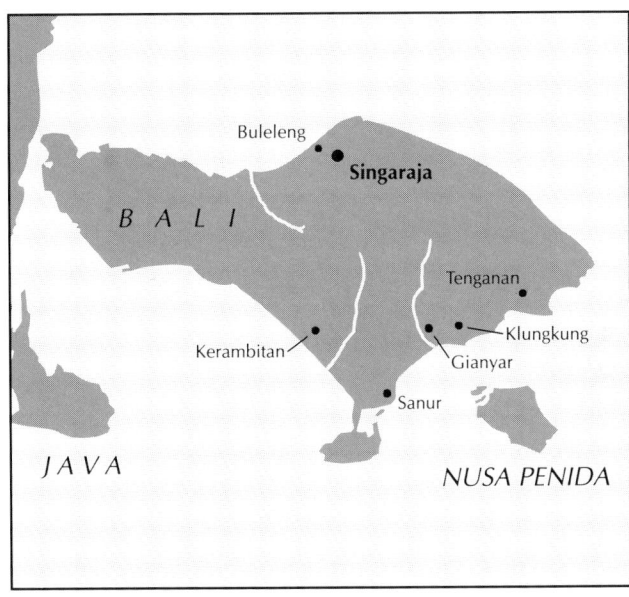

Bali and Nusa Penida.

In Balinese dramatic rituals, Rangda is the embodiment of black magic and the opponent of the mighty and protective Barong. An essential part of Rangda's traditional costume is the textile known as *kamben cepuk*, made of cotton or, less commonly, of silk (Pl. 28). It has a background of deep red, brick-red or brownish red, against which geometric and floral weft ikat designs are set within a strict framing structure of monochrome stripes and bands and ikat sections[1] (Pl. 29). The generic term *kamben cepuk* is composed of two elements: *kamben* (Indonesian, *kain panjang*) designates a long unsewn cloth, worn in Bali as a wraparound skirt over a second inner cloth, *tapih*; *cepuk* carries the meaning of "being brought face to face with someone" (passive form, *cepukang*), particularly with a divine power (Kersten 1984:216).

Uses of *Kamben Cepuk*

During ritual dramas, Rangda and her assistant witch, Rarung, wear the *cepuk* either wrapped as a skirt, *kamben*, over a yellow *tapih* (Pl. 28, Fig. 1), or draped over their shoulders under the mask (Fig. 2). In this context it is considered a strong magical attribute much like the white weapon-like cloth in Rangda's hands. The great protective and exorcistic power of *cepuk* cloths becomes evident through their role in nearly all forms of Balinese ritual—for the gods and for the living, for the deceased and for the demons who trouble the order of the world.

Because danger is most apt to be present in the transition from one life stage to another, *kamben cepuk* are used particularly in the rites of passage. At birth ceremonies, for example, if the newborn is thought to reincarnate an ancestor, sacred *cepuk* may be offered when a healer (*balian tenung*) has received the ancestor's request while in trance. At *otonin*, a ritual taking place on the 210th day after birth, small children may be wrapped in a *kamben cepuk* (Fig. 3).

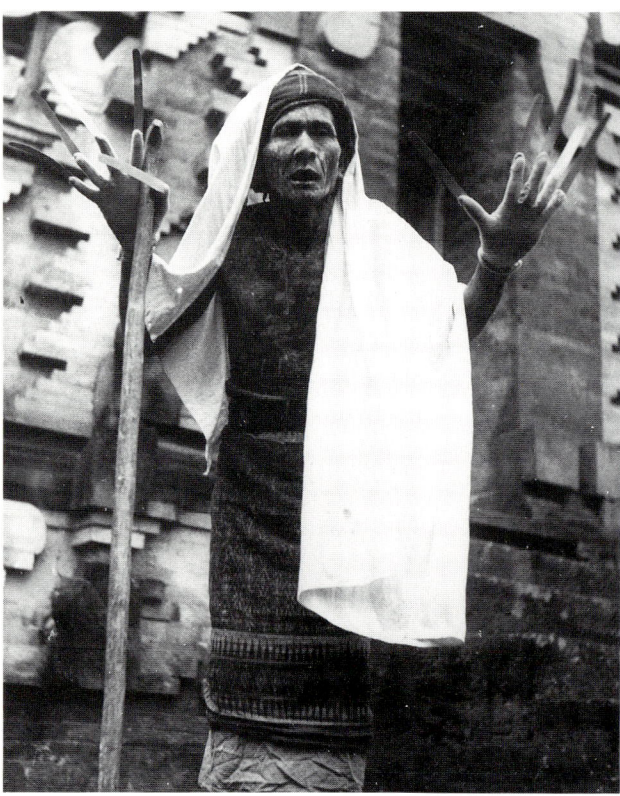

Figure 1. Rangda in her human form as destructive widow, danced by an old man in the Calon Arang drama. His skirtcloth is a kamben cepuk padang angket. Photographed by Theo Meier. Mawang Kaja, Gianyar district, South Bali, 1930s.

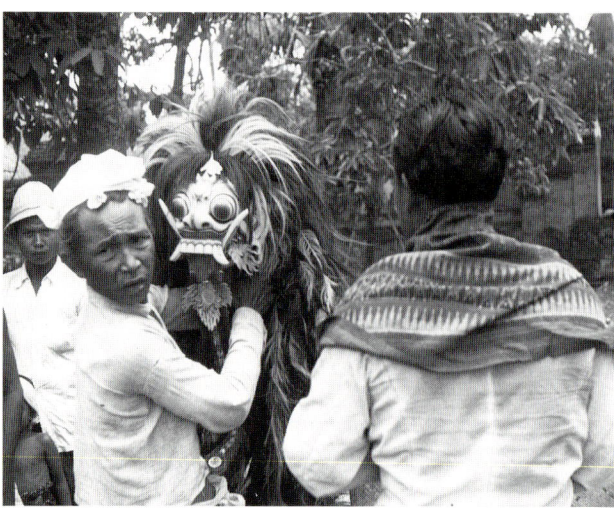

Figure 2. Man (right) preparing to don the Rangda mask, using kamben cepuk saksak as shouldercloth under the mask. Photographed by Theo Meier. Pagutan (?), South Bali, 1930s.

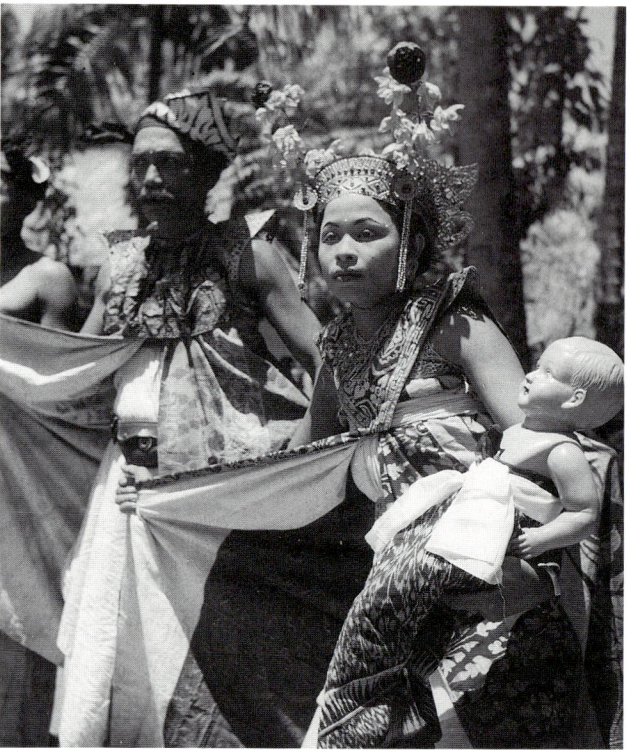

Figure 3. Princely couple with a doll (as "child") wrapped in a kamben cepuk. Probably from a scene in the Calon Arang drama. Photographed by Theo Meier. Pegog, South Bali, 1942-45.

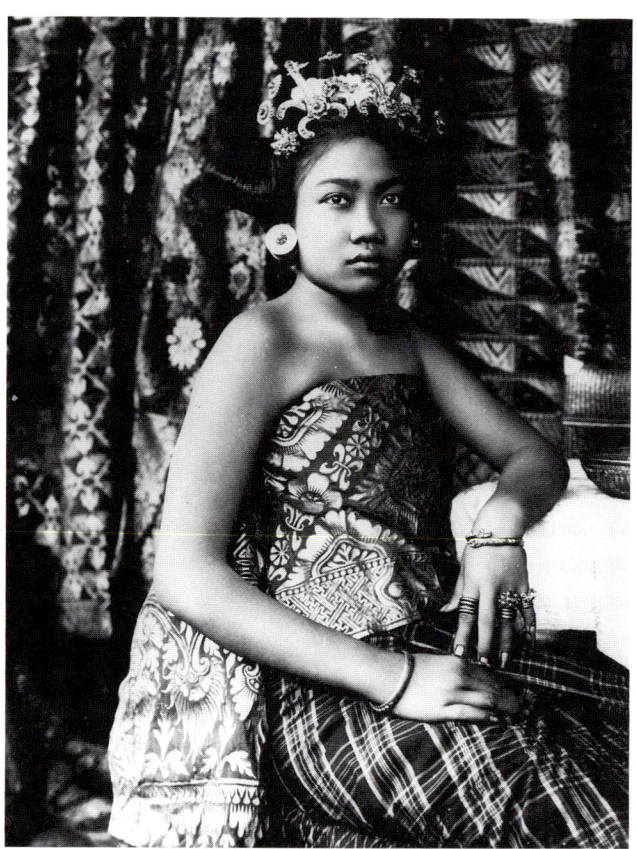

Figure 4. Bride sitting on a sacred cloth, kamben cepuk. Photographed by O. Kurkdjian. Bali, 1900-12.

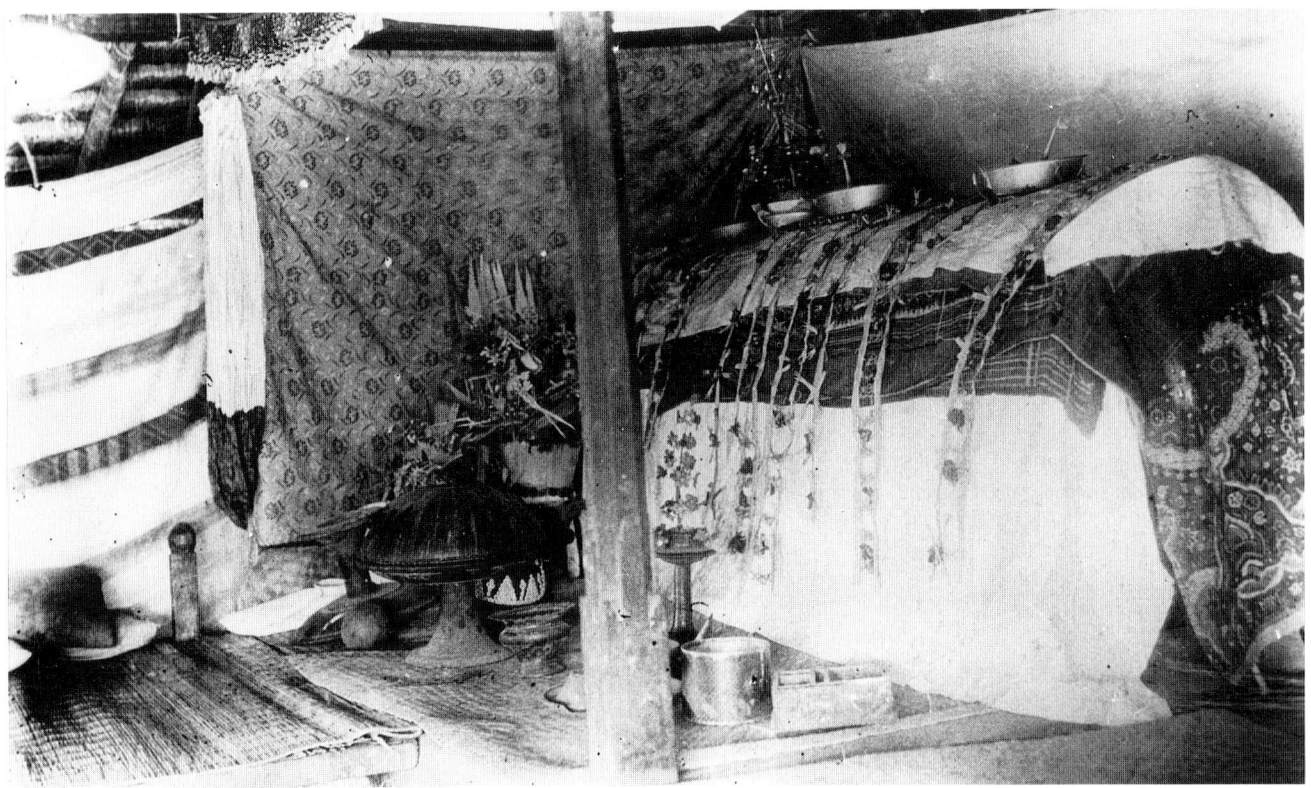

Figure 5. Coffin covered with kamben cepuk *and other textiles. Photographed by Augusta de Wit. Singaraja, Bali, circa 1900.*

Traditionally, sacred *cepuk* cloth also plays a role in puberty rites such as tooth filing and first menstruation rituals, performed particularly among upper classes. In both cases, *kamben cepuk* may be used to turn away dangerous powers from the young. For tooth filing, the candidate's head is laid on a folded cloth with flowering shrub motifs (*kamben cepuk angket*) or lotus-like ornaments (*kamben cepuk padma*). Girls at the menstruation ceremony wear cloths bearing certain blossom or grass motifs (*kamben cepuk cemara* and *padang derman* or *alija*). A photograph of a wedding ceremony at the turn of the century shows that *kamben cepuk* were also used to decorate the bride's seat (Fig. 4).

At Balinese death ceremonies, too, there are several traditional uses for *cepuk* cloth. Before cremation the embalmed body is kept in the house in a coffin covered with white cloths and a shroud, *kajang*, with drawings or symbols of sacred power. A photograph taken in 1900 in Singaraja by Augusta de Wit depicts a coffin shrouded with white cloth and two *kamben cepuk* (Fig. 5). *Cepuk* cloth also customarily serves to dress the effigy of the deceased (*sekah*), made for the soul-purifying rituals (*nyekah*) following the first cremation; this exorcism is considered necessary because through death a person has fallen into the power of the nether world. Additionally, *kamben cepuk* may be used in a special offering (*sangge*) at purification rituals for those dead who may have been ritually forgotten or for whom a former ceremony has not been properly performed. *Kamben cepuk padang angket* and *Semara guna* are mentioned in connection with purification rituals while a *kamben cepuk betola* could be used as a *kajang* of high castes, but never for low castes for fear of magical vengeance.

Sacred *cepuk* cloths are also important items in *rantasan*, sacrificial offerings to divine powers. They were used this way traditionally in Kerambitan; and today in the Klungkung area modern *cepuk* cloths from Nusa Penida still serve as *rantasan*. When the gods are taken to their ritual bath in the sea, *cepuk* are carried along, folded, and piled together on offering plates with other textiles. Another use of *kamben cepuk* was in the decoration of temples (Pelras 1962:219). In Tabanan, particularly, long *cepuk* cloths were draped around the household shrines.

During temple consecration or birth ceremonies, *kamben cepuk* are customarily worn by adepts who enter trance, enabling the divine powers to speak through them. If anyone else becomes unexpectedly possessed, he is immediately dressed in *kamben cepuk* so as to be protected from the mighty and dangerous powers that have entered him. Cultic statues as well may be dressed up in *kamben cepuk*; for example, the goddess of death, Betari Durga, is draped in a cloth

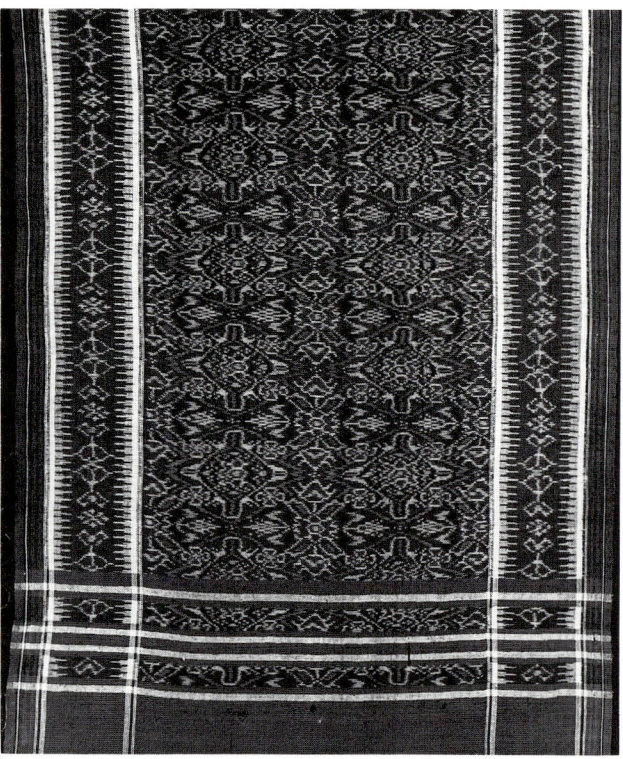

Figure 6. Balinese sacred cloth probably from Kerambitan, called kamben cepuk cendana kawi. Museum für Völkerkunde, Basel, IIc 2064.

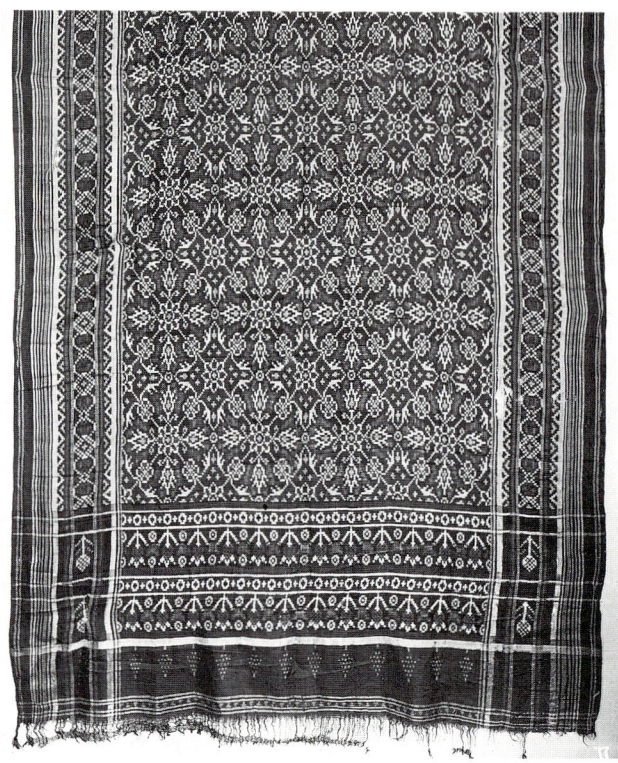

Figure 7. Indian patola cloth from Gujarat, called patolu chhabadi bhat. Museum für Völkerkunde, Basel, IIa 1677.

with an eight-pointed star motif, *kamben cepuk cendana kawi* (Fig. 6), or another type of *cepuk* cloth, as in Plate 31.

Origins of **Kamben Cepuk**

Sabuk cepuk, a *cepuk* sash, appears in East Javanese literature of the fourteenth and fifteenth centuries. It is mentioned in the *Malat*, the romances of the East Javanese hero Banji (in Balinese, Panji), where a *tapih cepuk* is explained as a "fabric with four colors" (Van der Tuuk 1897:650-51; Museum voor Land- en Volkenkunde1922/33:11).

In certain motifs and in design structure *kamben cepuk* seem to resemble silk fabrics known as patola (Figs. 6-9,23-31). Imported from Gujarat (in Gujarati, *patolu*, singular, *patola*, plural), these sophisticated double ikat fabrics and mordant-printed imitations, also from India, have been greatly esteemed throughout Indonesia and integrated into the indigenous cultures. In Bali particularly they have been used as noble women's garb, as temple decorations at religious festivals, for small sacrifices and as cures for serious diseases. A *lontar* (palm leaf) manuscript from the eighteenth century or even earlier "tells the sorcererer how to make a terrifying drawing, pronounce a mantra over it, wrap it up in *patowala* [sic] silk and throw it in the kitchen of the person at whom the sorcery is aimed.

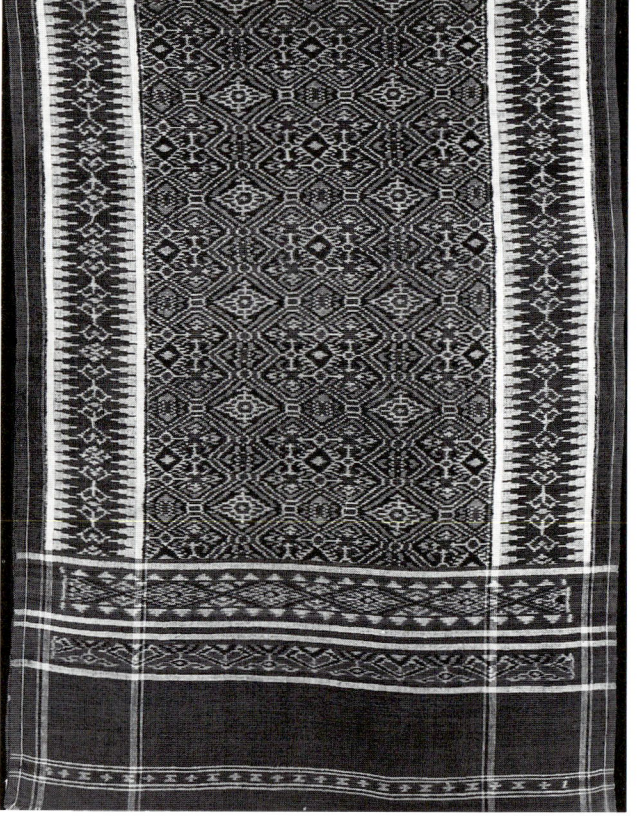

Figure 8. Balinese sacred cloth called kamben cepuk padma. Museum für Völkerkunde, Basel, IIc 14203. See also Plate 29.

Death will be the outcome for him" (Bühler and Fischer 1979:291; Hooykaas 1978:359). An early twentieth-century picture in De Zoete and Spies shows that Rangda could be dressed up in an outer skirtcloth of genuine patola (1938: pl. 58). In analyzing the various functions of *cepuk* and of patola silks it becomes obvious that *kamben cepuk* can be used as a substitute for real patola, and that the same exorcistic and magical ritual power in ceremonies and rituals are attributed to both kinds of cloth.

Common opinion holds that all *kamben cepuk* originate from the small island of Nusa Penida, south of Bali. To the contrary, in actuality it turns out that many of the cotton and all the silk specimens have been produced in Bali. Only certain types can be definitively assigned to Nusa Penida at the present time. But the frequent assertion by Balinese informants and dealers that all these textiles come from there might be rooted in traditional Balinese ideology, which orders the world on two antipodes: *kaja*, associated with the interior of the island of Bali, the mountains, the divine powers; and *kelod*, associated with the sea, the nether world, and its demonic forces. For the whole southern and southwestern half of Bali, *kelod* is also synonymous with the island of Nusa Penida, the lair of all evil, illness, and trouble. These are personified in Jero Gedé Mecaling, the fanged giant who comes to the south Balinese coast to release his evil forces, spreading disease. He is attended by many small demons, *omang*, which are, in the Balinese conception, of every color: red, yellow, blue, and white. *Kelod* is also the sphere of black magic, and Rangda's black witchcraft is highly *kelod*, while Barong has traits of *kaja* (Covarrubias 1937:10,335,356; Swellengrebel 1960:38,40; De Zoete and Spies 1938:99). Thus it becomes understandable why, for a Balinese, Rangda's magical *cepuk* has to come from Nusa Penida and nowhere else.

The Manufacture of *Kamben Cepuk*

Because the technical aspects of *kamben cepuk* manufacture have been described rather extensively earlier (Bühler 1943; Nabholz-Kartaschoff In Press), only the main features are summarized here. Up to the 1950s, handspun cotton yarn from Nusa Penida or Bali was used in weaving the *cepuk*. Industrially spun yarn started to appear in the 1920s, at first being used only for the warp and the plain weft sections (Gertis 1925:104; Korn 1944:99; Pelras 1962:235). The traditional dyes include red from the roots of *Morinda citrifolia* (*sunti*), yellow from curcuma (*kunyit*), blue from indigo (*taum*), and black from *kemiri* nuts (*Aleurites mollucana*) or from indigo mixed with kitchen soot. Red-dyeing with *sunti* involved complicated processes of mordanting and oiling.

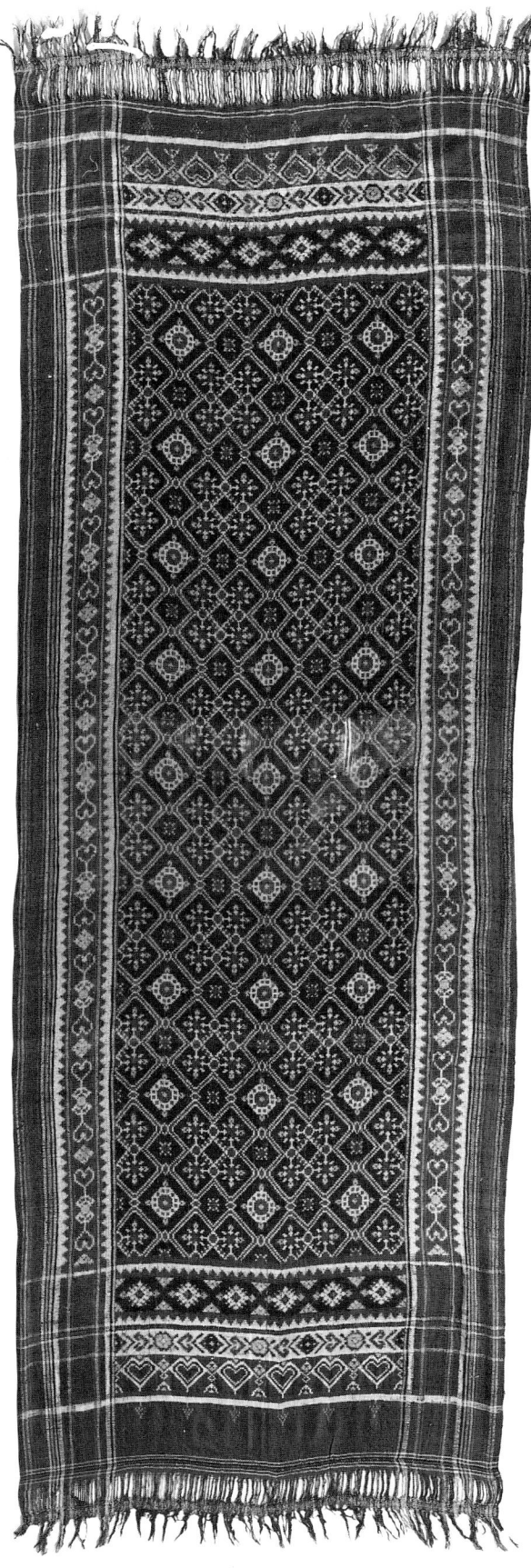

Figure 9. Indian patolu *from Gujarat, used in Bali. Museum für Völkerkunde, Basel, IIc 15626.*

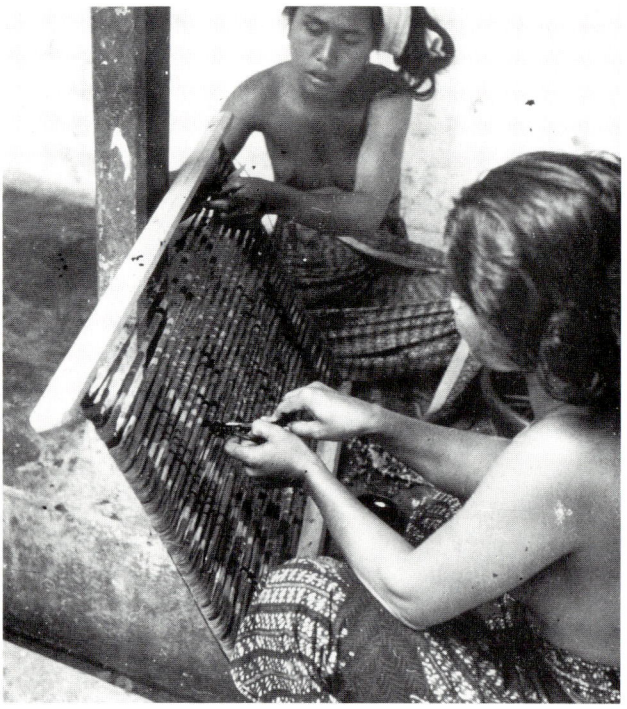

Figure 10. Painting synthetic dyes on weft yarn bundles with toothed sticks. Photographed by Theo Meier. Jeluk, Gianyar district, South Bali, 1930s.

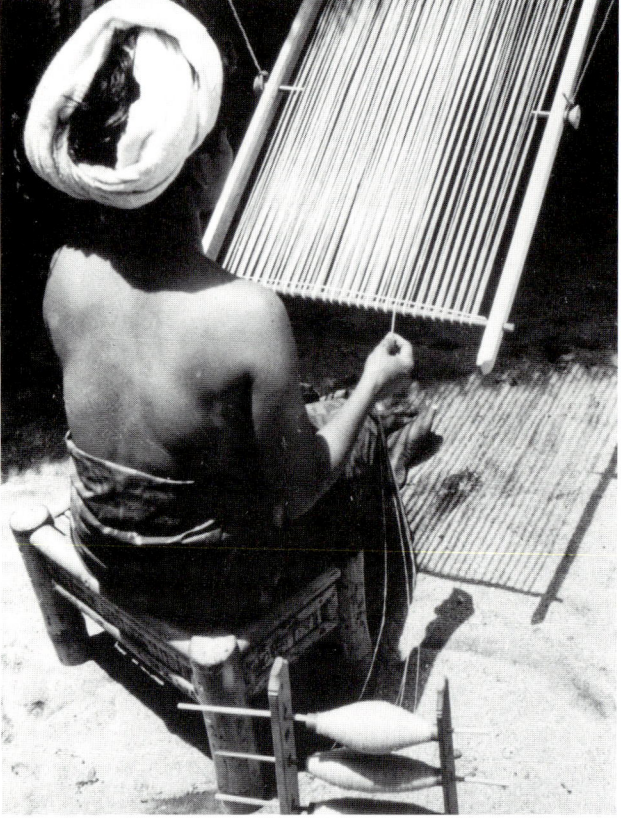

Figure 11. Winding weft yarn on tying frame. Photographed by Theo Meier. Jeluk, Gianyar district, South Bali, 1930s.

Green, purple, and brownish black shades were achieved by applying different dyes sequentially.

Synthetic dyes appear on Balinese silk weft ikats as early as 1908 and on cotton *kamben cepuk* from the 1920s on. The specimens in the Basel collection show that they were first used only for the warp and plain weft sections. For the ikatted weft yarns, synthetic dyes are applied directly on the stretched yarn with the help of small-toothed bamboo sticks (Fig. 10). Only the red color continues to be obtained by dipping the yarn in a dye bath. The weft yarn is stretched and grouped in bundles on a special tying frame according to the pattern (Fig. 11). A motif is usually built up from sixteen to sixty sets of four or six yarns each and repeated eleven to nineteen times over the centerfield. The resist wrapping is done with banana bast (*kubal*). For weaving the women use a loom with discontinuous warp and a reed, a type widely used in Balinese silk, cotton, and *songket* weaving (Fig. 12).

Basic Structure of *Kamben Cepuk*

All *kamben cepuk* manifest the same structural principle: they have vertical side borders and horizontal end panels, each arranged in a succession of bands and stripes. These frame a centerfield with a dominant overall weft ikat design. The structure is basically similar to the pattern arrangement of Indian patola (Bühler and Fischer 1979: figs. 2-4). Figure 13 illustrates all the elements of the *kamben cepuk*. The vertical side borders, horizontal end panels, and centerfield are made up of a number of smaller elements, each of which has a Balinese name.

The term *bibih* means "border," "seam," or "lip," and may refer to the selvedge or to the vertical side border as a whole (Fig 13a), including the red selvedge (Fig. 13b); three fine stripes, two blue and one white, known as *batis balang* or "legs of the grasshopper" (Fig. 13c); and two fine blue lines called *tembing manis*, "sweet" or "soft slope" (Fig. 13d). Together these fine lines are called *serati apit lawang*, a term also denoting the guardian figures on both sides of a temple door. The red sections in between are *capa*, which means the slanting parts of the upper part of a household shrine, *tugu capah*. Finally, the white and blue stripes framing the weft ikat border design that flanks the centerfield are termed *ganggong*, "socle of a household shrine" or *alis kening*, "eyebrows" (Fig. 13e). Just inside them, and also framing the weft ikat border design, are horizontal white triangles in weft ikat technique called *gigin Barong*, "teeth of Barong" (Fig. 13f).

The term *eled*, "head," denotes the end panel as a whole (Fig. 13g). The outer red border is again called *bibih* (Fig. 13h), while the white stripes just inside it are termed *serati*, "lines" (Fig. 13j). The broad red portion is *pelokan*, "a section of space" (Fig. 13k); the other red parts are called *manis*. The end panel ikat bands are termed *kenjung*, or "smile" (Fig. 13m).

The centerfield of a *kamben cepuk* (Fig. 13n) is filled with a geometric or stylized floral weft ikat design, parts of which may be repeated in the *kenjung* parts of the end panel. This ikat motif is frequently named after a flower, particularly a species used for offerings and in other rituals. The design is very often an exact copy or a close transposition of a genuine patola motif, and as mentioned above, its name often appears in the designation of a specific *kamben cepuk*.

These Balinese terms have referents on four different structural levels. A *kamben cepuk* is considered a human being with a head (*eled*), lips (*bibih*), a smile (*kenjung*), and eyebrows (*alis kening*). On the other hand, its whole framing structure is compared with architecture: designations like *serati*, *capa*, and *ganggong* refer to stepped profiles of architectural elements to be seen, for instance, on household shrines. *Serati apit lawang* associates parts

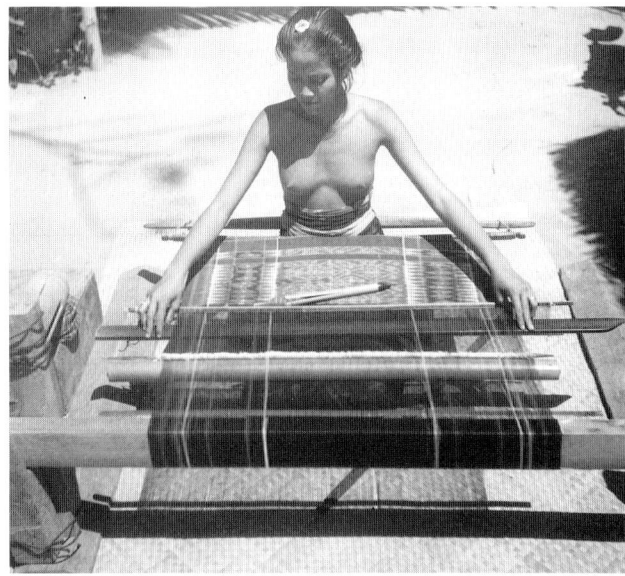

Figure 12. Weaving of a kamben cepuk. *Photographed by Theo Meier. Renon near Sanur, South Bali, 1930s.*

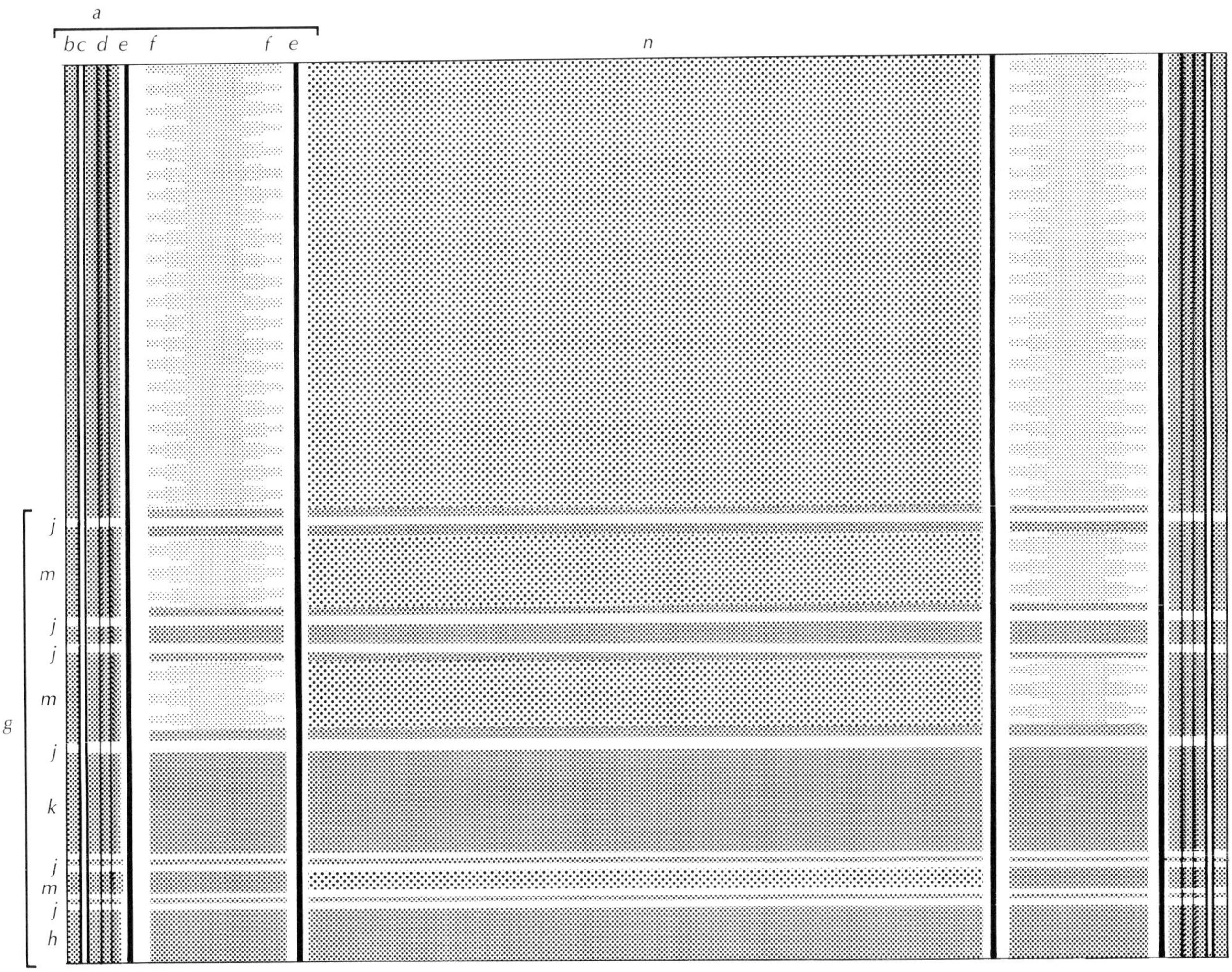

Figure 13. Basic structure of a kamben cepuk. *(a)* bibih—*whole side border (b)* bibih—*selvedge (c)* batis balang—"grasshopper legs" *(d)* tembing manis—"soft slope" *(e)* ganggong *or* alis kening—"socle" *or* "eyebrows" *(f)* gigin Barong—"Barong's teeth" *(g)* eled—"head" *(h)* bibih—*outer border (j)* serati—"lines" *(k)* pelokan—"section of space" *(m)* kenjung—"smile" [ikat bands] *(n)* centerfield—*overall ikat design. Museum für Völkerkunde, Basel, IIc 13940.*

Figure 14. Regional differences in basic structure of kamben cepuk:
a. (Upper left) Buleleng, North Bali.
b. (Upper right) Kerambitan, West Bali.
c. (Lower left) Nusa Penida.
Museum für Völkerkunde, Basel, IIc 13956, 2064, and 14630.

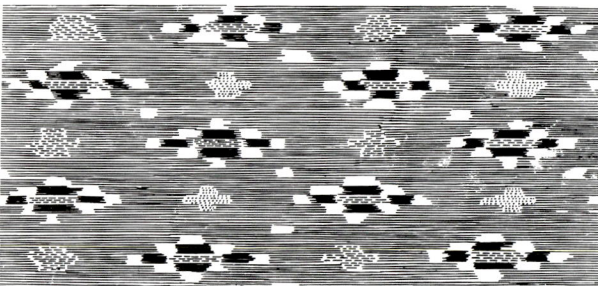

Figure 15. Blossom pattern in centerfield of kamben cepuk saksak. Museum für Völkerkunde, Basel, IIc 13985.

of the composition with the guardian figures at a temple door, while the names of different ikat motifs in the framing bands and centerfield refer to certain flowers, and particularly to those with a deep relation to ritual. *Gigin Barong*, the dominant and ubiquitous triangle design of the side border's innermost band, alludes to the mighty Barong, Rangda's opponent, and thus to the witch herself.

Particular ikat patterns cannot be attributed to specific places of origin at this time. However further investigation of the proportions of the basic format may establish regional variations. A comparison of *kamben cepuk* cloths from North Bali (Fig. 14a), West Bali (Fig. 14b) and Nusa Penida (Fig. 14c) reveals obvious differences. Examples from North Bali are slightly shorter with a narrower centerfield framed by prominent *gigin Barong*; their end panels are simpler, with narrow ikat bands. Those from West Bali are longer with a broader centerfield and finer *gigin Barong* triangles; the ikat bands within their end panels are more elaborate. *Kamben cepuk* from Nusa Penida are shorter, and frequently two or more smaller specimens are not cut, but rather left in one piece.

Typology of Centerfield Patterns

Within the approximately sixty *cepuk* cloths in the collection of the Museum für Völkerkunde, Basel, there are about twenty different types including variants. Most have specific names given by the ikat design of the centerfield.[2] *Kamben cepuk saksak* (Fig. 15) is a very simple pattern of regular horizontal rows with white, black and light red lozenges alternating with tiny blue crosses; *saksak* refers to the yellow blossom of *Wedelia mollucana*. In *kamben cepuk sambeh bintang* (Fig. 16), there are horizontal rows of alternating white and multicolored lozenges, between which are set small blue or green crosses; *sambeh bintang* means "dispersed small stars."

Kamben cepuk tangkariga (Fig. 17) is characterized by vertical rows of multicolored lozenges combined with a rhomboid motif made up of four small lozenges. The background is filled with tiny black and white rhombs and yellow arrow-head shapes; *tangkariga* is a species of coral. *Kamben cepuk sari* (Fig. 18) has a regular trellis pattern formed by white, blue, yellow and red lozenges with blue cross-shapes in the red spaces between; *sari* means "essence" or "flower."

In *kamben cepuk padang derman* or *padang alija* (Fig. 19), white lines form an overall regular lattice design which is filled with blue arrowheads, bright red crosses, and multicolored lozenges at the central intersections. A more elaborate variant of this design shows that this stylized filling was originally an eight-petaled flower (Fig. 20). *Padang alija* and *padang derman* are different grass species, the latter known as

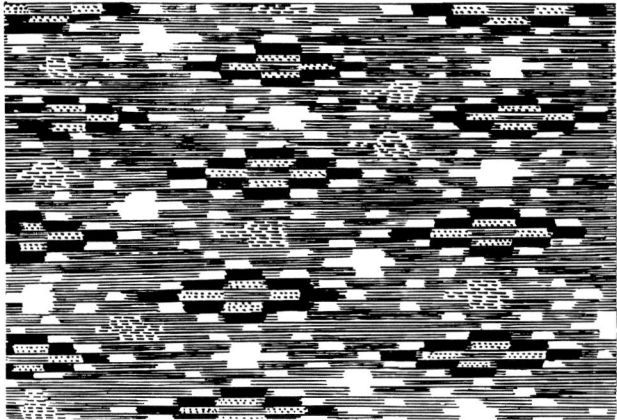

Figure 16. Dispersed-star pattern in centerfield of kamben cepuk sambeh bintang. *Museum für Völkerkunde, Basel, IIc 13945.*

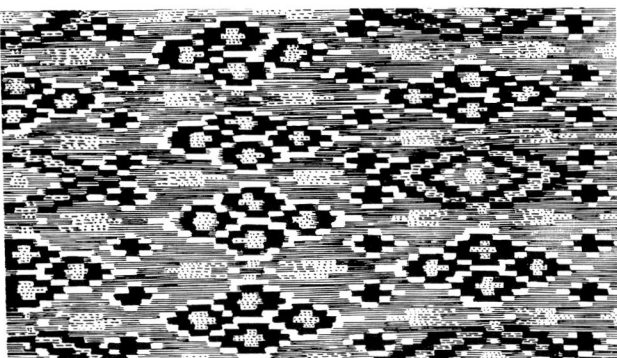

Figure 17. Coral pattern in centerfield of kamben cepuk tangkariga. *Museum für Völkerkunde, Basel, IIc 13939.*

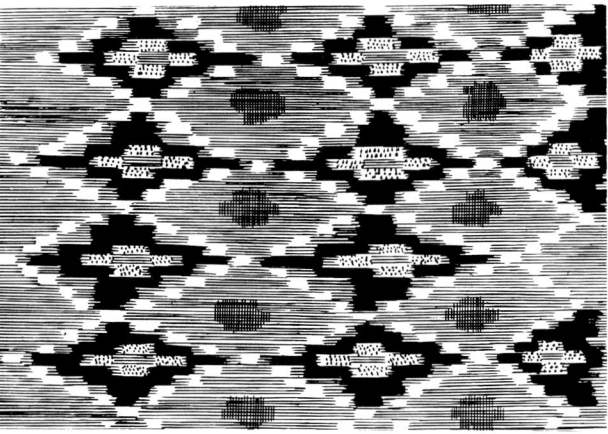

Figure 18. Flower pattern in centerfield of kamben cepuk sari. *Museum für Völkerkunde, Basel, IIc 13944.*

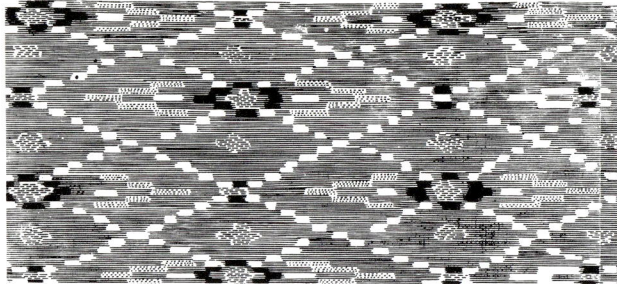

Figure 19. Flowering grass pattern in centerfield of kamben cepuk padang derman or padang alija. Museum für Völkerkunde, Basel, IIc 13956.

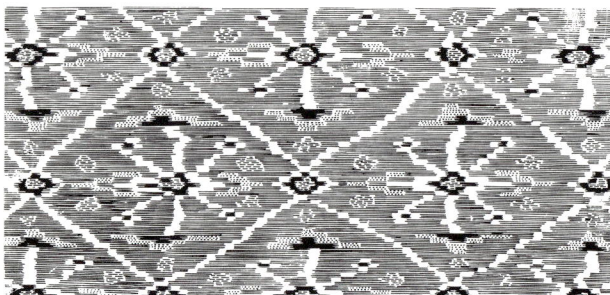

Figure 20. More elaborate variant of flowering grass pattern in centerfield of kamben cepuk padang derman or padang alija. Museum für Völkerkunde, Basel, IIc 13958.

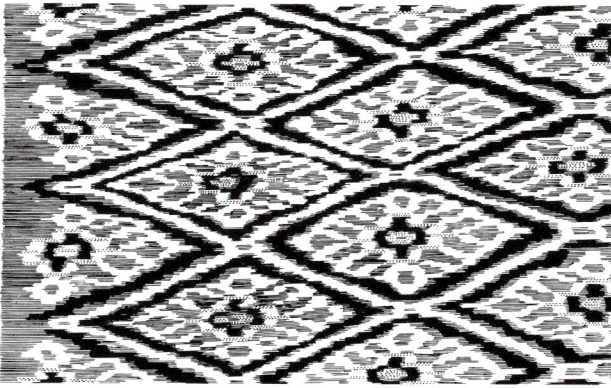

Figure 21. Flower pattern in centerfield of kamben cepuk sekar seroni. Museum für Völkerkunde, Basel, IIc 13937.

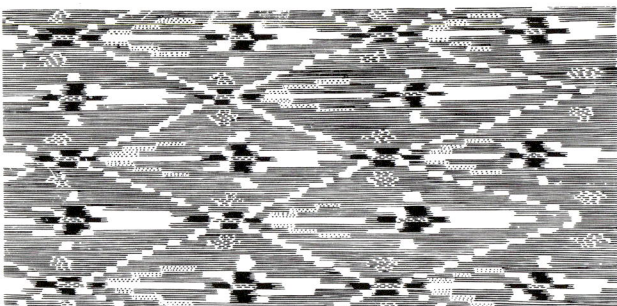

Figure 22. Flowering grass pattern with one blossom in centerfield of kamben cepuk padang angket. Museum für Völkerkunde, Basel, IIc 13951.

medicine against pustules. The same design is sometimes called *kamben cepuk beremara* or *cemara*, referring to the *cemara* tree (*Casuarina equisetifolia* or *Casuarina nodifera*). This particular *cepuk* form could be used as a shroud; it could also be worn by men of high or middle rank (i.e. iron and kris smiths) or used by girls as offerings during their puberty rites.

The overall design of *kamben cepuk sekar seroni* (Fig. 21) is filled with stylized yellow blossoms of rhomboid shape. *Sekar seroni* is a yellow flower, used for offerings, that grows in the region of the mountain Gunung Agung. This type of *cepuk* is sometimes given the name *kamben cepuk betola* (see below under *kamben cepuk cendana kawi*).

Kamben cepuk padang angket (Figs. 22,23,25) is a pattern of regular lozenges filled with a flowering shrub that has one, three, or five blossoms growing from a common stem with two basal opposite leaves. These shrubs either all face the same selvedge or are arranged in two directions. *Padang angket* is a grass species, *Physalis minima L.* There are many variations of this pattern, ranging from simple stylized ones to very elaborate ones. The flowering shrub motif is clearly derived from a traditional patola design (Figs. 24,26), one that was particularly favored both in Indonesia and in India (Bühler and Fischer 1979:33ff, 215, figs. 18ff). In India, patola designs with flowering shrubs are called *ful vadi bhat*, "floral field pattern," or more specifically *tran ful bhat* for the three-flower pattern, *panch ful bhat* for the five-flower pattern. Specimens of this type were especially popular in Bali and in the principalities of Central Java, where they were known as *sekar tanjung* and were used for ceremonial costumes, trousers, wraparound skirts, and sashes as well as for ritual bed decorations.

Kamben cepuk cendana kawi (Fig. 27) is a pattern combining two elements. At first sight, the vertical rows of lozenges with finger-like extensions command attention. Then, in between, the second motif becomes noticeable: an oval shape with a central flower, four four-petaled blossoms and four buds, arranged in the form of an eight-pointed star (Figs. 28,29). This is one of the classic patola patterns, called in India *chhabadi bhat* "basket design" (Bühler and Fischer 1979:68ff, 214, figs. 70,71,76, pls. VII-IX, 28-29). Patola textiles with this design have been exported to Indonesia and imitated in other techniques there. The motif appears on Javanese batiks, where it is called *jilamprang* or *jelamprang*, a term signifying the blossom of *Taluma elegans* or the wild magnolia *Michelia velutina*. Alternatively the design is called *kenanga*, after the flower of *Canaga odorata* (Bühler 1959:10; Bühler and Fischer 1979:283, pl. XXXII; Jasper and Pirngadie 1912:143ff; Rouffaer and Juynboll 1914:171).

When parts of this design are repeated in the ikat bands of the end border, the Balinese interpret them as

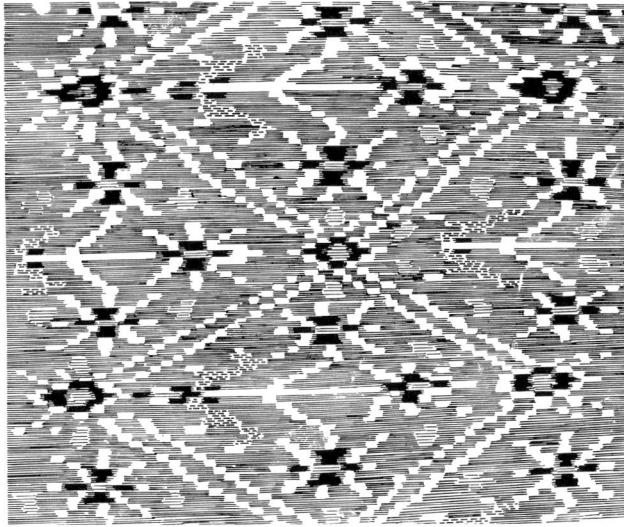

Figure 23. Flowering shrub pattern with three blossoms in centerfield of kamben cepuk padang angket. Museum für Völkerkunde, Basel, IIc 13963.

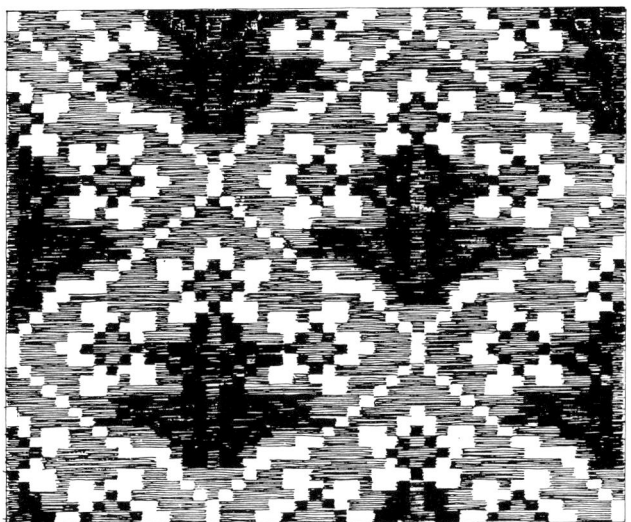

Figure 24. Indian patolu with three-blossom design, tran ful bhat. Museum für Völkerkunde, Basel, IIa 2389.

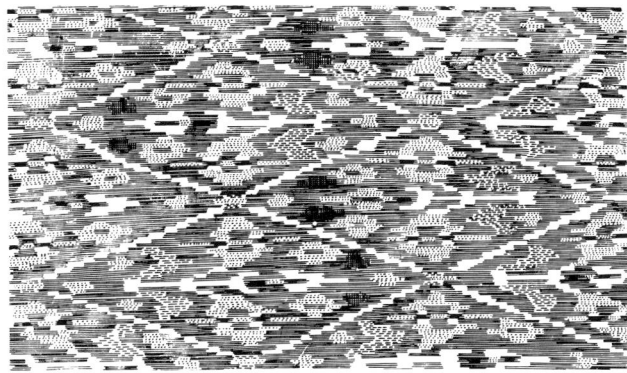

Figure 25. Flowering shrub pattern with five blossoms in centerfield of kamben cepuk padang angket. Museum für Völkerkunde, Basel, IIc 13981.

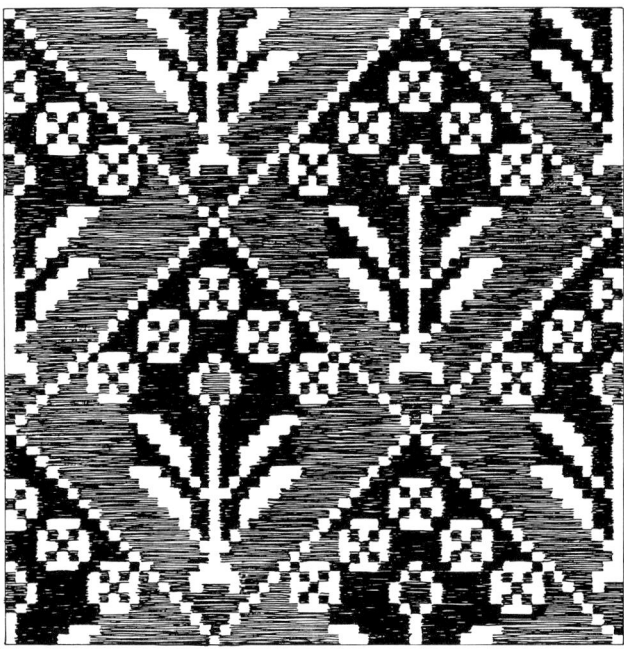

Figure 26. Indian patolu with five-blossom design, panch ful bhat (after a photograph by E. Fischer).

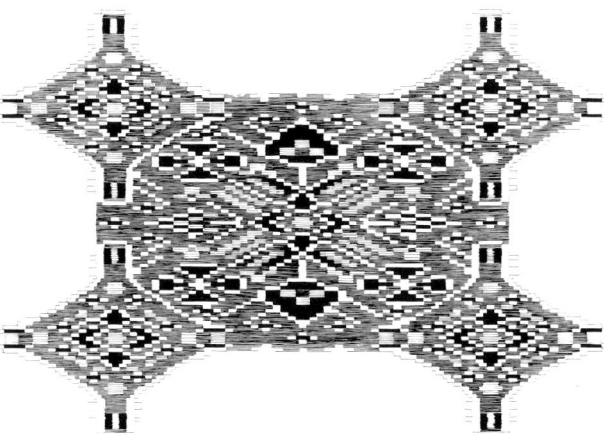

Figure 27. Lozenge-and-blossom pattern in centerfield of kamben cepuk cendana kawi. This is also a classic patola pattern, termed "basket design" (chhabadi bhat) in India. Museum für Völkerkunde, Basel, IIc 13940.

Figures 28. Design elements of Indian patola cloth with basket design, patolu chhabadi bhat. *Calico Museum of Textiles, Ahmedabad, India, 1695.*

Figure 29. Design elements of Indian patola cloth with basket design, patolu chhabadi bhat. *Museum für Völkerkunde, Basel, IIa 1677. See also Figure 7.*

representations of flowers: either as *sungsang*, which is the red Gloriosa lily associated with Rangda, or as *medori*, a flower often used in ancestral rituals. Other names for the same centerfield pattern, but combined with different border designs, are *kamben cepuk betola* (see above under *kamben cepuk sekar seroni*) or *kamben cepuk Semara guna*. The designation *betola* might be associated with *pitola*, the Balinese term for patola, but according to Balinese informants, *betola* is a creeping plant with brown stems and reddish green leaves; perhaps they mean the plant *Albizzia chinensis*. Semara is the god of love; *Semara guna* means "love-spell." An example of the same type in the Museum voor Land- en Volkenkunde in Rotterdam was collected by L.C. Heyting in 1922 under the designation *cepuk orti*. Orti is a form of offering made from *lontar* leaves and refers to an oval flower shape. *Kamben cepuk cendana kawi* is used to dress deities such as Betari Durga, goddess of death. It is also worn as an outer skirtcloth by men who channel divine power through trance-possession at temple or consecration ceremonies.

Kamben cepuk padma (Fig. 30, Pl. 29) shows two vertical rows of lozenges with rhomboid blossom-like ornaments, *padma* (lotus flowers); between them is a row of lozenges in groups of four, with star-shaped blossoms connected to form a diagonal cross in the center. This corresponds to another traditional patola design, hardly used in India, but very popular in the Malay archipelago (Fig. 31). It was frequently imitated on mordant-printed cotton fabrics produced in India for the Indonesian market, and was assimilated into the patterns of silk weft ikats made in Palembang, Sumatra. In Kerambitan, Bali, this same motif is called *angrek*, which is the name of an orchid species.

In most short *kamben cepuk* from Nusa Penida, the basic pattern is one in which four lozenges are joined to form a cross-like shape, repeated in rows (see Fig. 32). Half of the dark central cross rows are reiterated on both sides of the centerfield along the white *gigin Barong*, resulting in a vertical row of dark triangle forms that are typical for Nusa Penida even nowadays.

In certain *kamben cepuk* all weft ikat parts or only limited sections have an irregular design, without any visible pattern. These are *kamben cepuk* with the *nori reges* design (Fig. 33). Whether the yarn was intentionally prepared like this or whether the weaver used up yarn left from another textile or from a badly patterned lot is unknown. In Balinese, *nori* is a parrot with feathers of different colors; *reges* means "damaged" or "eaten by vermin." The design is therefore associated with the ruffled feathers of a parrot. It appears on specimens from Nusa Penida and from Bali. In Klungkung, small cloths with *nori reges* design in the centerfield are said to have been used as baby diapers (Fig. 34).

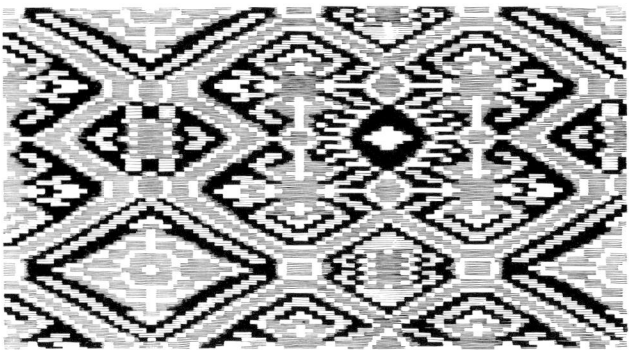

Figure 30. Lotus pattern in centerfield of kamben cepuk padma. *Museum für Völkerkunde, Basel, IIc 14203. See also Figure 8.*

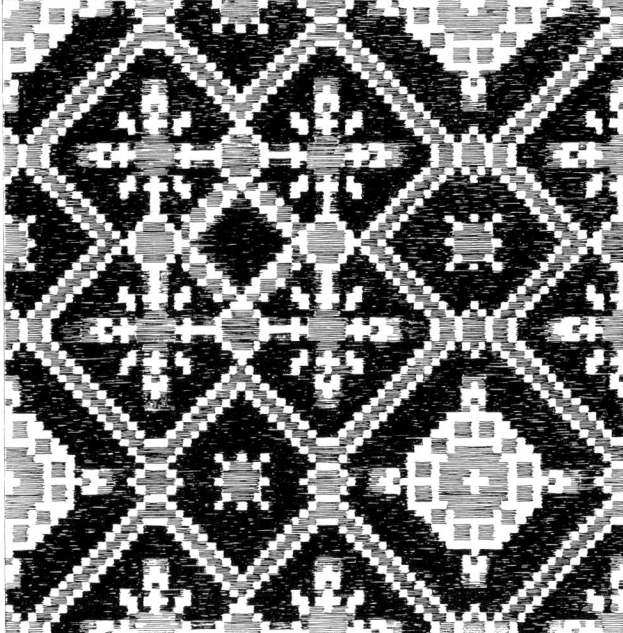

Figure 31. Indian patolu *with diagonal cross and rhomboid blossom design. Museum für Völkerkunde, Basel, IIc 15626. See also Figure 9.*

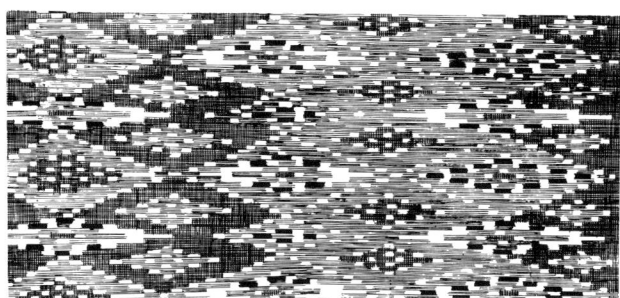

Figure 32. Typical design for kamben cepuk *from Nusa Penida. Museum für Völkerkunde, Basel, IIc 13943.*

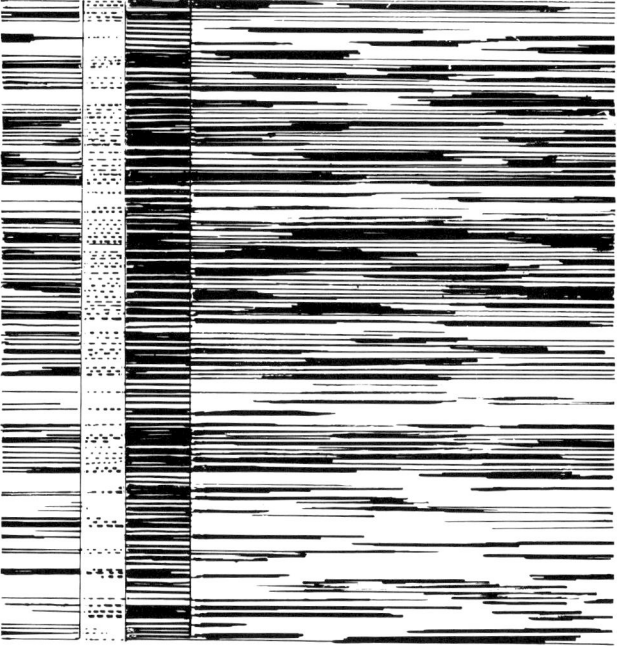

Figure 33. Ruffled parrot feathers (nori reges) *design. Museum für Völkerkunde, Basel, IIc 13941.*

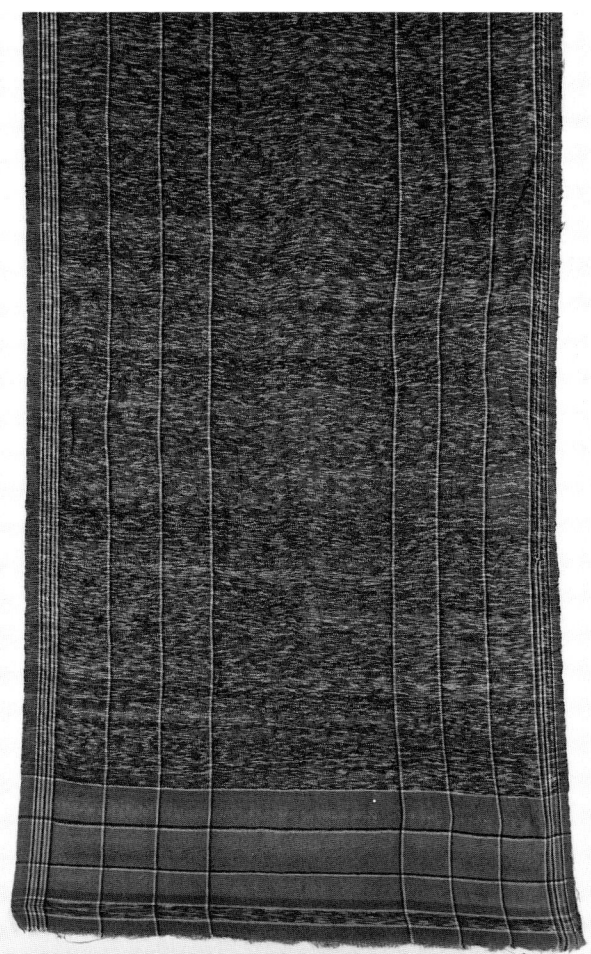

Figure 34. Small cepuk *cloth used as baby diaper. Klungkung, Bali, 1950s. Museum für Völkerkunde, Basel, IIc 20101.*

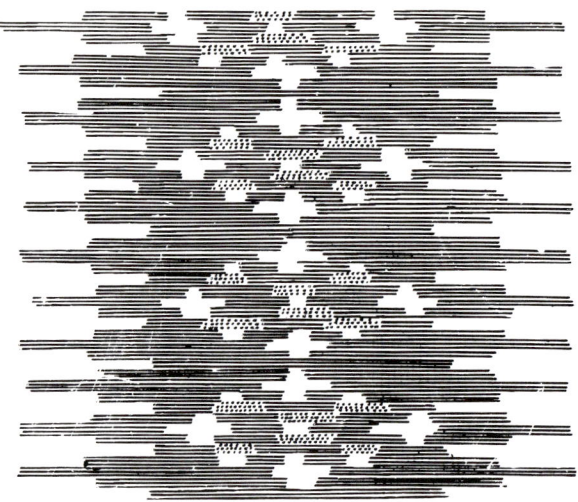

Figure 35. Side border lozenge pattern called bunga julit. *Museum für Völkerkunde, Basel, IIc 13939.*

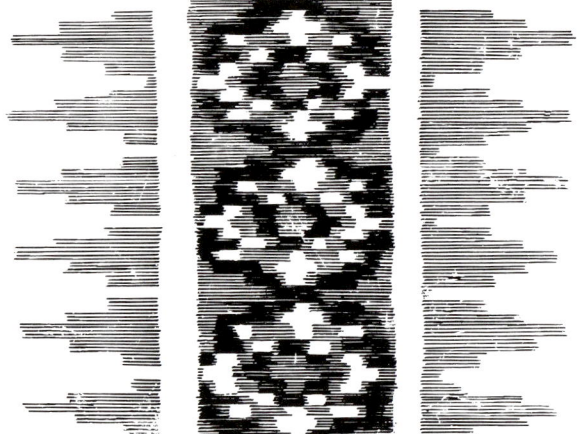

Figure 36. Side border lozenge pattern, name unknown. Museum für Völkerkunde, Basel, IIc 13956.

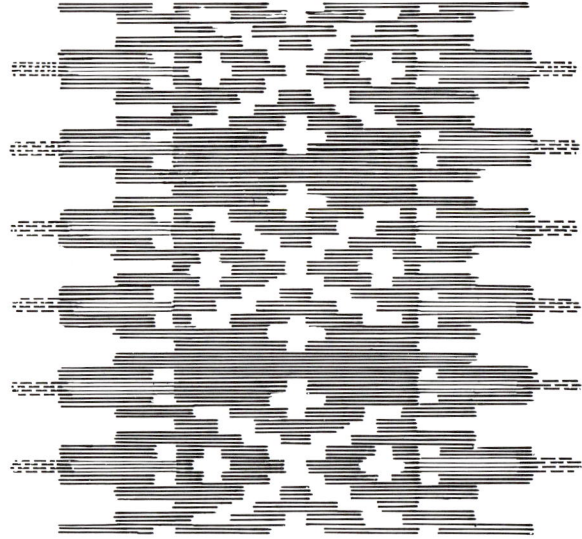

Figure 37. Side border pattern called "legs of a frog" (batis katak). *Museum für Völkerkunde, Basel, IIc 13937.*

Typology of Side Border Patterns

The sections in between the rows of white triangles (*gigin Barong*) on the side borders show a variety of weft ikat motifs. In many cases particular patterns are combined with certain centerfield designs; but there is no strict pairing. With one exception (Fig. 46), patterns cannot be attributed to specific regions. Only a few have been explicitly named by Balinese informants and in certain instances the same one may have different names. In general the names given to the side border pattern seem to be more descriptive than those applied to the centerfield.

Bunga julit (Fig. 35) is a border patterned with simple lozenges built up from small crosses and blocks. This design appears with the centerfield designs *cendana kawi*, *padma*, *sambeh bintang* and *sari*. Sometimes it is given the name of other flowers, for instance *saksak* (*Wedelia mollucana*), or *bakung* (*Grinum asiaticum*), a decorative plant with long leaves of the kind that are suspended from houses during certain rituals in Tenganan.

A pattern of unknown name (Fig. 36) consists of lozenges built up from small crosses, arrow-heads and blocks filled in and outlined with black or dark blue. It appears on *kamben cepuk padang derman* or *alija* and on *kamben cepuk beremara*. A border pattern made of X-shapes with four small crosses is termed *batis katak*, "legs of a frog" (Fig. 37). The term *batis katak* is sometimes completed by *bebintangan*, "sky full of stars." It can also be called *bunga bakung* (see above under *bunga julit*). This is the most frequent of all side border patterns to be seen on *kamben cepuk sekar seroni*, *cendana kawi* and other types. A more colorful variation of *batis katak*, called *kapukapu* (Fig. 38), is typical for *kamben cepuk padang alija*. *Kapukapu* was explained as a plant with black parts, growing in wet rice fields. Variants of *kapukapu* appear on different types of *kamben cepuk padang angket* (Figs. 39,40).

Another pattern combining aspects of the lozenge pattern (Fig. 36) and *batis katak* (Fig. 37) is frequently used to decorate the side bands of *kamben cepuk padang angket* side borders (Fig. 41). Variations of this design, with smaller lozenges and more elaborate X-shapes, appear on *kamben cepuk padang angket* and *padang derman* (Figs. 42,43). A pattern combining *batis katak* with two heart-shaped leaves and a dumbbell or hourglass form (Fig. 44) is the only one that corresponds exactly to a well-known patola border (Fig. 45). This pattern occurs on patola specimens with the lozenge design that has been assimilated in *kamben cepuk* (see above). It appears on *kamben cepuk padma* and *cendana kawi*.

The Nusa Penida design shown in Figure 46 is the only side border pattern whose specific regional

Sacred Cloth of Rangda

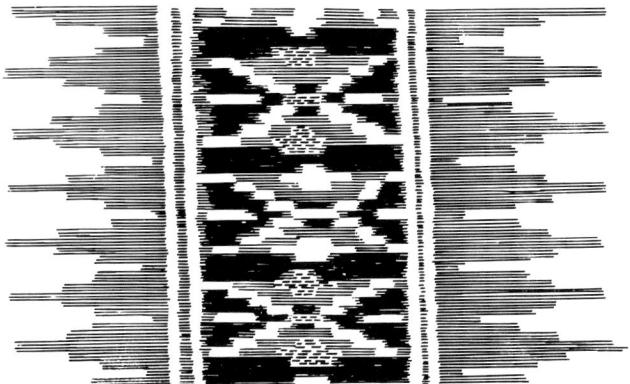

Figure 38. Variant of frog's leg side border pattern, called kapukapu, after a black plant that grows in rice fields. Museum für Völkerkunde, Basel, IIc 13955.

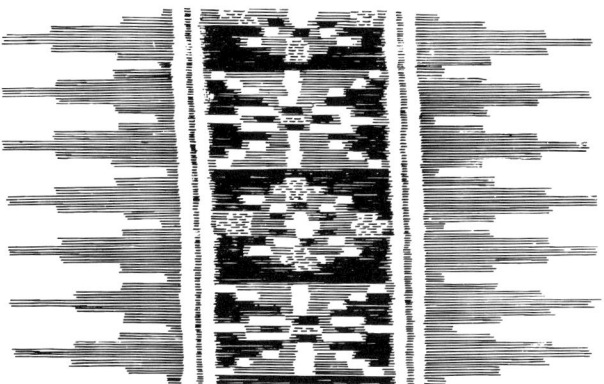

Figure 41. Side border pattern, name unknown, combining elements of Figures 36 and 37. Museum für Völkerkunde, Basel, IIc 13968.

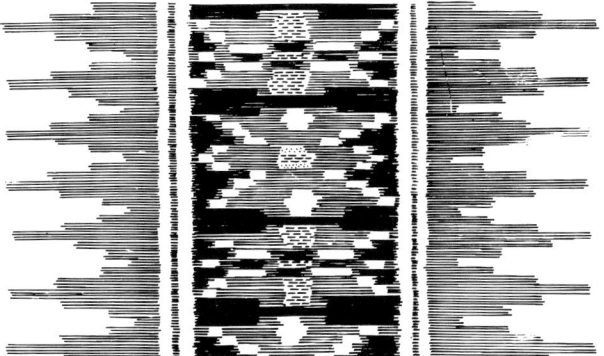

Figure 39. Variant of kapukapu (see above). Museum für Völkerkunde, Basel, IIc 13976.

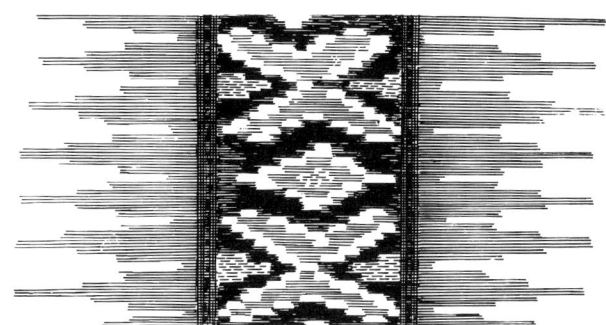

Figure 42. Variant of Figure 41. Museum für Völkerkunde, Basel, IIc 13957.

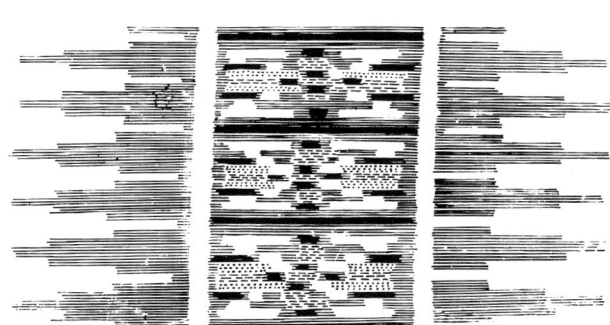

Figure 40. Variant of kapukapu (see above). Museum für Völkerkunde, Basel, IIc 13971.

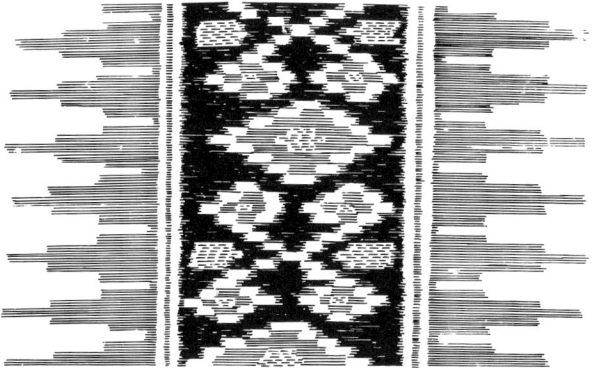

Figure 43. Variant of Figure 41. Museum für Völkerkunde, Basel, IIc 13974.

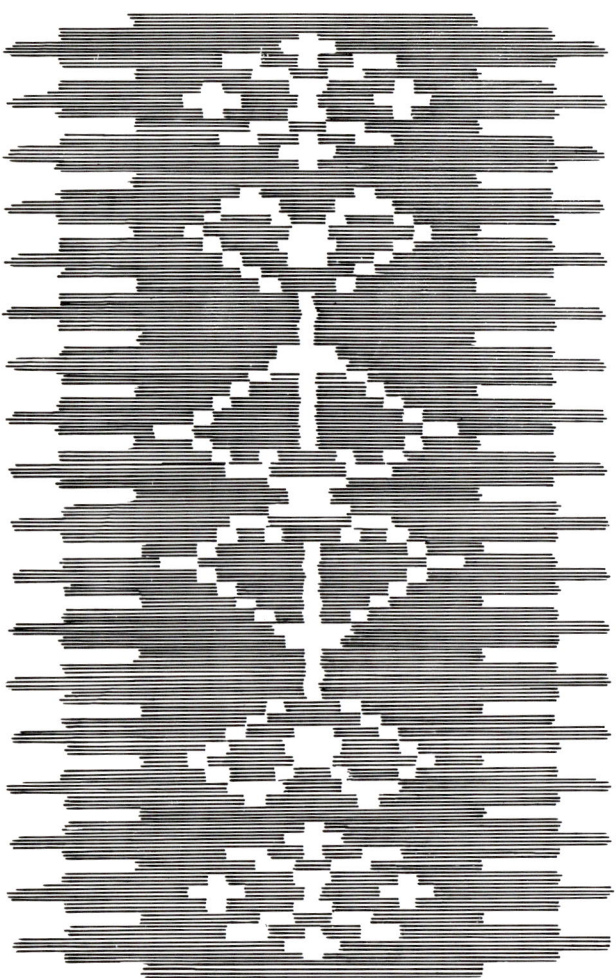

Figure 44. Combination of frog's leg side border pattern (batis katak) with two heart-shaped leaves and a dumbbell or sandglass form. Museum für Völkerkunde, Basel, IIc 2064.

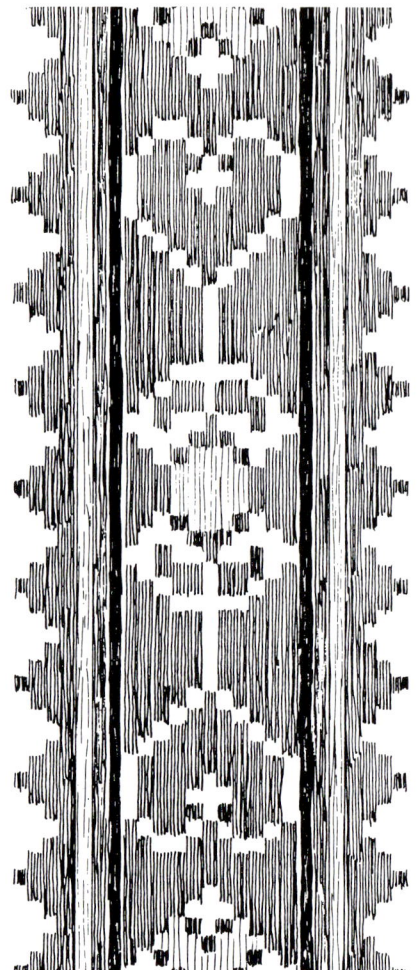

Figure 45. Indian patolu border design. Museum für Völkerkunde, Basel, IIc 15626. See Figure 9.

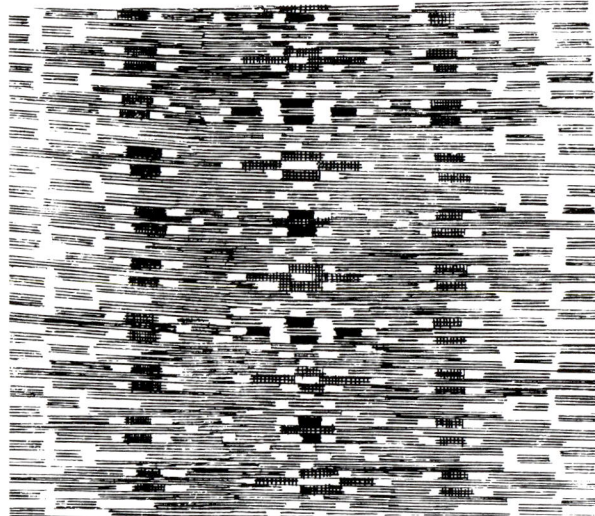

Figure 46. Typical Nusa Penida border design. Museum für Völkerkunde, Basel, IIc 13943.

provenience is certain. It consists of a vertical row of elongated lozenges built up by alternating small blocks, bigger forms and smaller forms. A name for this pattern is not known at present.

A Hierarchy of *Kamben Cepuk* Forms?

Information from the late 1930s on the use of certain forms of *kamben cepuk* in various context leads to the assumption that there existed a kind of formal hierarchy in design types. The highest forms seem to have been *kamben cepuk cendana kawi* and the related *kamben cepuk betola* and *Semara guna*. They were used as ceremonial garb for deities and persons in ritual trance-possession; they were also used in purification ceremonies and as shrouds (*kajang*) for people of high caste (though not for those of lower caste, lest there be magical reprisals). These same forms also appear as Rangda's cloth. Their common feature is the dominant oval flower design which shows the structure of an eight-pointed star (see Figs. 6,27).

In this connection it is interesting to pursue Van der Tuuk's translation of *cepuk* as a "fabric with four colors" (Van der Tuuk 1897:650). The connection may be understood in terms of another ritual cloth, *kekasang*, employed by Balinese priests for prayer, to honor the gods, and at hair cutting, tooth filing, and cremation rites; at post-cremation rituals *kekasang* are placed near an effigy of the deceased (Damsté 1926:254-64). The designs painted on them, called *sikep nawa sanga*, render the cosmic order by symbolizing the nine divine powers with their attributes in the form of an eight-pointed star with a center. Four main colors, four mixed colors, and the multicolored center correspond to the nine divine powers. Black or blue in the north corresponds to Wisnu; light blue in the northeast, to Sambu; white in the east, to Iswara; light red in the southeast, to Maheswara; deep red in the south, to Brahma; orange in the southwest, to Rudra; yellow in the west, to Mahadewa; green in the northwest, to Sanghara; and the multicolored center, to Siwa.

Given that the highly esteemed ritual *kekasang*, the patola with its eight-pointed star design, *jilamprang*, and the corresponding *cepuk* cloths of the type *kamben cepuk cendana kawi*, *betola* and *Semara guna* are all used exactly in the same ritual contexts, it does not seem presumptous to contend that there is an evident relationship between the representation of the cosmic order on *kekasang* and patola, and the code of colors on the *kamben cepuk*. This would be the deeper sense of the interpretation "fabric with four colors," and might explain why *kamben cepuk cendana kawi* is regarded the highest form of *cepuk* cloth and is preferred in rituals. It is interesting to note that the Balinese conceive of the small demons (*omang*) from Nusa Penida as being red, yellow, blue, and white.

Cepuk cloths of the *padma* type are worn by Rangda and Rarung and serve at tooth filing rituals. They also may be used by women as ritual garb. The vast group of flower patterns of the type *padang angket* has much broader use, as ceremonial dress for men, at tooth filing, for purification rituals, and as shrouds, for those of high and middle caste. They also are worn in ritual drama as dresses. Both *padma* and *padang angket* are considered less powerful and less magical than the *kamben cepuk cendana kawi*.

Of even lesser status, apparently, are simpler designs such as *cepuk saksak*, *sambeh bintang*, *sari*, and *padang derman* or *alija*. They can be worn by men at any ceremonial occasion, as a Balinese informant expressed it. More specifically, *padang derman* is allowed at menstruation rituals or as shrouds for people of middle castes. *Kamben cepuk sari* was explicitly mentioned in connection with the ritual for a newborn, but it could never be used for deities.

As a result we suggest—although this has to be confirmed by further investigations—that the forms nearer to genuine patola in design are considered of much higher status and can only be used in specific context of high ritual importance. The simpler types, which are farther away from original patola, are of lower status and can be used in a much broader sense and for different purposes of lower ritual importance.

NOTES

1. This chapter is based on a paper presented at the Symposium on Indonesian Textiles held in Cologne in Autumn 1985 (see Nabholz-Kartaschoff In Press). While the technical description has been reduced to a minimum, the section on designs and the illustrations and drawings have been enlarged. This article represents a preliminary note on an area of research that is just opening up; I am continuing investigations in the field. Most of the more than sixty *kamben cepuk* examples in the collection of the Museum für Völkerkunde, Basel, were assembled in 1949 by the late Professor Alfred Bühler with the assistance of the Swiss painter Theo Meier. Professor Bühler's notes on the inventory cards and his description of ikat weaving in South Bali (see Bühler 1943) were the main sources. I also was given precious information by Max Weber, a Swiss who during his stay of more than ten years in Bali gathered interesting information from Bali and Nusa Penida. I am indebted to my colleague, Dr. Urs Ramseyer, who patiently helped me trace the meaning of Balinese terms; and to Dr. David Stuart-Fox.

2. Controleur L.C. Heyting, who had collected *cepuk* cloths for the Museum voor Land- en Volkenkunde in Rotterdam mentioned that about ten sorts could be differentiated in the early 1920s; see Museum voor Land- en Volkenkunde 1922/33:11.

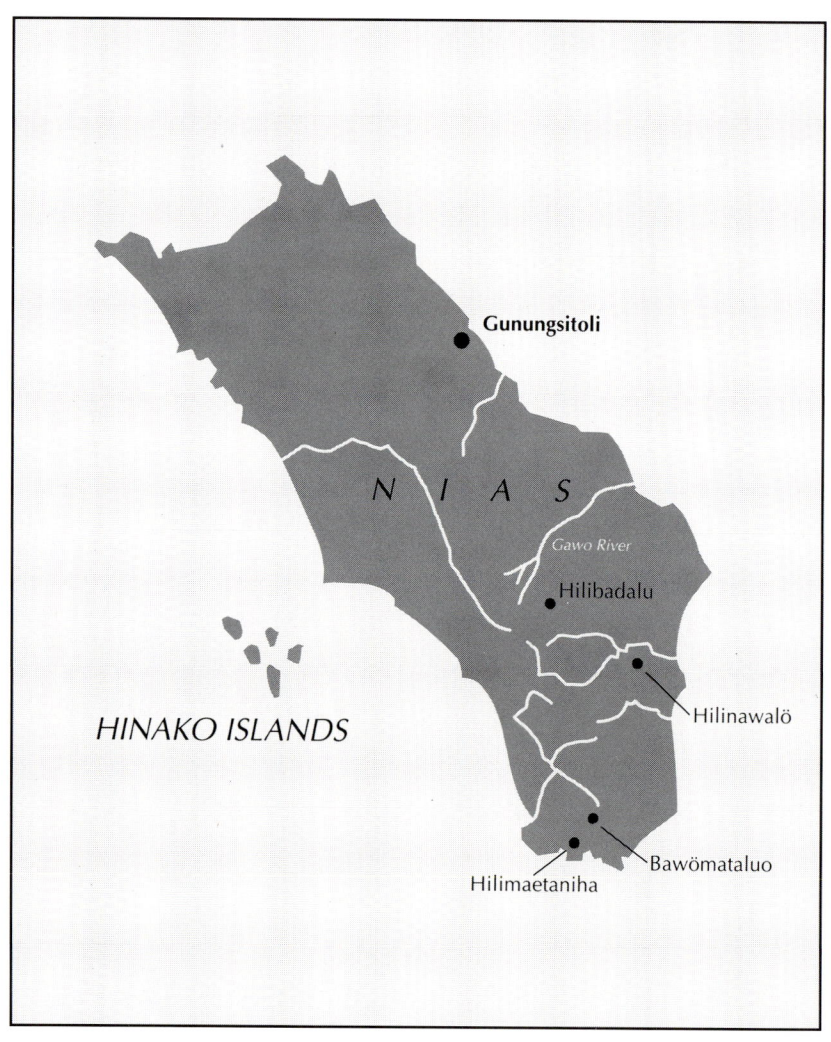
Nias and the Hinako Islands.

Ceremonial Attire in Nias

Jerome Feldman

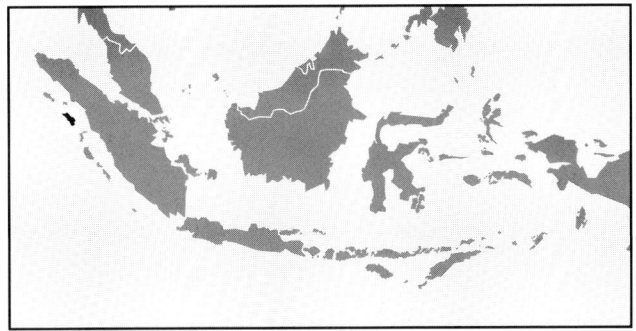

The people of Nias Island call themselves Ono Niha, the "Children of People." They call their island Tanö Niha, the "Land of People." The centrality of the human being in the conceptualizations of the Ono Niha is manifest in the emphasis upon human adornment in all regions of the island. In this place of rich architectural and sculptural traditions, the people themselves can be the most elaborate works of art.

This wealth of personal adornment occurs despite the paucity of techniques used in the production and patterning of fabrics. A few textiles are woven on back-tension looms and carry simple patterns in warp ikat stripes, but these are not common. Traditionally most textiles are of barkcloth fabricated from three types of *Ficus* and one variety of *Artocarpus* (Marschall 1976:86); however, since the beginning of the twentieth century, barkcloth has gradually been replaced with imported cotton. Its surface may be embroidered with gold yarn or appliquéd with geometric patterns in contrasting colored felt or imported cotton. Primary colors are most common and are used in a variety of combinations.

The Nias term *gamagama* in its broadest sense includes the totality of traditional attire. An individual never wears all elements at one time, but selects pieces as appropriate to the occasion. The richness of Nias ceremonial *gamagama* results from the configuration of clothing parts, gold jewelry, elaborate headgear; and sometimes from the use of iron or crocodile skin armor, deer antlers, masks, and a complicated system of weapons as well. It is the combination of these that conveys meaning in a ceremonial context.

Rank and social position are key in determining the magnificence of one's dress. Throughout Nias there are two classes, one of nobles and the other of commoners. The slaves of earlier times were considered possessions, not members of society; by the turn of this century they had been absorbed into the commoner class. The nobility is entitled to the most elaborate costumes with rich gold ornaments; yet these accoutrements can only be produced as part of an enormous cycle of feasts which require not only the gold necessary for the sponsor's crowns, earrings, and necklaces, but also an additional amount for the ceremonial distribution of gold within a village according to one's rank, and even to relations in other villages. Symbolic aspects of costume match the person's role in society. In South Nias, for example, warrior costumes differ from those of elders and nobles.

The style of attire varies regionally. The three regions of Nias correspond to broad ethnic and linguistic divisions in Nias culture.[1] North Nias comprises most of the island. The establishment of long term foreign residences marked both the early recording of North Nias culture and its early transformation. The Dutch had established their government headquarters here by 1840; and in 1865 the Germans founded and organized their missionary activities in the north. Since the first colonial accounts tend to be descriptive rather than interpretative, we can picture North Nias dress, but we have little information about its meaning. Central Nias, densely populated, is the area that most Ono Niha consider to be their homeland: it was here that traditional Nias culture began. Because it is the most poorly recorded region of Nias, we know very little about the appearance of ceremonial attire; but thanks to the recent works of Father Hämmerle, there are some data on the feasting and nomenclature required for certain types of *gamagama*. The southern tip of the island has the most spectacular and best preserved version of Nias culture. Fortunately, it has also been better recorded by scholars. This essay will therefore focus upon the *gamagama* traditions of South Nias, with particular reference to studies I conducted in Bawömataluo, the most elaborate traditional village in that region, and its related villages.[2]

North Nias

Traditionally in North Nias, the men and women of chiefly families adorn themselves with lavish gold crowns and sometimes enormous gold earrings. Women wear a short skirt (*götö*) over a long cloth, tied around the waist. The skirt is usually blue; the waistband is red and may be ornamented with beads (Rappard 1909:520). An illustration published in Rees shows a woman in such attire (Fig 1). She is also wearing a necklace of glass beads and two golden earrings. Her hair ornaments are probably made of gold, although Rees reports silver and coral beads (1866:37), and her bracelets, illustrated in Rogers (1985:274, nos. 8-10), would be of giant clamshell or copper (Nieuwenhuisen and Rosenberg 1863:30).

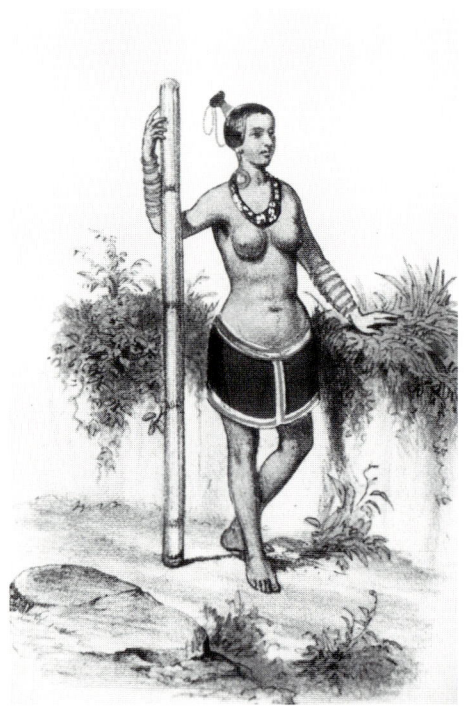

Figure 1. Woman from North Nias. From Rees 1866: opposite 37.

Evidence of an even more elaborate form of women's costume can be seen in Figure 2, from a photograph published in three different missionary sources (Anon. 1895:28; Lett 1901 IV:30; Sundermann 1905a:43). Exactly where it was taken is not known, but another photograph published by the missionary Lett shows similar headgear and clothing worn by women in the Hinako Islands, tiny islands to the west of Nias with a variant of North Nias culture (1901 IV:79). Their gold ornaments—particularly the crowns and necklaces—are identical to those worn by North Nias men as seen in other sources. (Their long garments and shawls, however, are quite different from those described as common to North Nias women.)

Male ceremonial attire of North Nias, also poorly recorded, must be understood primarily from engravings and photographs. Carvings constitute a secondary source of information: throughout Nias, golden ornaments are depicted with accuracy on ancestor figures. Textiles, on the other hand, are never portrayed in wood on old traditional carved figures, though actual textiles are often made to clothe them. These include miniature loincloths and, frequently, cloth attachments to the headgear. (From South Nias there are even a few examples of small jackets, *baru*, made for ancestor figures.[3])

A photograph published by Modigliani (1890: pl. 19), taken in a village in North Nias, gives us clear evidence of the crown type and other costume elements that were characteristic of that region.[4] A later photograph appearing in Witteborg illustrates a chief in a somewhat different costume but it may be assigned to North Nias because of the golden crown, or *saembu ana'a* (Fig. 3). In this excellent example, flat disks with conical bosses over them are arranged around the chief's headband. Above this, the crown structure rises to a point at the front of the head. Leaf-like forms emerge from the spire, terminating in a lozenge at the pinnacle.

In addition to his golden crown, the "old chief," as the missionary Witteborg called him, wears a single large golden earring called *gaule* (Modigliani 1890: 483-84; Rogers 1985:273, no. 2). In this he is typical of men throughout Nias, who adorn only their right ears. As a rule, asymmetry is for men and symmetry for women.[5] One item noticeably absent from Witteborg's chief, but normally included in the *gamagama* of a North Nias nobleman, is a necklace made of pleated gold sheet, very wide in the front and tapering to a hook at the back (see Rogers 1985:273, no. 5), commonly called *nifatöfatö* (Modigliani 1890:483). The old chief does, however, carry an item of swagger: in his hand he holds a small fan called *töritöri* or *turituri*, made of stiff, flag-like red cloth supported by a handle (Fig. 3). Characteristically, the *töritöri* would be used especially during processions.[6] Its handle would

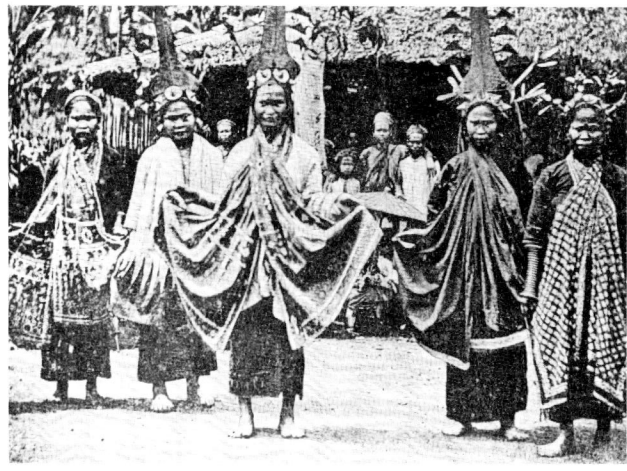

Figure 2. Women dancing during a marriage, possibly in the Hinako Islands. From Sundermann 1905a:43.

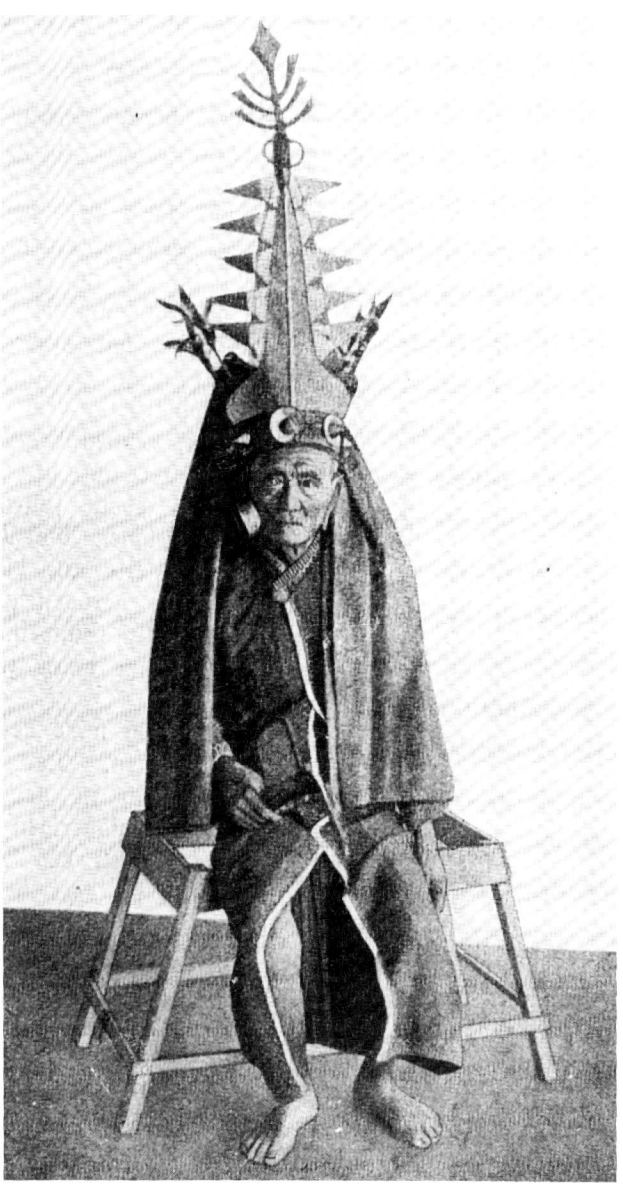

Figure 3. Chief from North Nias. From Witteborg 1909:11.

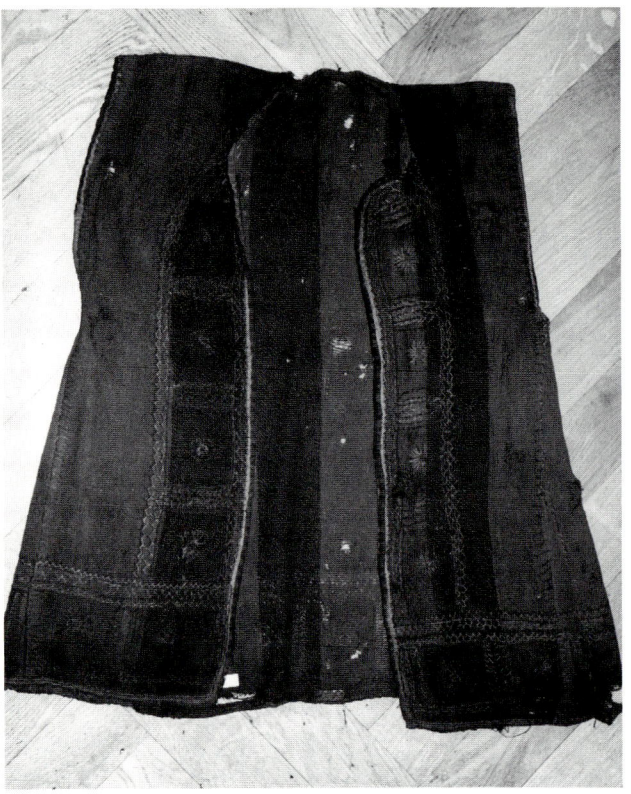

Figure 4. Chief's covering (baru luo), Sifalago Gomo, Central Nias. Danish National Museum C3381.

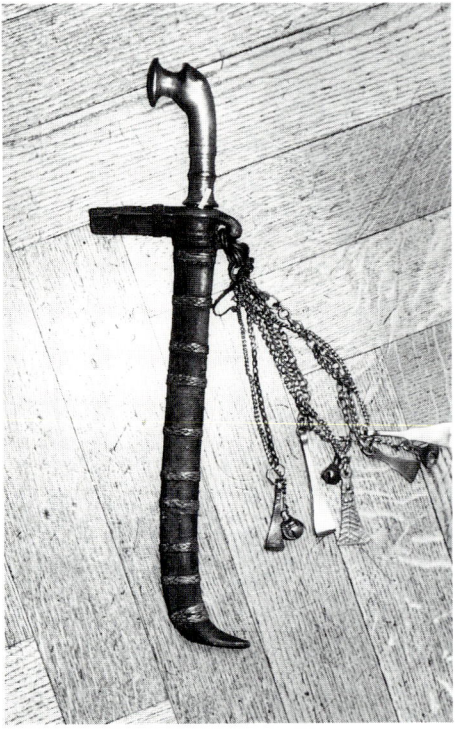

Figure 5. Dagger from Hilibadalu village, Gawo River, Central Nias. Danish National Museum C3415.

often be delicately incised and decorated with gold and small feathers (Schröder 1917:75). Another item of swagger could be a baton or walking stick made of dark palm wood (see Modigliani 1890: pl. 19). These can have incised or inlaid designs of mother of pearl (see Fischer 1909:22). Longer versions are carried by women as an emblem of authority (Modigliani 1890:488).

The textiles worn by the chief are of a kind rarely illustrated. A cape or cloth hangs from the top of his crown to the waist. He is also entirely clothed from his crown to his feet with a covering called *baru luo si handro tanö*, meaning, literally, "the sun jacket which reaches the ground." [7] Modigliani records that the example he studied was entirely of red cloth with fringes of pure white dentates (1890:482). The dual cosmic allusion to the heavens (sun) and the earth (ground) implies that the North Nias chief (*balugu* or *salawa*) embodies aspects of both. His clothing is a sign that he has given the entire cycle of feasts possible within the customary laws of his village. These references to the totality of the cosmos indicate the completeness of the individual.[8]

Central Nias

In Central Nias, the role of ceremonial costume is well documented; however, the costumes themselves are largely unrecorded. Many items of both ceremonial and daily wear require feasting to produce—evidence of the extremely high value placed upon body adornment. A practice illustrating the power of golden attire in Central Nias is documented by Schnitger. In the village of Lahusa[9] there is a vertical stone called *saita mbaru*, (literally, "hooks for the jacket"[10]). It is a pillar with a collar at the top adorned with hooks (1941-42: pl. 88, fig. 32). Schnitger records that when a ruler—in this case a certain Sebua Ana'a or "Big Gold"—had golden clothing and ornaments made, he had to contend with a curse that comes with the lusting for gold. Therefore a slave was made to wear the ornaments after they had been hung on the *saita mbaru*. This transferred the curse to the slave, who was then beheaded. His head was placed on top of the pillar, which was decorated with palm leaves. According to Schnitger, the *saita mbaru* represents "the tree of life," whose fertility and power is released through the severed head (1941-42:248).

The importance of ceremonial attire in the culture of Central Nias is also reflected in the complexity and variety of items used. Johannes Hämmerle published extensive descriptons of the most significant items (1982:70-71;1984:614-15). The list of men's wear includes a loincloth called *basöwa*, fifteen to twenty centimeters wide and two to three meters long, made of cloth or the bark of the Indian rubber tree (*basöwa gitö*), and several kinds of jackets. The golden jacket, *baru ana'a*, is one of the most prized possessions of a Central Nias chief. It is made of a material called *tafitafi*, the fine fiber mesh at the base of coconut leaves[11] which is rolled up, placed in a pot and cooked until supple. After felting, the fabric is cut and sewn into a sleeveless jacket, and gold thread or other gold items are worked into it, imparting a chiefly status. Another jacket (Fig. 4), also made of *tafitafi*, and usually fringed with red material, is called *baru nigözi* or *baru luo* (lit., "sun jacket"). It is analogous to the *baru luo si handro tanö* of North Nias, and its sun, whose rays are seen as golden, is perhaps a reference again to gold. Two simple daily jackets (*baru towa, baru gitö*), are worn at festivities because they have wide inner pockets for the storage of pork.

Hämmerle also describes items of jewelry and swagger for men. There is a gold headband (*ndrönö ana'a* or *böbö högö*); a golden earring for the right ear (*lulu ana'a*); and a golden necklace (*gamagama zabölö nidada*) whose many types are differentiated by weight.[12] A brass-handled dagger called *ekhe laoya* (Fig. 5) is used only by chiefs, who wear it tucked between stomach and loincloth.

Women, according to Hämmerle, also wear a number of special items during feasts (1982:72; 1984:615). Their sarongs include a golden one known as *u'i ana'a*, made of the same materials as the men's golden jacket (*baru ana'a*), and another one made of *ladari* grass, called *u'i ladari*. They also wear a blouse called *bairo* or *baru ndra alawe*. Women's accessories include a golden headband (*böbö högö ana'a*), a pair of golden earrings (*ana'a ba wiso*), a golden breastplate (*ana'a ba mbagi*) worn around the neck in the form of a half moon, pointed ends touching, and finally, golden necklaces (*uru mbagi, mbaugu*).

Evidence from ancestor figures, Hämmerle's descriptions, and a singular early photograph make it clear that the appearance of Central Nias nobility is quite impressive (Fig. 6). Noble men and women wear elaborate golden crowns featuring a high pointed front peak with two widely-flaring side pieces. A fourth vertical piece protrudes from the back of the crown. A broad horizontal golden mustache is also part of the attire and it appears from the photograph that whiskerlike elements protrude from the temples of the two men, suggesting something feline—perhaps a reference to a tiger or civet cat, both used at times as metaphors of chiefly power. The man on the right wears the *lulu ana'a*, or golden earring, and the large diameter golden necklace, *ana'a nifatali*. His brass-handled dagger, *ekhe laoya*, is also visible.

Little is known about the ceremonial costumes of priests in Nias. Three wooden faces from Central Nias, now distributed among the Tropenmuseum in Amsterdam, the Vereinigte Evangelische Missions

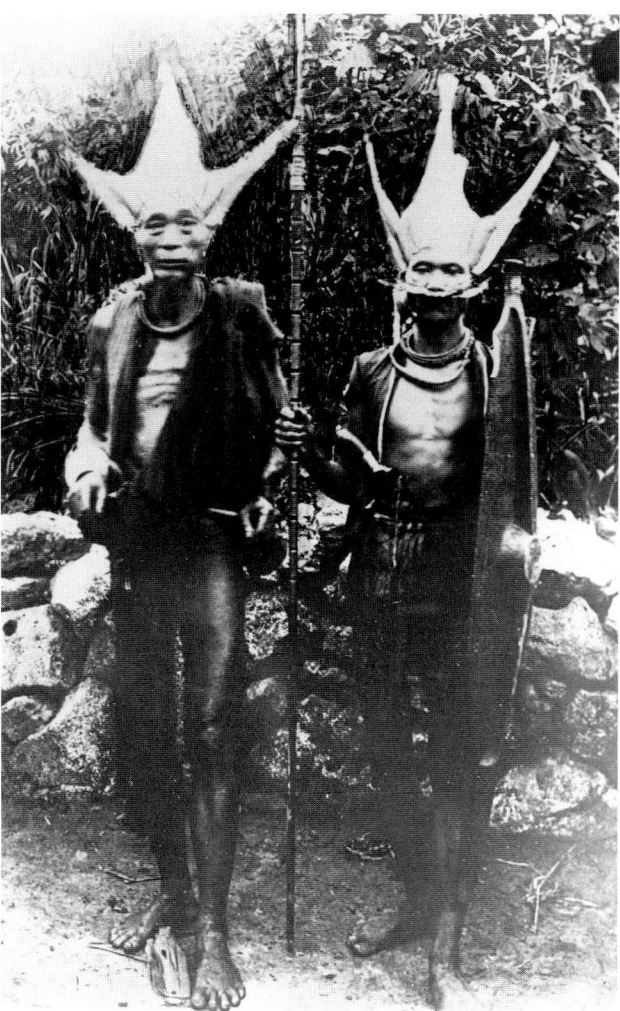

Figure 6. Two men from Central Nias wearing golden crowns. Photographed by F.C. Brust, circa 1912. Museum voor Volkenkunde, Rotterdam, F 2816/76.

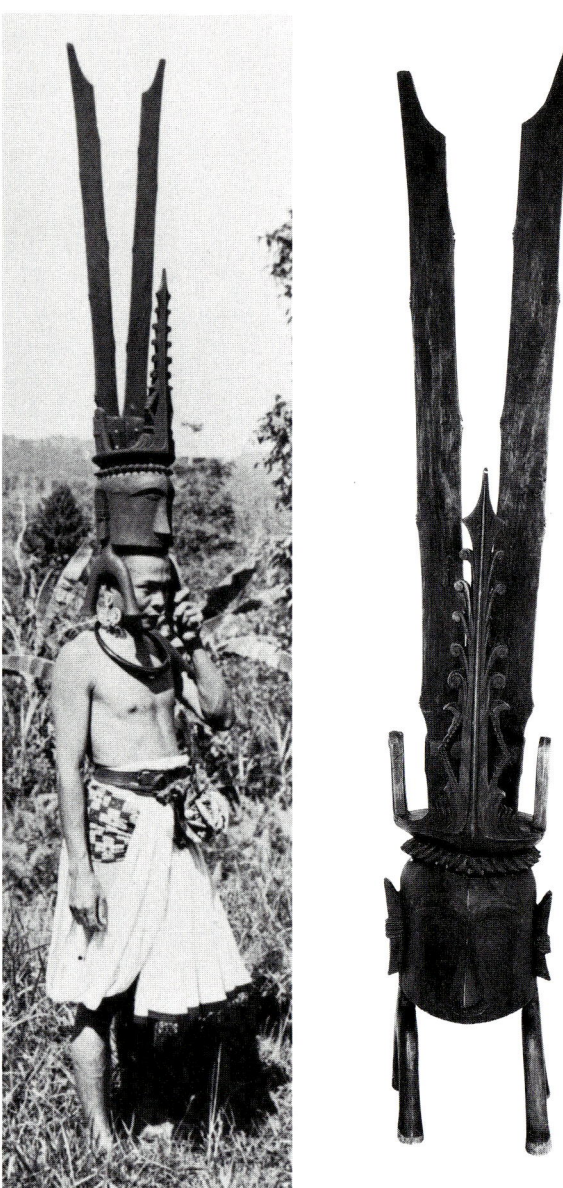

Figure 7. (a, left) Headgear called lötebulo, *from Central Nias, photographed in the field by W. Blanke, 1935. (b, right) Same headgear, now in the Tropenmuseum, Amsterdam, 1772.90.*

Museum in Wuppertal, and the Museum Nasional in Jakarta, are recorded as belonging to priests (see Anon. 1947:259, no. 25373). Strictly speaking, these are not masks but headgear since the wooden faces are worn above the head, the wooden props straddling the head of the priest (Fig. 7). The appearance would be that of a giant figure walking in the midst of the village. The largest of these structures, now in the Tropenmuseum in Amsterdam, is reported in the museum's archives as the "wooden headdress of the last priest king, Lôtoboelo,[13] the mightiest magician and sorcerer of all Nias." A recent publication of the museum indicates that "once every seven years he (Lotebulo) convened all village heads for a reconciliation feast lasting seven days. The headdress was his second face, allowing him to speak about phenomena of the spirit world" (Royal Tropical Institute 1987:262).

This description matches a seven year renewal festival held in North and Central Nias called Fondrakö. During this activity the priest reaffirms the customs and laws of his district. At the end of the ceremony, he stands upon a flat stone and recites phrases used to sanctify the reaffirmation of the laws as permanent, beginning with "*Me kara lö tebulo bulo,*" meaning "because rocks never change" (Laiya 1975:10-13). It is very likely that Lotebulo is a title that derives from the phrase *lö tebulo* and signifies "never changing."

The appearance of the entire costume would have closely resembled the largest of Central Nias wooden figures called *adu höro* (see Feldman 1985: figs. 31,33). These images are given offerings in order to ameliorate accumulated sins (see Møller 1934:129, fig. 12). Since the purpose of the Fondrakö ceremony is the reestablishment of order, it is possible that the priest acts, like the wooden image, to assuage previous transgressions of the law.

South Nias

The ceremonial attire of South Nias is spectacular. The wide variety of textiles and ornaments in astounding combinations create an effect, in the local context, that verges upon the magical.[14] This is best illustrated by a type of monument called "the ruler's clothes rack" (*naha gamagama nama*) or "the ruler's hat stand" (*naha dakula nama*), found in a number of prominent villages (Pl. 33). A stone with a somewhat phallic appearance, it is usually located at the ceremonial center of the village, *gorahua newali*. At times when the ruler is in danger, as when invasion is imminent, various items of his attire—usually including his ceremonial hat, sword, and jacket—are hung or draped around the stone. The chief is then free to seek safety outside of the village; meanwhile as long as his attire is on display the warriors remain under his command (see Feldman 1983:147, fig. 3). This monument at first appears related to the Central Nias stone, *saita mbaru*. But in South Nias, it is the attire itself that possesses the power to transfigure the stone into the ruler. There, the quest for golden ornaments is not considered problematic. In fact, it is required of a ruler, and is seen as a reason for celebratory feasting.

There are three broad types of ceremonial attire in South Nias. Women's dress forms one category. Men have two kinds of costume. They can appear in soft materials (Figs. 8,9) or in armor (Figs. 12,13). Similarly, there is a distinction on the basis of color. Colors are found primarily on soft costumes, while most warriors in armor are nearly entirely in black. Women never appear in armor but have an extensive and colorful set of jewelry and textiles of their own. There is a wide variety of subtypes within the three categories.

Men's Attire. From the Bawömataluo point of view, male ceremonial attire consists of armor (*öröba*) and attire which commemorates feasting (*gamagama tawila*). These correspond to hard and soft costumes. Men in soft attire, *gamagama tawila*, are the elite of the village, or experts in customary law. They may be of the nobility, *si'ulu*, or elders, *si'ila*, of the commoner class, *sato*. Plate 33 shows a man with golden ornaments befitting a high-ranking individual, but not that of the upper nobility. Figure 8, drawn from a photograph taken in the 1920s in Bawömataluo village, gives the form and terminology for the parts of the ceremonial attire reserved for the highest ranking *si'ulu*. Among the differences are the elaborate crown, the variety and weight of the gold jewelry, the jacket with long sleeves, the lengthy loincloth, and the extensive weapons. The colors are otherwise similar.

Colors in Bawömataluo have metaphorical associations. Black, *aito*, is associated with anger and fury (*fa'a budödö*). It is the color of armored warriors. Red, on the other hand, connotes expertise in ceremony and customary law (*adat* in Indonesian, *hada* in Nias). It also indicates blood, or that a person is capable of killing in war. Blue betokens victory (*fa'a möna*). White stands for purity and peace. Yellow is synonymous with gold, standing for royalty, wealth, power, grandeur, and such. The male costume imparts all of these qualities to the wearer. The color symbolism for women has not been recorded in detail, but the same sets of colors are associated with notions of wealth and class.[15]

There are other categories implied in the combination of elements in the costume. Nature appears in the form of birds, deer antlers, and plant motifs such as leaves, coiled ferns, and grass. These

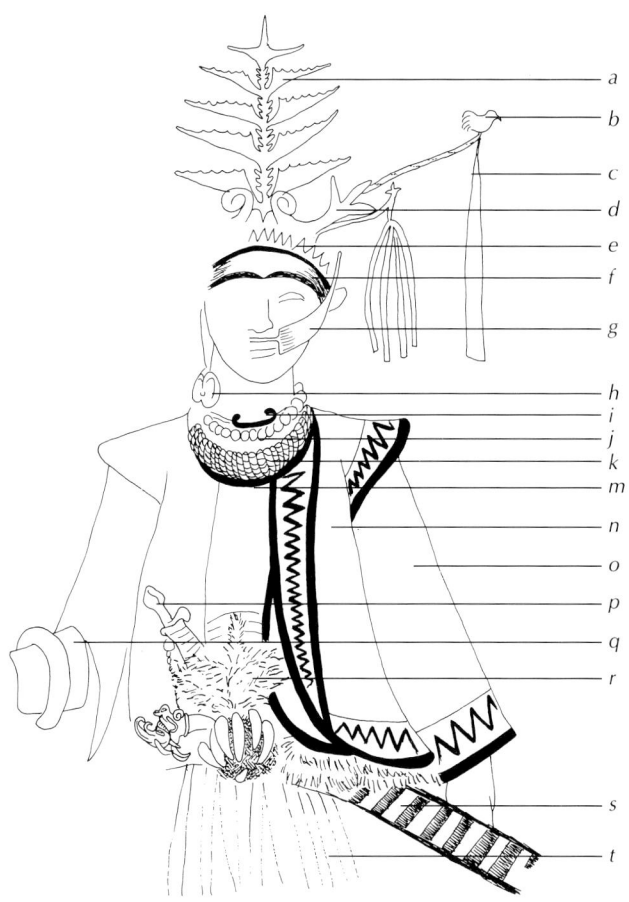

Figure 8. South Nias nobleman (si'ulu) in full ceremonial dress. After a photograph in the possession of the late Samögö Fau of Bawömataluo village.

a. *Leaf design called* bulu nadrulo; *the number of levels is proportionate to rank by birth and feasting.*
b. *Cock (*manu la'iya*), symbol of strength.*
c. *Horse hair (*rabu kuta*).*
d. *The horns of a deer (*sowahalaoyo*).*
e. *Golden headband (*böbödilau ana'a*).*
f. *Iron helmet (*takula tefau*). For one of higher rank this would be gold (*takula ana'a*).*
g. *Golden mustache (*bubewe ana'a*).*
h. *Male earring (*fondulu*). This earring can be used in pairs by women if a flat gold backing called* rusirusi *is attached.*
i. *Small mustache (*balabala bubawa*) said to be for daily use, normally worn over lip but seen here on neck as in photograph.*
j. *Wooden balls covered with gold leaf (*jolojolo ana'a*).*
k. Nifulufulu, *rope-like golden necklace weighing at least 100* pau, *for the ruler it must be at least 200* pau.
m. *Coconut shell and brass necklace (*kalabubu*) indicating valor in war.*
n. *Jacket (*baru*).*
o. *Jacket with long sleeves (*baru nifota'io*) worn under the* baru.
p. *Dagger (*balatu ria*).*
q. *Bracelet (*töla zaga*), usually of wood, covered with gold foil.*
r. *Leafy grass (*sobulu*).*
s. *Sword (*telögu*) with* lasara *head and tiger teeth on its amulet bundle,* ragö.
t. *Loincloth, usually consisting of three parts: (1) usual loincloth (*ödöra*). (2) support for the sword (*khaekhae mbalatu*). (3) special cloth,* hörö göra, *whose length is proportional to one's rank. Other combinations are possible. Information courtesy of Marlene Meyer-Patton.*

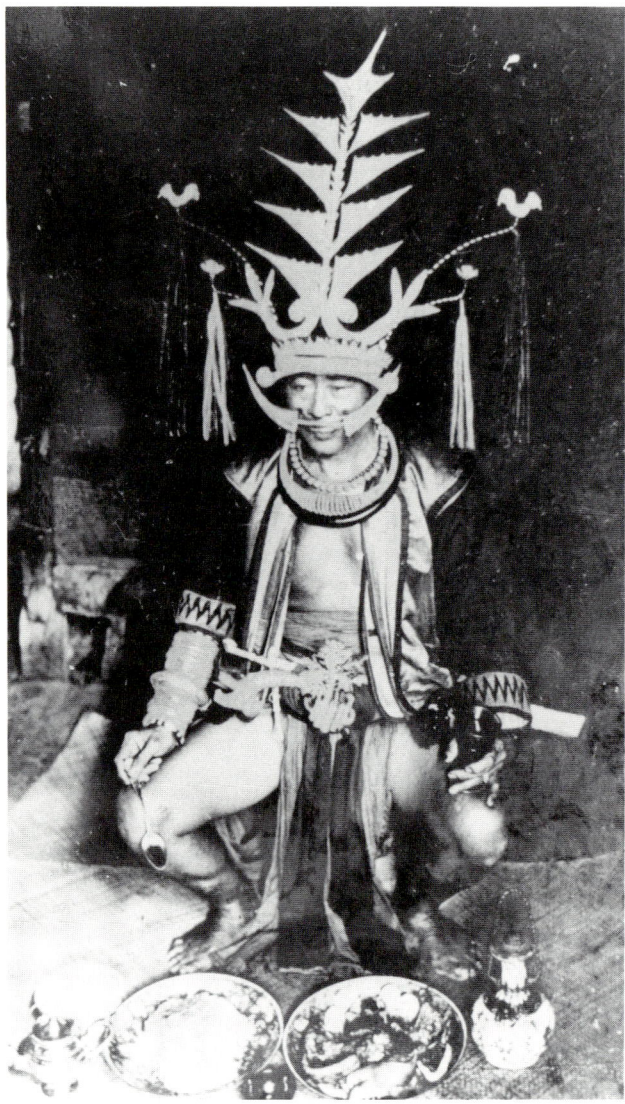

Figure 9. Ruler Ndröuzatarö, known as Golden Lord Ruler (Tuha Rajo Ana'a), seated as an ancestor image. Bawömataluo, 1920s (?). Photographer unknown (Agner Møller?). Collection of Buleni Fau.

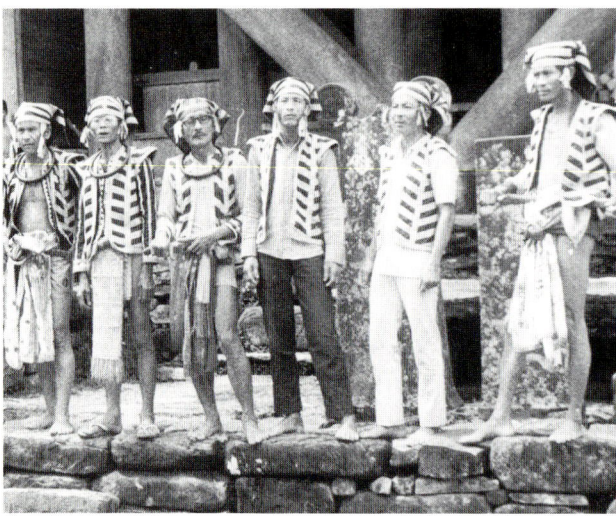

Figure 10. Men wearing the tiger attire. Hilinawalö village, 1982.

motifs are permissible only if one has given a long series of feasts. The titles resulting from such banquets confer upon the individual a completeness like that of the universe, whose wholeness with plants and animals is reflected in the carvings in one's house and the adornments to ceremonial costume. In fact there is a direct relationship between rank, as determined by birth and feasting, the grandeur of one's house, and the elaborateness of ceremonial costume (Feldman 1979:148-51).

This house/costume parallel goes even further. The house, especially the village ruler's house in Bawömataluo and other related villages, is an abstracted form of a costumed ancestor. Though details may vary, the roof is analogous to the headgear, the central living area to the body, and the pillars to the legs. The ancestor's curving mustache (*bubewe*) is echoed in the curving horizontal beam extensions (*sichöli*) of the house. Just as the ruler's sword (*telögu*) and supporting sash (*khaekhae*), his dagger (*mbalatu ria*), and the leafy plant at his waist (*sobulu*) provide protection, three images similarly clustered in front of a chief's house also function as a protective device (Feldman 1985:72-75). A large cane-like wooden form called *sokhaekhae* resembles the sword and sash (*khaekhae*); a somewhat taller forked image called *siraha salawa* conceptually parallels the dagger; and the leafy plant *sobulu* is there, too, exactly as in the ancestor costume.

In the same way that the chief's house (*omo sebua*) may represent an ancestor, so may the highest ranking noble, *si'ulu*, when in costume. An artificial beard and mustache are sometimes part of the full attire (Schröder 1917: fig. 48). These indicate age and are also attributes of sculptures of the most revered forebears, *adu zatua* (Feldman 1985: pl. 4). An astounding early photograph shows the ruler Ndröuzatarö, also known by his ceremonial title, Tuha Rajo Ana'a (Golden Lord Ruler), posing seated on his stool with a cup in his left hand, exactly paralleling the Bawömataluo *adu zatua* (Fig. 9). Thus fully costumed, the highest ranking individuals visually display the qualities of ancestors.

Nature motifs found both on house and costume include the abstract patterns on the jacket, *baru*. Sometimes these represent wild plants; sometimes they symbolize divided food as distributed during feasts, as in the case of the *ni'ogoli limo* (a sliced citrus fruit). The same patterns are painted on the facade of the *omo sebua*. As in Central Nias, the rare jackets with additional golden decoration are held in the highest esteem, and require enormous amounts of feasting.

A special renewal ritual involving tiger imagery inspires one variant of male soft costume. Every seven or fourteen years an enormous tiger effigy is constructed. The tiger, *harimao*, symbolizes the village ruler in its qualities of swiftness, cunning, strength, and so forth. Like the "ruler's clothes rack," the tiger effigy is a substitute for the ruler. It is thrown into the Gomo River as ransom and thereby destroyed, thus allowing the actual ruler to regain his power once it is exhausted (Feldman 1983; Hämmerle 1986). Tiger attire is recorded from Hilinawalö village, and may exist elsewhere. It consists of a striped kerchief (*laeru*) and a long-sleeved jacket called *baru so la'a harimao*, or the jacket with the colored patterns of the tiger (Fig. 10). Worn only by men, such costumes make symbolic references not to the qualities of the wearer, but to those of the ruler.[16]

Tiger allusions also appear on royal swords, *telögu*. The sheath often has stripes of inlaid silver or brass, and one of the distinctions between royalty and commoners is that tiger teeth are found exclusively on the protective amulet bundle (*ragö*) used by royalty. All others use crocodile teeth or pig tusks. The tiger teeth are arranged on the *ragö* in a pattern said to portray a kind of monster known as *lasara*, a royal protective being whose head also forms the handle of the sword. (Three *lasara* can also be seen on the facade of the ruler's house.)

Royal weaponry is replete with significant imagery. Above the *lasara* face on the handle of the *telögu*, there is a carving of a monkey[17]—another creature of nature carved likewise in the chief's house to indicate completeness. The sword's amulet bundle may also contain small wooden or ivory ancestor figures and small stone celts. These celts, called thunder stones, are found where lightning strikes and are associated with iron working (as in the sword blade) and protection. Other items, collectively called *daludalu balatu* (lit., "medicine sword") may be attached to the *ragö*.[18] A rather elaborate sword known as *balatu sala*, which is somewhat smaller than the *telögu*, is used by the ruler in daily wear. The monster on its handle is the *lawöle*, a village protector whose stone image is sometimes placed at the village entrance to ward off enemies. In addition to the sword, male ceremonial attire normally includes two more weapons, a spear and a shield. A long spear, called *toto'a doho*, is a prized possession whose size and fineness indicate rank. Spears are sometimes decorated with inlaid stripes, *niasak*.[19] Wooden shields, *baluse*, may represent stylized crocodiles whose hides are sometimes used for armor.[20]

Ornaments are also important in male attire. A black necklace called *kalabubu*, worn by nearly all men at ceremonial occasions, is a component of both soft and hard dress. A shiny black tapering cylinder, it is constructed of the polished disks of the inner shell of a coconut, tightly strung on a brass wire ring; at the back is a small brass disk. The *kalabubu* indicates valor in warfare and, according to some sources, signifies a successful headhunter (see Marschall 1976:85).

Soft attire is generally worn with golden ornaments. The names of these, and some of their characteristics, are given in Figure 8. The right to wear gold jewelry is earned through feasting; in fact the smithing of gold of specific weights is a requirement before an *omo sebua* (chief's house) can be built. Proof of this is carved on the side walls of every chief's house, where large relief carvings called *laso so hagu*, which imitate the golden forms, testify that the royal family possesses the required ornaments (Feldman 1977: figs. 105-7,117).[21] Separate *laso so hagu* are carved for male and female ornaments. At Bawömataluo wooden roosters (*la'iya*) hang in the back of the front room commemorating the feasting for women's gold ornaments, and dancing figures outside the trellis window memorialize feasts for male golden ornaments (Feldman 1985:70-71, figs. 55-57; Schröder 1917: fig. 147).

The most important golden ornaments are the headdress and the ropelike necklace, *nifulufulu*. The golden necklace must weigh at least 100 *pau*[22] for royalty, and 200 *pau* for the ruler (*tuha*, "lord" or *rajo*, "rajah") or his wife. Probably the greatest accumulation of such gold ornaments in South Nias was in the possession of the royalty of Bawömataluo village. It was stored in a treasure chest (*tabola gana'a*) in the rear room of the *omo sebua* (see Schröder 1917: fig. 145). In 1909, when Dutch authorities captured and imprisoned the last ruler of Bawömataluo, Saonigeho, they demanded all of the gold of the village as ransom for his release (Kruisheer 1932:226,319, 364-66).[23] The booty, including golden jackets and parasols, was never seen in public again. Though he did not reveal his source, Schnitger published drawings of some of the pieces of jewelry (Fig. 11). The labels that he provided help clarify their position in the traditional attire.

Armored warriors look quite different from their colorful unarmored counterparts (Figs. 12,13). Except for their loincloths and the banners above their heads, these figures appear entirely in black, which is all the more dramatic given the absence of golden ornaments. Armor, consisting of a helmet (*takula tefao*, iron helmet) and a jacket (*öröba*), can be made of crocodile skin, some other tough hide, or, most commonly, iron. Sometimes there are raised ridges down the spine of the jacket, resembling the bony spine of the crocodile. The armor can also be covered with long hairy strands of sugar palm fiber (*lema'a*). The effect of this is to convert the warrior into a frightful hairy being.[24]

Rulers, however, can have another version of the armor. If the requisite feasts are given, the armor may be gold-covered (Fig. 13). Gold, including jewelry, is apparently an exception made for the rulers from what would otherwise be a black costume. This *öröba ana'a* distinguishes them during actual battle and is no longer seen today even during ceremonial activity.

Feldman

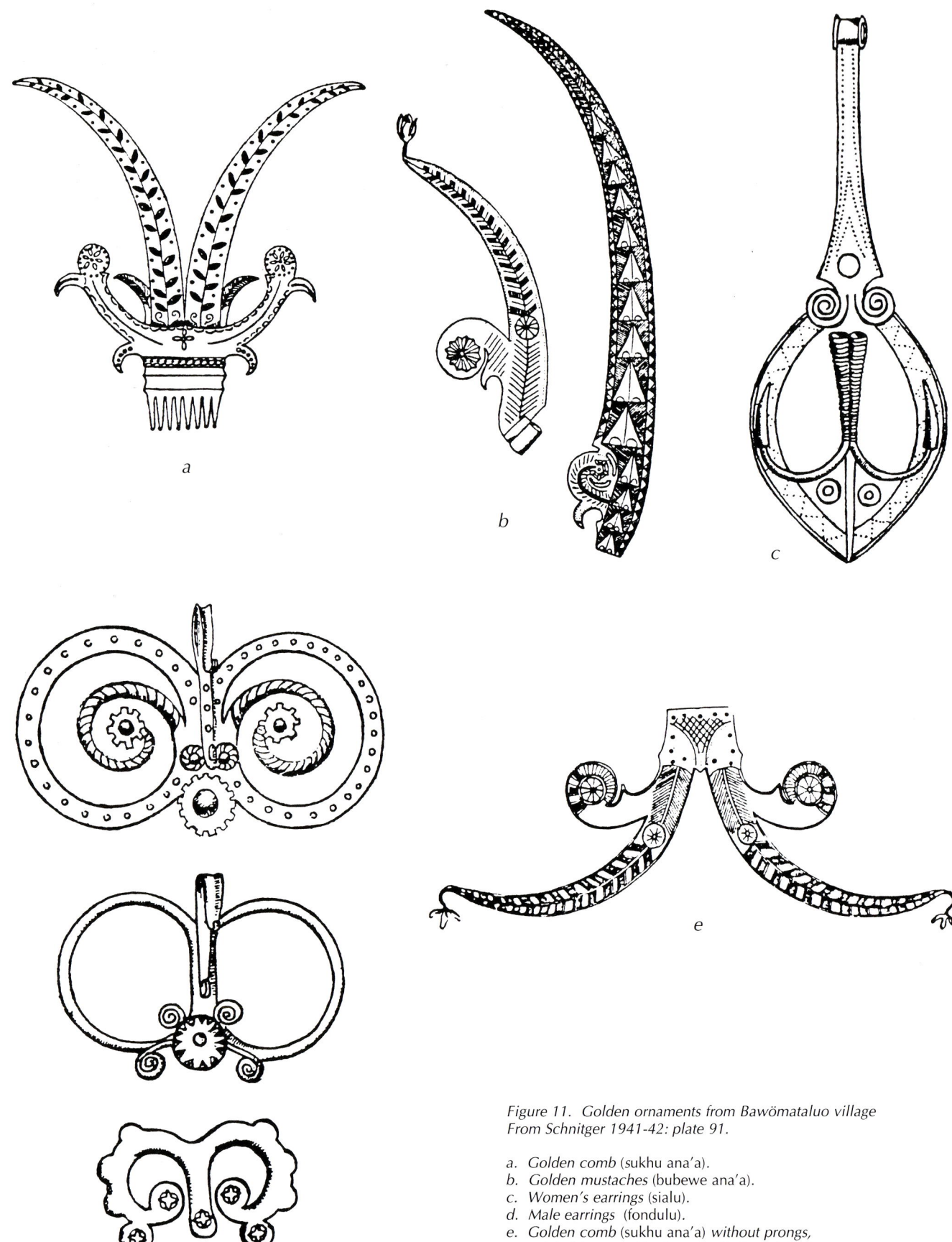

Figure 11. Golden ornaments from Bawömataluo village
From Schnitger 1941-42: plate 91.

a. Golden comb (sukhu ana'a).
b. Golden mustaches (bubewe ana'a).
c. Women's earrings (sialu).
d. Male earrings (fondulu).
e. Golden comb (sukhu ana'a) without prongs, printed here upside-down, as in the original.

Ceremonial Attire in Nias

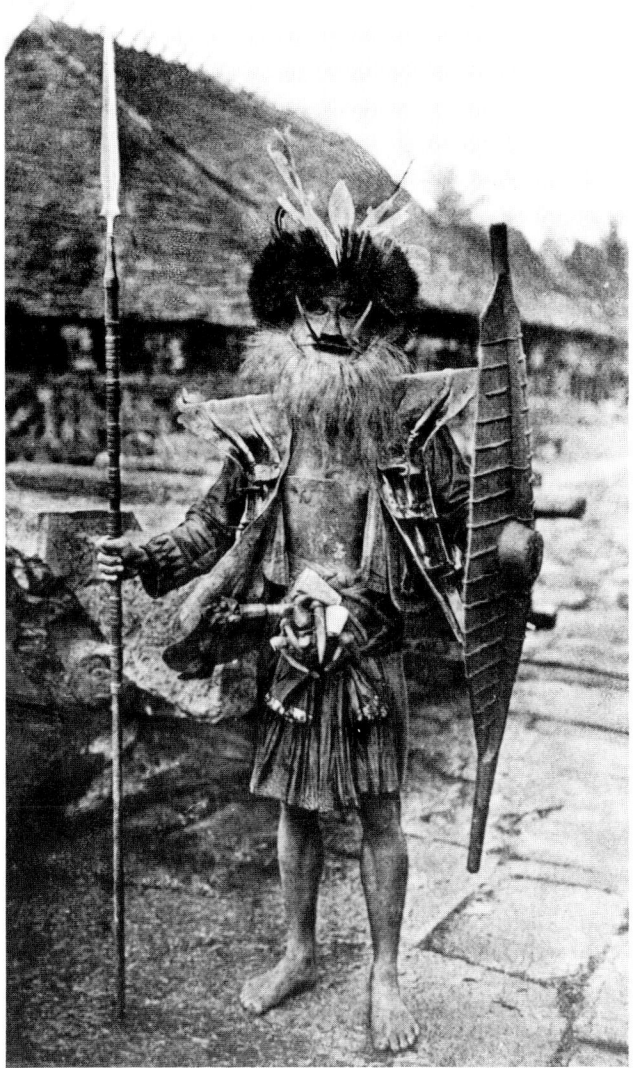

Figure 12. Armored warrior wearing bawa bekhu, *mask of an evil spirit of the dead. From Schröder 1917: figure 224.*

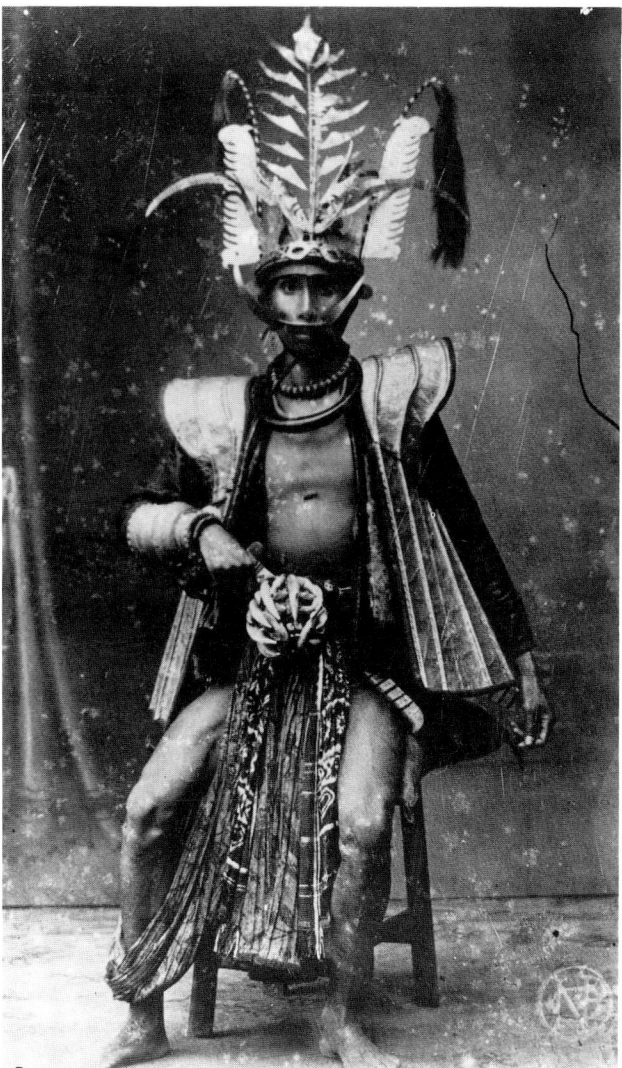

Figure 13. Nobleman (si'ulu) in golden armor, South Nias. Glass plate. Early 20th century. Photographer unknown.

Clearly the intent of the armor is not only to protect the warrior, but to demoralize the enemy. Helmets bristle with deer horns, sharp head protrusions, real hornbill beaks, iron birds, tigers, coiled ferns. Armored warriors all bear fearsome weapons. Some also wear *bawa bekhu*, the spirit masks of those who have died in unfortunate circumstances (Fig. 12). Such spirits can only be invoked for malevolent purposes; it is the job of the priestess in Bawömataluo to direct the *bawa bekhu* warriors against a foe (Feldman 1985:63).

Armored warriors are in many ways a counterpart to the unarmored. They always dance on the periphery of a dance formation while the unarmored men are in the center. Their low-pitched shouts with little verbal content punctuate the falsetto singing of the unarmored. They are black, bulky figures as compared to the brightly colored unarmored types. They often represent evil ancestors, whereas the brightly costumed men refer to, and sing about, the revered village founder.

Women's Attire. Women's ceremonial attire is as elaborate as men's. They wear long, monochrome skirts (*u'i*) in red, black, or blue, usually bordered by very elaborate geometric appliqué designs. Over it, they place a girdle (*awi*), often made of a fine mesh of brass wire. For important ceremonies, as in the past, noblewomen still wear blouses draped with necklaces, breastplates, and pendant earrings.[25] Women carry no weapons; their only handheld accessory is a purse called *bola nafo*, used to carry betel nut (Pl. 32). It is often made of plaitwork, and usually appliquéd with patterns representing the golden jewelry of a fully costumed woman. During ceremonial dances women move in slow motion in total silence as they present betel nut from the *bola nafo* to honored guests.

Figure 14, after a photograph from Møller, shows the noblewoman Fohinaya[26] in full ceremonial attire. While most of the items she wears are unique to women, a few are not. The women's *nifulufulu*

Feldman

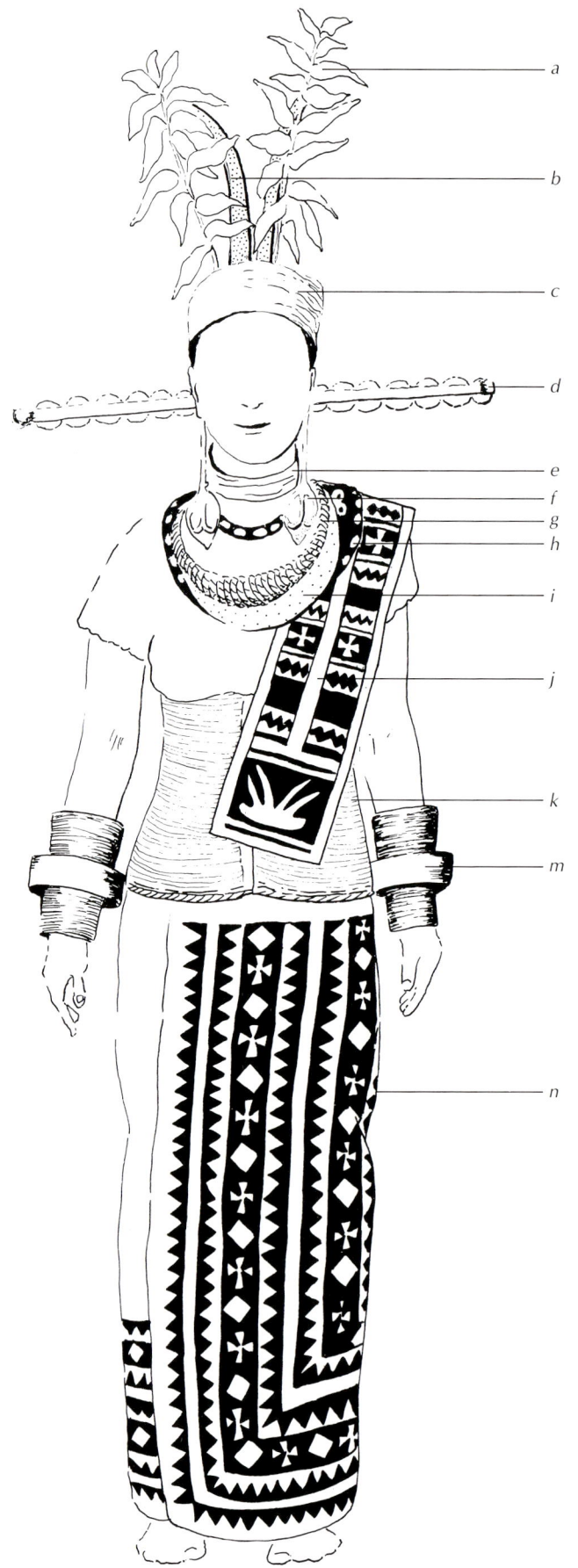

Figure 14. Women's ceremonial costume, Bawömataluo village. After a photograph of the noblewoman Fohinaya, in Møller 1934: figure 30.

a. *Golden tree-like ornaments* (rai salawa), *unique to royal women.*
b. *Golden comb* (sukhu ana'a).
c. *Golden headband* (saihögö or sanifi).
d. *Disk extensions from the back of the head* (taraho).
e. *Golden neckband* (baugu).
f. *Earrings* (sialu).
g. *Golden necklace* (nifulufulu) *identical to those worn by men.*
h. *Woven base for golden neck ornaments* (tubo baru).
i. *Golden breast plate* (kalambagi).
j. *Shouldercloth* (lembe).
k. *Girdle* (awi), *often made of a fine brass mesh.*
m. *Bracelets* (töla jaga).
n. *Long skirt* (u'i, or kabo).

necklace, earrings, and bracelets are in the same style as their male counterparts—though again it should be noted that men wear only a single earring and bracelet, on their right side. The *sukhu ana'a,* or golden comb (see Fig. 11a), though usually a female adornment, is sometimes worn by men (Schröder 1917: fig. 47). The cloth mat for the necklaces (*tubu baru*), the flat golden neck ornament (*kalambagi*), and the golden collar (*baugu*) are all distinctly female.²⁷ The same is true of the headband (*saihögö* or *sanifi*) and the tree-like ornament called *rai salawa,* which like many of these ceremonial items is also depicted in the relief carving of the chief's house. Perhaps the most unusual item is the *taraho,* a horizontal stick with a series of attached golden disks. Despite repeated efforts, I could find no information about it.

The one asymmetrical element in women's ceremonial attire is a long rectangle of red cloth worn over the left shoulder, called *lembe*²⁸ (Pl. 34). It is usually divided into small rectangular units each composed of small dentates or zigzags.²⁹ At its ends there is invariably an appliqué depicting the *sukhu ana'a,* or golden comb. Most of the *lembe* motifs are references to wealth, as is true of the rest of the costumes in Figure 14 and Plate 34. It is clear from early photographs taken in Bawömataluo that the *lembe* and the entire modern ceremonial women's attire were originally worn by priestesses, *ere* (see Schröder 1917: figs. 116,235). We do not know for sure if the shouldercloth was once used exclusively by the *ere,* but in early photographs those women who appear without the *lembe* are not said to be priestesses (Schröder 1917: figs. 17,25,26).

The *ere* of Bawömataluo had much power. They not only controlled the *bawa bechu,* but conducted rites sanctifying feasts (Schröder 1917:346, fig. 230), and made offerings to the ancestors for good fortune and curative purposes. They could cure disease, bless an undertaking, and send evil in the direction of the enemy. It was primarily in their curing role that they made contact with a female spirit intermediary called Silewe Nazarata. Silewe could bridge the distance between the Ono Niha and their deities—the god of the upperworld, Lowalani, and the god of the underworld, Lature Danö. As human contacts with Silewe the priestesses formed the vertical link to these gods. According to Møller, the name of Silewe means "she who wears a *lembe*" (1934:134); however he derives this information from North and Central Nias sources. Schröder relates that Silewe perched upon the Tora'a tree with a silk cloth *lembe* (1917:190). The Tora'a tree figures prominently in Central Nias mythology, but is not usually encountered in the South. Schröder only records the North and Central Nias conception of the *lembe* as a foreign, Malay-style shouldercloth (*selendang, slendang*) and does not use the term when describing South Nias attire (1917:48,51). Although priestesses were directly in contact with Silewe, there is no proof as yet of a link between the *lembe* and Silewe Nazarata in South Nias.

Although there are no longer any priestesses in South Nias, women wear the costumes of *ere* as ceremonial attire, and are given great deference. In Bawömataluo and many other South Nias villages, women walk in front of men as they enter and leave the village on ceremonial occasions. Although they do not participate directly in formal oratory (*orahu*), they are seated in a central position. During *orahu* at the chief's house, they are seated in a bower (*malige*) located near the rafters in the center of the building. This is the most exalted position as it is both central and high—locations always reserved for the most important dignitaries.

The Storage of Ceremonial Attire. When not in use, the ceremonial attire of Bawömataluo nobility is stored in special places in the private rear room (*föröma*) of the chief's house. On the left wall (as one faces the rear of the house), at a floor level used for sleeping (*bäto*), there is a finely made box called *tabola gamagama,* which contains ceremonial attire (Feldman 1979: fig. 43). In the same position along the right wall sits a massive chest made of a single piece of polished black *kafini* wood. This is the *tabola gana'a,* the container for gold (Feldman 1979: fig. 41). Daily attire is stored in a chest called *tabola nulu* which runs across the rear of the house. In a traditional Nias house, chests are placed on raised floor levels at front and rear. A parallel (as opposed to perpendicular) arrangement indicates that the owners have given a high level of feasts (Feldman 1979: fig. 6). Symmetry in the structure of the house is a sign of rank, whereas asymmetry shows lower status. Hard armor is usually hung in the rafters, perhaps because the smoke from the hearth will preserve and blacken it. The use of special places for the storage of ceremonial attire is another indication of its importance to the family who owns it.

In South Nias, ceremonial attire embodies meanings and powers that go much beyond the ordinary. Not only does it reflect one's social position; it also dramatically conveys one's cosmic status. Women as *ere* have a linkage to the gods. This could explain their position at the base of the symbolic upperworld in the *omo sebua.* Men in ceremonial dress embody spiritual forces that inhabit the Nias world. They may be glorious ancestors, or evil *bekhu.* They can assume the guise of the tiger, thus taking upon themselves the characteristics of the ruler. They are aided by powerful mythical creatures on their swords, the *lasara* and *lawöle.* They are even microcosms of the cosmos, with their references to the house of the ruler and the fertile land of the ancestors.

The attire of the ruler is so powerful that it can be substitute for the ruler himself.

Throughout North and Central Nias extraordinary meanings must also apply to ceremonial dress. The full significance of such attire is not clear. The fact that they express deeper meanings is implicit in the fineness and elaborateness of their design, as well as the extensive feasting and ceremonial activity encompassing them. These meanings extend beyond the normal connotations and powers of one's social status. If the ceremonial attire of Nias appears astounding to the outsider, the effect suggests that the artists who created the costume have successfully communicated something of the intended significance.

NOTES

1. A comprehensive explanation of Nias costume was proposed by Suzuki (1959:25-32). His thesis, based entirely on archival sources, suffers from an extensive blending of information from all regions of Nias. The result is that little of what is proposed is accurate when viewed in its actual context (see Hämmerle 1982:18-19; 1984:587; Marschall 1976:204).

2. Intensive research was conducted in South Nias in 1974 with a revisit in 1978. The author wishes to thank in particular Bazanalui Fau, Sarifiti Nehe, Mendruatönöni Manau and the late Samögö Fau of Bawömataluo village; Simaetöla Bu'ulölö of Hilinawalö Mazingö; and the many other Ono Niha who helped so generously. Additional field information was kindly provided by Marlene Meyer-Patton from her 1982 investigation of music. Although many of the customs and items described in this paper have vanished from Nias, many have not. Out of respect for a living tradition, the ethnographic present is being used.

3. An excellent example collected from South Nias before 1887 is said to represent a priest in full costume (ser. 1, no. 10, 1022, A. 3596 in the Tropenmuseum records, Amsterdam).

4. The photograph has been reproduced by Feldman (1977: fig. 15; 1985: fig. 15) and Barbier (1978: fig. 28).

5. This asymmetry is part of a system of dual oppostiions which are arbitrarily assigned within Nias culture. According to my South Nias informants, all cultural manifestations are expressed in dualistic terms. However there is not sufficient information on North Nias dualism to state this outright.

6. Fischer 1909:211, no. 1620/39; Modigliani 1890:481; Sundermann 1905b:220. The use of fan is also illustrated in Rees (1866: frontis.).

7. Unless otherwise noted all translations are by the author.

8. This interpretation is based upon the conceptions of the chief in South Nias (see Feldman 1979).

9. There are several villages named Lahusa. I presume this one is in the Gomo district.

10. Schnitger translates this as a hook for clothing.

11. Tafitafi is also used as a sieve for palm wine.

12. Necklace types are differentiated by their weight in batu, a standardized measure. Ana'a nifatali si felendrua batu (gold shaped like a rope), weighs 12 batu; ana'a nifatali si duawulu öfa batu, 24 batu; and ana'a nifatali si limawulu batu, 50 batu (Hämmerle 1982:71; 1984:615). For information on scales and weights see Roth 1985.

13. That old spelling reflected Dutch phonetics. An accurate rendering of the name would be Lötebulo; indeed a recent museum publication adopts this spelling, minus the diacritics.

14. For the techniques of textile manufacture in Nias see Marschall (1976:85-88, 105-10), Schröder (1917:224-25), and Fischer (1905:222; 1911-12:250-54).

15. The cosmic and social associations of colors suggested by Suzuki (1959:25) were firmly denied by field informants.

16. It is never worn by women as proposed by Suzuki (1959:31) and repeated by Khan Majlis (1984:20).

17. Another interpretation is that the small figure is a bekhu, an evil spirit. This was mentioned by some field informants as well as Modigliani (1890:249) and repeated by Lorm (1941a:1-3). The style of the tiny figure's head is exactly the same as a conventional monkey sculpture, even though it lacks a tail, and in no way resembles the bawa bekhu mask (see below). It may be a bekhu or a monkey according to informants.

18. Extensive descriptions of Nias swords and amulets were published by Modigliani (1890:238-53) and Lorm (1939;1941a;1941b). A theory that Nias sword handles are derived from scenes of Buddhist legends was proposed by Heine-Geldern (1925; 1937).

19. The names Suzuki offers in his classification of spear types (buluse, hulaoyo) are actually the names of spear points, not the entire spear (1959:29-30).

20. The idea that the shield represents a crocodile is stated by Suzuki (1959:27), based upon Schröder (1917:243), who derives his information from Fischer (1909:53), and ultimately a secondary source, Wilken (1891:263-492). Modigliani believes it is modeled after a banana leaf. He also illustrates an entirely different form of shield for North Nias called dagne (1889:214-17; 1890:230-33).

21. These are also depicted in Feldman (1979: figs. 22,24,30,31). Unfortunately Figure 30 was published upside down.

22. In the Bawömataluo system of standards, one pau is approximately ten grams.

23. This was the administration of Engelbertis Schröder, the author of the most important volumes on Nias.

24. Holt suggests that the basic form of Nias armor may have been inspired by Portuguese examples (1939:77).

25. A type of cloth that has disappeared from South Nias can be seen in Schröder (1917: fig. 16). The woman on the left has a long textile connected to her back and to her wrists. Her pose is precisely that of the sculptures that originally hung in the front of a chief's house commemorating feasts for golden ornaments (see Feldman 1985: fig. 57).

26. Grandmother of my informant, the late Samögö Fau.

27. For an illustration of a kalambagi see Rogers (1985:273, no.7).

28. A unique lembe in the Danish National Museum has two mirrors above the sukhu ana'a. It also does not have the rectangular central units. To my knowledge, this is the only lembe with a mirror on it and it is not found "often" (see Suzuki 1959:14). A cosmological interpretation of this was proposed by Suzuki (1959:30-31).

29. This design was deciphered by Fischer (1908:90) and has since been verified by field informants.

Batak Bags in Weft Twining

Rita Bolland

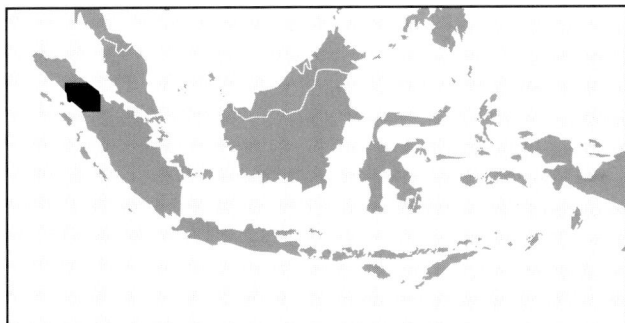

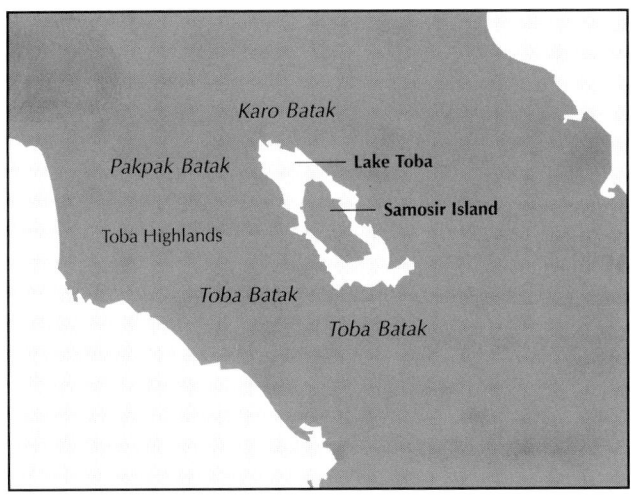

The Lake Toba region of North Sumatra.

Almost all Batak collections in anthropological museums include small bags in which men traditionally carried personal belongings, such as ingredients for smoking or chewing betel. They are usually plaited of pandanus leaves, sewn from cloth, or made of animal skin. Batak bags in weft twining are rare. One now belonging to The Textile Museum in Washington, D.C., which appeared in Gittinger's *Splendid Symbols* was probably the first such bag to be published. Its origin is given as "Batak region?" and regarding its technical structure the caption says: "This bag is not twined.... How all the warps interlock in the base area is not understood..." (1979a:101, pl. 64). Since then I have had an opportunity to study the Textile Museum bag (Fig. 1). It proved to be made in the weft-twining technique, just like three bags from the Toba Batak region, North Sumatra, in the Tropenmuseum in Amsterdam. My essay will deal with these rare and beautiful bags, made in such an interesting technique.

To make a fabric in weft twining, two basic elements are needed: a passive part, here called warp, and an active part, here called weft. Often the warp is thicker than the weft, which consists of two yarns that twist around each other as they enclose each warp in turn, as illustrated in Figure 3 (Emery 1966:201; Collingwood 1968:463; Burnham 1980:186). Twining can be done in an S- or a Z-twist (with reference to the dominant slant of twist). The Batak bags I know of are made in Z-twining. The structures and patterns on the front and back of the fabric are identical, but when two colors are twined together, the design appears in the reciprocal color on the reverse.

A pair of weft yarns may enclose more than one warp thread at a time, creating the potential for more complicated patterns as in Figure 4. However, only a limited number of warp ends can be enclosed at a time; if there are too many they tend to form a thick bundle instead of staying flat. When a long one-color line is needed in two-color twining, the required length must

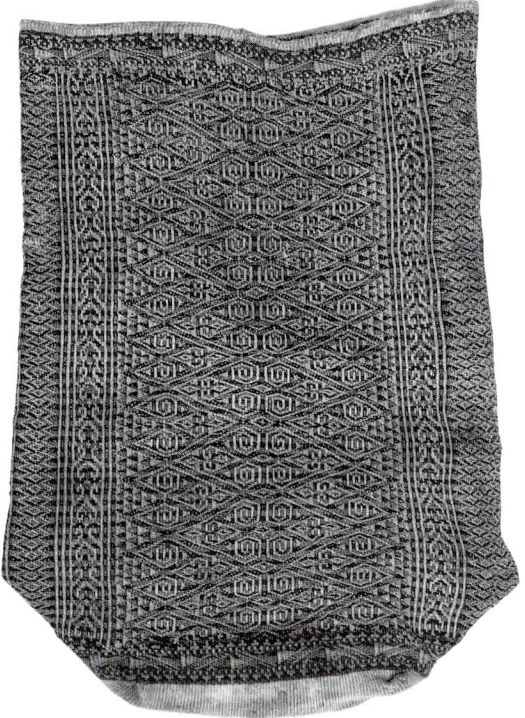

Figure 1. Weft-twined bag, front. Toba Batak, North Sumatra. Length, 28 cm., circumference 28 cm. The Textile Museum 1987.15.1. Gift of Fred and Rita M. Richman.

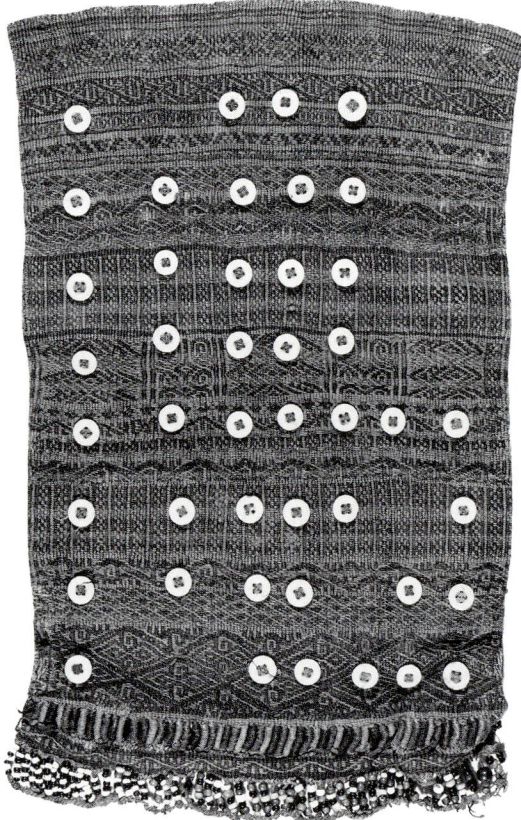

Figure 2. Weft-twined bag, front. Toba Batak, North Sumatra. Length 30.5 cm., width 19 cm. Tropenmuseum 153-39.

be worked in two or more smaller segments. The two weft yarns must make a full turn each time after enclosing three or four warp ends (Figs. 5,6). In the monochrome parts, these full-turn points are staggered. This can give the impression of fabric actually woven in twill or satin weave.

Three Weft-twined Batak Bags at the Tropenmuseum, Amsterdam

Each of the three weft-twined bags in the collection of the Tropenmuseum has a different shape. The bag shown in Figure 2 was a gift from D. van der Meulen in March 1922, recorded as *hadjoet nai borngin* (roughly, "a pouch from long ago," see below). It is a flat cotton bag with weft yarns of grey, red, and blue, and a nearly invisible warp of grey. One side is decorated with white porcelain buttons; the glass beads at the bottom are white, red, blue, and black.

This bag was started at the top along the rim (Fig. 7) and worked in spiraling rounds progressing downward. After twenty-six centimeters it was closed at the bottom by joining two warp ends—one from the front of the bag and one from the back—to act as a single warp element. Then five grey rows of twining were done, but now going back and forth instead of in spirals. Subsequently, sixty-one little bundles were made by tightly wrapping fourteen to sixteen warp elements with white, red, or blue cotton yarn. Then half the number of warp yarns in each bundle were cut away and those remaining were braided together to form a narrow band. After this braided interval a few rows of grey and blue were twined once more to lock the warp ends, and then the warps were braided again to create a second band. The remaining loose ends were twisted into fifty-six clusters and onto these were strung red, white, and blue (or black) beads. To create a final band the warps were braided a third time and then cut off.

The body of the bag was twined in alternating one- and two-color bands of grey and red or grey and blue. The rounds were so closely packed that the point at which a row shifts from one to two colors is almost invisible. Only careful study reveals that these changing points occur in a diagonal line, each staggered about one to one and a half centimeters past the preceding one. On the reverse of the fabric sometimes the pair of grey weft yarns may be carried from one grey band to the next, jumping over a distance of one to one and a half centimeters. This is not done with the two-color pair of weft yarns. How these yarns were cast off is not clear. They were probably cut close to the fabric; it is also possible that they were worked over a short distance into the adjacent twined round.

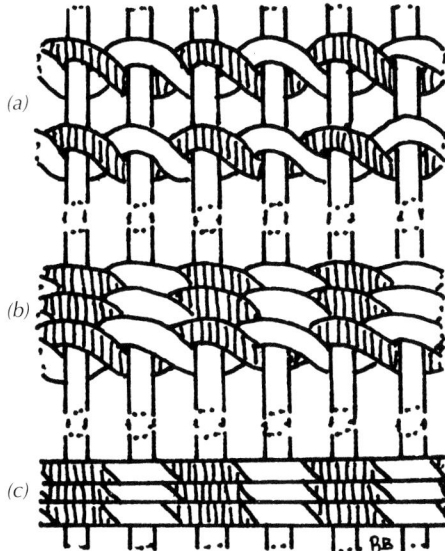

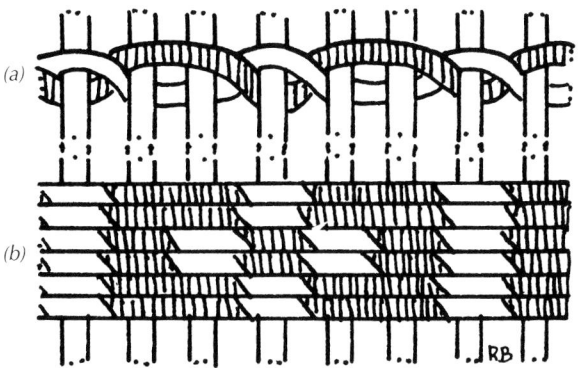

Figure 3. Weft twining, all Z-twist: (a) Two weft yarns go over and under a warp and over and around each other in a half turn. (b) The warp is completely covered by the closely packed weft yarns. (c) Diagram of a fabric in weft twining.

Figure 4. (a) A pair of twining weft yarns can enclose more than one warp end at a time. (b) When the weft yarns enclose more than a single warp end, more complicated patterns, such as this one, can result.

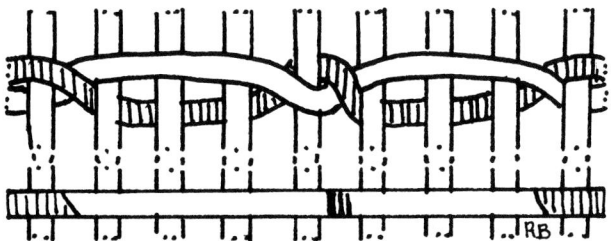

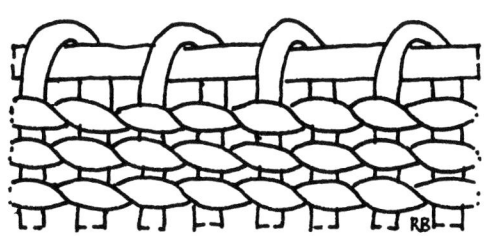

Figure 5. The two weft yarns make a full turn that breaks up the long one-color line.

Figure 7. Diagram of a Batak bag, Tropenmuseum 153-39, which was started at the top.

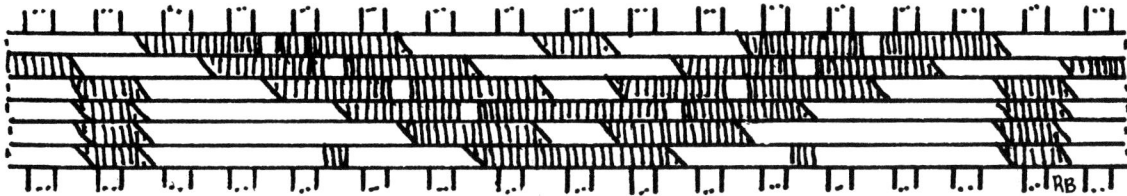

Figure 6. Diagram of a pattern from a Batak bag, Tropenmuseum 153-39. The twining weft yarns make half and full turns.

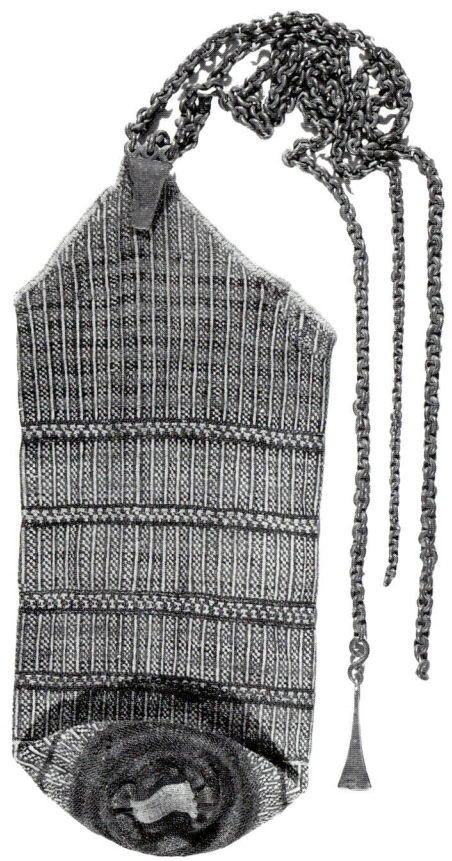

Figure 8. Weft-twined bag, Batak region, North Sumatra. Length 26-34 cm., circumference 29 cm. Tropenmuseum 2118-3.

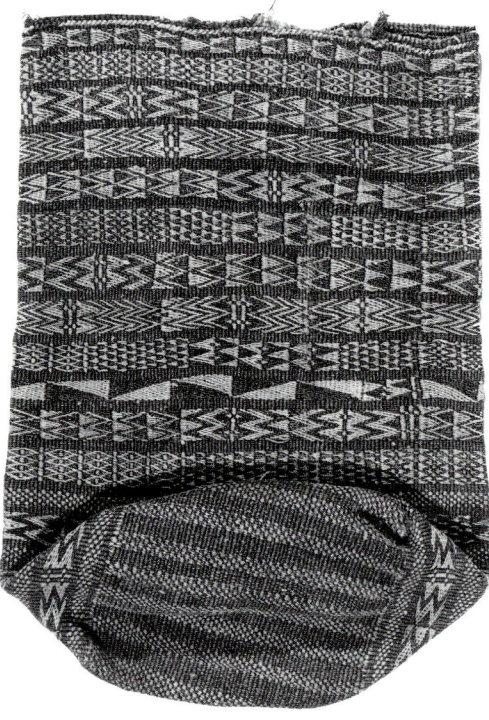

Figure 9. Weft-twined bag, Batak region, North Sumatra. Length 24.5 cm., circumference 37 cm. Tropenmuseum 2761-914.

The place at which the rows change color can indicate the direction in which the weft twining was worked. But it is not known how the bag was held for the twining process. If the warp yarns hung down, and each round was put under the last, the rows were done counterclockwise. If, however, the warp yarns were upright, or away from the worker, and each round was made on top of the last, the working direction was clockwise. Although the rim of this bag is damaged at some points, there is no indication that it ever had handles or a carrying string.

The tubular cotton bag shown in Figure 8 was a gift of the Koninklijk Militair Invalidetehuis "Bronbeek," the Royal Military Home for Retired Soldiers in Arnhem, in 1951.[1] The weft yarns are yellow-grey, brown-red, and blue; the warp is yellow-grey. The bag was worked from the bottom upward, starting with the rectangular yellow-grey bottom piece, made in rows of weft twining (Fig. 10). Then the double weft yarns that protruded from both sides of the fabric became warp elements, and the rest of the bag was done in spiraling rounds. Some of the weft yarns were immediately divided to make two single warps; other pairs were divided only gradually as appropriate, to increase the diameter of the "circular base." The spiraling rounds in blue and red-brown formed eight concentric bands, each four to five millimeters wide. When needed, a pair of warp yarns was added until the bottom had a more or less circular form, with a diameter about ten centimeters; then the tube was started.

Whether the spiraling rounds were worked clockwise or counterclockwise cannot be determined: the very tightly packed weft and the simple framed patterns make it impossible to see the pass-over from one round into the next. To the extended top lip of the bag, three brass chains are fastened by a brass plate in the shape of a horse head and a wooden pin (Fig. 11). Only one chain is complete, having a pair of tweezers at the end. Another ends in a hook, but is missing an implement. Of the third only forty-two centimeters remain. The rim of the bag is worked very tightly with yellow-grey cotton yarn (Fig. 12). The threads are close together, completely covering the twining work, so that it is impossible to tell how the twining was finished at this edge.

A third Batak bag at the Tropenmuseum (Fig. 9) is a gift from the Dutch Vrije Evangelische Gemeente (Free Evangelical Congregation), Amsterdam, in 1959. It was part of a collection made by Friederich Eigenbrod, from the Samosir Mission, at the request of the church. Eigenbrod started gathering Batak objects in 1919; the first shipment arrived in Amsterdam in 1923. The bag in question is of cotton and more or less tubular, with grey and blue weft yarns and a grey warp quite likely consisting of paired yarns. First a rectangular bottom was twined in back-and-forth rows, with grey and blue

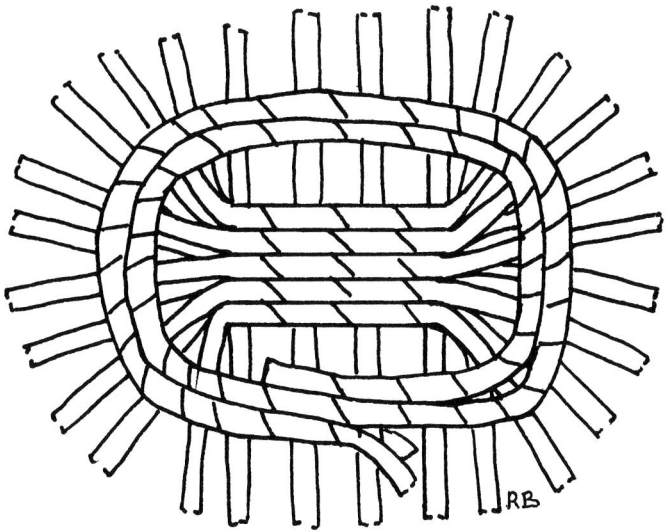

Figure 10. Diagram of a Batak bag, Tropenmuseum 2118-3, showing how it was started. The bottom area (1.7 x 3.2 cm.) was twined, and then the weft yarns turned into warp elements.

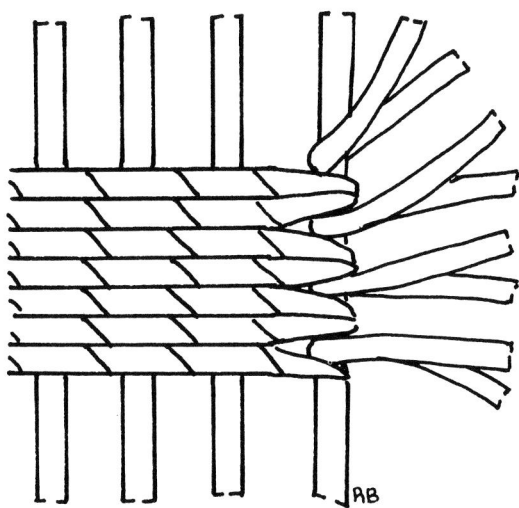

Figure 13. Diagram of a Batak bag, Tropenmuseum 2761-914. After the bottom piece (11 x 12 cm.) was twined new warp yarns were attached to the selvages.

(a)

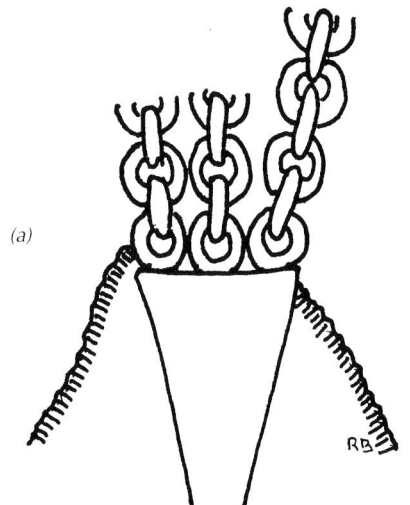

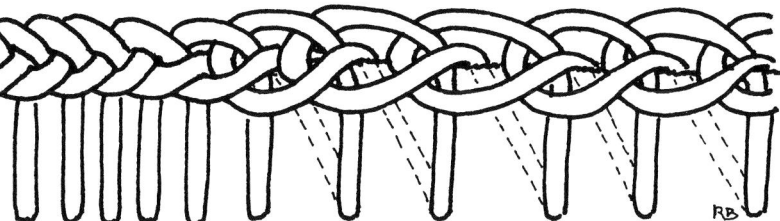

Figure 12. Diagram of a Batak bag, Tropenmuseum 2118-3. At the rim the fabric is finished off with a braiding stitch.

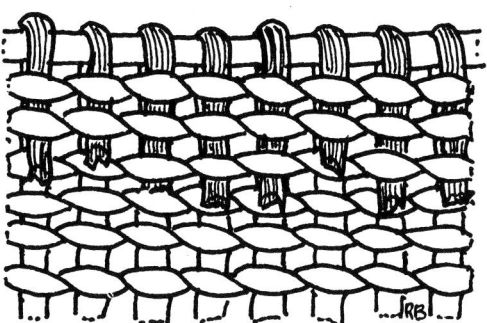

Figure 14. Diagram of a Batak bag, Tropenmuseum 2761-914, showing how the twined fabric was finished at the rim.

(b)

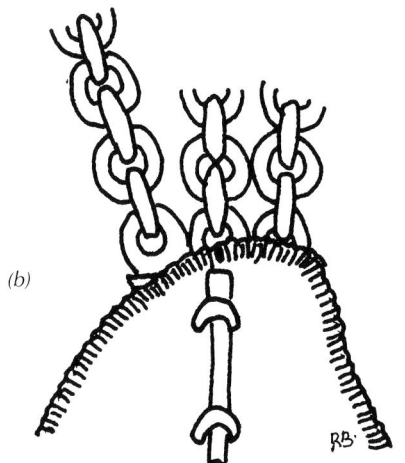

Figure 11. Diagram of a Batak bag, Tropenmuseum 2118-3, showing three brass chains attached to the rim by a horse head shaped brass plate. Chain lengths: 64 cm., 58 cm., and 42 cm. Only the first is complete. (a) Front. (b) Back.

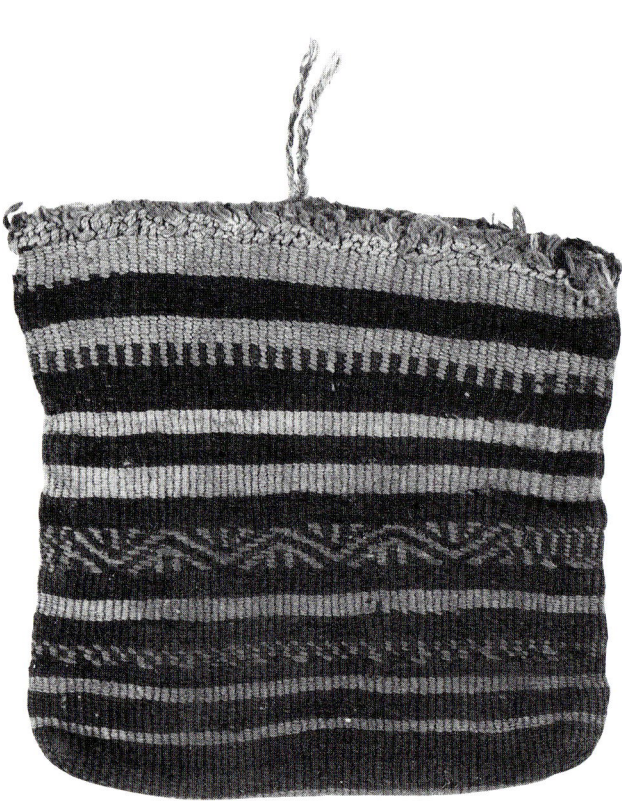

Figure 15. Weft-twined purse, Batak region, North Sumatra. Length 8 cm., width 9 cm. Tropenmuseum 2761-801.

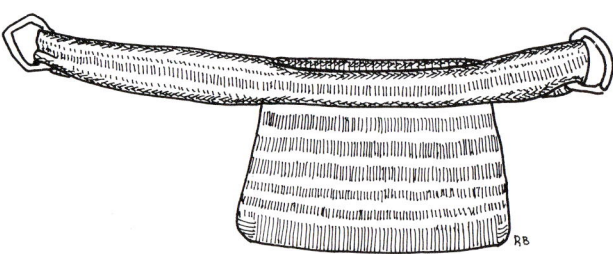

Figure 16. Diagram of a Batak purse, Tropenmuseum 2761-803, made in weft twining. Length 8 cm., width 12.5 cm. at base.

weft yarns making blue and blue-grey checkered stripes about six to seven millimeters wide; this formed a fabric eleven by twelve centimeters, with two selvages and long grey warp yarns hanging from two sides. New grey warp yarns were attached to the selvages (Fig. 13), and the spiraling rounds of twining weft yarns were started (whether this was done clockwise or counterclockwise is impossible to tell). The rim is partly damaged. As far as can be seen, the fabric is finished in the following way: after the last round of weft twining, a thick cotton cord was placed along the rim (see Fig. 14). Each warp end was folded backwards over this cord and worked into the previous three to four twined rounds (possibly the warp ends had been loosely folded over the thick cord before the twining of the last rounds). Then the backward-folded ends were pulled tight and cut off. There is no indication that the bag ever had handles, a string, or chains attached.

Three Weft-twined Purses in the Tropenmuseum Collection

In this same collection there are three flat cotton purses made in weft twining.[2] They are each eight centimeters long, and vary only slightly in width (see Figs. 15,16).[3] Each of the three has a long narrow base twined lengthwise in rows. As with the bag in Figure 9, new warp yarns have been attached to the selvages of all three purses. All have horizontal one-color bands in light blue, dark blue, and light brown. Only the first (Fig. 15) has a narrow patterned strip with tiny blocks, and a zig-zag line in the two colors in the dark blue band. The second (not shown here) is of the same shape as the third. It has a long narrow strip of cloth along the opening; the iron rings are missing. Of the three purses, the third is the most complete (Fig. 16). Along its opening is a weft-twined band. Most probably the two iron rings at both ends served to attach the purse to a man's belt. Its somewhat tapered shape results from the pairing of warp yarns at the "edge." This consolidation was done seven times on one edge and, in the same twining round, eight times on the opposite one, thus diminishing the width of the purse.

The Textile Museum Bag

An examination of the Textile Museum bag shown in Figure 1 leaves no doubt that it is from the Batak region, and made in the Z-twist weft-twining technique. The bag is more or less tubular. Its weft-twined bottom (fifteen by sixteen centimeters) was started first; then the bag was worked upward in spiraling rounds. All the warp yarns are light brown, as are the twined weft yarns of the bottom and the first centimeter of spiraling rounds. Therefore it is not easy to see in the very tightly worked fabric whether the bottom structure is like that of the Tropenmuseum bag illustrated in Figure 10, in which weft yarns become the warp, or like that of Figure 13, in which new warp yarns are attached to the selvages. The latter seems most probable, however, if we compare the structure and the shape of the bottom of these bags.

The colors of the Textile Museum bag are the same as those used in the bags at the Tropenmuseum. While the base and warp are light brown, the patterns are always in two colors, light brown with brown-red or light brown with blue; and some violet rounds are twined along the bottom. The rim of the bag is intact. After six light brown rounds each warp end is folded backwards, passing under and over the two warp ends just worked and then tucked into the last rounds (Fig. 17). The ends of the cut-off warp are visible on the reverse face. There is no sign that handles, a carrying string, or brass chains were ever attached to the rim. At one of the vertical stripes at the sides of the bag, between the two wide patterned panels, the pattern jumps (Fig. 18). It is here that one round passes over into the next one, which indicates that the weft-twining rounds were made clockwise (looking from the top down into the bag).

Up to now I know of only six additional Batak bags worked in weft twining: five are scattered among museums in Germany and Italy; the sixth is in a private collection.[4]

A Weft-twined Batak Bag at the Museum für Völkerkunde, Berlin

In 1899 the Museum für Völkerkunde, Berlin, acquired a bag collected by a Mr. Volz,[5] with accompanying documentation stating that it was used by the poor Toba Batak people living at the northern shore of Lake Toba. When it arrived at the museum it was filled with the personal belongings a man usually carries with him, including a flint and steel, tweezers to pull out beard hair, dice, and so forth. Judging from a photograph supplied by the Museum, the tubular bag seems to be the same type as the Tropenmuseum bag shown in Figure 8. Three incomplete brass chains are attached to the flap by a horse-head button. The bag was started from the base. First the square bottom was twined with light brown weft yarns over a light brown warp. This was followed by six concentric bands in alternating dark blue and light brown. The simple decoration gives narrow vertical stripes in blue and light brown, alternating with checkered stripes in the same colors. Most probably the rim was worked over in the same way as is done with the bag in Figure 8.

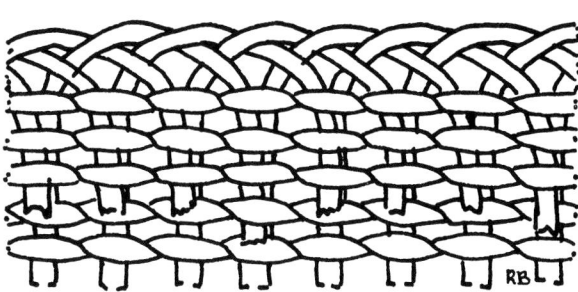

Figure 17. Diagram of a Batak bag, The Textile Museum 1987.15.1 showing how the twined fabric was finished at the rim.

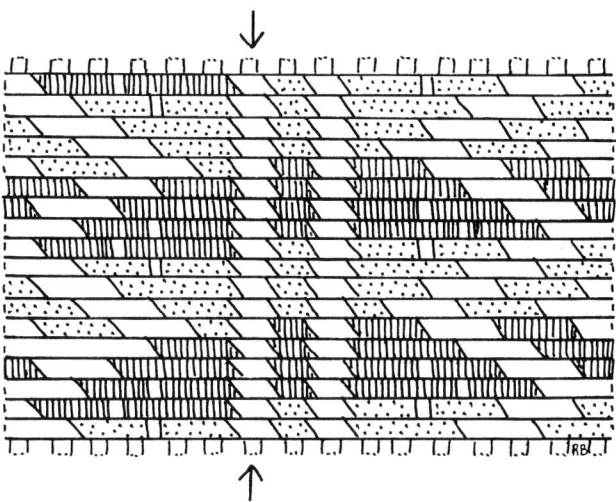

Figure 18. Diagram of a Batak bag, The Textile Museum 1987.15.1, showing a leap in the pattern that marks the place where each spiraling row passes over into the next one.

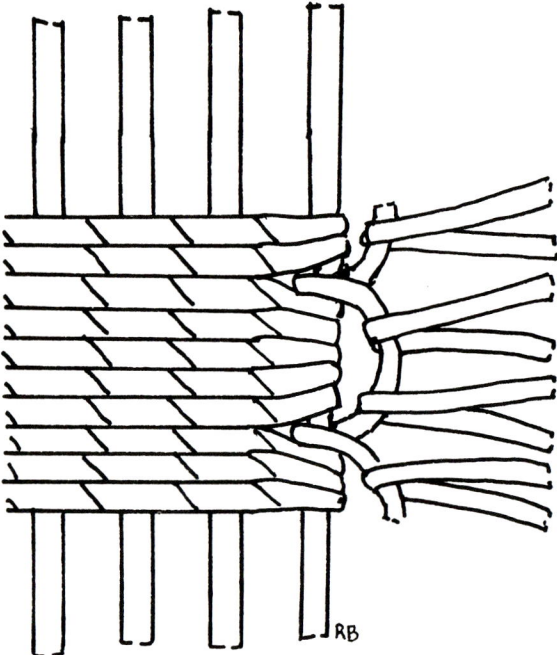

Figure 19. Diagram of a Batak bag, Frankfurt NS 10220. After the bottom piece was twined new warp yarns were folded around long stitches made along the selvages.

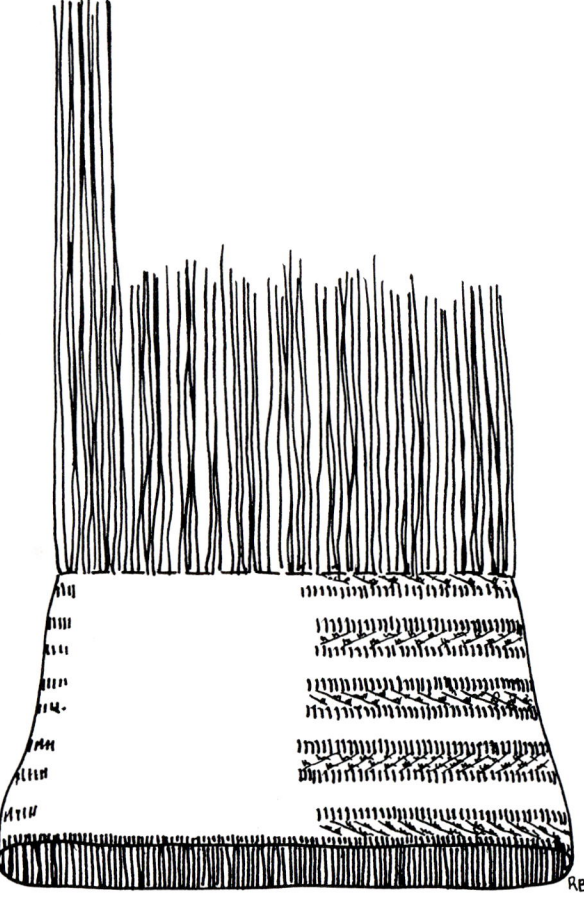

Figure 20. Diagram of a half-finished Batak bag or purse, Florence 11409, made in weft twining. Sketch after a photograph.

A Weft-twined Bag at the Museum für Völkerkunde, Frankfurt am Main

In 1908 a betel bag was purchased from Dr. F. Martin by the Museum für Völkerkunde, Frankfurt am Main.[6] Its greasy rim and bottom suggest it had been in use for a long time. This bag is of the same type as the Tropenmuseum bag shown in Figure 9, with two differences. First, the new warp yarns were attached to the light brown bottom (ten and a half centimeters square) in a different way: they were folded around long stitches that had been made along the selvages (see Fig. 19). Secondly, it has two complete brass chains (about eighty centimeters long) which are attached to the rim by a horse-head button exactly as in the Tropenmuseum bag seen in Figure 8. At each chain's end is a copper cent coin from the Dutch East Indies (Nederlandsch Oost Indië, the former Dutch colonies). The date 1857 is visible on one of the coins. The other one is more worn out; only the numbers "18.." can be deciphered. The weft twining is done in light brown with brown-red and light brown with dark blue. Horizontal bands and vertical stripes are filled with triangles, zig-zags, tiny blocks, and such.

Two Weft-twined Bags at the Staatliches Museum für Völkerkunde, Munich

There are two weft-twined bags in the collection of the Staatliches Museum für Völkerkunde in Munich.[7] These were among many textiles put on a table in the conference room on the last afternoon of the September 1985 symposium on Indonesian textiles at the Rautenstrauch-Joest Museum in Cologne. Not having had the opportunity to examine them closely I wrote the Museum in Munich for more information and received a copy of the catalogue card, which offers only: "betel bags, Batak, Sumatra, acquired from Martin," and a sketch of each bag with the length. No year is mentioned. On the basis of this and my own conference notes I have pieced together the following description: The first and longer of the two (seventeen and a half centimeters long) is of the same type as the Textile Museum bag. One complete cord with a coin is attached to the rim of the bag, though how is unknown. The second and shorter one (fourteen centimeters long) is of the same type as the Tropenmuseum bag in Figure 8. Two complete brass chains with coins from the Dutch East Indies, date unknown, are attached to the flap by a horse-head button. The weft twining was done in light brown, blue, and red. In the first, the simple geometric decorations were done in horizontal bands; in the second they were done in vertical stripes.

A Weft-twined Bag at the Museo di Antropologia e Etnologia, Florence

A half-finished weft-twined bag (Fig. 20) in the Museo di Antropologia e Etnologia, Florence, was collected by Elio Modigliani, who visited Batak country from October 1890 to April 1891. The bag shows a striking likeness to the Tropenmuseum purses, especially that seen in Figure 15. Both have the long, narrow, one-color rectangular bottom; and likewise both exhibit horizontal bands of light or dark brown and a narrow strip with a wing-like pattern. Though the size of the Florence bag is uncertain, a color photograph too poor to reproduce (one of two in my possession) enabled me to count the warp yarns in the light brown band. This gave the same number, nine to ten per centimeter, as the purse in Figure 15. It seems probable the photograph is life-sized and depicts a half-finished purse with a base width of nine and a length of four and a half centimeters. Without thorough examination it is impossible to understand why the dark brown warp yarns are of different lengths.

A Weft-twined Bag in the Holmgren and Spertus Collection

In 1983, a weft-twined bag entered the collection of Robert J. Holmgren and Anita E. Spertus, with the suggestion it could be a bag from the Toraja because of the pictures of men on horseback, women threshing rice, and a buffalo (Fig. 21a,b). A study of this bag leads to the conclusion that it is of the same type as the Textile Museum bag, the only difference being in the size of its base, which is narrow and rectangular (five by two centimeters). Warp and weft are of Z-spun and S-plied cotton yarns. The warp yarns are light brown, and the weft-twined patterns are in light brown with blue or brown-red. In some spots, especially in the bands with the men on horseback, the brown-red yarns are replaced by those of a violet-red color. A new piece of weft was knotted to the finished one, with a knot on the reverse face of the fabric. Sometimes two yarns were connected by twisting both ends together in a Z-twist. It was impossible to determine whether the spiraling rounds went clockwise or counterclockwise

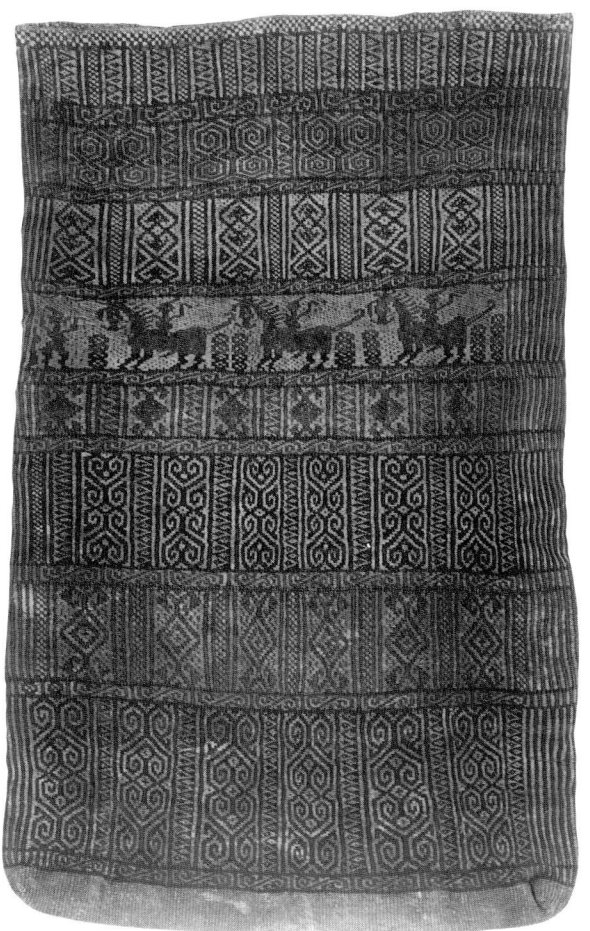

Figure 21a (above), b (right). Weft-twined bag. Batak region, North Sumatra. Length 23.5 cm., circumference about 42 cm. Collection of Robert J. Holmgren and Anita E. Spertus, New York.

from bottom to rim. The top of the bag is dirty and it looks as if the rim was once bordered by a red ribbon (was that the original finish of the rim or was that done later on?). Now only some tiny pieces of red (woolen?) fabric and some sewing stitches of white cotton thread remain. The parts of the rim that are complete reveal that the fabric is worked off in the same way as on the Tropenmuseum bag in Figure 9. It does not appear that handles, a string or chains were ever attached.

The provenance of this bag is problematic. It was bought in 1983 from a dealer in Europe. The decorations call to mind pictures often seen on the sacred cloths (sarita and maa') of the Sa'dan Toraja in south Sulawesi. However, the weft twining, yarns, and colors of this bag strongly suggest it was made in the Batak region, and its scenes are by no means unknown in Batak society. Women threshing rice is a common tableau and Batak men are good riders; their horses were famous and important as tradeware. The slaughter of a buffalo was the climax of the *bius* ceremonies connected with the cultivation of rice (Kreemer 1956:232). These animals also appear in decorations of the front wall of the Toba Batak house (Modigliani 1892). Considering all this, it becomes quite reasonable to assume that the Holmgren-Spertus bag was made in the Batak region.

General Comments about Batak Weft-Twined Bags

All the Batak bags and purses discussed here use rather stiff yarn, and their weft-twining rounds are very closely packed. Because it is therefore not easy to examine the single yarns, only some general remarks can be made. Regarding the weft elements, two or more Z-spun yarns are S-plied. As for the warp threads (as far as they are visible) some are double, some single. Occasionally the double warps (each one Z-spun and S-plied) will turn together with a Z-twist. The bags and purses are made of cotton. The yarns used for the Textile Museum bag are coarser than those of the others. On the Frankfurt bag described earlier (NS 10220) there is a small worn-out part where the horse-head button was once attached. The two or three warp yarns visible here are not made of cotton, but spun and plied of long fibers, probably palm leaf strips.

Museum documentation files do not give much information about the weft-twined Batak bags, nor does the literature. Scholars who have studied and traveled in Batak country, as well, could give me no information about these bags.[8] When they mention carrying bags, it is flat ones, sewn of cloth, woven of palm-leaf strips or made of animal skin. Bruch gives the most complete information following a description of the habit of chewing betel by women and men, young and old. Freely translated it says:

Old people use a small brass mortar to grind the leaves and pieces of betel nut....This mortar is kept in a shoulder bag together with containers for the ingredients to make the quid such as chalk, tobacco, betel nuts, etc. This bag can be made of rush or cloth or animal skin, (marten, cat, dog or calf skin), and hangs on a couple of brass chains over the shoulder. At the end of the chains, hanging in front, are as a rule, attached a flint, beard tweezers, coins or beads. Women, unmarried girls, and young men mostly use bags woven from rush; men, particularly of the rajah dignity use bags made of animal skin (1912:11; translation mine).

Volz reports that the Karo Batak, unlike their neighbors the Toba and Pakpak, hold the cordless bag under their arm (1909:291). Burton and Ward write:

When the men leave their villages, they carry with them a bag, made sometimes of mat, sometimes of goat's skin, containing tobacco, gambir, sirih, chunam, etc. To the neck of the bag is attached a thick brass chain, three or four feet in length, usually terminating with a pair of large flat iron nippers for plucking out the beard. This chain forms a counterpoise in front when the bag is thrown over the shoulder (1827:497).

The few early pictures that portray Batak men carrying a bag do not offer much information because the subject is always seen full face with only a small part of the shoulder bag visible. A bag carried over the left shoulder of a warrior depicted by Bruch (1912:87) looks like a flat woven one. Its two or three chains have coins at the end. Among a group of four sitting men shown in Modigliani (1892:113), one holds a flat rectangular bag under his right arm, while another has a kind of pouch hanging over his right shoulder.

As a matter of fact, in many parts of the Indonesian archipelago, men carry (or once carried) their personal belongings in a bag or pouch, attached to a cord or chain and slung over their shoulder. Hanging in front as a counterweight there may be coins, tweezers, little bronze or silver boxes for betel nut, and such. The donor of the Tropenmuseum bag in Figure 2 gave the native name, "*hadjoet nai borngin*," alas without any more information or translation. The dictionary says that *hadjoet* or *hajut* is a bag or a pouch to carry betel, etcetera. It can be made of a piece of cloth, woven of pandanus leaves, or sometimes made of animal skin (Van der Tuuk 1861:66,75). *Nai borngin* is more difficult to translate; in the Toba Batak language it means "from long ago, in older times, of old." In the opinion of H.J.A. Promés, who kindly gave me this information, *hadjoet nai borngin* only meant that it was a kind of bag which had been in use for a long time.

That the weft-twining technique is never mentioned does not mean that the betel bags seen by the observers or extant in collections could not have been made this way. To recognize the different techniques requires a thorough knowledge (Nooteboom 1948; Jager Gerlings 1952:32; Gittinger 1979a:180-83). Weft twining is well known in Indonesia. Three-dimensional objects made by this technique include, for instance, warrior jackets from Flores, central Sulawesi and central Kalimantan. From Timor we know of Meo headhunter garments done in a combination of weaving and weft twining, and a Molo betel bag in tapestry and weft twining.

Many Indonesian textiles have, at their fringed ends, two or more rows in this technique. There are, for example, textiles from the Dayaks in Kalimantan and from certain of the Nusa Tenggara Timor islands such as Timor, Flores, Savu, Sumba, and so forth. On a loom from Savu now in the Volkenkundig Museum Nusantara in Delft, it can be seen that the weft twining is done during the weaving process. The loom was on display at the International Colonial and Export Trade Exhibition at Amsterdam in 1883.[9] It is a back-strap loom of the heddle and shed stick type, with a circular continuous warp. Only about ten centimeters of the cotton ikat warp is woven. The weaver started with a strip of palm-leaf as the first pick. The second pick was a thick cotton thread. After this, on a closed shed, were two rows of weft twining. Following one more pick of thick cotton yarn, the actual weaving commenced. The two yarns used for the weft twining were not cut off; each still bears a bamboo bodkin, ten and eleven centimeters long, respectively, with a slot at the pointed end in which the thread is stuck.

On the Batak textiles, however, the narrow twined borders (*sirat*) are made after the weaving is finished and the remaining unwoven warp threads are cut. In former days this twining (called *manivat*) was done by men in their leisure time. Nowadays it is woman's work. Jasper tells how the *sirat* is made (Jasper and Pirngadie 1912:129-30). Some sixty years later Mattiebelle Gittinger saw it done in the same way (1975:16-17). According to her detailed description the woman sits on the floor with her right leg extended. The cloth on her lap is folded with one fringed end on top. A bamboo temple (*songkan*) keeps the last woven part at a constant width. Two yarns of different colors are tied into the fringes. To keep these threads stretched, the woman winds the ends around her right toe (Jasper tells us that the threads are wound round a little piece of bamboo that is hooked behind her toes). Each yarn passes through the holes at each end of the bamboo slat, which is eight to ten centimeters in length, and called *potir*, *hoting-hoting*, or per Jasper, *dopir*. It is used to twine the two yarns and to keep them separated. After each half or full turn of the *potir* the weaver slips a group of loose warp threads through this opening.

Was the twined Batak bag made in the same way as the *sirat*? On a small scale I tried replicating the twined bottom and the first rounds of the bag from the Tropenmuseum, depicted in Figure 8. I sat on the floor with my work in my lap and the two weft threads wound around a little stick that was hooked behind the toes of my stretched right leg. After each half turn of the *potir* I slipped a warp thread through the opening between the two threads. It worked very well round after round. It is quite possible that the bag was made in this way, but I am afraid that we shall never be sure. From the few known facts we may conclude that the weft-twined Batak bag was made and used in the Toba Batak region, but that about sixty to eighty years ago it went out of fashion and was not made any longer.

NOTES

1. It came into the collection with only the following documentation: "Nederlandsch Indië." The supposition, made in 1951, that it was a Batak bag has since proved correct.

2. They are consecutively numbered Tropenmuseum 2761- 801, 802, and 803.

3. The bag not shown, Tropenmuseum 2761-802, is 10 cm. in width.

4. There is possibly a seventh. The Rijksmuseum voor Volkenkunde at Leiden has a Batak betel bag (number 1926/ 867) that is described as a flat bag, 46 cm. long by 18 cm. wide, made of a dirty, stiff cotton fabric. It has a pointed part at one side on which a cord is attached. The name is *anak kampil*, "little bag," and the origin is probably up the Langkat River, northwest of Medan. It came into the collection in 1916 as a gift of the Bataviaasch Genootschap van Kunsten en Wetenschappen (Batavia Society for Art and Learning). I have a strong feeling that this is a weft-twined bag like the one in Figure 8 from the Tropenmuseum. To my disappointment I could not see this bag due to the renovations of the depot.

5. Museum für Völkerkunde, Berlin, IC-30832. Circumference, 30 cm.; total length, 44 cm.

6. Museum für Völkerkunde, Frankfurt am Main NS-10220. Length, 22 cm.; circumference, 28 cm.

7. Catalogue numbers 92.146 and 92.147.

8. Without the cooperation of the staff members of many museums in the Netherlands, other European countries and North America, and the help of Mattiebelle Gittinger (Washington, D.C.), Robert J. Holmgren and Anita Spertus (New York), Sandra A. Niessen (Leiden), H.J. Promés (Voorburg), Sitor Situmorang (Leiden), and P. Voorhoeve (Leiden) I could not have written this paper. Thank you all for your help.

9. The loom is No. 230-1180 at the Volkenkundig Museum Nusantara, and was shown in the catalogue accompanying the 1883 International Colonial and Export Trade Exhibition at Amsterdam (Instituut voor Onderwÿs...Delft 1888:98).

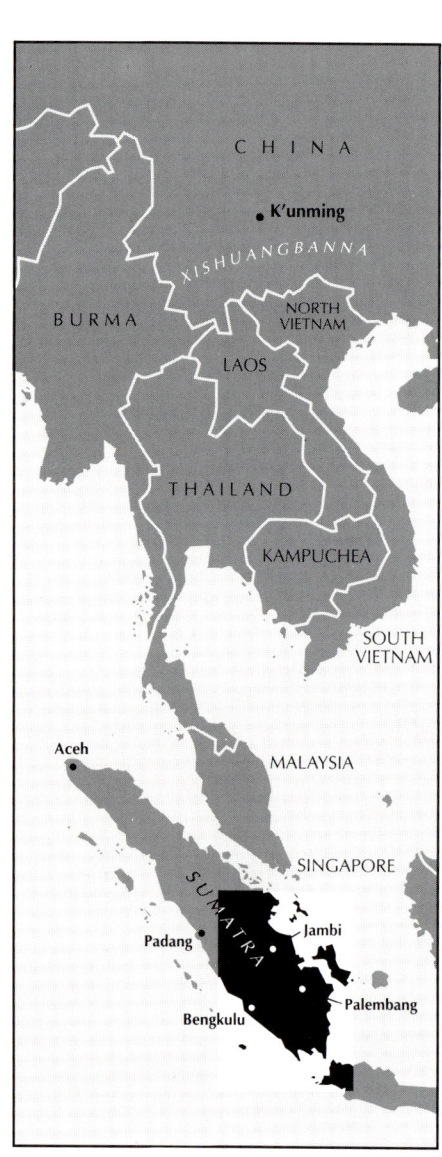

South Sumatra, relative to the Xishuangbanna region of China.

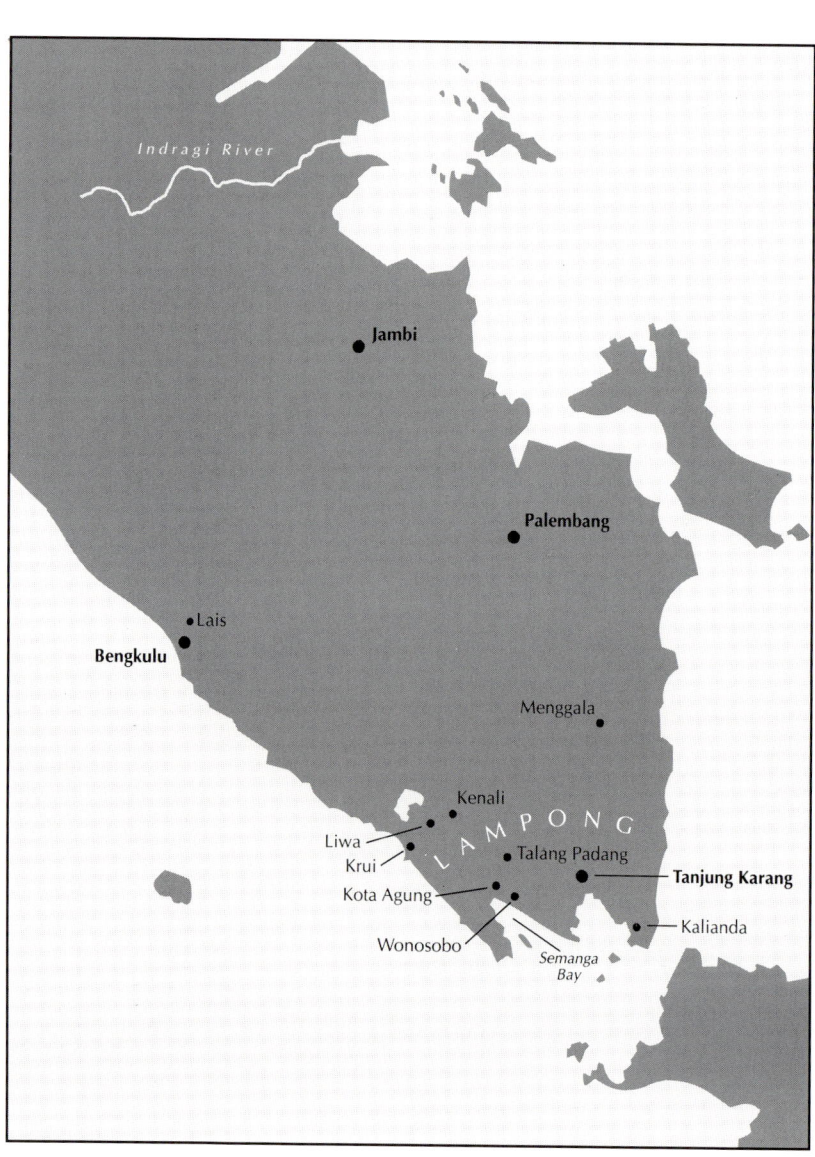

South Sumatra.

A Reassessment of the Tampan of South Sumatra

Mattiebelle Gittinger

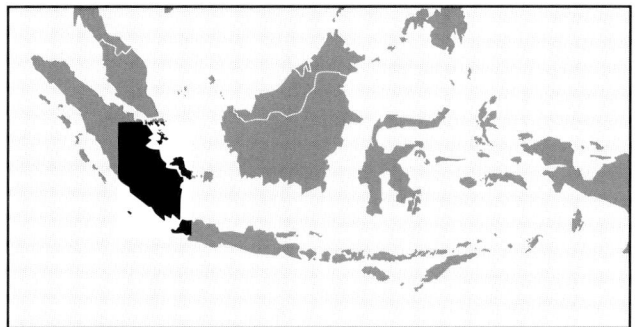

That there existed some sort of cultural continuum between central Thailand and Sumatra toward the end of first millennium is increasingly recognized. Historians from several disciplines have suggested these relationships which in regard to political and social spheres R.B. Smith summarizes: "...it is clear that by the eighth century at least there was a sort of cultural continuum stretching from north to south, between central Thailand and southern Sumatra, or between 'Dvaravati' and 'Srivijaya'"(1979:454).[1]

The following essay suggests that additional but contemporary evidence of this continuum resides in a type of cloth known as *tampan*, once woven in South Sumatra, and in certain textiles made by the T'ai people of the mainland. Parallels in technical structure, design, and function present compelling evidence of a relationship between these textiles. The mainland T'ai material, drawn from areas as dispersed as the Khorat Plateau, Laos, and the Xishuangbanna area of southern Yunnan, China, functions to a great degree in the service of Buddhism. This raises the possibility that the similarity perceived today between the textiles of Sumatra and the mainland exists because of shared roots that reach back to that cultural continuum of the first millennium, when Buddhism was an important factor in Sumatra as well as the mainland. While virtually impossible to prove, the hypothesis explains anomalies in the usage of certain Sumatran textiles and suggests new possibilities for interpreting certain designs.

The *Tampan* of South Sumatra

Tampan are relatively small rectangular cloths ranging from approximately 30 to 100 centimeters on a side (Figs. 1, 8-13). They have a plain weave cotton foundation patterned by supplementary wefts of cotton, or less commonly silk, and occasionally a combination of the two. Originally woven on back tension looms

225

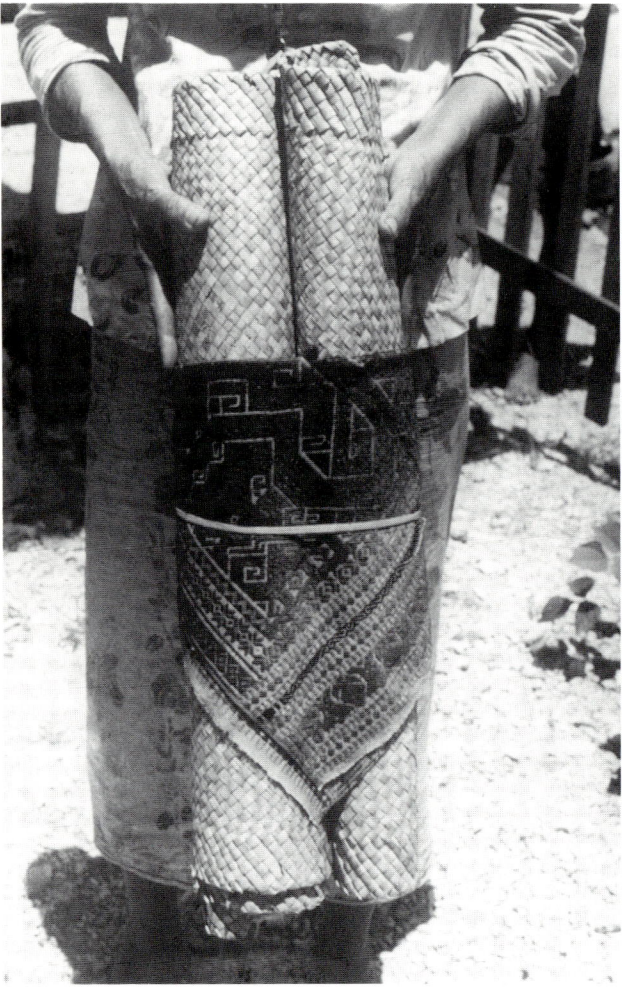

Figure 1. Along the west coast of Sumatra, in the Krui region, the ritual gift of a tampan and a mat (tikar) was given in this form, as photographed in 1970. This combination was once a required gift through much of South Sumatra.

that utilized a reed, their designs range from simple geometric patterns to imaginative abstractions, to highly vocal scenes. Elsewhere I have described these textiles and their functions in detail (see Gittinger 1972, 1974, and 1979a).

As late as 1970 a few *tampan* could be found among Redjang people inland from the Sumatran west coast village of Lais and south of this region among the Serawai. These groups knew them as *lamak*. Further south along the coast, where the term *tampan* was common, the textiles existed in more sizeable holdings among the Kauer people and among the Paminggir groups of the Krui region and inland areas of Liwa and Kenali. The greatest numbers, however, were among other Paminggir groups located all along the south coast, into the Kalianda peninsula.

The history of this southern region hides in the penumbra of more lustrous nearby centers. To the north, in the vicinity of present-day Palembang, the Kingdom of Srivijaya was the major economic, political, and religious power of insular Southeast Asia from the seventh to the eleventh century. Power later shifted north to the Jambi region and then to Java and the Malay peninsula. By the time of European contact, Bantam in West Java was the international trade center and it exercized suzerainty over much of South Sumatra in its attempt to monopolize the trade of that region's black pepper and cloves.

Such commercial crops exposed the southern rim of Sumatra to inter-island and international trade which brought a more varied array of stimuli than that known to the mountainous interior. This may be reflected in the *tampan* designs, which in the south seem to have had a more extensive range, varying from the very simple to highly complex, while in the interior and along the west coast the compositions were limited in number and included only a few of a complex nature.[2]

Elsewhere I have called these textiles "token textiles" because they have little practical utility yet appear to have assumed ritual roles traditionally claimed by wearable textiles elsewhere in the Indonesian archipelago. Just like the latter, *tampan* were once a primary element in gift exchange at life-crisis ceremonies, and served to identify ritual occasions, often being combined with other objects to create complex symbols. The usage of *tampan* differs slightly in detail from one region to another in South Sumatra, but there is little doubt they have a common cultural origin.

On initial consideration the *tampan* textile complex and its physical properties and functions within the social context appear to fit comfortably within the Indonesian scene. Yet to scholars familiar with other Indonesian textiles certain technical and functional aspects of these small cloths present disturbing anomalies that ask for specific resolution. One of these concerns the loom on which the textiles were woven. If *tampan* were an element in the very earliest cultural complex of this region, as their usage in gift exchange might suggest (when compared to the ritualized exchange between bride-givers and -takers among the Batak and Sumbanese[3]), one might expect them to be woven on the back tension loom utilizing a continuous warp but lacking a reed. Its distribution in the interior and more remote areas of Indonesia speaks for the antiquity of this type of loom. However, actual loom parts that remain in South Sumatra, as well as the dents still visible in many of the remaining textiles, prove that the *tampan* were woven on a loom utilizing a reed and, without doubt, one having a discontinuous warp. This loom is normally associated with silk weaving in coastal and court centers, rather than with cotton, the basic fiber of *tampan*. The proposition that weavers at some time changed looms does not seem to be viable, for it flies in the face of custom surrounding ritually important textiles. Does this suggest that *tampan* are not as old as the textiles of the Batak and others who use a loom with a continuous warp and no reed? Very probably. Does it mean the weaving of *tampan* developed at the same time as the weaving of silk and the loom normally associated with this? Possibly. Elsewhere I have suggested that silk weaving seems to have begun in Indonesia toward the end of the first millennium A.D. (Gittinger 1974:14). To propose the same date for the advent of *tampan* is consistent with other conclusions in this article.

Equally as perplexing as the nature of the loom is the pairing of the *tampan* with a mat—either the common palm leaf mat called *tikar* (Fig. 1) or the more prestigious *lampit*, made of split *rotan* lashed together in parallel rows. Together, the *tampan* and mat make a complementary set that is entirely unlike ritual gifts or prestige objects elsewhere in the archipelago. It seems to be unique to this region of Sumatra, at least in historical times.

Also puzzling are certain *tampan* designs. While the great majority are patterned with simple geometric forms, there are some with a complexity unique among the textiles of Indonesia. The imagery of these *tampan* has teased researchers with its implied narrative and symbolic forms (Holmgren and Spertus 1980:157-98; Gittinger 1974:3-18). These are the most obvious "problems" presented by the *tampan*. Comparison with certain textiles woven by the T'ai of mainland Southeast Asia suggests new ways to view the Sumatran cloths, and possibly, resolutions to some of the anomalies they present.

T'ai Textiles

There are several forms of T'ai textiles that relate to the Sumatran *tampan*. These include pillows, shawls, small rectangles, and banners (Figs. 2-7,16). All are patterned by supplementary wefts on a plain weave foundation similar to the *tampan*. A typical contemporary pillow from the Khorat Plateau in northeast Thailand (Fig. 2) illustrates characteristic construction: a decorated center panel of cotton joined to end pieces of plain cotton cloth. The patterned center panels (Fig. 3) are woven in long narrow continuous strips, which are cut into the appropriate rectangles as needed (see Lefferts 1980: item 80-47).

The long, narrow shawls of the Lao Neua, a T'ai people, have deep, patterned end borders that leave only about one third of the warp unpatterned in the center (Figs. 4-6). The ground and supplementary wefts are commonly silk except when blue occurs, in which case cotton is the usual fiber. Originally the textile was probably always woven as a single continuous piece, but today one sees examples in which old, finely woven end panels have been sewn to a plain silk center. There are also examples in which that section

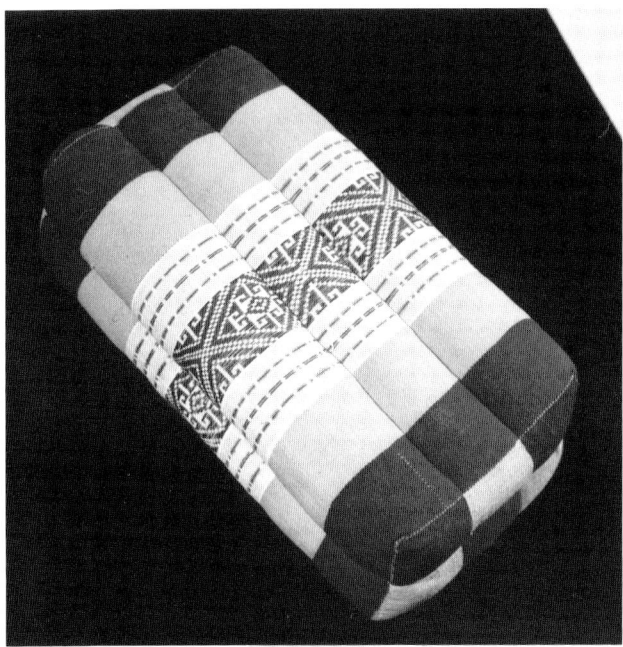

Figure 2. A pillow from the Khorat Plateau of Thailand. 30 x 20 x 14 cm. The Textile Museum 1976.27.2.

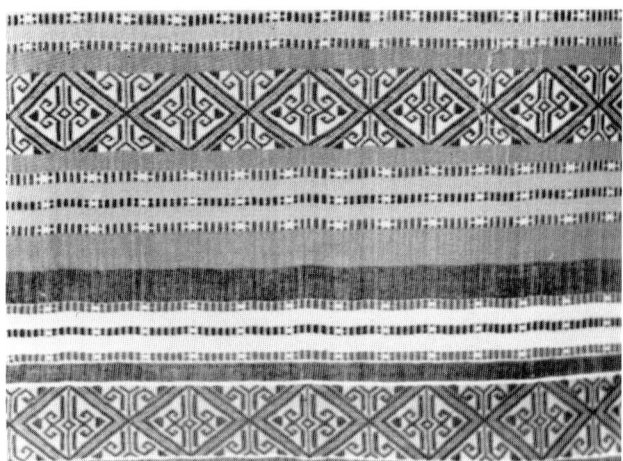

Figure 3. Detail of a pillow cover from Thailand. From Vimolphan 1973: plate 16.

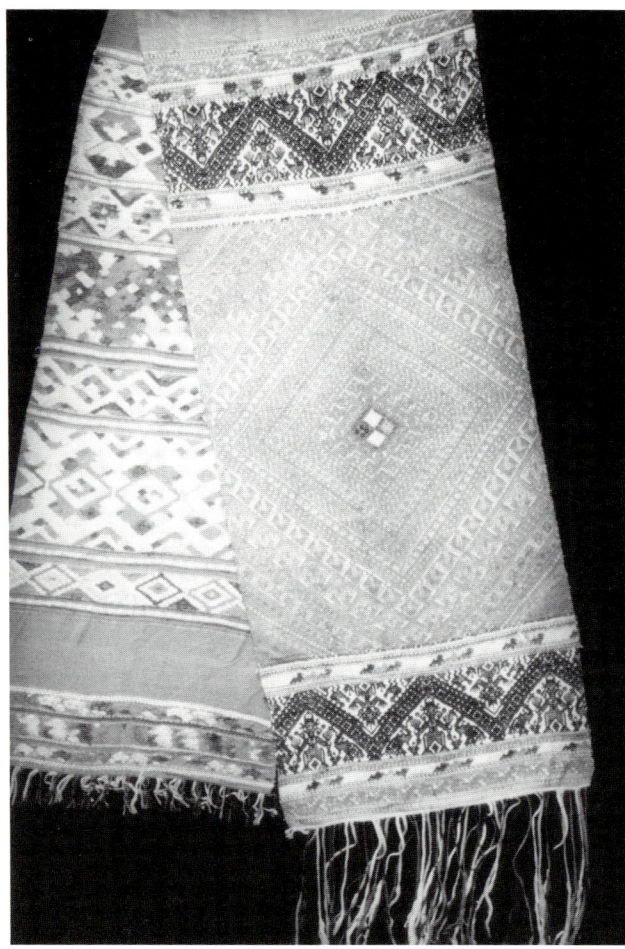

Figure 4. A shawl (pae beang) *made by the Lao Neua of northeast Thailand. 217 x 44 cm. The Textile Museum 1985.31.4.*

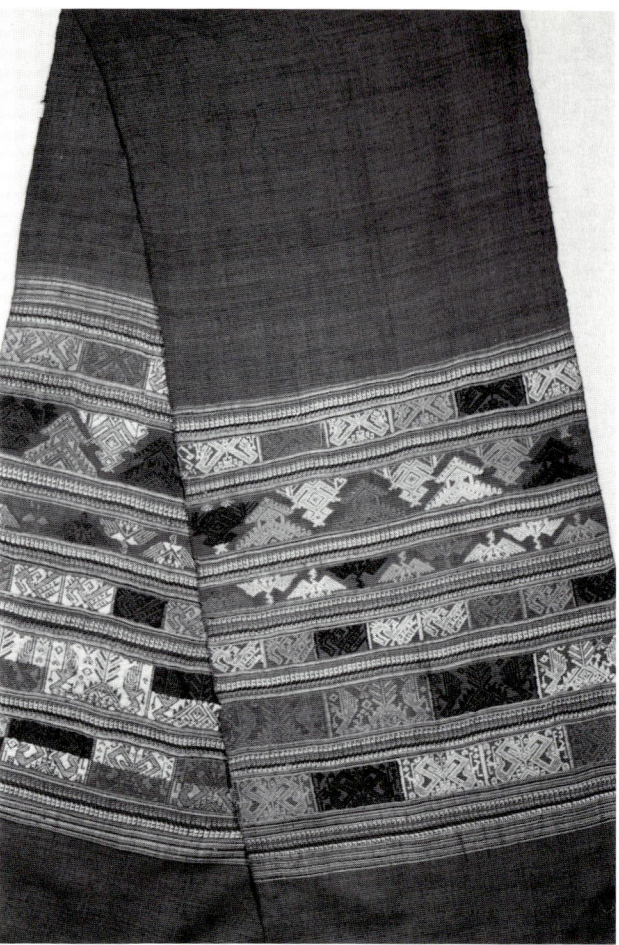

Figure 5. A shawl (pae beang) *made by the Lao Neua of northeast Thailand. 221 x 45 cm. The Textile Museum 1985.31.5.*

of the warp destined to become the ground of the end panels was tied or bound off with a resist, so that when the warp yarns were dyed red the areas protected by the resist remained white—the white of the silk fiber— and subsequently provided a white ground for the red supplementary patterning effected in the weaving. The two ends of the shawl tend to have different designs, one end carrying parallel rows of complex geometric forms and the other interspersing rows of geometric patterns with animal and possibly ship forms. Certain of these shouldercloths always have a diamond motif at one end; it is reiterated by concentric patterning that completely fills the center of the end panel (Figs. 4,6). This expanding diamond pattern is usually rendered in red silk and bordered at top and bottom with bands of blue bearing stylized animal or geometric motifs.

Among the weaving of the Lao Neua there are small rectangular textiles which in format and design replicate the shawl end with the expanding diamond pattern (Fig. 7). Some of these may actually be ends cut from a shawl, but others appear to have been woven as discrete objects (Pl. 30). It has been suggested these were used as aids to meditation by Buddhists (Cheesman 1982:123).

A fourth type of textile related to Sumatran weaving exists in the form of banners, called *tung*, made by T'ai people of north and northeast Thailand (Fig. 16). Used most frequently in association with accruing merit, they are hung at Buddhist temples. On the Khorat Plateau, where they are called *phaa tung*, these are long narrow patterned cotton strips in variable lengths (three collected in August 1980 measured 524 cm., 314 cm., and 55 cm., respectively[4]). A recent work on *tung* enumerates at least five categories, distinguished primarily by size and material.[5] Banners were also made for use in a Buddhist context by T'ai peoples in southern Yunnan, and the simplest examples are similar to the Dai textiles in Figure 19.

Design Parallels

Designs common to the T'ai textiles have direct parallels to those found on the *tampan* of South Sumatra. These are found not in the elaborate pictorial ones that most authors delight in publishing, but in the

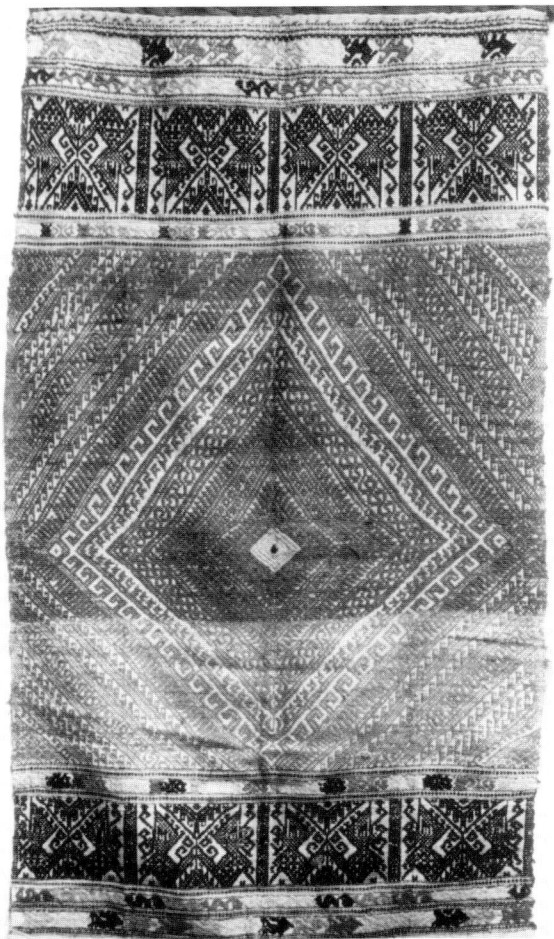

Figure 6. Detail of a Lao Neua shawl end. The entire cloth is 221 x 44 cm. The Textile Museum 1985.31.7.

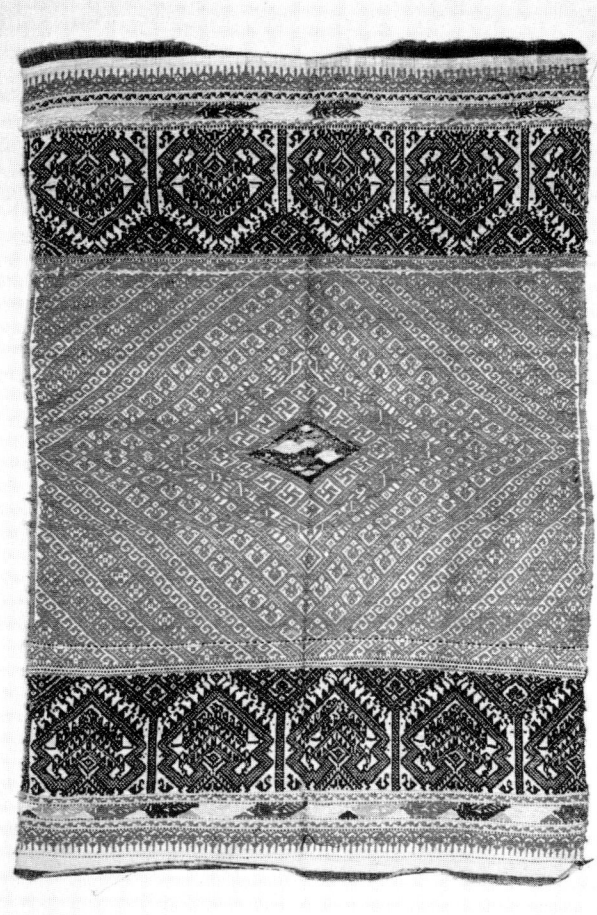

Figure 7. A small rectangle made by the Lao Neua. It is thought such pieces were aids to Buddhists' meditation. 67 x 47 cm. The Textile Museum 1985.31.1.

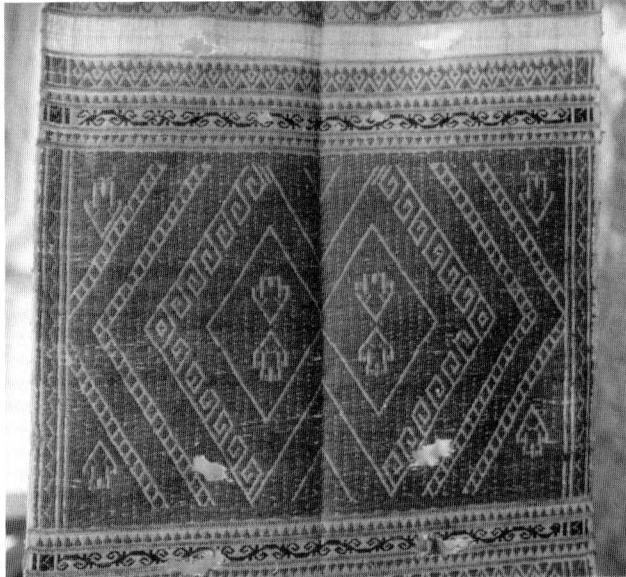

Figure 8. A tampan photographed in the Liwa area of South Sumatra in 1970.

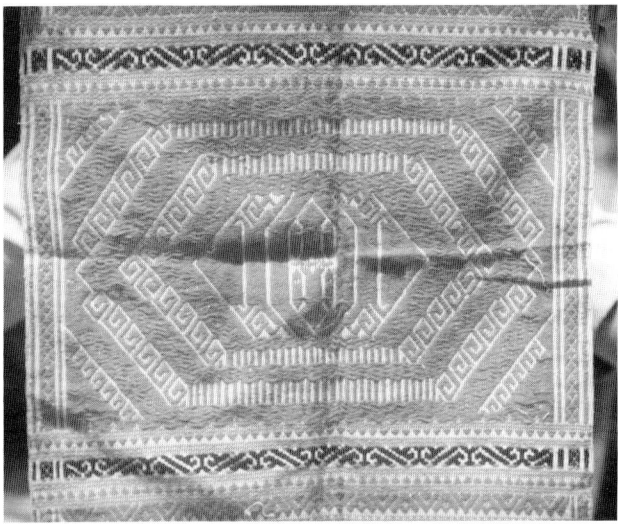

Figure 9. A tampan photographed in the Krui region on the west coast of South Sumatra in 1970.

Gittinger

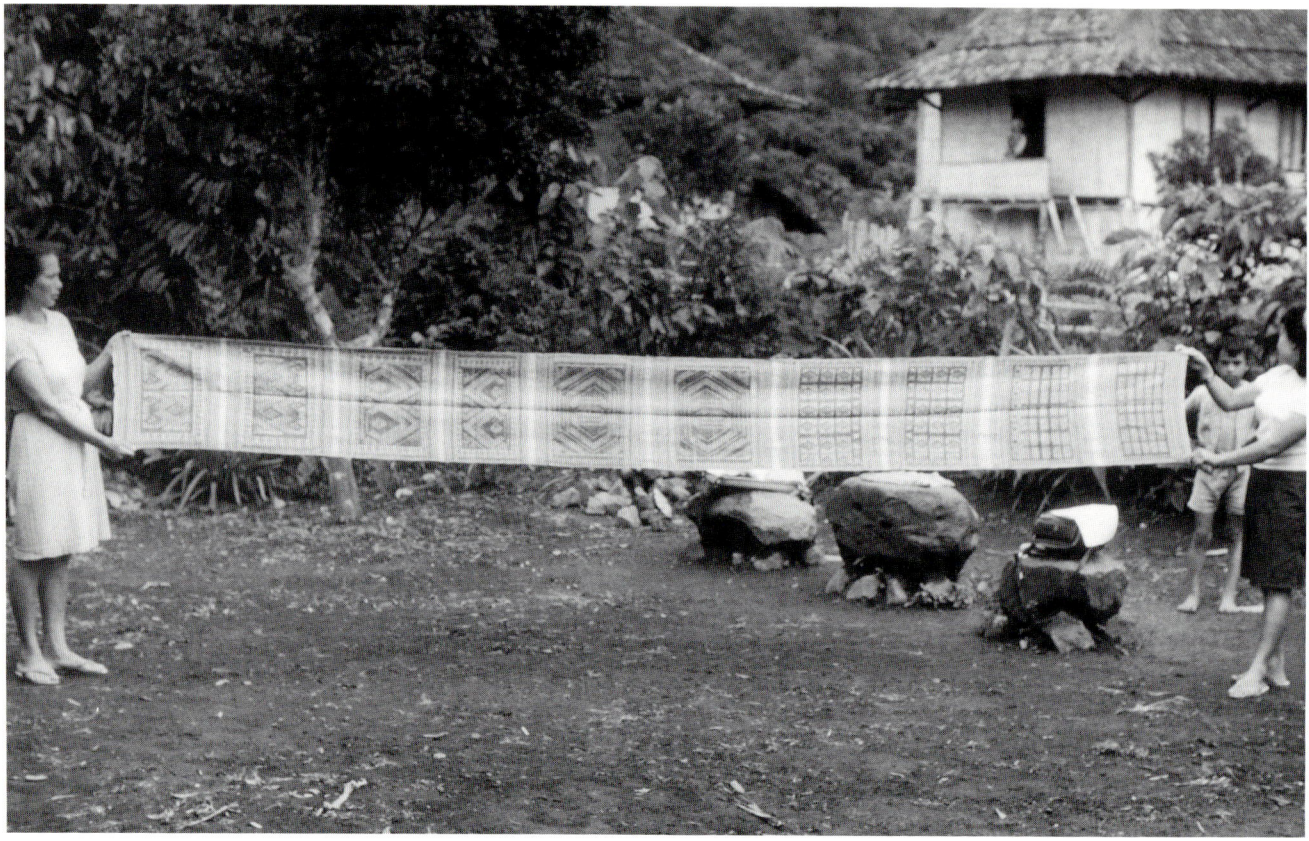

Figure 10. A strip of tampan not yet cut into separate pieces, photographed in the Liwa area of South Sumatra in 1970.

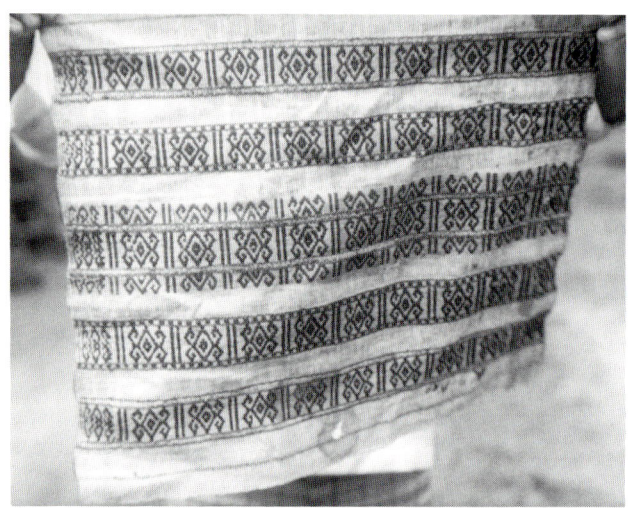

Figure 11. A tampan photographed in the Kalianda area of South Sumatra in 1971.

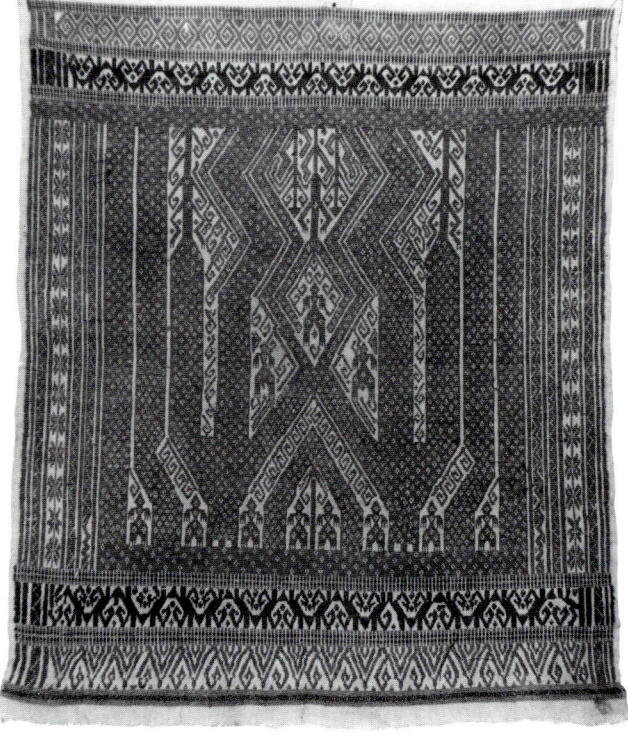

Figure 12. A tampan from the Kauer region of South Sumatra. Tampan of this design were common in the vicinity of Bintuhan in 1970. Tropenmuseum 2125-28.

dozens, even hundreds, of usual examples to be found in household treasuries. These less glamorous pieces, such as illustrated in Figures 8-12, are rarely published; yet they constitute the majority of *tampan* and should be thought to typify the core of this textile type. In format they have either parallel rows of geometric patterns or centerfields defined by upper and lower borders with guard stripes. The latter type (Fig. 8) almost always has a red or red-brown centerfield and blue borders. In format it directly parallels the Lao Neua meditating squares (Fig. 7) and shawl ends (Fig. 6). The other kind, with its parallel rows of geometric patterns (Fig. 10), recalls the strips woven for T'ai pillows (Fig. 3).

A wide range of similar geometric patterning appears in the textiles from each of these Sumatran and T'ai areas. Both kinds bear hooked lozenges (in simple and elaborate forms), key devices, s-scrolls, diamond configurations, and eight-pointed stars. Somewhat more complex is the border scheme of tangent-verted and inverted scallops as in the second line from the top of the T'ai banner in Figure 16 and the guard stripes in the *tampan* of Figures 8 and 12. This particular bordering design may be found in Dai material from Yunnan, T'ai banners, and *tampan* from all of southern Sumatra.

Of a much more complex nature is the complicated "ship" design (Figs. 13-16), a recurring element in each of these geographic areas, always rendered with elaborate high-rising bow and stern. In both Sumatran and T'ai examples the weaver may re-use her pattern sticks on the loom in inverted order, thus causing the design to appear in mirror image. When this is done immediately after the first rendering, a new design may appear to be formed, as can be seen by comparing the borders and centerfield of the *tampan* in Figure 13. Both the particular ship design element and the patterning technique were used by the Sumatrans and the T'ai. Figures 16 and 17 show that the birds in the T'ai and Sumatran weavings are depicted in a similar way. Figures 19 and 20 compare edge designs, revealing virtually identical elements in use on Dai and Sumatran textiles.

Functions

Those T'ai textiles that have been sewn into pillows are of immediate interest because they parallel the Sumatran *tampan* not only in their design, but in their function as a major item in gift giving. On the Khorat Plateau in northeast Thailand, when a young woman weaves a length of *phaa kit* (as the pillow covers are called), it signals that she is marriageable. After her engagement, as the date of the marriage approaches, this woven length is cut and sewn into pillows. On the wedding day many of these are given to the bride's in-

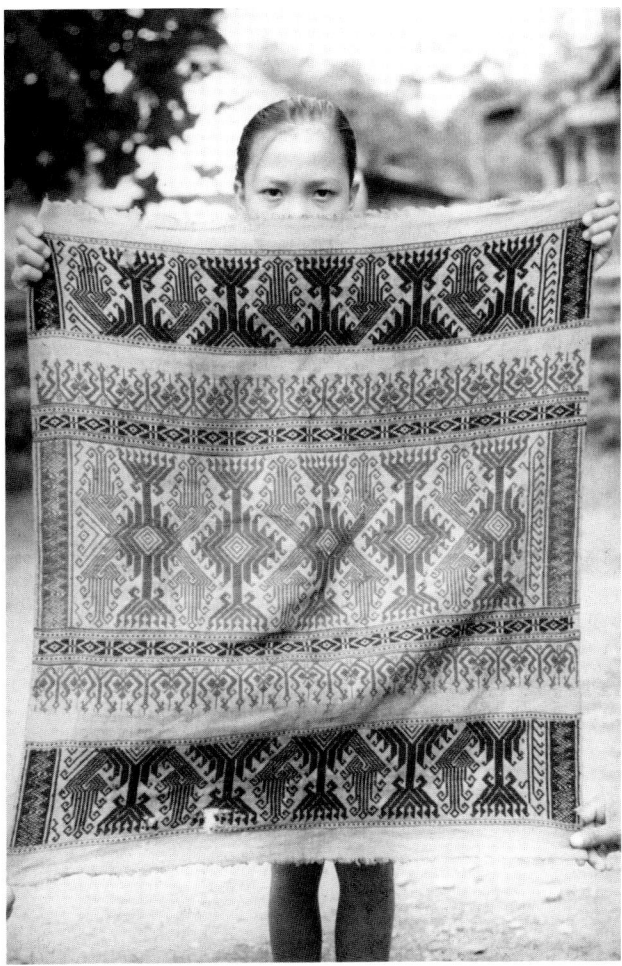

Figure 13. A tampan *photographed in the Talang Padang region of South Sumatra in 1971.*

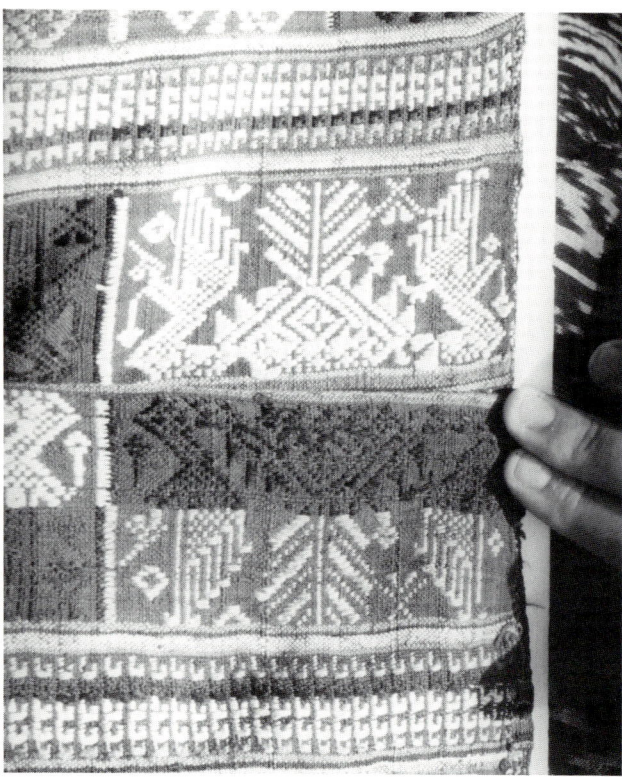

Figure 14. Detail of the Lao Neua shawl seen in Figure 5, showing ship design. The inverted ship done in a lower row has been placed next to the upright rendering. Ship motifs like this are found on the textiles from South Sumatra, Thailand, and southern Yunnan, China.

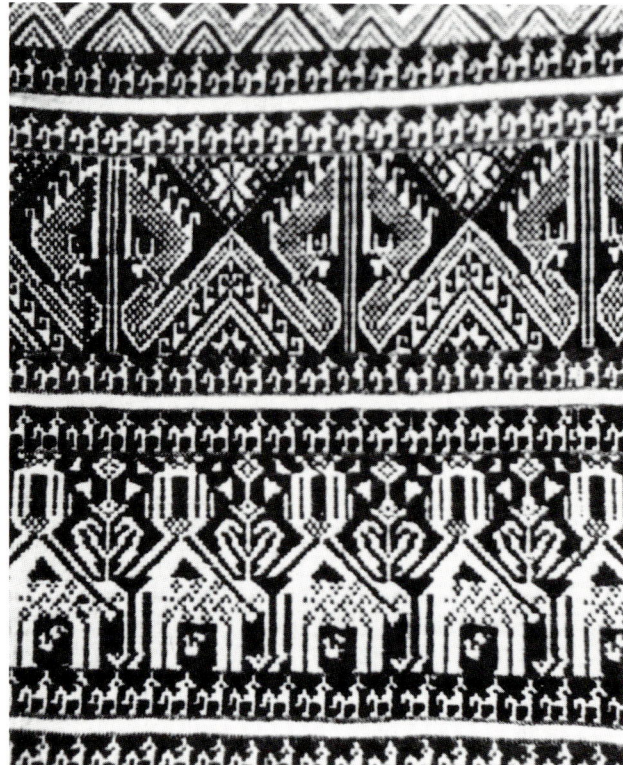

Figure 15. Detail of a Dai textile with ship motif, showing the reverse face of the textile. From a photograph in the Yunnan Provincial Museum, Kunming, Yunnan, China.

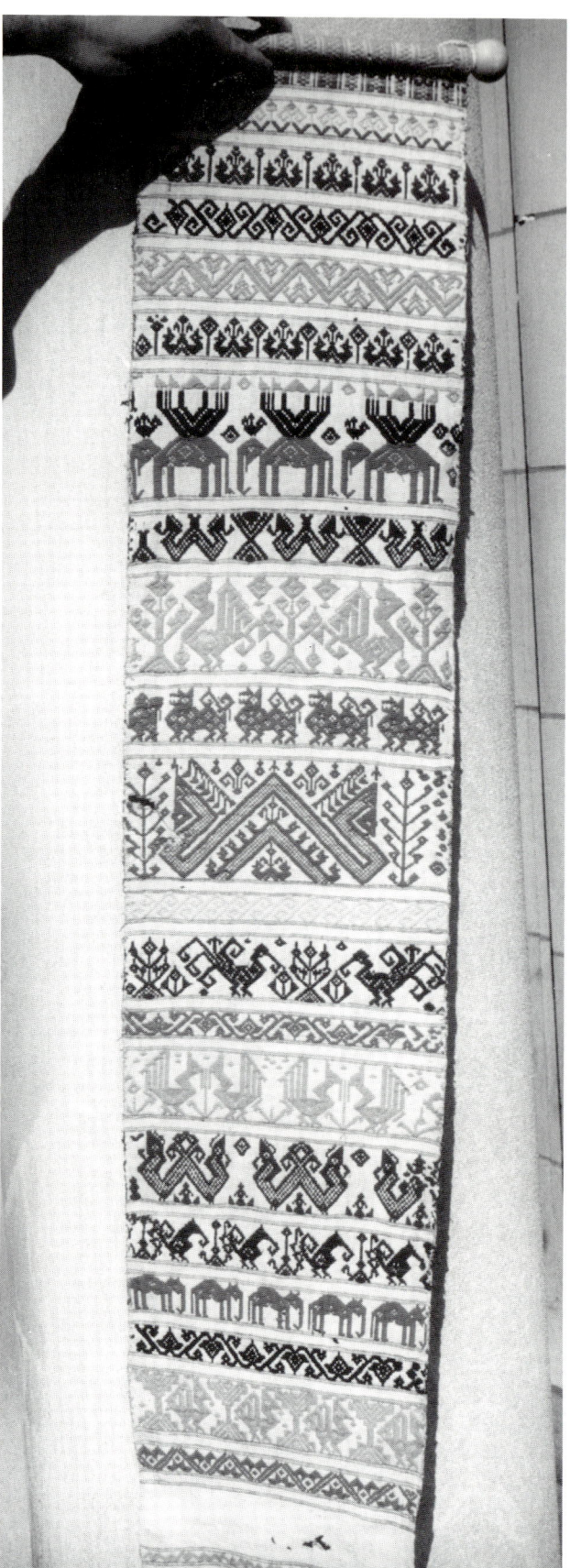

Figure 16. A T'ai banner (tung) probably made in northern Thailand. Collection of Burton Holtz.

laws in numbers carefully apportioned according to their relation to the groom. In addition, through much of her life, a good woman gives pillows to others as a sign of respect: to her elders (such as her father, mother, and paternal and maternal grandparents), friends, relatives, and household guests. Also, women earn merit by giving pillows to the Buddhist monastery (*sanga*) located in virtually every village (Vimolphan 1973:48-51; Lefferts 1980: items 80-29,30a-e,34a-h).

Among the Pai-yi, a Dai people of southern Yunnan, guests at a wedding must bring congratulatory gifts; in return the host must give presents of sheets, pillows, and cloth, whose value is proportionate to the closeness of the relation to the host. A very close relative is given a set of sheets and pillows, those of the next degree receive a pair of pillows, the next degree one pillow, and the next a piece of cloth. Chiang Ying-liang, the first anthropologist to work among the Dai in that region, reports: "Because of this custom, whenever there is a marriage among the chieftains, the families of the bride and groom prepare several hundred pillows" (1950:263). The Dai, he says, do not limit this pillow-giving custom to weddings, but offer them as a sign of respect to honored guests and particularly to the Buddha.[6] In Xishuangbanna today, small cotton rectangles resembling pillow covers, called *phaa chiit*, are used to wrap temple offerings (Fig.18). The sizeable numbers of these given to the temple may have replaced the earlier multiplicity of pillows.

Sumatran Parallels

In a ceremonial context the function of the Sumatran *tampan* was directly parallel to that of the T'ai *phaa kit* (pillow covers) except that in Sumatra, where weaving of the textiles ceased about the turn of the century, the textiles entering into the ritual exchanges were later returned to the original owner; and they were not employed to make pillows. *Tampan* were used to wrap either ceremonial food or a mat (Fig. 1). The combination of *tampan* and food was the gift most often associated with marriage. In the Kalianda region as many as 120 of these bundles were exchanged if the rank of the groom's father was sufficiently great (Gittinger 1972:26-28). The exchange of the *tampan*-wrapped food basically identified the multiplicity of new relationships created by a marriage. At subsequent ceremonies celebrating the bride's return home and presentation of a new child at the maternal grandparent's home, similar numbers of *tampan*-wrapped food packets were exchanged.

At boys' circumcision ceremonies and at funerals, food gifts were numerous, but the gift of a *tampan* in association with a mat (a *lampit* or a *tikar*) was the most significant element in gift giving. In the Krui region on the west coast apparently quite a large number of

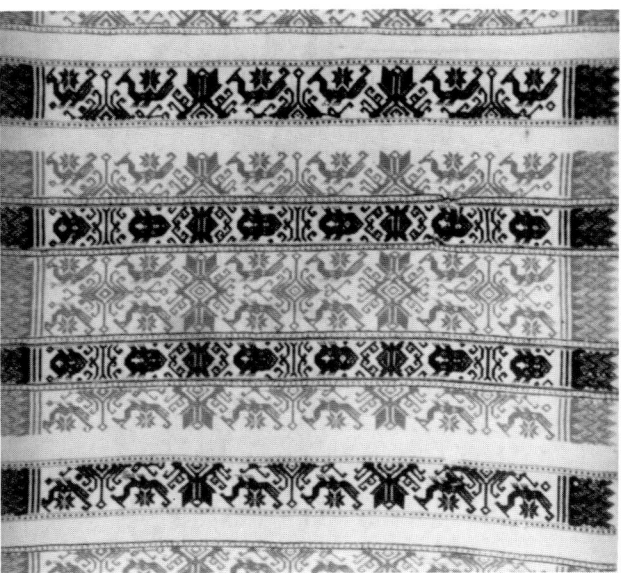

Figure 17. A tampan *showing birds similar to those on the banner seen in Figure 16. Tropenmuseum 2125/41.*

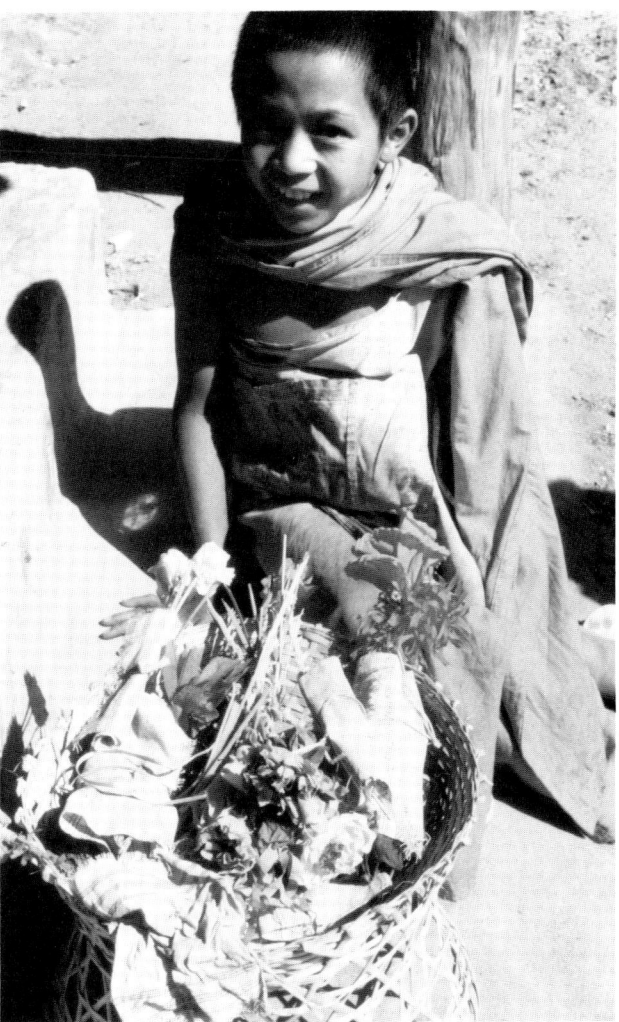

Figure 18. A Dai novice looks at temple offerings of candles and paper flowers, wrapped in cotton rectangles (phaa chiit) *with geometric designs. Near Menghai, Xishuangbanna, China, 1988.*

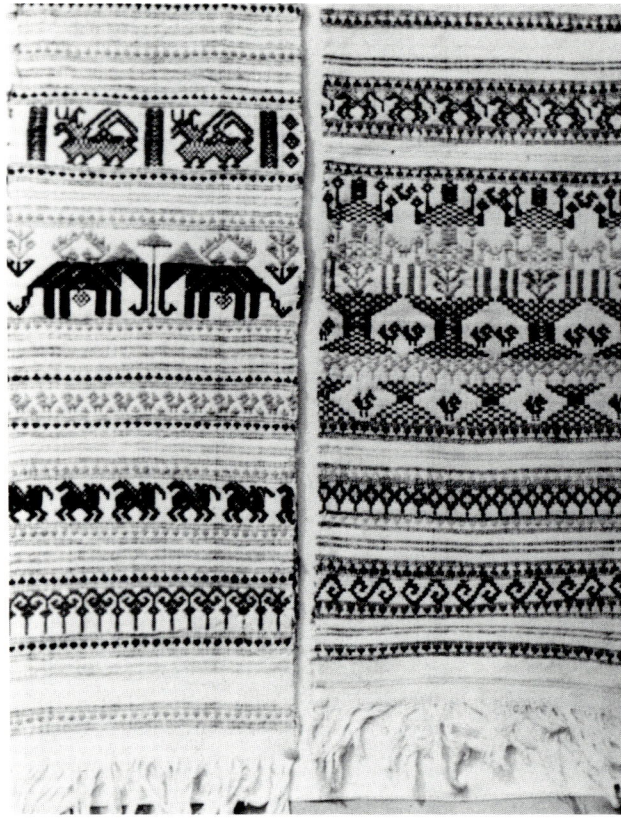

Figure 19. Details of two Dai textiles. From a photograph in the Yunnan Provincial Museum, Kunming, Yunnan, China.

people were obliged to present this combination at the time of death (Gittinger 1972:58-64). A *tampan* was placed beneath the head of the corpse while the body was washed, and a *tikar* served as a burial wrapping. Elsewhere, as in the Semangka Bay area, the *tampan-lampit* combination occurred as a required funeral gift, but did not have a practical function within the ceremonies. There, when the corpse was in state, a *lampit* mat bearing a *tampan* spread on a pillow were set to the side of the body as ritual objects.

In 1970, the South Sumatrans I interviewed immediately associated the *tampan*-and-mat gift with death and boys' circumcision ceremonies. However their responses to extensive questioning led me to believe that the *tampan-tikar* gift may have been obligatory for all rites of passage at one time. I suggested this in an earlier writing:

> The available evidence gives only a glimmer of how widespread such an exchange may have been. In the Liwa area older informants say a tampan-tikar gift, called *tampan-sulan*, must be delivered three days before the wedding ceremony to the house of the groom by an older brother of the groom, his father's oldest sister, and his *kelama* or maternal grandparents. In addition, the bride must give the religious leader who conducts the Moslem rite the same gift—in this instance called *sedekah kawin*. The sultan in Pekon Balak near Liwa reported that on the marriage day a married younger sister of the bride's father must give a tampan-tikar gift, called *djungan-sulan*, to the equivalent woman in the groom's family. This woman returns a gift of a new tikar and a different tampan. Thus while today this gift is associated predominantly with death, and many areas report no other occasions when it is given, there are indications that in earlier times, when the *tampan* were still woven the tampan-tikar served as an *adat* gift on many occasions (Gittinger 1972:63-64).

These strange partners of *tampan* and mat lose their eccentric character when viewed in what must have been their original form—as pillow and mat. The T'ai analogies suggest the logic of such an interpretation; in addition there are remnants of tradition in South Sumatra that reconstruct this pillow form. In the villages (*kampung*) of Kagungan and Menggala in the Wai Turgak area of South Sumatra, the bride and later the bride and groom sit in state on a seat formed from *tampan* spread over pillows and cushions (Gittinger 1972:45,50). In some areas circumcision was done on a *tampan* spread on a pillow (Gittinger 1972:56) while in others a *lampit* and a *tampan* spread on a pillow

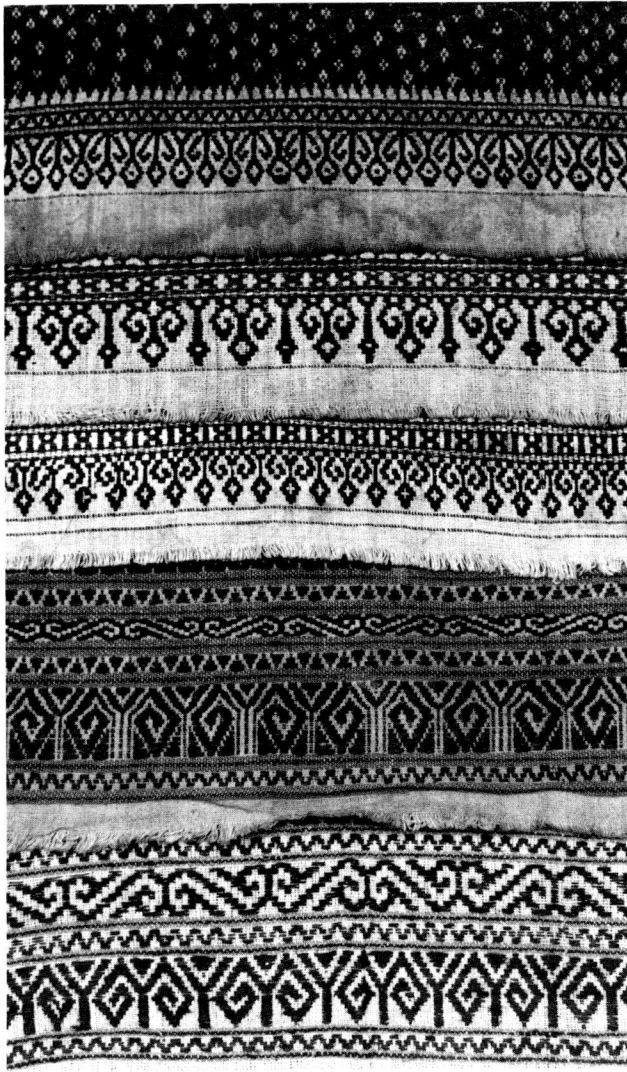

Figure 20. Border designs from five different tampan. *Similar borders appear on Dai textiles, as in Figure 19, and on Lao Neua ones, as in Figure 7.*

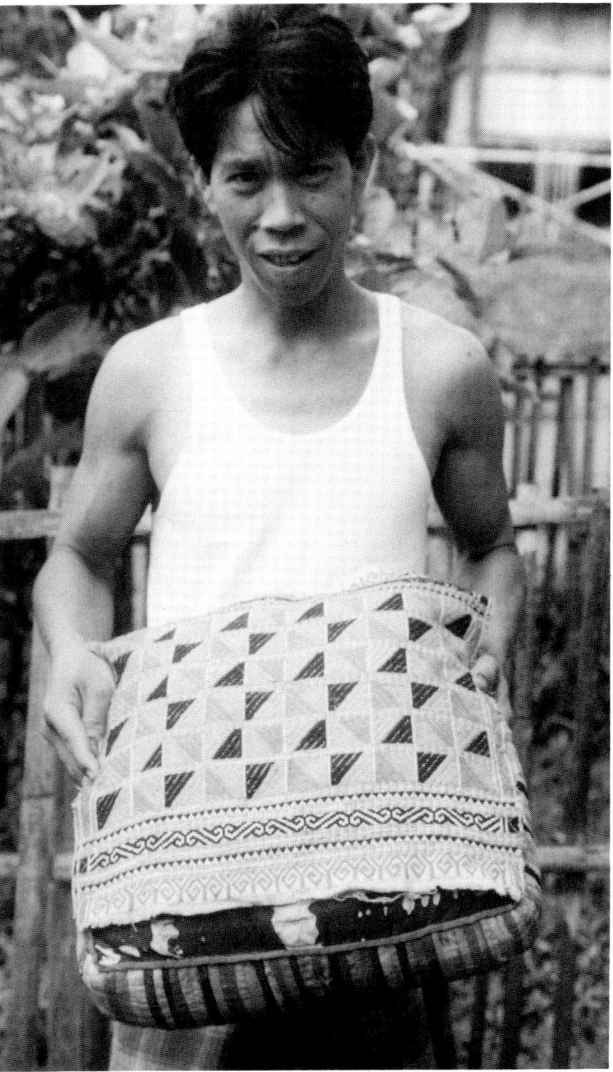

Figure 21. On ceremonial occasions to carry a tampan *on a pillow was the prerogative of certain families in South Sumatra. This one was photographed in Kota Agung, in the Wonosobo area, in 1971.*

were symbolic objects merely set out, but not used, at circumcision ceremonies and at funerals (Gittinger 1972:57,63). The right to carry a small wooden bench holding a pillow covered with a *tampan*, as in Figure 21, was a ceremonial privilege reserved by certain notable families in the south. Thus evidence remaining in South Sumatra as late as 1970 sustains the logic of the interpreting *tampan* as pillow covers. The broader significance of this will be discussed below.

Were all *tampan* originally woven to be used as pillow covers? Probably not. The association of the small cloths with ritual food gifts is so widespread throughout the South Sumatran region as to suggest it is not a recent adaptation, but has venerable roots. Also, the *tampan* had a synergetic effect when combined with other objects within a ceremonial context, creating broad symbols, and this argues that the textile had several functions beyond that of pillow cover alone.

At least one of these ritual images which *tampan* help create has parallels within T'ai customs.

In South Sumatra a most noteworthy ceremonial combination was the joining of the *tampan* with a spear, an umbrella, or a many-limbed ceremonial tree (*kayu ara*), to create the image of a tree-of-life. In the course of a marriage or circumcision ceremony these objects were ritually destroyed and the *tampan* given to an appropriate person as a sign of transition (Gittinger 1972:40-43,48-49).

Similar tree-of-life imagery is constructed with the banners (*tung*) of the T'ai. While used in conjunction with numerous festivals, the *tung* on the Khorat Plateau are particularly associated with Bun Phraawet/Bun Mahathat, a major village festival that celebrates the story of the Buddha in his penultimate birth before Buddhahood. The festival happily combines merit-making with secular interests, and in preparation a

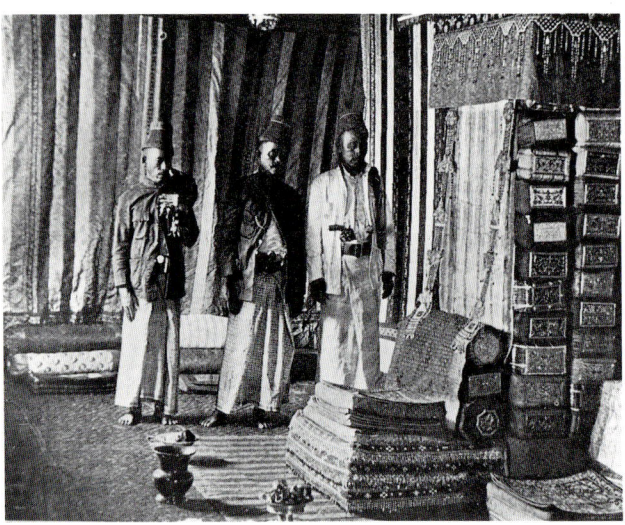

Figure 22. Along the coasts of Sumatra it was customary to use a ritual bed as a showcase for special textiles and pillows on the occasion of great ceremonies. This early photograph shows pillows piled on the bed to the right, and mats heaped on the temporary seat in front of it. The number of pillows and mats was determined by the relative rank of the family. Late 19th or early 20th century. Aceh, North Sumatra. Photographer unknown.

group of local women share in the endeavor of weaving up to eight banners. These are flown from tall poles placed at the cardinal directions and equal intervals in the courtyard of the local Buddhist monastery (Lefferts 1980: item 80-39). A basket at the base of each pole holds lotus leaves and blossoms and, at the time of a ritual circumambulation of the *sala* (temple), elderly men and women place rice balls, candles, and flowers in each basket. Tambiah, an anthropologist who has worked in this region, believes these poles are symbols for the Buddhist Wishing Tree, Kalpavriksha—the tree that gratifies the desires of man (1970:165). Thus in addition to sharing certain design parallels, the *tung* of the T'ai and the *tampan* of South Sumatra both have an important function involving sacred tree imagery.

Tung may serve other purposes. In an appeal for a prosperous life, a worshipper may present one as an offering to Buddha. They may be given as a memorial for a departed soul or be raised in celebration of a new temple, a public secular structure, or a religious monument (Tiparat 1986:5). In Dai Buddhist temples, banners play a role in feasts-of-merit. Traditionally these celebrations were accompanied by an extraordinary expenditure of money and, upon completion, entitled the sponsor to a new title (T'ien 1949:46). A major requirement of the feast was the making of beautiful banners. There is no detailed information about the ceremonial context in which they functioned, but ultimately they were hung in the local Buddhist temple. Chiang reports that there was intense competition in the design and craftsmanship of the banners and that they often required three to five months to complete (1950:331).

All the textiles of the T'ai people being examined here have in common their ties to Buddhism, but none more so than the small Lao Neua textile with the diamond pattern (Fig. 7), and very probably the related shawls that carry the same diamond motif at one end (Figs. 4,6). These small squares with the diamond pattern, called *duang tda* ("third eye") were used for meditation by Buddhists (Cheesman 1982:132). Unfortunately, there is little information on their precise use. Shawls are worn by women, but among the Lao of northern Thailand what may have been a shawl, or the small square which people now associate with Buddhist meditation, was used by Buddhist monks. Writing from four years of experience as a missionary among the Lao there, Lillian Johnson Curtis describes the costume of local monks in the early part of the century:

> . . . a cloth called a "bowing cloth" is caught into the folds (of the monk's robe) for use. This is to protect the monks' faces when they bow to the earth before an idol. This cloth is oftentimes richly ornamented with figures of

sacred shrines or royal umbrellas . . . If this cloth is so embroidered one will be sure to observe it in passing a monk, for he keeps it carefully folded outwards (1903:215).

Curtis's description surely pertains to the function of one or both of the Lao textile forms illustrated here. Each of the T'ai textile forms—the pillows given to earn merit, the banners offered in supplication to the Buddha, and the meditation squares (or shawls)—has a function within the context of Buddhism. Could the *tampan* have operated within a similar context at one time? There is enough circumstantial evidence to suggest that this may have been the case.

Buddhism in Sumatra

If the *tampan* of Sumatra, in addition to sharing design, technical structure, and functional elements with the T'ai textiles, also shared an association with Buddhism, their antecedents would have had to reach back to the time when South Sumatra was home to the great Buddhist learning center at Srivijaya, which was in existence at the end of the first millennium.

For several years between A.D. 671 and 695, the pilgrim-scholar I-Ching lived at the Srivijayan capital (thought to have been in the vicinity of present-day Palembang). He reported that 1,000 Buddhist priests resided there. As the religion of ruling powers, Buddhism must also have been a presence in some form in the hinterland[7] as well, and in regions having a vassal relationship with Srivijaya, such as Palas Pasemah in the Kalianda region. While K.R. Hall has argued convincingly that Buddhism was grafted onto Sumatran traditional values and existing systems (1976:79-93), it probably introduced new concepts and practices. It is through the office of Buddhism, whether it employed existing weaving skills and traditions or introduced new forms, that the correspondence between the T'ai and Sumatran textile complexes can be reconciled.

If *tampan* are placed in an earlier Buddhist context it is probable that at least some were used as pillow covers just as the T'ai examples are today. We know that pillows are mentioned by I-Ching, who wrote that in the ten islands of the Southern Seas, as well as in the five divisions of India, they did not use wooden pillows, as they did in his native China. He describes a pillow cover as being silk or linen: "the color varies according to one's own liking. It is sewed in a square bag one cubit long and a half cubit wide or approximately 45 centimeters by 22 centimeters." He adds that it is stuffed with any suitable home products (1966:112). Though he does not indicate that pillows were gifts nor that they were of particular import, by singling them out for mention at all, he implies some special regard.

As recently as the beginning of this century particular pillows were important status markers in Sumatran coastal centers, where families displayed them on ritual occasions within a showcase created by a ceremonial bed (Fig. 22). These status pillows, at least the visible ends, seem to be embroidered with silk and gold yarns and are probably not created from locally woven cloth. Their importance for the present discussion resides not in the designs, which suggest recent Chinese sources, but in the mere existence of pillows as culturally and ritually important objects. Obdeyn, a Dutch official writing earlier in the century about the Indragiri region, reports that the right to display a particular number of these pillows on the ceremonial bed on great ritual occasions was a jealously guarded prerogative tied to family rank. He speaks of guests abruptly leaving a wedding because the host family had presumed to display more pillows than entitled by rank (1929:122-24). Photographs from the end of the nineteenth century leave little doubt that the use of ceremonial pillows was a cultural manifestation found along Sumatra's east and north coasts and even among the Abung of the south. Paired with this in certain areas was the custom of having the bride sit on layers of mats, the number being determined by the rank of her family (Gittinger 1979a: 30,36, figs. 6-7,12).

This claim to numbers of pillows and mats seems ridiculous to the extreme unless it can be seen in an earlier context in which pillows entered into gift exchange and their numbers reflected the exchange network to which a family laid claim, just as among the great Xishuangbanna families in recent times. This gift exchange could have existed outside the framework of Buddhism, and obviously continued to exist after Buddhist power waned, but given the close ties between the giving of pillows and Buddhist merit-making on the mainland, there is a good argument that the strange customs surrounding pillows in coastal Sumatra share their origins with the T'ai and Dai phenomena.

If some *tampan* were once pillows, and a part of the Sumatran custom that associated prestige with pillows, it would help to explain practices in more recent times. The gift of a mat and a *tampan*, once customary on the Krui coast, could be seen as representing a mat and pillow. The obligatory gift assemblage came from a broad range of people having relationships to the principal just as clearly as the number of pillows and mats once displayed with a bride on Sumatra's east coast and the pillow gifts of the Dai of Xishuangbanna. There is a slight skewing or altering of custom, but surely they share a common origin. This interpretation and the antiquity it suggests would explain why *tampan* were temporarily spread on pillows for use by certain South Sumatran families at marriages and funerals, as mentioned earlier. It might also indicate why certain families would consider it their prerogative to carry or display a pillow and *tampan* supported on a small ceremonial bench. In these instances the original format was being reconstructed.

When or why the *tampan* was divorced from its pillow format in the Lampong area of South Sumatra is not apparent. Possibly the great wealth engendered by the lucrative pepper trade inflated the number of these gifts to such an unwieldy extent that the small woven panels alone came to represent the whole. It is apparent, however, that pillows and very probably paired pillows and mats were symbols of prestige from Aceh in the north, along the east coast and throughout the south. Originally the number of these very probably signaled the relative allegiance structure a family could command. Eventually this meaning became obscured along the east and north coasts, when locally woven covers were replaced by imported textiles, leaving the pillow form itself as the carrier of prestige. In the Lampong, however, where weaving of cotton continued into the beginning of this century, the covers remained available and so retained the ceremonial function.

There is little evidence, except the writings of such early visitors to Sumatra as I-Ching, to suggest what textiles were being used in Sumatra a thousand years ago. Unfortunately it is often not clear whether the items he mentions were from India, or Sumatra, or common to both. Occasionally, however, when an article was unusual he would specify its source. This was true regarding a shouldercloth of the Sumatran Buddhist monks. He writes:

> The priests of the Southern Sea islands keep a cloth three or five feet long, doubled up like a napkin, and they use it for kneeling on when they perform a salutation. They carry it on the shoulder when walking. Whenever Indian Bhikshus come to the islands, they cannot but smile when they see this custom (1966:111).

Even though I-Ching does not describe this textile further, it is important to know that the shouldercloth was an element in Buddhist costume in Sumatra and to learn of its function, particularly in light of the textile described by missionary Curtis (mentioned above) which evidently had similar use in much more recent times—at the turn of the century—among some mainland T'ai Buddhist monks. The proposition that the T'ai shawls have an ancient origin in common with those described by I-Ching would explain why the designs on the shouldercloths strongly parallel those on the *tampan*. All arise from the same historical period and share a cultural origin.

The present essay has suggested that *tampan* had a function in the days when Buddhism was a dominant influence in Sumatra. A corollary would be that certain enigmatic designs or compositions had a source in that period and its iconography. One design lending itself especially to this interpretation appears on an unusually accomplished group of *tampan* that display peacocks either singly or in confronting pairs, in small boats (Gittinger 1972:239-44). The choice of this particular bird has little meaning within the Sumatran context as we know it; nor is it a symbol found in the other arts and crafts of the area. It may, however, have been significant in the Buddhist context as a reference to the "Peacock" sutra. This is one of the *Pancaraksa* "Quintuple Protection" sutras. It honors a powerful spiritual force represented as a peacock, and offers to practitioners many talismanic formulae for protection against dangers, including appeals to local spirits.

A Chinese work from the early twelfth century records an emissary from San-fo-ch'i (possibly Jambi, by then the center of Srivijaya) reciting the Peacock sutra in Canton at a public feast, according to Wolters (1983:52-53). Wolters adds that I-Ching, who worked in Srivijaya in the latter half of the seventh century, had translated the sutra into Chinese, and surmizes that the Chinese scholar brought it with him from India. He points out that such tantric teachings were already known in Srivijaya at the time (1983:52-53). He hastens to add that none of the evidence suggests that the Peacock sutra was localized in South Sumatra by the seventh century, but that "the practice of invoking magical sanctions recommended in the sutra would certainly have made sense to Malays at that time" (1983:54). By the early twelfth century, however, as the Chinese work suggests, the sutra had become important in the tantric Buddhism of southeastern Sumatra. Hence it would not be unexpected to find symbolic representations in weaving—particularly on textiles critical to life-crisis situations when dangers seemed more imminent—that represented this protection or even acted as mnemonic devices for the sutra.

An examination of visual sources paired with Buddhist texts known to have been important in early Southeast Asia may lead to an understanding of still other *tampan* compositions. This may eventually include texts like the Vessantara Jataka, so favored in Thailand. It does not mean, however, that all representations on the *tampan* have referents in Buddhism. After Buddhism waned, new influences must surely have contributed designs to the repertoire available to the *tampan* weaver. However, the perceived efficacy of the older patterns would have been a powerful incentive for their continued replication by successive generations of weavers. Thus patterns woven as recently as the end of the nineteenth century may derive from sources centuries old.

To suggest that a textile complex persisted in South Sumatra with only slight modification for over a millennium may at first strain credulity, especially for historians accustomed to reconstructing prehistoric custom on the basis of evidence in stone and metal. But the comparison with textile forms from the T'ai people strongly argues that this is so, and the resulting conclusions resolve many of the anomalous features associated with textile practices in South Sumatra. The small square, the *tampan*, persisted because, while it may have arisen in the service of Buddhism, it ultimately became a counter in the complex web of alliances and reciprocal relationships. In societies such as those in Southeast Asia, where prestige and power has traditionally been defined by the numbers of people whose allegiance could be claimed, markers in that earnest game could well persist. The hypothesis opens interesting avenues of investigation in the textile arts and should be addressed seriously.[8]

NOTES

1. Srivijaya was the kingdom, centered more or less at present-day Palembang, that controlled sea trade through much of Indonesia for some 500 years. It arose in the seventh century and became a great power in the eighth, finally declining at the beginning of the eleventh. Dvaravati was an ancient kingdom in the central part of what we consider Thailand. Boisselier (1970:61) discusses related features in architectural decoration.

2. These conclusions are based on evidence remaining in South Sumatra in 1970. No *tampan* seem to have been woven in the sixty to seventy years previous to this.

3. For details of these exchanges see Niessen (1985) and Adams (1969).

4. Dr. Leedom Lefferts, the collector, has generously shared his information about the banners and pillows of the Khorat Plateau with me. I am deeply appreciative of his assistance. I would also like to thank Ms. Mary Jane Leland, Los Angeles, for first drawing my attention to the T'ai banners a number of years ago and for allowing me to photograph pieces in her collection.

5. Material on *tung* was presented by Pisal Tiparat at a seminar on Lanna Thai Art, Chiengmai, February 1-5, 1986. A digest of that material appears in Tiparat (1986:5-6).

6. Chiang (1950:263). I have used the Human Relations Area File translation of the original text. Moerman (1966:143) speaks of the Lue, a Dai group in northern Thailand, making pillows and banners as offerings.

7. Hall (1976:64-65) discusses the relationship of Srivijaya and its hinterland.

8. After this article was submitted for publication, the author had the opportunity to work among the Dai in the Xishuangbanna area. The textiles recorded show even closer parallels in design and function to the *tampan* of Sumatra than the present essay suggests. This material will be published in the future. In addition, the recent publication by Songsak Prangwatthanakun and Patricia Cheesman, *Lan Na Textiles* (Center for the Promotion of Arts and Culture, Chiang Mai University, Chiang Mai, Thailand, 1987), illustrates Lue men from Thailand wearing shouldercloths used in temple rites. These northern Thai textiles share technique and design vocabulary with the textiles discussed in this article.

Glossary

abang, red

adat, custom, customary law

alas-alasan, a forest motif with mountains, trees, plants, and animals (*alas*=forest)

badan, "body" (of a cloth) or centerfield; a sarong is usually composed of two parts, the *badan* and the *kepala* (head)

bangkudu (also *mengkudu*, *wungkudu*), *Morinda citrifolia*, a small tree whose cortical layer of roots is used extensively throughout Indonesia in the creation of red dye

batik, a resist-dye process in which the resist, usually wax, is applied to the cloth surface; when dyed, patterns are reserved in the colors of the foundation. Sequences of waxing and dyeing result in multiple color patterns

cåkrå, Wheel of the Law

cap, metal stamp used to apply molten wax to the cloth surface in one type of batik; also used to signify a brand name

cap-capan, stamped batiks (resist applied by stamp rather than by hand)

ceplok (also *ceplokan*), a lattice or grid pattern associated with Javanese batik

couched, a method of embroidery in which a decorative element is laid on the surface of cloth and tied down with a series of small anchoring stitches.

dodot, Javanese ceremonial court wrapper, now considered the ideal wedding costume

Garuda, carrier of the god Vishnu, sunbird of Indian mythology, adapted into Javanese legend

Garuda jaksa, a particular Javanese characterization of the Garuda

gamelan, Javanese or Balinese orchestra

gringsing, the name of a scale-like batik background pattern; also the name of the famous double-ikat cloth of Bali

gunungan, a tree/mountain puppet device used in *wayang* performance

ikat, (from Indonesian) lit., "string" or "band," and in its verb form "to tie" or "to bind." A term applied to a resist-dye process in which patterns are created in the warp or weft by tying off small bundles of yarns with a dye resistant material. The resists are cut away and/or new ones added for each color. When all are removed the yarns are patterned, ready for weaving.

ireng, blue-black

isen (*isen-isen*), the fillings or the inner part of batik motifs

kain, cloth, usually a cut rectangular piece

kain panjang, lit., "long cloth," traditionally a rectangular batik worn wrapped as an ankle-length skirt

kebaya, typical Javanese woman's blouse

kalamkari, lit., "penwork," referring to cotton textiles from India that are mordant-drawn or stamped and dyed

kekayon, shadow puppet element representing the cosmic tree

kemben, breastcloth

kepala, lit., "head," the decorative panel of the batik skirtcloth usually characterized by *tumpal* motifs

kraton, palace

kris, (from Malay *keris*), traditional Malay or Indonesian dagger or short sword with ridged serpentine blade

kuning, yellow

laid-in, term usually associated with a supplementary weft to indicate it lies in the same shed as the ground-weave weft.

lar, batik motif based on wings: a single-wing motif (cf. *sawat*)

lawon, plain, natural-colored cotton cloth used for batik

lurik, traditional Javanese handwoven cotton fabric, usually striped or plaid

maa', a type of textile sacred to the Toraja

mastiek, a paste used as a resist material in the batik process utilized in the Netherlands

merok, ritual of thanksgiving celebrated among the Toraja of Sulawesi, allotted to Eastern sphere, involving sacrifice of water buffalo

någå, mythical serpent, snake, or dragon

nila or *nula*, (from Sanskrit) indigo

pagi-soré, lit., "morning-evening"; in reference to batik, a cloth having different designs on each half, which can be worn to display either field

patola, (English, from Gujarati: *patolu*, sing., *patola*, plu.) an Indian silk textile patterned by double ikat.

parang, short sword

parang rusak, "broken sword," classical diagonal batik design motif

pembatik, person who does the batik hand-waxing

pinggir (or *sikilan*), decorative border at extremities of cloth

prada, applied gold-leaf glue-work

pusaka, sacred heirlooms

putih, white

sawat, batik motif based on wings, but in contrast to *lar*, having two wings and a tail

sarita, long narrow sacred textile of Toraja, patterned by a resist process

sarong, (English, from Indonesian *sarung*), tubular skirtcloth characterized by design zones known as "head" (*kepala*) and "body" (*badan*)

semen, (from *semi*, to sprout) the name of a classical batik design characterized by tendrils and foliage

sikilan, see *pinggir*

sirat, a border design, associated most often with twined border

slendang (also *selendang*), shouldercloth; also used as an all-purpose carrying sling, for babies, marketwares, etcetera

soga, brown dye used on Javanese batik, derived from several natural elements containing tannin, such as *Pelthophorum ferrugineum*

songket, supplementary weft cloth, usually made in Sumatra, Sulawesi and characteristically made with silver and gold metallic threads

supplementary warp or weft, decorative technique in weaving in which a pattern yarn is added between two regular foundation yarns. Supplementary warp yarns are usually continuous, extending the length of the warp

tampan, a small, rectangular textile used in ritual and ceremony in south Sumatra

tapestry weave, a textile structure in which the warps are concealed by the wefts which are worked back and forth in defined blocks. The variously colored wefts may interlock where the blocks join, or not, leaving slits in the patterning

tapi (also *tapis*, *tapih*), a length of cloth to be used as a wrapper

tarum (also *taum, tom*), Javanese term for indigo plant used for dyeing, usually *Indigofera* or *Marsdenia tinctoria*

tegerang (also *tegrang*), *Cudranus javanensis*, a yellow dyewood

tom gresi (also *tom presi*), see *tarum*

tongkonan, ancestral house and ritual center of a Toraja lineage

tritik, a resist dye process in which patterns are stitched and tightly gathered in the cloth to prevent substantial penetration of dye

tulis, lit., "hand-written, hand-drawn," the name for a batik, used when the resist has been hand-drawn rather than stamped

tumpal, patterns of isoceles triangles repeated in a row, associated with head (*kepala*) of a sarong and occasionally with other *kain*

twill weave, a textile structure characterized by a diagonal alignment of floats

warp, the longitudinal yarn elements, extended lengthwise, in parallel order on a loom

warp-faced, a textile structure in which the warps hide the wefts completely, thus dominating the appearance of the textile

wayang, traditional Javanese or Balinese theater, including leather, wooden, or shadow puppets, people, etcetera

weft-twined, a textile structure in which two or more weft elements are used in tandem and turned to enclose successive warp elements

Bibliography

Abdurachman, Paramita
1977 "Introduction." *Batik Exhibition of Chinese Designs.* Museum Tekstil and Himpunan Wastraprema. Jakarta.
1982 *Cerbon.* Jakarta.
1983 "Spinning a tale of yarn." *Garuda Magazine,* 3 (3): 22-27.

Adams, Marie Jeanne
1965 *Life and Death On Sumba.* Exhibition catalogue. Museum voor Land- en Volkenkunde. Rotterdam.
1969 *System and Meaning in East Sumba Textile Design.* Yale University Press. New Haven.
1970 "Symbolic Scenes in Javanese Batik." *Textile Museum Journal,* 3 (1): 25-40.
1971 "Work Patterns and Symbolic Structures in a Village Culture, East Sumba, Indonesia." *Southeast Asia,* 1 (4): 321-34.
1974 "Structural Aspects of a Village Art." *American Anthropologist,* 75 (1): 265-79.
1980 "Structural Aspects of East Sumbanese Art." In *The Flow of Life: Essays on Eastern Indonesia,* edited by J.J. Fox. Harvard University Press. Cambridge.
1983 "Indonesian Textiles: Silent Symbols and the Structure of Costume in Indonesia." Discussion Paper, Wenner-Green Foundation for Anthropological Research, an International Symposium.

Adriani, N. and Albert C. Kruyt
1912/14 *De Bare'e-sprekende Toradaja's van Midden Celebes.* Verhandelingen der Koninklijke Nederlandse Akademie van Wetenschappen. 3 volumes & Illustration volume. Batavia. [Republished in 1950-51 as *De Bare'e sprekende Torajas van Midden-Celebes.* Noord-Hollandsche Uitgeversmij. Amsterdam.]

Andaya, Leonard
1981 *The Heritage of Arung Palakka, A History of South Sulawesi (Celebes) in the Seventeenth Century.* Verhandelingen van het Koninklijk Instituut voor Taal-, Land- en Volkenkunde, no. 91. Martinus Nijhoff. The Hague.

Anderson, B.R.O'G.
1965 *Mythology and the Tolerance of the Javanese.* Modern Indonesia Project. Southeast Asia Program. Cornell University. Ithaca.

Anonymous
1895 "Tanzende Frauen auf Nias." In *Das Missionsblatt,* p. 28. Barmen.
1947 "De ethnografische verzameling." *Jaarboek van het Bataviaasch Genootschap,* 9:259.

Arndt, Paul
1933 *Li'onesisch-Deutsches Wörterbuch.* Arnoldus-Drukkerij. Ende, Flores.

Balai Penilitian Batik den Keradjinan
n.d. *Motief Batik.* Balai Penilitian Batik dan Keradjinan (Batik and Handicraft Research Center). Yogyakarta.

Baarda, M.J. van
1895 *Woordenlijst Galèlareesch-Hollandsch.* Martinus Nijhoff. The Hague.

Barbier, J.P.
1978 *Symbolique et motifs du Sud de Nias.* Publications de la Collection Barbier-Müller. Geneva.

Barnes, Robert H.
1974 *Kédang: A Study of the Collective Thought of an Eastern Indonesian People.* Clarendon Press. Oxford.
1977 "Mata in Austronesia." *Oceania,* 47:300-319.
1982 "Number and Number Use in Kédang, Indonesia." *Man,* 17:1-22.
1987 "Educated Fisherman: Social Consequences of Development in an Indonesian Whaling Community." *Bulletin de l'Ecole Française de l'Extrême Orient.*

Barnes, Ruth
1984 "The Ikat Textiles of Lamalera, Lembata within the Context of Eastern Indonesia Fabric Traditions." D.Phil. dissertation, Oxford.
1986 "Cloth in Lamelera, Indonesia, and the Adoption of Patola Patterns." In *Cloth and the Organization of Human Experience,* edited by J. Schneider and A.S. Weiner. Unpublished version.
1987 "Weaving and Non-Weaving among the Lamaholot." *Indonesia Circle,* 42:16-31.
1989 *The Ikat Textiles of Lamalera. A Study of an Eastern Indonesian Weaving Tradition.* E.J. Brill. Leiden.
In Press a "Patola in Southern Lembata." In *Proceedings of the Second Symposium on Indonesian Textiles, Köln 1985,* edited by Dr. Karin von Welck. Rautenstrauch-Joest-Museum. Cologne.

Barrett, D.
1953 "Sir Thomas Stamford Raffles." *British Museum Quarterly,*18:166-69. [Reprinted in *The Raffles Gamelan: A Historical Note,* edited by William Fagg, The British Museum, London 1970.]

Barrett Jones, Antoinette M.
1984 *Early Tenth Century Java From the Inscriptions. A study of economic, social and administrative conditions in the first quarter of the century.* Verhandelingen van het Koninklijk Instituut voor Taal-, Land- en Volkenkunde, 107. Foris. Dordrecht, Holland / Cinnamonson, U.S.A.

Basilio de Sá, Artur (editor)
1956 "Historia de Maluco no Tempo de Gonçalo

Pereira Marramague e Sancho de Vasconcellos...
1636. Fundação das Primeiras Cristanades nas
Ilhas de Solor e Timor... 1624-25."
*Documentaçao para a História das Missães do
Pradroada Português do Oriente, Insulíndia*, vol. 4.
Agencia Geral do Ultramar. Lisbon.

Bastin, John Sturgis and Pauline Rohatgi
1979 *Prints of S.E. Asia in the India Office Library: The East India Company in Malaysia and Indonesia 1786-1824*. H.M.S.O. London.

Beckering, J.D.H.
1911 "Beschrijving der eilanden Adonara en Lomblen, behoorende tot de Solor-groep." *Tijdschrift van het Koninklijk Nederlandsch Aardrijkskundig Genootschap*, 28 (2nd series): 167-202.

Bernet Kempers, August Johan
n.d. *Borobudur, mysteriegebeuren in steen. Verval en Restauratie. Oudjavaans volksleven*. Servire, Artibus. The Hague.

Boeren, A.
In Press "Warshields From South Irian Jaya, Style Differences and Principles of Ornamentation." In *Asmat Biwiptsj*, edited by P. Hanse. Heidelberg.

Boisselier, Jean
1970 "Récentes recherches à Nakhon Pathom." *Journal of the Siam Society*, 58 (2): 55-65.

Bolland, Rita
1956 "Weaving a Sumba Women's Skirt." In *Lamak and Malat in Bali and a Sumba Loom*, edited by T.P. Galestin, L. Langewis, and Rita Bolland. Royal Tropical Institute. Amsterdam.
1971 "A Comparison between the Looms Used in Bali and Lombok for Weaving Sacred Cloth." *Tropical Man*, 4:171-82.

Bondan, Molly
1982 *Candi in Central Java Indonesia*. Provincial Government of Central Java. Semarang.

Bondan, Molly, Teguh Djamal, Haryono Guritno & Pandam Guritno
1984 *Lordly Shades: Wayang Purwa Indonesia*. Jayakarta Agung. Jakarta.

Boow, Justine
1986 *Mbatik Manah. Symbols and Status in Central Javanese Batik Making*. Unpublished Ph.D. dissertation, University of Western Australia. Perth.

Bosch, Frederik David Kan
1948 *De Gouden Kiem*. Elsevier. Amsterdam/Brussels.

Brittain, J.
1979 *Needlecraft. Step-by step Encyclopaedia of --*. Good Housekeeping. Ebury Press. London.

Bruch, Alfred
1912 *Der Batak wie er leist und lebt, von seinem Geburt bis zum seinem Tod*. Bremen.

Bühler, Alfred
1941 "Turkey Red Dyeing in South and Southeast Asia." *Ciba Review*, 39:1423-26.
1943 "Materialien zur Kenntnis der Ikattechnik." *Internationales Archiv für Ethnographie*, 43: Supplement.
1959 "Patola Influences in Southeast Asia." *Journal of Indian Textile History*, 4:4-46.

Bühler, Alfred, and Eberhard Fischer
1979 *The Patola of Gujarat, Double Ikat in India*. 2 volumes. Krebs. Basel.

Bühler, Alfred, Urs Ramseyer, and Nicole Ramseyer-Gygi
1975-76 *Patola und Geringsing. Zeremonialtücher aus Indien und Indonesien. Führer durch das Museum für Völkerkunde und Schweizerisches Museum für Volkskunde Basel*. Museum für Völkerkunde und Schweizerisches Museum für Volkskunde. Basel.

Burnham, Dorothy K.
1980 *Warp and Weft. A Textile Terminology*. Royal Ontario Museum. Toronto.

Burton and Ward
1827 "Report of a Journey into the Batak Country in the Interior of Sumatra in the Year 1824." *Transactions of the Royal Asiatic Society*, 1:485-542. (London).

Campen, C.F.H.
1884 "Eenige mededeelingen over de Alfoeren van Hale-ma-hèra." *Bijdragen tot de Taal-, Land- en Volkenkunde*, 32 (2): 162-97; 32 (3): 511-16.

Cheesman, Patricia
1982 "The antique weavings of the Lao Neua." *Arts of Asia*, 12 (4): 120-25.

Chiang, Ying-liang
1950 *Pai-i te Sheng-huo Wen-hua* (The Life and Culture of the Pai-i). Human Relations Area File unpublished manuscript. Chunghua Book Co. Shanghai.

Chijs, J.A. van der
1885 *Catalogus der Ethnologische Verzameling van het Bataviaasch Genootschap van Kunsten en Wetenschappen*. Albrecht & Co. Batavia/Martinus Nijhoff. The Hague.

Clercq, F.S.A. de
1890 *Bijdragen tot de kennis der Residentie Ternate*. E.J. Brill. Leiden.

Collingwood, Peter
1968   *The Techniques of Rug Weaving.* Faber and Faber. London.

Cornets de Groot, A.D.
1822   "Statistiek van Java." *Residentie Grissee.* Manuscript H 379. Koninklijk Instituut voor Taal-, Land- en Volkenkunde. Leiden.

Covarrubias, Miguel
1937 [1965]   *Island of Bali.* London/ Toronto/ Melbourne/ Sydney. [A.A. Knopf. New York.]

Crouch, Harold
1978   *The Army and Politics in Indonesia.* Cornell University Press. Ithaca.

Cuisinier, J.
n.d.   *Fieldnotes: fiche textile 55.68.58.* Unpublished manuscript, Musée de l'Homme. Paris.

Curtis, Lillian Johnson
1903   *The Laos of North Siam.* The Westminster Press. Philadelphia.

Damsté, H.T.
1926   "Balische kleedjes en doeken, verband houdende met eeredienst en doodenzorg." In *Gedenkschrift uitgegeven ter gelegenheid van het 75-jarig bestaan van het Koninklijk Instituut voor de Taal-, Land- en Volkenkunde van Nederlansch-Indië te 's Gravenhage,* pp. 254-64. The Hague.

Daniell, Thomas, R.A
1795   *Oriental Scenery.* Part 1 of 6. London.

Daniell, Thomas, R.A., and William Daniell, A.R.A.
1795-1808   *Oriental Scenery.* Parts 2-6. London.
1810   *A Picturesque Voyage to India by the Way of China.* London.

Daubanton, J.D.
1922   *Beknopte beschrijving van de Batikindustrie op Java.* Rotterdam.

De Graaf, H.J.
1949   *Geschiedenis van Indonesië.* Van Hoeve. The Hague/ Bandung.

De Zoete, Beryl, and Walter Spies
1938   *Dance and Drama in Bali.* Faber and Faber. London.

Dempwolff, Otto
1938   *Austronesisches Wörterverzeichnis. Vergleichende Lautlehre des Austronesischen Wortschatzes,* vol. 3. Beiheft zur Zeitschrift für Eingeborenen-Sprachen, no. 19. Reimer. Berlin.

Departemen Pendidikan dan Kebudayaan
1977-78   *Adat dan Upacara Perkawinan Daerah Istimewa Yogyakarta* (*Yogyakarta Wedding Ceremony and Traditions*). Pusat Penelitian, Proyek Penelitian dan Pencatatan Kebudayaan Daerah. Departemen Pendidikan dan Kebudayaan, Republik Indonesia (Department of Education and Culture, Republic of Indonesia.) Jakarta.

Djoemena, Nian S.
1986   *Ungkapan Sehelai Batik: Its Mystery and Meaning.* (The Significance of a Piece of Batik: Its Mystery and Meaning). Penerbit Djambatan. Jakarta.

Does, A.M.D. de
1893   "Toestand der Nijverheid in de afdeling Bandjarnegara." *Tijdschrift voor Indische Taal-, Land- en Volkenkunde,* 36:1-112.

Drabbe, P.
1925   "Dood en begrafenis en spiritisme op Tanimbar." *Tijdschrift van het Koninklijk Nederlandsch Aardrijkskundig Genootschap,* 42:31-63.
1932   *Woordenboek der Fordaatsche taal.* Verhandelingen van het Koninklijk Bataviaasch Genootschap van Kunsten en Wetenschappen, 71 (2): 1-118.
1940   "Het leven van den Tanémbarees: ethnografische studië over het Tanémbareesche volk." *Internationales Archiv für Ethnographie,* 38: Supplement.

Eliade, Mircea
1975   *Myth and Reality.* Harper and Rowe. New York.

Ellen, G.J.
1942   "Adat en bijgeloof bij de bevolking der Westkust op het Noordelijk schiereiland van Halmahera." *Mededeelingen vanwege het Nederlandsch Zendeling-genootschap,* 85 (1): 53-75. [Oegstgeest.]

Elliot, I. McC.
1984   *Batik: Fabled Cloth of Java.* Clarkson N. Potter. New York.

Emery, Irene
1966   *The Primary Structures of Fabrics.* The Textile Museum. Washington, D.C.

Erp, Th. van
1923   *Voorstellingen van vaartuigen op de reliëfs van den Boroboedoer.* Monographieën over kunst en cultuur, no. 1. Adi Poestaka. The Hague. [Reprinted from *Nederlandsch-Indië Oud en Nieuw,* 8 (8).]

Fabricius, J.
1960[1959]   *De heilige paarden.* In memory of D.K. Wielenga. H.P. Leopolds. The Hague.

Fallick, R.
1983 "Tradition, Innovation and Struggle: Gerwani 1950-1965." Paper presented to the 2nd *Women in Asia Workshop*, Monash University (July). Melbourne.

Feith, Herbert
1962 *The Decline of Constitutional Democracy in Indonesia*. Cornell University Press. Ithaca.

Feldman, Jerome A.
1977 *The Architecture of Nias, Indonesia with Special Reference to Bawömataluo Village*. Ph.D. dissertation, Columbia University. New York.
1979 "The House as World in Bawömataluo, South Nias." In *Art, Ritual and Society in Indonesia*, edited by J. Becker and E. Bruner. International Studies: Southeast Asia Series, 53. Ohio University Center for International Studies. Athens, Ohio.
1983 "The High Tiger in South Nias, Indonesia." *Empirical Studies in the Arts*, 1 (2):143-56.
1985 "Ancestral Manifestations in the Art of Nias Island." In *The Eloquent Dead: Ancestors in the Sculpture of Indonesia and Southeast Asia*, edited by J. Feldman, pp. 45-78. Museum of Cultural History. Los Angeles.

Fischer, H.W.
1905 "Een houten klopper om boombast te bewerken van het eiland Nias." *Internationales Archiv für Ethnographie*, 17:222.
1908 "Mitteilungen über die Nias-Sammlung des Ethnographischen Reichsmuseums zu Leiden." *Internationales Archiv für Ethnographie*, 18:85-94.
1909 "Nias." In *Catalogus van 's Rijks Ethnografisch Museum*, 4:1-81, 199-222.
1911-12 "Weberei auf Nias." *Internationales Archiv für Ethnographie*, 20:250-54.

Fischer, J.
1979 *Threads of Tradition: Textiles of Indonesia and Sarawak*. University of California Press. Berkeley.

Fontein, J., R. Soekmono, and Satywati Suleiman
1971 *Kesenian Indonesia Purba: Zaman-zaman Djawa Tengah dan Djawa Timur*. The Asia Society. New York.

Forge, Anthony
In Press "Raffles and Daniell: The Illustrations for the History of Java."

Fortgens, J.
1913 "Het Saoe'sche doodenoffer en de maskerade." *Bijdragen tot de Taal-, Land- en Volkenkunde van Nederlandsch-Indië*, 68:508-20.

Foulcher, Keith
1986 *Social Commitment in Literature and the Arts: The Indonesian "Institute of People's Culture" 1950-1965*. Centre of Southeast Asian Studies, Monash University. Melbourne.
In Press "Category and Complement: Binary Ideologies and the Organization of Dualism in Eastern Indonesia." In *The Attraction of Opposites: Thought and Society in a Dualistic Mode*, edited by D. Maybury-Lewis and U. Almagor. Ann Arbor.

Fox, James J. (editor)
1980 *The Flow of Life: Essays on Eastern Indonesia*. Harvard University Press. Cambridge.

Geertz, Clifford
1960 [1969] *The Religion of Java*. The Free Press. Glencoe, Illinois/New York.
1968 *Islam Observed*. Yale University Press. New Haven.

Geirnaert [-Martin], Danielle C.
1983 "Ask Lurik Why Batik: A Structural Analysis of Textiles and Classifications (Central Java)." In *The Future of Structuralism—Papers of IUAES Intercongress, Amsterdam 1981*, edited by J.G. Oosten and A. de Ruijter. Göttingen. Amsterdam.
1986 Review of *Cloth and the Organization of Experience*, edited by Schneider and Weiner. In *Current Anthropology*, 27 (2).
1987 "Hunt Wild Pig and Grow Rice: On food exchanges and values in Laboya, West Sumba." In *The Leiden Tradition in Structural Anthropology. Essays in honor of P.E. de Josselin de Jong*, edited by R. de Ridder and J.A.J. Karremans. E.J. Brill. Leiden.
In Press a "Kijora: A Thing for Lost Souls." In *The Language of Things Symposium, 1984*. Bijdragen tot de Taal-, Land- en Volkenkunde. Koninklijk Instituut voor Taal-, Land- en Volkenkunde. Leiden.
In Press b "The Snake's Skin: Traditional Ikat in Kodi." In *Proceedings of the Second Symposium on Indonesian Textiles, Köln 1985*, edited by Dr. Karin von Welck. Rautenstrauch-Joest-Museum. Cologne.
Forthcoming *The Woven Land of Laboya: Socio-cosmological Values in West Sumba (Eastern Indonesia)*. Ph.D. dissertation. Leiden.

Geirnaert, D. C., and R. Heringa
1989 *The A.E.D.T.A. Batik Collection*. Association pour l'Etude et la Documentation des Textiles d'Asie. Paris.

Gerbrands, A.A.
1983 "Spiegelen, uitklappen en omkeren: een aspect van ethno-communicatie." *Liber Memorialis Prof. dr. P.J. Vandenhoute*. Leiden.

Gertis, A.
1925 "Enkele aanteekeningen omtrent Noesa Penida." *Jaarverslag van de Topographische Dienst van Nederlandsch-Indië over 1924*, 20: 101-10.

Gittinger, Mattiebelle [Stimson]
1972 *A Study of the Ship Cloths of South Sumatra: Their Design and Usage*." Ph.D. dissertation, Columbia University. University Microfilms, Ann Arbor.
1974 "Sumatran ship cloths as an expression of pan-Indonesian concepts." *Sumatran Research Bulletin*, 4 (1): 3-18.
1975 "Selected Batak Textiles: Techniques and Function." *Textiles Museum Journal* 4 (2): 13-25.
1976 "The ship textiles of South Sumatra: functions and design system." *Bijdragen tot de Taal-, Land- en Volkenkunde*,132 (2&3): 207-27.
1979a *Splendid Symbols: Textiles and Tradition in Indonesia*. The Textile Museum. Washington, D.C.
1979b "Conversations with a Batik Master." *Textile Museum Journal*, 18:25-32.
1982 *Master Dyers to the World*. The Textile Museum. Washington, D.C.

Gittinger, Mattiebelle (editor)
1980 *Indonesian Textiles. Irene Emery Roundtable on Museum Textiles, 1979 Proceedings*. The Textile Museum. Washington, D.C.

Gorkom, K.W. van
1881 *Oost-Indische cultures met betrekking tot handel en nijverheid*. 2 volumes. Amsterdam.

Graburn, N.H.H. (editor)
1976 *Ethnic and Tourist Arts*. University of California Press. Berkeley.

Gresshoff, M.
1894 *Nuttige Indische planten*. Amsterdam.

Haake, A.
1984 *Javanische Batik*. Schaper. Hannover.

Hall, Kenneth R.
1976 "State and Statecraft in Early Srivijaya." In *Explorations in Early Southeast Asian History: The Origins of Southeast Asian Statecraft*, edited by Kenneth R. Hall and John K. Whitmore. Center for South and Southeast Asian Studies, The University of Michigan. Ann Arbor.

Hämmerle, J.M.
1982 *Nias "Land der Menschen" Ein Beitrag aus Zentral-Nias*. Missionsprokur der Kapuziner. Munich.
1984 "Die Megalithkultur im Susua Gomo-Gebiet, Nias." *Anthropos*, 79:587-625.
1986 *Famato Harimao*. Abidin. Medan.

Hardjonagoro, K.R.T.
1980 "The Place of Batik in the History and Philosophy of Javanese Textiles: A Personal View." In *Indonesian Textiles. Irene Emery Roundtable on Museum Textiles, 1979 Proceedings*, edited by M. Gittinger. The Textile Museum. Washington, D.C.

Heine-Geldern, R.
1925 "Eine Szene aus dem Sutasoma-Jataka auf Hinterindischen und Indonesischen Schwertgriffen." *Ipek, Jahrbuch für Prähistorische und Ethnographische Kunst,* 1:198-238.
1937 "Sculptured Sword-Hilts Showing Scenes from Buddhist Legends." *Indian Society of Oriental Art Journal* (Jun-Dec):147-58.

Heringa, Rens
1985 "Kain Tuban. Een oude Javaanse indigotraditie." In *Indigo: Leven in een kleur*, edited by Loan Oei. Volume in honor of Rita Bolland. Amsterdam.
1988 "Textiel en wereldbeeld in Tuban. In *Indonesia, Apa kabar*, edited by Vincent Dekker, Nico de Jonge, and Reimar Schefold. Edu'Actief. Meppel. [Also published in English as "Textiles and Worldview in Tuban," in *Indonesia in Perspective*].
In Press a "Kapas Lawa. Brown Cotton." In *Proceedings of the Second Symposium on Indonesian Textiles*, edited by Dr. Karin von Welck. Rautenstrauch-Joest-Museum. Cologne.
In Press b "Textiles and the Social Fabric on Northeast Coastal Java." In *Proceedings of the Second Symposium on Indonesian Textiles, Köln 1985*, edited by Dr. Karin von Welck. Rautenstrauch-Joest-Museum. Cologne.

Heyne, K.
1927 *De nuttige planten van Nederlandsch-Indië*. 3 volumes. The Hague.

Hien, H.A. van
1912-13 *De Javaansche geestenwereld*. 2 volumes. Fifth printing. Bandung. Originally published in 1906.

Hindley, Donald
1966 *The Communist Party of Indonesia, 1951-1963*. University of California Press. Berkeley.

Holmgren, Robert J. and Anita E. Spertus.
1980 "Tampan Pasisir: Pictorial Documents of an Ancient Indonesian Coastal Culture." In *Indonesian Textiles. Irene Emery Roundtable on Museum Textiles, 1979 Proceedings*, edited by M. Gittinger. The Textile Museum. Washington, D.C.

Holt, Claire
1936 "Bandit Island: A Short Exploration Trip to Nusa Penida." *Djawa*, 16:67-84.
1939 "Costume de guerrier." In *Théâtre et danses aux Indes néerlandaises, XIIe Exposition des archives internationales de la danse*, pp. 77-78. G.P. Maisonneuve. Paris.

1967 *Art in Indonesia: Continuities and Change.*
    Cornell University Press. Ithaca.

Hooykaas, Christaan
 1974 *Cosmogony and Creation in Balinese Tradition.*
    The Hague.
 1978 "Patola and Gringsing: An Additional Note."
    Bijdragen tot de Taal-, Land- en Volkenkunde,
    134 (2-3): 356-59.

Hooykaas-van Leeuwen Boomkamp, Jacoba
 1955 "A Journey into the Realm of Death." *Bijdragen tot*
    de Taal-, Land- en Volkenkunde, 111 (3): 236-73.

Hueting, A.
 1922 "De Tobeloreezen in hun denken en doen."
    Bijdragen tot de Taal-, Land- en Volkenkunde,
    78:137-342.

I-Ching (I-Tsing)
 1966[1896] *A Record of the Buddhist Religion as Practised in*
    India and the Malay Archipelago (A.D. 671-695),
    translated by J. Takakusa. Munshiram Manoharlal.
    Delhi.

Instituut voor Onderwÿs...Delft
 1888 *Catalogus van de Ethnologische Verzameling van*
    het Instituut voor Onderwÿs in de Taal-, Land- en
    Volkenkunde van Nederlandsch Indië te Delft.
    Delft.

Jacobs, Hubert (editor)
 1974 "Fr. Baltasar Dias S.J. to Fr. Provincial António de
    Quadros S.J., Goa—Malacca, December 3, 1559."
    In *Documenta Malucensia,* vol. 1 (1542-77), pp.
    299-329. Monumenta Historica Societas Iesu.
    Rome.

Jager Gerlings, J.H.
 1952 *Sprekende weefsels.* Koninklijk Instituut voor de
    Tropen. Amsterdam.

Jansz, P.
 1906 *Practisch Javaansch-Nederlandsch woordenboek.*
    The Hague. Second printing.

Jasper, J.E., and Mas Pirngadie
 1912 *De weefkunst.* Vol. 2 of *De inlandsche*
    kunstnijverheid in Nederlandsch Indië. Mouton
    and Co. The Hague.
 1916 *De batikkunst.* Vol. 3 of *De inlandsche*
    kunstnijverheid in Nederlandsch Indië. Mouton
    and Co. The Hague.
 1927 *De guld- en zilversmeedkunst.* Vol. 4 *of De*
    inlandsche kunstnijverheid in Nederlandsch Indië.
    Mouton and Co. The Hague.

Joseph, L.C.
 1982 *Mengenal Tenun Tradisional Daerah Maluku.*
    P.N.R.I. Ambon.

Josselin de Jong, J.P.B. de
 1977 [1983] "The Malay Archipelago as a Field of Ethnological
    Study." [Original version 1935.] In *Structural*
    Anthropology in the Netherlands, edited by P.E. de
    Josselin de Jong. Koninklijk Instituut voor Taal-,
    Land- en Volkenkunde, translation series no 17.
    Martinus Nijhoff. The Hague.

Kadang, K.
 1960 *Ukiran Rumah Toradja.* Balai Pustaka. Jakarta.

Kapita, Oe H.
 1982 *Sumba/Kambera—Indonesia Dictionary.* Flores,
    Indonesia.

Kartiwa, S.
 1982 *Songket Indonesia.* Museum Nasional. Jakarta.
 1983 *Kain Tenun Donggala.* Donggala Press. Palu,
    Sulawesi Tengah.

Kats, J.
 1923 *Wajang Poerwa.* Vol. 1 of *Het Javaansche*
    tooneel. Commissie voor de Volkslectuur.
    Weltevreden.

Kaudern, W.
 1940 *The Noble Families of Maradika of Koelawi,*
    Central Celebes. Etnologiska Studier, vol. 11.
    Göteborg.

Keraf, Gregorius
 1977 "Status Bahasa-Bahasa di Flores Timur." *Dian,* 4
    (7-9, 13). [Ende, Flores.]
 1978 *Morfologi Dialek Lamalera.* Percetakan Offset
    Arnoldus. Ende, Flores.
 1983 "Economy and Social Change in Lamalera,
    Indonesia." Unpublished SSRC Project Report.

Kersten, J.
 1984 *Bahasa Bali.* Penerbit Nusa Indah. Ende, Flores.

Keuning, J.
 1938/49 *De tweede schipvaart.* 7 volumes. The Hague.

Khan Majlis, Brigitte
 1984 *Indonesische Textilien. Wege zu Göttern und*
    Ahnen. Bestandskatalog der Museen in
    Nordrhein-Westfalen. Rautenstrauch-Joest-
    Museum. Cologne.

Kiliaan, H.N.
 1892 "Inlandsche kunstnijverheid in de afdeling
    Patjitan." In *Tijdschrift van Nijverheid en*
    Landbouw in Nederlandsch Indië, 44: 333-62.

Koloniaal Verslag
 1892 "Bijlage C." In *Koloniaal Verslag.* ("Appendix C."
    In *Colonial Report.*)

Kooijman, S.
 1963 *Ornamented Bark-cloth in Indonesia.*

Mededelingen van het Rijksmuseum voor Volkenkunde, no.16. E.J. Brill. Leiden.

Korn, V.E.
1944 "Noesa Penida." *Cultureel Indië,* 6:97-109.

Kreemer, J.
1956 *De Karbouw, zijn betekenis voor de volken van de Indonesische Archipel.* Van Hoeve. The Hague.

Kroef, Justus M. van der
1965 *The Communist Party of Indonesia: Its History, Program and Tactics.* University of British Columbia. Vancouver.

Kruisheer, A.
1932 "Uit de pioniertijd. De vestiging van het Nederlandsche bestuur in Zuid Nias." *Orgaan der Nederlandsche Indische Officiersvereeniging*: 261-66,319-25,363-69,411-17,455-561,515-23.

Kruyt, Albertus Christiaan
1938 *De West-Toradjas op Midden-Celebes.* Verhandelingen der Koninklijke Nederlandsche Akademie van Wetenschappen, Afdeeling Letterkunde, nieuwe reeks, 40. Noord-Hollandsche Uitgeversmij. Amsterdam.

Kruyt, J.
1922 "Het weven der Toradja's." *Bijdragen tot de Taal-, Land- en Volkenkunde van Nederlandsche-Indië,* 78:403-25.

Kükenthal, W.
1896 *Forschungsreise in den Molukken und in Borneo.* Diesterweg. Frankfurt am Main.

Kuswadji, R.M. Kawindrasusanta
1984a "Motif Parang Rusak Justru Mengandung Perlambang Luhur" (The Parang Rusak Motif Actually Contains Symbols of an Illustrious Nature). *Buana Minggu,* 27 May.
1984b "Dalil Bobot-Bibit-Bebet Masih Perlu Diperhatikan" (The Bobot-Bibit-Bebet Theme Must Still Be Heeded). *Buana Minggu,* 12 August.

Laiya, B.
1975 "Sendi-sendi Masyarakat Nias" (The Basis of Nias Society). *Peninjau,* 2 (1): 3-19.

Langewis, Laurens, and Fritz A. Wagner
1964 *Decorative Art in Indonesian Textiles.* Van der Peet. Amsterdam.

Lapicque, Louis
[1895] "Voyage du yacht 'La Sémiramis' en 1892-1893." Unpublished ms., Musée de l'Homme. Paris.

Le Roux, C.C.F.M.
1930 "De rijksvlaggen van Bone." *Tijdschrift Bataviaasch Genootschap van Kunsten en Wetenschappen,* 70:205-67.

Lefferts, H. Leedom
1980 "A Collection of Northeast Thai Textiles." Unpublished Report submitted to the Department of Anthropology, The Smithsonian Institution. Washington, D.C.

Legge, J.D.
1972 *Sukarno: A Political Biography.* Allen Lane. Harmondsworth, U.K.

Lett, A.
1901 *Im Dienst des Evangeliums auf der Westküste von Nias.* 4 Parts. Verlag des Missionhauses. Barmen.

Leur, J.C. van
1960 *Indonesian Trade and Society.* Second edition. Sumur Bandung. Bandung.

Levi-Strauss, Claude
1974[1958] *Anthropologie Structurale.* Plon. Paris.
1979 *La Voie des Masques.* Plon. Paris.

Loebèr, J.A. Jr.
1914 *Textiele versieringen in Nederlandsch Indië.* Koloniaal Instituut. Amsterdam.
1921/1922 "Antikwiteiten op Java." *Nederlandsch Indië Oud & Nieuw,* 6:261-74.

Lorm, A.J.
1939 "Kantteekening bij eenige mesheften uit Nias." *Cultureel Indië,* 1:151.
1941a "Zwaardgrepen en mesheften van Nias." *Cultureel Indië,* 3:1-6.
1941b "Een merkwaardigheid van zwaardamuletten van Zuid-Nias." *Cultureel Indië,* 3:145-49.

Louwerse, P.
1894 *Geïllustreerde vaderlandsche geschiedenis.* Holkema en Warendorf. Amsterdam.

Marschall, W.
1976 *Der Berg des Herrn der Erde.* Deutscher Taschenbuch Verlag. Munich.

Maxwell, John R. and Robyn J. Maxwell
1976 *Textiles in Indonesia.* National Gallery of Victoria. Melbourne.

Maxwell, Robyn J.
1980 "Textile and Ethnic Configuration in Flores and the Solor Archipelago." In *Indonesian Textiles. Irene Emery Roundtable on Museum Textiles, 1979 Proceedings,* edited by M. Gittinger. The Textile Museum. Washington, D.C.
1981 "Textiles and Tusks: Some Observations on the Social Dimensions of Weaving in East Flores." In *Five Essays on the Indonesian Arts (Music, Theatre, Textiles, Painting and Literature),* edited by M.J. Kartomi, pp. 43-62. Monash University. Melbourne.

Mayer, L.Th.
1897　　Een blik in het Javaansche volksleven. 2 volumes. E.J. Brill. Leiden.

McCabe Elliott, I.
1984　　Batik, Fabled Cloth of Java. C.N. Potter. New York.

McKinnon, Susan
1983　　Hierarchy, Alliance, and Exchange in the Tanimbar Islands. Ph.D. dissertation. The University of Chicago, Illinois.

Meilink-Roelofsz, M.A.P.
1962　　Asian Trade and European Influence in the Indonesian Archipelago between 1500 and about 1630. Martinus Nijhoff. The Hague.

Merrill, E.D.
1917　　An Interpretation of Rumphius's Herbarium Amboinense. Manila.

Mills, R.F.
1975　　"The Reconstruction of Proto-South-Sulawesi." Archipel, 10:205-25.

Modelski, George (editor)
1963　　The New Emerging Forces. Canberra.

Modigliani, Elio
1889　　"Les boucliers des Nias." Internationales Archiv für Ethnographie, 2:214-17.
1890　　Un viaggio à Nias. Treves. Milan.
1892　　Fra i Batachi indipendenti. Società Geografica Italiana. Rome.

Moerman, Michael
1966　　"Ban Ping's Temple: The Center of a 'Loosely Structured' Society." In Anthropological Studies in Theravada Buddhism, edited by Manning Nash. Yale University Southeast Asian Studies Cultural Report Series, 13. New Haven.

Møller, A.
1934　　"Beitrag zur Beleuchtung des Religiösen Lebens der Niasser." Internationales Archiv für Ethnographie, 32:121-66.

Museum Tekstil
1980　　Puspita Warni: Pameran Kain Batik Koleksi Pribadi Gusti Kanjeng Putri Mangkunegoro VIII (1923-1978). Himpunan Pencinta Kain Tenun dan Batik Wastraprema/ Museum Tekstil. Jakarta.

Museum voor Land- en Volkenkunde, Rotterdam
1922/33　　Verslag omtrent den toestand van het Museum voor Land- en Volkenkunde en Maritiem Museum 'Prins Hendrik'. Rotterdam.

Musschenbroek, S.C.J.W. van
1878　　Iets over de inlandsche wijze van katoenverven op Midden Java; naar Javaansche bronnen bewerkt. Leiden.

Nabholz-Kartaschoff, Marie-Louise
In Press　　"Preliminary Approach to Cepuk Cloths From South Bali and Nusa Penida." In Proceedings of the Second Symposium on Indonesian Textiles, Köln 1985, edited by Dr. Karin von Welck. Rautenstrauch-Joest-Museum. Cologne.

Niessen, S.A.
1982　　"A Few Observations about Indigenous Toba Batak Dyeing Techniques." Unpublished manuscript.
1985 [1984]　　Motifs of Life in Toba Batak Texts and Textiles. Verhandelingen van het Koninklijk Instituut van Taal-, Land- en Volkenkunde, no. 140. Foris Publications. Dordrecht, Holland/ Cinnaminson, U.S.A. [Originally a Ph.D. dissertation, Leiden University.]

Nieuwenhuisen, J.T., and H.C.B. von Rosenberg
1863　　Verslag omtrent het eiland Nias en deszelfs bewoners. Verhandelingen van het Bataviaasch Genootschap van Kunsten en Wetenschappen, 30.

Nieuwenkamp, W.O.J.
1906/10　　Bali en Lombok. Reisherinneringen en studies omtrent land en volk, kunst en kunstnijverheid. Edam.

Nooteboom, C.
1948　　Quelques techniques de tissage des petites îles de la Sonde. Mededelingen van het Rijksmuseum voor Volkenkunde, 3. Leiden.

Nooy-Palm, Hetty
1979　　The Sa'dan-Toraja. A Study of their Social Life and Religion. Vol. 1 of Organization, Symbols and Beliefs. Verhandelingen van het Koninklijk Instituut voor Taal-, Land- en Volkenkunde, 87. Martinus Nijhoff. Leiden.
1980　　"The Role of Sacred Cloths in the Mythology and Ritual of the Sa'dan-Toraja of Sulawesi, Indonesia." In Indonesian Textiles. Irene Emery Roundtable on Museum Textiles, 1979 Proceedings, edited by M. Gittinger. The Textile Museum. Washington, D.C.
1986　　The Sa'dan-Toraja. A Study of their Social Life and Religion. Vol. 2 of Rituals of the East and West. Verhandelingen van het Koninklijk Instituut voor Taal-, Land- en Volkenkunde, 118. Foris Publications. Dordrecht, Holland/Cinnaminson, USA.

Nouhuys, J.W. van
1925-26　　"Was-batik in Midden-Celebes." Nederlandsch Indië Oud en Nieuw, 10 (4): 10 ff.

Obdeyn, V.
1929　　"Indragirische weefkunst." Tijdschrift van het

Koninlijk Bataviaasch Genootschap van Kunsten en Wetenschappen, 68:92-124.

Orsoy de Flines, E.W. van
1939 *Verslag omtrent een reis voor onderzoek en studie van de antieke uitheemsche keramiek, voorkomende in Zuid en Midden Celebes, van eind maart tot begin mei 1939*. Stenciled report.

Ossenbruggen, F.D.E. van
1983 [1977] "Java's Monca-pat: Origins of a Primitive Classification System." In *Structural Anthropology in the Netherlands*, edited by P.E. de Josselin de Jong. Martinus Nijhoff. The Hague.

Pakan, L.
1973 [1961] *Rahasia Ukiran Toradja. The Secret of Typical Toradja Patterns*. Macassar.

Platenkamp, J.D.M.
1984 "The Tobelo of Eastern Halmaheira in the Context of the Field of Anthropological Study." In *Unity in Diversity: Indonesia as a field of anthropological study*, edited by P.E. de Josselin de Jong. Verhandelingen van het Koninklijk Instituut voor Taal-, Land- en Volkenkunde, 103. Foris Pub. Dordrecht, Holland/ Cinnamonson, USA.

Pelras, C.
1962 "Tissages Balinais." *Objets et Mondes*, 2 (1): 215-39.
1972 "Contribution à la géographie et à l'ethnologie du métier à tisser en Indonésie." In *Langues et techniques, nature et société, 2. Approche ethnologique, approche naturaliste*, pp. 81-97. Paris.

Pigeaud, Th.G.Th.
1967-70 *The Literature of Java*. 3 volumes. The Hague.
1977 "Javanese Divination and Classification." *Structural Anthropology in the Netherlands*, edited by P.E. de Josselin de Jong. Martinus Hijhoff. The Hague.

1982 *Javaans Nederlands woordenboek*. The Hague. [Reprint.]

Poensen, C.
1876-77 "Iets over de kleeding der Javanen." *Mededelingen van het Nederlandsch Zendeling-genootschap*, 20, 21.

Pranata
1984 *Mencari Jodoh dan Upacara Perkawinan Adat Jawa* (Match-making and the Javanese Wedding Ceremony). P.T. Yudha Corporation. Jakarta.

Raffles, T.S.
1812 *Factory Records, East India Company*. Letter dated 29 October.

1817 [1978] *The History of Java*. 2 volumes. Black, Parbury and Allen. London. [Reprint, Oxford University Press, Kuala Lumpur.]

Rappard, T.C.
1909 "Het eiland Nias en zijne bewoners." *Bijdragen tot de Taal-, Land- en Volkenkunde*, 62:477-648.

Rees, H.A. van
1866 *De Pioniers der beschaving in Neerlands Indië, verhall eenige Krijgstogten op de buitenbezittingern*. D.A. Thieme. Arnhem.

Rogers, S.
1985 *Power and Gold, Jewelry from Indonesia, Malaysia, and the Philippines from the Collection of the Barbier-Müller Museum, Geneva*. Barbier-Müller Museum. Geneva.

Rosenberg, H.C.B. von
1878 "Die Insel Nias." In *Der Malayische Archipel: Land und Leute in Schilderungen gesammelt während eine dreissigjährigen Aufenthaltes in den Kolonien*, pp. 123-76. J.H. de Bussy. Amsterdam.

Roth, R.
1985 "Object als Symbol: Bulu gana'a eine Goldwaage aus Süd-Nias (Indonesien)." *Tribus*, 34:121-44.

Rouffaer, G.P.
1900 *Over Indische batikkunst vooral die op Java*. Haarlem.

Rouffaer, G.P., and H.H. Juynboll
1914 *De batik-kunst in Nederlandsch Indië en hare geschiedenis.* [*Die Indische Batikkunst und ihre Geschichte.*] Vol. 3 [Issued in 6 parts,1900-1914]. Publicaties van 's Rijks Ethnographisch Museum, ser. 2, no. 1. Utrecht/Haarlem.

Royal Tropical Institute (Koninklijk Instituut voor de Tropen)
1987 *Budaya-Indonesia: Arts and Crafts in Indonesia*, Tropenmuseum, Drukkerij de Lange/van Leer bv., Deventer.

Rumphius, G.E.
1750/55 *Het Amboinsche Kruydboek*. 4 volumes, 7 parts. Second printing.

Sastroamidjojo, S.
1964 *Renungan Tentang Pertunjukan Wayang Kulit* (Contemplations on the Leather Puppet Show). P.T. Kinta. Jakarta.

Schnitger, F.M.
1941/42 "Megalithen vom Batakland und Nias," *Ipek, Jahrbuch für prähistorische und ethnographische Kunst*, 16: 220-52.

Schouten, Wouter
1676 *Wouter Schoutens Oostindische Voyagie*. Meurs and Van Someren. Amsterdam.

Schröder, E.E.W.Gs
1917 *Nias: Ethnographische, geographische en historische aanteekeningen en studiën.* 2 volumes. E.J. Brill. Leiden.

Schulte Nordholt, H.G.
1971 *The Political System of the Atoni of Timor.* Verhandelingen van het Koninklijk Instituut voor Taal-, Land- en Volkenkunde, 60. Martinus Nijhoff. The Hague.
1980 "The Symbolic Classification of the Atoni of Timor." In *The Flow of Life: Essays on Eastern Indonesia*, edited by J.J. Fox. Harvard University Press. Cambridge.

Scott-Kemball, J.
1970 *Javanese Shadow-Puppets: The Raffles Collection in the British Museum.* The British Museum. London.

Smith, R.B.
1979 "Mainland South East Asia in the Seventh and Eighth Centuries." In *Early South East Asia*, edited by R.B. Smith and W. Watson. Oxford University Press. New York / Kuala Lumpur.

Snodgrass, A.
1985 *The Symbolism of the Stupa.* Studies on Southeast Asia, South-East Asian Program. Cornell University. New York.

Solyom, Bronwen, and Garret Solyom
1978 *The World of the Javanese Keris.* East-West Center. Honolulu.
1980a "Cosmic Symbolism in *Semèn* and *Alasalasan* Patterns in Javanese Textiles." In *Indonesian Textiles. Irene Emery Roundtable on Museum Textiles, 1979 Proceedings*, edited by M. Gittinger. The Textile Museum. Washington, D.C.
1980b "A Note on Some Rare Javanese Court Textiles in Indonesian Textiles." In *Indonesian Textiles. Irene Emery Roundtable on Museum Textiles, 1979 Proceedings*, edited by M. Gittinger. The Textile Museum. Washington, D.C.

Spertus, Anita, and Robert J. Holmgren
1977 "Celebes." In *Textile Traditions of Indonesia*, edited by Mary Hunt Kahlenberg. Los Angeles County Museum of Art. Los Angeles.

's Rijks Ethnografisch Museum
1920 *Catalogus van 's Rijks Ethnografisch Museum*, 14. Sumatra-Supplement. Leiden.

Stapel, F.W.
1930 *Geschiedenis van Nederlansch-Indië.* J.M. Meulenhoff. Amsterdam.

Steinmann, A.
1947 "Batik Designs." *Ciba Review*, 58:2110-20.

1958 *Batik, A Survey of Batik Design.* Leigh-on-Sea, U.K.

Sundermann, H.
1905a *Die Insel Nias und die Mission daselbst.* Verlag des Missionhauses. Barmen.
1905b *Niassisch-Deutches Wörterbuch.* Bataviaasch Genootschap van Kunsten en Wetenschappen. Moers.

Suripto
n.d. *Ibu Tien Soeharto: Ibu Negara Jang Ramah Tamah.* Pantja Pudjibangun. Surabaya.

Suzuki, P.
1959 *The Religious System and Culture of Nias, Indonesia.* Ph.D. dissertation, Leiden University. Excelsior. The Hague.

Swellengrebel, J.L.
1960 "Introduction." In *Bali: Studies in Life, Thought, and Ritual.* Van Hoeve. The Hague/ Bandung.
1977 "Some Characteristic Features of the Korawasrama Story." In *Structural Anthropology in the Netherlands*, edited by P.E. de Josselin de Jong. Martinus Nijhoff. The Hague.

Tambiah, S.J.
1970 *Buddhism and the Spirit Cults in North-east Thailand.* Cambridge University Press. Cambridge.

T'ien, Ju-K'ang
1949 "Pai Cults and Social Age in the Tai tribes of the Yunnan-Burma border." *American Anthropologist*, 51:46-57.

Tiparat, Pisal
1986 "'Tung' in the Cultural Life of the Northern People." *Thai Cultural Newsletter*, 3 (5): 5-6.

Tirtaamidjaja, N., J. Marzuki and B.R.O'G. Anderson
1966 *Batik: pola dan corak—pattern & motif.* Djambatan. Jakarta.

Tobias, J.H.
1857 [1980] *Memorie van Overgave. Ternate.* Arsip Nasional Republik Indonesia. Jakarta.

Traube, E.
1980 "Affines and the Dead: Mambai Rituals of Alliance." *Bijdragen tot de Taal-, Land- en Volkenkunde*, 136:90-115.

Ulbricht, H.
1972 *Wayang Purwa: Shadows of the Past.* Oxford in Asia. Kuala Lumpur.

Van der Tuuk, H.N.
1861 *Bataksch - Nederduitsch woordenboek.* Friederich Muller. Amsterdam.

1897   *Kawi-Balineesch-Nederlandsch woordenboek.* Batavia.

Varadarajan, Lokita
1978   "Towards a Definition of Kalamkari." *Marg,* 31 (4): 19-21.

Vatter, Ernst
1932   *Ata Kiwan: unbekannte Bergvölker im tropischen Holland.* Bibliographisches Institut. Leipzig.

Veen, H. van der
1965   *The Merok Feast of the Sa'dan-Toradja.* Verhandelingen van het Koninklijk Instituut voor Taal-, Land- en Volkenkunde, 45. Martinus Nijhoff. The Hague.

Veldhuisen, H.
1980   *Blauw en bont. Chinese en Europese invloed in de Batik van Java.* Delft.
1985   "De commerciële Noordkustbatik van Java." *Indigo,* edited by Loan Oei. Amsterdam.

Veldhuisen-Djajasoebrata, Alit
1980   "On the Origin and Nature of Larangan: Forbidden Batik Patterns from the Central Javanese Principalities." In *Indonesian Textiles. Irene Emery Roundtable on Museum Textiles, 1979 Proceedings,* edited by M. Gittinger. The Textile Museum. Washington, D.C.
1984   *Bloemen van het heelal: De kleurrijke wereld van de textiel op Java.* Sijthoff. Amsterdam/ Museum voor Land- en Volkenkunde. Rotterdam.
1985   "De bangun tulak van Midden-Java." In *Indigo,* edited by Loan Oei. Amsterdam.

Viallett, N. (editor)
1971   *Tapisserie: méthode et vocabulaire. Principes d'analyse scientifique.* Ministère des Affaires Culturelles. Imprimerie Nationale. Paris.

Vimolphan Peetathawatchai
1973   *Esarn Cloth Design.* Faculty of Education, Khon Kaen University. Khon Kaen, Thailand.

Visser, Leontine E.
1984   "Mijn tuin is mijn kind." Ph.D. dissertation. Rijksuniversiteit te Leiden.

Volz, Wilhelm
1909   *Nord Sumatra, Bd. I, Die Batakländer.* Reimer. Berlin.

Vroklage, B.A.G.
1953   *Ethnographie der Belu in Zentral-Timor.* 3 volumes. E.J. Brill. Leiden.

Wahyono, M.
1979   *Lurik Daerah Jogyakarta dalam perbandingan.* Unpublished stencilled manuscript. Jakarta.

Warming, W. and M. Gaworski
1981   *The World of Indonesian Textiles.* Kodansha. Tokyo/ New York.

Weatherbee, D. E.
1966   *Ideology in Indonesia: Sukarno's Indonesian Revolution.* Southeast Asia Studies no. 8. Yale University. New Haven.

Wilken, G.A.
1891   "De hagedis in het volksgeloof der Malayo-Polynesiërs." *Bijdragen tot de Taal-, Land- en Volkenkunde,* 40:473-92.

Winter, C.F.
1843   "Serat Manikmaya." (Dutch translation). *Tijdschrift voor Nederlandsch-Indië,* 5 (1).

Witteborg, P.
1909   *Ein frühvollendetes Missionarsleben.* Verlag des Missionshauses. Barmen.

Wolters, O.W.
1983   "A few miscellaneous Pi-chi jottings on early Indonesia." *Indonesia,* 36 (October): 49-65.

Yamin, Mr. Muh.
1954   *6000 Tahun Sang Merah-Putih* (6000 Years of the Red-and-White). Penerbit Siguntang. Jakarta.

Yoshimoto, S.
1977   *Indoneshia Senshoku Taikei I.* Kyoto.

Zainu'ddin, A.
1980   *A Short History of Indonesia.* Second edition. Cassell. Melbourne.

Zerner, Charles
1981   "Signs of the Spirits, Signature of the Smith: Iron forging in Tana Toraja." *Indonesia,* 31:89-112.

Zoetmulder, P.J.
1982   *Old Javanese-English Dictionary.* Vol. 1. Martinus Nijhoff. The Hague.

Contributors

Judi Achjadi was born in Canada but became an Indonesian citizen in the late 1950s when she moved to Jakarta with her diplomat husband. There her longtime interest in ethnic dress, sewing, art, and history found a new outlet in the study of Indonesian culture and language. Her specialty is Indonesian women's dress and wedding ceremonies. She has written several books and articles on Indonesian costumes, crafts, textiles, and other cultural themes and has translated some dozen publications on a variety of Indonesian subjects. Judi is presently living in Washington, D.C.

Ruth Barnes, born in Germany, has lived in Great Britain since 1974 and in Oxford since 1978. Her interest in Indonesian textiles and Southeast Asian art was first awakened when she accompanied her husband to Kédang, Lembata, from 1969 to 1971, for his field research in cultural anthropology. Upon return she began graduate work in art history, first at UCLA and then at the University of Edinburgh, where she earned an M.A. Honors. During two subsequent visits to Lembata in 1979 and 1982—now with two children—Ruth spent nine months investigating textiles there. The result was a doctoral dissertation for Oxford in 1984, recently published by E.J. Brill, Leiden. Future research plans include a comprehensive catalogue and interpretation in historical context of the Ernst-Vatter Collection in Frankfurt, Germany. Ruth plans a book on the vast textile collection from the Naga Hills in the Pitt Rivers Museum, Oxford.

As Curator of Textiles at the Tropenmuseum in Amsterdam, **Rita Bolland** worked with the textiles, looms, and related material from tropical countries, and helped prepare numerous exhibitions on these subjects. The total renovation of the Tropenmuseum, completed in 1979, gave her the opportunity to mount a permanent textile show. Her publications deal mainly with the technical aspects of looms and fabrics. Since her retirement in 1984, she has been able to devote more time to her special interest, the study of looms of the heddle and shedstick type.

Following undergraduate work at City College in New York, **Jerome Feldman** received his M.A. from the University of Hawaii, and his Ph.D. from Columbia University in Art History. He has done field research in Nias and other parts of Indonesia as well as in American Samoa. His activities include publications and consultation for exhibitions on Indonesian and Micronesian Art at UCLA, the University of Hawaii, the Metropolitan Museum of Art, and currently at the Smithsonian Institution. He is Associate Professor of Art History at Hawaii Loa College.

Anthony Forge is Professor of Anthropology at Australian National University. He has done extensive work on the art of the Abelam people of the Sepik River in Papua New Guinea. More recently he has worked in Bali and other parts of Indonesia on art and ritual. He was editor as well as a contributor to *Primitive Art and Society*, published in London (Oxford University Press) in 1974 and is also the author of *Balinese Traditional Painting*, published in Sydney in 1980.

Mattiebelle S. Gittinger is an art historian concerned with the religious and cultural usage of ethnographic textiles. She is Research Associate for Southeast Asian Textiles at The Textile Museum in Washington, D.C., where she has organized numerous exhibitions. Her writings include *Splendid Symbols: Textiles and Tradition in Indonesia* and *Master Dyers to the World*. She has investigated textile usage in Indonesia, India, and most recently in mainland Southeast Asia, among the T'ai people. Dr. Gittinger is a founding member of the Textile Society of America and serves on its Directing Council.

Rens Heringa has been involved with Indonesian textiles for twenty years. An initial interest in the craft of batik led to scholarly studies and museum work. While living in Indonesia she taught batik courses in Surabaya, and did field research with a special focus on traditional work methods. She also served as executive secretary of the Society of Friends at the Jakarta Textile Museum. Presently living and studying in Leiden, she has completed several annotated catalogues of private and museum collections and a series of contributions to publications on Indonesia, Indonesian textiles and textile history. The relationship between the social and the economic exchange systems of village textiles forms her main current interest and is the subject of another year of fieldwork on Java.

John and Robyn Maxwell first became interested in Indonesian traditional textiles while teaching at Pajajaran University in Bandung, West Java, in the early 1970s. A jointly awarded Myer Foundation Asia and Pacific Grant-in-Aid enabled them to conduct extensive research into the textile cultures of the Indonesian archipelago from 1976 to 1978. This was carried out under the auspices of the Indonesian Institute of Sciences and the Institute of Textile Technology, Bandung. A Netherlands Government Scholarship in 1983 permitted a thorough examination of the collections of Indonesian textiles and related objects in European ethnographic museums. The Maxwells have written a number of articles on Indonesian art, culture and politics. **Robyn Maxwell**, as Visiting Curator of Asian Textiles at the Australian National Gallery, has recently completed a major study of Southeast Asian textiles, *Tradition, Trade, and Transformation: The Textiles of Southeast Asia.* **John Maxwell,** with the Department of Political and Social Change in the Research School of Pacific Studies at the Australian National University, is especially interested in post-independence Indonesian political biography.

Susan McKinnon received her M.A. and Ph.D. in anthropology from the University of Chicago. She conducted pre-doctoral field research on marriage and exchange in the Tanimbar Islands (eastern Indonesia) in 1978-80, and returned there in 1983-84 to conduct post-doctoral research on headhunting, warfare, and inter-village alliance rituals. She is currently on the faculty in the Department of Anthropology at the University of Virginia in Charlottesville.

Marie-Louise Nabholz-Kartaschoff, born in 1939, received her doctorate in ethnology, prehistory, and classical archaeology from the University of Basel in 1967; there she studied European ikat textiles under the supervision of Dr. Alfred Bühler. Since 1968 she has been Keeper of Asian Textiles and East Asia at the Museum für Völkerkunde und Schweizerisches Museum für Volkskunde. From 1970-79 she was Lecturer in Ethno-technology at the University of Basel. She did field work in India in 1975 and 1979, and in Indonesia in 1982 and 1988. She has published on a variety of textile subjects, including plangi, batik, Indian textiles, technical aspects of rugs and flat weaves. She has also curated exhibitions at the Museum für Völkerkunde on a variety of subjects including plangi, batik, American quilts, golden textiles from Indonesia, textile techniques, and embroidery from India.

Hetty Nooy-Palm, born in 1921, is an emeritus professor of Museology and Material Culture of the University of Amsterdam. Her interest in Indonesia dates back to the years following World War Two, when she did fieldwork in Java, Sumatra, and Sulawesi. Most of her research was done in the Sa'dan-Toraja area, where she focused on the ritual and symbolic significance of material objects in Toraja culture. For her 1955 doctoral dissertation, *Polynesische Migraties*, she analyzed Polynesian migrations. From 1952-57 she was a curator of the Ethnological and Historical section of the Museum of the Batavian Society for Arts and Sciences (Bataviaasch Genootschap van Kunsten en Wetenschappen), now known as Museum Nasional, in Jakarta. During the subsequent three years she studied the closed community of Staphorst, Netherlands, examining the traditional women's costume and its role in Staphorst culture. From 1958 to 1983 she was a senior research fellow of the Koninklijk Instituut voor de Tropen, or Royal Tropical Institute, Amsterdam.

Leontine E. Visser studied anthropology at Leiden University (Rijksuniversiteit te Leiden). Her doctoral fieldwork on Halmahera (1979-80) concentrated on social organization and agricultural practice. She graduated from Leiden in 1984 and from 1985-87 was engaged in several development projects in Indonesia. Since 1987 she has been a staff member of the Department of Public Administration at Leiden, and in charge of the non-Western section.

Credits

COVER: Susan Einstein.

FRONTISPIECE: Mattiebelle Gittinger.

COLOR PLATES:
Plates 1,2, Susan McKinnon.
Plates 3,4,5, Ruth Barnes.
Plates 6,7,8,9,10, Leontine E. Visser.
Plates 11,12,13,15,16, Danielle Geirnaert.
Plate 14, A.A. Gerbrands.
Plates 17,18, Anthony Forge.
Plates 19, 20a&c, Rijksuniversiteit te Leiden.
Plates 23,24,25, Judi Achjadi.
Plates 26a&b,27, Wismar.
Plate 28, Urs Ramseyer.
Plate 29, M.L. Nabholz-Kartaschoff.
Plate 30, Mattiebelle Gittinger.
Plate 31, Peter Horner.
Plates 33,34, Jerome Feldman.

McKINNON:
Figure 5, Koninklijk Instituut voor de Tropen.
Figures 2-4,6-19, Susan McKinnon.

BARNES:
Figures 3,6,8,10, Tony Kluck.
Figures 1,2,4,5,7,9,11-16, Ruth Barnes.

GEIRNAERT:
Figures 13,15,16,19,27, A.A. Gerbrands.
Figures 1,2,3,26, Tony Kluck.
Figures 4-9,11,12,14,17,18,20,22-25, Danielle Geirnaert.

VISSER:
Figures 1-9, Leontine E. Visser.

FORGE:
Figures 3-5,7-17, Tom Forge.
Figures 1,2,6, Anthony Forge.

MAXWELL AND MAXWELL:
Figures 1-3,5,8-13, Australian National Gallery, Canberra.
Figure 7, Hugh O'Neill.

HERINGA:
Figures 2,4,5,6,11,17, Theo Vlaar.
Figures 8,12-15,18, Pramono Sutikno.
Figures 1,3,7,9,10,16,19-22, Rens Heringa.

ACHJADI:
Figures 4a&b,8, Wismar.
Figures 1,2,3,6,10, Courtesy of Ibu Maktal.
Figures 5,7,9a,b, Tony Kluck.

NOOY-PALM:
Figures 1,2, Richard Todd.
Figure 3, Koninklijk Instituut voor de Tropen, Amsterdam.
Figures 5a-e, Vlisco B.V., Helmond, Netherlands.
Figures 4,6,7,13, Hetty Nooy-Palm, courtesy of Koninklijk Instituut voor de Tropen, Amsterdam.
Figure 9a&b, Mary Hunt Kahlenburg, Textile Arts, New Mexico.
Figure 10, Victoria and Albert Museum, courtesy of the Board of Trustees.
Figures 11a&b, Rob Kok, Galerie Mabuhay, Amsterdam.

NABHOLZ-KARTASCHOFF:
Figure 4, Museum voor Land- en Volkenkunde, Rotterdam.
Figures 1-3, 5,6-12, Museum für Völkerkunde, Basel.
Figures 25,27,29,30,32,45, Christina Schaublin, courtesy of Museum für Völkerkunde, Basel.
Figures 14,15a-c,28,31,34,37,44, Eva Weber, courtesy of Museum für Völkerkunde, Basel.
Figures 16-24,26, 28,33,35,36,38-43,46, Unknown designer, (Theo Meier?), courtesy of Museum für Völkerkunde, Basel.

FELDMAN:
Figures 4,5, Jerome Feldman.
Figure 6, Museum voor Volkenkunde, Rotterdam.
Figure 7b, Koninklijk Instituut voor de Tropen, Amsterdam.
Figure 9, Courtesy of Buleni Fau.
Figures 7a,13, Museum Nasional, Jakarta.
Figure 10, Marlene Meyer-Patton.
Figures 8,14, Aileen Matsuyama-Feldman.

BOLLAND:
Figure 1, The Textile Museum, Washington, D.C.
Figures 2,8,9,15,16, Koninklijk Instituut voor de Tropen, Amsterdam.
Figure 21a&b, Robert J. Holmgren and Anita E. Spertus, New York.
Figures 3-7,10-14,17-20, Rita Bolland.

GITTINGER:
Figures 2,4-7,14, The Textile Museum, Washington, D.C.
Figures 15,19, Yunnan Provincial Museum, Kunming, Yunnan, China.
Figures 12,17,22, Koninklijk Instituut voor de Tropen, Amsterdam.
Figures 1,8-11,13,16,18,20,21, Mattiebelle Gittinger.

Museum Staff

Christopher B. Donnan, *Director*
Doran H. Ross, *Associate Director*
Patricia B. Altman, *Curator of Folk Art and Textiles*
Patricia Anawalt, *Consulting Curator of Costumes and Textiles*
Millicent Besser, *Accountant*
Daniel R. Brauer, *Director of Publications*
Jack Carter, *Exhibition Designer*
Robin Blair Chamberlin, *Conservator*
Robert Childs, *Collections Manager*
Richard Chute, *Development Coordinator*
Henrietta Cosentino, *Editor*

Mary E. Doyle, *Librarian*
Betsy Escandor, *Administrative Assistant*
Paul Farnsworth, *Curator of Archaeology*
Sarah Jane Kennington, *Registrar*
Virginia Miska, *Assistant Accountant*
Owen Moore, *Assistant Collections Manager*
Paulette Parker, *Assistant Registrar*
Betsy D. Quick, *Director of Education*
Gene Riggs, *Exhibition Staff*
Don Simmons, *Exhibition Staff*
Barbara Underwood, *Administrative Analyst*

Presentation

Henrietta Cosentino, *Editing*
Daniel R. Brauer, *Design*
Richard Todd, *MCH Photography*
Tony Kluck, *Maps*
Dai Nippon Printing Co., Ltd., *Printing and Binding*
Supertype, *Headline Typography*

Typesetting and layout were accomplished by the Editor and the Designer on Macintosh computers using Aldus PageMaker 3.01.
The text is set in Optima, an Adobe Font.
Headline type is Nordia medium and bold.